THE
STYLE
SOURCEBOOK

THE
STYLE
SOURCEBOOK

THE DEFINITIVE ILLUSTRATED DIRECTORY OF
FABRICS WALLPAPERS **PAINTS** FLOORING **TILES**

REVISED EDITION

JUDITH MILLER

FIREFLY BOOKS

A FIREFLY BOOK

Published by Firefly Books Ltd. 2003
First published in Great Britain in 1998 by Mitchell Beazley, an imprint
of Octopus Publishing Group Ltd

First printing

Publisher Cataloging-in-Publication Data   (U.S.)
Miller, Judith.
    The style sourcebook : the definitive illustrated directory of fabrics,
wallpapers, paints, flooring, tiles : revised edition / Judith Miller.
  [402] p. : col. ill ;   cm.
Originally published: New York: Stewart, Tabori & Chang, 1998.
Includes index.
Summary: Sourcebook for selecting and ordering fabrics, trimmings,
wallpapers, paint, tiles and flooring for interior design.
ISBN 1-55297-791-9
1. Decoration and ornament -- Directories.   I. Title.
745.4/029/473 21   NK1705.M56 2003

National Library of Canada Cataloguing in Publication
Miller, Judith
    The style sourcebook : the definitive illustrated directory of fabrics,
wallpapers, paints, flooring and tiles/ Judith Miller.—Rev. ed.
Includes index.
ISBN 1-55297-791-9
    1. Decoration and ornament--Directories. 2. Decoration and
ornament--Information services--Directories. I. Title.

NK1705.M56 2003   745.4'029'4   C2003-900401-5

Published in the United States in 2003 by
Firefly Books (U.S.) Inc.
P.O. Box 1338, Ellicott Station
Buffalo, New York 14205

Published in Canada in 2003 by
Firefly Books Ltd.
3680 Victoria Park Avenue
Toronto, Ontario, M2H 3K1

Printed and bound in China

Original edition

Chief Contributor	John Wainwright
Contributors	Chris Blanchett, Penny McGuire, Olga Moyle
Consultants	Jill Draper, David Gunton, Tessa Smith-Agassi, Michael Szell, Christine Woods
Senior Editor	Penelope Cream
Senior Art Editor	Emma Boys
Editor	Julia North
Designer	Kenny Grant
Editorial Assistants	Patrick Evans, Anna Nicholas
Design Assistant	Estelle Bayllis
Production Controllers	Rachel Staveley, Kate Thomas
Picture Researchers	Sally Claxton, Lois Charlton
Executive Editor	Judith More
Executive Art Editor	Janis Utton
Special Photography	Steve Tanner
Special Location Photography	James Merrell

Revised edition

Chief Contributor	John Wainwright
Project Editor	Emma Clegg
Editorial Coordinator	Catherine Emslie
Caption Researcher	Caroline Dyas
Proofreader	Libby Willis
Indexer	Helen Snaith
Executive Art Editor	Auberon Hedgecoe
Designers	Peter Gerrish and John Round
Production Controller	Gary Hayes
Picture Researcher	Emma O'Neill
Special Photography	Roger Dixon

Contents

Foreword

We produced the first *Style Sourcebook* in 1998. Our intention then was to provide something previously unavailable: namely, a comprehensive guide to fabrics, wallpapers, tiles, paints and floor coverings that located particular materials, motifs, patterns and colours within specific historical periods. Judging by our readers' comments and subsequent sales, it proved a major success – a very pleasing, but not surprising outcome. As I noted at the time, there had been a substantial growth of interest in interior decoration since the Second World War. Initially, the opening up of many historically important houses had introduced a wider public to the finest examples of the art. Subsequently, diverse books, magazines and television programmes illustrating both historical and contemporary interiors demonstrated the tremendous decorative potential of all our homes. The result: what in previous centuries had been largely the preserve of a wealthy minority had become the one art form practised by virtually everyone.

Much, of course, has happened in the five years since our initial publication. First and foremost, interest in interior decoration has become even more intense and widespread. Secondly, on-going research has brought to light many new patterns, motifs and colours employed in different historical periods. Thirdly, numerous new designs for contemporary styles of decoration have been conceived. And fourthly, manufacturers have responded by producing the essential decorative media in ever more extensive ranges of historical and contemporary patterns and colourways.

To guide you through all these developments we have produced a thoroughly revised *Style Sourcebook* that encompasses through myriad samples – more than 60 per cent of which are new – fashionable styles of decoration from the Middle Ages to the present day. Judging by the reception of our original title, I am convinced you will find this new book informative, inspirational, user-friendly and, above all, an invaluable guide when choosing decorative schemes for your period or modern home, whether your preferences are historical or contemporary.

Judith Miller

Using *The Style Sourcebook*

Over 2,000 samples, from the widest possible range of international designs, provide inspiration for selecting the ingredients for any interior scheme, from medieval to modern. The Style Guide presents an historical overview of interior design and major stylistic developments, while the chapters that follow contain hundreds of samples of every style, colour and pattern, divided into the main design types, such as florals, geometrics and motifs. Each design type or material is further categorized by period, from medieval to early 21st century, enabling you to select your favourite designs and colours, item by item and era by era.

Useful Features

Various easy-to-use design features on every page make the information in *The Style Sourcebook* highly accessible. Colour-coded bands, each indicating a particular century, lie on the edge of every page to help you to turn instantly to a specific era. The same colour is used in the border of the special feature boxes, linking them with their most relevant period.

Each sample is accompanied by a detailed caption listing all the information needed for ordering, such as name, code number (if applicable) and the colourway shown. Sizes, repeat and composition are also indicated, together with any relevant symbols for usage, special applications and other information (*see* Key to Symbols, left).

Further Information

The samples in the book have been obtained from a wide variety of international manufacturers and suppliers, whose details are listed in the Directory of Suppliers (*see* page 401). The Glossary provides further information about the technical, artistic and historical terms mentioned in the book.

STYLE AND DATE HEADING
Every spread of samples is identified by the type of design and the date of the decorative style. A detailed introduction provides an overview of the era.

DESIGN OVERVIEW
Each design type is discussed with reference to its specific use in interior decoration, and is illustrated with colour examples of room settings and furniture.

KEY DESIGNS
The most significant designs are highlighted and their historical, cultural and artistic importance discussed.

COLOUR BANDS
Easily identifiable colour bands represent the different historical periods, allowing designs of a particular era to be found quickly across all chapters.

CAPTIONS
Every sample illustrated has a detailed caption that provides all the information necessary for ordering the featured design and colourway required.

SCALE BAR
A scale bar beneath the sample indicates the size at which it is reproduced. The largest samples are life size, while the smallest are at 25 per cent of their actual size.

BOX FEATURE
Important historical or technical topics are discussed in detail within a box. The box is colour-coded according to the appropriate corresponding date.

The Samples

FABRICS

Osborne & Little/Dufy Velvet F5151 Colour **01**
Alt. colours **yes** Composition **59% viscose,
41% cotton** Width **132cm/51¾in** Repeat
59cm/23in Price ★★★★ 🛋️ LC 🛋️

Price Guide	per metre/yard
£1–20	★
£21–50	★★
£51–100	★★★
£101–150	★★★★
£150+	★★★★★

The samples shown in the Fabrics section (*see* pages 60–201) are categorized by design or pattern type and historical period. The composition of each fabric is shown by fibre type and expressed in terms of percentages.

The price of each fabric is given by the metre/yard; this may vary slightly depending on where and when it is bought. Suggested uses and any special features are indicated at the end of each caption.

Also included in the Fabrics section are the Braids & Trimmings pages. Described here are the different types of braids, ribbons, fringes and tassels.

WALLPAPERS

Bradbury & Bradbury/Glasgow Panel Colour
natural Alt. colours **yes** Width **68.5cm/27in**
Length **2m/2⅛yd** Repeat - Price ★

Price Guide	per metre/yard
£1-5	★
£6–10	★★
£11–20	★★★
£21–35	★★★★
£35+	★★★★★

The Wallpapers section (*see* pages 202–283) is divided by design type and then by historical period. Full-size wallpapers as well as borders and friezes are illustrated, and the latter can be combined with plainer designs.

Prices for wallpapers are shown by the metre/yard, and the symbol ♣ indicates those that are hand-printed or hand-blocked (these are generally more expensive than the machine-printed designs).

Certain wallpapers need painting or finishing after hanging, and this requirement is also indicated by the relevant caption symbol.

PAINTS & FINISHES

Liberon Waxes Colour **gilt cream chantilly**
Composition and finish *spirit-based:* **satin
sheen** Price ★★★★ ◨ 🔲

Price Guide	per litre/gallon
£1–5	★
£6–10	★★
£11–30	★★★
£30+	★★★★

The divisions within the Paints & Finishes section (*see* pages 284–309) concentrate on the application material, such as regular paints, special paints and wood finishes, which is then categorized by date where applicable.

Prices for the samples in this section are per litre/gallon; however, certain finishes such as gilt waxes are needed only in tiny amounts and so may be supplied in smaller quantities.

The composition and finish of each paint is given; many colours are available in a variety of finishes, each suitable for a different use.

TILES

Original Style/Rose and Trellis 6970A Colour
multi Alt. colours **no** Composition **ceramic** Size
15 x 15cm x 7mm/6 x 6 x ¼in Price ★ W

Price Guide	per tile/set
£1–5	★
£6–10	★★
£11–20	★★★
£21–35	★★★★
£35+	★★★★★

The measurements given for the samples in the Tiles section (*see* pages 310–359) signify the longest side by the shortest side(s). This is not an indication of which way up a tile should be positioned – some tile designs can be placed horizontally, vertically or even diagonally.

Prices are given for each tile, or, where the design consists of a number of tiles, for the price of the total set or panel. The tiles are shown without scale bars, and wherever possible each tile is shown in its entirety. Some tiles are available in a variety of sizes and this is indicated by the symbol ⊞.

FLOORING

Kahrs/Alder Monte Carlo Colour **natural**
Alt. colours **no** Composition **alder** Width
20cm/8in Repeat - Price ★★

Price Guide	per square metre/yard
£1–20	★
£21–50	★★
£51–100	★★★
£101–150	★★★★
£150+	★★★★★

The Flooring section (*see* pages 360–397) is split first into the type of flooring material – wood, carpet, matting and sheet flooring – and then into different historical periods. Certain types of flooring were available earlier than others, and this is reflected in the era divisions.

Prices in this section are given per square metre/yard (except in the case of some of the borders, which are sold by the linear metre/yard, so check with the supplier before ordering). Inlaid wooden flooring is often made up on commission to fit the area required, so is priced according to space and type.

USING THE SCALE BAR

Most of the samples in the book, apart from those such as tiles and paints that may vary in size or are not measured by area, have a scale bar beneath them. This scale bar has four divisions which are shaded according to the relative size of the sample shown, in proportion to its actual size.

A single shaded division indicates that the sample is illustrated at a quarter (or 25 per cent) of its full size; two shaded divisions mean that the sample is at half (or 50 per cent) its actual size; three shaded divisions indicate that the sample is at three-quarters of its actual size (or 75 per cent), while a completely shaded bar means that the sample is shown at actual size (100 per cent).

25%

50%

75%

100%

Style Guide

Medieval to pre-16th Century

During the Middle Ages, interior decoration was the preserve of the seigneurial classes. They alone had the money and time to devote to this domestic preoccupation, and what is now called "Medieval style" was confined to their stone-built or timber-framed castles and manor houses.

Medieval interiors were sparsely furnished, so the architectural shell played a major role in the decoration. Floors at ground level consisted of bricks, stone flags or tiles, and upper floors of oak or elm boards. Ceilings were often coffered, and the stone walls left exposed or covered with coarse plaster (the latter limewashed and often painted with stencilled motifs). The wooden studs and braces of timber-framed walls were exposed and the wattle-and-daub panels in between were limewashed and sometimes stencilled. Battened plank doors were set under flat or four-centred arches – as were most mullion windows.

Furniture was mostly of oak, elm or chestnut. Tables were wooden boards supported on trestles, seating largely consisted of benches and stools, and beds were simple pallets or canopied four-posters. Soft furnishings included silk, woollen and tapestry bed- and wall-hangings, embroidered quilts, floor cushions, rush- and straw-matting floor-coverings and, in the grandest households, oriental carpets which were used as table-coverings.

Throughout the Middle Ages, the decorative motifs that adorned furniture, woodwork, tiles and textiles were derived from three vocabularies of ornament: Romanesque, Gothic and Heraldic. The Romanesque combined Classical Roman, oriental, pagan and Christian motifs, and included chevrons, foliage, people and beasts. Gothic ornament included architectural elements such as lancets, foils and tracery, as well as flora and fauna and human figures. Heraldic decoration consisted of motifs and emblems such as cyphers, the "Tree of Life", and human and animal figures.

ABOVE & RIGHT
Monogrammed silk bed- and wall-hangings, and a matching hand-woven rug and chair throw, dominate this Medieval-style bedroom at Leeds Castle, in Kent, England. Prior to the 18th century, monograms were the preserve of the aristocracy and were used to denote ownership or patronage. The colourways here are typical of grand Medieval and early Renaissance interiors.

LEFT Limewashed walls and monogrammed silk hangings provide the backdrop for a military-style, sheer-draped tented washtub at Leeds Castle, England. The woven rush matting provides a near-authentic substitute for the loose rushes that were often laid over wooden floorboards before the 17th century.

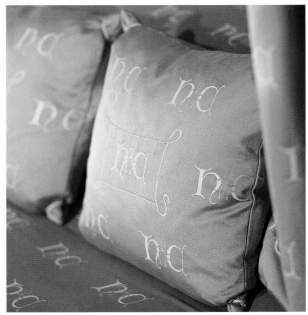

16th & 17th Centuries

During the 16th and 17th centuries, interior decoration was marked by an ever-increasing emphasis on domestic comfort, reflecting the spread of prosperity beyond the nobility to the rapidly expanding merchant classes of both Europe and the newly established American colonies. Stylistically, the most significant development was the widespread adoption of Classical (mainly Roman) forms of ornament. Originating in Renaissance Italy, the Classical style was often loosely interpreted in Europe (and later America) via engraved treatises and pattern books. Classical ornament was sometimes combined with Medieval (especially Gothic and Heraldic) types during the 16th century, but virtually supplanted them in the elaborate Baroque interiors of the 17th century. Oriental styles of decoration became popular in the late 17th century as trading links with China and India strengthened.

Architecturally, the 16th century saw the incorporation of geometrically patterned marble, and elaborate marquetry and parquetry floors on the ground level of grander houses; bricks, tiles, stone flags and wooden boards were still in widespread use in most homes. Ceilings still consisted of exposed beams and joists, infilled with limewashed plaster panels. Coarse-plastered and limewashed stone walls were much in evidence, as was exposed studwork in timber-framed houses. However, there was a much greater use of wainscoting throughout the period, either full height or to frieze or dado level. Carved or applied decoration was highly fashionable, with linenfold patterns, arabesques, strapwork and roundels being especially favoured. Panelling made from hardwoods was either left untreated, stained or limed; softwood panelling (particularly prevalent in America) was either flat-painted or, especially in the 17th century, grained in imitation of expensive hardwoods. By the late 16th century transomed

ABOVE The hangings and draperies on this 16th-century bed at Parham House, in Sussex, England, include flamestitch-pattern drapes (c. 1615) on the posts, and an embroidered coverlet, back, canopy and mattress valance hand-stitched by Mary, Queen of Scots, c. 1585.

RIGHT This wall at St Mary's in Sussex, England, features wood-grained, *trompe l'oeil* arcading, executed by a Flemish painter-stainer for the visit of Queen Elizabeth I of England in 1585.

FAR RIGHT Set against limed oak doors and panelling, the 17th-century furniture at Parham House includes an armchair upholstered with Flemish needlework. The pictorial covering features designs typical of the period.

windows had become as common as Medieval mullions, with diagonally arranged quarries being superseded during the 17th century by larger, rectangular panes.

The most significant development in furniture design was the introduction of upholstery, mostly in the form of back stools and armchairs covered in turkeywork, leather, velvet or tapestry. Such fabrics, together with elaborate crewelwork, damasks, lace and, in the late 17th century, imported cottons (*indiennes*), were also in widespread use as bed- and wall-hangings. Although rush matting was the main form of floor-covering, oriental carpets began to appear on floors at this time, having previously been confined to tabletops.

ABOVE Upholstered seating first appeared in Europe in the 1620s. Favoured fabrics during the 17th century included leather, velvet and, as shown here, flame-stitched tapestry.

LEFT Pale burgundy-painted wall-panelling and stained and polished wooden floor-boards provide a foil for gilt and ebony framed portraits, *chinoiserie* lacquered chairs and Chinese vases.

Early 18th Century

ABOVE Pale colours, such as straw and pearl grey, were popular in the first half of the 18th century. In this New York apartment they provide an understated backdrop for a symmetrical display of botanical watercolours and Queen Anne walnut furniture.

LEFT Rococo elements in this early 18th-century English interior include silk *chinoiserie* upholstery, a swagged nut garland, scallop-shell candle shields and Classical carvings on the furniture and woodwork.

Two quite distinct styles of architecture and decoration dominated the first half of the 18th century. The first, Palladianism, was derived from the writings and engravings of the 16th-century Italian architect Andrea Palladio, and was especially popular in Europe and, from the 1740s, the United States. Classical Roman in origin, the style in its purest form was characterized by bold, austere and, in the grandest houses, large architectural elements, such as Venetian windows. It was also notable for its harmony of proportion and detail. Floorboards were bare wood, augmented with sisal matting or with oriental or turkeywork carpets, and ceilings were plain-plastered or coffered with plaster mouldings. Walls were fully panelled and flat-painted (often in grey and green), wood-grained, or plaster-covered with either silk hangings or hand-painted wallpapers – all providing the backdrop for paintings, prints or engravings. Furniture, much of it made of solid or veneered walnut, was generally sparse. Typical pieces included bureau-bookcases, tripod tables, upholstered armchairs, and occasional and dining chairs. The seating was often upholstered in a fabric that co-ordinated with the window treatment.

In continental Europe, the austerity of Palladian Classicism was superseded from as early as the 1720s by the second distinctive style – Rococo. This was a lighter, exotic, even frivolous look that first appeared in informal buildings such as tea pavilions and garden grottoes. Primarily decorative rather than structural, Rococo was characterized by the use of *rocaille*, *chinoiserie*, *singeries* and Turkish and Indian figures, combined with flowers and foliage, and with light scrollwork and diaper patterns. In England, Rococo was combined with Gothick style, a romanticized revival of elements of Gothic style, such as ogee arches and quatre-foils. However, neither pure Rococo, nor Rococo-Gothick, made a significant impact in America.

ABOVE The window and bed draperies in a bedroom at the Château de Morsan in France are embellished with patterns and motifs inspired by Indian styles of ornament. The walls are hand-painted with delftware-style designs.

RIGHT This painted Rococo settee with ornate *rocaille* and scrolled-leaf carvings has a buttoned velvet squab and is flanked by pairs of topiary sentinels and Kang Hsi vases. The Classical window treatment is typical of early to mid-18th-century reception rooms, and incorporates swagged pull-up sheers, pleated and tied-back yellow silk drapes and a swagged and tailed pelmet embellished with bullion fringing, tassels and fabric rosettes. The plain panelled walls are painted a light yellow – a fashionable colour of the era.

Late 18th Century

While *chinoiserie* and Gothick remained much in evidence during the second half of the 18th century, especially in Britain, the predominant style of ornament and decoration during this period was Neo-classicism. It emerged in Europe in the 1750s as a reaction to the flamboyant and often frivolous Rococo style, and reached the United States in the 1780s. In many respects it can be seen as a natural development of early 18th-century Palladianism. Like Palladian style, Neo-classicism drew for inspiration on Classical Roman architecture but, unlike Palladianism, it also encompassed ancient Greek ornament. Neo-classicism was drawn from direct observations of Roman and Greek architecture and ornament, made possible by a series of archaeological excavations – notably in Rome, Pompeii and Herculaneum – and the subsequent publication of the illustrated accounts and pattern books of influential architects and designers, such as Robert and James Adam, who visited these sites.

Neo-classical interiors were characterized by an elegance and lightness of style, and a general preference for linear decoration – in marked contrast to the heavier, sculptural qualities of Palladian interiors. For example, plain butt-jointed wooden floorboards, which had been in widespread use in upper storeys for centuries, were now used at ground level. When made from finely figured hardwoods, they were often stained and polished and left uncovered; when of softwoods (such as pine or fir) they were invariably covered with pile carpet which, in the grandest of houses, came from the factories at Savonnerie or Aubusson in France, or Wilton in England. Ceilings were usually smooth, painted plaster, augmented with simple cornice mouldings. However, the grandest featured Neo-classical motifs on painted and gilded plaster panels. Most walls were divided by a dado rail, and either flat-painted or covered

ABOVE The most striking feature of this late 18th-century-style New York apartment is the brightly coloured wallpaper. Exotic blooms, birds and insects characterize *chinoiserie* papers of this period.

LEFT Classical Roman motifs embellish the gilded architectural fixtures and fittings and furniture in the French Empire-style *faux*-marble-walled Grand Salon at the Château de Compiègne.

RIGHT Here the bare pine floorboards, grey-white walls divided with cobalt-blue stripes, furniture and striped bed- and window-hangings epitomize late 18th-century Swedish style.

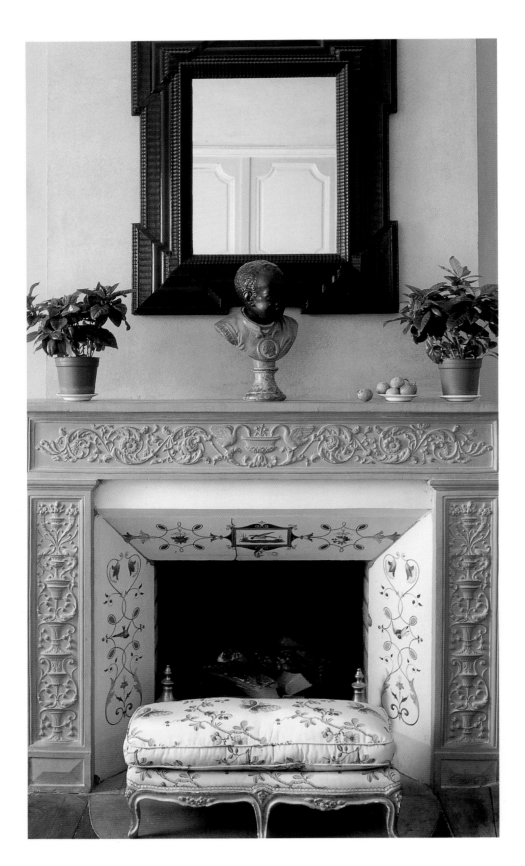

with intricately patterned papers also displaying Neo-classical imagery. Engravings or prints, as well as traditional gilt-framed portrait and landscape paintings, were hung on the walls.

The lightness of ornament that characterized Neo-classicism was mirrored in the furniture of the period – the leading designers of which were Thomas Sheraton and George Hepplewhite. The most fashionable pieces were veneered in satinwood; the most decorative embellished with painted swags of flowers, ornamental bows, and cupids and other mythological or pastoral scenes set in panels. Pieces were usually made from solid or veneered mahogany.

The influence of Neo-classicism spread to 18th-century soft furnishings. Swagged-and-tailed drapes were a common window treatment, while Neo-classical motifs and patterns were featured on both window- and bed-hangings and on upholstered furniture whenever plain fabrics were not used. However, the most striking characteristic of the soft furnishings of the period was the eschewing of lavish, heavyweight fabrics – such as tapestries and woollen velvets – in favour of lightweight silks, printed cottons and sheers.

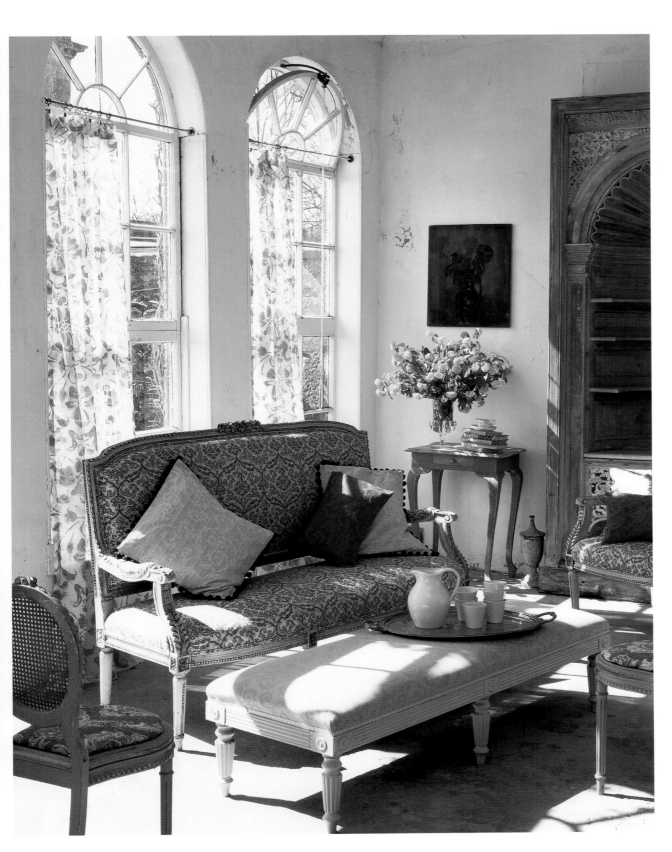

FAR LEFT Floral-patterned tile slips were often fitted in later 18th-century chimney-pieces, and usually either matched or echoed the floral designs found on upholstery and textile hangings.

CENTRE LEFT Chinese and European styles of ornament are evident in the upholstery and wallpaper in this reconstruction of a late 18th-century French interior. Highly fashionable at the time were flowers, birds and animals, set against vivid yellow grounds.

LEFT The curtain and upholstery fabrics in this late 18th-century drawing room are embellished with plant-form imagery typical of the period. While the top-covers on the painted and gilded chairs and settee show intricate and stylized floral and vegetal patterns, the curtains display naturalistic floral forms that were fashionable from the late 1760s onward.

PREVIOUS PAGES This late-18th-century, Rococo-style French bedroom has been reconstructed in a New York mansion apartment. The pale green walls and ceiling provide a complementary backdrop for a display of engraved fashion plates (published during the reign of Louis XVI of France) and embroidered silk panels. The tasselled draperies on the *lit à la polonaise* are striped and floral Belgian cotton, taken from a documentary design, and are colour co-ordinated with the walls and the floral-patterned table cover.

Early 19th Century

During the early 19th century, interior decoration was still essentially Neo-classical. However, the predominant styles of the period – Empire and Regency – contrasted with the often intricate detailing of late 18th-century Neo-classicism in their employment of purer, simpler Classical forms. They drew inspiration not only from ancient Roman and Greek ornament, but also, in celebration of Napoleon's conquests, from ancient Egyptian and contemporary military motifs.

Empire style originated in France during the late 1790s in the post-revolutionary restorations of French palaces. The basic architectural style of these palaces was Classical, and mostly derived from Imperial Roman rather than Greek examples. Typical motifs applied to architectural fixtures and fittings, furniture and drapery included laurel wreaths, medallions and imperial eagles, as well as animals such as swans and lions.

From c. 1820, regional variations began to appear. These included the gradual transformation of American Empire style into a Greek Revival, in which motifs and imagery of Roman origin were supplanted by those of Greek derivation, and, in Britain, the introduction of Regency style, which had much in common with French Empire but which drew more heavily on Greek ornament and incorporated elements of *chinoiserie*. In Austria and Germany a simpler, more functional version of French Empire – known as Biedermeier style – grew in popularity.

A key element of these early 19th-century Neo-classical styles included an increase in the use of fitted cut-pile or Brussels-weave carpets. In most houses, ceilings were generally lower than before and of plain plaster, embellished with a central medallion or garland (from which a chandelier was hung). In larger houses, walls were often divided into frieze, field and dado; in smaller ones the frieze was often omitted in favour of a simple cornice.

ABOVE Striped fabrics, often embellished with trailing flowers or floral repeats, were the height of fashion in Neo-classical American, English and, as here, French interiors during the early 19th century.

RIGHT & LEFT These two early 19th-century interiors at the Morris Jumel Mansion in New York are decorated and furnished in Empire style. Both feature Neo-classical wallpapers, applied to make a tripartite division of the walls. The day-bed and *lit-en-bateau* are decorated with Classical and Egyptian motifs.

Fashionable wall-coverings included flat paint, textiles and wallpapers (mainly pictorial). Swagged and tailed or festooned draperies were also popular, and were usually tied back to flank embroidered lace under-curtains or plain silk blinds. Favoured fabrics for draperies included lightweight silks and floral-patterned chintzes, while damasks and reps proved popular for upholstered seating. Painted *faux* finishes – marbles, porphyries, bronze and woodgrains – were also much in evidence.

Neo-classical furniture was mostly made from mahogany, maple and rosewood. Popular styles included sofa, Pembroke, Loo, and combined work-and-games tables, bow-fronted sideboards and *chiffoniers*, sabre-leg chairs, and *lit-en-bateau* and *chaises-longues*. A new development was the permanent groupings of chairs and tables in reception rooms to facilitate conversation.

ABOVE Re-decorated in its original colour scheme of mauve and yellow, this bedroom in an early 19th-century American mansion in New York features a Federal four-poster bed with an elegant tented and swagged silk canopy.

RIGHT A collection of Duncan Phyfe furniture stands on a hand-woven fitted Savonnerie carpet. The Neo-classical furnishings are enhanced by *faux* marble panelling on the walls.

PREVIOUS PAGES This Welsh interior features a velvet-upholstered *chaise-longue* and a floral-patterned French Aubusson carpet.

FOLLOWING PAGES Vivid yellow walls, drapes and upholstery provide strong colour contrast to the mahogany and ebony furniture in this typical early 19th-century reception room.

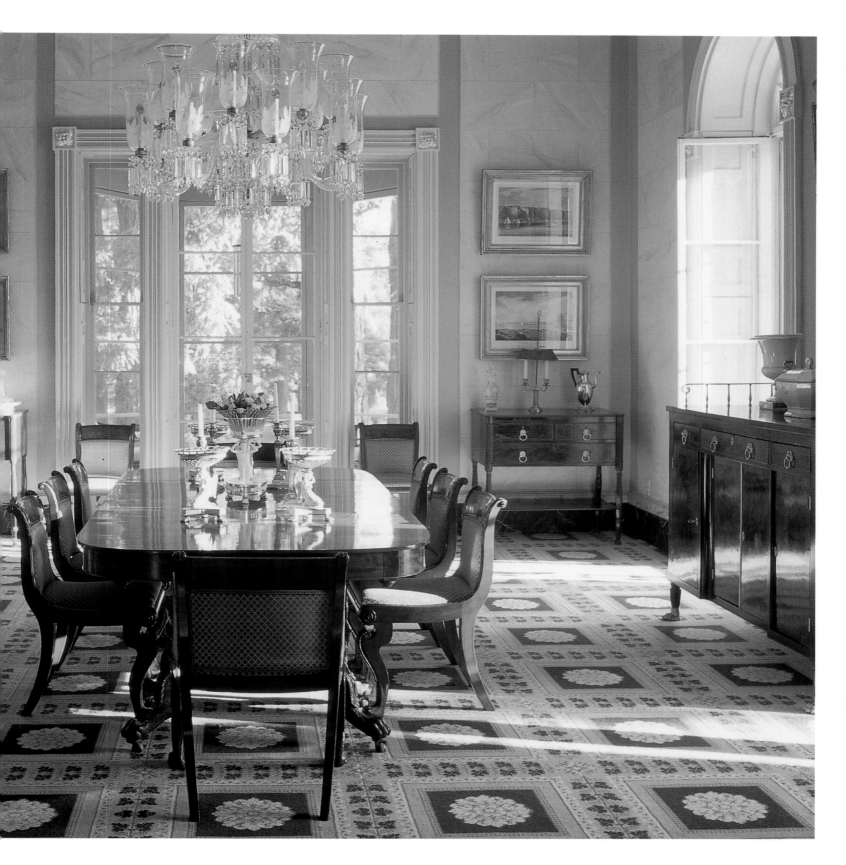

STYLE GUIDE: EARLY 19TH CENTURY

Mid-19th Century

During the middle of the 19th century, an eclectic mix of decorative styles was fashionable on both sides of the Atlantic, the majority of which were revivals of popular styles from previous centuries. They included a Renaissance Revival, based on the 16th-century use of Classical forms (mainly Roman) and relics of Medieval Gothic style; a Baroque Revival (known as Second Empire style in France), which followed the Renaissance Revival and employed Classical architectural detailing, imagery and motifs that were very similar to those employed in the original Baroque style of the 17th century; and a Rococo Revival, derived from the flamboyant 18th-century French Rococo, especially favoured in boudoirs, bedrooms and ladies' drawing rooms. There was also a Greek Revival, a strand of early 19th-century Neo-classicism particularly fashionable in the United States and Britain, and a Gothic Revival, which, unlike the romanticized Gothick style of the late 18th century, was characterized by historically accurate re-creations of Medieval Gothic styles of ornament. In addition to these historic revivals, styles appeared that included motifs and imagery derived from Chinese, Persian, Indian and Arabic ornament, and from primitive African and South American art. These were brought about through increased trade, as well as the travels of architects and ornamentists such as Owen Jones, whose *Grammar of Ornament* (1856) was highly influential.

Although the range of revival or "historical" styles was extensive, and different styles were often employed in different rooms within the same house, most mid-19th-century interiors incorporated a number of common decorative elements. For example, in grander houses, marble slabs or tiles were used on the floors of entrance areas, while in less affluent dwellings simulations of these in linoleum provided a cheaper alternative. However, in most rooms, wooden floorboards were the norm;

ABOVE The smoking room at Cedar Grove, a mid-19th-century American mansion, features a pair of deep red, gold-fringed velvet drapes with elaborate swagged and tailed valances. The carpet is also red and gold – a popular colour combination in mid-Victorian interiors.

RIGHT Ceramic tiles and marble slabs were often employed as floor-coverings in the entrance areas and ground-level hallways of Victorian houses. Geometric patterns were fashionable in the mid-19th century.

LEFT Eclectic groupings of red and yellow damask and striped plush upholstered chairs were often to be found in mid- and late Victorian interiors. However, the dominant feature of this English, Gothic Revival room is the magnificent chimney-piece with its gilded wood and plaster mouldings.

RIGHT Large-scale panoramic or scenic papers were very popular in grander houses in the United States during the middle of the 19th century. Most of them were designed in France by companies such as Zuber, and they were exported in considerable numbers after the fall of Napoleon in 1815. This example shows a sight-seeing tour on a steamboat to the bottom of Niagara Falls.

LEFT The parlour of the 19th-century Monmouth House, in Natchez, Mississippi, USA, is furnished with mid-19th-century mahogany furniture. This armchair, like the rest of the suite, is upholstered with a pale blue silk damask patterned with vases, urns and plant forms derived from Graeco-Roman Classical ornament. The drapes behind are made from the same fabric and secured with rope-and-tassel tie-backs.

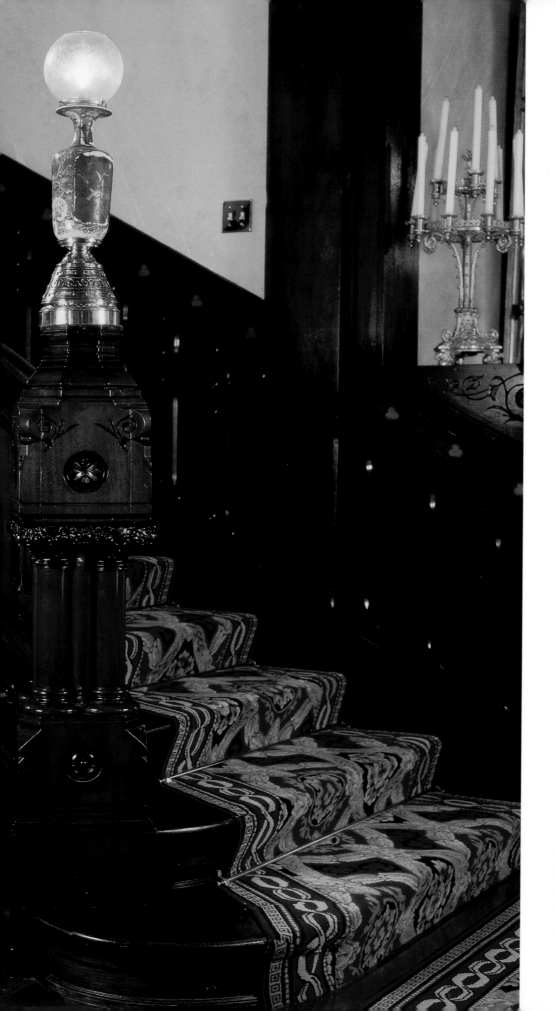

these were covered with either a centrally placed, patterned carpet or floorcloth, with the borders stained and polished, stencilled, flat-painted or laid as parquet. Plaster mouldings (cornices and central medallions) – often highly elaborate – also came back into fashion and, while many were flat-painted in a single colour, others were vibrantly polychromatic.

After c. 1860, most walls were divided into the classic division of frieze, field and dado. Silk hangings remained a fashionable, if expensive, choice in affluent households, and flat-painting (often augmented with repeat stencil motifs at dado- and picture-rail height) was also employed. However, wallpaper was the principal form of covering following the development of mass-production printing techniques, which made it affordable for the rapidly expanding middle classes.

Faux marble and woodgrained finishes were much in evidence on doors and other woodwork, and on softwood fire-surrounds – the latter a more economical substitute for surrounds made of marble, granite, cast iron and hardwoods such as mahogany. Solid and veneered hardwood furniture was also produced in vast quantities during this period to complement the numerous historical styles. However, the most characteristic pieces were upholstered chairs, settees and sofas, mostly sumptuously stuffed, often deep-buttoned and augmented with cushions, and found in large numbers. The fashion for heavyweight fabrics was extended to the elaborate, layered window treatments of the period, with lined damask, velvet (or plush) and rep much in evidence, topped by large pelmets and drawn or tied back over lace or muslin insertions (either plain or intricately patterned). There was also a profusion of paintings, prints and collections of decorative artefacts, the latter displayed on mantelshelves, in glass-fronted cabinets or on built-in open shelving.

ABOVE This New York interior bears all the hallmarks of the mid-19th-century American Gothic Revival style: these include subdued lighting and ranks of gilt-framed paintings hung against a diaper-pattern wallpaper.

LEFT Standing on a tiled floor in the hall of a manoir near Bordeaux in France, this mid-19th-century mahogany armchair retains its original floral-pattern, cut-velvet upholstery.

FAR LEFT Many stair runners in mid-19th-century houses, as in this American example, displayed either stylized or naturalistic floral patterns set within borders that featured repeated geometric motifs.

Late 19th Century

During the last three decades of the 19th century, the fashion for employing different historical or period-revival styles in different rooms of the same house was still prevalent in Europe and America. It was not unusual to find a Medieval dining room, a Louis XIV drawing room, a Rococo parlour, a Gothic library and a Moresque boudoir under the same roof. However, in the late 1860s a reaction to this eclecticism began to emerge among leading artists and designers, such as William Morris and Charles Eastlake. They wished not only to reintroduce a more coherent decorative style, but also to reduce the "clutter" of Victorian interiors and to re-establish the aesthetic and constructional qualities of pre-industrial, hand-crafted furnishings in the wake of the plethora of poorly designed factory-made goods.

The two closely related styles at the forefront of this reaction to eclectism were the Aesthetic and the Arts and Crafts movements. Both were primarily styles of decoration dependent almost entirely for effect upon colour and pattern, rather than on a particular architectural style. They were successfully applied to houses as architecturally diverse as 15th- or 16th-century, stone-built or timber-framed manor houses, 18th-century townhouses and 19th-century terraces.

The motifs and imagery that appeared on Aesthetic and Arts and Crafts wallpapers, tiles, furniture, soft furnishings and artefacts were derived from Classical, Medieval (Gothic), Renaissance and Chinese and Japanese vocabularies of ornament, with oriental artefacts and motifs being especially favoured by Aesthetic movement designers. Apart from design and good craftsmanship, key elements in Aesthetic and Arts and Crafts schemes included a tripartite division of the walls into frieze, field and dado using three interrelated but distinct wallpaper patterns; colour co-ordination of overmantels to match either the walls or furniture; stained or

ABOVE Swagged, bullion-fringed, silk damask drapes hang in the sitting room at the Calhoun Mansion built in the 1870s in South Carolina, USA.

RIGHT A silk canopy, lace hangings and a lace bedspread furnish this rosewood and walnut half-tester bed in the Garth Woodside Mansion, in Hannibal, Missouri, USA.

LEFT The window treatment at the Calhoun Mansion features silk drapes secured with bullion-fringed tie-backs. It has an elaborate pelmet swagged with matching silk. The deep-buttoned upholstery is also typical of later Victorian interiors.

flat-painted woodwork that acted as a foil for brightly coloured, vegetable- and mineral-dyed papers and fabrics; oriental rugs and carpets, or rush matting, laid over bare wooden floorboards; and groupings of furniture, pictures and ornaments.

In the 1890s, Art Nouveau emerged in Europe and Britain. Peaking in popularity around the turn of the century, and generally out of favour by 1910, the movement took two distinct stylistic paths: one based on austerely elegant, elongated rectilinear forms and tight, precise floral ornament; the other composed of wild, flowing curvilinear elements characterized by restless whiplash lines. Design elements included the use of deep friezes and fields, and a revival in the use of stencilled decoration. "Greenery-yallery" colours such as olive, sage green and mustard were employed, as well as browns, lilacs, violets and muted purples. Stylized vegetal and bird motifs were popular, and there was a preference for artefacts such as ceramics and metalware over pictures. Window treatments were simple, with curtains of plain or mute-patterned fabrics, or abandoned altogether.

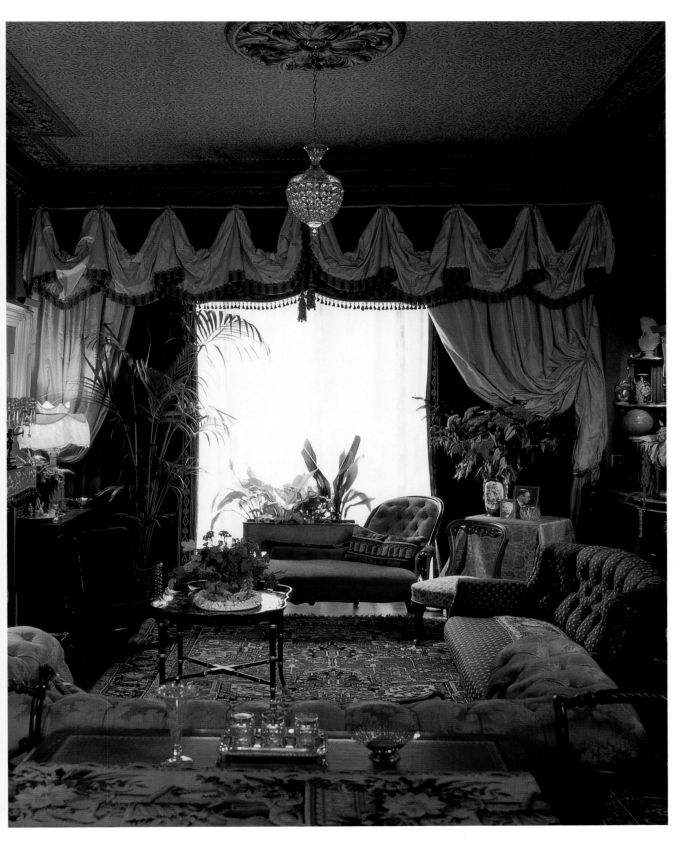

LEFT The eclectic nature of many Victorian interiors is shown here. Classical influence is evident in the window treatment and plaster mouldings, while Egyptian motifs adorn the canvaswork panel. The pile-woven rug is Middle Eastern and the upholstery is 19th-century European in style. The willow pattern featured on the ceiling paper is derived from Japanese ornament.

CENTRE LEFT This armchair is covered with a printed paisley pattern fabric that was very popular in late 19th-century interiors. The design is based on pinecones and small incidental motifs found on Indian fabrics. The leopard-spot cushion cover is a typical example of the exotic *faux* animal-skin fabrics favoured at this time.

FAR LEFT The late 19th-century fascination with oriental ornament can be seen in Françoise Lafon's Egyptian-style bedroom. The striped wallpaper and flat-weave carpet are inspired by patterns found on Egyptian textiles. The sand-yellow, pale blue and green colour scheme is also quintessentially Egyptian – the green being *eau-de-nil* (Nile-water green).

PREVIOUS PAGES The Arts and Crafts movement was as influential in the United States in the late 19th century as it was in England, its country of origin. The oak furniture and wall-panelling in this American interior are highly representative of the style. The wallpaper frieze illustrates the extent to which Medieval styles of decoration were rekindled in Arts and Crafts designs.

Early 20th Century

ABOVE This Art Deco living room is in the Geffrye Museum in London, England. It includes abstract-patterned carpeting, geometrically patterned upholstery and an asymmetrical, mottled-tile fire-surround.

LEFT Chocolate brown, black, cream and yellow are recurring colours in Art Deco interiors. The zebra-skin rug laid over a complementary coloured carpet is also typical of the style.

A number of revivalist styles were fashionable in the early 20th century on both sides of the Atlantic. However, the two styles that dominated the period were Art Deco and Modernism.

The term Art Deco was first coined in 1925, and used to describe the displays at the *Exposition Internationale des Arts Décoratifs et Industriels Modernes*. The style was derived from elements in the work of the Deutscher Werkbund and the Wiener Werkstätte, from the early 20th-century art movements of Cubism, Expressionism, Futurism and Fauvism, and from African and native South American art. Prior to the mid-1920s, Art Deco was characterized by the use of rounded and romantic motifs such as garlands and rosebuds. However, during the late 1920s and 1930s these were superseded by abstract and geometric motifs, Egyptian imagery, South American stepped shapes and sun motifs, and emblems suggesting speed and dynamism. Art Deco style was epitomized by clean lines and smooth planes in walls, ceilings, floors and joinery; by contrasting-coloured walls and woodwork; by textiles with geometric or bold floral patterns; and by plump, upholstered sofas and armchairs and other furniture, often veneered with exotic woods or lacquered in black, scarlet or pale yellow and embellished with *chinoiserie* motifs.

Modernist architecture and decoration, avidly adopted on both sides of the Atlantic between the First and Second World Wars, was based upon a desire to render the home, in the words of architect and designer Le Corbusier, a "machine for living in". In practice, this involved shunning unnecessary ornament and highlighting the industrial origins of modern building materials, furniture and textiles. Elements included the use of chrome and glass furniture and fittings, pale walls and ceilings, abstract- or geometric-patterned curtains and carpets (often laid over parquet flooring), and the minimum of displayed artefacts.

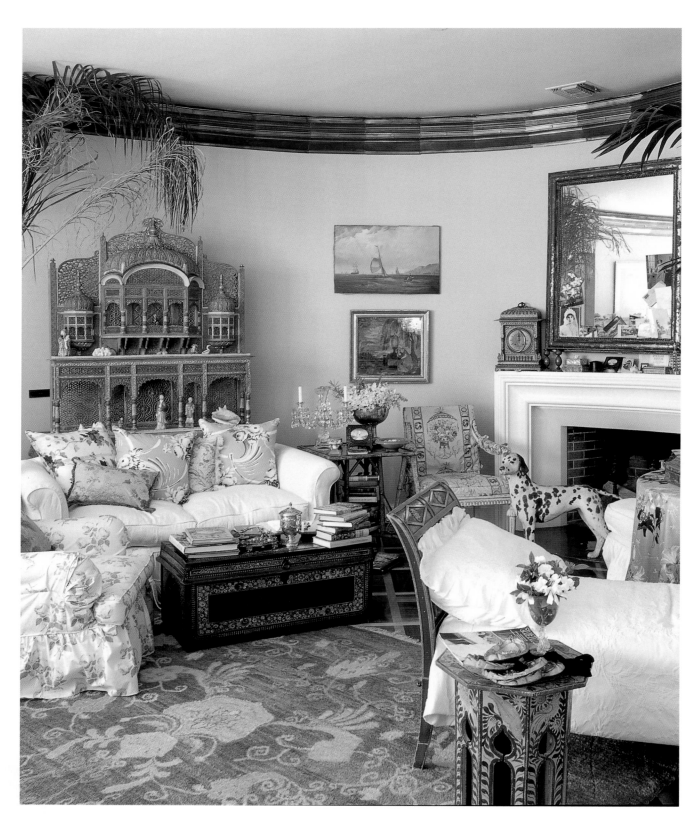

LEFT Light colour schemes were very fashionable during the early 20th century. In this eclectic interior, the mint-green painted walls and ceiling provide an unobtrusive and complementary background for the furnishings. Oriental influence is evident in the display cabinet, table-covering and in the stylized plant forms on the rug. African ornament is represented by the *faux* leopard-skin lamp shades, and in the Egyptian motifs on the upholstered chair by the fireplace. The latter is also embellished with Neo-classical floral motifs.

RIGHT Traditional striped and floral patterns remained fashionable for wallpapers during the first half of the 20th century. In this bedroom they are combined in a paper that displays broad blue and white stripes embellished with naturalistic blooms and bouquets (some depicted in Classical Graeco-Roman vases) inspired by 18th-century French decoration.

Late 20th and Early 21st Century

Two broad, discernible trends have been apparent in interior design and decoration since the end of the Second World War: one largely retrospective, the other essentially futuristic. Within the latter category, many architects, designers and manufacturers have enthusiastically embraced new imagery to create innovative styles that simply have not been seen before. The most prominent examples of this appeared from the late 1950s to the mid-1970s, and primarily involved the depiction on fabrics and wallpapers of cellular structures newly exposed by microphotography, and of striking figural, geometric and abstract motifs derived from Pop and Op fine art and Psychedelia. At the same time, new synthetic fibres, plastics and alloys were rapidly adapted to the manufacture of not only textiles and wallpaper, but also furniture – a constantly evolving process.

In contrast, the retrospective movement has been both more extensive and diverse. Comprising a range of historical-revival styles that have been either replications, adaptations or reinterpretations of the originals, it was initially fuelled by an aesthetic rejection of the unremitting rationality and

ABOVE Minimalism inspired by traditional Japanese interiors has been fashionable in the West since the late 20th century. This bedroom is characterized by clean lines, simplicity and lack of clutter.

LEFT The walls of Charles Jencks's 1980s Post-Modernist London residence are painted with colours – and stencilled with small motifs – symbolic of the four seasons. Both the fireplace and mantelshelf columns are *faux*-marbled.

RIGHT This Provençal sitting room, with its yellow-painted, rough-plastered walls, rush seating and earth-coloured upholstery, conveys a sophisticated view of rural calm and simplicity.

minimal use of colour and pattern that characterized Modernist interiors earlier in the 20th century. In many cases this has involved restoring period homes to their original decorative styles, and in many others it has taken the form of often strikingly inventive recolouring and patterning of originally plain, unornamented, Modernist architectural shells.

Specific examples of style revivals in Britain and Europe have included an Art Nouveau revival in the 1960s and early 1970s, and an Art Deco revival in the 1970s and 1980s, while in America Colonial and Federal styles proved fashionable once again during the 1980s and 1990s. Less specific examples have included the "country-house" look, based on the comfortable, chintz-covered rural interiors of the late 19th and early 20th century, but now applied to both urban and rural houses, and a general revival of medieval and, especially, Classical motifs and imagery – Classicism, in all its manifestations, being the least faddish and most enduringly fashionable style of the late 20th and early 21st century.

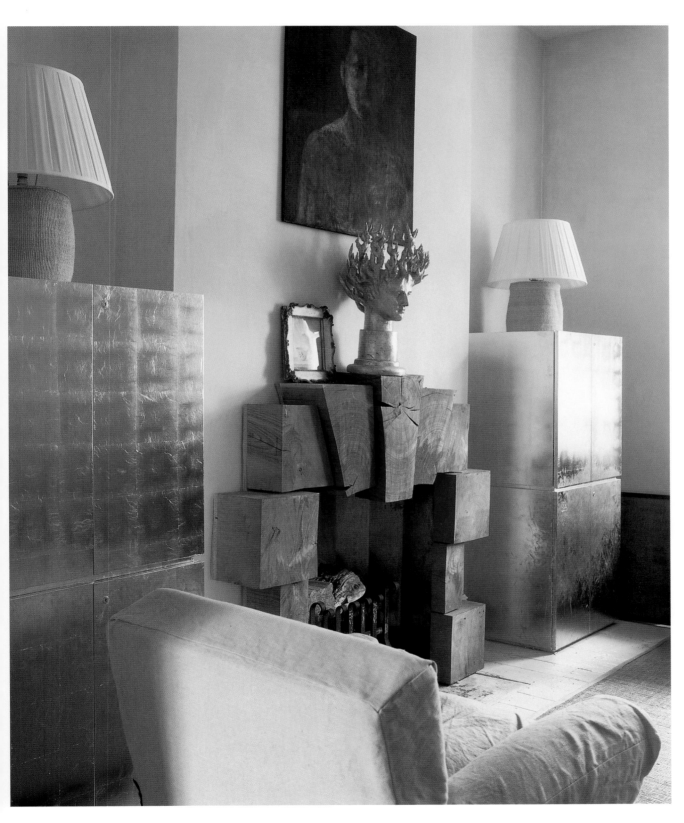

LEFT Colours, textures and geometric forms, rather than applied patterns, lie at the heart of this late 20th-century decorative scheme. The most striking features of the room are a stone-block fire-surround and a pair of storage cabinets finished with gold leaf. These have been set against an unobtrusive backdrop of mottled green and yellow.

CENTRE LEFT Pale colour schemes incorporating plain or delicate floral-patterned fabrics proved a fashionable treatment for bedrooms for much of the 20th century, particularly from the 1980s.

FAR LEFT During the latter years of the 20th century, some fabric manufacturers, such as Liberty, took traditional patterns and motifs and re-presented them in exciting new colourways. The leaf and sprig motifs on the upholstered chairs boast hot pink and yellow grounds, a theme taken up in the bold, floral-striped curtains and in the coordinated floral-check runner on the table.

In addition to the revival of styles associated with a particular historical period or periods, there has also been a surge in the adoption of the traditional decorative styles of other geographical areas or cultures. Notable imports from the 1980s onward include Japanese-style minimalism – the Post-Modern Modernism; the southern Mediterranean palette, with its luminous whites, dusty terracottas and splashes of pure, vibrant colour; the earth tones and hot candy hues of old rural and modern urban Mexican architecture; and the cooling and/or exotic interiors of North and West Africa.

Significantly, successful reinterpretations or re-creations of all these traditional decorative styles have been made ever more feasible by responsive manufacturers and importers. Quite simply, the ranges of suitable fabrics, wallpapers, tiles, paints and flooring – the building blocks of style – are now more extensive than ever before.

LEFT The understated elegance of African Ivory and Gold Coast interiors is recreated by the designer Decarpentrie in his house in Brussels, Belgium. Flagstone floors, off-white walls, muted-colour textiles and dark-brown wooden furniture and architectural fixtures (the latter often intricately carved) create a cool colour scheme that would offer respite in the fiercest of climates.

BELOW LEFT Late 18th- and early 19th-century Neo-classical style is revived in the living room of Bill Blass's New York apartment. The butt-jointed floorboards, dentilled cornice, marble columns, classical busts and late-Georgian furniture (including daybeds upholstered in a typical Regency stripe) are all period authentic. The colour scheme of whites, creams and shades of brown carried over from the architectural shell to the soft furnishings recalls the elegant simplicity of many Directoire interiors.

FAR LEFT North African Moorish style resonates throughout Zaza Van Hulle's Paris apartment. Geometric-patterned floor tiles, brass trays and lamps, Moroccan-style banquettes, vegetable-dyed kelims and floor cushions, and a profusion of towering vegetation transport the owner from temperate, northern European reality.

FOLLOWING PAGES Classical inspiration is also evident in this sitting room by French designer Yves Gastou. Inherent in the linear symmetry of the architectural shell, it is reinforced by marble statuary and wall-hung torchères, and echoed in the scroll motifs of the carpet. The painting firmly establishes the room as late-20th to early 21st century. However, its yellow, mauve and blue colours – like the rust-reds, terracottas, greys and greens of the soft furnishings – also recall the earth and vegetable pigments of classical antiquity.

Fabrics

Plain Fabrics

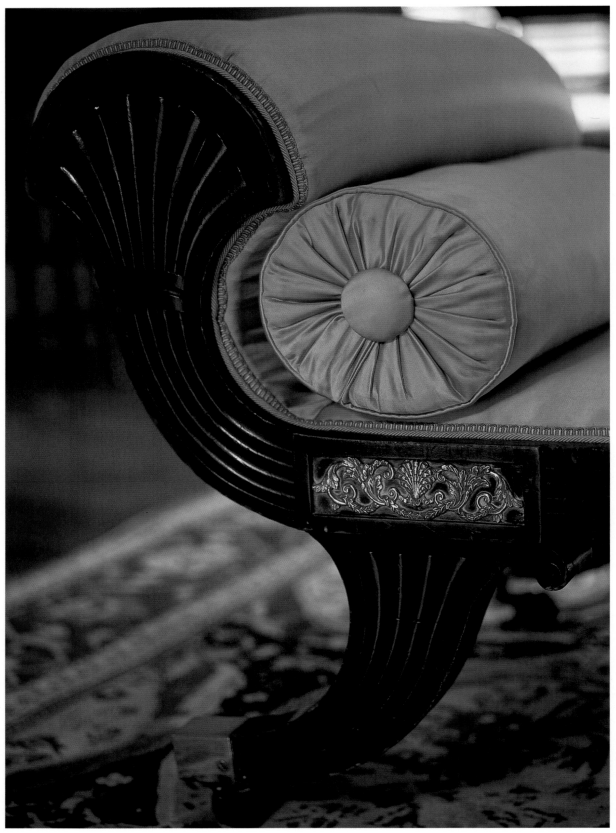

Single-colour cloths not embellished with woven or printed patterns are known collectively as "plains", their appeal residing in their colour or texture, or both. Plains include taffetas, cambric, canvas, calico and some tweeds, which have a plain ("tabby") weave of uniform warp and weft threads that pass alternately over and under one another. However, many other fabrics traditionally ascribed to the plains category belie the description "plain" in one of three ways.

First, many "plains" are "self-patterned" by variations within their weave: these include seersuckers, in which alternate bands of tight and slack warps create a puckered effect; ribbed fabrics, such as poplin and rep, which have thick and thin yarns; and zig-zag herringbones. Second, many neutral-colour fabrics, such as slubby silks and noiles, display more than one colour as a result of the presence of naturally occurring "specks" in the fibres. And third, some "plains", such as silk moirés, are dyed one colour, but show variations in tone as a result of "hot-pressing" during the manufacturing process.

LEFT A detail of an Empire-style mahogany daybed, made *c.* 1815 in New York for Nathaniel Russell House, in South Carolina, USA. The bed and its matching bolster are upholstered with a plain yellow silk top-cover that complements the carved and gilded panels (scrolling foliage and shell motifs) along the sides of the bed.

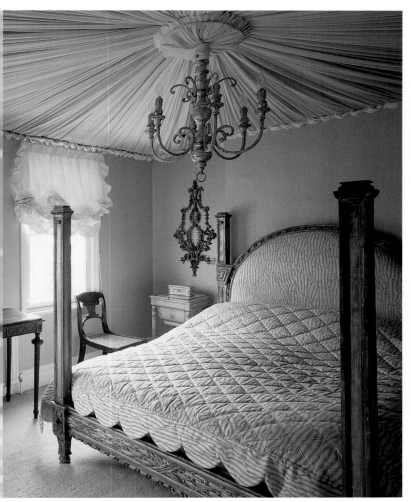

ABOVE Tented ceilings were particularly fashionable in France and England in the early 19th century. They have their origins in the military camps and tournaments of the Middle Ages, and were revived during the Napoleonic wars. The ruched yellow silk example shown here is in a 20th-century re-creation of a Regency bedroom.

COTTON DUCK

Although most fabrics are used for the same purposes today as they were in centuries past, some are now employed in ways never originally intended. For example, cotton duck – the name is derived from the glazed surface which sheds water – is a strong, thick cloth (finer than canvas). During the 19th century it was made of linen and was used to make sails, cooks' aprons, tents and physicians' coats. Nowadays, however, it is often made up into durable slip-covers for chairs and sofas.

KEY DESIGNS

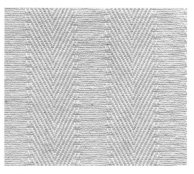

1 Plain-woven fabrics have been made from durable coarse and fine linen since the Middle Ages. Slight stiffness and ease of creasing has made linen weaves better suited to upholstery than to draping.

2 Plain or neutral-coloured herringbones are subtly "self-patterned". Usually made from cotton or linen, they have become increasingly fashionable for upholstery and hangings during the 20th century.

3 Plain-coloured pile fabrics, such as cut or uncut velvets and velours, have been favoured since the Renaissance, and used for upholstered furniture in particular in mid-19th-century interiors.

4 Many plains are employed for their texture as much as for their colour – coarseness of texture being determined by type of weave and thickness of yarn(s), in this case a cotton-viscose mix.

5 Fine plain-weave cottons are well-suited to monochromatic dyeing – both vegetable and synthetic. As they drape well they are often employed for window- and bed-hangings, and for loose covers.

6 Plain-weave silks are also ideal for monochromatic dyeing, and display pure, saturated colours that have been exploited by interior designers from the Renaissance to the present day.

1 De Le Cuona/Hopsack Moss Colour **F4** Alt. colours **yes** Composition **100% linen** Width **140cm/55in** Repeat – Price ★★ 🛋️ LC 🪑

2 Ian Mankin/Stripe Jacquard Colour **natural** Alt. colours **no** Composition **100% cotton** Width **137cm/54in** Repeat – Price ★ LC 🪑 ▦ 🛋️

3 Jab/Maharadscha Colour **red** Alt. colours **yes** Composition **100% silk** Width **122cm/ 48in** Repeat – Price ★★ 🪑 ▦ 🛋️

4 Harlequin/Assisi/Siena Colour **433** Alt. colours **yes** Composition **13% cotton, 87% viscose** Width **140cm/55in** Repeat – Price ★★ 🛋️ 🪑

5 Olicana/Calypso Colour **cayman blue** Alt. colours **yes** Composition **100% cotton** Width **145cm/57in** Repeat – Price ★★ 🪑 🛋️

6 Seamoor Fabrics/Kaleidoscope Colour **crushed rose** Alt. colours **yes** Composition **100% cotton** Width **120cm/47in** Repeat – Price ★ 🪑

Plains

Some plain neutral-coloured furnishing fabrics are produced by tinting the fibres from which they are made with pale dyes (either vegetable or synthetic). Other "neutrals", such as cambric, are bleached to whiten the fibres. However, many of the "neutrals" considered fashionable in this and previous centuries rely for colour on the natural pigmentation of their fibre(s). Notable examples include unbleached calico, which is a creamy colour relieved by small brown flecks of cottonseed that remain in the cotton yarn; brown Holland, an unbleached, closely woven, pale brown linen popular for window shades during the 18th and 19th centuries; black and white horsehair fabrics, woven from unadulterated horsehair of those colours and favoured for upholstery since the 18th century; neutral-coloured slub silks and noiles, which display the grainy brown specks inherent in natural, unbleached silk fibre; and Tussah silk, produced from cocoons spun by wild silkworms, which produce a textured, pale brown yarn.

1

2

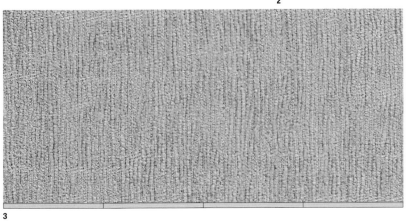

3

1 **De Le Cuona/Storm Italian Straw** Colour **NN2** Alt. colours **yes** Composition **100% linen** Width **140cm/55in** Repeat – Price ★★★ 🛋

2 **De Le Cuona/Peasant Cloth String** Colour **AA1** Alt. colours **yes** Composition **100% linen** Width **135cm/53in** Repeat – Price ★★★ LC 🗔🗔🛋

3 **Harlequin/Assissi/Siena** Colour **431** Alt. colours **yes** Composition **13% cotton, 87% viscose** Width **140cm/55in** Repeat – Price ★★ 🛋🗔

4 **De Le Cuona/Shale Butterscotch** Colour **BB3** Alt. colours **yes** Composition **100% linen** Width **150cm/59in** Repeat – Price ★★★ 🗔

5 **Ian Sanderson/Sophia** Colour **creme** Alt. colours **yes** Composition **83% viscose, 17% cotton** Width **140cm/55in** Repeat – Price ★★ 🛋

4

5

6 **Malabar/Flote** Colour **Caramel** Alt. colours **yes** Composition **72% cotton, 28% viscose** Width **135cm/53in** Repeat – Price ★★ 🗔🗔🛋

7 **De Le Cuona/Coast Jade** Colour **H1** Alt. colours **yes** Composition **100% linen** Width **148cm/58¼in** Repeat – Price ★★★ 🗔🛋LC

8 **Ian Sanderson/Verity Silk** Colour **Duck Egg** Alt. colours **yes** Composition **55% silk, 45% linen** Width **140cm/55in** Repeat – Price ★★ 🗔🗔W

6

HORSEHAIR FABRIC

Woven from horse mane and tail hairs on a silk, cotton, linen or wool warp, horsehair fabric has been used for upholstery since the early 18th century, on Chippendale and Hepplewhite chairs notably. Favoured colours have included black, green, grey, gold, red and ivory.

John Boyd Textiles/Ricana RI/620/6 Colour **ivory** Alt. colours **yes** Composition **68% horsehair, 32% cotton** Width **56cm/22in** Repeat – Price ★★★ 🛋W

John Boyd Textiles/Criollo CR/227 Colour **light grey** Alt. colours **yes** Composition **68% horsehair, 32% cotton** Width **65cm/25½in** Repeat – Price ★★★ 🛋W

7

8

9

10

9 **De Le Cuona/Magma Velvet Sable** Colour **Y2** Alt. colours **yes** Composition **100% linen** Width **140cm/55in** Repeat – Price ★★★ ⌷LC⌷ 🛋 🛋

10 **Ian Mankin/Pavilion Jacquard** Colour **natural** Alt. colours **no** Composition **100% cotton** Width **137cm/54in** Repeat **2cm/¾in** Price ★ 🛋 🛋

11 **Hodsoll McKenzie/Plain Repp 356/101-106** Colour **natural** Alt. colours **yes** Composition **76% cotton, 24% silk** Width **127cm/50in** Repeat – Price ★★★ 🛋 🛋 ⌷W⌷

12 **Brunschwig & Fils/Petassoun Matelassé 89462** Colour **008 ivory** Alt. colours **yes** Composition **72% cotton, 28% viscose** Width **147cm/ 58in** Repeat **36cm/14in** Price ★★★ 🛋

13 **Marvic Textiles/Misa Moiré Plain 6565-54** Colour **daisy** Alt. colours **yes** Composition **52% linen, 48% viscose** Width **140cm/55in** Repeat – Price ★★ 🛋 🛋

11

12   13

14

14 **Olicana/Finistere** Colour **white** Alt. colours **no** Composition **100% cotton** Width **130cm/51in** Repeat – Price ★★ 🛋 🛋

15 **De Le Cuona/Hornbuckle Milk** Colour **NNN4** Alt. colours **yes** Composition **50% wool, 50% polyester** Width **150cm/59in** Repeat – Price ★★ 🛋

16 **De Le Cuona/Shale True Taupe** Colour **BB5** Alt. colours **yes** Composition **100% linen** Width **150cm/59in** Repeat – Price ★★★ 🛋

17 **Harlequin/Metzo** Colour **690** Alt. colours **yes** Composition **92% polyester, 8% viscose** Width **140cm/55in** Repeat – Price ★★ 🛋

18 **Larsen/Cybele L8565** Colour **10 Silver Dust** Alt. colours **yes** Composition **51% nylon, 49% polyester** Width **150cm/ 59in** Repeat – Price ★★ 🛋

19 **Marvic Textiles/Moiré Celeste 47-4** Colour **primula** Alt. colours **yes** Composition **39% cotton, 35% viscose, 26% linen** Width **150cm/59in** Repeat – Price ★★ 🛋 🛋 ⌷W⌷

15   16

17   18

19

Plains

Plain fabrics rely heavily on both their colour and their texture for decorative effect. The appearance of any particular colour is affected by a number of factors, ranging from the texture of the fabric and the nature of the weave to the angle and intensity of natural or artificial light to which the fabric is exposed. In other words, the same coloured dye will look markedly different on a ribbed wool or worsted rep (a closely woven ribbed fabric) from how it will on a smooth satin-weave silk. However, the look of colour is affected by more than the physical properties of the fibres to which the colour is applied and the environmental conditions under which the fabrics are used and displayed. The nature of the pigments used also contributes to the appearance of a plain fabric. For example, in the mid-19th century synthetic aniline dyes were developed by extracting benzine oil from coal tar and combining it with acids. The result was a wide range of new, vibrantly coloured pigments that appeared gradually from the 1850s to the 1880s. Notable among them were "mauveine", magenta, various purple-blues and greens, Manchester brown and yellow, Congo blue and a synthetic substitute for indigo.

Jab/Maharadscha 6943-211 Colour **orange** Alt. colours **yes** Composition **100% silk** Width **122cm/48in** Repeat – Price ★★

Osborne & Little/Ghillie Wool F1241 Colour **02** Alt. colours **yes** Composition **92% wool, 8% nylon** Width **140cm/55in** Repeat – Price ★★★

Zimmer & Rohde/Option 1910 Colour **162** Alt. colours **yes** Composition **52% cotton, 48% polyester** Width **140cm/55in** Repeat – Price ★★★

Abbott & Boyd/Albarracin 9740-0 Colour **cream** Alt. colours **yes** Composition **70% cotton, 28% viscose, 2% polyester** Width **138cm/54in** Repeat – Price ★★★

Scalamandré/Adriatic Antique Taffeta 5870-028 Colour **maize** Alt. colours **yes** Composition **100% silk** Width **142cm/55¾in** Repeat – Price ★★★

Monkwell/MF 5787 Colour **806 Bison Cherry** Alt. colours **yes** Composition **98% polyester, 2% cotton** Width **137cm/53¾in** Repeat – Price ★

Olicana/Yachting Cotton Colour **red rag** Alt. colours **yes** Composition **100% cotton** Width **137cm/54in** Repeat – Price ★★

Zimmer & Rohde/Priya 6989-226 Colour **tan** Alt. colours **yes** Composition **100% silk** Width **120cm/47in** Repeat – Price ★★★

Osborne & Little/Nomad Plain Moiré F1281 Colour **02** Alt. colours **yes** Composition **36% viscose, 32% wool, 16% cotton, 16% polyamide** Width **140cm/55in** Repeat – Price ★★★ 🛋

Abbott & Boyd/Traviata Colour **05** Alt. colours **yes** Composition **77% viscose, 23% polyamide** Width **140cm/55in** Repeat – Price ★★★★ 🪟 🛋

Harlequin/Assisi/Siena Colour **436** Alt. colours **yes** Composition **13% cotton, 87% viscose** Width **140cm/55in** Repeat – Price ★★ 🛋🪟

Donghia/Piega 0488/9325 Colour **18** Alt. colours **yes** Composition **55% cotton, 23% polyester, 13% polyacrylic, 9% viscose** Width **133cm/52in** Repeat – Price ★★★★ 🛋

Osborne & Little/F5023 Colour **05** Alt. colours **yes** Composition **82% (poly)cotton, 18% polyester/viscose** Width **145cm/57in** Repeat – Price ★★★ 🪟 🛋

Ian Sanderson/Sophia Colour **sungold** Alt. colours **yes** Composition **83% viscose, 17% cotton** Width **140cm/55in** Repeat – Price ★★ 🪟 🛋

Jab/Tosca 1-6048 Colour **449** Alt. colours **yes** Composition **100% silk** Width **140cm/55in** Repeat – Price ★★★ 🪟

Zimmer & Rohde/Tango 9215 Colour **371** Alt. colours **yes** Composition **100% viscose** Width **140cm/55in** Repeat – Price ★★ 🛋 Ⓦ

Plains

Synthetic dyes and colours were first introduced in the 1850s and continued to be developed and used during the 20th century. However, many consider that they can never match the chromatic intensity and purity of colour obtained from traditional vegetable dyes – a contemporary view that echoes William Morris's negative reaction to the artificiality and "garishness" of the aniline dyes of the 19th century and his advocacy of a return to the use of vegetable and mineral dyes.

There is no doubt that, when it comes to colour, new technology and increased industrialization do not automatically equate to higher quality. Indeed, the brilliance, intensity, subtle variation and diversity of hue of vegetable dyes used from the Middle Ages to the mid-19th century (and enjoying a revival today) will probably never be matched synthetically. For example, during the 17th century "drugs" from the Orient and the Americas, such as saffron, indigo, quercitron and brazilwood, were employed to produce a vast spectrum of tints, including greens as diverse as parakeet, emerald, carnation, duck and moss, and a palette of 12 different shades of blue.

6

1

3

4

5

7

8

9

1 Antico Setificio Fiorentino/ Tela di Seta T1 Colour green/gold Alt. colours yes Composition 100% silk Width 120cm/47in Repeat – Price ★★★ LC 🛋️ 🪑 W

2 Zimmer & Rohde/Donna 5083 Colour 583 Alt. colours yes Composition 77% cotton, 18% silk Width 132cm/51¾in Repeat – Price ★★★ 🛋️

3 Zoffany/Boston Plain BOS0101 Colour 6 Alt. colours yes Composition 95% viscose, 5% silk Width 144cm/56½in Repeat – Price ★★ LC 🛋️ 🪑🛋️

4 George Spencer Designs/ Strie 011L/09 Colour lime Alt. colours yes Composition 79% linen, 21% silk Width 140cm/55in Repeat – Price ★★★ 🛋️🪑

5 Designers Guild/Diagonale F563/11 Colour green Alt. colours yes Composition 100% cotton Width 140cm/55in Repeat – Price ★★ 🪑

6 Liberty Furnishings/Savile Weaves/Plain LF4171 Colour 10 Alt. colours yes Composition 100% wool Width 130cm/51in Repeat – Price ★★★ LC 🛋️ 🪑🪑 W

7 Antico Setificio Fiorentino/ Spinone Melangé 52 Colour green Alt. colours yes Composition 60% silk, 40% linen Width 130cm/51in Repeat – Price ★★★ 🛋️🪑

8 Marvic Textiles/Misa Moiré Plain 6565-56 Colour jungle Alt. colours yes Composition 52% linen, 48% viscose Width 140cm/55in Repeat – Price ★★ 🛋️🪑 W

9 Zimmer & Rohde/Alto 1928 Colour 718 Alt. colours yes Composition 53% cotton, 34% fleece wool, 13% polyester Width 140cm/55in Repeat – Price ★★★🪑

10

12

10 Malabar/Jutka Colour **sky** Alt. colours **yes** Composition **50% cotton, 50% linen** Width **137cm/53¾in** Repeat – Price ★★ 🔲 ▦ LC 🛋

11 Today Interiors/Silki SK 23 Colour **windsor blue** Alt. colours **yes** Composition **57% viscose, 31% cotton, 12% polyester** Width **140cm/55in** Repeat – Price ★★ 🔲 🛋

12 Zimmer & Rohde/Corela 1913 Colour **663** Alt. colours **yes** Composition **57% cotton, 43% viscose** Width **140cm/55in** Repeat – Price ★★ 🛋

13 Malabar/Suliman Colour **cochineal** Alt. colours **yes** Composition **100% silk** Width **122cm/48in** Repeat – Price ★★ 🔲 ▦

14 Olicana/Calypso Colour **paradisian pink** Alt. colours **yes** Composition **100% cotton** Width **145cm/57in** Repeat – Price ★★ 🔲 🛋

15 Liberty Furnishings/Plume Chenille LF4280 Colour **18** Alt. colours **yes** Composition **45% viscose, 30% cotton, 25% polyester** Width **146cm/57½in** Repeat – Price ★★ LC 🔲 🛋

13   14   15

16

MOIRÉS

Fashionable since the early 18th century, moirés are ribbed fabrics on to which clouded or watered (wave-like) effects are imposed by passing them between heavy iron or copper rollers. Traditionally, the fabric is left dry while it is subjected to intense, uneven pressure from the rollers. However, liquid and heat can also be applied. Most moirés are made of heavy silk, but some are wool or worsted. From the 20th century moirés have often been made from rayon or are a mixture of cotton and viscose.

Marvic Textiles/Marvic Moiré 45-27 Colour **leman** Alt. colours **yes** Composition **58% cotton, 42% viscose** Width **136cm/53½in** Repeat – Price ★★ 🔲 🛋 W

17

18   19

16 Zimmer & Rohde/Idris 6991-556 Colour **blue** Alt. colours **yes** Composition **100% silk** Width **135cm/53in** Repeat – Price ★★★ 🔲 🛋

17 Designers Guild/Laelia F558/01 Colour **blue** Alt. colours **yes** Composition **100% cotton** Width **137cm/54in** Repeat – Price ★★ 🛋

18 Today Interiors/Palio/Drago CH850027 Colour **27** Alt. colours **yes** Composition **40% cotton, 42% viscose, 10% linen, 8% nylon** Width **140cm/55in** Repeat **1.7cm/⅝in** Price ★★ 🔲 🛋

19 Today Interiors/Kariba KB 4078 Colour **green** Alt. colours **yes** Composition **71% viscose, 21% cotton, 8% polyester** Width **140cm/55in** Repeat – Price ★★★ 🔲 🛋

Patterned Pile

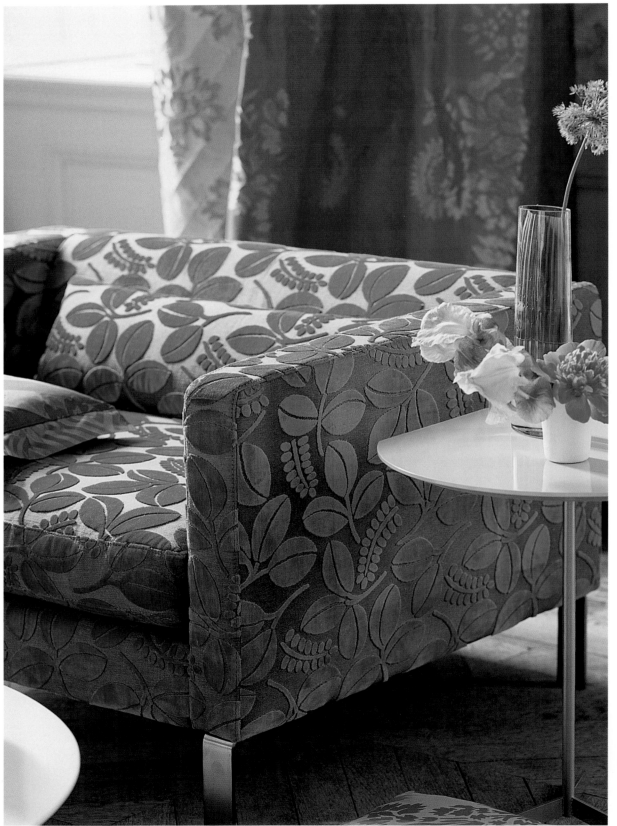

Traditionally woven from silk, mohair, wool, worsted or cotton, pile fabrics have been produced for drapery since the Middle Ages, and for upholstery since the 17th century. The best-known are Genoa, Utrecht and *gaufrage* velvets. Related types include moquette ("mock velvet"), chenille ("poor man's velvet"), plush (a wool velvet), Manchester velvet (a cotton variety), velour (cotton) and corduroy (also cotton). All are distinguished by their raised pile, which consists of rows of loops woven into a simple ground weave. The loops can be cut, which gives them a fur-like texture, or left uncut. The direction of the pile, and the angle at which light strikes it, determine the density and sheen of the colours, which can vary from dark matt to bright and shimmering. Patterns are created during weaving, or stamped on afterward with a metal plate or cylinder. If the pattern is woven leaving areas of ground weave exposed, the fabric is referred to as "voided"; alternatively, if the ground is completely covered with patterned pile, the fabric is described as "solid".

LEFT This modern square-framed armchair is covered with "Murskaya" fabric from the Designers Guild Inessa collection. Leaf patterns have been popular for centuries, but this colour combination – a vibrant electric blue against a pale earthy hue – is very 21st century. Typically, the use of a voided ground enhances the three-dimensionality of the raised-pile leaf motifs.

ABOVE This 19th-century painted chair from France has been reupholstered with a flamboyant cut-pile velvet. The naturalistic red and green flower-and-leaf pattern is well defined by a contrasting pale yellow ground weave. The back of the chair nestles into a pair of heavy yellow silk damask curtains.

SELF-PATTERNS

When recreating this typical mid-19th-century interior, Swiss designer Christophe Gollut used a voided cut-pile velvet to upholster the mahogany seating. With the ground weave exposed, a voided pattern will allow the manufacturer to produce a self-coloured pattern in the pile, so creating a damask effect (*see* pages 76–85), and giving the pattern increased texture and definition.

KEY DESIGNS

1 Naturalistic floral patterns have been a recurring theme in patterned pile fabrics. Here raised-pile flowers and leaves are rendered in golden yellow, sage green and pale brown on a rust-brown ground.

2 Stylized foliage is among the most traditional of pile-fabric patterns. This example has a woven pile, but *gaufrage* (stamped) foliage patterns have also proved popular since the 16th century.

3 Overall pattern repeats of small motifs, such as the plant forms on this Empire-style chenille, became easier to produce following the invention of the dobby loom in 1824.

4 Such formalized fruit and foliage patterns as this were derived from oriental and classical ornament. They have appeared on patterned pile fabrics since the Renaissance.

5 Inspired by military bunting, striped velvets were very fashionable in the late 18th and early 19th century. This example features a cut blue-stripe pile on a sage-green ground.

6 Multi-coloured chequerboard-pattern pile fabrics such as this one were popular during the Renaissance, and came back into vogue during the latter part of the 20th century.

---

1 **Monkwell/MF 5859** Colour **800 rust** Alt. colours **yes** Composition **48% acrylic, 28% cotton, 24% polyester** Width **137cm/53¾in** Repeat **56cm/22in** Price ★★

2 **Mulberry/Baroque Vine FD338** Colour **J103 cream** Alt. colours **yes** Composition **85% cotton, 10% viscose, 5% polyamide** Width **145cm/57in** Repeat **40cm/15¾in** Price ★★★

3 **Hodsoll McKenzie/Empire Chenille 093/124** Colour **124** Alt. colours **yes** Composition **100% cotton** Width **127cm/50in** Repeat **5.5cm/2¼in** Price ★★★

4 **Lelièvre/Ravenne 647** Colour **02** Alt. colours **yes** Composition **39% cotton, 32% viscose, 29% Bemberg** Width **130cm/51in** Repeat **57cm/22¼in** Price ★★★★★

5 **Percheron/Robespierre** Colour **green/blue** Alt. colours **yes** Composition **69% viscose, 31% cotton** Width **130cm/51in** Repeat – Price ★★

6 **Old World Weavers/San Marco Square** Colour **multi** Alt. colours **yes** Composition **69% cotton, 31% silk** Width **130cm/51in** Repeat – Price ★★★★★

Patterned Pile: **Pre-20th century**

Prior to the 20th century, pile fabrics were produced in numerous colours and patterns. Silk Genoa velvet (made since the Renaissance) has always been the most expensive. It features a multi-coloured pile (cut or uncut) on a satin ground and is patterned during weaving. Less costly Utrecht and *gaufrage* velvets have patterns produced by a stamping process. Alternatives include: moquette (produced since the 16th century), which has a wool warp pile (usually cut) on a linen ground, and woven or stamped patterns; chenille (first seen in the 19th century), a fabric woven from cut and twisted woven cloth, with a fuzzy pile; plush (from the late 17th century), which is a double-warp fabric, of wool and hair (or silk) with woven or stamped patterns and a longer but less dense pile than velvet; and, since the 18th century, Manchester velvet (*see* page 70) and velour (the latter having a short lustrous cotton-warp pile).

5 The Silk Gallery/Cantabile Colour **maroon silk, gold chenille** Alt. colours **yes** Composition **83% cotton, 17% silk** Width **127cm/ 50in** Repeat **38cm/15in** Price ★★★ 🎨🛋

6 Old World Weavers/Aracelis Colour **wine** Alt. colours **yes** Composition **54% viscose, 43% acrylic, 3% polypropylene** Width **137cm/54in** Repeat **24cm/9½in** Price ★★★ 🛋

7 Ian Sanderson/Pendragon Colour **coral** Alt. colours **yes** Composition **58% cotton, 24% polyacrylic, 18% viscose** Width **140cm/55in** Repeat **63cm/ 24¾in** Price ★★★ 🎨🛋

8 Old World Weavers/Corda Matisse Colour **gold** Alt. colours **yes** Composition **67% viscose, 33% cotton** Width **130cm/51in** Repeat **66cm/26in** Price ★★★★ 🛋

1 Old World Weavers/Sahara SX 02342149 Colour **beige and green** Alt. colours **yes** Composition **47% rayon, 32% acrylic, 21% cotton** Width **140cm/55in** Repeat **47cm/18½in** Price ★★★ 🛋

2 Beaumont & Fletcher/Augustus Chenille 1005C Colour **red/grey** Alt. colours **yes** Composition **90% cotton, 10% wool** Width **140cm/55in** Repeat **28.5cm/11in** Price ★★★ 🛋

3 Hodsoll McKenzie/Turkish Flower 303/101 Colour **coral** Alt. colours **yes** Composition **100% cotton** Width **127cm/ 50in** Repeat **8cm/3in** Price ★★★ 🎨🛋 Ⓦ

4 Lelièvre/Ravenne 647-01 Colour **emeraude** Alt. colours **yes** Composition **39% cotton, 32% viscose, 29% Bemberg** Width **130cm/ 51in** Repeat **57cm/22½in** Price ★★★★★ 🅛🅒🎨⊞🛋

9

10

9 The Silk Gallery/Chenille II
Colour **henna and gold** Alt.
colours **yes** Composition
83% cotton, 17% silk Width
127cm/50in Repeat –
Price ★★★ 🛋

10 Old World Weavers/Leopard
Velvet Y00 6900001 Colour
gold and brown Alt. colours
no Composition **57% silk,
30% cotton, 13% viscose** Width
132cm/51¾in Repeat **73.5cm/
28¾in** Price ★★★★★ 🛋

11 Hodsoll McKenzie/Star Chenille
301 Colour **106** Alt. colours
yes Composition **100%
cotton** Width **127cm/50in**
Repeat **10.5cm/4in**
Price ★★★ 🛋🛋 W

12 Watts of Westminster/Pine
Colour **brick and leaf green**
Alt. colours **yes** Composition
100% cotton chenille Width
124cm/48¾in Repeat **79cm/31in**
Price ★★★★ 🛋🛋

13 Mulberry/Aubusson Chenille
FD001/508 Colour **S103** Alt.
colours **yes** Composition
75% cotton, 25% wool Width
150cm/59in Repeat **131cm/
51½in** Price ★★★ 🛋⊞🛋

14 Old World Weavers/Velours
Marmara FV6 7028007 Colour
green Alt. colours **yes**
Composition **75% rayon,
25% cotton** Width **135cm/53in**
Repeat – Price ★★★ 🛋

11

12

13

14

15 Zoffany/La Scala VRS
Colour **07** Alt. colours **yes**
Composition **66% linen,
34% cotton** Width **130cm/51in**
Repeat – Price ★★★ 🛋🛋

16 Zimmer & Rohde/Filion 1278
Colour **184** Alt. colours **yes**
Composition **64% polyester,
36% viscose** Width **144cm/
56½in** Repeat **5cm/2in**
Price ★★★★ 🛋

17 Sahco Hesslein/Eroica 04630
Colour **green and yellow**
Alt. colours **yes** Composition
57% cotton, 43% viscose
Width **130cm/51in** Repeat –
Price ★★★★ LC🛋

18 Scalamandré/Billingsley
26594-007 Colour **beige, rust**
Alt. colours **yes** Composition
**55% wool, 45% acrylic
chenille** Width **152cm/
60in** Repeat **59cm/23in**
Price ★★★★ LC🛋🛋

15

16

17

18

Patterned Pile: 20th–early 21st century

Toward the end of the 19th century, patterned pile fabrics suffered a dip in popularity. Because of their densely woven pile, they were viewed by many arbiters of household taste as dust-traps, particularly when heavily draped around beds, over doors or at windows; at the latter, they were also deemed to hinder the entrance of "health-giving" sunlight. In reality, such views were less a concern for health and more an aesthetic reaction to overfurnished and often gloomy "High Victorian" interiors. Patterned pile fabrics enjoyed a resurgence of popularity at the beginning of the 20th century, and, except in minimal Modernist interiors, their use has been sustained to this day.

Manufacturers have continued to produce a wide range of patterned pile fabrics, notably Genoa and *gaufrage* velvets, as well as chenille and velour. Most are intended for curtains and as top-covers for upholstery. Generally, patterns have remained traditional, with floral, leaf or fruit motifs, and stripes and checks being most in demand. As in previous centuries, silk, mohair, wool and cotton yarns are still used in the production of pile fabrics, although, since 1945, synthetic yarns, such as Dralon, have also been employed.

Donghia/Rugose 0556/6480-10 Colour **cavolo-cream** Alt. colours **yes** Composition **80% viscose, 12% polyester, 8% polyacrylic** Width **133cm/52in** Repeat **9cm/3½in** Price ★★★★★ 🛋

Mulberry/Valais Chenille FD348 Colour **J103 cream** Alt. colours **yes** Composition **100% cotton** Width **130cm/51in** Repeat **31cm/12in** Price ★★★ 🛋

Zimmer & Rohde/Dido 1258 Colour **989** Alt. colours **yes** Composition **100% cotton** Width **140cm/55in** Repeat **22cm/8½in** Price ★★★ 🛋

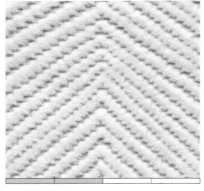

Sahco Hesslein/Akka 04614 Colour **cream** Alt. colours **no** Composition **100% cotton** Width **140cm/55in** Repeat – Price ★★★ 🛋

Zimmer & Rohde/Dina 1260 989 Colour **black and cream** Alt. colours **yes** Composition **100% cotton** Width **140cm/55in** Repeat **2cm/¾in** Price ★★★ 🛋

Bentley & Spens/Lilies Colour **black/grey** Alt. colours **no** Composition **100% cotton** Width **130cm/51in** Repeat **49cm/19¼in** Price ★★★★★ (special order) 🛋

Sahco Hesslein/Akkord 04625 Colour **cream** Alt. colours **no** Composition **68% cotton, 32% viscose** Width **140cm/55in** Repeat **13cm/5in** Price ★★★ 🛋

POPULAR ANIMAL MOTIFS

Although animal motifs have been regularly used to ornament fabrics since the Middle Ages, they have proved to be particularly popular since the last quarter of the 19th century. The patterned-pile upholstered armchair shown here displays a pride of lions. Although the textile design was created in the late 20th century, it strongly echoes the fabrics embellished with antelopes, gazelles, lions and other exotic African animals that were in vogue throughout much of Europe during the 1920s and 1930s.

Andrew Martin/Pride Colour **taupe** Alt. colours **yes** Composition **face: 100% cotton; back: 72% polyester, 28% rayon** Width **140cm/55in** Repeat **30cm/11¾in** Price ★★ 🛋

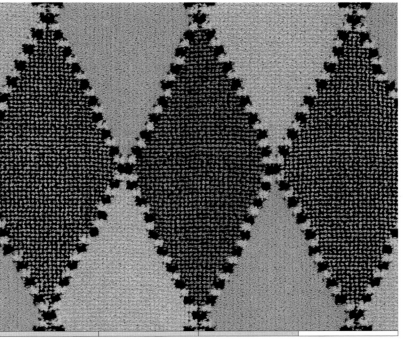

Pierre Frey/Brigitte Bardot/Rivoli 2150 Colour **anthracite** Alt. colours **yes** Composition **77% viscose, 23% cotton** Width **130cm/51in** Repeat **2cm/¾in** Price ★★★ 🛋🛏

Giant/Labyrinth 9020 Colour **aqua** Alt. colours **yes** Composition **100% cotton** Width **130cm/51in** Repeat – Price ★★★★ 🛋

Brunschwig & Fils/Altena Velvet 53293 Colour **01** Alt. colours **yes** Composition **78% polyester, 22% cotton** Width **140cm/55in** Repeat **23cm/9in** Price ★★★★ 🛋

Brunschwig & Fils/Bichon Chenille Plaid 46091 Colour **02** Alt. colours **yes** Composition **60% rayon, 40% cotton** Width **142cm/55¾in** Repeat **15cm/6in** Price ★★★★ 🛋

Jab/Studio 1-3024-138 Colour **green 138** Alt. colours **yes** Composition **100% cotton** Width **140cm/55in** Repeat – Price ★★★ 🛋▣

Jab/Tampa 1-2011-581 Colour **green and blue** Alt. colours **yes** Composition **100% cotton** Width **140cm/55in** Repeat – Price ★★★ 🛋

Giant/Chaine 3050 Colour **grape 08** Alt. colours **yes** Composition **100% cotton** Width **130cm/51in** Repeat – Price ★★★★ 🛋

Zimmer & Rhode/Bamboo 5096 Colour **349** Alt. colours **yes** Composition **83% viscose, 17% cotton** Width **138cm/54in** Repeat **34cm/13½in** Price ★★★★ 🛋

Ian Sanderson/Jester Colour **Harvest** Alt. colours **yes** Composition **84% viscose, 16% cotton** Width **140cm/55in** Repeat **42cm/16½in** Price ★★★ ▢▦🛋

Old World Weavers/Cubic PWO 0930005 Colour **rust/putty** Alt. colours **yes** Composition **60% cotton, 40% rayon** Width **140cm/55in** Repeat – Price ★★★ 🛋

Brunschwig & Fils/Brigham Mohair Figured Velvet 32 38 01 Colour **5** Alt. colours **yes** Composition **50% cotton, 50% mohair** Width **130cm/51in** Repeat – Price ★★★★ 🛋

Damask & Brocade

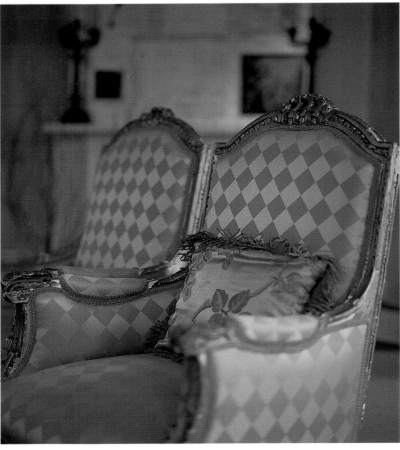

ABOVE Residing in the drawing room of a house in Charleston, South Carolina, USA, this pair of 18th-century French gilt armchairs have been re-covered in a 20th-century, chequer-pattern silk damask – the geometric design inspired by upholstery fabrics fashionable in France since the 17th century.

Damasks were first produced in the Syrian capital, Damascus, during the 4th century AD. The first European damasks were made in Italy during the 15th century, and thereafter mostly in the Netherlands, France, Ireland, Switzerland and Britain. True damask is a monochrome reversible fabric displaying fluid but formal patterns created by the contrast between a shiny satin-weave ground and matt sateen-weave figuring. However, damasks incorporating two or more colours have also been produced. Originally, damasks were made of silk, but linen, wool, cotton and man-made fibres have also been used. Traditional motifs include stylized flowers and leaves, and exotic fruits such as the pomegranate.

Brocatelle is a variant of damask and incorporates a satin or twill figuring that is contrasted with a plain- or satin-weave ground.

Brocade is also damask-based, but is distinguished from true damask by the figured patterns raised against the ground by the embroidery-like technique of spooling additional coloured threads through the weave.

FLORAL DAMASK

The late 18th-century French armchair shown here has been sympathetically reupholstered in a rose-pattern silk damask. Floral patterns have proved to be among the most enduringly popular of damask designs since they were first produced in Europe during the early Renaissance. Many of the examples produced since then have featured designs of stylized and often exotic flowers and vegetation. However, during the late 18th century the floral patterns, as here, tended to be more naturalistic depictions of cultivated and wild flowers that were native to the European countryside.

RIGHT A detail of one of a pair of heavy yellow silk damask curtains, with silk rope-and-tassel tie-backs, in Rosalie, a mid-19th-century house in Natchez, Mississippi, USA. The floral-pattern damask is late 20th century, but copied from the fabric originally used in the house when it was first furnished and decorated.

1 Stylized interlaced foliage patterns (arabesques) were derived from Near-Eastern ornament, and favoured on European (and later American) damasks since the mid-16th to early 17th century.

2 Vegetal patterns incorporating ripening fruit or berries (as here), or seed pods, are among the most traditional of damask designs. They were first used during the early Renaissance.

3 While shading has sometimes been employed on damasks to give the design a more naturalistic "three-dimensional" quality, most flower and leaf patterns are flat and highly stylized.

4 Damasks and brocades embellished with small repeated motifs became increasingly popular from the early 19th century – particularly on fabrics intended for use on upholstered seating.

5 Diaper-patterned damasks, such as this small trellis design with stylized flowers, have been produced since the Renaissance, but were a notable feature of 19th-century Victorian interiors.

6 While true damasks are monochromatic, multi-coloured examples are also produced. On floral or faunal patterns, the use of multiple colours almost invariably enhances the naturalistic qualities.

---

1 Lelièvre/Damask Orion 4120 Colour **05 agate** Alt. colours **yes** Composition **65% cotton, 35% silk** Width **130cm/51in** Repeat **80cm/31⅛in** Price ★★★★ ⬚ ⊞

2 Scalamandré/Newport Damask Colour **vermeil** Alt. colours **yes** Composition **100% silk** Width **140cm/55in** Repeat **47cm/18½in** Price ★★★★★ ⬚ W

3 Zoffany/Tours DUP7400 Colour **3** Alt. colours **yes** Composition **100% cotton** Width **138cm/54in** Repeat **64cm/25in** Price ★★ ⬚

4 John Wilman/Laurel Colour **celadon** Alt. colours **yes** Composition **63% cotton, 37% polyester** Width **137cm/54in** Repeat **7cm/2¾in** Price ★ ⬚ ⌂

5 Gainsborough Silk Weaving/F841 Colour **gold** Alt. colours **yes** Composition **100% cotton** Width **127cm/50in** Repeat **9.5cm/3¾in** Price ★★★ LC ⬚ ⊞ ⌂

6 Brunschwig & Fils/Lady's Slipper Lampas 89481 Colour **876** Alt. colours **yes** Composition **55% silk, 45% cotton** Width **140cm/55in** Repeat **41cm/16in** Price ★★★★★ ⬚ ⌂ ⊞

Damask & Brocade: **Pre-18th century**

During the Renaissance, Italy led the way in the production of silk damasks and heavier silk brocatelles and brocades, the latter often being augmented with gold and silver thread. Favoured designs – stylized flowers, fruits and leaves – had large pattern repeats particularly suitable for wall-, bed-, window- and door-hangings in grander interiors. After the Netherlands began large-scale production in the late 15th century, less expensive linen weaves became fashionable. During the 16th century, Flemish weavers also introduced new designs, such as hunting scenes, and made traditional patterns with smaller repeats, better suited for upholstery. By the early 17th century, production had spread to France, notably the Huguenot city of Lyons, and, following the emigration of the Huguenots to England, Ireland and Switzerland in the late 17th century, these countries also began to produce large quantities of silk, linen, and even cheaper woollen and worsted weaves for use as both hangings and upholstery.

4 **Gainsborough Silk Weaving/ F832** Colour **8** Alt. colours **yes** Composition **85% cotton, 15% viscose** Width **127cm/ 50in** Repeat **66cm/26in** Price ★★ 🛋

5 **Watts of Westminster/Crevelli** Colour **gold and pearl** Alt. colours **yes** Composition **51% cotton, 29% lumiyarn, 20% silk** Width **124cm/48¾in** Repeat **88cm/34½in** Price ★★★★★ 🪟🛋

6 **Ian Sanderson/Fontaine** Colour **cranberry** Alt. colours **yes** Composition **54% cotton, 46% viscose** Width **140cm/ 55in** Repeat **62cm/24¼in** Price ★★★ LC 🪟🛋

7 **Stuart Interiors/Fiori** Colour **burgundy and gold** Alt. colours **yes** Composition **60% wool, 40% linen** Width **175cm/68¾in** Repeat **60cm/23¾in** Price ★★★★ LC 🪟🛋 W

8 **Stuart Interiors/Medici** Colour **gold, red/gold** Alt. colours **yes** Composition **100% wool** Width **170cm/67in** Repeat **47cm/18½in** Price ★★★ LC 🪟🛋 W

1 **Claremont/Stanhope Damask** Colour **eau de nil** Alt. colours **yes** Composition **100% silk** Width **130cm/51in** Repeat **55cm/21½in** Price ★★★★ 🪟

2 **The Silk Gallery/Ceres Damask** Colour **ivory/antique green** Alt. colours **yes** Composition **82% silk, 18% cotton** Width **127cm/50in** Repeat **38cm/15in** Price ★★★★ 🪟🛋

3 **Antico Setificio Fiorentino/Doria D1** Colour **green on green** Alt. colours **yes** Composition **100% silk** Width **120cm/47in** Repeat **55cm/21½in** Price ★★★★★ 🪟🛋 W

BIRDS

Usually shown in flight or sitting in foliage, birds are among the most traditional of damask and brocade motifs. "Uccellini" dates from the 16th century and is typical of Florentine Renaissance design – similar examples being found in the drapery of paintings by Domenico Ghirlandaio or Benozzo Gozzoli. "Love Bird" is from the 17th century and is representative of the symbolism of birds in fabric patterns. For example, two birds in a tree were emblematic of the Holy Ghost and the Virgin Mary.

Antico Setificio Fiorentino/Uccellini UC1 Colour **silver/green** Alt. colours **yes** Composition **100% silk** Width **130cm/51in** Repeat **11cm/4¼in** Price ★★★★★ 🪟🛋 W

Scalamandré/Love Bird 1098m Colour **old ivory** Alt. colours **yes** Composition **100% silk** Width **127cm/50in** Repeat **46cm/18in** Price ★★★★★ 🪟🛋

9

13

9 **Crowson/Rousillon Damasks/
Ferdinand** Colour **7** Alt.
colours **yes** Composition
100% cotton Width **137cm/
54in** Repeat **42cm/16½in**
Price ★★ 🗌 ⊞ 🛋

10 **Stuart Interiors/Genoa** Colour
blue and rust Alt. colours
yes Composition **100%
wool** Width **124cm/48¾in**
Repeat **88cm/34½in**
Price ★★★ LC 🗌 🛋 W

11 **Zoffany/Flower 334405**
Colour **blue** Alt. colours
yes Composition **61% wool,
29% cotton, 10% nylon** Width
145cm/57in Repeat **10.5cm/4in**
Price ★★ 🛋

12 **Zimmer & Rohde/Evangeline
9204** Colour **813** Alt. colours
yes Composition **60% linen,
40% cotton** Width **140cm/
55in** Repeat **21cm/8¼in**
Price ★★★ 🗌

13 **Jab/Adora 1-7327** Colour **180**
Alt. colours **yes** Composition
**65% cotton, 26% silk, 9%
polyester** Width **140cm/55in**
Repeat **44cm/17in**
Price ★★★★ 🗌

14

15

16

14 **Sahco Hesslein/Lilian 08888**
Colour **red and gold** Alt.
colours **yes** Composition **57%
linen, 43% cotton** Width **140cm/
55in** Repeat **68cm/26¾in**
Price ★★★ 🗌 🛋

15 **Watts of Westminster/Holbein
F0012-02/G4** Colour **Canterbury
blue** Alt. colours **yes**
Composition **100% silk**
Width **124cm/48¾in** Repeat
33cm/13in Price ★★★★ 🛋

16 **Sahco Hesslein/Eleganza 1806**
Colour **02** Alt. colours **yes**
Composition **73% wool, 27%
silk** Width **138cm/54in**
Repeat **84cm/33in**
Price ★★★ 🛋 🛋

17 **Zimmer & Rohde/Solista
5077** Colour **184** Alt. colours
yes Composition **24% silk,
24% linen, 20% acetate**
Width **140cm/55in** Repeat
55cm/21½in Price ★★★ 🗌

18 **Zoffany/Knole Drawing Room
NTF0200** Colour **5** Alt.
colours **yes** Composition
100% cotton Width **138cm/
54in** Repeat **82cm/32⅓in**
Price ★★★ 🗌 LC 🛋

10

11

12

17

18

Damask & Brocade: **18th century**

The increased production of damasks during the second half of the 17th century was sustained throughout the 18th century. Silk and linen damask upholstery was a feature of Palladian, Rococo-style and Neo-classical interiors in Britain and Europe, and often employed *en suite* with wall-hangings and curtains. Damask upholstery and hangings, mostly of a woollen or worsted variety imported from Britain, were also fashionable in North American Adam-style interiors of the late 18th century.

Favoured colours of the period included magenta and crimson, deep green, dark blue, and pastel pinks and blues. Flower, leaf and fruit patterns remained fashionable, although pastoral designs in which traditional motifs were combined with musical instruments and birds also came into vogue. In grander interiors silk brocade hangings were much in evidence. Many were multi-coloured, with exotic designs such as coral motifs and Indo-*chinoiserie* patterns featuring elephants and buddhas.

Donghia/Sogno 0387/9315 Colour 09 Alt. colours yes Composition **38% silk, 35% linen, 27% cotton** Width **137cm/54in** Repeat **79cm/31in** Price ★★★★★

Andrew Martin/Avignon Colour **black** Alt. colours **yes** Composition **100% cotton** Width **136cm/53½in** Repeat **67cm/26¼in** Price ★★

Scalamandré/Wicklow 20427 Colour **Red Strie** Alt. colours **yes** Composition **83% silk, 17% cotton** Width **140cm/55in** Repeat **60.5cm/24in** Price ★★★★

Beaumont & Fletcher/Marlowe 1012b Colour **gold/red** Alt. colours **yes** Composition **92% wool, 8% nylon** Width **140cm/55in** Repeat **45cm/17½in** Price ★★★

Gainsborough/S590 Colour **22** Alt. colours **yes** Composition **61% cotton, 39% silk** Width **127cm/50in** Repeat **69cm/27in** Price ★★★★★

John Wilman/Laurel 170177 Colour **salmon** Alt. colours **yes** Composition **63% cotton, 37% polyester** Width **137cm/54in** Repeat **7cm/2¾in** Price ★★ 🗆🗆

Garin/Anna Maria 3589 Colour **rojo** Alt. colours **yes** Composition **100% cotton** Width **140cm/55in** Repeat **69cm/27in** Price ★★ 🗆🗆

Marvic Textiles/Damask Rosario 5210-4 Colour **rose** Alt. colours **yes** Composition **71% cotton, 29% silk** Width **130cm/51in** Repeat **47cm/18½in** Price ★★★ 🗆🗆

Hodsoll McKenzie/Turkish Tulip 357/101-109 Colour **natural** Alt. colours **yes** Composition **100% silk** Width **127cm/50in** Repeat **65cm/25½in** Price ★★★★ 🗆🗆 W

Gainsborough/F954 Colour **1** Alt. colours **yes** Composition **61% cotton, 39% silk** Width **127cm/50in** Repeat **51cm/21in** Price ★★★★★ T LC 🗆🗆

Warner Fabrics/Hilliard T 114004 Colour **cedar** Alt. colours **yes** Composition **100% silk** Width **140cm/55in** Repeat **38cm/15in** Price ★★★ 🗆🗆

The Silk Gallery/Campana Colour **henna/cedar ground** Alt. colours **yes** Composition **82% silk, 18% cotton** Width **127cm/50in** Repeat **60cm/23¾in** Price ★★★★ 🗆🗆

Hodsoll McKenzie/Venetian Damask 352/101 Colour **dusty pink** Alt. colours **yes** Composition **61% flax, 26% cotton, 13% silk** Width **127cm/50in** Repeat **66cm/26in** Price ★★★★ 🗆

Damask & Brocade: **Early 19th century**

The most significant development in the production of woven fabrics during the first half of the 19th century was technological. The invention, in 1805, of the automated Jacquard loom resulted in a speeding up of the weaving process and, by reducing the number of operators needed, a cut in labour costs. Damasks, brocatelles and, to a lesser extent, partly hand-worked brocades, therefore became more affordable than before, and damask-covered upholstery gradually found its way into middle-class homes – particularly on sofas and chairs. The "dobby" loom, invented in 1824 and designed to supplement the Jacquard loom, also made it easier to produce patterns with smaller repeats – the type most suited to upholstering furniture.

While linen, woollen and worsted damasks, brocatelles and brocades became cheaper and more accessible, more expensive silk versions continued to be produced not only for upholstery but also for wall- and bed-hangings, curtains and lambrequins. During this period, the new looms of Genoa in Italy, Lyons in France and Spitalfields in England turned out increasingly complex and elaborate patterns well suited to the grander French Empire, English Regency and American Federal interiors.

2

1 Watts of Westminster/Gaheris F0048-01/N6 Colour **rose/linen** Alt. colours **yes** Composition **64% cotton, 36% linen** Width **140cm/55in** Repeat **18cm/7in** Price ★★★

2 Guy Evans/Palmerston Damask Colour **red/gold** Alt. colours **yes** Composition **50% wool, 50% silk** Width **107cm/42in** Repeat **49.5cm/19¼in** Price ★★★★

3 Garin/Beatriz Colour **azul** Alt. colours **yes** Composition **55% cotton, 45% viscose** Width **140cm/55in** Repeat **57cm/22in** Price ★★★

4 Scalamandré/Kilfane 26531 Colour **lime 007** Alt. colours **yes** Composition **38% linen, 34% cotton, 28% silk** Width **144cm/56½in** Repeat **67.3cm/ 26½in** Price ★★★★

5 Jab/Mornay 7233 Colour **blue** Alt. colours **yes** Composition **52% cotton, 48% polyester** Width **140cm/55in** Repeat **53cm/21in** Price ★★

6 Garin/Anna Maria 3591 Colour **crudo** Alt. colours **yes** Composition **100% cotton** Width **140cm/55in** Repeat **69cm/27in** Price ★★

3

5

1

4

6

7 Today Interiors/Court Weaves FRW 1332 Colour **gold** Alt. colours **yes** Composition **52% modacrylic, 36% cotton, 12% nylon** Width **140cm/ 55in** Repeat **6.5cm/2½in** Price ★★ ⬚⬚ ⊞ 🛋

8 Harlequin/Assisi/Castina Colour **709** Alt. colours **yes** Composition **13% cotton, 87% viscose** Width **140cm/ 55in** Repeat **57.5cm/23in** Price ★★ ⬚⬚

9 Northwood Designs/Jupiter Colour **7863** Alt. colours **yes** Composition **100% Trevira CS** Width **280cm/ 110in** Repeat **37cm/14½in** Price ★★★ ⬚⬚ 🛋 ᵣᵉ

9

10

11

12

10 Watts of Westminster/Giovanna Damask F0052-01/B4 Colour **white/butter** Alt. colours **yes** Composition **100% silk** Width **124cm/48¾in** Repeat **20cm/8in** Price ★★★★ ⬚⬚ 🛋

11 Dedar/Paris Colour **04** Alt. colours **yes** Composition **70% cotton, 30% viscose** Width **140cm/55in** Repeat **56cm/22in** Price ★★ LC 🛋

12 Mulberry/Lysander Weave FD403 Colour **oyster blue** Alt. colours **yes** Composition **73% cotton, 20% rayon, 7% nylon** Width **127cm/50in** Repeat **106cm/42in** Price ★★ LC ⬚⬚ ⊞ 🛋

13 Crowson/Rousillon Damasks/ Corin Colour **10** Alt. colours **yes** Composition **100% cotton** Width **137cm/54in** Repeat **15cm/6in** Price ★★ LC ⊞ 🛋

8

13

Damask & Brocade: Late 19th–21st century

From the mid-19th century to the present day, damasks, brocatelles and brocades have remained in widespread use, with coloured damasks particularly favoured for upholstery, and brocades primarily produced as curtain fabrics. Traditional white linen damask tablecloths and napkins, the preserve of the aristocracy during the 16th and 17th centuries, can also now be found in numerous households. However, damask wall-, bed- and door-hangings tend to be confined to grander period-style interiors.

Over the past 150 years, silk, linen and wool have continued to be used for the manufacture of these fabrics, although cotton damask has become increasingly popular (particularly for upholstery). Traditional designs have also remained fashionable: stylized flowers and leaves, pomegranates and acorns, and, recently, Napoleonic motifs (such as swans, bees and Ns encircled by laurel wreaths) are all much in demand. However, there have been design innovations of note, including late 19th-century Gothic-style polychrome brocatelles incorporating traditional motifs set within geometric grids, 1920s gold brocades featuring stylized floral motifs overprinted with Jazz Age motifs in black, and post-1940s damasks with abstract figuring and designs inspired by 16th- and 17th-century needlework patterns.

Nina Campbell/NCF3440 Falaise Colour **07** Alt. colours **yes** Composition **65% viscose, 19% polyester, 16% cotton** Width **134cm/52½in** Repeat **71cm/28in** Price ★★★ LC

Watts of Westminster/Hilliard F0011-07/J4 Colour **old gold and Medici** Alt. colours **yes** Composition **100% silk** Width **124cm/48¾in** Repeat **22cm/8½in** Price ★★★★

Scalamandré/20432 Colour **005** Alt. colours **yes** Composition **72% linen, 28% silk** Width **140cm/55in** Repeat **15cm/6in** Price ★★★

Garin/Damjan 97985051 Colour **Barquillo** Alt. colours **yes** Composition **70% cotton, 30% viscose** Width **140cm/55in** Repeat **56cm/22in** Price ★★

Claremont/Fortuny/Corone Colour **Bayou green and beige** Alt. colours **yes** Composition **100% cotton** Width **120cm/47in** Repeat **100cm/39¼in** Price ★★★★★ LC

Scalamandré/Lucia 26476 Colour **001** Alt. colours **yes** Composition **100% silk** Width **130cm/51in** Repeat **36.5cm/14¾in** Price ★★★★★

Watts of Westminster/Flame F0007-02/J17 Colour **gold** Alt. colours **yes** Composition **51% cotton, 29% lumiyarn, 20% rayon** Width **124cm/48¾in** Repeat **21cm/8¼in** Price ★★★

Donghia/Omen 9418 Colour **taupe** Alt. colours **yes** Composition **59% cotton, 29% viscose, 15% polyester** Width **137cm/53¼in** Repeat **30cm/11¾in** Price ★★★★ LC

Gainsborough Silk Weaving/S590 Colour **19** Alt. colours **yes** Composition **61% silk, 39% cotton** Width **127cm/50in** Repeat **69cm/27in** Price ★★★

G.P. & J. Baker/Arabica K0240 Colour **118** Alt. colours **yes** Composition **57% cotton, 43% modacrylic** Width **145cm/57in** Repeat **2cm/¾in** Price ★★

Jab/Rigaud 7232 Colour **blue** Alt. colours **yes** Composition **52% cotton, 48% polyester** Width **140cm/55in** Repeat **6cm/2½in** Price ★★

MATELASSÉ

Derived from the French verb *matelasser*, which means to quilt or wad, matelassé is a term used to describe double-woven damasks (and other fabrics) that incorporate raised figures or motifs on their surface. The decorative puckered effect, which looks like machine quilting, is achieved by weaving in an interlocking "wadding weft" to accentuate relief. The "Magnolia" design shown here is typical of the floral patterns fashionable during the 19th, 20th and early 21st centuries.

Northwood Designs/Magnolia 18184 Colour **tourmaline 018** Alt. colours **yes** Composition **100% cotton** Width **280cm/110in** Repeat **81cm/32in** Price ★★★ LC

Bentley & Spens/Day By Night BS09 Colour **natural** Alt. colours **no** Composition **50% linen, 50% cotton** Width **135cm/53in** Repeat **71cm/28in** Price ★★

Jab/Janai 1-7243 Colour **254** Alt. colours **yes** Composition **86% silk, 14% wool** Width **140cm/55in** Repeat **66cm/26in** Price ★★★

Tapestry

A heavy, durable material, similar in appearance to embroidery, tapestry has been used since the Middle Ages for wall-hangings, bed-hangings, portières, screens and cushion covers; since the 17th century it has also been utilized as a top-cover for upholstered furniture. Tapestry consists of different-coloured warp and weft threads woven to form motifs or, more commonly, narrative accounts of important religious or historical events or scenes from everyday life. The designs were often based on drawings or paintings that were followed as a guide. Prior to the late 19th century, all tapestry was hand-woven with bobbins, and worked on a loom, but since then many tapestries have been machine-made (jacquard-woven).

The traditional yarns used include wool, linen and cotton. The grandest tapestries incorporate silk or gilt thread, while in recent years man-made fibres, such as viscose, have also been employed. The number of colours in any one tapestry can range from as few as eight to as many as 300.

LEFT A pictorial tapestry portière hangs in an arch-top doorway at Parham House, in Sussex, England. Since the Middle Ages, heavier-weight fabrics, including tapestry, velvet and brocatelle, have been favoured for portières because of their draught- and sound-proofing qualities. However, lighter fabrics, such as chintz and silk taffeta, have also been employed, particularly in the better-insulated houses of the 20th century.

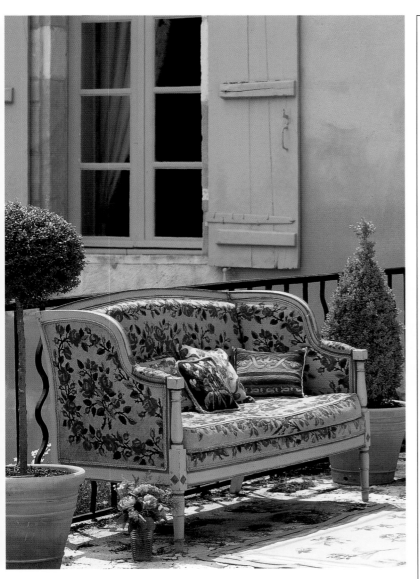

ABOVE The tapestry upholstery on this 19th-century painted French canapé, temporarily displayed on the terrace of a medieval *manoir* in Monflanquin, France, is original and particularly well preserved. The floral rose pattern is typical of the period.

KEY DESIGNS

1 Over the centuries many tapestry wall-hangings have featured patterns simulating architectural fixtures and fittings, such as pilasters, cornices, dados or, as here, windows.

2 Scenes of Indian origin, such as these elephants, first appeared on early 17th-century tapestries, and were fashionable again during the second half of both the 18th and the 19th centuries.

3 Elaborate floral-patterned tapestries designed for hangings and upholstery were especially popular during the 17th, the first half of the 18th, and the second half of the 19th century.

4 Tapestries feature an array of heraldic motifs; the lion, featured on medieval, Renaissance, early 18th-century and 20th-century Classical Revival tapestries, symbolizes majesty, courage and pride.

1 Brunschwig & Fils/Tristan Figured Woven **89528** Colour **833** Alt. colours **yes** Composition **100% spun rayon** Width **140cm/55in** Repeat **50cm/19½in** Price ★★★

2 Nobilis-Fontan/Les Animaux **8071** Colour **amber on green** Alt. colours **yes** Composition **89% cotton, 11% polyester** Width **130cm/51in** Repeat **78cm/30¾in** Price ★★★★★

3 Brunschwig & Fils/Animalitos Woven Tapestry **89477** Colour **150** Alt. colours **yes** Composition **100% cotton** Width **145cm/57in** Repeat **74cm/29in** Price ★★★

4 Watts of Westminster/Parisian Lions Colour **rust** Alt. colours **yes** Composition **58% viscose, 21% polyester, 21% cotton** Width **140cm/55in** Repeat **59cm/23in** Price ★★★

TAPESTRY UPHOLSTERY

When chairs with upholstered seats and backs, such as English "farthingales", first appeared in the 1620s, many were covered with hand-woven tapestry. Providing comfort and durability, tapestry remained a popular top-cover on chairs and settees until the Classical and Neo-classical Revivals of the late 18th century and early 19th century. Tapestry-upholstered seating came back into fashion in Gothic Revival, Arts and Crafts and Jacobean Revival interiors from the 1860s to the 1920s, and has remained popular ever since.

ABOVE Classical mythology and pastoralism are combined in the 19th-century scallop-edged tapestry that extends the canopy to the headboard of this fruitwood four-poster. The bed resides in an 18th-century French hunting lodge.

Tapestry: **Pre-19th century**

Prior to the 17th century, the majority of tapestries were narrative pictorials produced for wall-, bed- and door-hangings. However, non-narrative tapestries were also woven, with fashionable patterns including animals, scrolled ribbons and *mille fleurs*. During the 17th and 18th centuries, tapestry also became a popular top-cover on upholstered furniture. Production increased throughout the world – notably in Flanders, at Aubusson, Gobelins and Beauvais in France, and at Mortlake and Worcester in England. "Picturesque" designs ranged from military conflicts, cities and castles to scenes from nature and Aesop's fables. Elaborate floral arrangements also remained fashionable, while in the 18th century *chinoiserie* and *verdure* tapestries came into vogue.

Changing tastes and the preference for wallpaper over wall-hangings resulted in a decline in tapestry production toward the end of the 18th century that was to last until the second half of the 19th century.

Brunschwig & Fils/89381 Colour **M26** Alt. colours **yes** Composition **12% cotton, 87% viscose, 1% polyester** Width **140cm/55in** Repeat **39cm/15¼in** Price ★★★★★ LC

Turnell & Gigon/Perceval 14862 Colour **blue** Alt. colours **yes** Composition **73% cotton, 25% acrylic, 2% rayon** Width **130cm/51in** Repeat **38cm/15in** Price ★★★★

Watts of Westminster/Jacobean Brocade Colour **beige and terracotta** Alt. colours **yes** Composition **66% viscose, 34% cotton** Width **136cm/53¼in** Repeat **61cm/24in** Price ★★★★ LC

Watts of Westminster/Tea Rose BCF0045-01/J25 Colour **multi** Alt. colours **no** Composition **66% cotton, 34% acrylic** Width **135cm/53in** Repeat **34cm/13½in** Price ★★★ LC

Fired Earth/Carolean Colour **red** Alt. colours **no** Composition **100% cotton** Width **146cm/57½in** Repeat **45cm/17½in** Price ★★

Stuart Interiors/Rose & Pansy Colour **gold background** Alt. colours **yes** Composition **100% wool** Width **145cm/57in** Repeat **29cm/11¼in** Price ★★★★ LC W

AUTHENTIC EARLY COLOURS

The design of this tapestry-woven fabric is based upon an early 17th-century embroidered bed-hanging. The pattern is produced in a limited colour range on a plain ground and contains rudimentary areas of shading. In these respects it bears a much closer resemblance to the flat and highly stylized tapestries of the Middle Ages than to the multi-coloured and subtly shaded "three-dimensional" realism of the style of tapestry that began to be produced during the Renaissance. The thistles and birds-of-prey depicted in the pattern of this fabric are motifs that recur frequently in English and French medieval tapestries.

Watts of Westminster/Windsor F0033-01/23 Colour **Windsor** Alt. colours **yes** Composition **100% cotton** Width **124cm/48¾in** Repeat **57cm/22½in** Price ★★★

Stuart Interiors/Tree of Life Colour **D** Alt. colours **yes** Composition **60% wool, 40% cotton** Width **125cm/49¼in** Repeat **90cm/35½in** Price ★★★★ 🛋️ LC ⧄ ⊞

Fired Earth/Medieval Rose FE9021 Colour **1** Alt. colours **no 53% polyester** Composition **25% cotton, 18% modacrylic, 4% polypropile** Width **138cm/54in** Repeat **34cm/ 13½in** Price ★★ 🛋️

Northwood Designs/Fidelio M063N2 Colour **06** Alt. colours **yes** Composition **56% cotton, 44% polyester** Width **140cm/55in** Repeat **36.5cm/14½in** Price ★★★ ⧄ LC ⊞ 🛋️

Fired Earth/Sunflower Colour **1** Alt. colours **no** Composition **100% cotton** Width **147cm/58in** Repeat **39cm/15¼** Price ★★ ⊞ ⧄

Old World Weavers/Beethoven BD648/0001 Colour **brown** Alt. colours **no** Composition **86% cotton, 14% rayon** Width **140cm/ 55in** Repeat **86.5cm/34in** Price ★★★ 🛋️

John Lewis/Dean Fr 1 V1229-44 Colour **reds on sand** Alt. colours **yes** Composition **66% cotton, 34% modacrylic** Width **140cm/55in** Repeat **42cm/16½in** Price ★★★★★ **(special order)** 🛋️

Old World Weavers/Clermont ND495 40088 Colour **gold/green/beige** Alt. colours **yes** Composition **100% cotton** Width **127cm/50in** Repeat **72cm/28¼in** Price ★★★★ 🛋️

Tapestry: 19th–early 21st century

After a 50-year decline, tapestry production enjoyed a resurgence during the late 19th century. Medieval-style designs were predominant, although hanging baskets of flowers set within scrolling wreaths and cartouches also proved highly popular.

Most 20th- and early 21st-century tapestries are machine-made. Heavy and durable, they tend to be more flexible than their hand-woven counterparts and are thus suitable for curtains, although they are also designed specifically for upholstery. Many of the *verdure* tapestries favoured in the early 20th-century Baronial-style and Jacobean Revival interiors featured foliage in soft greens, tans and browns on a dark blue background. Similarly, numerous contemporary tapestries display stylized floral-and-trellis or geometric patterns. Machine-made and hand-woven pictorial tapestries are still produced, primarily as wall-hangings. However, in terms of artistic approach, hand-woven designs have changed. Instigated early in the century at Aubusson, by Frenchman Jean Lurçat, there has been a gradual move away from narrative pictorial realism. Many designs rely on the interaction between the textures and colours used, and in this respect mirror the innovation and developments of modern art.

19th century

20th & 21st century

1

2

1 **Marvic Textiles/Criss Cross 3903-5** Colour **russet** Alt. colours **yes** Composition **100% cotton** Width **140cm/ 55in** Repeat **7cm/2¾in** Price ★★★ LC ⌂

2 **Marvic Textiles/Maple Leaf 3902-5** Colour **russet** Alt. colours **yes** Composition **100% cotton** Width **140cm/ 55in** Repeat **8.5cm/3¼in** Price ★★★ LC ⌂

3

4

5

3 **Watts of Westminster/Parisian Lions** Colour **green** Alt. colours **yes** Composition **58% viscose, 21% polyester, 21% cotton** Width **140cm/55in** Repeat **59cm/23in** Price ★★★ 🪟

4 **Fired Earth/Mulberry Tree** Colour **1** Alt. colours **no** Composition **100% cotton** Width **140cm/55in** Repeat **69.5cm/27¼in** Price ★★ 🪟 ⊞ ⌂

5 **Old World Weavers/Boboli TV 25240001** Colour **cinnabar** Alt. colours **yes** Composition **50% rayon, 47% acrylic, 3% cotton** Width **140cm/55in** Repeat **119cm/46¾in** Price ★★★★ ⌂

6 **Watts of Westminster/Flora** Colour **multi** Alt. colours **no** Composition **100% cotton** Width **138cm/ 54in** Repeat **61cm/24in** Price ★★★ ⌂ LC 🪟

7 **Watts of Westminster/Benson** Colour **Westminster** Alt. colours **yes** Composition **62% cotton, 38% silk** Width **124cm/48¾in** Repeat **63cm/ 24¾in** Price ★★★★★ 🪟

6

7

8

10

11

8 Watts of Westminster/Damme
Colour **multi** Alt. colours **no**
Composition **86% cotton,
12% viscose** Width **140cm/
55in** Repeat **69cm/27in**
Price ★★★ LC 〔〕🛋

9 Brunschwig & Fils/89477
Colour **333** Alt. colours
yes Composition **100%
cotton** Width **145cm/57in**
Repeat **74cm/29in**
Price ★★★ 🛋

9

10 Brunschwig & Fils/89247
Colour **402** Alt. colours
yes Composition **100%
cotton** Width **150cm/59in**
Repeat **100cm/39¼in**
Price ★★★★ 🛋

11 Brunschwig & Fils/89528
Colour **239** Alt. colours
yes Composition **100%
spun rayon** Width **140cm/
55in** Repeat **50cm/19½in**
Price ★★★ 〔〕 LC 🛋

12 Fired Earth/Oakleaf Colour **1**
Alt. colours **no** Composition
100% cotton Width **157cm/
61¾in** Repeat **45cm/17½in**
Price ★★★ 〔〕 ⊞ 🛋

**13 Brunschwig & Fils/Jacinthe
Tapestry 53122.01** Colour
ultramarine Alt. colours **yes**
Composition **100% cotton**
Width **137cm/54in** Repeat
11.5cm/4½in Price ★★★ 🛋

14 Marvic Textiles/Grapes 3901-3
Colour **yellow** Alt. colours **yes**
Composition **100% cotton**
Width **140cm/55in** Repeat
23cm/9in Price ★★★ LC 🛋

ART NOUVEAU

The revival in tapestry
production that took
place during the Arts and
Crafts movement was
also evident in the output
of the designers who
were working in the Art
Nouveau style from the
late 19th century to the
early years of the 20th
century. Liberty of
London commissioned a
number of designs, one
of which was the late
19th-century tapestry-
weave "Ianthe", shown
here. Typical of Art
Nouveau and its strong
fascination with the forms
of nature, the pattern
depicts stylized stems,
roots, elongated blooms
and foliage within highly
sinuous, interlaced lines.

Arts and Crafts Home/Ianthe 1095022 Colour **E** Alt. colours
no Composition **53% linen, 35% cotton, 12% nylon**
Width **137cm/54in** Repeat **31cm/12in**
Price ★★ LC 〔〕🛋

12

13

14

19th century

20th & 21st century

Motif Fabrics

Woven and printed cloths displaying patterns made up of systematically repeated images are traditionally referred to as "motif fabrics". Their enduring appeal through the centuries is largely explained by decorative qualities such as strong visual repetition, and by the ease with which they allow hangings, upholstery and floor-coverings to be coordinated *en suite* not only with each other, but also with architectural fixtures and fittings and pieces of furniture embellished with the same motifs. The attractiveness of such fabrics also resides in the huge variety of motifs that can be represented; a catalogue of architectural, mythological, animal and plant-form imagery, both stylized and naturalistic, steadily accumulated from around the globe from the Middle Ages onward, much of it being disseminated via pattern books in circulation from the late Renaissance until the early 20th century.

The inherent symbolism of most motifs is particularly appealing to fabric designers because it allows them to convey "hidden meanings" via the pattern. For example, a wreath motif is not merely a "still life" of bound laurel, oak or olive leaves – it is also a symbol of sovereignty, honour, glory, poetic achievement or victory over death.

ABOVE The silk top-cover of this early 19th-century sabre-legged mahogany "tub" chair from France features a repeat wreath motif. Consisting of a garland or crown of leaves (laurel, oak or olive), the wreath was a popular motif during the early Renaissance, and was revived under the Neo-classical Empire style of the late 18th and early 19th centuries – the Emperor Napoleon chose a golden wreath of laurel for his coronation to recall the sovereignty, honour, glory and victories of the ancient Roman emperors.

LEFT "Palmiers", the yellow linen-cotton top-cover on this late 18th-century French settee and footstool, displays a repeat palm tree motif. The pattern was derived and adapted by Comoglio from an 18th-century Marseilles pattern book. Naturalistic and stylized palm trees – a species native to North Africa – became fashionable fabric motifs during the late 18th and early 19th centuries following Napoleon's military campaigns in Egypt.

CYPHERS

Traditionally, cyphers – initials interwoven to form a flat linear design – are used on fabrics to denote ownership or patronage. Prior to the 18th century, they were the almost exclusive preserve of monarchies – a notable example being the interlaced Ls of Louis XI of France. However, following the publication in 1726 of Samuel Sympson's *A New Book of Cyphers*, which contained "every possible combination of two intertwining scrolling letters embellished with flourishes of foliage", they were increasingly commissioned by other sections of society on both sides of the Atlantic, and proved especially popular in 19th-century Gothic Revival interiors.

KEY DESIGNS

1 Used primarily as symbols of nature and the cycle of life, insects such as grasshoppers, bees, butterflies, moths and beetles have been popular motifs ever since the Middle Ages.

2 Originally from France, the fleur-de-lis (a stylized three- or five-petal lily) has been one of the most popular of all motifs, and was prominent in medieval, Renaissance and Gothic Revival interiors.

3 The wreath – a crown or garland of leaves – symbolized sovereignty, honour, glory and victory in ancient Greece and Rome. Fashionable in the Renaissance, it was revived under Empire style.

4 The swan was associated with Apollo (music) and Venus (love) in classical mythology, and was widely used as a motif on medieval, Empire, Biedermeier, Regency and Art Nouveau fabrics.

5 This pear motif is early 21st century, but pear and other fruit motifs – from apples and raspberries to figs and pineapples – have been favoured on textiles since the Middle Ages.

6 The oak leaf symbolizes civic virtue and steadfastness and has appeared on numerous fabrics, notably in ancient Roman, Gothic, Renaissance, Neo-classical and Arts and Crafts interiors.

---

1 Brunschwig & Fils/89518 Colour **005** Alt. colours **yes** Composition **71% cotton, 29% rayon** Width **140cm/55in** Repeat **6cm/2¼in** Price ★★★

2 Warner Fabrics/Poitiers T6800 Colour **red** Alt. colours **yes** Composition **69% viscose, 31% cotton** Width **140cm/55in** Repeat – Price ★★

3 Scalamandré/Rosecliff NW Bedroom 20221 Colour **cranberry** Alt. colours **yes** Composition **100% silk** Width **140cm/55in** Repeat **16.5cm/ 6½in** Price ★★★★★

4 Stuart Interiors/Medieval Swans Colour **blue and gold** Alt. colours **yes** Composition **100% wool** Width **145cm/57in** Repeat **16cm/6¼in** Price ★★★★

5 Harlequin/Notebook/Poire 00181 Colour **181** Alt. colours **yes** Composition **36% cotton, 52% linen, 12% nylon** Width **137cm/54in** Repeat **91.5cm/36in** Price ★★

6 Lee Jofa/Oak Leaf Weave 854252 Colour **hunter green** Alt. colours **yes** Composition **85% rayon, 15% cotton** Width **132cm/51¾in** Repeat **8cm/3in** Price ★★★★

Motifs: **Pre-18th century**

In addition to Islamic ornament, such as arabesques, favoured European motifs of the Middle Ages included stylized heraldic decorations and naturalistic depictions of animals and plant forms – particularly *mille fleurs* (roses, violas, anemones, pinks and columbines), ivy, grapevines, wild strawberries, chestnuts and acorns. Heraldic motifs remained fashionable during the Renaissance, as did military and emblematic symbols. However, Renaissance fabrics were largely characterized by sculptural-like classical forms, such as swags, festoons, dolphins and scallop shells, and realistically depicted acanthus leaves, scrolling foliage, pomegranates, thistles and other plant forms. During the later Renaissance rambling foliage, luxuriant blooms and exotic fruits and birds also embellished imported Indian chintzes. The classical ornamentation of the Renaissance was further consolidated in the Baroque interiors of the 17th century, with fabric motifs including angels, cupids, human figures, scrolls, urns, flaming torches, swags and leafy scrolls. Vying with the classical, however, were *chinoiserie* pagodas, bells, mandarins, dragons and birds, which were very popular in the late 17th century following the publication in several languages of J. Nieuhof's illustrated travel book, *Atlas Chinois* (1665).

1
2
3
5

1 **The Silk Gallery/Fleur Weave** Colour **antique gold and green** Alt. colours **yes** Composition **68% silk, 32% polyester** Width **127cm/ 50in** Repeat **6cm/2¼in** Price ★★★

2 **Elizabeth Eaton/Saighton** Colour **green on white** Alt. colours **yes** Composition **100% linen** Width **122cm/ 48in** Repeat **5cm/2in** Price ★★

3 **Les Olivades/Indianaire TRT 0064** Colour **yellow/blue** Alt. colours **yes** Composition **100% cotton** Width **150cm/ 59in** Repeat **3cm/1¼in** Price ★★

4 **Stuart Interiors/Heraldic Beasts** Colour **rust/beige** Alt. colours **yes** Composition **70% wool, 30% linen** Width **172cm/ 67½in** Repeat **89cm/35in** Price ★★★★

5 **Stuart Interiors/Fleur de Lys** Colour **blue** Alt. colours **yes** Composition **75% wool, 25% silk** Width **145cm/ 57in** Repeat **25cm/9¾in** Price ★★★★

6 **Jason D'Souza/Siena SIE01** Colour **coral** Alt. colours **yes** Composition **51% modacrylic, 37% cotton, 12% nylon** Width **135cm/53in** Repeat **4cm/1½in** Price ★★

7 **Zoffany/Rosa GRD8600** Colour **1** Alt. colours **yes** Composition **37% cotton, 13% linen, 50% viscose** Width **140cm/55in** Repeat **14cm/5½in** Price ★★★

8 **Andrew Martin/Parasol** Colour **Alloy** Alt. colours **yes** Composition **56% polyester, 44% viscose** Width **140cm/ 55in** Repeat **10.5cm/4in** Price ★★★

4
6
7
8

9

10

9 **Zoffany/Leaf PCW0300** Colour **1**
Alt. colours **yes** Composition
**73% cotton, 14% viscose, 12%
nylon, 1% silk** Width **145cm/
57in** Repeat **4.5cm/1¾in**
Price ★★ LC 🗗🗗🛋

10 **Zoffany/Este DUP7600** Colour **2**
Alt. colours **yes** Composition
100% cotton Width **138cm/
54in** Repeat **32cm/12½in**
Price ★★ 🗗🗗

11 **The Silk Gallery/Dis Print**
Colour **stone 235** Alt. colours
yes Composition **100% silk**
Width **127cm/50in** Repeat
14cm/5½in Price ★★★ 🗗🗗

12 **Bernard Thorp & Co/Daisy Time**
Colour **blue** Alt. colours **yes**
Composition **100% jute** Width
120cm/47in Repeat **53cm/21in**
Price ★★ 🗗🗗🛋

13 **Zoffany/Hardwick High Great
Chamber NTF0100** Colour **1**
Alt. colours **yes** Composition
47% cotton, 53% viscose Width
141cm/55½in Repeat **81cm/32in**
Price ★★★ 🛋🗗🗗

14 **Harlequin/Navaril/Nadir**
Colour **736** Alt. colours
yes Composition **100%
cotton** Width **137cm/54in**
Repeat **64cm/25in**
Price ★★ LC 🗗🗗🛋

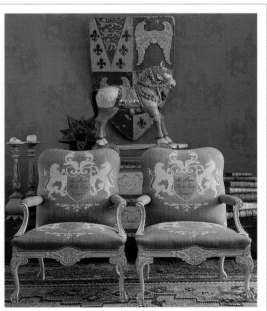

11

12

13

14

HERALDIC MOTIFS

First used in the 12th
century to denote
position and status in a
feudal society, heraldic
emblems rapidly became
a form of decoration that
also conveyed pride of
ownership and pedigree.
Typical motifs, often
within achievements-
of-arms, include helmets
and shields, cyphers
and draperies. Stylized
beasts, such as stags,
dogs, porcupines or
lions, griffins or harpies,
unicorns, and enfields
or ypotrylls were also
very popular.

Andrew Martin/Magna Carta Colour
red Alt. colours **yes** Composition
100% cotton Width **133cm/
52in** Repeat **112cm/44in**
Price ★★ 🗗🗗🛋

Heraldic motifs have been frequently utilized by
manufacturers as inspiration for their fabric designs.
The central shield on the fabric shown here bears a
Latin inscription that translates as: "One does not
value things easily obtained."

Motifs: **18th century**

Access to the numerous pattern books in international circulation during the 18th century enabled fabric designers to draw on a rich and varied catalogue of historical ornamentation. Early in the century, fabrics adorning Palladian interiors featured herms, eagles, dolphins and masks inspired by classical Roman and Renaissance ornament, while fabrics in Picturesque schemes displayed pastoral and rustic scenes and *fêtes galantes* – the latter also appearing on the Rococo-style fabrics in vogue until the middle of the century. Other motifs typical of the Rococo period included *singeries*, *rocaille*, scrollwork and *chinoiserie* birds and lanterns. In the Neo-classical Adam- and Federal-style schemes of the late 18th century, Roman motifs – lion masks, rosettes, urns, vases, griffins and delicate scrolling foliage – were prevalent, while the Gothick Revival at the end of the century saw Gothic ornament, such as flora, fauna, the seasons and portraits of masons and clerics, portrayed in an historically accurate manner.

5 Colefax and Fowler/Osterley 2063/03 Colour **coral and green** Alt. colours **yes** Composition **52% linen, 36% cotton, 12% nylon** Width **134cm/52½in** Repeat **41cm/16in** Price ★★ 🗹 🛋

6 G.P. & J. Baker/Pineapple Colour **2** Alt. colours **yes** Composition **60% linen, 20% cotton** Width **134cm/52½in** Repeat **56cm/22in** Price ★★ LC 🗹 ⊞🛋LC

7 Busby & Busby/Amaretti 4913 Colour **gold, crimson and stone** Alt. colours **yes** Composition **100% cotton** Width **140cm/55in** Repeat **64cm/25in** Price ★★ 🗹🛋

5

1 Hodsoll McKenzie/Toile d'Avignon 221/105 Colour **red/blue** Alt. colours **yes** Composition **50% rayon, 50% cotton** Width **127cm/50in** Repeat **40.5cm/16in** Price ★★★ 🗹🛋 W

2 Brunschwig & Fils/Canton Cotton Print 79512.04 Colour **blue fish on white** Alt. colours **yes** Composition **100% cotton** Width **134cm/52½in** Repeat **64cm/25in** Price ★★ 🗹🛋

3 Timney Fowler/Ornamental Stripe Colour **01 black & white** Alt. colours **yes** Composition **100% cotton** Width **140cm/55in** Repeat **90cm/35½in** Price ★★ 🗹 ⊞

4 Mulberry/Oberon Chenille/FD402 Colour **stone/jade** Alt. colours **yes** Composition **87% cotton, 13% viscose/flax** Width **127cm/50in** Repeat **165cm/67in** Price ★★★ 🗹 ⊞🛋

6

1

2

3

7

8 **Apenn/Hampton Linen
LN 476-8/9** Colour **red-blue**
Alt. colours **yes** Composition
100% linen Width **125cm/49¼in**
Repeat **20cm/8in**
Price ★★ 🪑🛋

9 **The Isle Mill/Red Fintry/FIN006**
Colour **red** Alt. colours **yes**
Composition **100% wool** Width
137cm/54in Repeat **6cm/2¼in**
Price ★★ LC 🪑🛋

10 **Thomas Dare/Providence 958**
Colour **234** Alt. colours **yes**
Composition **93% cotton, 7%
rayon** Width **137cm/54in**
Repeat **32.5cm/12¾in**
Price ★★ 🪑 ⊞🛋 W

11 **Brunschwig & Fils/89513**
Colour **647** Alt. colours **yes**
Composition **100% Trevira CS**
Width **140cm/55in**
Repeat **63cm/24¾in**
Price ★★★ 🪑 LC🛋 W

12 **Brunschwig & Fils/89511**
Colour **409** Alt. colours **yes**
Composition **100% Trevira CS**
Width **140cm/55in**
Repeat **4cm/1½in**
Price ★★★ 🪑 LC🛋

13

14   15

16   17

13 **Bennison Fabrics/China Birds**
Colour **1** Alt. colours **yes**
Composition **70% linen, 30%
cotton** Width **118cm/46¼in**
Repeat **43cm/16¾in**
Price ★★ 🪑🛋

14 **Marvic Textiles/Pineapple Plaid
414-10** Colour **holly** Alt. colours
yes Composition **62% linen,
23% cotton, 15% viscose** Width
130cm/51in Repeat **6.5cm/2½in**
Price ★★🛋

15 **Scalamandré/Strawberry Design
205-003** Colour **multi on blue
and ivory** Alt. colours **yes**
Composition **100% silk** Width
127cm/50in Repeat **6.5cm/2½in**
Price ★★★★★ 🪑🛋

16 **Timney Fowler/Scroll Stripe
TF0304** Colour **black & white**
Alt. colours **yes** Composition
100% cotton Width **140cm/55in**
Repeat **21.5cm/8½in**
Price ★★ 🪑 ⊞

17 **Ian Sanderson/Amy Check**
Colour **brick** Alt. colours **yes**
Composition **37% polyester,
35% cotton, 28% viscose** Width
135cm/53in Repeat **1.5cm/⅝in**
Price ★★ 🪑🛋

18 **Timney Fowler/Roman Heads
TF0027.04** Colour **red and ecru**
Alt. colours **yes** Composition
100% cotton Width **120cm/47in**
Repeat **108cm/42½in**
Price ★★🛋

NEO-CLASSICISM

This Louis XVI-style
lampas was designed
in 1779 and used to
upholster chairs in Marie
Antoinette's apartments
at the Château de
Versailles near Paris,
France. In 1859 it was
reproduced for Empress
Eugénie's apartments in
the Palais des Tuileries.
The predominantly floral
pattern, in the centre
of which lies an oval
medallion encompassing
a stylized fluted torch
encircled with flowers
and entwined with
crumpled ribbons, is
typical of late 18th-
century Neo-classicism.

Lelièvre/Lampas – Marie Antoinette 10481 Colour **2** Alt. colours
yes Composition **100% silk** Width **130cm/51in** Repeat **2cm/¾in**
Price ★★★★★ 🪑🛋

18

Motifs: **Early 19th century**

Underpinning the Empire, Regency and Federal styles of decoration prevalent during the early 19th century was a revival of Classicism in its original purity. Initiated in France by architects Percier and Fontaine (under the patronage of Napoleon), Empire style was encapsulated in their influential book *Recueil des Décorations Intérieures* (1801), rapidly spread to Federal America and was strongly reflected in the Regency interiors of England. Early 19th-century Classicism was made up of two major historical strands: "le Style Etrusque" and Roman. Favoured Etruscan motifs for fabrics included palmettes, palm leaves and anthemions, as well as vases, medallions, winged lions and eagles. Roman motifs and emblems proved even more popular, especially in France, largely owing to Napoleon's desire to identify the country with the greatness of the Roman Empire. Therefore laurel and oak wreaths, lances, arrows and fasces, griffins, winged torches, and figures of victory and fame were much in evidence. An additional historical influence was fuelled by archaeological excavations in Egypt and by Napoleon's Nile campaign, ancient Egyptian motifs, such as scarabs, sphinxes, lotus flowers and hieroglyphics appearing soon after being copied from drawings in Baron Denon's *Voyages dans la Basse et la Haute Egypte* (1802–3).

7

6 Ramm, Son & Crocker/Floris Colour **aqua** Alt. colours **yes** Composition **52% linen, 36% cotton, 12% nylon** Width **140cm/55in** Repeat **10cm/4in** Price ★★

7 Scalamandré/26546 Colour **005** Alt. colours **yes** Composition **50% cotton, 50% viscose** Width **130cm/51in** Repeat **8cm/3in** Price ★★★★

8 Today Interiors/Samadhi/Tulipa Colour **SAF308** Alt. colours **yes** Composition **88% linen, 12% nylon** Width **137cm/ 54in** Repeat **48cm/19in** Price ★★

9 Lelièvre/Prudhon 4147 07 Colour **marine** Alt. colours **yes** Composition **55% cotton, 45% silk** Width **130cm/51in** Repeat **22cm/8½in** Price ★★★

1

2

6

(detail with floral and vase motifs)

3   4

1 Brunschwig & Fils/Lindsey's Garden Lisère 53451 Colour **01** Alt. colours **yes** Composition **55% cotton, 45% rayon** Width **137cm/54in** Repeat **17cm/6¾in** Price ★★★

2 Northwood Designs/Romeo/ M061Y6 Colour **pistache** Alt. colours **yes** Composition **100% cotton** Width **290cm/114¼in** Repeat **8.5cm/3¼in** Price ★★

3 Warner Fabrics/Little Acorns CS 336080 Colour **petrol/buff** Alt. colours **yes** Composition **100% cotton** Width **137cm/54in** Repeat **10cm/4in** Price ★★

4 Mulberry/Signal Silk/FD421 Colour **yellow/pink T125** Alt. colours **yes** Composition **83% acetate, 17% silk** Width **148cm/ 58¼in** Repeat **24cm/9½in** Price ★★★★

5 Laura Ashley/Marlborough Colour **raspberry** Alt. colours **yes** Composition **70% viscose, 20% cotton, 10% nylon** Width **130cm/51in** Repeat **44cm/17in** Price ★★

5   9

11

10

12

NAPOLEONIC MOTIFS

Three recurring Napoleonic motifs are the bee, the swan and the palm tree. Napoleon adopted the bee as his emblem primarily because it was an ancient Greek symbol of order and industry, but also because metal bees found in the tomb of Chilperic I (a 6th-century Frankish king) provided a link with early French rulers. The black swan was the Empress Josephine's emblem, chosen because swans pulled the chariot of Venus. The palm tree was an emblem of fame and victory, and, being indigenous to Africa, served as a symbol of Napoleon's Egyptian campaigns.

1

2

10 Scalamandré/Lampas – Rosecliff Laurel 20221-007 Colour **cranberry** Alt. colours **yes** Composition **100% silk** Width **140cm/55in** Repeat **17cm/6¾in** Price ★★★★ 🛋🛏

11 G.P. & J. Baker/Laurel Colour **red** Alt. colours **yes** Composition **67% cotton, 33% modacrylic** Width **140cm/55in** Repeat **6cm/2⅜in** Price ★★ 🛋🛏

12 Lelièvre/Vernet 414606 Colour **bleu** Alt. colours **yes** Composition **55% cotton, 45% silk** Width **130cm/51in** Repeat **16cm/6¼in** Price ★★★★ 🛋🛏

13 G.P. & J. Baker/Eccleston Colour **terracotta** Alt. colours **yes** Composition **100% lightly glazed cotton** Width **137cm/54in** Repeat **81cm/31¾in** Price ★★ 🛋🛏

14 Zoffany/Neo Classique Colour **red** Alt. colours **yes** Composition **53.9% viscose, 46.1% cotton** Width **142cm/55¾in** Repeat **86cm/33¾in** Price ★★🛏

13

14

1 Scalamandré/Bee 213-002 Colour **multi on cream ground** Alt. colours **yes** Composition **100% silk** Width **127cm/50in** Repeat **5.5cm/2¼in** Price ★★★★★ 🛋

2 Turnell & Gigon/Les Cygnes 18429 Colour **green and red** Alt. colours **yes** Composition **60% viscose, 40% cotton** Width **130cm/51in** Repeat **32cm/12½in** Price ★★★★★ 🛋🛏

3 Pierre Frey/Palmiers 2525 Colour **original** Alt. colours **yes** Composition **64% linen, 36% cotton** Width **136cm/53½in** Repeat **25.5cm/10in** Price ★★★★ 🛋🛏

3

Motifs: **Mid-19th century**

The majority of fabric motifs favoured in the middle of the 19th century fell into one of two stylistic categories – Classical Revival and Gothic Revival – and in this respect mirrored the "battle of the styles" that was taking place in contemporary architecture. Typical Gothic Revival motifs – employed by noted designers such as the English architect A.W.N. Pugin – included stylized scrolling leaves and heraldic motifs (such as fleur-de-lis), usually set within a flat pattern of basic ogival structure. Mythical beasts, gargoyles and patrons of the arts, presented within medallions, were also recurring motifs of the style.

Classical ornamentation of the period was wide ranging. In Renaissance Revival interiors, Roman-influenced acanthus leaves, scrolling foliage, swags and festoons vied with grotesques and *grisaille* panels incorporating the Elements and the Muses; while in the Baroque Revival (Second Empire) designs that followed, leafy scrolls, swags, urns, flaming torches, angels and putti were all much in evidence. Further enriching the ornamentation of fabrics during this period were Moorish motifs, such as arabesques, and Indian designs, such as the paisley patterns derived from Kashmiri shawls and consisting of formalized representations of pine cones, palms and almonds.

Borderline/Forget Me Not Colour **A** Alt. colours **yes** Composition **100% cotton** Width **137cm/54in** Repeat **37.5cm/14¾in** Price ★★ 🪑

George Spencer Decorations/ Elizabeth 017L Colour **apricot** Alt. colours **yes** Composition **60% cotton, 40% linen** Width **138cm/54in** Repeat **20cm/8in** Price ★★★★ 🪑🛋

Donghia/Vicenza/4906 Colour **10 silver** Alt. colours **yes** Composition **81% viscose, 19% linen** Width **140cm/55in** Repeat **43cm/16¾in** Price ★★★★ 🪑🛋

Jab/Mukarnas CA 7212 Colour **003** Alt. colours **yes** Composition **46% cotton, 30% viscose, 12% polyacrylic, 12% linen** Width **140cm/55in** Repeat **73cm/28½in** Price ★★★ 🛋🪑

Sheila Coombes/Lindale Colour **76 Sea Holly** Alt. colours **yes** Composition **47% wool, 31% cotton, 12% viscose, 10% nylon** Width **137cm/54in** Repeat **7cm/2¾in** Price ★★ 🪑🛋

Bennison Fabrics/Jubilee Stripe Colour **red** Alt. colours **yes** Composition **70% linen, 30% cotton** Width **139cm/54¾in** Repeat **43.5cm/17in** Price ★★★ 🪑🛋

Watts of Westminster/Tudor Badge F0026-01/U1 Colour **lichen/old gold** Alt. colours **yes** Composition **100% cotton** Width **124cm/48⅞in** Repeat **14cm/5½in** Price ★★★ 🪑🛋

Watts of Westminster/Trellis Z1TR/M30FR Colour **bottle green** Alt. colours **yes** Composition **56% cotton, 44% polycotton** Width **140cm/55in** Repeat **18cm/7in** Price ★★★🛋

Mary Fox Linton/Fedra Colour **01** Alt. colours **yes** Composition **54% cotton, 28% viscose, 18% polyester** Width **140cm/55in** Repeat **16cm/6¼in** Price ★★★ 🪑

Watts of Westminster/Wexford Welby 21WWB/3 Colour **Geneva** Alt. colours **yes** Composition **100% cotton** Width **124cm/48¾in** Repeat **21cm/8¼in** Price ★★★ 🪑🛋

Abbott & Boyd/Objetos Colour **blue/red** Alt. colours **yes** Composition **100%** Width **155cm/61¼in** Repeat **19cm/7½in** Price ★★ 🪑🛋

Mulberry/Cartouche FD336 Colour **T31 gold/blue** Alt. colours **yes** Composition **65% viscose, 25% cotton, 10% polymide** Width **146cm/57½in** Repeat **30cm/11¾in** Price ★★ 🪑 LC🛋 W

Weymss Houlès/Minster/Canterbury Colour **303** Alt. colours **yes** Composition **56% linen, 33% cotton, 11% nylon** Width **137cm/54in** Repeat — Price ★ 🪑

Zoffany/Dup7600 Este Colour **1** Alt. colours **yes** Composition **100% cotton** Width **138cm/54in** Repeat **32cm/12½in** Price ★★ LC🪑🛋

Zuber/Chateau de Blois/Alcove Chambre de la Reine T9222 Colour **1** Alt. colours **no** Composition **100% cotton** Width **130cm/51in** Repeat **74cm/29in** Price ★★★★ 🪑🗗🛋 W

Motifs: Late 19th century

The diversity of fabric motifs in evidence during the late 19th century was as wide ranging as the contemporary styles of architecture and decoration. On both sides of the Atlantic, an eclectic mix of revivalist styles, such as Gothic, Louis XIV, Rococo and Pompeiian, were often employed in different rooms throughout the same house. However, a reaction to this jumbled diversity of ornamentation set in, and more uniform decorative schemes derived from the Aesthetic, Arts and Crafts and Art Nouveau movements emerged.

Fabric motifs favoured by the Aesthetic movement included flowers (particularly sunflowers), mostly depicted in a conventionalized, flat, circular form, but sometimes with almost botanical accuracy; Japanese-style sparrows, kingfishers and peacocks; Renaissance-style putti, dolphins and grotesques, and scrollwork inspired by Turkish, Persian and Cretan embroideries. Arts and Crafts fabrics – the most popular of the period – featured flowers and birds, rhythmically presented within a medieval-style pattern structure. Stylized birds, and floral and vegetative motifs, notably scrolling acanthus leaves, were also favoured by Art Nouveau designers. However, these were more sinuously illustrated than their Arts and Crafts counterparts.

1 Bennison Fabrics/India Stripe
Colour **red** Alt. colours **yes**
Composition **70% linen,
30% cotton** Width **122cm/
48in** Repeat **49cm/19¼in**
Price ★★★ 🪑🛋

**2 Watts of Westminster/Malvern
WF0016-03/T5** Colour **brick/
rust/old gold** Alt. colours **yes**
Composition **63% cotton,
37% flax** Width **130cm/51in**
Repeat **124cm/48¾in**
Price ★★★★ 🪑🛋

**3 Kravet/Joseph Abboud/
Cavendisa 19836** Colour
916 mink Alt. colours **yes**
Composition **100% cotton**
Width **137cm/54in**
Repeat **68cm/26¾in**
Price ★★★★★ 🪑 LC 🪟🛋

**4 Liberty Furnishings/Allerton
LF4190** Colour **06** Alt. colours
yes Composition **91% cotton,
9% nylon** Width **140cm/55in**
Repeat **62cm/24¼in**
Price ★★ LC 🪑

**5 Hodsoll McKenzie/Small
Ottoman 263/101-106** Colour
blue Alt. colours **yes**
Composition **100% cotton**
Width **127cm/50in** Repeat
21cm/8¼in Price ★★★ 🪑

**6 Liberty Furnishings/Lodden
1069622** Colour **C** Alt. colours
yes Composition **100% cotton**
Width **137cm/54in**
Repeat **46cm/18in**
Price ★★ 🪑 LC 🪟

**7 Scalamandré/Coeur de Lion
26315-002** Colour **crimson**
Alt. colours **yes** Composition
52% acrylic, 48% cotton Width
142cm/55¾in Repeat **18cm/7in**
Price ★★★ 🪟🪑

**8 Watts of Westminster/Memlinc
F0017-07/A5** Colour **taupe/
oatmeal** Alt. colours **yes**
Composition **100% cotton**
Width **124cm/48¾in**
Repeat **98cm/38¾in**
Price ★★★ 🪟🪑

**9 Warner Fabrics/Etiennes Folly
CS 8060** Colour **stone/cream**
Alt. colours **yes** Composition
68% linen, 32% cotton Width
137cm/54in Repeat **62cm/24¼in**
Price ★★ 🪟🪑

4

5

6

7

8

9

19th century

FABRICS: *MOTIFS* **103**

Motifs: **Early 20th century**

For the first five years of the 20th century, Art Nouveau motifs such as stems, roots, elongated blooms and dream-like figures of women retained their popularity, while Arts and Crafts fabrics, featuring daisies, wild roses and medieval motifs such as the fleur-de-lis, remained fashionable well into the 1930s. Tudor Revival and Jacobean Revival fabrics were also in vogue, ornamented with birds of paradise, the "Tree of Life", Tudor roses and furled, banner-like ribbons.

Less revivalist and more innovative were the designs on the Art Deco fabrics. The earliest examples were embellished with rounded and romantic motifs, such as garlands and baskets of flowers, stylized rosebuds, fawns, doves and ropes of pearls. Such images were gradually superseded by Egyptian motifs, including the scarab, and Aztec symbols, such as stepped shapes and sun motifs. However, these motifs were in turn supplanted by streamlined geometric and abstract images that provoked French designer Paul Iribe to observe: "They [have] sacrificed the flower on the altar of Cubism and the machine."

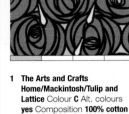

1

2

1   **The Arts and Crafts Home/Mackintosh/Tulip and Lattice** Colour **C** Alt. colours **yes** Composition **100% cotton** Width **122cm/48in** Repeat **16cm/6¼in** Price ★★★ LC 🛋

2   **The Arts and Crafts Home/Mackintosh/Rose and Teardrop** Colour **D** Alt. colours **yes** Composition **100% cotton,** Width **122cm/48in** Repeat **24cm/9½in** Price ★★★ LC 🛋

3

4

3   **Wemyss/Earlswood** Colour **1P.172** Alt. colours **yes** Composition **49% modacrylic, 39% cotton, 20% nylon** Width **140cm/55in** Repeat **19cm/7½in** Price ★★ LC ✂ ⊞🛋

4   **Lee Jofa/Gadesden HAD** Colour **1210** Alt. colours **yes** Composition **100% linen** Width **132cm/51¾in** Repeat **96cm/37¾in** Price ★★★ ✂

5   **Today Interiors/Samadhi/ Samara** Colour **SAF3079** Alt. colours **yes** Composition **88% linen, 12% nylon** Width **137cm/54in** Repeat **62cm/ 24¼in** Price ★★ 🛋 LC W

6   **Mulberry/Daisy Daisy FD084** Colour **J103 Cream** Alt. colours **yes** Composition **75% cotton, 25% viscose** Width **150cm/59in** Repeat **13.5cm/5¼in** Price ★★★ ✂ ⊞

7   **Hill & Knowles/Lorian/Oakham C4265** Colour **65** Alt. colours **yes** Composition **52% linen, 48% cotton** Width **140cm/ 55in** Repeat **63cm/24¾in** Price ★★ ✂ LC ⊞🛋

5

6

7

8

9

10

8 **Donghia/Fleur d'Hiver 0475/ 3310** Colour **01** Alt. colours **yes** Composition **88% cotton, 12% viscose** Width **137cm/ 54in** Repeat **68cm/26¾in** Price ★★★★

9 **Hill & Knowles/Lorian/Teal C4482** Colour **82** Alt. colours **yes** Composition **52%linen, 48% cotton** Width **140cm/ 55in** Repeat **35.5cm/14in** Price ★★

10 **Brunschwig & Fils/Sycamore Floral Plaid 53373.01** Colour **mandarin plaid** Alt. colours **yes** Composition **100% cotton** Width **130cm/51in** Repeat **16cm/6¼in** Price ★★

11 **Zoffany/Provence Check PLP0500** Colour **1** Alt. colours **yes** Composition **100% cotton** Width **137cm/ 54in** Repeat **6cm/2½in** Price ★★

12 **Celia Birtwell/Orphée 1013** Colour **beige** Alt. colours **yes** Composition **100% silk** Width **140cm/55in** Repeat **91cm/35¾in** Price ★★★

13

14

11

12

THE OAK LEAF

The fabric shown here is adapted from a hand-blocked tapestry woven in the Arthur H. Lee factory in Birkenhead, England, until the early 1970s, when the factory closed. The pattern dates from the early 20th century. However, the oak-leaf motif was first used much earlier than that – for example, in ancient Rome as a symbol of civic virtue, and in naturalistic decorations of the Middle Ages and the Renaissance. Similarly, the acorn – a symbol of life, fecundity and immortality – notably recurs in ancient Roman, Celtic and Scandinavian designs, and has been consistently favoured since the Middle Ages.

Lee Jofa/Oak Leaf Weave 854252 Colour **carmine** Alt. colours **yes** Composition **85% rayon, 15% cotton** Width **132cm/51¼in** Repeat **8.5cm/3¼in** Price ★★★★

15

13 **Abbott & Boyd/Medina** Colour **verde** Alt. colours **yes** Composition **100% cotton** Width **160cm/63in** Repeat **40cm/15¾in** Price ★★

14 **Zoffany/Florette PLP0100** Colour **1** Alt. colours **yes** Composition **100% cotton** Width **137cm/54in** Repeat **21.5cm/8½in** Price ★★

15 **J. Robert Scott/Floating Petals 3451** Colour **green tea** Alt. colours **yes** Composition **66% wool, 34% silk** Width **135cm/53in** Repeat **45.5cm/ 17¾in** Price ★★★

20th century

Motifs: Late 20th–early 21st century

Fashionable fabric motifs of the 1950s included abstract, geometric and Cubist-inspired images, as well as crystal-like shapes derived from scientific observations under the microscope and produced by designers working in a style known as Organic Modernism. Small repeat motifs of fruits such as apples and pears were also popular. Depicted in both stylized and naturalistic form, and often set on a plain background, they remained in demand for much of the rest of the century.

The 1960s gave rise to a profusion of decorative styles and accompanying motifs: Art Nouveau fabrics (harbouring sinuous plant stems and roots and elongated blooms) enjoyed a great revival; foliage, flowers, animals, birds and insects appeared in repeating patterns taken from Persian paintings and ceramics; Renaissance-style classical figures, vases and urns – sometimes set within geometric patterns and sometimes in mosaic form – came into vogue, and Pop Art crossed over from canvas and concrete to textiles. As the 1960s drew to a close, a new ruralism emerged, significant consequences of which were the enduring "country-house look" and the accompanying revival in the manufacture of chintzes incorporating traditional foliage, flower, fruit and bird motifs.

1

2

1 Monkwell/Estrella MF5821
Colour **sand 404** Alt. colours
yes Composition **47%
modacrylic, 43% cotton,
10% nylon** Width **137cm/
54in** Repeat **6cm/2⅜in**
Price ★★

2 Knowles & Christou/Posey
Colour **porceline** Alt. colours
yes Composition **100%
silk** Width **152cm/59¾in**
Repeat **40cm/15¾in**
Price ★★★

3 Sahco Hesslein/Minerva 1831
Colour **03** Alt. colours **yes**
Composition **74% cotton,
18% silk, 5% acrylic, 3%
viscose** Width **130cm/51in**
Repeat **25cm/9¾in**
Price ★★★

**4 Nina Campbell/Nina's Garden/
Rock Pool NCF3133/03**
Colour **red** Alt. colours **yes**
Composition **100% cotton**
Width **140cm/55in** Repeat
30cm/11¾in Price ★★

5 Malabar/Bo Leaf TAPR22
Colour **silver** Alt. colours
no Composition **100% silk**
Width **140cm/55in**
Repeat **49cm/19¼in**
Price ★★★

6 Brunschwig & Fils/89418
Colour **honey beige 069**
Alt. colours **yes** Composition
100% cotton Width **137cm/
54in** Repeat **63.5cm/25in**
Price ★★

3

4

5

6

7

10

11

7 Donghia/Crown Jewels 2000
Colour **18** Alt. colours **yes**
Composition **81% rayon,**
19% polyester Width **137cm/**
54in Repeat **32cm/12½in**
Price ★★★★★ 🛋

8 Textra/Okaya Colour **cream,**
orange Alt. colours **yes**
Composition **100% linen**
Width **138cm/54in** Repeat
32cm/12½in Price ★★ 🛋

9 Abbott & Boyd/Est Complemento
Flora Colour **antillana verde**
Alt. colours **no** Composition
100% Width **150cm/59in**
Repeat **35cm/13¾in**
Price ★★ 🛋

10 Nina Campbell/Manihiki
Prints/Vanuta NCF3362-04
Colour **04** Alt. colours **yes**
Composition **100% cotton**
Width **140cm/55in**
Repeat **45cm/17⅛in**
Price ★★ 🛋

12

11 Osborne & Little/Rondo F1413
Colour **02** Alt. colours **yes**
Composition **57% cotton, 43%**
viscose Width **140cm/55in**
Repeat **36cm/14in**
Price ★★★ 🛋

12 Montgomery/Jasmine
Colour **beige 12** Alt. colours
yes Composition **67% polyester,**
26% viscose, 7% linen Width
140cm/55in Repeat **64cm/25in**
Price ★ 🛋

13 Harlequin/Notebook/Tilia Colour
apple green 177 Alt. colours **yes**
Composition **36% cotton,**
52% linen, 12% nylon Width
137cm/54in Repeat **64cm/25in**
Price ★★ 🛋

8

9

13

Motifs: Late 20th–early 21st century

Many of the fabric motifs favoured since the late 1960s have reflected a widespread nostalgia for previous eras and the accompanying boom in "period-style" interiors. Apart from chintz-style flowers, foliage and birds, revivals have included late 19th-century William Morris- and other Arts and Crafts-style flowers, animal motifs derived from 16th- and 17th-century needlework patterns and, in America, "Native Orders", first popular in the late 18th and 19th centuries. Significant among the latter were corncobs, tobacco and cotton balls, stars, turkeys and bald eagles, as well as Native American motifs including feathered arrowshafts, bison and bison horns. Some of the most striking motifs are classical architectural elements rendered in black and white. At the same time, more short-term nostalgia resulted in "space age" motifs inspired by the Apollo programme and the moon landings.

Internationally, the late 20th and early 21st century also witnessed a further consolidation of the links between contemporary fine art and fabric design, with fashionable motifs featuring artistic images of fruits and berries, a diverse range of domestic artefacts ranging from crockery to buttons, and photographic images and photocopied prints.

Pierre Frey/Minton 1962 Colour **rose ancien 5** Alt. colours **yes** Composition **100% cotton** Width **138cm/54in** Repeat **77cm/30¼in** Price ★★★★ ⟨⟩

Mulberry/Tea Rose/FD441 Colour **red** Alt. colours **yes** Composition **61% silk, 39% polyester** Width **127cm/50in** Repeat **13cm/5¼in** Price ★★ 🛋

Harlequin/Divine/Sense Colour **197** Alt. colours **yes** Composition **100% cotton** Width **137cm/54in** Repeat **64cm/25in** Price ★ ⟨⟩ 🛋

Today Interiors/Aymara/Mirage Colour **3313** Alt. colours **yes** Composition **52% linen, 48% cotton** Width **137cm/54in** Repeat **50.5cm/20in** Price ★★ LC ⟨⟩ 🛋

Today Interiors/Taffetas/Pensee Colour **4041** Alt. colours **yes** Composition **100% acetate (flowers - polyester/viscose)** Width **150cm/59in** Repeat **20cm/8in** Price ★★ ⊞

Timney Fowler/Porticos TF0203/03 Colour **03** Alt. colours **yes** Composition **100% cotton** Width **137cm/54in** Repeat **96.5cm/38in** Price ★★ ⟨⟩ 🛋

Brunschwig & Fils 79529 Colour **761** Alt. colours **yes** Composition **100% cotton** Width **142.5cm/56in** Repeat **46cm/18in** Price ★★ 🛋️LC 〈〉

Montgomery/Samurai Colour **12** Alt. colours **yes** Composition **100% cotton** Width **140cm/55in** Repeat **64cm/25in** Price ★ 〈〉 ⊞

Manuel Canovas/Tilda 4423/21 Colour **rose/jaune** Alt. colours **yes** Composition **73% viscose, 27% cotton** Width **140cm/55in** Repeat **8.5cm/3¼in** Price ★★ 〈〉🛋️

Malabar/Jutis Colour **01** Alt. colours **yes** Composition **90% cotton, 10% jute** Width **137cm/54in** Repeat – Price ★★ 〈〉🛋️⊞

Liberty Furnishings/Bellini LF4290 Colour **03** Alt. colours **yes** Composition **45% polyester, 35% viscose, 15% acrylic, 5% polyamide** Width **144cm/56½in** Repeat **10cm/4in** Price ★★ 〈〉 ⊞

Malabar/Alula Colour **02** Alt. colours **no** Composition **80% silk, 20% wool** Width **140cm/55in** Repeat **70cm/27½in** Price ★ 🛋️

Abbott & Boyd/Est el Jardin Verde Colour **green on cream** Alt. colours **no** Composition **100% cotton** Width **160cm/63in** Repeat **66cm/26in** Price ★★ 〈〉⊞

Anna French/Chalice Colour **28** Alt. colours **yes** Composition **100% cotton** Width **137cm/54in** Repeat **64cm/25in** Price ★★ 〈〉🛋️

Floral Fabrics

Throughout history, textile designers have made extensive use of plant motifs and floral subjects. In Europe, before the end of the 16th century, floral patterns were featured on a wide variety of fabrics, including tapestry, embroidery and woven damasks and velvets. However, the accurate depiction of the many and diverse plants in existence was restricted by the limitations of early weaving techniques and by a lack of botanical reference material.

Two events were to occur that resulted in a proliferation of floral-patterned fabrics that has endured to this day. The first event was the publication in 1586 of *La Clef des Champs*, by French artist and traveller Jacques le Moyne de Morgues. Depicting flowers, fruits and animals in a simple but accurate style, this early pattern book provided textile designers with a wealth of inspiration, and also set the precedent for more extensive publications in the future. The second was the importation of the first colourfast, hand-blocked calicoes (*indiennes*) from India, which confirmed that floral decoration could be most dramatically exploited on printed fabrics.

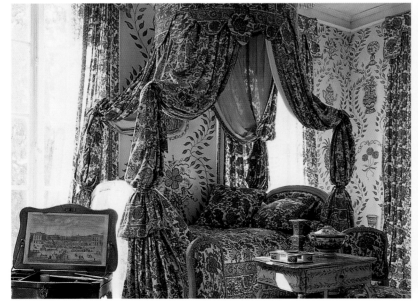

LEFT Printed cotton curtains grace the window of a medieval house in a *bastide* in the Lot-et-Garonne region, France. The floral design, augmented with a pattern of foliage and birds, is elegantly rendered in white, red and shades of pink.

BELOW LEFT *Chinoiserie* patterns on 17th- and 18th-century delftware provided the inspiration for the bed-hangings and upholstered seating in this bedroom at the Château de Morsan, France.

BELOW The walls of this room, designed by Roger Banks-Pye, are decorated with a machine-woven, crewelwork fabric, its stylized floral pattern inspired by 17th-century Eastern designs. The various blue-and-white and black-and-white checks covering the cushions and screen stand out sharply against this contrasting background.

ROSE MOTIFS

Rich in symbolism, the rose has been one of the most enduringly popular of the floral motifs. In Christian iconography it is an attribute of the Virgin Mary and paradise, while in classical mythology it is a token of Venus (and love), and of secrecy (*sub rosa*). Other notable associations of the rose include martyrdom (red rose) and piety (white rose). Over the centuries wild and cultivated roses have inspired fabric designs, wild roses being closely associated with medieval, Jacobean and Arts and Crafts fabrics and cultivated roses appearing on Victorian and Edwardian designs.

KEY DESIGNS

1 Naturalistic floral patterns were especially popular in the 18th and 19th centuries, but first began to appear in the 17th century as designers gained access to illustrated botanical studies.

2 Flowering-vine patterns were prevalent in ancient Egyptian, Roman and early eastern Mediterranean decorations, and were favoured on Renaissance and 17th-, 18th- and mid-19th-century fabrics.

3 Stylized floral patterns have been seen since the Middle Ages. They were particularly popular during the late 19th century, and were a feature of Arts and Crafts and Art Nouveau fabrics.

4 Flowers are a feature of *chinoiserie* and *japonaiserie* fabrics, many of which were derived from traditional porcelain designs. Popular imagery included blossom sprigs, peonies and chrysanthemums.

5 Patterns of densely packed blooms and foliage were highly fashionable in Victorian interiors, especially on chintzes, and were to come back into fashion in the Art Deco schemes of the 20th century.

6 Since the Middle Ages, typical embellishments to naturalistic and stylized floral patterns have included trelliswork, hanging baskets and, as in this rose pattern, decorative ribbons.

1 Bennett Silks/Basket and Ribbon Colour **multi** Alt. colours **yes** Composition **100% silk** Width **130cm/51in** Repeat **61cm/24in** Price ★★★

2 Schumacher/Imperial Vine 168360 Colour **document cream and multi** Alt. colours **yes** Composition **100% cotton** Width **137cm/54in** Repeat **64.5cm/25¼in** Price ★★★

3 Morris & Co/Golden Lily PR7702 Colour **4** Alt. colours **yes** Composition **53% linen, 35% cotton, 12% nylon** Width **137cm/54in** Repeat **53cm/21in** Price ★★

4 Old World Weavers/Lasalle Colour **multi/ brown** Alt. colours **yes** Composition **100% rayon** Width **140cm/55in** Repeat **64cm/25in** Price ★★★

5 Jason D'Souza/Blenheim Colour **plum/rust** Alt. colours **yes** Composition **64% linen, 36% cotton** Width **135cm/53in** Repeat **92cm/36in** Price ★★★

6 Lelièvre/Watteau Colour **ivoire** Alt. colours **yes** Composition **68% viscose, 32% silk** Width **130cm/51in** Repeat **8cm/3in** Price ★★★

Florals: **Pre-18th century**

With the notable exception of the often highly naturalistic *mille fleurs* in medieval tapestries, the majority of floral-patterned fabrics produced before the 17th century featured stylized flowers. Most Renaissance damasks and velvets employed symmetrical floral designs, and the brightly coloured calicoes (*indiennes*) imported from India at the end of the 16th century portrayed stylized flowers (as did the European copies that followed). However, during the 17th century naturalistic renderings of an ever-greater number of flowers became increasingly common as knowledge of plant forms grew and pattern books on the subject proliferated. Influential publications included Pierre Vallet's *Le Jardin du Roi* (1608), which introduced many species, such as the tulip, and P.A. Ducerceau's *Bouquets Propres pour les Etoffes de Tours* (c.1660–70). The latter was specifically intended for silk designers and included species as diverse as narcissi, snake's-head and crown fritillaries, lilies, orchids, roses, pinks, clematis and campanula.

1

2

3

1 **Hodsoll McKenzie/English Crewelwork 220/103** Colour **olive** Alt. colours **yes** Composition **60% rayon, 40% cotton** Width **127cm/ 50in** Repeat **62cm/24¼in** Price ★★★ 🛋 W

2 **Chelsea Textiles/Queen Anne F101A** Colour **rust** Alt. colours **yes** Composition **60% linen, 40% cotton with cotton crewelwork** Width **114cm/ 44½in** Repeat **107cm/42in** Price ★★★★ LC 🛋 ⊞ W

3 **Zimmer & Rohde/Zagara 5093** Colour **214** Alt. colours **yes** Composition **80% cotton, 20% viscose** Width **140cm/55in** Repeat **116cm/45¾** Price ★★★ 🛋

4

5

4 **Watts of Westminster/Langton F0064-01/ZIF** Colour **natural** Alt. colours **yes** Composition **100% linen** Width **125cm/ 49in** Repeat **80cm/31½in** Price ★★★ 🛋

5 **Jane Churchill/Florian Damask J254F** Colour **caramel** Alt. colours **yes** Composition **100% cotton** Width **143cm/ 56in** Repeat **28cm/11in** Price ★★ LC 🛋

6 **Chelsea Textiles/Grapes Fine Crewelwork F032** Colour **multi** Alt. colours **yes** Composition **100% cotton with wool crewelwork** Width **150cm/ 59in** Repeat **96cm/37¾in** Price ★★★★ 🛋 ⊞

6

SYMBOLISM

The inspiration for "Darnley" came from a 16th-century needlework panel attributed to Mary, Queen of Scots and now part of the historic Hardwick Hall collection in Derbyshire, England. It features interlaced lilies, thistles, and roses, symbolic respectively of Mary's double crown of France and Scotland and of her claim to the throne of England. The fabric is woven in muted shades of the original (but now faded) ivory, gold, rose and green.

Stuart Interiors/Darnley Colour **ivory** Alt. colours **yes** Composition **60% wool, 40% cotton** Width **125cm/ 49in** Repeat **30cm/11¾in** Price ★★★★ LC 🛋 ⊞ W

CREWELWORK

A form of outline embroidery, crewelwork was fashionable during the 17th and 18th centuries and enjoyed revivals in the late 19th and 20th century. Stitched with crewel, a loose-spun worsted yarn, on a linen or cotton ground, crewelwork is traditionally used for bed furnishings and cushion covers, and sometimes rugs. Popular stitches for outlining include stem, double-back or chain, while satin, buttonhole, rope coral or French knot are used for fillings. Motifs are generally Eastern in origin, and include naïvely depicted flowers, leaves, animals and birds.

Marvic Textiles/Purna Colour **1213-1 red** Alt. colours **yes** Composition **58% wool, 42% cotton** Width **150cm/59in** Repeat **71cm/28in** Price ★★★★ 🔲 ⊞

7 **Jason D'Souza/Medici MED03** Colour **burgundy/ blue** Alt. colours **yes** Composition **70% linen, 30% cotton** Width **136cm/ 53½in** Repeat **49.5cm/19¼in** Price ★★★ 🛋

8 **Bernard Thorp & Co/Jane** Colour **blue and red** Alt. colours **yes** Composition **100% jute** Width **120cm/ 47in** Repeat **84cm/33in** Price ★★ 🔲 W

9 **Zimmer & Rohde/Perle d'Or 9210 371** Colour **red and cream** Alt. colours **yes** Composition **100% cotton** Width **140cm/55in** Repeat **61cm/24in** Price ★★★ 🔲

10 **Beaumont & Fletcher/Tyger 2337a** Colour **madder/indigo** Alt. colours **yes** Composition **52% linen, 36% cotton, 12% nylon** Width **133.5cm/52½in** Repeat **80cm/31½in** Price ★★★ 🔲 🛋

11 **Liberty/Moray LF4010** Colour **02** Alt. colours **yes** Composition **100% cotton** Width **140cm/ 55in** Repeat **39cm/15¼in** Price ★★ 🛋

12 **Abbott & Boyd/Floralia Barroca 45314-5** Colour **deep multi on grey** Alt. colours **no** Composition **100% linen** Width **140cm/55in** Repeat **110cm/43in** Price ★★★ 🔲 🛋

13 **Fired Earth/FE9013 Papaver** Colour **6 Coral** Alt. colours **yes** Composition **60% linen, 20% cotton, 20% modal** Width **134cm/52½in** Repeat **50cm/9¼in** Price ★★ LC 🔲 ⊞ 🛋

Florals: **Early 18th century**

The first half of the 18th century saw developments in the design of floral-patterned fabrics. A new influence came from the East in the form of Chinese lacquer wares and ceramics showing exotic floral ornamentation. These provided the inspiration to copy unfamiliar flowers, such as the chrysanthemum, and to produce *chinoiserie* designs that imitated oriental compositions, notably the *famille rose* and *Kakiemon* patterns. During the Rococo period pursuit of the exotic even extended to the devising of imaginary species, such as the "umbrella" flower.

Running parallel to the adoption of Chinese forms of decoration was a growth in the production of French and English floral chintzes (developed from the imported Indian calicoes, or *indiennes*, of the previous century). By 1721 these printed cotton fabrics were sufficiently popular to threaten the future of woven fabrics, and in England an Act of Parliament forbade their manufacture for the home market. However, owing to popular demand, the English cotton industry was allowed to renew production in the 1730s (restrictions being removed totally in the 1770s), using a linen-cotton cloth known as fustian. Similar legislation was introduced in France in the 1680s but rescinded in 1759.

1 **Beaumont & Fletcher/Aubusson Rose 2209** Colour **coral** Alt. colours **yes** Composition **52% linen, 36% cotton, 12% nylon** Width **133.5cm/52½in** Repeat **84cm/33in** Price ★★★

2 **Jab/Excelsa-Rose 1-7318** Colour **cream 270** Alt. colours **yes** Composition **100% silk** Width **135cm/53in** Repeat **19cm/7½in** Price ★

3 **Hodsoll McKenzie/Indian Iris 105/501** Colour **red/blue** Alt. colours **yes** Composition **52% linen, 36% cotton, 12% nylon** Width **137cm/54in** Repeat **20cm/8in** Price ★★

4 **Marvic Textiles/Baronscourt 474** Colour **4** Alt. colours **yes** Composition **35% viscose, 39% cotton, 26% linen** Width **136cm/53½in** Repeat **150cm/59in** Price ★★

5 **Scalamandré/Louis XV 2770M-005** Colour **Chinese red** Alt. colours **yes** Composition **100% silk** Width **140cm/55in** Repeat **53cm/21in** Price ★★★★★

6 **Zoffany/Gold Flowers AMB0500** Colour **1** Alt. colours **yes** Composition **100% cotton** Width **138cm/54in** Repeat **73cm/28½in** Price ★★

7 Jason D'Souza/Verona Colour **pink and blue** Alt. colours **yes** Composition **70% linen, 30% cotton** Width **136cm/53½in** Repeat **74cm/29in** Price ★★★

8 Garin/Janini 96455041 Colour **rojo** Alt. colours **yes** Composition **69% cotton, 21% viscose, 10% linen** Width **150cm/59in** Repeat **56cm/22in** Price ★★★

9 Lee Jofa/Hollyhock Minor Print 849010-16 Colour **mocha** Alt. colours **yes** Composition **100% cotton** Width **132cm/51¾in** Repeat **58cm/22¾in** Price ★★

10 Zoffany/Emily FRN0100 Colour **1** Alt. colours **yes** Composition **51% linen, 49% cotton** Width **137cm/53¾in** Repeat **56cm/22in** Price ★★

11 Jason D'Souza/Colonne Fleurie CF1 Colour **tonal pink** Alt. colours **yes** Composition **70% linen, 30% cotton** Width **121cm/47½in** Repeat **47cm/18½in** Price ★★★

7

8

9

10

11

12

12 Zimmer & Rohde/Adrastos 2556 Colour **184** Alt. colours **yes** Composition **70% cotton, 30% viscose** Width **138cm/54in** Repeat **36cm/14in** Price ★★★

13 Colefax and Fowler/Lincoln 2061/03 Colour **cream and aqua** Alt. colours **yes** Composition **60% linen, 20% cotton, 20% modacrylic** Width **135cm/53in** Repeat **35cm/13¾in** Price ★★

14 Chelsea Textiles/Wisteria Pink F057P Colour **pink** Alt. colours **yes** Composition **55% linen, 45% cotton with cotton embroidery** Width **120cm/47in** Repeat **20cm/8in** Price ★★★ LC

15 Old World Weavers/Lisere Romano II AO 27513222 Colour **rose/green** Alt. colours **yes** Composition **100% silk** Width **50cm/19½in** Repeat **35cm/13¾in** Price ★★★★★

16 Hodsoll McKenzie/English Ribbon 223/101-108 Colour **blue** Alt. colours **yes** Composition **61% spun rayon, 39% cotton** Width **127cm/50in** Repeat **20.5cm/8in** Price ★★★ W

15

13

14

16

Florals: Late 18th century

The proliferation of floral-patterned fabrics in Europe was further fuelled during the latter half of the 18th century by the British government's removal, in the 1770s, of previously imposed restrictions on the manufacture of cotton chintzes. Moreover, the development of copperplate printing in the 1750s had revolutionized the fabric industry by increasing output, reducing costs and improving the quality of designs. By the end of the 18th century, Americans were also producing their own chintzes thanks to the emigration of a number of English printers to Philadelphia.

Aesthetically, floral patterns of the second half of the century were characterized by a move away from the exotic toward naturalistic renditions of less complicated (often wild) flowers. Typical examples included larkspurs, roses, carnations, poppies and cornflowers, as well as the daisies, stocks, violets and anemones embellishing many of the fabrics used in 1768 to decorate Marie Antoinette's bedroom at the Petit Trianon in Versailles, France.

5

1　　　　2

3

7

6

1 Wemyss Houlès/Wellbeck
Colour **18** Alt. colours **yes**
Composition **53% viscose, 35% cotton, 12% nylon** Width **140cm/55in** Repeat **24cm/9½in** Price ★★

2 Lennox Money/Miramar 2433C
Colour **green and yellow** Alt. colours **yes** Composition **100% cotton** Width **136.5cm/ 53¾in** Repeat **119cm/46¾in** Price ★★

3 Bennison Fabrics/Corne Fleurie
Colour **blue and yellow** Alt. colours **yes** Composition **70% linen, 30% cotton** Width **129cm/51in** Repeat **42cm/16½in** Price ★★★

4 Watts of Westminster/Edenwood F0063-02/N15 Colour **Dorchester** Alt. colours **yes** Composition **100% linen** Width **127cm/50in** Repeat **76cm/30in** Price ★★★★

5 Zoffany/China Rose FRN0300
Colour **1** Alt. colours **yes** Composition **100% cotton** Width **138cm/54in** Repeat **55cm/21½in** Price ★★★

6 Hodsoll McKenzie/Roots 926/ 502 Colour **blue** Alt. colours **yes** Composition **52% linen, 36% cotton, 12% nylon** Width **137cm/53¾in** Repeat **13cm/5in** Price ★★★

7 Brunschwig & Fils/65346.01
Colour **6** Alt. colours **yes** Composition **100% cotton** Width **137cm/54in** Repeat **151cm/59½in** Price ★★★★

18th century

8 Jane Churchill/Rose Toile
J240F Colour **03 Aqua** Alt.
colours **yes** Composition
100% cotton Width **137cm/**
54in Repeat **18cm/7in**
Price ★★ LC ⟨⟩ 🛋

9 Zoffany/Sweet Briar FRN0500
Colour **1** Alt. colours **yes**
Composition **100% silk**
Width **136cm/53½in**
Repeat **84cm/33in**
Price ★★★ ⟨⟩

10 Anne & Robert Swaffer/Amy
Colour **32** Alt. colours
yes Composition **100%**
cotton Width **140cm/55in**
Repeat **22cm/8½in**
Price ★ ⟨⟩ ⊞ 🛋

11 Brunschwig & Fils/36465.01
Colour **5** Alt. colours **yes**
Composition **100% wool**
Width **122cm/48in**
Repeat **16cm/6¼in**
Price ★★★ ⟨⟩ LC 🛋

12 Bennison Fabrics/Wheatflower
Colour **1** Alt. colours **yes**
Composition **70% linen,**
30% cotton Width **126cm/**
49in Repeat **57.5cm/22½in**
Price ★★★ ⟨⟩ 🛋

13 Brunschwig & Fils/Empress of
China Stripe 51305 Colour **01**
Alt. colours **yes** Composition
100% cotton Width **140cm/**
55in Repeat **107cm/42in**
Price ★★★ ⟨⟩ 🛋

14 Lennox Money/Chekian Lotus
Colour **1** Alt. colours **no**
Composition **100% cotton**
Width **135cm/53in**
Repeat **64cm/25in**
Price ★★★ LC ⟨⟩ W

8

9

10

11 12

13

14

DOCUMENTARY DESIGNS
A "document" is used to describe an historic fabric that serves as the source for a reproduction – a documentary fabric. In its purest form a documentary fabric is an exact copy of the fibres, width, repeat, colours and every detail of the original design. However, if one or more of the original elements is altered (as is often the case), the reproduction is referred to as an "adaptation". Typical examples include a change from silk to synthetic fibres, adjustments of scale to accommodate modern power looms, and variations in colour caused by different dyes or printing techniques.

The fabrics below are based on the original documents shown above, with some modifications: alteration to the size of the pattern and, in the case of "Tulip Stripe", replacement of some of the roses with a broken stripe.

Apenn/Surrey Rose Garland AV464-1/2/3 Colour **1** Alt. colours **yes**
Composition **100% cotton** Width **122cm/48in** Repeat **48cm/19in**
Price ★★ ⟨⟩ 🛋

Apenn/Tulip Stripe AV466-1/2/3 Colour **red and blue** Alt. colours **yes**
Composition **100% cotton** Width **124cm/ 48¾in** Repeat **23cm/9in**
Price ★★ ⟨⟩ 🛋

Florals: **Early 19th century**

During the early 19th century, the naturalistically rendered flowers that had been a feature of 18th-century Neo-classical ornamentation remained fashionable – although in Empire-style interiors they were eventually abandoned in favour of militaristic motifs and mythical beasts. At the beginning of the century, many French, British and American chintzes with a glazed finish did show flowers in stylized form. However, they too became ever more naturalistic as the century progressed.

As before, the realistic depiction of flowers was aided by the publication of botanical reference books, with the Kensington nurseryman Robert Furber's late 18th-century seed catalogue *The Flower Garden Display'd* still proving a useful source of inspiration. Technical advances – notably the discovery of mineral colours, such as manganese bronze, antimony orange and a "solid" green (instead of indigo pencilled over yellow) – also made more realistic representations of flowers possible. On a more esoteric level, floral patterns in general were further popularized by the publication, from the 1820s, of numerous books on "floral emblems" and "flower language", although the symbolic meaning attributed to particular flowers was often rather tenuous. For example, the poppy, known to induce sleep, represented consolation.

Brunschwig & Fils/36350 Colour **0** Alt. colours **yes** Composition **100% cotton** Width **165cm/65in** Repeat **90cm/35½in** Price ★★★★★

Scalamandré/Amazonia 16232 Colour **001** Alt. colours **yes** Composition **100% cotton** Width **140cm/55in** Repeat **91.5cm/36in** Price ★★★★

Brunschwig & Fils/50005 Colour **5** Alt. colours **yes** Composition **100% cotton** Width **135cm/53in** Repeat **53cm/21in** Price ★★★

Brunschwig & Fils/Candace Glazed Chintz 79442 Colour **04** Alt. colours **yes** Composition **100% cotton** Width **137cm/54in** Repeat **91.5cm/36in** Price ★★

Donghia/Stella/Casement 0375 Colour **03** Alt. colours **yes** Composition **66% linen, 34% cotton** Width **150cm/59in** Repeat **40cm/15¾in** Price ★★★★★

Garin/Alameda 66823853 Colour **Isabelino** Alt. colours **yes** Composition **42% rayon, 37% cotton, 21% silk** Width **130cm/51in** Repeat **72cm/28¼in** Price ★★★★

G.P. & J. Baker/Directoire Stripe B0851 03 Colour **mustard on white** Alt. colours **yes** Composition **100% cotton** Width **137cm/54in** Repeat **63cm/24¾in** Price ★★

19th century

EVOLVING PRINTING TECHNIQUES

Nowadays, an ever-increasing number of textile manufacturers are producing less expensive screen-printed versions of their hand-blocked documentary fabrics. "Althea" (taken from the Latin for hollyhock) is Lee Jofa's screen-printed alternative to its classic hand-blocked "Hollyhock", which was adapted for printing in the 1920s from an early 19th-century document.

Hamilton Weston/Swakely 6137175 Colour **pink** Alt. colours **yes** Composition **100% cotton** Width **137cm/54in** Repeat **36cm/14in** Price ★★ LC 〚〛 🛋

Lee Jofa/Hollyhock Handblock Print 7129 Colour **white/coral/blue** Alt. colours **yes** Composition **100% linen** Width **120cm/47in** Repeat **102cm/40in** Price ★★★★★ 〚〛 🛋

Lee Jofa/Althea 879001 Colour **beige/leaf green on ivory** Alt. colours **yes** Composition **100% cotton** Width **132cm/51¼in** Repeat **130cm/51in** Price ★★★ 〚〛 ⊞ 🛋

Hodsoll McKenzie/Exotic Column 009/413 Colour **grey** Alt. colours **yes** Composition **100% cotton** Width **137cm/54in** Repeat **37cm/14½in** Price ★★ LC 〚〛 🛋 W

Warner Fabrics/Chintz Garden CS 4620 Colour **multi/stone** Alt. colours **yes** Composition **100% cotton** Width **137cm/54in** Repeat **82cm/32in** Price ★★ LC 〚〛

Bennison Fabrics/Dragon Flower Colour **terracotta/green on beige** Alt. colours **yes** Composition **70% linen, 30% cotton** Width **140cm/55in** Repeat **78cm/30¾in** Price ★★★ 〚〛 🛋

Borderline/Kirmani 2340 Colour **blue** Alt. colours **yes** Composition **61% linen, 39% cotton** Width **137cm/54in** Repeat **45.5cm/18in** Price ★ LC 〚〛 🛋

Garin/Janini Colour **verde** Alt. colours **yes** Composition **70% cotton, 20% viscose, 10% linen** Width **140cm/55in** Repeat **56cm/22in** Price ★★★ LC 〚〛 W

Nina Campbell/Viola NCF3132 Colour **03** Alt. colours **yes** Composition **100% cotton** Width **140cm/55in** Repeat **40cm/15¾in** Price ★★ 🛋

Florals: Mid-19th century

Two technological developments served to expand the production and popularity of floral-patterned fabrics during the middle of the 19th century. The first was the introduction of the power loom, which had come into widespread use during the mid-1820s and served to increase the speed as well as reduce the costs of production. The second development was the discovery of coal tar and aniline dyes in the mid-1850s, which enabled manufacturers to produce deeper and more vivid colours. The result was an outburst of naturalistic, often overblown, floral ornament. For example, many Rococo-style ("Louis Quatorze") fabrics displayed floral patterns augmented with scrolls and cartouches shaded for "three-dimensional effect". Similarly, a typical mid-19th-century chintz incorporated "three-dimensional" scrolling acanthus leaves and flowers in various shades of green, blue, white, violet and yellow. The rationale of this heightened naturalism was expressed by the Jury of the Great Exhibition, held in London, England, in 1851: "The task is to cover the surface almost entirely with large, coarse flowers: dahlias, hollyhocks, roses, hydrangeas, or others which give scope for strong or vivid colouring, and which are often magnified by the designer much beyond the scale of nature."

5

1

2

3

4

6

7

1 **Nina Campbell/Rosenkavalier NCF3432** Colour **04** Alt. colours **yes** Composition **84% linen, 16% nylon** Width **140cm/ 55in** Repeat **62cm/24¼in** Price ★★ LC

2 **Beaumont & Fletcher/Baroque Floral 2239b** Colour **rose** Alt. colours **yes** Composition **52% linen, 36% cotton, 12% nylon** Width **133.5cm/ 52½in** Repeat **52cm/20½in** Price ★★★

3 **Borderline/Indica 2463** Colour **blue and yellow** Alt. colours **yes** Composition **100% wool** Width **137cm/54in** Repeat **24.5cm/9¾in** Price ★ LC

4 **George Spencer Designs/ Thistle 108L** Colour **red** Alt. colours **yes** Composition **100% linen** Width **120cm/47in** Repeat **47cm/18½in** Price ★★★

5 **Lee Jofa/Floral Bouquet 889300** Colour **white** Alt. colours **yes** Composition **100% cotton** Width **134cm/ 52½in** Repeat **84cm/33in** Price ★★★

6 **Sanderson/Bloom PR8510** Colour **2** Alt. colours **yes** Composition **100% cotton** Width **137cm/54in** Repeat **32cm/12½in** Price ★★

7 **Colefax and Fowler/Coniston F1314/01** Colour **stone** Alt. colours **yes** Composition **52% linen, 36% cotton, 12% nylon** Width **135cm/ 53in** Repeat **43cm/17in** Price ★ LC

8 Warner Fabrics/Montpelier Chintz CS8611 Colour **blue ribbon** Alt. colours **yes** Composition **100% cotton** Width **137cm/54in** Repeat **44cm/17¼in** Price ★★★

9 Jane Churchill/Country Rose Stripe J237F Colour **red/ green 01** Alt. colours **yes** Composition **37% cotton, 51% linen, 2% nylon** Width **140cm/55in** Repeat **34cm/ 13¼in** Price ★★

10 Brunschwig & Fils/79489 Colour **015** Alt. colours **yes** Composition **100% cotton** Width **137cm/ 54in** Repeat **107cm/42in** Price ★★★

11 Jim Thompson/Montague 1055 Colour **04** Alt. colours **yes** Composition **100% silk** Width **122cm/48in** Repeat **46cm/18in** Price ★★★★

8

9

10

FADED CHINTZ

One of the most attractive characteristics of chintz is that its original bright colours gradually mellow and fade – a process that is caused by exposure to sunlight, laundering and general usage. This explains why 18th- and 19th-century chintzes are sought after today, and why, since the 1970s, designers and manufacturers have been producing "artificially aged" chintzes to meet the demand. Soaking the fabric in a weak solution of tea is a simple method of achieving subtle discoloration, and sandwashing produces fading. However, most manufacturers make adjustments in the dyes they use and employ chemical solutions to achieve the desired effect.

Bennison Fabrics/Rosevine Colour **faded pink, green** Alt. colours **yes** Composition **70% linen, 30% cotton** Width **132cm/51¾in** Repeat **49cm/19¼in** Price ★★★

Bennison Fabrics/Damask Rose Colour **green/pink** Alt. colours **yes** Composition **70% linen, 30% cotton** Width **119cm/46¾in** Repeat **63cm/24¾in** Price ★★★

Hodsoll McKenzie/Faded Bouquet 110/403 Colour **blue** Alt. colours **yes** Composition **100% cotton** Width **137cm/54in** Repeat **59.5cm/23¼in** Price ★★★

11

Florals: Late 19th century

The last two decades of the 19th century witnessed a reaction to the highly naturalistic floral patterns favoured earlier. For example, the Aesthetic movement espoused the use of simple flowers, such as the lotus (a Japanese influence), pinks and sunflowers – the latter appearing as a recurring motif in the designs (some highly stylized, some botanically accurate) of Walter Crane. Similarly, William Morris and the Arts and Crafts movement promoted a return to simple, uncomplicated flowers – as illustrated in medieval herbals – and the use of traditional vegetable, rather than chemical, dyes.

Morris's designs included columbines, poppies, honeysuckle, pinks, anemones, marigolds, daisies and jasmine, and had a rhythmical, sensuous quality absent from the flat, static patterns produced by many followers of the Aesthetic movement. This sensuousness was later reflected in the work of some Art Nouveau designers. Many of them had rejected floral forms altogether and turned to vegetal motifs (roots, buds and seedpods) to fit the dynamic lines of Art Nouveau. However, others – such as E.A. Séguy in his *Les Fleurs et Leurs Applications Décoratives* (1899) – employed a wide selection of sinuous plant forms, such as passionflowers, poppies, wisteria and waterlilies.

5

1

2

6

7

3

4

1 Morris & Co/Fruit RR8048
Colour **1** Alt. colours **yes**
Composition **100% cotton**
Width **137cm/54in** Repeat
64cm/25in Price ★ 🛏🛋

2 G.P. & J. Baker/Avalon R1285
02 Colour **greens** Alt. colours
yes Composition **60% linen,
22% cotton, 18% viscose**
Width **137cm/54in**
Repeat **62cm/24¼in**
Price ★★ LC 🛏🛋

3 Old World Weavers/Vera Linen
B1886L01 Colour **07 multi**
Alt. colours **yes** Composition
58% linen, 42% cotton Width
140cm/55in Repeat **96cm/37¾in**
Price ★★★★ 🛏🛋

4 Lee Jofa/Kingsworthy Print
929070 Colour **eggshell** Alt.
colours **yes** Composition
100% linen Width **132cm/
51¼in** Repeat **50cm/19½in**
Price ★★★★ LC 🛏🛋

5 Brunschwig & Fils/Ogden
House Cotton Print 79308
Colour **176 pomegranate**
Alt. colours **yes** Composition
100% cotton Width **138cm/
54in** Repeat **38cm/15in**
Price ★★★ 🛏

6 Borderline/Pomegranate 2170B
Colour **jade/pink** Alt. colours
yes Composition **60% linen,
40% cotton** Width **14.5cm/
5¾in** Repeat **30cm/11¾in**
Price ★ 🛏🛋

7 Beaumont & Fletcher/Wistaria
& Rose 2196A Colour **rust/tan**
Alt. colours **yes** Composition
**52% linen, 36% cotton, 12%
nylon** Width **134cm/52½in**
Repeat **71cm/28in**
Price ★★★ 🛏🛋

8 **Lelièvre/Bouquet Champêtre
4317** Colour **ivory 01** Alt.
colours **yes** Composition
100% silk Width **130cm/51in**
Repeat **103cm/40½in**
Price ★★★★★ 🛋

9 **Lelièvre/Les Tulipes 4138**
Colour **ivoire 01** Alt. colours
no Composition **100% silk**
Width **130cm/51in**
Repeat **53cm/21in**
Price ★★★★★ 🛋🛋

10 **Scalamandré/Newport – Moiréd
Lisère 96495** Colour **multi
on beige and salmon stripe**
Alt. colours **yes** Composition
100% silk Width **127cm/
50in** Repeat **8cm/3in**
Price ★★★★★ 🛋🛋

11 **Lee Jofa/Southdown Rose
909403** Colour **03** Alt.
colours **yes** Composition
100% cotton Width **132cm/
51¾in** Repeat **45cm/17½in**
Price ★★ 🛋🛋

12 **Jim Thompson/Botanica
PDB 3014** Colour **A** Alt.
colours **yes** Composition
100% silk Width **122cm/48in**
Repeat **91.5cm/36in**
Price ★★★★ 🛋🛋

13 **Marvic Textiles/Baudouin 8247**
Colour **blue 6** Alt. colours
yes Composition **52% linen,
48% viscose** Width **140cm/
55in** Repeat **69cm/27in**
Price ★★ 🛋🛋 w

11

8

9 | **10**

12 | **13**

ARTS & CRAFTS STYLE
"Anyone wanting to produce
dyed textiles with any artistic
quality in them must forego
the modern and commercial
methods in favour of those
that are at least as old as
Pliny, who speaks of them
as being old in his time"
(William Morris). For Morris
(and the other Arts and
Crafts designers) this meant
using block- rather than
roller-printing, and vegetable
rather than chemical dyes.
The rhythmical and elaborate
patterns of these designers
incorporate simple but
sinuous flowers and other
plant forms, and have
remained fashionable to
the present day.

Liberty Furnishings/Burnham 1064616 Colour **L** Alt. colours **yes**
Composition **100% cotton** Width **137cm/54in** Repeat **51cm/20in**
Price ★ 🛋🛋

Liberty Furnishings/Snakeshead 1095020 Colour **blue/green** Alt. colours **yes** Composition
53% linen, 35% cotton, 12% polyacrylic Width **137cm/54in** Repeat **44cm/17in**
Price ★★ 🛋⊞🛋

Florals: Early 20th century

Despite the earlier protestations of the Aesthetic movement, largely on the grounds of "poor taste", naturalistically depicted floral chintzes remained highly popular among the general public around the end of the 19th century. However, the majority of the Art Deco fabrics that were fashionable during the early 20th century incorporated stylized flowers – although they were usually confined (in the "classical style") to baskets, festoons or garlands, or were densely packed. For example, E.A. Séguy's highly influential *Bouquets de Fronaisons*, first published in Paris, France, in 1927, showed illustrations of tightly packed rosebuds and composites such as daisies, marguerites and zinnias.

William Morris's floral designs (*see* pages 122-3) remained fashionable in the later Arts and Crafts interiors of the first three decades of the century, as did the cheaper, machine-printed copies of his designs that were produced. However, the designers of fabrics in the Modernist style largely rejected floral ornamentation altogether.

Mulberry/Parrot Tulips FD309/713 Colour **Light Red V139** Alt. colours **yes** Composition **51% silk, 49% cotton** Width **127cm/50in** Repeat **59cm/23in** Price ★★★★

Clarence House/Flowering Quince 33944 Colour **green** Alt. colours **yes** Composition **100% linen** Width **137cm/54in** Repeat **100cm/39¼in** Price ★★★

Ramm, Son & Crocker/Iris & Geranium Colour **red/taupe** Alt. colours **yes** Composition **84% linen, 16% nylon** Width **140cm/55in** Repeat **65cm/25½in** Price ★★

Mulberry/Secret Garden Linen Union FD181 Colour **Red V106** Alt. colours **yes** Composition **51% linen, 37% cotton, 12% nylon** Width **137cm/54in** Repeat **61cm/24in** Price ★★

G.P. & J. Baker/Peony & Blossom R1368 Colour **6** Alt. colours **yes** Composition **100% linen** Width **137cm/54in** Repeat **80cm/31½in** Price ★★

Brunschwig & Fils/79494.051 Colour **4** Alt. colours **yes** Composition **100% cotton** Width **135cm/53in** Repeat **106cm/41½in** Price ★★★

Brunschwig & Fils/Sconset Quilted Floral 32833.01 Colour **gold and red** Alt. colours **yes** Composition **100% cotton** Width **140cm/55in** Repeat **48cm/19in** Price ★★★

Brunschwig & Fils/Highland Rose 7989.04 Colour **ivory** Alt. colours **no** Composition **100% cotton** Width **137cm/54in** Repeat **36cm/14in** Price ★★

Anna French/Rosebud Colour **71** Alt. colours **yes** Composition **100% cotton** Width **137cm/54in** Repeat **14.5cm/5¾in** Price ★

Lee Jofa/Harrogate Handblock 697115 Colour **natural** Alt. colours **no** Composition **100% linen** Width **122cm/48in** Repeat **76cm/30in** Price ★★★

Manuel Canovas/Serendip 11300 Colour **Ecru/95** Alt. colours **yes** Composition **100% cotton** Width **135cm/53in** Repeat **155cm/61in** Price ★★★★

Warner Fabrics/Edwardian Roses CS 336910 Colour **pink/blue/cream** Alt. colours **no** Composition **100% cotton** Width **137cm/54in** Repeat **64cm/25in** Price ★★

Jane Churchill/Country Rose Sprig J238F Colour **05 Russet** Alt. colours **yes** Composition **100% cotton** Width **137cm/54in** Repeat **20cm/8in** Price ★

Florals: Late 20th–early 21st century

Floral chintzes became less popular after the Second World War, fading away as abstract and geometric patterns started to come into vogue. Chintzes remained largely out of favour for some 40 years, but during the late 1980s there was a revival of interest in them, particularly for use in bedrooms. Consequently, many companies are now producing reproductions of 19th-century chintzes, with original patterns and colours virtually unchanged, while many contemporary designers have returned to nature for inspiration and are producing floral chintzes in "new" pastel colourways. Demand for woven floral damasks has also increased recently, especially for use in upholstery. William Morris designs are highly fashionable once again, as are some of the designs originated by Sybil Colefax and John Fowler in the mid-20th century. Also epitomizing late 20th and early 21st-century tastes in florals are flowerheads, petals, posies and garlands rendered in bright, strong colours.

1

1 Manuel Canovas/Clelia
Colour **celadon** Alt. colours
yes Composition **100% cotton**
Width **146cm/57½in** Repeat
68cm/26¾in Price ★ ⬚ ⊞

2 Laura Ashley/Charlotte
Colour **cowslip/multi white**
Alt. colours **yes** Composition
100% cotton Width **122cm/**
48in Repeat **32cm/12½in**
Price ★ ⬚

3 Laura Ashley/Kelmscott
Colour **delphinium** Alt. colours
yes Composition **100% cotton**
Width **138cm/54¼in** Repeat
57cm/22½in Price ★★ ⬚ LC

4 Nicholas Herbert/Toile
de Rosa 121 Colour **03 green**
Alt. colours **yes** Composition
100% cotton Width **137cm/**
54in Repeat **25cm/9¾in**
Price ★★ ⬚ LC ⌂

5 Nina Campbell/Manihiki
Prints/Futuna NCF3364
Colour **03** Alt. colours **yes**
Composition **84% cotton,**
16% nylon Width **140cm/**
55in Repeat **62cm/24¼in**
Price ★★ LC ⬚ ⊞⌂

6 J. Robert Scott/Floating Petals
3452 Colour **cardamom** Alt.
colours **yes** Composition
66% wool, 34% silk Width
135cm/53in Repeat **44cm/**
17in Price ★★★ ⬚

7 Lelièvre/Nougatine 5983
Colour **ivoire** Alt. colours **yes**
Composition **90% viscose,**
10% linen Width **138cm/**
54in Repeat **68cm/26¾in**
Price ★★★ LC ⬚

4

5

6

7

8

8 Manuel Canovas/Pali 11146
Colour **bleu 59** Alt. colours
yes Composition **100%
cotton** Width **130cm/
51in** Repeat **103cm/40½in**
Price ★★★★★

9 Brunschwig & Fils/78790
Colour **04** Alt. colours
yes Composition **100%
cotton** Width **137cm/
54in** Repeat **69cm/27in**
Price ★★★

10 Claremont Fabrics/Sunbury
Colour **wine** Alt. colours
yes Composition **100%
polyester** Width **140cm/
55in** Repeat **60cm/23¾in**
Price ★

11 Mulberry/Tuileries FD341
Colour **natural K101** Alt.
colours **yes** Composition
**55% cotton, 45% viscose
spun rayon** Width **145cm/
57in** Repeat **26cm/10¼in**
Price ★★ LC

12 Fired Earth/Autumn Fall
Colour **coral** Alt. colours
yes Composition **89% cotton,
11% nylon** Width **136cm/
53½in** Repeat **63cm/24¾in**
Price ★★ LC

14

13

13 Laura Ashley/Roundswood
Colour **pale lavender** Alt.
colours **yes** Composition
68% cotton, 32% linen
Width **140cm/55in** Repeat
32cm/12½in Price ★

14 Claremont Fabrics/Octavia
P99013 Colour **sapphire** Alt.
colours **yes** Composition
100% cotton Width **137cm/
54in** Repeat **68cm/26¾in**
Price ★

15 Claremont Fabrics/Sunbury
Flower S03 Colour **wine**
Alt. colours **yes** Composition
100% polyester Width **140cm/
55in** Repeat **45.5cm/17¾in**
Price ★

16 Osborne & Little/Turfan F1162
Colour **04** Alt. colours **yes**
Composition **100% cotton**
Width **140cm/55in** Repeat
44cm/17in Price ★★

15

11

12

16

9

10

Pictorial Fabrics

Pictorial fabrics have appeared in various guises since the Middle Ages. The best known are woven tapestries and printed *toiles de Jouy*; others of note include Chinese and Middle-Eastern pictorial silks, Indonesian batiks, Indian calicoes (*indiennes*), European chintzes, ethnic African weaves and prints, and European and American hand-blocked or screen-printed synthetics.

Long regarded as a mirror of civilization, narrative pictorial fabrics depict a wide range of human activities (both real and mythical) from biblical scenes, military conquests and political events, to harvesting, hunting, pastoral gatherings and theatregoing. However, this reflection of life is also evident in non-narrative pictorials, such as "still-life" fruits and flowers, views of animals on the move, birds in flight and "drawings" of architectural components. In each case the subject matter, the manner in which it is portrayed and the techniques used to reproduce it reflect both the preoccupations of, and the styles of ornament available to, different cultures at different times.

LEFT A detail of a late 18th-century oval-back, gilt open armchair in a manor house in Norfolk, England. The top-cover is original, exquisitely worked in petit-point, and depicts cherubs at play – a popular subject for the pictorial fabrics used in classical interiors on both sides of the Atlantic during the latter part of the 18th century.

INDUSTRIAL ESPIONAGE

Toile de Jouy fabrics originated in 1770, in a factory established by the German Oberkampf brothers in the French village of Jouy-en-Josas. Intent on expansion, the brothers travelled to England in 1810 in an attempt to find out the secret advances made in copperplate printing techniques. They managed to smuggle out the information by writing it on cotton percale fabric using an alum solution tinted with madder dye, then dipping the fabric in vinegar to render the writing invisible. Once back in France, they immersed the fabric in madder dye to retrieve the concealed information.

This late 20th-century settee is upholstered with a hand-printed, modern pictorial bric designed by Janet Milner. The hairdressing imagery, particularly the exaggerated eehive" hairdo, is wryly amusing, but the design is potentially classic – largely thanks to e sophisticated combination of black, cream and caramel colouring.

KEY DESIGNS

1 Historically significant naval and land battles were popular subjects for pictorial fabrics, particularly medieval and Renaissance tapestries and 18th- and 19th-century printed toiles.

2 Oriental scenes incorporating human figures, buildings and exotic animals, birds and plant forms, appeared on numerous European textiles from the mid-17th century to the late 19th century.

3 Printed cottons and linens featuring pictorial patterns copied from or inspired by Chinese export porcelain and delftware were highly fashionable in Europe during the 18th century.

4 Fabrics patterned with a series of scenes, framed within decorative plaques or cartouches, have been popular since the Renaissance. This Empire-style print displays classical imagery.

5 Ethnic weaves and prints have been a recurring source of inspiration for 20th- and early 21st-century European and American pictorial textiles.

6 This playing-card pattern is early-21st century, but its portrayal of royalty and theatrical figures is within a genre that extends back to the Middle Ages.

1 **Manuel Canovas/Hispaniola** Colour **groseille/ ecru 05** Alt. colours **yes** Composition **100% cotton** Width **178cm/70in** Repeat **96cm/37¾in** Price ★★

2 **Apenn/Chelworth Linen** Colour **heather/navy blue** Alt. colours **yes** Composition **60% linen, 30% cotton, 10% nylon** Width **122cm/48in** Repeat **83cm** **32½in** Price ★★★

3 **Bennison Fabrics/Chinese Toile** Colour **blue and white** Alt. colours **yes** Composition **70% linen, 30% cotton** Width **122cm/ 48in** Repeat **45cm/17½in** Price ★★★

4 **Marvic Textiles/Empire 5220-007** Colour **red on sand** Alt. colours **yes** Composition **100% cotton** Width **140cm/55in** Repeat **74cm/ 29in** Price ★★

5 **Fired Earth/Indienne Sapphire** Colour **sapphire blue** Alt. colours **yes** Composition **44% viscose, 41% polyacrylic, 15% modacrylic** Width **141cm/55½in** Repeat **33cm/13in** Price ★★

6 **Scalamandré/Royal Flush 16392-003** Colour **red and brown** Alt. colours **yes** Composition **100% linen** Width **138.5cm/54½in** Repeat **86.5cm/34in** Price ★★★

Pictorials: **Pre-18th century**

Medieval pictorial fabrics – mostly tapestry wall-hangings – depicted subject matter from and were executed in a style that bore close resemblance to illustrated manuscripts of the period. Typical subjects ranged from ecclesiastical scenes and narratives of significant matters of state, to everyday life at court. Pageantry was also shown, including military sieges, parades and tournaments (often augmented with motifs such as coats-of-arms). Hunting scenes, featuring stylized heraldic beasts, such as stags, dogs, lions, griffins, unicorns and enfields, were also widely portrayed.

Much of the subject matter of medieval pictorial fabrics, particularly hunting and battle scenes, also appeared during the Renaissance. However, biblical stories, classical mythology and pastoral images became increasingly fashionable, and all images were rendered with a much greater use and understanding of perspective. By the 17th century, pictorial wall-hangings had become even more spectacular and sophisticated in terms of both colour and realism – especially in the grandest French and English Baroque interiors, where classical, mythological, historical, religious and pastoral images remained popular (and often appeared *en suite* on upholstered furniture).

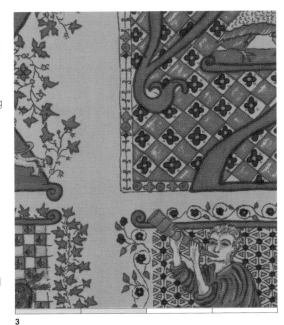

3

3 Mulberry/Medieval Alphabet F142/608 Colour **red, blue, gold and green** Alt. colours **yes** Composition **100% cotton** Width **132cm/51¾in** Repeat **21cm/8¼in** Price ★★ 🎨 ▥ 🛋

4 Brunschwig & Fils/Palio Cotton and Linen Print 79821.04 Colour **rosso** Alt. colours **yes** Composition **54% linen, 46% cotton** Width **137cm/54in** Repeat **46cm/18in** Price ★★★★ 🎨 🛋

5 Fired Earth/Calligraphy Colour **red** Alt. colours **yes** Composition **44% viscose, 41% polyacrylic, 15% modacrylic** Width **140cm/55in** Repeat **68cm/26¾in** Price ★★ 🇱🇨 🎨 ▥ 🛋

1

4

5

1 Claremont Fabrics/Merrydown C74 M53 Colour **chintz** Alt. colours **yes** Composition **100% cotton** Width **137cm/54in** Repeat **68cm/26¾in** Price ★ 🎨 🛋

2 Fired Earth/Gryphon Colour **cream on red** Alt. colours **yes** Composition **75% cotton, 25% wool** Width **155cm/61in** Repeat **60cm/23¾in** Price ★★★ 🇱🇨 🎨 ▥ 🛋

2

BATIK STYLE

During the 17th century, imported Indonesian cottons displaying pictorial patterns of stylized buildings, human figures, animals and birds came into vogue in Europe. These fabrics were produced by "batik", a form of printing that involves applying hot wax to the cotton around the pattern before applying dyes or inks. The wax resists the dyes or inks, which adhere to the unwaxed areas, and the pattern is revealed once the wax is removed with hot water.

Monkwell/Batumi 09358 Colour **5** Alt. colours **yes** Composition **100% cotton** Width **137cm/54in** Repeat **62cm/24¼in** Price ★★ 🎨 🛋

6

6 Stuart Interiors/English Needlework Design Colour **multi** Alt. colours **no** Composition **40% cotton, 60% wool** Width **126cm/ 49¾in** Repeat **57cm/22½in** Price ★★★★ 🎨 ▦ 🛋

7 Mulberry/Tudor Animals FD101/521 Colour **natural** Alt. colours **yes** Composition **56% linen, 22% cotton, 22% viscose** Width **137cm/54in** Repeat **82cm/32⅛in** Price ★★★ 🎨 🛋

8 Celia Birtwell/Beasties Colour **green** Alt. colours **yes** Composition **100% cotton** Width **140cm/55in** Repeat **64cm/25in** Price ★★ 🎨 🛋

9 Abbott & Boyd/Escritura 47658 Colour **4** Alt. colours **yes** Composition **100% cotton** Width **160cm/63in** Repeat **64cm/25in** Price ★★ 🎨 🛋

10 Monkwell/Salamanca 09371CU/004 Colour **gold on blue/green** Alt. colours **yes** Composition **100% cotton** Width **137cm/54in** Repeat **82cm/32⅛in** Price ★★ 🎨 🛋

7

8

9

10

11 Monkwell/Tamburlaine 09370 Colour **red and green** Alt. colours **yes** Composition **100% cotton** Width **137cm/ 54in** Repeat **64cm/25in** Price ★★ LC 🎨 🛋

12 Abbott & Boyd/Caciera Medieval 49009 Colour **yellow/beige ground** Alt. colours **no** Composition **100% cotton** Width **160cm/ 63in** Repeat **68cm/26¾in** Price ★★ 🎨 🛋

13 Abbott & Boyd/Cenera Medieval 49131 Colour **yellow/beige ground** Alt. colours **no** Composition **100% cotton** Width **160cm/ 63in** Repeat **96cm/37¾in** Price ★★ 🎨 🛋

14 Brunschwig & Fils 89496 Colour **940** Alt. colours **yes** Composition **65% cotton, 26% silk, 9% polyester** Width **140cm/55in** Repeat **62cm/ 24¼in** Price ★★★ 🎨 LC 🛋

15 Lee Jofa/Stuart Tree Print 858271 Colour **tapestry blue** Alt. colours **yes** Composition **100% linen** Width **137cm/ 54in** Repeat **73cm/28½in** Price ★★★ 🎨 🛋

11

12   **13**

14

15

Pictorials: **Early 18th century**

Stylistically, some of the pictorial fabrics produced during the early 18th century were rather heavy and sombre in appearance, and echoed the Baroque ornamentation of the previous century. The vast majority, however, increasingly reflected the lighter-hearted and less formal, more colourful and often frivolous approach of the Rococo style that became fashionable across most of Europe as the century progressed.

Much of this change of style can be attributed to an expansion of trade with the Orient and the importation of Chinese silks, ceramics and wallpapers, and hand-painted and hand-printed Indian calicoes (*indiennes*) – all of which provided inspiration for European pictorial silk, cotton and tapestry hangings. Typical subject matter included interpretations of Chinese, Indian, Arabian, Moorish and Persian landscapes filled with indigenous flora and fauna. Also common were native figures engaged in a diverse range of activities including hunting, fishing, harvesting, tax collecting, taking tea, playing musical instruments and bartering with colonial traders. Trading ships in the South China seas were much in evidence, then, and, as the first half of the century drew to a close, images of life in the English countryside began to appear.

1

2

1 **Brunschwig & Fils/Clipper Ships 79680.04** Colour cream Alt. colours **yes** Composition **55% linen, 45% cotton** Width **135cm/53in** Repeat **113.5cm/44½in** Price ★★★ 🛋

2 **Clarence House/Las Palmas 33976/2** Colour **green** Alt. colours **yes** Composition **100% cotton** Width **137cm/ 54in** Repeat **86cm/33¾in** Price ★★★★★

3

4

EASTERN INFLUENCE
Inspired by imported Chinese goods, 18th-century designers such as Antoine Watteau and Jean Pillement devised *chinoiserie* patterns for textiles and wallpapers. Their popularity at the time was reflected in Lady Mary Wortley Montagu's observation of 1740: "Sick of Grecian eloquence and symmetry or Gothic grandeur, we must all seek the barbarous gaudy gout of the Chinese." Similar designs, suitable for 18th-century interiors, are being produced today.

Nina Campbell/Zembla/Manchu NCF3403 Colour **01** Alt. colours **yes** Composition **100% linen** Width **140cm/55in** Repeat **88cm/34½in** Price ★★ LC

3 **Timney Fowler/Librarian TF0175** Colour **15** Alt. colours **yes** Composition **100% cotton** Width **133cm/ 52in** Repeat **58cm/22¾in** Price ★★★

4 **Timney Fowler/Studies TF0177** Colour **15** Alt. colours **yes** Composition **100% cotton** Width **133cm/ 52in** Repeat **73.5cm/28¾in** Price ★★★

5 **Brunschwig & Fils/Fishing Lady 79654.04** Colour **stone green** Alt. colours **yes** Composition **65% linen, 35% cotton** Width **137cm/ 54in** Repeat **81cm/31¾in** Price ★★

6 **Rubelli/Vasco Da Gama 7469** Colour **1 rosso/verde** Alt. colours **yes** Composition **100% cotton** Width **140cm/ 55in** Repeat **100cm/39¼in** Price ★★

5

6

7

11

7 **Old World Weavers/Voyage en Chine FBA 02A 0002** Colour **black** Alt. colours **yes** Composition **59% linen, 41% cotton** Width **137cm/ 54in** Repeat **114cm/ 44⅞in** Price ★★★ 🔲🛋

8 **Brunschwig & Fils/Chinoiserie Glazed Chintz 75460.04** Colour **lacquer red** Alt. colours **yes** Composition **100% cotton** Width **122cm/ 48in** Repeat **91.5cm/36in** Price ★★ 🔲

9 **Rubelli/Planter Café 7135** Colour **tabac/blue** Alt. colours **yes** Composition **100% cotton** Width **135cm/ 53in** Repeat **96cm/37⅞in** Price ★★★ 🔲🛋

10 **Zoffany/Reveillon Miniature PLP0700** Colour **5** Alt. colours **yes** Composition **100% cotton** Width **137cm/54in** Repeat **50cm/19½in** Price ★★ 🔲⊞🛋

8

9

10

12

11 **Rubelli/Tea Introduction 7134** Colour **famille rose** Alt. colours **yes** Composition **100% cotton** Width **135cm/ 53in** Repeat **12cm/4¾in** Price ★★★ 🔲🛋

12 **Brunschwig & Fils/West Indies Toile Cotton 79522.04** Colour **blue on white** Alt. colours **yes** Composition **100% cotton** Width **134cm/52½in** Repeat **87cm/34¼in** Price ★★ 🔲

13 **Busby & Busby/Serenata 4956** Colour **red/gold** Alt. colours **yes** Composition **100% cotton** Width **140cm/55in** Repeat **91cm/35¾in** Price ★★ 🔲🛋

14 **Brunschwig & Fils/Bromley Hall Toile 50151.01** Colour **red** Alt. colours **yes** Composition **100% cotton** Width **106.5cm/ 41¾in** Repeat **91.5cm/36in** Price ★★★ 🔲

13   **14**

Pictorials: Late 18th century

As pictorial tapestry production declined during the second half of the 18th century, the manufacture of pictorial silks and printed calicoes (particularly from Jouy in France) increased. Much of the subject matter favoured in earlier Rococo interiors remained fashionable, except in America where the style never really took root. The *chinoiserie* and Indian scenes produced were more authentically depicted than previously, because fabric designers now had greater access to the illustrated recollections of Europeans who had travelled to the Orient.

In addition, pastoral and rustic images, such as *fêtes galantes*, were much in evidence. This was also the case with theatrical scenes and accounts of contemporary events, such as the American War of Independence, the French Revolution and the first ascents by hot-air balloon. Mythological and ancient Roman and Greek subjects also returned to favour in the Neo-classical interiors that came into vogue during the latter part of the century.

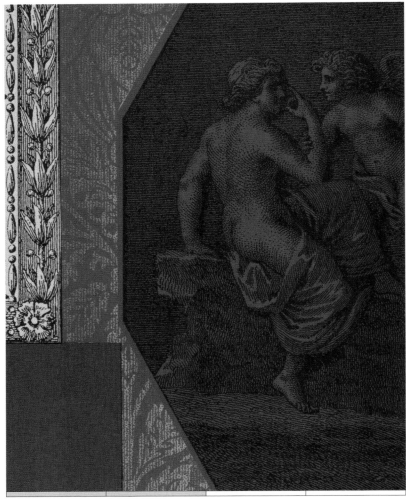

Timney Fowler/Draughtsman's Collage TF0172 Colour 20 Alt. colours no Composition 100% cotton Width 133cm/52in Repeat 110cm/43in Price ★★★

Anne & Robert Swaffer/Boulebard/Valencay 440 Colour 440 Alt. colours yes Composition 100% cotton Width 140cm/55in Repeat 64cm/25in Price ★★

Abbott & Boyd/Elefantes 47654 Colour 2 Alt. colours yes Composition 100% cotton Width 145cm/57in Repeat 56cm/22in Price ★★

The Design Archives/Stove Tiles 54139 Colour blue on cream Alt. colours yes Composition 100% cotton Width 137cm/54in Repeat 80cm/31½in Price ★★

Brunschwig & Fils/79575 Colour 829 Alt. colours yes Composition 100% cotton Width 131cm/51½in Repeat 91.5cm/36in Price ★★

Mulberry/Flights of Fantasy FD140/604 Colour navy/red F108 Alt. colours yes Composition 100% cotton Width 135cm/53in Repeat 50cm/19½in Price ★★

The Design Archives/Gustavian Cameo Colour black and grey on yellow Alt. colours yes Composition 100% cotton Width 137cm/54in Repeat 49cm/19¼in Price ★★

Brunschwig & Fils/79327.01 Colour 331 Alt. colours yes Composition 100% cotton Width 137cm/54in Repeat 42cm/16¼in Price ★★★

Marvic Textiles/Le Jardin Anglais 7702-4 Colour dusky rose Alt. colours yes Composition 100% cotton Width 138cm/54in Repeat 79cm/31in Price ★★

Nina Campbell/Canton Cargo NCF674 Colour 02 Alt. colours yes Composition 100% cotton Width 140cm/55in Repeat 91cm/35¾in Price ★★

The Design Archives/Pavilions 54138 Colour red and green Alt. colours yes Composition 100% cotton Width 137cm/54in Repeat 62cm/24¼in Price ★★

Lee Jofa/Chanteloup Brocade 2000182 Colour pomegranate 19 Alt. colours yes Composition 52% cotton, 34% viscose, 14% silk Width 139cm/54¾in Repeat 46.5cm/18¼in Price ★★★★★

TOILE DE JOUY

The majority of printed cottons, or toiles, made at the famous Jouy factory in France prior to 1775 were one of two design types – either striped or floral. After this time, however, an enormous variety of narrative patterns were produced. Apart from *chinoiserie*, the most popular subject matter for the fabric designs included idealized or romanticized depictions of rural life and well-known scenes from the theatre. Such patterns were to remain popular in both Europe and America well into the 19th century.

Laura Ashley/Toile Colour raspberry Alt. colours yes Composition 100% cotton Width 140cm/55in Repeat 46cm/18in Price ★★

Marvic Textiles/Les Fables de La Fontaine 7704-3 Colour carmine Alt. colours yes Composition 100% cotton Width 137cm/54in Repeat 59cm/23in Price ★★

Timney Fowler/Passage of Time TF0200/02 Colour neutral Alt. colours yes Composition 100% cotton Width 137cm/54in Repeat 84cm/33in Price ★★

The Design Archives/Liaisons 54044 Colour brown on cream Alt. colours yes Composition 100% cotton Width 137cm/54in Repeat 46cm/18in Price ★★

Marvic Textiles/Les Enfants 5440-005 Colour black on sand Alt. colours yes Composition 100% cotton Width 140cm/55in Repeat 88cm/34½in Price ★★

Pictorials: Early 19th century

The first three decades of the 19th century saw a further expansion of the printed-cotton industry to meet the ever-increasing demand for pictorial *toiles* (and floral chintzes). Moreover, advances in copperplate printing techniques, when combined with traditional pigments, such as madder (pinks and reds), indigo and woad (blues), and newly discovered mineral dyes, such as manganese (bronze) and antimony (orange), enabled manufacturers to produce increasingly ambitious and sophisticated images.

Chinoiserie, Indian and similarly exotic scenes retained their popularity from the previous century, while narratives depicting Napoleon's campaigns in Egypt became widespread. However, in keeping with the Neo-classical styles of decoration fashionable on both sides of the Atlantic, mythological and classical subjects proved the most popular. Typically elaborate toiles consisted of medallions or cartouches incorporating classical figures or ancient buildings, framed by allegorical figures, animals, scrolls and trophies of arms, linked by scrolling flowers or sheaves of wheat – imagery that drew heavily on the motifs and styles of ornamentation that had been unearthed during archaeological excavations at Pompeii and Herculaneum in the late 18th century.

1

1 **Timney Fowler/Diana TF0300** Colour **01** Alt. colours **no** Composition **100% cotton** Width **140cm/55in** Repeat **105cm/41¼in** Price ★★

2 **Timney Fowler/Regency Toile TF0302** Colour **01** Alt. colours **no** Composition **100% cotton** Width **140cm/55in** Repeat **102cm/40in** Price ★★

3 **Rubelli/Bises Novità/Maradjah 21883** Colour **avorio** Alt. colours **yes** Composition **78% cotton, 18% silk, 4% viscose** Width **130cm/51in** Repeat **64cm/25in** Price ★★★

2

3

4 **Marvic Textiles/Les Amours 5330-007** Colour **blues on off-white** Alt. colours **yes** Composition **100% cotton** Width **140cm/55in** Repeat **50.5cm/20in** Price ★★

5 **Marvic Textiles/Les Vues de Paris 6203-6** Colour **charcoal** Alt. colours **yes** Composition **100% cotton** Width **140cm/55in** Repeat **47cm/18½in** Price ★★

6 **Brunschwig & Fils/Mount Vernon 79668.04** Colour **wheat** Alt. colours **yes** Composition **100% cotton** Width **137cm/54in** Repeat **91.5cm/36in** Price ★★

4

5

7

8

9

7 **Brunschwig & Fils/79584**
Colour **845** Alt. colours
yes Composition **100%
cotton** Width **137cm/54in**
Repeat **75cm/29½in**
Price ★★ ⬚🛋

8 **Brunschwig & Fils/Hunting
Toile 70932.04** Colour **blue**
Alt. colours **yes** Composition
50% cotton, 50% linen Width
122cm/48in Repeat **28.5cm/
11in** Price ★★★ ⬚

9 **Brunschwig & Fils/Bunny
Business Glazed Chintz 79781**
Colour **04** Alt. colours **yes**
Composition **100% cotton**
Width **137cm/54in** Repeat
71cm/28in Price ★★★ ⬚

10 **Busby & Busby/Amaretti**
Colour **blue/stone** Alt. colours
yes Composition **100% cotton**
Width **140cm/55in** Repeat
64cm/25in Price ★★ ⬚

11 **Nicholas Herbert/Le Pecheur
113** Colour **01** Alt. colours
yes Composition **100%
cotton** Width **100cm/
39¼in** Repeat **65cm/25½in**
Price ★★ ⬚ LC ⬚🛋

10

11

12

13

12 **G.P. & J. Baker/Directoire
Parrot B0849** Colour **01** Alt.
colours **yes** Composition
100% cotton Width **137cm/
54in** Repeat **64cm/25in**
Price ★★ LC ⬚🛋

13 **Nicholas Herbert/Corinthia
109** Colour **05** Alt. colours
yes Composition **100%
cotton** Width **130cm/51in**
Repeat **94cm/36½in**
Price ★★★ ⬚ LC ⬚🛋

14 **Timney Fowler/Lady in Waiting**
Colour **multi** Alt. colours **yes**
Composition **100% cotton**
Width **133cm/52in** Repeat
117cm/46in Price ★★ ⬚🛋

BRIGHTON

The printed cotton fabric shown here was inspired by fabric wall-panels commissioned in 1801 by the Prince of Wales (subsequently Prince Regent, and then George IV, of England) for the Brighton Pavilion. Like many French and English printed cottons of the late 18th and early 19th centuries, the pattern includes "birds of paradise", exotic insects (dragonflies and butterflies), colourful flowers and luxuriant foliage. They are depicted in a style that owes much to contemporary imported Indian textiles and even more to the ornamentation found on imported Chinese artefacts.

Scalamandré/Brighton 16121-002 Colour **multi
on framboise** Alt. colours **yes** Composition
100% cotton Width **137cm/54in**
Repeat **101cm/39¾in**
Price ★★★★★ ⬚

14

Pictorials: **Mid-19th century**

To meet the requirements of the increasingly numerous middle classes on both sides of the Atlantic, printed pictorial cottons continued to be produced in quantity in the mid-19th century. However, one consequence of the Gothic Revival was a renewed demand for woven pictorial fabrics – notably tapestries – depicting medieval images. Gothic-arched windows with elaborate tracery provided typical subject matter, and were often augmented with heraldic motifs such as banners, emblems and achievements-of-arms.

As far as printed pictorials were concerned, *chinoiserie*, Indian and African scenes maintained their popularity, and featured exotic and indigenous figures, animals, birds and plant forms. In grander European and American Renaissance Revival interiors, classical ornamentation was the height of fashion, with some of the most interesting pictorial hangings inspired by della Robbia earthenware plaques (made in 15th-century Florence and decorated with festoons of fruit and flowers and white figures on pale blue grounds). Garish in comparison were the pictorial designs of children and animals that found favour in more ordinary households, but were despised for their sentimentality by the emerging Aesthetic and Arts and Crafts movements.

2

3

4

6

1

1 **Scalamandré/Daktari 26270** Colour **002** Alt. colours **yes** Composition **65% cotton, 30% rayon, 5% polyester** Width **137cm/54in** Repeat **41cm/16in** Price ★★★

2 **Nicholas Herbert/Hunting Lodge 117** Colour **red** Alt. colours **yes** Composition **100% cotton** Width **139cm/ 54¾in** Repeat **51cm/20in** Price ★★★

3 **Timney Fowler/Parks & Gardens TF0204** Colour **03** Alt. colours **yes** Composition **100% cotton** Width **137cm/ 54in** Repeat **84.5cm/33in** Price ★★★

4 **Nina Campbell/Sir Oliphant NCF 3124** Colour **04** Alt. colours **yes** Composition **60% linen, 20% cotton, 20% viscose** Width **140cm/55in** Repeat **50cm/19½in** Price ★★

5 **Nina Campbell/Lord Lyon NCF 3120** Colour **06** Alt. colours **yes** Composition **100% cotton** Width **140cm/ 55in** Repeat **64cm/25in** Price ★★

6 **Marvic Textiles/Vivarais 7542-001** Colour **blue on red** Alt. colours **yes** Composition **100% cotton** Width **150cm/ 59in** Repeat **28.5cm/11in** Price ★★

7

8

9

10

11

12

12 G.P. & J. Baker/The Floating Pavillion A2109 Colour **4** Alt. colours **yes** Composition **60% hemp, 40% silk** Width **140cm/55in** Repeat **115cm/45in** Price ★★★ ◻

13 Timney Fowler/Dante TF0198 Colour **yellow** Alt. colours **yes** Composition **100% cotton** Width **133cm/52in** Repeat **80.5cm/31¾in** Price ★★★ ◻ ⊞

14 Bentley & Spens/Animal Magic Colour **pale green** Alt. colours **yes** Composition **70% linen, 30% cotton** Width **135cm/53in** Repeat **106cm/41½in** Price ★★ LC ◻ 🛋 W

13

7 Busby & Busby/Fête 4936 Colour **charcoal** Alt. colours **yes** Composition **100% cotton** Width **140cm/55in** Repeat **91cm/35¾in** Price ★★ 🛋

8 G.P. & J. Baker/Blush China R1361 Colour **1** Alt. colours **yes** Composition **100% linen** Width **137cm/54in** Repeat **69cm/27in** Price ★★ ◻ 🛋

9 Rubelli/Black Pepper 7137 Colour **jaune/rose** Alt. colours **yes** Composition **100% cotton** Width **135cm/53in** Repeat **112cm/44in** Price ★★★ ◻ 🛋

10 Abbott & Boyd/Flora Antilana 48076 Colour **9** Alt. colours **no** Composition **100% cotton** Width **150cm/59in** Repeat **96cm/37¾in** Price ★★ ◻

11 Timney Fowler/Adam & Eve TF0197 Colour **blue** Alt. colours **yes** Composition **100% cotton** Width **133cm/52in** Repeat **79cm/31in** Price ★★★ ◻ ⊞

14

Pictorials: Late 19th century

Although the leading exponents of the Aesthetic and Arts and Crafts movements dismissed many of the mass-produced, aniline-dyed pictorial fabrics fashionable since the mid-19th century as garish and sentimental, such designs still found favour outside the confines of these aesthetic elites. Woven and printed pictorials of cats, dogs, horses, children and railway trains were still much in evidence in ordinary homes until the end of the century. Conversely, Aesthetic movement *japonaiserie* fabrics, displaying images of dragons, birds (sparrows, kingfishers, peacocks) and flowers (chrysanthemum, prunus blossom) derived from *Kakiemon*-pattern porcelain, were rarely admired except by the artistically minded.

More universally popular were the Gothic Revival pictorials that drew inspiration from medieval ornamentation. Notable among these were the vegetable-dyed Arts and Crafts designs, many of which depicted human figures set against a floral ground. Similarly, *chinoiserie*, Indian and African pictorials remained in vogue, as did classically inspired architectural prints rendered in black and white. The most innovative pictorials were produced by Art Nouveau designers: dream-like figures of women, set among sinuous, entwining plant forms (*femmes fleurs*), became a recurring theme of their work.

1

2

3

1 Brunschwig & Fils/79561-207 Colour **207** Alt. colours **yes** Composition **59% linen, 41% cotton** Width **137cm/ 54in** Repeat **64cm/25in** Price ★★★

2 Jim Thompson/Chinoiserie PMS **2991** Colour **B** Alt. colours **yes** Composition **100% silk** Width **122cm/48in** Repeat **91.5cm/36in** Price ★★★

3 Dedar/Dulcina Colour **02** Alt. colours **yes** Composition **100% cotton** Width **140cm/ 55in** Repeat **132cm/51¾in** Price ★★★

4 Marvic Textiles/Elizabeth 5205 Colour **gold 2** Alt. colours **yes** Composition **60% cotton, 40% viscose** Width **140cm/ 55in** Repeat **76cm/30in** Price ★★★

5 Colefax and Fowler/Ditchley F1508/06 Colour **yellow** Alt. colours **yes** Composition **52% linen, 36% cotton, 12% nylon** Width **136cm/53½in** Repeat **71.5cm/28¼in** Price ★★

6 Abbott & Boyd/Pentagramma **45832** Colour **8** Alt. colours **yes** Composition **100% cotton** Width **150cm/59in** Repeat **96cm/37¾in** Price ★★

7 Timney Fowler/Agra Ironwork TF0004 Colour **black & white 01** Alt. colours **yes** Composition **100% cotton** Width **140cm/ 55in** Repeat **28cm/10¾in** Price ★★

8 Timney Fowler/Ceiling Rose TF0218 Colour **01** Alt. colours **yes** Composition **100% cotton** Width **140cm/55in** Repeat **69cm/27in** Price ★★

9 **Borderline/Palmyra 2303** Colour
A Alt. colours **yes** Composition
52% linen, 48% cotton Width
137cm/54in Repeat **56cm/22in**
Price ★★ 🔲

10 **Mulberry/Doublet Silk FD089-
675** Colour **red V106** Alt.
colours **yes** Composition
62% silk, 38% polyester
Width **130cm/51in**
Repeat **15.5cm/6¼in**
Price ★★★ 🔲

11 **Timney Fowler/Tunnel Plan
TF0055** Colour **black and white**
Alt. colours **yes** Composition
100% cotton Width **120cm/47in**
Repeat **53cm/21in**
Price ★★ 🔲🛋

12 **Borderline/Samarkand 2341A**
Colour **burgundy** Alt. colours
yes Composition **52% linen,
36% cotton, 12% nylon** Width
137cm/54in Repeat **52cm/20½in**
Price ★★ 🔲🛋

13 **Borderline/Water Garden** Colour
blue Alt. colours **yes**
Composition **100% cotton**
Width **125cm/49¼in** Repeat
42.5cm/16¾in Price ★ 🔲🛋

12

13

14

15

14 **Mulberry/Final Furlong FD200**
Colour **parchment J107** Alt.
colours **yes** Composition
64% linen, 36% cotton Width
139cm/54¾in Repeat **60.5cm/
24in** Price ★★ 🔲 ⊞🛋

15 **Mulberry/Gazebo Sheer FD423**
Colour **moss R107** Alt. colours
yes Composition **100% linen**
Width **330cm/130in** Repeat
125cm/49¼in Price ★★★ 🔲

16 **Borderline/Otaka 2424** Colour
blue/pink Alt. colours **yes**
Composition **100% cotton**
Width **137cm/54in**
Repeat **48cm/19in**
Price ★★ 🔲

16

17 **Mulberry/Naval Ensigns
FD116/569 V113** Colour
red/navy Alt. colours **yes**
Composition **100% cotton**
Width **135cm/53in** Repeat
66cm/26in Price ★★ 🔲🛋

17

Pictorials: **Early 20th century**

Although rarely employed in Art Deco and Modernist interiors, pictorial furnishing fabrics continued to be produced in considerable quantities and in a diverse range of styles during the first half of the 20th century. Prominent examples included chintzes that were either reproductions of or inspired by the "Tree of Life" and "birds of paradise" designs favoured during the 17th and 18th centuries. Primarily used in Jacobean Revival interiors, they tended to be made in more sombre and muted colours than the flamboyant originals. Pictorial tapestries also appeared in some Jacobean- and Arts and Crafts-style schemes, although most of the tapestries created during this period departed from the pictorial tradition and displayed geometric and abstract designs. In addition to birds of paradise, animals and fish also proved fashionable in scenes. Especially popular were printed examples primarily intended for use in kitchens and bathrooms, many of them appearing in stylized form and often humorously augmented with pertinent objects, such as items of kitchenalia and vegetables, or perfume bottles, tablets of soap and shaving equipment. Exotic animals, notably African elephants and Indian tigers, were also in vogue, as were groups of "humanized" animals derived from nursery stories, designed for children's rooms.

3

4

4 **Scalamandré/Kilkenny Cats 16259-004** Colour **pink** Alt. colours **yes** Composition **100% cotton** Width **137cm/ 54in** Repeat **88cm/34½in** Price ★★ ⬚

5 **Lee Jofa/Delia's Trousseau Print 2000224** Colour **715 pastel** Alt. colours **yes** Composition **100% cotton** Width **137cm/ 54in** Repeat **46cm/18in** Price ★★ ⬚

6 **Mulberry/Round the Island FD201** Colour **marine blue** Alt. colours **yes** Composition **62% cotton, 38% jute** Width **143cm/ 56in** Repeat **82cm/32⅓in** Price ★★ ⬚ ⊞

1

1 **Liberty Furnishings/Dante 1095015** Colour **A** Alt. colours **yes** Composition **53% linen, 35% cotton, 12% polyacrylic** Width **137cm/54in** Repeat **33cm/13in** Price ★★ ⬚⬚

2 **Scalamandré/Under the Ice 16263-003** Colour **multi on sky blue** Alt. colours **yes** Composition **51% linen, 37% cotton, 12% nylon** Width **138.5cm/54½in** Repeat **88cm/34½in** Price ★★★ ⬚⬚

3 **Warner Fabrics/Souvenir d'Afrique CS6140** Colour **straw yellow** Alt. colours **yes** Composition **100% cotton** Width **137cm/54in** Repeat **64cm/25in** Price ★★ LC ⬚ ⊞

2

5

6

7

8

10

11

7 **Rubelli/Friday 7470** Colour **oceano 1** Alt. colours **yes** Composition **100% cotton** Width **140cm/55in** Repeat **96cm/37⅞in** Price ★★★ LC ⬚⬚⬚⬚⬚

8 **Scalamandré/Akbar's Stables 6236-004** Colour **tan and black** Alt. colours **yes** Composition **100% cotton** Width **140cm/55in** Repeat **68.5cm/27in** Price ★★★ ⬚

9 **Celia Birtwell/Mademoiselle/ Isabella** Colour **red/white/ grey/aqua** Alt. colours **no** Composition **100% cotton twill** Width **140cm/55in** Repeat **42cm/16½in** Price ★★ ⬚⬚⬚

10 **Mulberry/Jibe Stripe FD153-661** Colour **marine blue H103** Alt. colours **yes** Composition **100% cotton** Width **142cm/ 55¾in** Repeat **15.5cm/6⅛in** Price ★★ LC ⬚⬚⬚

11 **Clarence House/Jungle Book 33977** Colour **sand 1** Alt. colours **no** Composition **100% cotton** Width **137cm/ 54in** Repeat **99.5cm/39in** Price ★★★★ ⬚⬚

TREE OF LIFE

This hand-blocked linen fabric incorporates an early 20th-century version of the "Tree of Life" design. The original pattern, which has at its centre a tree symbolizing the "life force", was first seen in ancient Persian and Indian fabrics. However, the manner in which it is depicted here – with branches and shoots, and with exotic flowers and fruits interwoven with birds of paradise – is in the style of the English "Tree of Life" designs developed during the 17th century and most commonly found on contemporary Jacobean crewelwork and on 19th-century Jacobean Revival chintzes.

Lee Jofa/Tree of Life 667069 Colour **multi** Alt. colours **no** Composition **100% linen** Width **127cm/50in** Repeat **252cm/99in** Price ★★★★★ ⬚ W W

Pictorials: Late 20th–early 21st century

Much of the subject matter depicted in the pictorial fabrics favoured during the first half of the 20th century has remained popular to the present day – particularly stylized and naturalistic, and Indian-influenced, animal scenes and Persian-style hunting scenes. Printed classical and Neo-classical images inspired by or adapted from designs that were first produced during the Renaissance and the 17th and 18th centuries have also come into vogue. Typical examples include ancient biblical events, as well as ancient Roman and Greek figures in architectural settings – many of which have been produced in black and white or shades of grey. A large number of fabric manufacturers have also mass-produced machine-printed pictorials in the style of 18th- and 19th-century hand-printed toiles (see pages 134–7). Innovations include highly stylized medieval scenes (such as knights on horseback), nursery stories, diverse landscapes and still lifes in styles that mirror the developments of 20th-century fine art.

1 **Bentley & Spens/Fruit with Bowls** Colour **red** Alt. colours **yes** Composition **55% linen, 34% cotton, 11% nylon** Width **117cm/46in** Repeat **162cm/65in** Price ★★★

2 **Timney Fowler/Draughtsman's Collage TF0172/20** Colour **multi** Alt. colours **yes** Composition **100% cotton** Width **133cm/52in** Repeat **110cm/43in** Price ★★

3 **Turnell & Gigon/Newmarket 10005** Colour **1** Alt. colours **yes** Composition **100% cotton** Width **133cm/52in** Repeat **61cm/24in** Price ★★★

4 **Ivo Prints/Cox** Colour **black, white and green** Alt. colours **yes** Composition **100% cotton** Width **120cm/47in** Repeat **40cm/15¾in** Price ★★

5 **Timney Fowler/Madonna TF0196** Colour **black and white** Alt. colours **yes** Composition **100% cotton** Width **133cm/52in** Repeat **65cm/25½in** Price ★★

6 **Osborne & Little/Toad Hall F1178** Colour **2** Alt. colours **yes** Composition **100% cotton** Width **140cm/55in** Repeat **91cm/35¾in** Price ★★

Sandberg/Saga 300 Colour **24**
Alt. colours **yes** Composition
100% cotton Width **147cm/
58in** Repeat **90.5cm/35⅝in**
Price ★★ 🏷

**Jane Churchill/Jousting JY32F-
03** Colour **dark red** Alt.
colours **yes** Composition
100% cotton Width **141cm/
55½in** Repeat **40.5cm/16in**
Price ★★ 🏷🛋

Anna French/Treasure Island
Colour **24** Alt. colours **yes**
Composition **100% cotton**
Width **137cm/54in** Repeat
82cm/32⅛in Price ★★ 🏷⊞

7

10

9

11

12

10 Anna French/Fairies Colour **33**
Alt. colours **yes** Composition
100% cotton Width **137cm/
54in** Repeat **82cm/32⅛in**
Price ★★★ 🏷⊞🛋

11 Anna French/Tea for Teddies
Colour **22** Alt. colours
yes Composition **100%
cotton** Width **137cm/54in**
Repeat **82cm/32⅛in**
Price ★★ 🏷⊞

**12 Donghia/Housepets 0450/5850-
18** Colour **nana** Alt. colours
yes Composition **100%
cotton** Width **137cm/54in**
Repeat **34cm/13⅓in**
Price ★★★★★🛋

13 Andrew Martin/Mungo Park
Colour **blue and red** Alt.
colours **yes** Composition
60% cotton, 40% jute Width
132cm/51¾in Repeat **94cm/
36½in** Price ★★ LC ⊞

**14 G.P. & J. Baker/Tiger Tiger
J0248** Colour **green** Alt.
colours **yes** Composition
100% silk Width **140cm/
55in** Repeat **63cm/24¾in**
Price ★★★★ 🏷🛋

8

14

Overall Pattern

Of all the imagery that has provided inspiration for fabric patterns from the Middle Ages to the present day, organic forms – especially plants – have proved the most universal. Fabrics with floral patterns have been produced in such diverse styles that they merit discussion and illustration elsewhere (*see* pages 110–27). However, running a close second to floral designs are the patterns based on fruits, buds, stems, leaves, shoots, roots and organic forms such as animal skins and bird feathers.

Most plant ornament – both naturalistic and stylized – can be traced to specific cultures or periods. For example, the pomegranate is Middle Eastern in origin, the palm Asian and African, and the anthemion ancient Greek and oriental. Since the Renaissance, however, the expansion of export trade in fabrics has "internationalized" these forms, a development that has also been fuelled by archaeological discoveries of ancient civilizations, more extensive travel overseas and the publication of botanical studies and pattern books.

ABOVE A flame-stitch pattern fabric has been glued to the walls in this contemporary re-creation of a turn-of-the-18th-century English interior. Hand-woven flame-stitch fabrics were fashionable, especially in America, during the late 18th and early 19th centuries. The example shown here is machine-woven.

BLOCK-PRINTING

One of the oldest methods of printing designs on textiles (and still used today) involves hand-pressuring wooden blocks against the surface of the fabric – the pattern having been carved in relief on to the underside of the blocks, and the dyes or inks being carried on the raised sections of the carving. The number of blocks required depends on the complexity of the design, and can range from one for a simple repeat monochrome to up to a thousand or more for incredibly complex, multi-coloured pictorial patterns. Many scrolling, vegetal patterns have been produced in this way.

RIGHT The windows and seating in this 19th-century interior are furnished with late 20th-century woven and printed fabrics. The window sheers, the jacquard-woven top-covers on the daybed and oval-back painted armchair, and the jacquard-woven curtains all feature traditional trailing-foliage patterns. The fabrics covering the screen and foreground cushion display fruit-and-foliage patterns printed in complementary colourways.

1 Stylized interlaced foliage, scrolling or trailing, has been one of the most popular fabric patterns since the late Middle Ages. This scrolling leaf pattern was designed in the late 20th century.

2 Paisley patterns – stylized pinecones surrounded by vegetation – are derived from oriental decoration. Paisley fabrics have been fashionable on both sides of the Atlantic since the mid-19th century.

3 Historically, most interlaced foliage patterns have been highly stylized. However, naturalistic renderings have also been produced, particularly during the early 19th and 20th centuries.

4 Symbolizing immortality, foresight and beauty, peacock feathers are often found on oriental textiles. Other notable applications include Renaissance silks and Aesthetic movement fabrics.

5 Fabric designers have often drawn inspiration from decorative architectural mouldings. Typical examples since the Renaissance include fluting, *guilloche*, and as here, S- and C-scroll patterns.

6 Woven and printed fabric patterns simulating exotic animal skins, such as zebra, tiger and leopard, became fashionable from the middle of the 19th century onward, particularly in Europe.

---

1 Nina Campbell/Wilingdon NCF3411 Colour **06** Alt. colours **yes** Composition **56% rayon, 44% cotton** Width **129cm/51in** Repeat **22cm/8½in** Price ★★ LC ⬚⬚⬛

2 De Le Cuona/Grosvenor No11 Colour **coffee** Alt. colours **yes** Composition **60% wool, 40% cotton** Width **140cm/55in** Repeat – Price ★★★ ⬚⬚⬛⬛

3 Bennison Fabrics/Oakleaf Colour **green** Alt. colours **yes** Composition **70% linen, 30% cotton** Width **141cm/55½in** Repeat **28.5cm/11in** Price ★★★ ⬚⬚ W

4 Liberty Furnishings/Hera Colour **green** Alt. colours **yes** Composition **53% linen, 35% cotton, 12% nylon** Width **137cm/54in** Repeat **36cm/14in** Price ★ ⬚⬚⬛⬛

5 Sahco Hesslein/Tidepool 1871 Colour **01** Alt. colours **yes** Composition **75% silk, 25% wool** Width **140cm/55in** Repeat **32cm/12½in** Price ★★★ ⬚⬚

6 Chase Erwin/Ultrasuede Colour **zebra** Alt. colours **yes** Composition **100% polyester** Width **120cm/47in** Repeat **76cm/30in** Price ★★★ ⬛LC T ⬛

Overall Pattern: **Pre-18th century**

Prior to the 18th century, the vast majority of overall-patterned fabrics were decorated with stylized or naturalistic plant forms. During the Middle Ages, the ability of European fabric designers to depict such images accurately was restricted by the limitations of early weaving techniques and by a scarcity of botanical reference material (medieval herbals). Nevertheless, patterns based on grapevines, ivy, parsley, water leaves, oak leaves and acorns were much in evidence, as were palms – which were adopted as an heraldic emblem after the Crusades.

During the Renaissance, European fabric designers began to gain access to a much wider catalogue of plant ornament, notably those forms used in classical Graeco-Roman and Middle-Eastern decoration. These included the stylized pomegranate and pine forms set within repeat leaf patterns, favoured for damasks and velvets, and classical scrolling foliage patterns based on the acanthus leaf. In the 17th century, the proliferation of botanical pattern books, such as Guillaume Toulouze's *Livre de Fleurs, Feuilles et Oyzéaus* (1656), further fuelled the fashion for overall plant-form patterns, and made possible highly naturalistic renderings of fruit and extravagant scrolling foliage.

1

1 Warwick/Marseille 105461506-620 Colour **burgundy** Alt. colours **yes** Composition **100% cotton** Width **137cm/ 54in** Repeat **64cm/25in** Price ★★

2 Bernard Thorp & Co/Faisan Colour **multi** Alt. colours **yes** Composition **88% flax, 12% silk** Width **120cm/47in** Repeat **96.5cm/38in** Price ★★★

3 Jason D'Souza/Riccio RIC04 Colour **peach** Alt. colours **yes** Composition **50% linen, 50% cotton** Width **136cm/ 53½in** Repeat **17cm/6¾in** Price ★★

4 Ramm, Son & Crocker/ Fontaine R12074 Colour **willow** Alt. colours **yes** Composition **84% linen, 16% nylon** Width **140cm/ 55in** Repeat **49cm/19¼in** Price ★★

5 Bernard Thorp & Co/Lucien Colour **multi** Alt. colours **yes** Composition **58% flax, 42% cotton** Width **120cm/ 47in** Repeat **37cm/14½in** Price ★★

2

3

5

6 Montgomery/Kashmir Colour **gold 03** Alt. colours **yes** Composition **53% polyester, 47% cotton** Width **137cm/ 54in** Repeat **21cm/8¼in** Price ★ 🔲 ⊞

7 Garin/Samarkanda Colour **oro/azul** Alt. colours **yes** Composition **75% cotton, 25% viscose** Width **140cm/ 55in** Repeat **47cm/18½in** Price ★★★ 🔲 🛋

8 Rubelli/San Marco 1220 Colour **blue 5** Alt. colours **yes** Composition **100% silk** Width **125cm/49¼in** Repeat **63cm/24¾in** Price ★★★★★ 🔲

6

8

7

MORESQUE

The fabric shown here is derived from a panel of English, ivory and white silk damask overworked in embroidery, dated c.1554. The pattern is "moresque", a term used to describe the stylized foliage patterns that were fashionable in Europe from the mid-16th century to the early 17th century. Also known as "arabesques", these patterns originated in the damascened and engraved metalwork of Mesopotamia, Persia and Syria, and were introduced into Europe by Muslim craftsmen who settled in Venice during the 15th century.

Stuart Interiors/Walsingham MC/LA Colour **ecru, bottle and cherry** Alt. colours **yes** Composition **60% wool, 40% cotton** Width **145cm/57in** Repeat **60cm/23¾in** Price ★★★ 🔲 ⊞ 🛋

Overall Pattern: **18th century**

The library of plant forms utilized by fabric designers was substantially augmented during the 18th century. The factors fuelling this included a greater understanding of plant ornament used in classical Rome and Greece, following significant archaeological discoveries; the importation of Chinese silks and ceramics and Indian chintzes decorated with oriental plant forms; and the increasing fashionableness of horticulture and gardening, and the attendant publication of botanical pattern books such as J.G. Huquier's *Nouveau Livre de Trophées de Fleurs Etrangers* (c. 1750) and Philip Miller's *Figures of the Most Beautiful and Uncommon Plants* (1752). Many plant-form patterns on fabrics in Palladian interiors were based on the acanthus and the water leaf, while in Rococo schemes designs were based on light, scrolling foliage, palms, *chinoiserie* and Indian lotus leaves, artichokes and cauliflower florets. In the Neo-classical interiors of the second half of the century, anthemia, laurels, lotus leaves, oak leaves, palmettes and seaweed were fashionable – the latter often combined with coral on silk damasks. Ivy patterns also became popular in Gothick schemes, as the plant's association with ruined buildings made it well suited to the Gothick taste for images of rustic decay. *Guilloche* patterns (*see* page 160) were also very popular.

1   **The Silk Gallery/Persephone** Colour **new gold 278** Alt. colours **yes** Composition **100% silk** Width **127cm/ 50in** Repeat **90cm/35½in** Price ★★★

2   **Knowles & Christou/Ferns** Colour **fudge** Alt. colours **yes** Composition **100% linen** Width **132cm/51¾in** Repeat **67cm/27in** Price ★★★

3   **Zoffany/Silk Lampas SLA68** Colour **003** Alt. colours **yes** Composition **84% viscose, 16% silk** Width **128cm/50½in** Repeat **85cm/33½in** Price ★★★

4   **Timney Fowler/Agra Ironwork TF004/3** Colour **green and ecru** Alt. colours **yes** Composition **100% cotton** Width **135cm/ 53in** Repeat **28cm/11in** Price ★★

5   **Watts of Westminster/Alwyne Zial** Colour **beige/oatmeal** Alt. colours **yes** Composition **100% cotton** Width **124cm/ 48¾in** Repeat **96.5cm/38in** Price ★★★

6 Apenn/Hayward AV469-1
Colour **green** Alt. colours **yes**
Composition **100% cotton**
Width **121cm/47½in** Repeat
8cm/3in Price ★★ 🗋🛋

7 Brunschwig & Fils/Benoa
Contrefond Cotton Print 51251
Colour **01** Alt. colours **yes**
Composition **100% cotton**
Width **135cm/53in** Repeat
17.5cm/7in Price ★★ 🗋

8 Marvic Textiles/Oakley 7335
Colour **juniper** Alt. colours
yes Composition **74% cotton,**
26% viscose Width **142cm/**
55¾in Repeat **16.5cm/6½in**
Price ★★ 🗋 LC 🛋

9 Zoffany/Vine 347706 Colour
Swedish blue Alt. colours **yes**
Composition **45% modacrylic,**
41% cotton, 14% nylon Width
137cm/54in Repeat **10cm/4in**
Price ★★ 🗋🛋

10 Brunschwig & Fils/Rampur
Stripe Cotton Print 79637
Colour **04** Alt. colours **yes**
Composition **100% cotton**
Width **137cm/54in** Repeat
46cm/18in Price ★★★🛋

11 Bennison Fabrics/Cinnabar
Colour **sienna on beige** Alt.
colours **yes** Composition
70% linen, 30% cotton
Width **138cm/54in**
Repeat **49cm/19¼in**
Price ★★★ 🗋🛋

12 Warner/Templeton Field
Colour **grass** Alt. colours
yes Composition **100%**
cotton Width **137cm/**
54in Repeat **2cm/¾in**
Price ★ 🗋🛋

13 Zoffany/Mirandola DUP7100
Colour **1** Alt. colours **yes**
Composition **100% cotton**
Width **131cm/51½in**
Repeat **46cm/18in**
Price ★★ 🗋

6

7

8

9

10

11

12

13

Overall Pattern: **Early 19th century**

In early 19th-century Neo-classical interiors, fashionable plant-form-patterned fabrics were based on stylized anthemia (especially popular in France and America), laurels, Egyptian-style lotus and palm leaves, seaweed and the water leaf. However, as the century progressed increasingly naturalistic renderings of plant patterns were produced. Sometimes "sculptured" with shading, favoured patterns included acanthus leaf, grapevine, oak leaf, thistle and various fruits.

Around the middle of the century, there was a reaction to naturalistic patterns, with influential designers such as A.W.N. Pugin and Owen Jones producing heavily stylized designs. For example, many of the fabrics designed by Pugin in the 1840s were "flat-patterned" with a basic ogival structure featuring scrolling leaves and fleurs-de-lis, while Jones's designs incorporated stylized classical and Moorish ornament. Abstract patterns derived from motifs were also popular at this time, as were "ironwork" designs.

1

2

4

3

5

1 **Nicholas Herbert/Loose Leaves 104** Colour **blue** Alt. colours **yes** Composition **66% linen, 34% cotton** Width **130cm/ 51in** Repeat **8.5cm/3¼in** Price ★★★

2 **Wemyss Houlès/Kingsbury/ Kensington** Colour **18** Alt. colours **yes** Composition **43% cotton, 43% modacrylic, 14% nylon** Width **138cm/ 54in** Repeat **32cm/12½in** Price ★★

3 **Lennox Money/Araz 2149A** Colour **beige on green** Alt. colours **yes** Composition **100% cotton** Width **140cm/ 55in** Repeat **120cm/47in** Price ★★

4 **Brunschwig & Fils/Coraux Glazed Chintz 62702.01** Colour **blueberry** Alt. colours **yes** Composition **100% cotton** Width **140cm/55in** Repeat **14cm/5½in** Price ★★

5 **Hodsoll McKenzie/Arabesque 222/105** Colour **green** Alt. colours **yes** Composition **56% cotton, 44% rayon** Width **127cm/50in** Repeat **36.5cm/ 14¼in** Price ★★★

6 **Marvic Textiles/Astor 4557**
Colour **cardinal** Alt. colours
yes Composition **100%
cotton** Width **140cm/55in**
Repeat **70cm/27½in**
Price ★★★ 🔲 LC🛋

7 **Busby & Busby/Fontmell 6476**
Colour **stone** Alt. colours **yes**
Composition **100% cotton**
Width **140cm/55in** Repeat
64cm/25in Price ★★ 🔲

8 **Anne & Robert Swaffer/
Cotterstock/Allington** Colour **19**
Alt. colours **yes** Composition
100% textured cotton Width
140cm/55in Repeat **64cm/25in**
Price ★★ 🔲 LC ⊞ 🛋

9 **Nina Campbell/Ferronnier
Chenilles/Rateau NCF3350**
Colour **02** Alt. colours **yes**
Composition **51% rayon,
49% cotton** Width **132cm/
51¼in** Repeat **71cm/28in**
Price ★★★ 🔲 ⊞

10 **Rubelli/Bises Novità/
Sheerazade 2193** Colour
crena 1 Alt. colours **yes**
Composition **41% linen,
25% cotton, 20% silk, 14%
viscose** Width **130cm/51in**
Repeat **50cm/19½in**
Price ★★★ 🔲 ⊞

11

12

6

7   **8**   **9**

11 **Andrew Martin/Cabaret/
Arabesque** Colour **arabesque**
Alt. colours **no** Composition
100% viscose Width **132cm/
51¼in** Repeat **41cm/16in**
Price ★★ 🔲 ⊞ 🛋

12 **Montgomery/Halkidiki** Colour **6**
Alt. colours **yes** Composition
100% cotton Width **140cm/
55in** Repeat **64cm/25in**
Price ★ 🔲 LC🛋⊞

13 **Howe/Hydrangea** Colour
hydrangea Alt. colours
no Composition **100%
cotton** Width **125cm/49¼in**
Repeat **40cm/15¾in**
Price ★★ 🔲 ⊞🛋

10   **13**

FABRICS: *OVERALL PATTERN*   **153**

Overall Pattern: Late 19th century

Although naturalistically rendered plant-form patterns continued to appear on fabrics during the second half of the 19th century, stylized versions proved more fashionable. For example, designers of the Aesthetic movement drew inspiration from classical, medieval, Renaissance, Middle-Eastern and Japanese flat-patterns and plant motifs. These include E.W. Godwin's rigid geometric designs that incorporate highly conventionalized flowers and leaves reduced to flat, circular forms, and Christopher Dresser's formalized lotus patterns. Many Arts and Crafts fabrics also featured stylized, rhythmical plant forms, such as the willow, worked within medieval-style pattern structures, while Art Nouveau fabrics displayed sinuous vegetal patterns based on pomegranates, thistles, buds and seedpods, and leaf-like peacock feathers.

Of special note during the second half of the century were the paisley-pattern fabrics widely employed in English and American Victorian interiors, and also popular in France. Inspired by imported Kashmiri shawls, they featured formalized representations of pine cones infilled with small, incidental motifs commonly found in Indian textile designs, and surrounded by stylized vegetation based on palms, cypress and other plant forms.

1 **Lennox Money/Mangosteen 2152c** Colour **dark green on beige** Alt. colours **yes** Composition **100% cotton** Width **138cm/54in** Repeat **113cm/44in** Price ★★

2 **Zoffany/Palmette AMB0300** Colour **1** Alt. colours **yes** Composition **60% linen, 20% cotton, 20% modacrylic** Width **138cm/54in** Repeat **104cm/40½in** Price ★★

3 **Zuber/Arabesque/Volutes 30005** Colour **celadon** Alt. colours **yes** Composition **100% cotton** Width **130cm/51in** Repeat **43.5cm/17in** Price ★★★

4 **Watts of Westminster/Bodley F0041** Colour **English beige** Alt. colours **yes** Composition **54% cotton, 46% Velicren** Width **140cm/55in** Repeat **36cm/14in** Price ★★★

5 **Watts of Westminster/Grange Grosmont Shrewsbury F0040-01/M7** Colour **bottle green** Alt. colours **yes** Composition **54% cotton, 46% Velicren** Width **140cm/55in** Repeat **79cm/31in** Price ★★★

19th century

6 Borderline/Juniper 2528a
Colour **red** Alt. colours **yes**
Composition **100% wool**
Width **137cm/54in** Repeat
44cm/17in Price ★★ LC 🛋

7 Bennison Fabrics/Pacific Willow
Colour **beige** Alt. colours **yes**
Composition **70% linen, 30%
cotton** Width **133cm/52in**
Repeat **13cm/5in**
Price ★★★ 🛋

**8 Nina Campbell/Curzon Chenilles/
Dalhousie/NCF3412** Colour **02**
Alt. colours **yes** Composition
**74% rayon, 23% cotton, 3%
polyester** Width **131cm/51½in**
Repeat **70cm/27½in**
Price ★★★

6

9

10

7

8

11

9 Marvic Textiles/Khaipur 5818-1
Colour **claret** Alt. colours **yes**
Composition **40% acryllic, 40%
viscose, 20% cotton** Width
150cm/59in Repeat **35.5cm/
14in** Price ★★★

**10 Morris & Co/Garden Tulip
PR8539** Colour **1** Alt. colours
yes Composition **53% linen,
35% cotton, 12% nylon** Width
137cm/54in Repeat **44.5cm/
17¼in** Price ★★ LC

**11 Liberty Furnishings/Hera
1067032** Colour **G** Alt. colours
yes Composition **100% cotton**
Width **137cm/54in** Repeat
36cm/14in Price ★

12 Mulberry/Cartouche FD336
Colour **soft green/brick** Alt.
colours **yes** Composition
**65% viscose, 25% cotton, 10%
polyamide** Width **146cm/
57½in** Repeat **30cm/11¾in**
Price ★★★ LC

FLAME STITCH

The flame stitch pattern
enjoyed a resurgence of
popularity during the late
19th century and, as a
consequence, machine-
made versions were
produced to meet the
demand. A form of
embroidery that was
primarily used as a cover
for chairs, sofas and fire-
screens, flame stitch
consists of "flames" of
colour. The technique, by
which large areas of
backing canvas can be
covered rapidly and to
dramatic effect, was a
fashionable pastime in
Britain and America
during the 18th century.

Brunschwig & Fils 89381 Colour **M46** Alt. colours **yes** Composition
87% viscose, 12% cotton, 1% polyester Width **140cm/55in** Repeat
39cm/15¼in Price ★★★★★ LC

12

Overall Pattern: **Early 20th century**

Woven and printed fabric patterns consisting of stylized plant forms remained very fashionable during the first half of the 20th century. For example, sinuously depicted foliage was an important element in later designs of the Art Nouveau period, and thistle, poppy, wisteria and waterlily patterns were especially favoured. Similarly, Arts and Crafts designers continued to explore new areas of plant ornament. L.F. Day, whose influential *Nature and Ornament* was published 1908–9, noted: "The rose has been variously treated but comparatively little use has been made...[to date]...of the fruit, or of the thorns, or of the broad stipules at the base of the leaves."

More traditional plant-form patterns were also much in evidence during the first half of the century. Significant examples included the Renaissance-style pomegranate- and acorn-patterned damasks that were found in Tudor Revival and Jacobean Revival interiors. Also prevalent were the classical Graeco-Roman palms and palmettes that appeared on some of the Art Deco fabrics. However, the increasing influence of fine art on textile design resulted in the appearance of radically new organic forms, such as abstract depictions of aquaria and pond life.

3

1

2

4

5

6

1 **Northwood Designs/Lampen M06352** Colour **03** Alt. colours **yes** Composition **61% cotton, 39% viscose** Width **140cm/ 55in** Repeat **10.5cm/4in** Price ★★★

2 **Zuber/Tissus Anciens III/ Chambord Brodé 10174** Colour **white/gold** Alt. colours **yes** Composition **100% cotton** Width **140cm/ 55in** Repeat **67cm/26¼in** Price ★★★★★

3 **Monkwell/MF 5883** Colour **ananda** Alt. colours **yes** Composition **37% acrylic chenille, 27% polyester, 14% viscose, 14% polyester chenille, 8% cotton** Width **140cm/ 55in** Repeat **46cm/18in** Price ★★

4 **Monkwell/MP 9556** Colour **brick** Alt. colours **yes** Composition **58% linen, 31% cotton, 11% nylon** Width **137cm/ 54in** Repeat **11cm/4¼in** Price ★★

5 **Nina Campbell/Ferronnier Chenilles/Poiret NCF3352** Colour **03** Alt. colours **yes** Composition **66% cotton, 34% rayon** Width **137cm/ 54in** Repeat **19cm/7½in** Price ★★★

6 **Donghia/Magic 0392/5725-03** Colour **harvest** Alt. colours **yes** Composition **100% silk** Width **140cm/55in** Repeat **13cm/5in** Price ★★★★★

7 Lee Jofa/Pardah Print 919301
Colour **persian red/indgo** Alt.
colours **yes** Composition
**52% linen, 36% cotton,
12% nylon** Width 137cm/
54in Repeat **72cm/28¼in**
Price ★★

8 Brunschwig & Fils/89507
Colour **247** Alt. colours
yes Composition **100%
rayon** Width **140cm/
55in** Repeat **18.5cm/7¼in**
Price ★★★

**9 Warner Fabrics/Aquarium
GW32903** Colour **orange** Alt.
colours **yes** Composition
100% cotton Width **137cm/
54in** Repeat **72cm/28¼in**
Price ★★ [LC]

10 Scalamandré/16316 Colour **001**
Alt. colours **yes** Composition
100% cotton Width **54cm/
21½in** Repeat **25cm/10in**
Price ★★★★★

11 Zimmer & Rohde/Lyra 6997
Colour **717** Alt. colours **yes**
Composition **100% silk** Width
140cm/55in Repeat **9cm/3½in**
Price ★★★★

**12 Northwood Designs/Spirale
P074B7** Colour **03** Alt.
colours **yes** Composition
100% cotton Width **140cm/
55in** Repeat **32cm/12½in**
Price ★★★

**13 Brunschwig & Fils/Involve
Silk Texture 53462.01** Colour
imperial blue Alt. colours
yes Composition **76% silk,
24% cotton** Width **140cm/
55in** Repeat **31cm/12in**
Price ★★★

**14 Osborne & Little/Dufy Velvet
F5151** Colour **01** Alt. colours
yes Composition **59% viscose,
41% cotton** Width **132cm/
51¾in** Repeat **59cm/23in**
Price ★★★★ [LC]

10 **11** **12**

9

13

15 Malabar/Taprabane/Rubra Leaf
Colour **silver** Alt. colours **no**
Composition **100% silk** Width
140cm/55in Repeat **12cm/4¾in**
Price ★★★

**16 Manuel Canovas/Kapsan
1420** Colour **36** Alt. colours
yes Composition **100% cotton**
Width **139cm/54¾in** Repeat
36.5cm/14¼in Price ★★

4

15 **16**

Overall Pattern: **Late 20th–early 21st century**

Woven and printed fabrics with traditional-style leaf patterns have been much in demand during the late 20th and early 21st century. Highly stylized – sometimes shaded, sometimes flat – they have often been presented on a contrasting plain ground to give them a contemporary feel. Sinuous Art Nouveau and rhythmical Arts and Crafts plant-form patterns (*see* pages 154-7) came back into fashion in the 1960s and the 1980s respectively. Pointillist-style patterns comprising small repeated fruit motifs such as strawberries and raspberries have also found favour, while stylized and naturalistic animal prints have proved popular, especially as top-covers for upholstered seating.

Among recent and important additions to the catalogue of organic ornamentation are colourful woven fabrics showing stylized "three-dimensional" wickerwork patterns, and literally three-dimensional fabrics that are comprised of plain- or neutral-coloured grounds "embroidered" with highly textured threadwork.

1

2

4

5

6

3

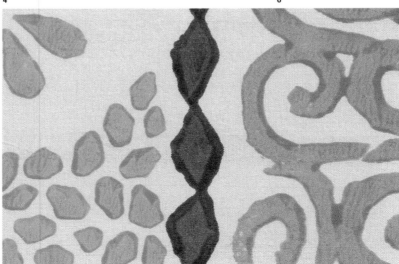

7

1 **Clarence House/Zambezi 33975/3** Colour **multi** Alt. colours **yes** Composition **72% linen, 17% cotton, 11% polyester** Width **130cm/51in** Repeat **94.5cm/36½in** Price ★★★★★ 🛋

2 **Nya Nordiska/Pavonia** Colour **bronze 06** Alt. colours **yes** Composition **40% polyester, 30% polyamid, 30% acetate** Width **160cm/63in** Repeat **21cm/8¼in** Price ★★★ 🔲🛋

3 **Monkwell/Vellum MP 9495** Colour **baked** Alt. colours **yes** Composition **100% cotton** Width **137cm/54in** Repeat **32cm/12½in** Price ★★ 🔲⊞

4 **Garin/Kaisery** Colour **arena** Alt. colours **yes** Composition **100% cotton** Width **140cm/55in** Repeat **47cm/18½in** Price ★★★ 🛋 LC

5 **Donghia/Casino 10025** Colour **01** Alt. colours **yes** Composition **56% rayon, 44% cotton** Width **140cm/55in** Repeat **18.5cm/7¼in** Price ★★★★ 🔲🛋 LC

6 **Knowles & Christou/Cabouchon KG403a** Colour **opal and lilac** Alt. colours **yes** Composition **100% cotton** Width **132cm/51¾in** Repeat **10cm/4in** Price ★★★ 🔲🛋 W

7 **Galbraith & Paul/Mosaic** Colour **silver** Alt. colours **yes** Composition **100% shantung silk** Width **134cm/52½in** Repeat **46cm/18in** Price ★★★★ 🔲

Mulberry/Ice Dance FD387
Colour **pink W106** Alt. colours **yes** Composition **73% cotton, 20% rayon, 7% nylon** Width **130cm/51in** Repeat **43cm/16⅞in** Price ★★★ [LC] [icons]

Lelièvre/Damasquine 909
Colour **cuivre 02** Alt. colours **no** Composition **95% cotton, 5% polyamide** Width **136cm/53½in** Repeat **12cm/4¾in** Price ★★★ [icons]

Jim Thompson/Image 1023
Colour **07** Alt. colours **yes** Composition **100% cotton** Width **142cm/55¾in** Repeat – Price ★★★ [icons]

Knowles & Christou/Wicker
Colour **blue** Alt. colours **yes** Composition **100% linen** Width **132cm/51¾in** Repeat **3cm/1⅛in** Price ★★★ [icons] [W]

Marvic Textiles/Le Croc/5924-2
Colour **blue** Alt. colours **yes** Composition **100% cotton** Width **136cm/53½in** Repeat **27cm/10⅝in** Price ★★★ [icons]

8

9

12

"ANIMAL SKIN" FABRIC

Distinctively patterned animal skins provided fashionable covers for chairs and sofas during the 19th century, particularly in Britain and France as they expanded their empires into Africa. However, even then demand outstripped supply and thus *faux* skins made of both woven and printed fabrics were also produced for upholstery.

With animals such as the leopard, tiger, panther and some species of zebra now hunted close to extinction, it is the fabric substitutes that have enjoyed a resurgence in popularity during the second half of the 20th century.

G.P. & J. Baker/Panther JO257-220 Colour **black and cream** Alt. colours **yes** Composition **86% cotton, 14% polyacrylic** Width **138cm/54in** Repeat **38cm/15in** Price ★★ [LC] [icons]

Jim Thompson/Leopard PDB 2798A Colour **A** Alt. colours **no** Composition **100% silk** Width **122cm/48in** Repeat **46cm/18in** Price ★★★★ [icons]

Geometric Fabrics

A wide range of geometric-patterned fabrics, woven and printed, has been produced from the Middle Ages to the present day. Much of the geometric ornament employed originated in ancient classical and oriental civilizations or in medieval Europe.

Stylistically, fabrics with geometric patterns can usually be divided into two basic categories. In the first the pattern consists of geometric or linear forms; in the second a basic geometric pattern, sometimes comprised of non-geometric repeat motifs, frames the non-geometric imagery or provides the ground against which it is set.

Patterns classified as "pure" geometrics include woven or printed stripes; checks, such as woven tartans and printed madras; and combinations of irregular geometric forms that were inspired by Cubist art. "Loosely" geometric-based patterns include trellis- or latticework, and *guilloche* – an overall repeating pattern (*see* pages 146–59) of interlacing curved bands, sometimes forming circles enriched with floral motifs.

LEFT The squab seat of the lyre-back chair in the background is upholstered with a red horsehair-weave, cut-pile velvet, while the armchair in the foreground is covered with a red-and-gold trellis-pattern silk lampas by Scalamandré. Both chairs date from the early to mid-19th century, and are in the parlour of the 19th-century Andrew Low House, Georgia, USA.

BOVE Linear-stripe patterns are particularly suitable for pull-up, pull-down window blinds, nd were very fashionable in late 18th- and early 19th-century interiors. These Roman blinds re in a late Georgian house in Brighton, England.

TICKING

This 19th-century French wirework child's bed has been converted into a small bench seat – with a bolster added for extra comfort. The squab and bolster are both covered with a modern blue-and-white striped bed ticking – a fabric that has been produced in various patterns over the centuries, although striped examples are certainly the most common. Blue-and-white striped ticking such as this, woven in either cotton or linen, has changed very little in appearance since the late 18th century, and has remained fashionable on both sides of the Atlantic for a variety of uses.

KEY DESIGNS

1 Popular since the 19th century, checked ginghams have vertical and horizontal stripes of equal width. They are woven from only two colours, but display a third colour where these overlap.

2 Thick-textured, multi-coloured fabrics patterned with woven stripes of various alternating widths were much in evidence during the Renaissance, as well as appearing in 20th-century interiors.

3 Striped fabrics incorporating alternating weaves and colourways have been popular since the Middle Ages, but were especially fashionable during the late 18th and early 19th centuries.

4 Tartans have been widely used as furnishing fabrics since the 19th century. They are produced in various patterns and colourways ("setts"), each associated with a particular Scottish clan.

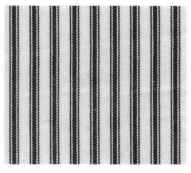

5 Diaper patterns have consistently appeared on fabrics since the Middle Ages. Favoured designs include trellis or lattice frameworks containing repeated geometric or non-geometric motifs.

6 Originally a mattress covering, striped herringbone-weave ticking is now widely employed for hangings and upholstery. Classic colourways are black, green, blue or red on white or beige.

1 **Manuel Canovas/Passy 4261** Colour **96** Alt. colours **yes** Composition **100% viscose** Width **130cm/51in** Repeat **2cm/¾in** Price ★★

2 **Thomas Dare/Sarawak** Colour **multi/orange** Alt. colours **yes** Composition **100% cotton** Width **137cm/54in** Repeat – Price ★★

3 **Nobilis-Fontan/Rodolphe 9937** Colour **red** Alt. colours **yes** Composition **56% cotton, 44% viscose** Width **130cm/51in** Repeat – Price ★★★

4 **The Isle Mill/Tullochcan STR009** Colour **multi** Alt. colours **yes** Composition **100% wool** Width **140cm/55in** Repeat **25cm/9¾in** Price ★★★

5 **G.P. & J. Baker/Roi Soleil** Colour **green** Alt. colours **yes** Composition **57% cotton, 43% modacrylic** Width **145cm/57in** Repeat **6cm/2½in** Price ★★

6 **Ian Mankin/Ticking 01** Colour **black** Alt. colours **yes** Composition **100% cotton** Width **137cm/54in** Repeat – Price ★

Geometrics: **Pre-18th century**

During the Middle Ages, diaper patterns were often employed on woven fabrics, and usually took the form of trellis grounds filled with motifs, such as lozenges, squares, scales or formalized flowers and leaves. Chequer patterns – regularly spaced squares of alternating colours – were also popular, as were chevrons (V-shapes, used either singly in vertical series, or strung to form zig-zags), nailheads (small pyramid forms) and powdered ornament (evenly spaced scatterings of small flowers or stars).

Diaper, chequer and nailhead patterns continued to appear on Renaissance fabrics. Strapwork patterns (twisted and intertwined bands similar to ribbons or strips of leather) were also fashionable, and Islamic influence was notable in *guilloches* (repeated interlacing curved bands, sometimes forming circles and usually enriched with floral motifs). However, aside from tartans (*see* opposite), which were primarily used for clothing and blankets during this period, the most notable late 16th- and 17th-century addition to this rich catalogue of geometric ornament was jewelled strapwork: an elaboration of its plainer forerunner in which increasingly intricate banding was embellished with studs or lozenges shaded in imitation of faceted, prismatic jewels.

1 Jason D'Souza/Stripe 561
Colour **green** Alt. colours **yes**
Composition **50% linen, 50% cotton** Width **137cm/54in**
Repeat **8cm/3in**
Price ★★ 🪑 ⊞ 🛋

2 Today Interiors/Checkmate/ Check FR3501 Colour **1** Alt. colours **yes** Composition **100% cotton** Width **137cm/54in** Repeat **51cm/20in** Price ★★
LC 🪑 ⊞ 🛋

3 Jason D'Souza/San Marco SAN 01 Colour **walnut and coral** Alt. colours **yes** Composition **50% linen, 50% cotton** Width **133cm/52in** Repeat **5.5cm/2¼in** Price ★★ ⊞ 🛋

4 John Boyd Textiles/Squares 682/5 Colour **purple/black** Alt. colours **yes** Composition **68% horsehair, 32% cotton** Width **56cm/22in** Repeat **-** Price ★★★ LC 🪑 ⊞ 🛋

5 John Boyd Textiles/Jutland JU/609 Colour **brown/black** Alt. colours **yes** Composition **68% horsehair, 32% cotton** Width **65cm/25½in** Repeat **-** Price ★★★ 🛋 W

6 Zoffany/Cottage Garden ORC0500 Colour **1** Alt. colours **yes** Composition **56% linen, 36% cotton, 8% nylon** Width **138cm/54⅓in** Repeat **8cm/3in** Price ★★ LC 🪑 🛋

10 Zoffany/Mosaic VEN9600 Colour **1** Alt. colours **yes** Composition 37% wool, 3% nylon, 60% modacrylic Width **137cm/54in** Repeat **13cm/5in** Price ★★ LC 🛋

11 Anta/Ballone 955 Colour **blue/green** Alt. colours **no** Composition 100% wool Width **90cm/35½in** Repeat **50cm/19½in** Price ★★★★ 🛋

10

7

Wemyss Houlès/Minster/ Winchester Colour **blue** Alt. colours **yes** Composition 56% linen, 33% cotton, 11% nylon Width **138cm/54¼in** Repeat - Price ★★ 〈〉 LC 🛋 ▦

Montgomery/Dot.Com Colour **blue 1** Alt. colours **yes** Composition 53% cotton, 47% polyester Width **137cm/54in** Repeat **2cm/¾in** Price ★ 〈〉 ▦

Zoffany/Bark NAT2900 Colour **1** Alt. colours **yes** Composition 52% polyester, 48% cotton Width **125cm/49¼in** Repeat **23cm/9in** Price ★★ 〈〉

8

11

TARTAN

In the 19th century, when tartans became fashionable furnishing fabrics, many manufacturers outside Scotland produced them in setts (patterns and colours) that sometimes bore little resemblance to the authentic designs of the Scottish clans. This development was fuelled by three factors: financial opportunism, the use of synthetic aniline rather than vegetable dyes, and a lack of knowledge. Many of the pre-18th-century setts were never recorded, but were instead passed down by generations of Scottish dyers and weavers.

Seamoor Fabrics/Hay Tartan 96720/22 Colour **red and black** Alt. colours **no** Composition 100% cotton Width **140cm/55in** Repeat **11cm/4¼in** Price ★ LC 〈〉 🛋 W

Seamoor Fabrics/Macalpine Tartan 96720/27 Colour **green and cream** Alt. colours **no** Composition 100% cotton Width **140cm/55in** Repeat **11cm/4¼in** Price ★ LC 〈〉 🛋 W

Geometrics: **Early 18th century**

Diaper ornament continued to appear on furnishing fabrics produced during the first half of the 18th century. Indeed, early Rococo-style fabrics were characterized by trellis and latticework patterns (often constructed from leaf motifs), while bandwork (the 18th-century term for strapwork) was also much in evidence, and usually provided the ground for light, scrolling foliage. Other medieval and Renaissance geometric patterns that either remained popular or were revived included V-shape chevrons (particularly prevalent in mid-18th-century Gothick interiors), dogteeth (symmetrically arranged, star-like decorations developed from pyramid-shaped nailheads – *see* page 162), and, to a lesser extent, tartans.

Also increasingly popular during the early 18th century were vertical-stripe patterns. Varied in width, alternated in two or more colours and sometimes incorporating additional small motifs, the stripes either made up the main body of the pattern, or were superimposed over other patterns (often floral) in the weave.

Crowson/Valentino Santi Colour **4** Alt. colours **yes** Composition **38% cotton chenille, 32% polyester, 30% acetate** Width **137cm/54in** Repeat **stripe** Price ★★ 🗔🛋

Scalamandré/Province 154-007 Colour **yellow and pale blue** Alt. colours **yes** Composition **100% silk** Width **127cm/50in** Repeat **2.5cm/1in** Price ★★★★★ 🗔🛋

George Spencer Decorations/Check 001C/11 Colour **green/plum** Alt. colours **yes** Composition **100% cotton** Width **120cm/47in** Repeat **2cm/¾in** Price ★★ 🗔🛋

Bennett Silks/Manhattan/Waldorf Colour **65** Alt. colours **yes** Composition **100% silk** Width **140cm/55in** Repeat – Price ★★★ 🗔 🅛🅒 ⊞🛋

John Wilman/Aida 888201 Colour **petrol** Alt. colours **yes** Composition **100% cotton satin** Width **137cm/54in** Repeat **2cm/¾in** Price ★🛋

The Isle Mill/Black Watch MW 801 Colour **black and green** Alt. colours **no** Composition **100% wool** Width **140cm/55in** Repeat **25cm/9¾in** Price ★★★ LC ⊞ 🛋

The Isle Mill/Campbell Ancient Muted MW 1203 Colour **green and blue** Alt. colours **no** Composition **100% wool** Width **140cm/55in** Repeat **30cm/11¾in** Price ★★★ LC ⊞ 🛋

Zimmer & Rohde/Arena 6996 684 Colour **green and yellow** Alt. colours **yes** Composition **54% cotton, 46% viscose** Width **140cm/55in** Repeat **3cm/1¼in** Price ★★★ 🔲 🛋

Tiffany/Petites Fleurs FWE3100 Colour **1** Alt. colours **yes** Composition **69.2% cotton, 18.8% viscose, 12% nylon** Width **142cm/55¾in** Repeat **14cm/5½in** Price ★★ 🔲 LC 🛋

Jab/Ragione 1-2300 Colour **117** Alt. colours **yes** Composition **55% polyester, 37% cotton, 8% polyacrylic** Width **140cm/55in** Repeat **3cm/1¼in** Price ★★★ 🛋

Brunschwig & Fils/89511 Colour **409** Alt. colours **yes** Composition **100% Trevira CS** Width **140cm/55in** Repeat **4cm/1½in** Price ★★★ LC 🔲 🛋

TRELLIS PATTERNS

The trellis pattern was a much-favoured fabric design in both Rococo and Neo-classical interiors throughout the 18th century, most notably in Sweden and especially for upholstered furniture. Although the majority of trellis designs were made up of small interlocking leaves, some consisted of small interlaced flowers or buds or, more exceptionally, feather-like motifs. Particularly fashionable colours throughout the century included pale shades of brown or green, straw yellows, pearl greys and muted dark or pale blues.

Today Interiors/Taffetas/Frou Frou TAF4025 Colour **25** Alt. colours **yes** Composition **100% acetate; nylon yarn trim** Width **150cm/59in** Repeat **15cm/6in** Price ★★ ⊞

John Wilman/Figaro 888065 Colour **granite** Alt. colours **yes** Composition **100% cotton** Width **137cm/54in** Repeat **–** Price ★ 🛋

Geometrics: Late 18th century

Striped fabrics were found in many Neo-classical interiors during the second half of the 18th century. The alternation of the widths and colours of woven stripes also became increasingly sophisticated following technical improvements made to the looms. Typical designs included thin bands of vertically stacked single chevrons alternating with contrasting-coloured wider bands of horizontally linked pairs of chevrons; Etruscan-style vertical stripes composed of leaves, tripods, urns, chimeras, half-figures and other classical motifs; and overall *guilloche* patterns (*see* pages 150–1).

In Greek Revival interiors, the Greek key pattern was often used as a border on fabrics – the interlocking right-angled and vertical lines often doubled up to create a perspective effect – sometimes intermittently embellished with either *paterae* or rosettes. Latticework patterns were also fashionable, often as grounds for *chinoiserie* and Indian motifs, as were multi-coloured woven checks, their squares sometimes decorated with small classical or floral motifs. Toward the end of the century, ticking, too, became popular. Initially employed as a cover for feather mattresses – its herringbone-weave stripes designed to keep feathers in and ticks out – its use subsequently spread to furnishings.

4

1

5

6

2

3

1 Wemyss Houlès/Kingsbury/Windsor Colour **05** Alt. colours **yes** Composition **43% cotton, 43% modacrylic, 14% nylon** Width **138cm/54in** Repeat **32cm/12½in** Price ★★

2 Sahco Hesslein/Bellevue 14790 Colour **brown** Alt. colours **yes** Composition **71% cotton, 29% silk** Width **130cm/51in** Repeat – Price ★★★★

3 Ian Sanderson/Pym Stripe Colour **brick** Alt. colours **yes** Composition **100% cotton** Width **140cm/55in** Repeat – Price ★★

4 Zimmer & Rohde/Stradino 4818 Colour **245** Alt. colours **yes** Composition **100% silk** Width **140cm/55in** Repeat **2cm/¾in** Price ★★★

5 Zoffany/Paysanne Stripe FWE3200 Colour **1** Alt. colours **yes** Composition **55.2% cotton, 44.8% viscose** Width **144cm/56½in** Repeat – Price ★★

6 Ian Sanderson/Laura Stripe Colour **brick** Alt. colours **yes** Composition **40% polyester, 34% viscose, 26% cotton** Width **135cm/53in** Repeat **6cm/2½in** Price ★★

7 Zimmer & Rohde/Calicantus 5097 Colour **188** Alt. colours **yes** Composition **82% cotton, 18% silk** Width **140cm/55in** Repeat **35cm/13¾in** Price ★★★

8 Sahco Hesslein/Etoile 1919 Colour **02** Alt. colours **yes** Composition **67% cotton, 33% nylon** Width **140cm/55in** Repeat – Price ★★★

8

18th century

9 **Bennett Silks/Selby** Colour **1131** Alt. colours **yes** Composition **100% silk** Width **150cm/ 59in** Repeat **21cm/8¼in** Price ★★★ 🗡 🄻🄲🛋⊞

10 **Zimmer & Rohde/Sciro 4819 707** Colour **13** Alt. colours **yes** Composition **100% silk** Width **140cm/55in** Repeat **16.5cm/ 6½in** Price ★★★ 🗡🛋

11 **Colefax and Fowler/Maplehurst Check F1305/03** Colour **green** Alt. colours **yes** Composition **45% cotton, 47% modacrylic, 8% linen** Width **137cm/54in** Repeat **5cm/2½in** Price ★★ 🗡🛋

12 **Manuel Canovas/Vivaldi 4464** Colour **22** Alt. colours **yes** Composition **100% silk** Width **138.5cm/54½in** Repeat **35cm/13¾in** Price ★★★ 🗡

13 **Today Interiors/Capella/Zaniah ZF2886** Colour **86** Alt. colours **yes** Composition **100% cotton** Width **137cm/54in** Repeat **20cm/8in** Price ★★ 🛋🄻🄲

14 **Scalamandré/Roma 1205- 001** Colour **multi on ivory** Alt. colours **yes** Composition **100% silk** Width **127cm/ 50in** Repeat **12cm/4¾in** Price ★★★★★ 🛋

15 **Old World Weavers/Ombre Thien JN00030001** Colour **multi/gold** Alt. colours **yes** Composition **100% silk** Width **122cm/48in** Repeat – Price ★★★★ 🗡🛋

9

12

10

11

13

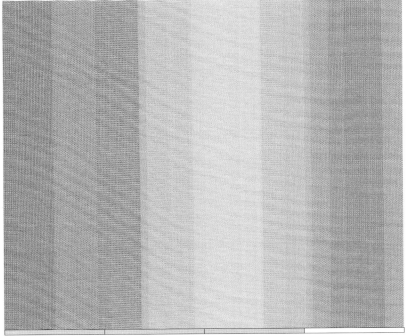

15

14

ANTICO SETIFICIO FIORENTINO

The Italian cloth factory Antico Setificio Fiorentino has produced woven fabrics since the Renaissance, and makes most of its document fabrics on the original looms – some of which were donated by the Grand Duke of Tuscany in 1780. The factory also retains an ancient thread-winding machine based on a design by Leonardo da Vinci. It is not at all surprising, therefore, that ordering a brocade or damask made there has been described as similar to ordering a custom-made Ferrari.

Antico Setificio Fiorentino/Le Roy Colour **gold/orange/bright beige** Alt. colours **yes** Composition **100% silk** Width **120cm/47in** Repeat **29cm/11¼in** Price ★★★ 🗡🛋 🅆

Geometrics: **Early 19th century**

Stripes were very fashionable until the 1830s, particularly for upholstered seating (*see* "Striped Fabrics", opposite), while during the 1840s jewelled strapwork patterns and powdered ornament (*see* page 162) reappeared in Gothic Revival interiors. However, in addition, a tremendous range of check-patterned fabrics was produced throughout the first half of the 19th century. For example, rectangular shapes surrounding small Neo-classical and Napoleonic motifs were popular for use in Empire-style interiors, and twill-weave tartans began to be more widely employed as furnishing fabrics in both Britain and America.

Typical of the printed checks that became increasingly fashionable were the imported Indian ginghams. These were lightweight cottons, brightly coloured with vegetable dyes. Unfortunately, they were not colourfast, a problem that also affected silk and cotton, and especially red-and-black-check Indian madras – known as "bleeding madras" because of the instability of its colours.

1

2

1 **The Isle Mill/Macnaughton Muted MW1229** Colour **red and green** Alt. colours **no** Composition **100% wool** Width **140cm/55in** Repeat **25cm/9¾in** Price ★★★ LC ▦

2 **Ian Sanderson/Keswick** Colour **pippin red** Alt. colours **yes** Composition **100% wool** Width **140cm/55in** Repeat **17cm/6¾in** Price ★★ LC 🛋🪑

3

4

3 **Zoffany/Veneto Check CW4700** Colour **1** Alt. colours **yes** Composition **46% cotton, 5% nylon, 49% modacrylic** Width **140cm/55in** Repeat **6cm/2½in** Price ★★ LC 🪑 ▦ 🛋

4 **Marvic Textiles/Fabiola 8249-5** Colour **olive** Alt. colours **yes** Composition **52% linen, 48% viscose** Width **140cm/55in** Repeat – Price ★★ LC 🪑 ▦ 🛋

5 **Baer & Ingram/Daisy DSF 05** Colour **dark pink** Alt. colours **yes** Composition **100% cotton** Width **140cm/55in** Repeat **11cm/4¼in** Price ★★ 🪑 🛋

6 **Nina Campbell/Violet Plaid NCF3131** Colour **01** Alt. colours **yes** Composition **100% cotton** Width **140cm/55in** Repeat **9cm/3½in** Price ★★ 🪑 🛋

7 **Ian Mankin/Empire 1** Colour **Air Force** Alt. colours **yes** Composition **100% cotton** Width **137cm/54in** Repeat – Price ★ 🪑 🛋

5

6

7

19th century

8 **Scalamandré/Simbolo 90010-001** Colour **multi on peach** Alt. colours **yes** Composition **100% silk** Width **127cm/50in** Repeat **43cm/16¾in** Price ★★★★ 🪑 🛋

9 **Garin/Aral** Colour **celeste** Alt. colours **yes** Composition **50% silk, 50% cotton** Width **140cm/55in** Repeat **–** Price ★★★ 🪑

10 **Brunschwig & Fils/Valmy Lisère Stripe 32482.01** Colour **blue stripe** Alt. colours **yes** Composition **100% cotton** Width **130cm/51in** Repeat **7cm/2¾in** Price ★★★ 🛋

11 **The Silk Gallery/Pergamon** Colour **henna and Italian gold** Alt. colours **yes** Composition **68% silk, 32% polyester** Width **127cm/50in** Repeat **–** Price ★★★ 🪑 🛋 Ⓦ

12 **Hodsoll McKenzie/Campaign Stripe 353/103** Colour **red/green** Alt. colours **yes** Composition **76% cotton, 24% silk** Width **127cm/50in** Repeat **–** Price ★★★ 🪑 🛋 Ⓦ

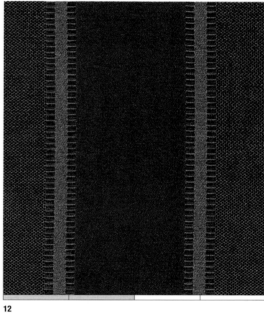

STRIPED FABRICS

Silk, linen and cotton fabrics in striped designs first became fashionable in France during the early years of the 19th century. They were initially inspired by the striped bunting hung from the exteriors of buildings to celebrate the Emperor Napoleon's victories on the battlefield against other European powers.

Striped textile hangings and upholstery fabrics proved just as popular in America and elsewhere in Europe, particularly Britain, until the 1830s. In Britain the range of colourful woven and printed striped fabrics produced during this period (in the Regency and then reign of George IV) came to be known as "Regency stripes".

1 **Jim Thompson/Flotilla II 1002** Colour **02** Alt. colours **yes** Composition **100% silk** Width **122cm/48in** Repeat **10cm/4in** Price ★★★ 🪑

2 **Marvic Textiles/Emilio FR 1302-7** Colour **red/black** Alt. colours **yes** Composition **63% viscose, 37% modacrylic** Width **140cm/55in** Repeat **–** Price ★★ Ⓛⓒ 🪑 🛋 Ⓦ

Geometrics: **Late 19th century**

Proposition Eight of Owen Jones's *Grammar of Ornament* (published in 1856 and reprinted until 1910) stipulated that "all ornament should be based on geometric construction". Jones's view, much shaped by his studies of Chinese, Japanese, Indian, Indonesian, African, South American, Celtic and medieval patterns, proved highly influential during the second half of the 19th century, particularly among designers in the Aesthetic and Arts and Crafts movements. Many of Jones's and these designers' theories of ornament also found favour with the general public once translated on to fabrics.

Typical examples included trelliswork, latticework and other diaper patterns, used as frames or grounds for medieval, Jacobean or oriental motifs, such as fleur-de-lis, thistles and pomegranates. Jewelled strapwork, chevrons, stripes and powdered ornament (*see* page 162) were fashionable, as were Celtic triquetra and triskele. Imported Indonesian *ikats*, featuring kaleidoscopic blocks, circles and stripes, and Indian checked gingham and madras were also much in evidence. Extremely fashionable, however, were the striped and checked tartans now widely employed for hangings and covers – a trend fuelled by Queen Victoria's establishment of a royal residence in Balmoral, Scotland.

4

1

2   3

4 **Hodsoll McKenzie/Ottoman Stripe 262/106** Colour **coral/green** Alt. colours **yes** Composition **100% cotton** Width **127cm/ 50in** Repeat **11cm/4¼in** Price ★★★ 🪑🛋️ Ⓦ

5 **Hill & Knowles/Highland/Elgin 01/CA02** Colour **stone** Alt. colours **yes** Composition **100% cotton** Width **140cm/ 55in** Repeat **2cm/¾in** Price ★★ 🛋️

6 **John Boyd Textiles/ Fredericksborg FR/605/14** Colour **green and black** Alt. colours **yes** Composition **68% horsehair, 32% cotton** Width **65cm/25½in** Repeat **4.5cm/1¾in** Price ★★★ 🛋️

1 **Old World Weavers/Feltre EB35660001** Colour **green and rust** Alt. colours **yes** Composition **50% rayon, 49% cotton, 1% nylon** Width **130cm/51in** Repeat **10cm/ 4in** Price ★★★★ 🛋️

2 **Mary Fox Linton/Montallegro** Colour **18** Alt. colours **yes** Composition **60% cotton, 40% viscose** Width **135cm/ 53in** Repeat **2.5cm/1in** Price ★★★ 🪑🛋️

3 **Antico Setificio Fiorentino/ Cordellone C1** Colour **ecru, red, pink** Alt. colours **yes** Composition **80% linen, 20% silk** Width **120cm/ 47in** Repeat **14cm/5½in** Price ★★★ 🪑🛋️ Ⓦ

6

7 The Isle Mill/Duke of Fife MW509 Colour **red, green and black** Alt. colours **yes** Composition **100% wool** Width **140cm/55in** Repeat **16cm/6¼in** Price ★★★ 🛋

8 Sahco Hesslein/Duke 1267 Colour **07** Alt. colours **yes** Composition **100% cotton** Width **140cm/ 55in** Repeat **17cm/6¾in** Price ★★★ 🛋 LC

7

8

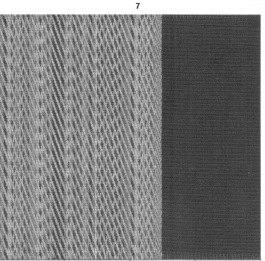

9 Zimmer & Rohde/Agave 5091 Colour **387** Alt. colours **yes** Composition **70% viscose, 30% cotton** Width **140cm/ 55in** Repeat **35cm/13¾in** Price ★★★★ LC 🛋

10 Dedar/Manon Colour **cream and black** Alt. colours **yes** Composition **50% cotton, 50% viscose** Width **140cm/55in** Repeat – Price ★★★ 🔀

11 Nina Campbell/Stratford Weaves/Othello NCF3281 Colour **02** Alt. colours **yes** Composition **62% viscose, 38% cotton** Width **140cm/55in** Repeat – Price ★★ 🔀 ⊞

12 Old World Weavers/Shantung Albatross SB14862201 Colour **multi** Alt. colours **no** Composition **100% silk** Width **140cm/55in** Repeat **34cm/13½in** Price ★★★★★ 🔀 🛋

13 Antico Setificio Fiorentino/ Spinato SP1 Colour **orange, green, yellow, blue** Alt. colours **yes** Composition **70% silk, 30% linen** Width **120cm/ 47in** Repeat **16cm/6¼in** Price ★★★ 🔀 🛋 W

14 John Boyd Textiles/Neapolitan NE/637/2 Colour **green and beige** Alt. colours **yes** Composition **68% horsehair, 32% cotton** Width **65cm/ 25½in** Repeat **5cm/2in** Price ★★★ 🛋

11

12

13

9

10

14

Geometrics: **Early 20th century**

Geometrically patterned fabrics remained very fashionable from the end of the 19th century until the outbreak of the Second World War. Many of these had been popular in previous centuries: striped and checked tartans in Baronial-style interiors; strapwork and jewelled strapwork patterns in Elizabethan Revival and Jacobean Revival schemes; and chevrons, Aztec-stepped shapes and prismatic triangles in Art Deco rooms. Herringbone-weave ticking also began to be used increasingly for curtains, upholstery and blinds.

However, the most innovative fabric patterns of the period were designed by artists bridging the gap between fine and applied art. Examples included the woodblock-printed, Cubist-inspired, irregular shapes of Raoul Dufy in the first two decades of the 20th century; the strong geometric forms and bold stripes, often combined with abstract floral forms, produced by Paul Poiret in 1911; and the colourful shapes and lines of Sonia Delaunay in the 1920s and 1930s.

1 **Bennison Fabrics/Tooth Check**
Colour **greens** Alt. colours
yes Composition **70% linen, 30% cotton** Width **138cm/ 54in** Repeat **16cm/6¼in**
Price ★★★

2 **John Boyd Textiles/Dales**
Colour **black/yellow** Alt. colours **yes** Composition **68% horsehair, 32% cotton** Width **65cm/25½in** Repeat –
Price ★★★★

3 **G.P. & J. Baker/Gallery J0242**
Colour **755** Alt. colours **yes** Composition **100% silk** Width **140cm/55in** Repeat **18cm/ 7in** Price ★★★

4 **Donghia/Righe 9305** Colour **05** Alt. colours **yes** Composition **100% silk** Width **140cm/ 55in** Repeat **5cm/2in** Price ★★★★★

5 **Ian Mankin/Lincoln Stripe** Colour **slate** Alt. colours **yes** Composition **100% cotton** Width **137cm/54in** Repeat – Price ★

6 **Marvic Textiles/Josephine 6102-1** Colour **yellow/leaf** Alt. colours **yes** Composition **100% cotton** Width **140cm/ 55in** Repeat **4.5cm/1¾in** Price ★★★

7 **Manuel Canovas/Vita 4424** Colour **pêche, veronse** Alt. colours **yes** Composition **58% viscose, 42% cotton** Width **130cm/51in** Repeat **4cm/1½in** Price ★★★

8

9

11

8 **Brunschwig & Fils/89516**
Colour **235** Alt. colours **yes**
Composition **100% cotton**
Width **142cm/55⅞in** Repeat –
Price ★★ 🛋 LC 🗠 ⊞

9 **Nina Campbell/Wide Stripe NCF
3140** Colour **01** Alt. colours
yes Composition **60% cotton,
40% modacrylic** Width **140cm/
55in** Repeat – Price ★★ 🛋

10 **Sahco Hesslein/Ambassador
15013** Colour **green** Alt. colours
yes Composition **70% wool,
25% silk, 5% polyester** Width
130cm/51in Repeat **22cm/
8½in** Price ★★★★ 🗠 ⊞

11 **Jab/Till 1-7421** Colour **199**
Alt. colours **yes** Composition
100% cotton Width **140cm/
55in** Repeat – Price ★★ 🗠

12 **Garin/Bolero 66754441** Colour
cream, black Alt. colours **yes**
Composition **100% cotton**
Width **140cm/55in** Repeat
1cm/⅜in Price ★★ 🛋

13 **The Isle Mill/Glen Morar GT112**
Colour **blue, red and cream**
Alt. colours **yes** Composition
100% wool Width **140cm/
55in** Repeat **6cm/2⅜in**
Price ★★ LC ⊞

14 **Osborne & Little/Modello
Trattino F5051** Colour **07** Alt.
colours **yes** Composition
50% cotton, 50% viscose
Width **130cm/51in** Repeat
1cm/⅜in Price ★★ 🗠 ⊞

12

10

13

14

15

15 **Jane Churchill/Carousel Check
J137f** Colour **red** Alt. colours
yes Composition **100% cotton**
Width **140cm/55in** Repeat
1cm/⅜in Price ★★ 🗠

16 **Ian Mankin/Satin Check**
Colour **eau de nil** Alt. colours
yes Composition **100% cotton**
Width **137cm/54in** Repeat
11.5cm/4½in Price ★ 🗠

17 **Bennett Silks/Margot**
Colour **59X** Alt. colours
yes Composition **100% silk**
Width **150cm/59in** Repeat –
Price ★★★ 🗠 ⊞

16

17

Geometrics: **Late 20th–early 21st century**

Many of the geometrically patterned fabrics that have proved fashionable for drapes and upholstery at the end of the 20th and in the early 21st century have originated from European and American designers. In the 1950s and 1960s, for example, numerous late Modernist-style fabrics were embellished with schematized geometric or abstract patterns; these consisted of modified versions of the irregular geometric forms found in Cubist paintings from earlier in the century. Crystalline structures (such as insulin viewed under a microscope) presented within diaper-ground patterns also provided inspiration for many designs of the period, and symmetrically spaced triangles, squares and dots were much in evidence.

Among the imported fabrics that have become increasingly desirable are ginghams, *ikats* and madras. Indonesian *ikats*, woven in either silk or fine cotton yarn, have been particularly appreciated for the way in which their geometric blocks, circles and stripes are softened by a vegetable-dyeing process – a procedure that feathers the edges of the colours into one another. Similarly, silk, cotton and rayon check madras, at one time dyed only black and red, has become much more popular as other vibrant colourways have been produced.

5

1

2

3

6

7

8

1 Thomas Dare/Jermyn 891
Colour **pistachio** Alt. colours **yes** Composition **100% cotton** Width **137cm/54in** Repeat **6.5cm/2½in** Price ★★

2 Brunschwig & Fils/42535
Colour **02** Alt. colours **yes** Composition **86% rayon, 14% dacron** Width **132cm/51¼in** Repeat **4cm/1½in** Price ★★

3 Zoffany/Check PCW0200
Colour **9** Alt. colours **yes** Composition **73% cotton, 14% viscose, 12% nylon, 1% silk** Width **145cm/57in** Repeat **7cm/2¾in** Price ★★

4 Donghia/Quadri 0375/9300
Colour **05** Alt. colours **yes** Composition **100% silk** Width **140cm/55in** Repeat **3cm/1¼in** Price ★★★★★

5 Today Interiors/Palio/Lupa CH85032 Colour **8** Alt. colours **yes** Composition **40% cotton, 42% viscose, 10% linen, 8% nylon** Width **140cm/55in** Repeat **3cm/1¼in** Price ★★

6 Wemyss Houlès/Orient/Java Colour **2E149** Alt. colours **yes** Composition **48% modacrylic, 39% cotton, 13% nylon** Width **138cm/54in** Repeat – Price ★★

7 Today Interiors/Palio/Lupa CH85032 Colour **4** Alt. colours **yes** Composition **40% cotton, 42% viscose, 10% linen, 8% nylon** Width **140cm/55in** Repeat **3cm/1¼in** Price ★★

8 Scalamandré/26656 Colour **007** Alt. colours **yes** Composition **53% cotton, 33% viscose, 14% linen** Width **140cm/55in** Repeat **10cm/4in** Price ★★★

9 Monkwell/Mistri 05413 CU/012 Colour **red and gold** Alt. colours **yes** Composition **88% cotton, 12% polyacrylic** Width **137cm/54in** Repeat **9cm/3½in** Price ★★

9

10 Larsen/Coffee Bean L8680
Colour **07 steel** Alt. colours
yes Composition **51%
polyester, 31% acrylic,
18% silk** Width **123cm/
48½in** Repeat **2.5cm/1in**
Price ★★★ ⊞ ⟦⟧

11 Nya Nordiska/Pila Colour
05 copper Alt. colours **yes**
Composition **50% linen,
40% polyester** Width **155cm/
61in** Repeat **7cm/2¾in**
Price ★★★ ⟦⟧

**12 Marvic Textiles/Valencia
Stripe 5013** Colour **browns**
Alt. colours **no** Composition
54% viscose, 46% linen Width
140cm/55in Repeat –
Price ★★ LC ⊞ ⌂

**13 Turnell & Gigon/Ascot Taffeta
HAP 10001** Colour **cream
ground** Alt. colours **yes**
Composition **57% viscose,
43% cotton** Width **130cm/51in**
Repeat – Price ★★ ⌂

14 The Isle Mill/Kildonan STR016
Colour **blue/gold/rust** Alt.
colours **yes** Composition
100% wool Width **140cm/
55in** Repeat **14cm/5¼in**
Price ★★★ LC ⊞

15

16

17

12

13

**15 John Boyd Textiles/Ardennais
AR/SK 100/72** Colour **beige/
black/red** Alt. colours **yes**
Composition **68% horsehair,
32% cotton** Width **56cm/
22in** Repeat **8cm/3in**
Price ★★★★ ⌂

16 Percheron/Corfu 7246-2 Colour
junior navy 2 Alt. colours **yes**
Composition **43% viscose,
39% cotton, 18% linen** Width
140cm/55in Repeat **12cm/4¾in**
Price ★★★ LC ⊞

17 Zimmer & Rohde/Askuni 2557
Colour **347** Alt. colours **yes**
Composition **52% viscose,
29% cotton, 19% linen** Width
139cm/54¾in Repeat **35cm/
13¾in** Price ★★★ ⟦⟧ ⌂

**18 Ottilie Stevenson/Monty Check
VF0052** Colour **mustard** Alt.
colours **yes** Composition
100% cotton Width **137cm/54in**
Repeat – Price ★★ ⟦⟧ ⌂

18

Geometrics: Late 20th–early 21st century

The late 20th and early 21st century has seen a strong growth in the number and type of geometric designs. Many of these have been created through innovative weaving techniques, often producing pattern by means of texture and colour. Other fabrics have included several imports, such as the various ethnic weaves and prints from Africa. Notable among these are the woven "kente" silks and cottons, particularly from Ghana and Nigeria, which display brightly coloured, eclectic combinations of stripes, checks, chevrons and other geometric forms. South American weaves, with geometric, abstract and iconographic patterns derived from ancient Aztec and Inca cultures, have been in demand, too, and have provided inspiration for European and North American designers.

Also fashionable during the late 20th and early 21st century have been striped and checked tartans, and printed fabrics embellished with repeat classical motifs framed by traditional diaper grounds, or set within vertical stripes resembling strips of cine-film.

1

2

3

4

1 **Bentley & Spens/New Geometrics** Colour **natural** Alt. colours **no** Composition **50% linen, 50% cotton** Width **135cm/53in** Repeat **42cm/16½in** Price ★★ 🛏️🛋️ⓦ

2 **Today Interiors/Taffetas/Soprano 4055** Colour **55** Alt. colours **yes** Composition **88% acetate, 12% acrylic** Width **150cm/59in** Repeat **2cm/¾in** Price ★★ 🛏️

3 **Thomas Dare/Savile** Colour **teal** Alt. colours **yes** Composition **100% cotton** Width **140cm/55in** Repeat **17.5cm/7in** Price ★★ 🛏️🛋️▦

4 **Today Interiors/Aymara/Axis AYF 3330** Colour **30** Alt. colours **yes** Composition **51% linen, 37% cotton, 2% nylon** Width **137cm/54in** Repeat **40cm/15¾in** Price ★★ LC🛋️

1

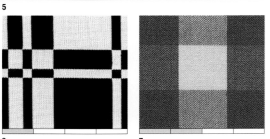

5

5 **Jim Thompson/Mirage Check P4011** Colour **taupe** Alt. colours **yes** Composition **100% silk** Width **122cm/48in** Repeat **4cm/1½in** Price ★★★★ 🛏️🛋️

6 **Lee Jofa/Bill's Plaid 2002194** Colour **8 black** Alt. colours **yes** Composition **100% cotton** Width **143cm/56in** Repeat **19cm/7½in** Price ★★★ LC🛋️

7 **Ian Sanderson/Box Check** Colour **cornflower** Alt. colours **yes** Composition **100% cotton** Width **140cm/55in** Repeat **2.5cm/1in** Price ★★ 🛏️🛋️

8 **Jim Thompson/Pavilion Cloth 1018** Colour **01** Alt. colours **yes** Composition **60% silk, 40% cotton** Width **122cm/48in** Repeat **1cm/¾in** Price ★★★ 🛏️🛋️

8

6   7

9 Osborne & Little/Valdepero
F5022 Colour **06** Alt. colours
yes Composition **45%**
polyester, 28% viscose,
27% cotton Width **143cm/**
56in Repeat **31cm/12in**
Price ★★ 🗔 ⊞

10 Nya Nordiska/Baccara Colour
84 purple Alt. colours **yes**
Composition **85% viscose,**
15% silk Width **140cm/**
55in Repeat **31cm/12in**
Price ★★★ ⊞ LC 🗔 🛋

9   10

Knowles & Christou/Tambour
KG208 Colour **topaz** Alt.
colours **yes** Composition
100% cotton Width **132cm/**
51¼in. Repeat **15cm/6in**
Price ★★★ 🗔 🛋 W

Knowles & Christou/Taffeta
Silk Stripe Colour **date** Alt.
colours **yes** Composition
100% silk Width **120cm/**
47in Repeat **16cm/6¼in**
Price ★★★ ⊞ W

John Boyd Textiles/Ardennais
AR/SK107/2 Colour **black/**
red/beige Alt. colours **yes**
Composition **56% horsehair,**
44% silk Width **65cm/25½in**
Repeat – Price ★★★★ 🛋 W

Anna French/Blanket Colour **29**
Alt. colours **yes** Composition
100% cotton Width **137cm/**
54in Repeat **64cm/25in**
Price ★★ 🛋

Nya Nordiska/Trapunta Colour
13 copper Alt. colours **yes**
Composition **50% viscose,**
26% polyester, 24% silk Width
140cm/55in Repeat **8cm/**
3in Price ★★★ 🛋 LC 🗔

Larsen/Sugar Cane L8681
Colour **08 amethyst** Alt. colours
yes Composition **51% polyester,**
31% acrylic, 18% silk Width
125cm/49¼in Repeat –
Price ★★★ 🗔 ⊞

11

12

13

17

17 Scalamandré/26577 Colour **001**
Alt. colours **yes** Composition
62% viscose, 38% cotton
Width **137cm/54in** Repeat –
Price ★★★★ 🛋 LC

18 Elizabeth Eaton/Lanka Check
Colour **pink** Alt. colours **no**
Composition **100% cotton**
Width **127cm/50in** Repeat
2.5cm/1in Price ★★ 🗔 🛋

14

15   16   18

20th & 21st century

Lace & Sheers

Lace is an ornamental openwork fabric that is traditionally made from flaxen thread or silk, wool or cotton yarns. Before the late 18th century it was exclusively hand-made, by buttonhole stitching with a needle and thread ("needle" lace), or by twisting bobbins carrying the threads around pins outlining the pattern and stuck into a pillow ("bobbin" lace). A less expensive alternative is machine-woven Nottingham (or "Swiss") lace, which was first produced in quantity during the early 19th century.

Lace has been used as decorative bed and table covers, but also as bed-hangings and under-curtains designed to diffuse sunlight, provide a degree of privacy and keep out insects. Other materials used for this purpose, known as "sheers", include muslin, a soft, open-mesh fabric woven from finely spun cotton or silk; organza, a stiffer version of muslin; *voile*, a crisp and finely woven fabric made from cotton, silk or synthetics; and leno, a cross-woven gauze made from natural or man-made fibres.

RIGHT The use of lace and sheers as both under-curtains ("insertions") and the main drapes in a window treatment has flourished during the 20th century, especially in bedrooms. Here laces are simply pleated for the insertions, tassel-fringed and tied back for the main drapes, and elaborately swagged and tailed for the heading. They are coordinated with the bed-hangings, cushion covers and bedspread – a fashion that dates back to the late 17th century.

ABOVE These lace under-curtains ("insertions") are in a 19th-century American house. Their sage-green stylized flower-and-leaf pattern was particularly fashionable toward the end of the 19th century. Like much of the lace used in American interiors during this period, these examples are machine-made and imported from Brussels, Belgium.

"ANTIQUING" LACE

Pre-20th-century hand-made lace is highly sought after today; it can be bought from specialist antiques dealers and at textile auctions. However, it is becoming more and more expensive. Consequently, when asked to create a period look on a tight budget, many interior designers mimic the appearance and feel of hand-made antique lace simply by soaking inexpensive, white machine-made lace in a weak solution of cold tea (or coffee). The lace emerges with a subtle, straw-coloured tint and a softer, less crisp texture than it had before the treatment.

KEY DESIGNS

1 While many coloured sheers are literally plain, others – such as this early 21st-century silk sheer – incorporate for decorative effect soft gradations of colour and/or subtle abstract patterns in the weave.

2 Stylized birds, particularly exotic oriental species, as well as architectural components, such as pillars and arches, have been frequent embellishments to lace and sheers since the 19th century.

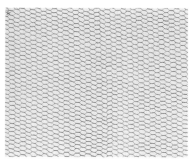

3 Silk bobbin net ("tulle") was first produced in France at the end of the 18th century; it has been used primarily for insertions and bed-hangings, notably in hot climates as an insect barrier.

4 Repeats of small woven or printed dots have been used to embellish sheers and semi-sheers since the 18th century – imported Indian muslins were among the first to display such patterns.

5 During the course of the 20th century, increasingly colourful patterns – mostly printed, like this floral-and-leaf-patterned voile – have been employed on sheers and semi-sheers. They offer a decorative screen that allows light to filter through.

6 Before the 20th century, finely woven voiles were made from cotton or silk; thereafter, synthetic yarns have also been used. Voiles in coloured stripes were especially fashionable during the early 19th century.

1 **Nina Campbell/Loire Silks/Touraine Sheer NCF3391** Colour **04** Alt. colours **yes** Composition **100% silk** Width **140cm/ 55in** Repeat **95cm/37in** Price ★★ 🗔

2 **G.P. & J. Baker/My Lady's Garden** Colour **white** Alt. colours **yes** Composition **93% cotton, 7% polyester** Width **150cm/59in** Repeat **64cm/25in** Price ★ 🗔

3 **Bennett Silks/Annelle** Colour **91** Alt. colours **yes** Composition **100% silk** Width **175cm/68¾in** Repeat – Price ★★ 🗔

4 **Abbott & Boyd/Visillo Plumeti** Colour **white** Alt. colours **yes** Composition **100% polyester** Width **300cm/118in** Repeat **2cm/¾in** Price ★★ 🗔

5 **Anna French/Moss Rose Voile** Colour **32** Alt. colours **yes** Composition **100% cotton** Width **137cm/54in** Repeat **82cm/32⅛in** Price ★★ 🗔

6 **Liberty Furnishings/Irisa Prints/Isadora LF4202** Colour **02** Alt. colours **yes** Composition **70% viscose, 30% polyester** Width **142cm/55⅞in** Repeat – Price ★★ 🗔

Lace & Sheers: **Pre-19th century**

Leading centres of lace production were established in Italy (in Venice, Genoa and Milan), the Netherlands (in Brussels, Mechlin and Antwerp), and Spain and Portugal during the 16th century; then in France (in Alençon, Argenton, Paris and Chantilly) and England (in Honiton) during the 17th century. Lace production in America took hold during the 18th century, notably in Ipswich, Massachusetts. Fashionable needle lace included *punto in aria*, *gros point*, *point plat*, *point de neige* ("Venetian"), *point de France* and *hollie point*. From the early 17th century, bobbin lace was produced in greater quantity and was equally sought after. Popular patterns included stylized flowers linked by scrolling stems, and Moorish geometric designs such as the wheel and the sun.

Throughout this period, hand-made lace was used for bed and table covers and bed-hangings, but rarely for under-curtains. However, many shutterless 17th- and 18th-century windows were covered with "sashes" (thin silks or linens stretched over frames and soaked with oil to make them transparent). Sheers draped at 18th-century windows included "quinze-seize" (thin taffeta), "leno" (a gauze often painted with Indian motifs) and Indian muslin (white or cream and sometimes woven with a ribbed stripe or small motif).

1

3

4

1 Interdesign/Rio Fleur de Lys 2301/3 Colour **white** Alt. colours **yes** Composition **100% linen** Width **210cm/82½in** Repeat – Price ★★★★

2 Knowles & Christou/Cardoban Lion KSC03 Colour **white** Alt. colours **yes** Composition **60% polyester, 40% cotton** Width **120cm/47in** Repeat **24cm/9½in** Price ★★

3 Knowles & Christou/Angels KSC05 Colour **white** Alt. colours **yes** Composition **60% polyester, 40% cotton** Width **120cm/47in** Repeat **24cm/9½in** Price ★★

4 Claremont Fabrics/Campanile JOA COA Colour **green** Alt. colours **yes** Composition **40% polyester, 60% cotton** Width **140cm/55in** Repeat **69cm/27in** Price ★

5 Laura Ashley/Thirlmere Colour **delphinium** Alt. colours **no** Composition **63% polyester, 37% cotton** Width **144cm/56½in** Repeat **71cm/28in** Price ★

6 Larsen/Luminescence L7480 Colour **04** Alt. colours **yes** Composition **70% copper, 18% cotton, 12% polyester** Width **147cm/58in** Repeat **2cm/¾in** Price ★★★

7 Crowson/Script Colour **6** Alt. colours **yes** Composition **67% polyester, 33% cotton** Width **137cm/54in** Repeat **64cm/25in** Price ★

2

5

6

7

8 Malabar/Indian Organza NSIL28
Colour gold Alt. colours
no Composition 100% silk
Width 137cm/54in Repeat
2cm/⅜in Price ★★

9 Zoffany/Floraison Leaf FRN0700
Colour 1 Alt. colours yes
Composition 64% linen,
36% polyester Width 160cm/
63in Repeat 10cm/4in
Price ★★

10 Zoffany/Lotus Voile MB0700
Colour 1 Alt. colours yes
Composition 100% cotton
Width 131.5cm/51¾in
Repeat 105.5cm/41½in
Price ★★

**11 Rose's Mill/Venus Lace
Panel** Colour antique ivory
Alt. colours no Composition
100% cotton Width 260cm/102in
Repeat - Price ★★★★★

8

9

10

11

12

13

14

**12 Today Interiors/Taffetas/Pique
TAF4049** Colour purple/
burgundy Alt. colours yes
Composition inner 100%
polyester, outer 77% polyester,
23% nylon Width 150cm/59in
Repeat 15cm/6in Price ★★

13 Mulberry/Chenille RIB FD356
Colour cream J103 Alt.
colours no Composition
53% cotton, 47% polyester
Width 300cm/118in Repeat
1cm/⅜in Price ★★★

**14 Bernard Thorp & Co/French
Damask** Colour white Alt.
colours yes Composition
91% polyester, 9% flax/
linen Width 120cm/47in
Repeat 87cm/34¼in
Price ★★

**15 Rose's Mill/Holyrood Lace
Panel** Colour pure white Alt.
colours yes Composition
100% cotton Width 91cm/
35¾in Repeat – Price ★★

16 Mulberry/Venetian Stripe FD377
Colour red Alt. colours yes
Composition 80% cotton,
20% polyester Width 322cm/
127in Repeat 20cm/8in
Price ★★

17 Bennett Silks/Como 5111DC
Colour 54/70L Alt. colours
yes Composition 100% silk
Width 105cm/41¼in Repeat
54cm/21½in Price ★★★

15

16

17

FABRICS: *LACE & SHEERS* **181**

Lace & Sheers: **19th century**

By the early 19th century, under-curtains had become a fairly standard window treatment in fashionable European (particularly English Regency and French Empire) and American Federal interiors. Thin silks or muslin (the latter by this time made in Europe and America, as well as in India) were the preferred choice, and in many cases they were augmented with delicate fringing or border designs in contrasting colours – green or yellow on white being a popular combination.

The production of lace underwent a revolution throughout Europe and America at the end of the 18th century. Costly hand-made lace was still being manufactured in traditional centres of production (*see* page 180), but the invention of cheaper, machine-woven lace dramatically expanded the market to include less affluent homeowners. Made in large quantities in Nottingham, England, machine-woven lace was largely intended for use as more decorative under-curtains and bed-hangings, and featured exuberant patterns of hothouse flowers and other designs derived from 16th- and 17th-century hand-made lace.

5

6

7

2

3

4

8

1 **Old World Weavers/Vera Sheer B/1886S0108** Colour **multi** Alt. colours **yes** Composition **100% cotton** Width **139cm/54¼in** Repeat **97cm/38¼in** Price ★★★★ ⟦⟧

2 **Sahco Hesslein/Mizar 16012** Colour **white** Alt. colours **no** Composition **70% cotton, 30% polyester** Width **300cm/118in** Repeat **63cm/24¾in** Price ★★★ ⟦⟧

3 **Anna French/Fondant Lace** Colour **68** Alt. colours **yes** Composition **100% cotton** Width **150cm/59in** Repeat **72cm/28¼in** Price ★★ ⟦⟧

4 **Hill & Knowles/Voiles IV/ Feather Dance VF86F** Colour **gold on cream** Alt. colours **yes** Composition **67% polyester, 33% cotton** Width **145cm/57in** Repeat **64cm/25in** Price ★ ⟦⟧

5 **Elizabeth Eaton 9550/3609** Colour **white** Alt. colours **yes** Composition **100% cotton** Width **150cm/59in** Repeat **22cm/8½in** Price ★★★ ⟦⟧

6 **Rose's Mill/Secret Garden Lace Panel** Colour **natural white** Alt. colours **yes** Composition **95% cotton, 5% polyester** Width **137cm/54in** Repeat – Price ★★ ⟦⟧

7 **Elizabeth Eaton/Muslin 9550/3837** Colour **white** Alt. colours **no** Composition **100% cotton** Width **150cm/ 59in** Repeat **11cm/4¼in** Price ★★ ⟦⟧

8 **Interdesign/Ric Api 2301/09** Colour **tan** Alt. colours **yes** Composition **100% linen** Width **160cm/63in** Repeat **12cm/4¾in** Price ★★★★ ⟦⟧ ⊞

9 **Sahco Hesslein/Mirabelle 16005**
Colour **white** Alt. colours **no**
Composition **90% polyester,
10% linen** Width **330cm/130in**
Repeat **5cm/2in**
Price ★★★★ 🖫

10 **Bennett Silks/1502 CHR** Colour
53/55 Alt. colours **no**
Composition **100% silk** Width
105cm/41in Repeat **34cm/13½in**
Price ★★ 🖫

11 **Bennett Silks/1502 CHB** Colour
53/55 Alt. colours **no**
Composition **100% silk**
Width **105cm/41in** Repeat
34cm/13½in Price ★★ 🖫

12 **Ian Sanderson/Hope Plain**
Colour **champagne** Alt. colours
yes Composition **100% linen**
Width **140cm/55in** Repeat –
Price ★★ 🖫

13 **Jane Churchill/Country Rose
Sprig Voile J239F** Colour
yellow/blue 02 Alt. colours **yes**
Composition **100% cotton**
Width **133cm/52in** Repeat
20cm/8in Price ★★ 🖫

14 **Sanderson/Bloom Sheer PR8537**
Colour **3** Alt. colours **yes**
Composition **70% polyester,
30% viscose** Width **150cm/
59in** Repeat **60.5cm/24in**
Price ★ 🖫

15 **Bentley & Spens/Animal Magic
Sheer** Colour **white on white**
Alt. colours **no** Composition
100% cotton voile
Width **135cm/53in** Repeat
106cm/41½in Price ★★ 🖫

16 **Bennett Silks/Ravena 5111D101**
Colour **89** Alt. colours **yes**
Composition **100% silk** Width
105cm/41in Repeat **18cm/7in**
Price ★★ 🖫

19th century

Lace & Sheers: Early 20th century

Around the beginning of the 20th century, a reaction set in to the extensive use of lace and sheers in 19th-century interiors. In some quarters this was an aesthetic judgement – the American writer Edith Wharton dismissed them, particularly at windows, on the grounds that "lingerie effects do not commune well with architecture". Other commentators were more concerned with the welfare of the homeowner. For example, the English architect and writer Charles Eastlake believed it was healthier to sleep without being surrounded by layers of (dust-trap) draperies, and thus recommended metal or wooden bedsteads without hangings – although he did make an exception for warm, humid climates, such as those of Australia and the southern states of America, where muslin or organza could be draped over a four-poster or half-tester, or from a corona, to protect the occupant from mosquitoes and other insects.

However, with the exception of Eastlake, whose views proved highly influential in America, most householders during the first half of the 20th century chose to ignore such arbiters and continued to use sheers such as muslin, organza and voile at windows. Favoured patterns included woven stripes, and woven or printed spots and figurative patterns.

1

2

3

4

5

6

1 **Marvic Textiles/Plume 4540** Colour **bronze 3** Alt. colours **yes** Composition **50% silk, 50% linen** Width **140cm/55in** Repeat **51cm/20in** Price ★★★★ 🎴

2 **Zoffany/Pollen PLP0900** Colour **2** Alt. colours **yes** Composition **67% polyester, 33% cotton** Width **150cm/59in** Repeat **4cm/1½** Price ★ 🎴

3 **Osbourne & Little/Hespera/Brume F1642/05** Colour **05** Alt. colours **yes** Composition **100% cotton** Width **140cm/55in** Repeat **5cm/2in** Price ★★ 🎴 LC ⊞ 🛋

4 **Osborne & Little/Jivala Silks/Avani Sheer F1963** Colour **01** Alt. colours **yes** Composition **100% silk** Width **137cm/54in** Repeat **40cm/15¾in** Price ★★★ 🎴

5 **Scalamandré/Angus 26366** Colour **white 001** Alt. colours **no** Composition **95% cotton, 5% polyester** Width **151cm/59½in** Repeat – Price ★★★ 🎴

6 **Scalamandré/Madeira 16318** Colour **swan 001** Alt. colours **yes** Composition **100% cotton** Width **137cm/54in** Repeat **97cm/38¼in** Price ★★★★ 🎴

20th century

COLOURED SHEERS

Historically, most sheers – particularly muslins and organzas – have been produced in either white or off-white colours. However, coloured versions have proved very fashionable, notably during the 20th century. While pale pastel colours are generally widely available, it is worth remembering that when exposed to strong sunlight their colouring can be rendered overly subtle. To compensate for this, slightly stronger tones, such as the yellow and green shown below, can be employed.

7 Ian Sanderson/Faith Stripe
Colour **thyme** Alt. colours **yes** Composition **100% linen** Width **140cm/55in** Repeat – Price ★★ ⟨⟩

8 Donghia/Rete 0378/9335-10
Colour **ecru** Alt. colours **yes** Composition **100% linen** Width **130cm/51in** Repeat – Price ★★★★ ⟨⟩

9 Liberty Furnishings/Irisa Prints LF 4204 Colour **carlotta** Alt. colours **yes** Composition **70% cotton, 30% polyester** Width **140cm/55in** Repeat **31cm/12in** Price ★★★ ⟨⟩

10 Mulberry/Orchard Linen FD366 Colour **cream** Alt. colours **yes** Composition **95% linen, 5% cotton**, Width **140cm/ 55in** Repeat **32cm/12½in** Price ★★★ ⟨⟩

11 Ian Sanderson/Charity Check Colour **thyme** Alt. colours **yes** Composition **100% linen** Width **140cm/55in** Repeat **7cm/2¾in** Price ★★ ⟨⟩

Crowson/Monticelli Colour **yellow** Alt. colours **yes** Composition **100% polyester** Width **150cm/59in** Repeat – Price ★ ⟨⟩

Liberty Furnishings/Zari Weaves/Zari Plain LF4254 Colour **14** Alt. colours **yes** Composition **100% cotton** Width **142cm/55¾in** Repeat – Price ★★ ⟨⟩

Lace & Sheers: Late 20th century

During the second half of the 20th century, there was a renewed demand for traditional hand-made lace, particularly for decorative bed covers. Machine-woven lace, notably incorporating floral, animal and bird patterns, was a popular choice for under-curtains in period houses, while plain or patterned muslin, organza and voile sheers (the latter often made from synthetic fibres) were widely employed as bed-hangings.

Although these fabrics had been used to some extent in the first half of the century, manufacturers increasingly produced coloured versions, such as pastel lemons, plaster pinks, pale blues, blue-greys, and warm hues. Other trends included stretching sheers over wooden frames to make screens or room dividers – similar to traditional Japanese *shojis*, and well suited to large warehouse conversions and loft apartments. The 19th-century practice of bordering sheers, such as muslin, with contrasting fabrics was further developed by some 20th-century designers, who alternated and joined strips of semi-transparent muslin with strips of closely woven fabrics, such as damask or leather, to produce web-like effects.

1

1 **Malabar/Tarlatan** Colour **grey 03** Alt. colours **yes** Composition **100% polyester** Width **135cm/53in** Repeat **80cm/31½in** Price ★★★ ⬚⬚

2 **Elizabeth Eaton/Muslin** Colour **white** Alt. colours **yes** Composition **100% cotton** Width **150cm/59in** Repeat **12cm/4¾in** Price ★★ ⬚⬚

3 **Bentley & Spens/Cornelli Sheers** Colour **white on white** Alt. colours **no** Composition **100% cotton voile** Width **130cm/51in** Repeat **60cm/23¾in** Price ★★ ⬚⬚

4 **Laura Ashley/Mimosa** Colour **ecru** Alt. colours **yes** Composition **embroidered voile, 63% polyester, 37% cotton** Width **144cm/56½in** Repeat **15cm/6in** Price ★ ⬚⬚

5 **Hill & Knowles/Columbine Star VG97F** Colour **gold/cream** Alt. colours **yes** Composition **67% polyester, 33% cotton** Width **150cm/59in** Repeat **32cm/12½in** Price ★ ⬚⬚

2

3

4

SEMI-SHEERS

The main difference between sheer and semi-sheer fabrics is a matter of translucency. Sheers such as muslin, organza and voile are highly translucent and allow considerable quantities of diffused light to enter a room. At the same time, sheers can also provide a certain degree of privacy without obliterating the view entirely. The more opaque semi-sheers are generally produced from fabrics such as half-silks and taffetas, as well as open-weave linens, cottons and synthetics.

1

2

1 **Jack Lenor Larsen/Luminescence** Colour **topaz** Alt. colours **yes** Composition **66% metal, 22% cotton, 12% polyester** Width **140cm/55in** Repeat – Price ★★★ ⬚⬚

2 **Sahco Hesslein/Caprice 50262** Colour **gold** Alt. colours **yes** Composition **50% viscose, 21% silk, 15% acrylic, 14% linen** Width **140cm/55in** Repeat – Price ★★★ ⬚⬚

5

Larsen/Pinion Sheer L7412
Colour **old ivory** Alt. colours
no Composition **76% cotton,
24% linen** Width **150cm/
59in** Repeat **10cm/4in**
Price ★★★ 🔲

Larsen/Mercury L2509
Colour **silver** Alt. colours
yes Composition **100% silk**
Width **140cm/55in** Repeat
68cm/26¾in Price ★ 🔲

Hill & Knowles/Naturals C5326
Colour **slate 26** Alt. colours
yes Composition **100% cotton**
Width **137cm/54in** Repeat
5cm/2in Price ★★ 🔲

Interdesign/Ricamati 2301/11
Colour **natural** Alt. colours
yes Composition **100% cotton**
Width **270cm/106in** Repeat
12cm/4¾in Price ★★★★ 🔲 ▦

Larsen/Chevalier L7367
Colour **old ivory** Alt. colours
no Composition **51% linen,
49% cotton** Width **150cm/
59in** Repeat **23cm/9in**
Price ★★★ 🔲

**Bentley & Spens/Shells
B5044 Voile** Colour **bronze,
silver and white** Alt. colours **no**
Composition **100% cotton**
Width **134cm/52½in** Repeat
65cm/25½in Price ★★ 🔲

12 Anna French/Polka Dot Voile
Colour **red on white V8** Alt.
colours **yes** Composition
100% cotton Width **137cm/
54in** Repeat **10cm/4in**
Price ★★ 🔲

13 Designers Guild/Oola F495/08
Colour **fuchsia** Alt. colours
yes Composition **100% cotton**
Width **115cm/45¼in** Repeat
10cm/4in Price ★ 🔲

**14 Jack Lenor Larsen/Fielding
7478-01** Colour **hazelnut**
Alt. colours **yes** Composition
100% polyester Width **112cm/
44in** Repeat **6cm/2¼in**
Price ★★ 🔲

15 Marvic Textiles/Raindrop 4541
Colour **damson** Alt. colours
yes Composition **100% silk**
Width **140cm/55in** Repeat
35cm/13¾in Price ★★★ 🔲

Lace & Sheers: **Early 21st century**

The late 20th-century revival of interest in lace and sheers has, if anything, gathered further momentum during the early years of the 21st century. In terms of usage, there has been a marked increase in the deployment of sheers as bed-hangings, especially canopied from the ceiling above. Equally, many homeowners who had previously shunned their use at windows on grounds of fashion have come to appreciate the light- and heat-diffusing qualities of sheers in this context; they have also realized that coloured sheers can be called on to subtly alter the colour of natural light and therefore the ambience of an interior.

The majority of new designs that have emerged during the early 21st century have been geometric in pattern. Stripes or bands of subtly contrasting weave or colour have proved particularly popular – both two-tone and polychromatic. Also, whether configured vertically or horizontally, the stripes or bands have rarely been run as neat, crisp parallels: meandering courses, irregular edges and even random acute angles have all been preferred. In contrast to the predominant geometrical patterns (which have also included spherical and rectangular repeats), there has also been a vogue for repeat foliate and insect-like motifs – these often stylized to the point of abstraction.

5

1

1 **Larsen/Hologram Square L7430** Colour **bronze 02** Alt. colours **no** Composition **56% silk, 44% linen** Width **140cm/ 55in** Repeat **11cm/4¼in** Price ★★★

2 **Larsen/Billows L7481** Colour **autumn haze 03** Alt. colours **yes** Composition **100% polyester** Width **165cm/65in** Repeat – Price ★★★

3 **Nya Nordiska/Tre-De** Colour **pyrite 05** Alt. colours **yes** Composition **58% viscose, 36% polyester, 6% linen** Width **150cm/59in** Repeat **14-16cm/5½-6¼in** Price ★★★

4 **Sahco Hesslein/Ulf Moritz/ Tzar 1842** Colour **01** Alt. colours **yes** Composition **66% horsehair, 23% metal, 11% linen** Width **147cm/58in** Repeat – Price ★★★

2

6

7

3

4

8

5 **Interdesign/Missoni Sheers/ Cajun** Colour **51** Alt. colours **yes** Width **295cm/116in** Composition **64% viscose, 36% polyester** Repeat **62cm/ 24¼in** Price ★★★

6 **Osborne & Little/Hespera/ Boreal F1643** Colour **02** Alt. colours. **yes** Composition **65% polyester, 35% cotton** Width **150cm/59in** Repeat **11cm/4¼in** Price ★★

7 **Bennett Silks/Kashi/1508C** Colour **54** Alt. colours **yes** Composition **87% rayon, 13% silk** Width **42cm/16½in** Repeat – Price ★

8 **Sahco Hesslein/Chess 1905** Colour **01** Alt. colours **yes** Composition **65% cotton, 35% polyester** Width **295cm/ 116in** Repeat **24cm/9½in** Price ★★★

21st century

Sahco Hesslein/Ulf Moritz/ Tuscany 1883 Colour **01** Alt. colours **yes** Composition **47% paper, 33% polyester, 20% viscose** Width **300cm/118in** Repeat – Price ★★★★

Larsen/Merlin L2507 Colour **beige 01** Alt. colours **yes** Composition **100% silk** Width **140cm/55in** Repeat **4.5cm/ 1¾in** Price ★★★

Larsen/Reflection L7633 Colour **slate 01** Alt. colours **no** Composition **60% polyester, 25% linen, 15% cotton** Width **140cm/55in** Repeat – Price ★★★

9

10

12 Larsen/Cumulus L7456 Colour **mist 07** Alt. colours **no** Composition **80% saran, 20% polyethylene** Width **137cm/54in** Repeat – Price ★★★

13 Chase Erwin/Silk Organza Colour **sunset** Alt. colours **yes** Composition **80% metallic, 20% silk** Width **110cm/43in** Repeat – Price ★★

14 Osborne & Little/Hespera/ Cirrus F1640 Colour **05** Alt. colours **yes** Composition **50% cotton, 50% polyester** Width **140cm/55in** Repeat – Price ★★

15 Malabar/Indian Silk/Gold Book Colour **NSIL34** Alt. colours **yes** Composition **100% silk** Width **137cm/54in** Repeat **2.5cm/1in** Price ★★

16 Liberty Furnishings/Silvani Weaves/Selkie LF4243 Colour **06** Alt. colours **yes** Composition **92% polyester, 8% cotton** Width **300cm/118in** Repeat – Price ★★

17 Sahco Hesslein/Ulf Moritz/ Azteka 1915 Colour **11** Alt. colours **yes** Composition **74% linen, 23% polyester, 3% nylon** Width **168cm/66in** Repeat – Price ★★★

14

15

16

17

Braids & Trimmings

Decorative hand-sewn trimmings (*passements*) such as tassels, fringing braids and galloons (tapes and ribbons), were originally designed to disguise the seams and edges of wall-, bed- and window-hangings. In the 15th and 16th centuries *passements* were popular in Italy but rarely used elsewhere. However, following the emigration of skilled Milanese textile workers to the court of Louis XIV of France during the 17th century, *passements* became fashionable among the French nobility.

As window drapes and upholstered furniture became common in the houses of other sections of society during the 17th century, demand for decorative trimmings grew. Much of this was met by the French Huguenot communities who, in order to escape religious persecution, emigrated to England, Ireland, the Netherlands, Germany and Switzerland at the end of the 17th century, taking their skills in the art of *passementerie* with them. The result was a proliferation of intricate trimmings throughout Europe and, later, America, during the 18th and 19th centuries.

LEFT This oval-backed gilt armchair in the Calhoun Mansion in Charleston, South Carolina, USA, features edging braid around the pink moiré silk upholstery. It is coordinated with the wire-braid tiebacks and the deep bullion fringing on the silk damask curtains.

ABOVE These silk damask curtains at the 19th-century Calhoun Mansion were designed to imitate mid-19th-century originals. They are edged with multi-coloured, rope-twist bullion fringing made from silk.

CAMPAIGN FRINGE

Numerous styles of decorative trimmings for drapes and upholstery have been produced since the 15th century, including fringes made up of braid (or sometimes rope), from which hangs a row (or rows) of tassels. Often highly elaborate, most tassels were worked around wooden forms carved in a variety of shapes, such as arrows, domes and balls. However, the most enduringly popular type of edging has proved to be the "campaign" fringe. First devised in Italy in the 17th century, it is so called because the tassels have a bell-like shape – the Italian for bell being *campana*.

KEY DESIGNS

1 While the tops of many of the tassels produced since the Renaissance have been worked around plain wooden forms, some have been enclosed within decorative forms made from carved wood, cut glass, or engraved or plain metal. This tassel is made of jute and bound with a simple tin band.

2 Elaborately worked silk-tasselled tie-backs were a favoured means of securing hangings during the 18th and 19th centuries. They remain among the most intricate examples of the *passementier*'s art.

3 Bullion fringe, originally made from gold or silver thread, has been in widespread use as a decorative edging for drapes, pelmets and upholstery since the mid-19th century.

4 Decorative braid edgings, such as this "campaign-fringed" example, featured prominently on curtains, pelmets, upholstery, cushions and lamp shades in Victorian interiors.

5 Ribbons and ribbon-braids (galloons) have been produced in numerous patterns and colourways since the Renaissance. This example is designed as a disguise for upholstery seams.

6 Multi-coloured, interlaced braids were especially popular during the last quarter of the 19th century. This particular design, however, can be traced back to 17th-century France.

---

1 V.V. Rouleaux/Tin Tassel Colour **jute** Alt. colour **yes** Composition **jute and tin** Depth **15cm/6in** Width – Price ★ 🪑

2 Scalamandré/T2906-010 Colour **multi** Alt. colour **yes** Composition **90% silk, 10% wood** Depth **60cm/23¾in** Width – Price ★★★ 🪑

3 Henry Newbery & Co/Melrose/Selkirk **Bullion Fringe** Colour **4** Alt. colour **yes** Composition **mixed fibres** Depth **20cm/8in** Width – Price ★★ 🪑🛋

4 Henry Newbery & Co/Portobello/Portobello **Tassel Fringe** Colour **12** Alt. colour **yes** Composition **100% viscose** Depth **6cm/ 2⅜in** Width – Price ★★ 🪑🪑

5 Abbott & Boyd/Braid Colour **bottle green, golden maize and silver grey** Alt. colour **yes** Composition **100% cotton** Depth – Width **4cm/1½in** Price ★ 🛋

6 Clarence House/Richelieu Braid 110420 Colour **752** Alt. colour **yes** Composition **100% rayon** Depth – Width **4cm/1½in** Price ★★★★ 🪑🪑

Tassels & Tie-backs

Decorative tassels and tie-backs have been used to embellish drapery since the Renaissance. At their simplest, tassels are ornamental tufts of thread incorporated into fringing and edgings (*see* pages 196–201) applied to bed-hangings, window drapes, lambrequins, pelmets, portières and upholstery. However, many of the more elaborate tassels – notably those employed as, or as part of, tie-backs for bed- and window-hangings and portières – are among the most intricate examples of the *passementier*'s art. Working around flat-, dome-, arrow-, ball- or screw-shaped wooden forms covered with fabrics such as silk or velvet, the *passementier* could apply a range of embellishments, such as braid or cord edgings, appliquéd motifs and long or short skirts (many of which were made of gold- or silver-thread fringing). During the 18th century, relatively small arrow- and rectangular-shaped heads were popular, as were proportionately short skirts trimmed with appliquéd bows or smaller, fabric-covered wooden forms. Such ornamentation, however, was discreet when compared to the elaborate tassels produced during the 19th century.

1 **V.V. Rouleaux/Acorns** Colour **emerald, gold and blue** Alt. colours **yes** Composition **100% polyester** Depth **3.5cm/1¼in** Width – Price ★

2 **V.V. Rouleaux/MOK-05-L** Colour **black and silver** Alt. colours **yes** Composition **70% rayon, 30% polyester** Depth **3.5cm/1¼in** Width – Price ★

3

4

5

6

3 **V.V. Rouleaux/Waxed Turk Hen Knot Tassel** Colour **navy** Alt. colours **yes** Composition **100% acrylic** Depth **3.5cm/1¼in** Width – Price ★★ (special order)

4 **Mulberry/Bishop Tie-back FC004/000** Colour **Natural K101** Alt. colours **yes** Composition **wood and wool** Depth **32.5cm/12¾in** Width – Price ★★★

5 **Mulberry/Hayrick Jute Tie-back FC028/084** Colour **natural K101** Alt. colours **yes** Composition **100% jute** Depth **36cm/14in** Width – Price ★★

6 **Mulberry/Bishop Painted Wood Silky Tie-back FC049/087** Colour **soft gold T106** Alt. colours **yes** Composition **wood & wool** Depth **32.5cm/12¾in** Width – Price ★★★★

7 **Mulberry/Bishop Tie-back FC004/000** Colour **cream J103** Alt. colours **yes** Composition **wood & wool** Depth **32.5cm/12¾in** Width – Price ★★★

8 **Henry Newbery & Co/ Cambridge Tie-back** Colour **wine (1)** Alt. colours **yes** Composition **100% Dralon** Depth **20cm/8in** Width – Price ★★★

7

8

RENAISSANCE INFLUENCE

The manufacture of decorative trimmings (known as *passements*) for furnishings has remained a specialist activity since the Renaissance. However, as far as the design of these often exquisite trimmings is concerned, there has always been considerable cross-fertilization of ideas that exist between different areas of textile production. These elaborate tassels are inspired by dressmakers' embellishments and key fobs that were considered the height of fashion in Italy during the Renaissance.

1

2

1 **Wendy Cushing Trimmings/ Traditional Key Tassel 39112** Colour **silver** Alt. colours **yes** Composition **100% cotton** Depth **10cm/4in** Width – Price ★★

2 **V.V. Rouleaux/Terracotta Tassel** Colour **burgundy & gold** Alt. colours **yes** Composition **50% rayon, 50% acrylic** Depth **24cm/9½in** Width – Price ★★★★★

9

10

11

14

9 **Abbott & Boyd/Single Tassel Tie-back 613** Colour **jute and red** Alt. colours **yes** Composition **50% jute, 50% cotton** Depth **30cm/ 11¾in** Width – Price ★★

10 **Henry Newbery & Co/Fitzherbert Tie-back** Colour **wine and aquamarine** Alt. colours **yes** Composition **100% viscose** Depth **16.5cm/6½in** Width – Price ★★★

11 **Wendy Cushing Trimmings/ Gothic Tie-backs 39033** Colour **black and white** Alt. colours **yes** Composition **100% cotton** Depth **17.75cm/7in** Width – Price ★★★★★

12 **Zoë Barlow Passementerie/ Mexicana Mex/P2/M** Colour **green, blue, yellow and rust** Alt. colours **yes** Composition **cotton and wood** Depth **11.5cm/4½in** Width – Price ★★★★★

13 **V.V. Rouleaux/OP-8612** Colour **light blue 63** Alt. colours **yes** Composition **100% polyester** Depth **14cm/5½in** Width – Price ★

14 **Abbott & Boyd/Double Tassel Tie-back 614** Colour **jute** Alt. colours **yes** Composition **50% jute, 50% cotton** Depth **30cm/11¾in** Width – Price ★★★

13

12

ROSETTES

Strictly defined as a circular, formalized flower ornament, but generally accepted as any type of circular ornament with decorative elements radiating from its centre, the rosette has been frequently employed as a trimming for drapery and upholstery since the Renaissance. As shown here, the basic circular shape is frequently augmented with tassels. Since the early Renaissance it has recurred on Classical and Neo-classical furnishing, yet this almost universal motif can be traced back to both ancient Greece and to the Mesopotamian civilization of *c.* 2500 BC, where it was frequently applied to furnishings and other decorative and religious artefacts.

2

3

1 **Zoë Barlow Passementerie/ Button and Tassel EP/P20/ Sg/Sp** Colour **pink & green** Alt. colours **yes** Composition **cotton & wood** Depth **55cm/ 21½in** Width – Price ★★★★

2 **Zoë Barlow Passementerie/ Button Med/D10/Sp** Colour **pastel** Alt. colours **yes** Composition **cotton & wood** Depth **30cm/11¾in** Width – Price ★★★

3 **V.V. Rouleaux/Cherry Ball** Colour **neutral** Alt. colours **no** Composition **100% jute** Depth **13cm/5in** Width – Price ★

1

Tassels & Tie-backs

During the 19th century, tassels generally became more ornate and played an even more prominent role in the furnishing of interiors. As in previous centuries, they were incorporated into fringes and edgings on drapes, lambrequins, pelmets and upholstery. However, the most elaborate examples tended to be reserved for tie-backs and – a new use – bellpulls. In this context their increased complexity mirrored that of related items, such as the bronze and gilt rosettes, discs and cloakpins that were used to secure the tie-backs. Notable examples from the 19th century included multi-tiered tassels worked around a maximum of six carved or turned wooden forms. Arrow- and dome-shaped heads, appliquéd with golden leaves or shells, proved very popular, as did long, onion-shaped skirts.

During the Art Deco and Modernist periods of the 20th century, tassels became smaller and simpler than before, although there were some innovations, including the use of heads made from uncovered cut-glass. More recently, to meet renewed demand, manufacturers and designers have once again begun to produce highly intricate and elaborate tassels, based on, or inspired by, authentic period designs.

1

2   3

4   5   6

7

1 **Zoë Barlow Passementerie/ Tropical Fish/Purple Angel** Colour **purple, yellow and orange** Alt. colours **yes** Composition **wood, cotton and rayon** Depth **31cm/12in** Width – Price ★★★★★ ⬚

2 **Scalamandré/Tassel Tie T2906-10** Colour **black and sand** Alt. colours **yes** Composition **100% silk** Depth **15cm/6in** Width – Price ★★★★★ ⬚

3 **Henry Newbery & Co/Melrose – Single Tassel** Colour **pink** Alt. colours **yes** Composition **100% viscose** Depth **17.5cm/ 7in** Width – Price ★★★ ⬚

4 **Wendy Cushing Trimmings/ Celtic Tie-back 39063** Colour **blue** Alt. colours **yes** Composition **50% cotton, 50% artificial silk** Depth **23cm/9in** Width – Price ★★★★★ ⬚

5 **Scalamandré/T2790-12** Colour **green and gold** Alt. colours **yes** Composition **100% silk** Depth **18cm/7in** Width – Price ★★★★★ ⬚

6 **Henry Newbery & Co/Alpha Tie-back** Colour **green and sand** Alt. colours **yes** Composition **100% viscose** Depth **24cm/9½in** Width – Price ★★★ ⬚

7 **Claremont/Embrasse Neker Guirlande** Colour **blue and gold** Alt. colours **yes** Composition **100% fibranne** Depth **29cm/11¼in** Width – Price ★★★★★ ⬚ T

8 **Zoë Barlow Passementerie/ Tassel Electric Blue** Colour **blue** Alt. colours **yes** Composition **100% cotton, wood** Depth **28cm/10¾in** Width – Price ★★★★ 🔲

9 **Henry Newbery & Co/Beta** Colour **bright gold** Alt. colours **yes** Composition **47% cotton, 43% metallic thread, 10% wood** Depth **27cm/10½in** Width – Price ★★★★ 🔲

10 **V.V. Rouleaux/Mosaic Tassel** Colour **multi** Alt. colours **yes** Composition **100% acrylic, coloured glass, iron** Depth **to order** Width – Price ★★★★★ (special order) 🔲

11 **Zoë Barlow Passementerie/ Double Tie-back Tassel MEX/ P2/M** Colour **blue, green, yellow & rust** Alt. colours **yes** Composition **100% cotton, wood** Depth **11.5cm/ 4½in** Width – Price ★★★★★ 🔲

12 **Claremont/Embrasse Raisins** Colour **green** Alt. colours **yes** Composition **100% fibranne** Depth **18cm/7in** Width – Price ★★★★★ 🔲 🔲

13 **Zoë Barlow Passementerie/ Tassel Siamese Fighting Fish (A)** Colour **rusty orange & bottle green** Alt. colours **yes** Composition **100% cotton, wood** Depth **22.5cm/8¾in** Width – Price ★★★★★ 🔲

14 **V.V. Rouleaux/Sev – Special** Colour **red and gold** Alt. colours **yes** Composition **100% acrylic** Depth **40cm/15¾in** Width – Price ★★★★★ 🔲

TIE-BACKS

Historically, the majority of tie-backs used to restrain window drapes, bed-hangings and portières have been embellished with intricately worked *passements*. However, relatively simple arrangements have also found favour. For example, during the 17th century most tie-backs consisted merely of plaited rope cords made from fibres as diverse as silk, cotton and hemp. Ribbons or "galloons" proved popular during the 18th century, and plain cords re-emerged during the 19th century – albeit some as thick as an elephant's trunk.

1 **Mulberry/'Silk' Sash Tie-back FC056** Colour **soft gold T106** Alt. colours **yes** Composition **100% viscose rayon** Length **85cm/ 33½in** Width **35cm/13¾in** Price ★★★ 🔲

2 **Claremont/S & S Cable Tie-back** Colour **green, pink and white** Alt. colours **yes** Composition **100% cotton** Length **75cm/29½in** Width **5cm/2in** Price ★★★ 🔲 🔲

3 **Nobilis-Fontan/Embrasses Club 1201.87** Colour **gold and blue** Alt. colours **yes** Composition **70% viscose, 15% silk, 15% cotton** Length **90cm/35½in** Width **3cm/1¼in** Price ★★ 🔲

4 **Abbott & Boyd/211** Colour **58** Alt. colours **yes** Composition **95% cotton, 5% viscose** Length **73cm/28½in** Width **3cm/1¼in** Price ★ 🔲

Fringes

As the influential 19th-century English architect, designer and ornamentist A.W.N. Pugin once noted, fringe was at one time "nothing more than the threads of a silk or woollen stuff knotted together at a ragged edge, to prevent it unravelling further". In terms of its original purpose, this was undeniably true. However, since the 17th century fringe has been produced in a wide variety of styles, some of which have been simple and functional, others highly elaborate and decorative (*see pages 198–9*).

During the 19th century, extremely ornate upholstery fringing was the height of fashion. Prior to that time, fringes were often relatively plain, with typical examples consisting of braid (or sometimes lace) tops hung with simple tufts or tassels. The depth of such fringes essentially depended on their purpose: shorter versions (which did not droop) were designed for the vertical edges of hangings and upholstered seating, while longer fringes were intended for the bottom edges. Some simple fringes were also made during this period, specifically for the leading edges of mantelshelves (*tours de cheminées*) and bookcases, the purpose of the latter being to dust a book each time it was removed from and returned to its shelf.

4

5

1

6

7

8

3

9

1 **Wemyss Houlès/Toinette 33127** Colour **royal blue (light blue) with white** Alt. colours **yes** Composition **100% viscose** Depth **7cm/2¾in** Width – Price ★

2 **Scalamandré/Cut Fringe FC1195** Colour **red and parchment** Alt. colours **yes** Composition **90% silk, 10% rayon** Depth **9.5cm/3¾in** Width – Price ★★★

3 **Wendy Cushing Trimmings/Roll Top Bullion Fringe** Colour **black and white** Alt. colours **yes** Composition **100% rayon** Depth **12cm/4¾in** Width – Price ★★

4 **Wendy Cushing Trimmings/Silk Bullion with Gimp Heading and Silk Acorns 39120** Colour **silver** Alt. colours **yes** Composition **100% silk** Depth **10cm/4in** Width – Price ★★★★★

5 **Mulberry/Cotton Tassel Fringe FC013/000** Colour **gold T102** Alt. colours **yes** Composition **100% cotton** Depth **3cm/ 1⅛in** Width **7.5cm/2¾in** Price ★★

6 **Claremont/Block Fringe Long** Colour **mauve, mustard and green** Alt. colours **yes** Composition **100% fibranne** Depth **6.5cm/2½in** Width – Price ★★

7 **Turnell & Gigon/Effilé Naturel 906** Colour **two-tone natural (3)** Alt. colours **yes** Composition **93% linen, 7% viscose** Depth **6cm/2¼in** Width – Price ★★

8 **Henry Newbery & Co/Portobello Bayswater Fan Edge** Colour **12** Alt. colours **yes** Composition **100% viscose** Depth **2.5cm/1in** Width – Price ★

9 **Henry Newbery & Co/Opera Fringe/Callas Looped Ruche** Colour **2** Alt. colours **yes** Composition **80% viscose, 20% wool** Depth **5cm/2in** Width – Price ★

BULLION FRINGE

So called because its twisted lengths of hanging rope were often made from gold, silver or metallic fibres, bullion fringe was particularly fashionable during the mid-19th century. Its primary use was as a skirt for the base of upholstered armchairs and sofas. Single- and multi-coloured linen and cotton versions also proved popular in mid-20th-century "country-house" style interiors.

1 Ian Sanderson/Zanzibar Trimmings/Bullion Fringe Colour **spice** Alt. colours **yes** Composition **59% viscose, 40% acrylic, 1% polyester** Depth **15cm/6in** Width **–** Price ★★ ⬚ ⬚

2 Clarence House/Vérone Frange Torse 119612 Colour **green, gold, red & brown (859)** Alt. colours **yes** Composition **100% viscose** Depth **12cm/4¾in** Width **–** Price ★★ ⬚ ⬚ ⬚

10 Claremont/Frange Guirlande Colour **blue and gold** Alt. colours **yes** Composition **100% fibranne** Depth **17cm/6¾in** Width **–** Price ★★★★★ ⬚ ⬚ ⬚

11 Wendy Cushing Trimmings/ Spiral Silk Fringe with Hangers 39121 Colour **grey** Alt. colours **yes** Composition **100% silk** Depth **10cm/4in** Width **–** Price ★★★★★ ⬚

12 Clarence House/Cut Fringe Richelieu 110421 Colour **navy and gold** Alt. colours **yes** Composition **100% viscose** Depth **12cm/4¾in** Width **–** Price ★★★★ ⬚ ⬚

13 Wemyss Houlès/Samurai 33063 Colour **9582** Alt. colours **yes** Composition **100% viscose** Depth **6.5cm/ 2½in** Width **–** Price ★★ ⬚

14 V.V. Rouleaux/Feather Trim Colour **brown and black** Alt. colours **yes** Composition **100% feathers** Depth **16cm/ 6¼in** Width **–** Price ★★★ ⬚

Fringes

During the late 18th and early 19th centuries, fringe was generally regarded as unfashionable. Napoleon I, for example, described it as a "useless" ornament and banned it from his apartments at the Tuileries in Paris. There was also a reaction against it among the followers of the Aesthetic movement during the second half of the 19th century. However, for most of the Victorian era and for much of the 20th century an enormous variety of intricate and highly elaborate fringing was employed on drapes and upholstery. For example, from the 1830s to the 1850s long spiral and bullion fringes, embellished with appliquéd flowers and topped with picot or gimp braids, were very fashionable. In the second half of the 19th century, Persian fringe incorporating a wide braid border supporting fabric-covered balls ("teardrops") was popular, and during the 20th century many Art Deco and Modernist furnishings featured long, skirt-like fringes with deep, crochetwork headings. These are but a few of the many types of fringing that have enjoyed a vogue. Other significant types include "inch", "caul", "block", "campaign", "vellum", "trellis", "butterfly", "snailing", "tufted", "twisted", "knotted", "netted", "fagoted" (sic) and "swagged", all of which are still produced by the *passementiers* of today.

7

8 9

10

1

2 3

11

1 Henry Newbery & Co/Blenheim
Colour **green and beige (2)**
Alt. colours **yes** Composition
90% acrylic, 10% rayon
Depth **7cm/2¾in** Width –
Price ★★

2 Zoffany/Pompom Tassel Fringe
TRM0900 Colour **3** Alt. colours
yes Composition **100% viscose**
Depth **6.5cm/2½in** Width –
Price ★★

3 Scalamandré/Tassel Fringe
FT44 Colour **1** Alt. colours
yes Composition **100% silk**
Depth **6cm/2½in** Width –
Price ★★★★

4 Wemyss Houlès/Cap-Ferret
33385 Colour **yellow-maize and
green** Alt. colours **yes**
Composition **82% viscose,
18% wool** Depth **7.5cm/2¾in**
Width – Price ★★

5 Zoffany/3¼" Tassel Fringe
TRM0800 Colour **3** Alt.
colours **yes** Composition
100% viscose Depth **8.5cm/
3¼in** Width – Price ★★

6 Brunschwig & Fils/Applause
Tassled Fringe 30429-mmm
Colour **multi** Alt. colours **yes**
Composition **100% viscose**
Depth **8cm/3in** Width –
Price ★★

7 Clarence House/Richelieu –
Fringe & Mèches 110422
Colour **752** Alt. colours **yes**
Composition **100% viscose**
Depth **11cm/4¼in** Width –
Price ★★★★★

8 Wemyss Houlès/Cordelia 33376
Colour **9573** Alt. colours
yes Composition **85% wool,
15% viscose** Depth **9cm/3½in**
Width – Price ★★★★

9 Wemyss Houlès/Sultane 33379
Colour **9574** Alt. colours **yes**
Composition **90% viscose,
5% cotton, 5% metal** Depth
6.5cm/2½in Width –
Price ★★★★

10 Henry Newbery & Co/Capricorn/
Salvador Bullion Fringe Colour
rosebud Alt. colours **yes**
Composition **80% viscose,
20% acrylic chenille** Depth
20cm/8in Width –
Price ★★★

11 Henry Newbery & Co/Capricorn/
Capricorn Tassel Fringe Colour
rosebud Alt. colours **yes**
Composition **93% viscose,
7% acrylic chenille** Depth
7cm/2¾in Width –
Price ★★

12 Wendy Cushing Trimmings/ Gilded Bell Hanger Fringe 39045 Colour **gold** Alt. colours **yes** Composition **50% cotton, 50% wool** Depth **10cm/4in** Width – Price ★★★★★

13 V.V. Rouleaux/3-Drop Bauble Fringe Colour **terracotta** Alt. colours **yes** Composition **75% cotton, 25% jute** Depth **10cm/4in** Width – Price ★★

14 Brunschwig & Fils/Paulina Beaded Fringe 905861.05 Colour **creme** Alt. colours **yes** Composition **50% silk, 50% glass** Depth **6cm/2½in** Width – Price ★★★★

15 Scalamandré/Clear Crystal Fringe ST5401 Colour **white** Alt. colours **yes** Composition **50% rayon, 50% lucite** Depth **4cm/1½in** Width – Price ★★

6 Henry Newbery & Co/Carlos Fringe Colour **4** Alt. colours **yes** Composition **100% acrylic** Depth **10cm/4in** Width – Price ★★

7 Brunschwig & Fils/Tourner Wood Mould Fringe 90580. 05/2 Colour **natural** Alt. colours **yes** Composition **74% wood, 25% cotton, 1% metal** Depth **9cm/3½in** Width – Price ★★★★

8 Henry Newbery & Co/Opera Colour **4** Alt. colours **yes** Composition **100% viscose** Depth **5cm/2in** Width – Price ★★★

9 V.V. Rouleaux/3 Bauble Drop R5 Colour **oyster** Alt. colours **yes** Composition **100% polyester** Depth **15cm/6in** Width – Price ★★★★ (special order)

0 Wendy Cushing Trimmings/ Classical Hanger Fringe 39052 Colour **green, red & gold** Alt. colours **yes** Composition **silk & wood** Depth **10cm/4in** Width – Price ★★

FABRICS: *FRINGES* **199**

Braids & Ribbons

Primarily used to disguise seams and raw edges, braids – flat, narrow, woven textiles – also serve to add decorative embellishments to drapes and upholstery, often in conjunction with tassels and fringing. In the 17th century, braids of plaited silk and gold thread were fashionable, as were velour braids that featured stylized flowers and lozenges. From the 18th century, many tie-backs were edged with substantial braids embellished with flowers, bows, rosettes and butterfly shapes, and picot or gimp braids served as headings for fringing. Early 19th-century braids tended to be delicate, while mid-century examples were generally larger, and end-of-century braids were often multi-coloured, curved and interlaced. In the 20th century, neater, straighter braids with geometric motifs have been favoured.

Decorative ribbons ("galloons") have also been widely used for embellishments. In Paris, France, there were more than 700 *rubaniers* producing bows and artificial flowers from ribbons during the mid-18th century. These were used as trims on drapes, pelmets, valances, tie-backs and table coverings. Many examples, such as "à la cocque", "au mirlton", "à la quadrille" and "à l'allure", took their names from current events, personalities, popular songs and dances, and are still available today.

7

9

1

1

2

3

4

5

6

11

12

13

14

1 Claremont/Galon Chenille Colour **pink, green, cream and black** Alt. colours **yes** Composition **100% cotton** Depth – Width **5cm/2in** Price ★★ ⊞ ⛊ T

2 Henry Newbury & Co/Windsor Gimp Colour **17** Alt. colours **yes** Composition **70% rayon, 30% acrylic** Depth – Width **1cm/⅜in** Price ★ ⊞⛊

3 Wendy Cushing Trimmings/ Tabby Braid 39038 Colour **black and cream** Alt. colours **yes** Composition **50% cotton, 30% silk, 20% rayon** Depth – Width **1.5cm/⅝in** Price ★★ ⊞⛊

4 Henry Newbury & Co/Norfolk Picot Braid Colour **16** Alt. colours **yes** Composition **100% cotton** Depth – Width **2.5cm/1in** Price ★ ⊞⛊

5 Henry Newbury & Co/Kingston Braid Colour **82** Alt. colours **yes** Composition **80% viscose, 20% cotton** Depth – Width **2cm/¾in** Price ★ ⛊⛊⊞

6 Wemyss Houlès/Cap-Ferret 32179 Colour **9171** Alt. colours **yes** Composition **100% viscose** Depth – Width **4cm/1½in** Price ★ ⊞⛊

7 Nobilis-Fontan/Galon et Boutons de Roses 1404 Colour **blue and white** Alt. colours **yes** Composition **100% viscose** Depth – Width **4.5cm/1¾in** Price ★★★⛊

8 George Spencer Designs/ Check Braid 506 Colour **manila and terracotta** Alt. colours **yes** Composition **100% cotton** Depth – Width **6cm/2½in** Price ★★ ⊞ ⛊

9 Scalamandré/Military Ribbon V161-48 Colour **jade green, maize and old glory red** Alt. colours **yes** Composition **100% rayon** Depth – Width **2cm/¾in** Price ★★ ⛊⛊

10 Abbott & Boyd/Braid 621 Colour **jute and white** Alt. colours **yes** Composition **70% jute, 30% cotton** Depth – Width **3.5cm/1¼in** Price ★ ⊞⛊

11 Claremont/Galon Colour **burgundy, green and cream** Alt. colours **yes** Composition **100% fibranne** Depth – Width **13cm/5in** Price ★★★⛊T

12 V.V. Rouleaux/Indian Figure of Eight Colour **jute** Alt. colours **no** Composition **100% jute** Depth – Width **6cm/2½in** Price ★ ⊞⛊

13 V.V. Rouleaux/Petersham Colour **6** Alt. colours **yes** Composition **64% viscose, 36% cotton** Depth – Width **2cm/¾in** Price ★ ⊞⛊

14 Claremont/Greek Key Border Colour **gold, white and black** Alt. colours **yes** Composition **100% fibranne** Depth – Width **5.5cm/2¼in** Price ★★ ⊞⛊T

5 Scalamandré/Braid V635-4
Colour **seaspray, teal blue and cream** Alt. colours **yes** Composition **100% silk** Depth – Width **5cm/2in** Price ★★ LC 🛋

6 Brunschwig & Fils/30434-M21
Colour **wine, red, turquoise, cream and gold mix** Alt. colours **yes** Composition **100% viscose** Depth – Width **5cm/2in** Price ★ 🛋 ⊞

7 Scalamandré/Braid V713-4
Colour **taupe and pink** Alt. colours **yes** Composition **90% silk, 5% rayon, 5% Bemberg** Depth – Width **5cm/2in** Price ★★★ LC 🛋

8 Scalamandré/Braid V417-12
Colour **salmon pink, tarragon and parchment** Alt. colours **yes** Composition **100% silk** Depth – Width **4cm/1½in** Price ★★★ ⊞ 🛋

15

16

17

18

21

3

24

5

19 Zoffany/Flower Braid TRM0700
Colour **3** Alt. colours **yes** Composition **100% viscose** Depth – Width **1.5cm/⅝in** Price ★ 🛋 ⊠

19

20 Claremont/Galon d'Olives Colour **red museum** Alt. colours **yes** Composition **100% wool** Depth – Width **3cm/1¼in** Price ★★ ⊞ 🛋 T

21 Claremont/Palmette Colour **tan, green and black** Alt. colours **yes** Composition **100% viscose** Depth – Width **4cm/1½in** Price ★★ ⊠ T

20

22 V.V. Rouleaux/Mokuba – Flower Tape 9313 Colour **yellow, blue and red** Alt. colours **yes** Composition **85% rayon, 15% polyester** Depth – Width **7mm/¼in** Price ★★ ⊞ 🛋

23 V.V. Rouleaux/1359 No. 12 Colour **7** Alt. colours **yes** Composition **100% silk** Depth – Width **5cm/2in** Price ★ 🛋

24 V.V. Rouleaux/Mokuba Ribbon Colour **moss green 16** Alt. colours **yes** Composition **100% polyester** Depth – Width **5cm/2in** Price ★ 🛋

25 Ian Sanderson/Etosha Trimmings/Lacy Leather Trim Colour **earth** Alt. colours **yes** Composition **100% leather** Depth – Width **4cm/1½in** Price ★ 🛋

26 V.V. Rouleaux/Ribbon Picot Edge Colour **cayenne, green and cream** Alt. colours **yes** Composition **100% polyester** Depth – Width **2.5cm/1in** Price ★ ⊞ 🛋

26

UPHOLSTERY BRAIDS

Braid was first extensively employed as a means of decoratively masking the seams and raw edges of drapes and pelmets during the reign of Louis XIV of France. However, the profusion of braid designs that emerged from the late 17th to the end of the 19th century largely resulted from the development of numerous styles of upholstered seating during this period. Braid provided a complementary (or contrasting) edging material, and served to define the diverse shapes of seating as varied as wing and bergère chairs, occasional and corner chairs, and settees and chaise-longues.

1

2

3

1 Henry Newbury & Co/Capricorn/Phoenix Border Colour **leopard** Alt. colours **yes** Composition **90% viscose, 10% acrylic** Depth – Width **4.5cm/1¾in** Price ★ 🛋 ⊠ ⊞

2 Zoffany/Picot Braid TRM1400 Colour **5** Alt. colours **yes** Composition **100% cotton** Depth – Width **1cm/⅜in** Price ★ LC 🛋 ⊠

3 Scalamandré/Braid V780-7 Colour **royal blue, wine and gold** Alt. colours **yes** Composition **90% cotton, 10% rayon** Depth – Width **2.5cm/1in** Price ★★★ ⊞ 🛋

Wallpapers

Plain Wallpapers

Although most wallpapers made since the 15th century have been embellished with patterns and motifs, a significant minority have been produced in plain or mottled colours. The plainest present a solid expanse of a single colour. The types of dyes and inks – animal, vegetable, mineral, aniline and chemical – used to print them, as well as the method of printing, have varied, and have determined the purity, strength and vivacity of colour available (*see* page 206). However, the primary purpose of these plain papers has always been to introduce colour into a room while providing an uncluttered and complementary backdrop for architectural fixtures and fittings, furniture and soft furnishings. Also found within the plains category are those papers that exhibit subtle gradations or mottling of colour. Some are purely abstract, such as many 20th-century Modernist papers, but others are intended as simulations of stone, wood and textiles, such as hessian and tweed. Many papers of this type have been produced since the Renaissance, and a few also exhibit embossing or applied texturing across their surface.

RIGHT In the Victorian era, pictures were often displayed against plain wallpapers. Crimson and magenta papers were deemed appropriate as they accentuated the warm glow of gilded and polished wooden picture frames while providing a contrasting ground for ebony and black-lacquered frames.

PAINT-EFFECT PAPERS

Wallpapers that reproduce the appearance of decorative paint effects have been famously popular since the 1980s. Most are imitations of colourwashing, ragging, rag-rolling, sponging and stippling. Known as "broken-colour techniques", all these effects display, to varying degrees, subtle gradations and patterning of colour. Some – such as sponging or rag-rolling – are often used in re-creations of period interiors. They simulate the mottling that occurred in many pre-20th-century paint finishes as a result of a chemical breakdown in their pigments following exposure to light.

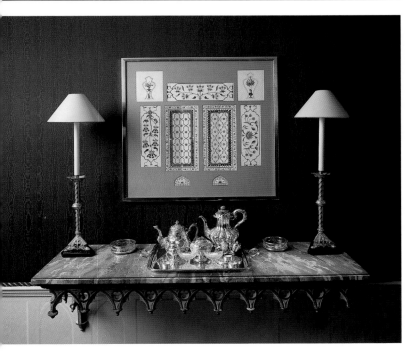

ABOVE Since the late 19th century, dark blue papered walls have often been used as complementary backdrops for displays of silverware and grey marble and granite artefacts.

KEY DESIGNS

1 Many plain papers have been produced in imitation of plain-woven fabrics. This early 21st-century example imitates the warp and weft of the weave in its two-colour surface printing.

2 Finely figured hardwoods are often simulated in wallpapers. This modern design displays the configurations and mottled colouring associated with stained and polished walnut.

3 During the 19th and 20th centuries, a number of papers were produced in imitation of leather wall-hangings. Some, like this taupe-coloured paper, do actually have the texture of leather.

4 This *faux*-limewash paper exhibits the subtle gradations and luminosities of colour associated with this traditional paint finish. Paint-effect papers have proved very popular since the 1980s.

5 Some plain wallpapers suggest the appearance of stonework or patinated metal surfaces. They can also display subtle and random variations in tonality that can be appreciated in their own right.

6 Grass cloths have been used as wall coverings for centuries, particularly in Japan and Korea. They were very fashionable in Europe and America from the 1960s until the 1980s.

1 **Harlequin/Notebook** Colour **45664** Alt. colours **yes** Width **52cm/20½in** Length **10m/11yd** Repeat – Price ★

2 **Maya Romanoff/Patina MR-T35-176-G** Colour **golden taupe** Alt. colours **yes** Width **76cm/30in** Length **to order** Repeat – Price ★★★★★

3 **Today Interiors/FX/Leather FXV342** Colour **1** Alt. colours **yes** Width **53cm/21in** Length **10m/11yd** Repeat **53cm/21in** Price ★

4 **Zoffany/Limewash NTW070** Colour **07** Alt. colours **yes** Width **52cm/ 20½in** Length **10m/11yd** Repeat – Price ★

5 **Osborne & Little/Glissando W1443/01** Colour **silver** Alt. colours **yes** Width **52cm/20½in** Length **10m/11yd** Repeat – Price ★

6 **Donghia/Hemps Wallcovering G970/01** Colour **red** Alt. colours **yes** Width **91cm/35¾in** Length **3.5m/3¾yd** Repeat – Price ★★★★★

Plains

Forerunners of wallpapers, printed with a single block of colour (usually blues, reds and greens), appeared in the 15th century as grounds for paper cutouts of religious and heraldic imagery. During the 18th century, plain blue, crimson and yellow wallpapers were used in "print rooms" (*see* page 245). In 19th-century interiors, single-coloured wallpapers (especially in shades of red) were favoured for displaying ebony- and gilt-framed pictures, while in the 20th century plain-coloured papers have proved particularly suitable for Modernist and post-Modernist interiors.

Prior to the 1850s, papers that had been hand-blocked with animal, vegetable or mineral dyes exhibited a notable delicacy and purity of colour. In comparison, the hand-blocked or roller-printed aniline dyes of the mid- and late 19th century were more vibrant, but sometimes rather garish. The synthetic chemical dyes of the 20th and 21st centuries have increased the colour range but, partly owing to the slight loss of crispness associated with photogravure and screen-printing, have often failed to match the even coverage given by vegetable dyes – a fact that explains the revival of hand-blocking with traditional vegetable and mineral dyes that began in the late 20th century.

Nina Campbell/Lawn NCW2025/06 Colour **yellow** Alt. colours **yes** Width **52cm/20½in** Length **10m/11yd** Repeat – Price ★

G.P. & J. Baker/Carrara W0110-01 Colour **01** Alt. colours **yes** Width **52cm/20½in** Length **10m/11yd** Repeat – Price ★★

Maya Romanoff/Washi Tsuchikabe MR-RW3018 Colour **green** Alt. colours **yes** Width **93cm/36in** Length **to order** Repeat – Price ★★★★

Zoffany/Stucco PC81905 Colour **05** Alt. colours **yes** Width **52cm/20½in** Length **10m/11yd** Repeat – Price ★

Ornamenta/Lysander Cirrus GIR306 Colour **grey** Alt. colours **yes** Width **52cm/20½in** Length **10m/11yd** Repeat – Price ★★★★★

Today Interiors/FX/Fresco FXV343 Colour **2** Alt. colours **yes** Width **53cm/21in** Length **10m/11yd** Repeat – Price ★

Crowson/Sparta Colour **45** Alt. colours **yes** Width **53cm/21in** Length **10m/11yd** Repeat – Price ★

Maya Romanoff/Patina MR-T35-163 Colour **mustard** Alt. colours **yes** Width **77cm/30½in** Length **to order** Repeat – Price ★★★★★

Ornamenta/Woodgrain WGR808 Colour beige, pink and rose Alt. colours yes Width 53cm/21in Length 10m/11yd Repeat – Price ★★★★★ 🪣

Anya Larkin/Moondust Teapaper Colour 236 pueblo Alt. colours yes Width 102cm/40in Length 3m/3⅓yd Repeat – Price ★★★★★ 🪣

Andrew Martin/Raffia Medium Colour natural Alt. colours no Width 91cm/35¾in Length 6m/6½yd Repeat – Price ★★

Anya Larkin/Concertina Colour 430 ivory Alt. colours yes Width 74cm/29in Length 3m/3⅓yd Repeat – Price ★★★★★ 🪣

Harlequin/Navari Colour 45808 Alt. colours yes Width 52cm/20½in Length 10m/11yd Repeat 52cm/20½in Price ★

Nobilis/Tassili Colour TAS214 Alt. colours yes Width 68cm/26¾in Length 10m/11yd Repeat – Price ★★

Anya Larkin/Flat Teapaper Colour 104 gold Alt. colours yes Width 102cm/40in Length 3m/3⅓yd Repeat – Price ★★★★★ 🪣

GRASS CLOTHS

Textured wallpapers with a "natural" look have been popular since the mid-1960s, especially in northern Europe and Scandinavia. Typical examples include loose-weave hessian (laminated to a paper backing), suedes and grass cloths (shown here). The latter, which consist of parallel strips of dried grass (or seaweed) glued or woven to a coarse paper ground, had been used as wall-coverings in Korea and Japan for centuries. Many of the grass cloths included in Western interiors are imported from the Far East, but some are produced in Europe (notably France), and these often have a flame-retardant coating.

Donghia/Grasscloth G946-04 Colour 04 seaweed Alt. colours yes Width 91cm/35¾in Length 3.5m/3⅞yd Repeat – Price ★★

Plains

Wallpapers displaying subtle mottling and gradations of colour printed in imitation of stonework, such as marble, limestone, granite and porphyry, were produced in Italy and France as early as the 16th century. As a cheaper substitute for the often unavailable raw material, they have remained in widespread use ever since. Papers simulating the colours, figuring and grain of hardwoods, such as mahogany, oak, maple and birch, have also proved fashionable since the 17th century and have been primarily employed as a substitute for expensive dado panelling, or half- or full-height wall-panelling. Throughout the 20th century and in the early 21st, other special-effect papers have appeared featuring abstract patterns not dissimilar to *faux* stone and wood. Among the most notable and influential are the Modernist papers of the 1930s, which displayed blurred, streaky patches of graduated colour and were sometimes enlivened with gilt powders.

4 **Fardis/Les Ochres 89840** Colour **54** Alt. colours **yes** Width **70cm/27½in** Length **10m/11yd** Repeat **35cm/13¾in** Price ★

5 **Graham & Brown 11525** Colour **yellow** Alt. colours **yes** Width **52cm/20½in** Length **10m/11yd** Repeat – Price ★

6 **Graham & Brown 11522** Colour **terracotta** Alt. colours **yes** Width **52cm/20½in** Length **10m/11yd** Repeat – Price ★

1 **Coloroll/Firenze Texture 27-109B** Colour **buttermilk** Alt. colours **yes** Width **52cm/20½in** Length **10m/11yd** Repeat **64cm/25in** Price ★

2 **De Gournay/"E" Red Silk** Colour **red** Alt. colours **yes** Width **93cm/36in** Length **3m/3⅓yd** Repeat – Price ★★★ 🖌

3 **Fardis/San Marco/Les Rouges 85800** Colour **031** Alt. colours **yes** Width **70cm/27½in** Length **10m/11yd** Repeat **40cm/15¾in** Price ★

8

9

7 **Harlequin/Arc** Colour **45123**
Alt. colours **yes** Width **52cm/
20½in** Length **10m/11yd**
Repeat – Price ★

8 **Nobilis/Tassili TAS218** Colour
gold Alt. colours **yes** Width
58cm/22¾in Length **10m/
11yd** Repeat – Price ★

9 **Harlequin/Navari** Colour
45802 Alt. colours **yes** Width
52cm/20½in Length **10m/
11yd** Repeat **52cm/20½in**
Price ★

10 **Osborne & Little/Adagio
W1444/05** Colour **yellow**
Alt. colours **yes** Width **52cm/
20½in** Length **10m/11yd**
Repeat – Price ★

11 **Crowson/Nimbus** Colour
45 Alt. colours **yes** Width
53cm/21in Length **10m/
11yd** Repeat **52cm/20½in**
Price ★

11

12 **Ornamenta/Pompeiian OMP500**
Colour **black** Alt. colours **yes**
Width **65cm/25½in** Length
10m/11yd Repeat –
Price ★★★★★

13 **Paint and Paper Library/David
Oliver/Stardust** Colour **brick**
Alt. colours **yes** Width **52cm/
20½in** Length **10m/11yd**
Repeat **53cm/21in**
Price ★

13

Plains

Over the centuries, but particularly since the mid-19th century, wallpapers produced in imitation of plain textiles have proved just as popular as those simulating the appearance of wood and stone (see page 208).

Favoured "fabrics" during this period have included canvas, cambric, calico, hessian, tweed, seersuckers, moiré silks and lurex. In many cases the simulation is achieved by flat-printing the weave and subtle gradations of colour that characterize the fabrics. Screen-printing and photogravure have proved highly suitable for simulating texture, the latter achieving this *trompe l'oeil* effect by building up the finish with a series of small coloured dots of varying degrees of opacity (see page 281).

However, some of the *faux* fabrics produced – notably pile fabrics such as velvet and corduroy – have actually been textured, either by embossing the paper or by flocking it, while other fabric papers, such as Korean and European grass cloths (see page 207) are textured in their own right.

1 **Today Interiors/FX/Linen FXV345** Colour **8** Alt. colours **yes** Width **53cm/21in** Length **10m/11yd** Repeat – Price ★

2 **Graham & Brown 11527** Colour **blue** Alt. colours **yes** Width **52cm/20½in** Length **10m/11yd** Repeat – Price ★

3 **Today Interiors/FX/Basket Weave FXV341** Colour **9** Alt. colours **yes** Width **53cm/21in** Length **10m/11yd** Repeat – Price ★

4 **Jane Churchill/Eliot JY60W-04** Colour **blue** Alt. colours **yes** Width **52cm/20½in** Length **10m/11yd** Repeat – Price ★

5 **Ornamenta/Pompeiian OMP508** Colour **blue** Alt. colours **yes** Width **65cm/25½in** Length **10m/11yd** Repeat – Price ★★★★★

6 **Today Interiors/Zaniah ZW283** Colour **6** Alt. colours **yes** Width **53cm/21in** Length **10m/11yd** Repeat – Price ★

7 **Today Interiors/Zaniah ZW2821** Colour **1** Alt. colours **yes** Width **53cm/21in** Length **10m/11yd** Repeat – Price ★

8 **Crowson/Eclipse/Moonshine** Colour **50** Alt. colours **yes** Width **52cm/20½in** Length **10m/11yd** Repeat – Price ★

9 **Crowson/Willowmead** Colour **40** Alt. colours **yes** Width **52cm/20½in** Length **10m/11yd** Repeat – Price ★

10 **Cole & Son/Jaspé 57/2513** Colour **aqua** Alt. colours **yes** Width **52cm/20½in** Length **10m/11yd** Repeat – Price ★

11 J.W. Bollom/Brushed Suede
Colour **purple** Alt. colours **yes**
Width **138cm/54in** Length **10m/
11yd** Repeat – Price ★★

12 Ornamenta/Pompeiian OMP509
Colour **green** Alt. colours **yes**
Width **65cm/25½in** Length
10m/11yd Repeat –
Price ★★★★★

13 Graham & Brown 11523 Colour
purple Alt. colours **yes** Width
52cm/20½in Length **10m/
11yd** Repeat – Price ★

**14 Today Interiors/Samadhi
SAW305** Colour **2** Alt. colours
yes Width **53cm/21in** Length
10m/11yd Repeat – Price ★

15 Anna French/Eden/Galiska
Colour **GALNW072** Alt. colours
yes Width **52cm/20½in** Length
10m/11yd Repeat **64cm/25in**
Price ★

16 Mauny/Faux Marbres FM14
Colour **pink** Alt. colours **yes**
Width **56cm/22in** Length
10m/11yd Repeat –
Price ★★★ 🖌

17 Sheila Coombes/Wray W612
Colour **5** Alt. colours **yes**
Width **53cm/21in** Length
10m/11yd Repeat –
Price ★★★★

**18 Today Interiors/FX/Papyrus
FXV340** Colour **2** Alt. colours
yes Width **53cm/21in** Length
10m/11yd Repeat –
Price ★

Motif Wallpapers

The vast catalogue of motifs that wallpaper designers have been able to draw on has accumulated since the late Middle Ages as oriental, Asian and African styles of ornament have gradually been added to those of European origin. In addition, the types of motif favoured at different periods have invariably reflected the cultural, aesthetic and political preoccupations of the time.

For example, heraldic imagery remained much in evidence during the early Renaissance, and resurfaced during the Gothic Revival of the 19th century. Classical motifs began to appear during the Renaissance, and were added to and refined until the mid-19th century as knowledge of ancient Greek and Roman civilizations increased. Chinese motifs were adopted as European fascination with the Orient developed through trade from the late 17th century onward. Egyptian motifs were assimilated during Napoleon's military campaigns in the early 19th century and, during the 20th century, Cubist, Pop Art and Constructivist imagery found its way on to wallpapers

LEFT This grand, 19th-century American dining room displays the papered tripartite division of walls – frieze, field and dado – that was the height of fashion in reception rooms during this period. The ceiling is also compartmentalized with complementary papers in imitation of polychromatic plaster mouldings. The motifs, which include stars and shells, are of classical origin.

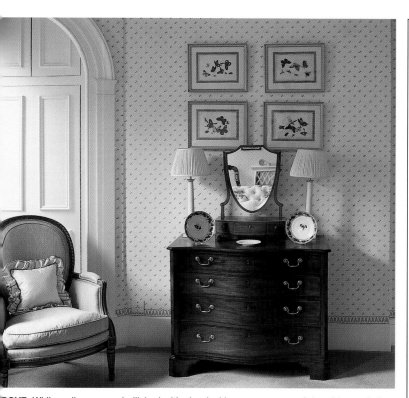

While wallpapers embellished with classical imagery were much in evidence during e late 18th and early 19th century, patterns made up of small, regularly spaced leaf motifs, milar in appearance to medieval powdered ornament, were also fashionable.

WATTS OF WESTMINSTER

The British architects G.F. Bodley, Thomas Garner and Gilbert Scott the Younger founded Watts & Company in 1874 to produce wallpapers, textiles, needlework and furniture in the Gothic Revival and early English Renaissance style – furnishings they were unable to obtain elsewhere. Many of their hand-blocked wallpapers were inspired by A.W.N. Pugin's Gothic Revival designs, of which this diaper-patterned paper with floral motifs is a typical example. It is representative of what was to become the accepted decorative style of the Church of England and the British Establishment.

KEY DESIGNS

1 Highly conventionalized leaves and flowers, combined with repeat geometric motifs in imitation of Islamic tiles, featured on many late Victorian papers, notably those by Christopher Dresser.

2 The stylized, three-petalled lily flower – or fleur-de-lis – is an heraldic motif that has been in widespread use since the Middle Ages. It appeared on many 19th-century Gothic Revival papers.

3 An heraldic symbol, also much used in Islamic ornament, the star has often appeared on papers, notably in Regency England and in America during the early years of independence.

4 Animal motifs, such as those derived from heraldic ornament, were frequently depicted on papers in 18th-century, Neo-classical and Victorian interiors. The lion is a symbol of strength and pride.

5 Medieval and early Renaissance motifs, such as the rose and the coronet, appeared on many Gothic Revival papers of the 19th century. This example was designed by A.W.N. Pugin.

6 Etruscan motifs of urns, festoons, scrolling leaf forms and palmettes were discovered in Pompeiian wall paintings in the mid-18th century and were popularized in England by Robert Adam.

1 **Bradbury & Bradbury/Algernon AGW** Colour **210** Alt. colours **yes** Width **68.5cm/27in** Length **4.5m/5yd** Repeat **34.5cm/ 13½in** Price ★★★ ♣

2 **Graham & Brown 12835** Colour **red** Alt. colours **yes** Width **52cm/20½in** Length **10m/11yd** Repeat **16cm/6¼in** Price ★

3 **Watts Of Westminster/Cleopatra Star W0012** Colour **Llewellyn** Alt. colours **yes** Width **54cm/21¼in** Length **10m/11yd** Repeat **8cm/3in** Price ★

4 **Zuber/Documents III/Lions 40028** Colour **gris et vert** Alt. colours **yes** Width **47cm/ 18¼in** Length **10m/11yd** Repeat **23cm/ 9in** Price ★★★ ♣

5 **Watts of Westminster/Tudor Badge W0058-04/B11** Colour **14** Alt. colours **yes** Width **52cm/20½in** Length **10m/ 11yd** Repeat **13cm/5in** Price ★

6 **Laura Ashley/Chaville 3167 759** Colour **raspberry and gold** Alt. colours **yes** Width **52cm/20½in** Length **10m/11yd** Repeat **64cm/25in** Price ★

Motifs: **Pre-19th century**

The most commonly used motifs on late 15th- and 16th-century papers were heraldic and floral, and were mainly woodcut-printed or stencilled. Typical of the heraldic imagery were coats-of-arms, emblems, cyphers and fleurs-de-lis, while notable flowers and plant forms included Tudor roses, anemones, columbines, thistles, chestnuts and acorns, stylized pomegranates and pinecones derived from European damasks. On many papers these motifs were applied to plain grounds, but on others they were printed on *faux*-marble grounds or framed by simple diaper patterns. Heraldic motifs and stylized plant forms remained fashionable during the 17th century. Naturalistic flowers, fruits, caterpillars and butterflies, as found on "Spanish stitch" textiles, were also in evidence, as were classical motifs, such as cupids, putti, vases and urns. Classical imagery remained popular throughout the 18th century, when it also included eagles, dolphins, masks, rosettes, griffins and architectural components inspired by archaeological discoveries at Herculaneum and Pompeii. Also often found in the late 17th and 18th century were motifs taken from oriental pictorials; these included pagodas, dragons and exotic birds and flowers (*see* pages 132–133).

1 **Graham & Brown 12842** Colour **gold** Alt. colours **yes** Width **52cm/20½in** Length **10m/11yd** Repeat **2cm/¾in** Price ★

2 **Hamilton Weston/Archway House** Colour **white, green and black on grey** Alt. colours **yes** Width **52cm/20½in** Length **10m/11yd** Repeat **9cm/3½in** Price ★★ ♣

3 **Elizabeth Eaton/Saighton** Colour **No. 4** Alt. colours **yes** Width **57cm/22½in** Length **10m/11yd** Repeat **5cm/2in** Price ★★

4 **Cole & Son/Temple Newsam** Colour **special** Alt. colours **yes** Width **52cm/20½in** Length **10m/11yd** Repeat **54cm/21½in** Price ★★★ ♣

1

2

3

4

5 Hamilton Weston/Guilloche BD43 Colour **document** Alt. colours **yes** Width **4cm/1½in** Length **10m/11yd** Repeat – Price ★ ♣

6 The Design Archives/Delphi 58020 Colour **3** Alt. colours **yes** Width **52cm/20½in** Length **10m/11yd** Repeat **4.5cm/1¾in** Price ★

7 Hamilton Weston/Embroidery BD21 Colour **grey** Alt. colours **yes** Width **4cm/1½in** Length **10m/11yd** Repeat – Price ★ ♣

8 Anna French/Eden/Gobi Colour **GOBNW044** Alt. colours **yes** Width **52cm/20½in** Length **10m/11yd** Repeat **4cm/1½in** Price ★

9 Ornamenta/Gothick Shadow GTK 408 Colour **beige** Alt. colours **yes** Width **52cm/20½in** Length **10m/11yd** Repeat **30cm/11¾in** Price ★★★★★ ♣

10 Laura Ashley/Embleton Border 1045 111 Colour **brick** Alt. colours **no** Width **13cm/5in** Length **10m/11yd** Repeat **19.5cm/7¾in** Price ★

11 Zoffany/Brittany 36BY03 Colour **03** Alt. colours **yes** Width **52cm/20½in** Length **10m/11yd** Repeat **8cm/3in** Price ★

Motifs: Early 19th century

Many of the early 19th-century papers patterned with repeat motifs were printed in Britain, where, unlike in France, a stringent government tax based on the weight of the wallpaper inhibited the production of large pictorial designs that required heavier paper. The majority of motif patterns that were produced for the French Empire, English Regency and American Federal interiors of the first 30 years of the century were derived from the classical vocabulary of ornament, particularly Roman and Etruscan. Egyptian motifs, including scarabs, sphinxes and lotus flowers, were also much in evidence after the Peninsular War fought between France and England.

Typical Roman motifs, popular in America and Europe (especially in France under the rule of Napoleon Bonaparte), included laurel, oak and olive wreaths, rosettes, arrows and lances, winged torches, lions, eagles and griffins. Favoured Etruscan motifs – which were in fact ancient Greek in origin – included palm leaves, anthemions, festoons, vases, medallions and chimeras, while Egyptian influence was evident in lotus flowers, scarabs and sphinxes. Also liked during this period were *trompe l'oeil* border papers made in imitation of acanthus leaf, Greek key, rope, dentil and egg-and-dart plaster or stucco mouldings.

1

2

3

4

1 **Alexander Beauchamp/Egg and Dart Border** Colour **grey** Alt. colours **yes** Width **6.5cm/2½in** Length **25m/27½yd** Repeat **5cm/2in** Price ★★★★ ♣

2 **G.P. & J. Baker/Keystone Border W0122-02** Colour **02** Alt. colours **yes** Width **6cm/2½in** Length **10m/11yd** Repeat **8cm/3in** Price ★

3 **Zuber/Documents III/Petits Lauriers 40084** Colour **JSD** Alt. colours **yes** Width **47cm/18½in** Length **10m/11yd** Repeat **55cm/21½in** Price ★★★

4 **Laura Ashley/Burgess Border 1635 275** Colour **gold** Alt. colours **yes** Width **13cm/5in** Length **10m/11yd** Repeat **8cm/3in** Price ★

5 **Zuber/Document III 40066** Colour **gold** Alt. colours **yes** Width **47cm/18½in** Length **10m/11yd** Repeat **60cm/23¾in** Price ★★★★★ ♣

6 **Laura Ashley/Lexington Border 5417 522** Colour **gold** Alt. colours **yes** Width **8cm/3in** Length **10m/11yd** Repeat **6.5cm/2½in** Price ★

7 **Hamilton Weston/Anthemion Border** Colour **beige** Alt. colours **yes** Width **4cm/1½in** Length **10m/11yd** Repeat – Price ★ ♣

5

6

7

8 Graham & Brown 91204 Colour **terracotta** Alt. colours **yes** Width **13cm/5in** Length **5m/5½yd** Repeat – Price ★

9 Hamilton Weston/Green Park Colour **210** Alt. colours **yes** Width **52cm/20½in** Length **10m/11yd** Repeat **4cm/1½in** Price ★★

10 Jane Churchill/Colbrooke Sprig JY58W-07 Colour **yellow** Alt. colours **yes** Width **52cm/20½in** Length **10m/11yd** Repeat **4.5cm/1¾in** Price ★

11 G.P. & J. Baker/Heraldic Damask W0113-02 Colour **02** Alt. colours **yes** Width **52cm/20½in** Length **10m/11yd** Repeat **53cm/21in** Price ★

10

12

13

12 Hamilton Weston/Regency Rosette Colour **mint green on pale green** Alt. colours **yes** Width **52cm/20½in** Length **10m/11yd** Repeat **5cm/2in** Price ★★ ♣

13 Cole & Son/Victorian Star 55/3017/PR Colour **gold on red** Alt. colours **yes** Width **52cm/20½in** Length **10m/11yd** Repeat **4.5cm/1¾in** Price ★

14 Zoffany/Blois V322 Colour **01** Alt. colours **yes** Width **52cm/20½in** Length **10m/11yd** Repeat **9cm/3½in** Price ★

15 Graham & Brown 91186 Colour **beige** Alt. colours **yes** Width **18cm/7in** Length **5m/5½yd** Repeat – Price ★

14

15

Motifs: **Mid-19th century**

The majority of classical motifs that had appeared on wallpapers during the early 19th century also found favour in the Renaissance and Baroque Revival interiors fashionable on both sides of the Atlantic around the middle of the century. In contrast to these predominantly naturalistic and often "three-dimensionalized" classical motifs were the stylized, flat motifs on Gothic Revival wallpapers throughout Europe – notably those devised by influential English designers such as A.W.N. Pugin (*see* opposite) and Owen Jones.

Conventionalized plant forms, often presented within a geometrical pattern structure, lay at the heart of many of Pugin's and Jones's designs. However, while Pugin drew heavily and precisely from the Gothic and heraldic vocabulary of ornament prevalent during the Middle Ages and the early Renaissance, Jones's sources were more wide-ranging; they were primarily oriental – Chinese, Far Eastern, Persian, Indian, Arabic and Moorish – while also embracing medieval imagery and primitive art.

Graham & Brown 11645 Colour **yellow** Alt. colours **yes** Width **52cm/20½in** Length **10m/11yd** Repeat **32cm/12½in** Price ★

Hodsoll McKenzie/Fleur de Lys 504/631 Colour **yellow** Alt. colours **yes** Width **52cm/20½in** Length **10m/11yd** Repeat **7.5cm/2¾in** Price ★

Watts of Westminster/Pineapple W0039-03/I12 Colour **Seton** Alt. colours **yes** Width **54cm/21½in** Length **10m/11yd** Repeat **27cm/10½in** Price ★★

Zuber/Chateau de Blois/Alcove Chambre de la Reine 9222 Colour **gold, terracotta and grey** Alt. colours **no** Width **51cm/20in** Length **9m/10yd** Repeat **88cm/34½in** Price ★★★

Cole & Son/The Strawberry OEW0141 Colour **white** Alt. colours **yes** Width **52cm/20½in** Length **10m/11yd** Repeat **37cm/14½in** Price ★★★★ ♣

Laura Ashley/Farnley Border 155 241 Colour **dark brick** Alt. colours **no** Width **9cm/3½in** Length **10m/11yd** Repeat **–** Price ★

Sandberg/Erik 933 Colour **24** Alt. colours **yes** Width **3.5cm/1¼in** Length **10m/11yd** Repeat **22cm/8½in** Price ★

Cole & Son/Block 015 Colour **yellow on green** Alt. colours **yes** Width **52cm/20½in** Length **10m/11yd** Repeat **–** Price ★★★ ♣

Watts of Westminster/Rose and Coronet Colour **Stuart** Alt. colours **yes** Width **54cm/21¼in** Length **10m/11yd** Repeat **45cm/17½in** Price ★★

Hamilton Weston/Uppark Mock Emboss Colour **document** Alt. colours **yes** Width **52cm/20½in** Length **10m/11yd** Repeat **48cm/19in** Price ★★ ♣

Watts of Westminster/Shrewsbury W0050 Colour **Walton** Alt. colours **yes** Width **54cm/21¼in** Length **10m/11yd** Repeat **47cm/18½in** Price ★★

Osbourne & Little/Durbar/Rajura W1012 Colour **03** Alt. colours **yes** Width **52cm/20½in** Length **10m/11yd** Repeat **20cm/8in** Price ★

Zoffany/Gothic Flower 36GF04 Colour **04** Alt. colours **yes** Width **52cm/20½in** Length **10m/11yd** Repeat **32cm/12½in** Price ★

PUGIN PAPERS

The influential English architect A.W.N. Pugin (1812–52) designed hundreds of wallpapers in the mid-19th century, notably for the New Palace of Westminster, in London, England. Dismissive of eclecticism, and scornful of *trompe l'oeil* papers for creating "dishonest" illusions of depth on two-dimensional surfaces, his flat and conventionalized treatments of imagery were derived from Gothic art. Typical patterns included heraldic emblems and stylized fruit and foliage forms found on medieval manuscripts and textiles, as well as geometric patterns based on medieval tiles and stencilling.

Watts of Westminster/Trellis W0056-06/I12 Colour **Padgett** Alt. colours **yes** Width **54cm/21¼in** Length **10m/11yd** Repeat **18cm/7in** Price ★★

Watts of Westminster/Triad W5057-15/A13 Colour **Amsterdam** Alt. colours **yes** Width **54cm/21¼in** Length **10m/11yd** Repeat **80cm/31¼in** Price ★★

Motifs: **Late 19th century**

The tremendous variety of motifs employed on wallpapers during the last three decades of the 19th century reflected the eclectic mixture of decorative styles favoured at this time in both Europe and America. Classical and Pompeiian motifs typical of the 18th century (*see* pages 214–215) re-emerged, while A.W.N. Pugin's Gothic Revival imagery endured, especially in Britain, and the oriental- and Moresque-based patterns of Owen Jones remained internationally influential.

However, the most distinctive, and in many respects the most innovative, wallpapers of the late 19th century were produced by designers working under the umbrellas of the Arts and Crafts, Aesthetic or Art Nouveau movements. Many Arts and Crafts patterned wallpapers, particularly those devised by William Morris, were characterized by stylized, rhythmical plant forms – usually English, floral and medieval in origin. Conventionalized as well as naturalistic plant forms, together with exotic bird and insect motifs, were also an important feature of both Aesthetic and Art Nouveau papers, and were inspired not only by medieval imagery but also by Renaissance, Rococo, Chinese and, especially, Japanese styles of ornament.

1 **Zuber/Documents III/Fleur de Lys 4805 BRD** Colour **blue** Alt. colours **yes** Width **47cm/18½in** Length **10m/11yd** Repeat **33cm/13in** Price ★★★

2 **Hamilton Weston/Victorian Leaf Quatrefoil** Colour **cream, grey and grey/blue** Alt. colours **yes** Width **52cm/20½in** Length **10m/11yd** Repeat **15cm/6in** Price ★★ ♣

3 **Zoffany/Maple V43805** Colour **05** Alt. colours **yes** Width **52cm/20½in** Length **10m/11yd** Repeat – Price ★

4 **Zoffany/Lennel BLY02** Colour **02** Alt. colours **yes** Width **52cm/20½in** Length **10m/11yd** Repeat **32cm/12½in** Price ★

5 **G.P. & J. Baker/Fleur de Lys W0097-09** Colour **red** Alt. colours **yes** Width **52cm/20½in** Length **10m/11yd** Repeat **5cm/2in** Price ★

6

7

8

**Bradbury & Bradbury/Roland
RLW-130** Colour **130** Alt.
colours **yes** Width **68cm/
26¾in** Length **4.5m/5yd**
Repeat **27cm/10½in**
Price ★★ 🖌

**Laura Ashley/Ashton 3162
283** Colour **plum and natural**
Alt. colours **yes** Width
52cm/20½in Length **10m/11yd**
Repeat **16cm/6¼in** Price ★

**Watts of Westminster/Gaheris
WW0017-02/E12** Colour
Garbot Alt. colours **yes**
Width **47cm/18½in** Length
10m/11yd Repeat **19cm/
7½in** Price ★★

**Cole & Son/Butterflies
54/4717/PR** Colour **red
on green** Alt. colours **yes**
Width **52cm/20½in** Length
10m/11yd Repeat **30.5cm/
12in** Price ★

9

**10 Today Interiors/Odonata/
Dragonfly ODW 3654**
Colour **4** Alt. colours **yes**
Width **53cm/21in** Length
10m/11yd Repeat **52cm/20½in**
Price ★

11 Zoffany/Florentine Lily ZV0503
Colour **03** Alt. colours **yes**
Width **52cm/20½in** Length
10m/11yd Repeat **8cm/3in**
Price ★

11

19th century

WALLPAPERS: *MOTIFS* **221**

Motifs: Early 20th century

Although plant-form motifs were generally excluded from Modernist designs, they were widely employed in the other fashionable decorative styles of the early 20th century. For example, Art Nouveau wallpapers featured roots, stems and elongated blooms, while small leaves, fruits and cup-shaped blossoms appeared on Deutscher Werkbund papers. Arts and Crafts papers were characterized by conventionalized flowers and leaves, while early Art Deco designs incorporated stylized floral motifs (see pages 124–125). Many wallpapers were also produced in imitation of 18th- and 19th-century floral chintzes. Even the highly mathematical Cubist-patterned papers of the 1920s and 1930s were sometimes softened with small flower or leaf motifs.

Egyptian motifs (see opposite); heraldic imagery on Tudor Revival papers; and bows, swags, shells, insects and architectural scrollwork inspired by 18th-century, French Rococo and Neo-classical decoration were all to be seen. The majority of other fashionable motifs were either geometric or abstract in form. These included medieval and oriental diaper patterns, the stepped shapes and overlapping squares and oblongs of Art Deco, and the shaded circles, triangles and rectangles inspired by Constructivist principles of painting.

1

1 Graham & Brown/51506 Colour **beige** Alt. colours **yes** Width **52cm/20½in** Length **10m/11yd** Repeat **53cm/21in** Price ★

2 Bradbury & Bradbury/Neo-Grecian Dado NGD-210 Colour **210** Alt. colours **yes** Width **69cm/27in** Length **to order** Repeat **35cm/13¾in** Price ★★★ ♣

3 Coloroll/Ironwork Motif 27-026 Colour **terracotta** Alt. colours **yes** Width **52cm/20½in** Length **10m/11yd** Repeat **64cm/25in** Price ★

4 Alexander Beauchamp/Florence Colour **red, gold and black** Alt. colours **yes** Width **53cm/21in** Length **10m/11yd** Repeat **76cm/30in** Price ★★★ ♣

4

FINISHING LINCRUSTA

Machine-embossed Lincrusta papers – a composite of linseed oil, gum, resins and wood-pulp on canvas (see page 239) – provided a substantially cheaper alternative to traditional wood, plaster, leather and tile panelling and mouldings. Lincrusta was particularly suited to avant-garde use – the example shown here was designed for dado panelling and features a stylized flower and foliage pattern typical of early 20th-century Art Nouveau. Its *faux* tile finish was created by lightly distressing a blue-green oil-based glaze, which was applied over a bronze-gold basecoat.

IHDG/Edwardian Dado RD1950 Colour **white** Alt. colours **no** Width **61cm/24in** Length **102cm/40in** Repeat – Price ★★★ 🔲

EGYPTIAN MOTIFS

Wallpapers patterned with Egyptian motifs first became fashionable in early 19th-century Neo-classical interiors, particularly in France and Britain, after Napoleon Bonaparte's military campaigns in Egypt. They also appeared on British wallpapers during the last quarter of the 19th century as the British Empire consolidated its rule over Egypt. During the first half of the 20th century, Egyptian motifs, such as scarabs, sphinxes, lotus leaves and (as shown here) palm trees and camels, enjoyed a further revival. Egyptian elements and features were also frequently included in Art Deco schemes of the period.

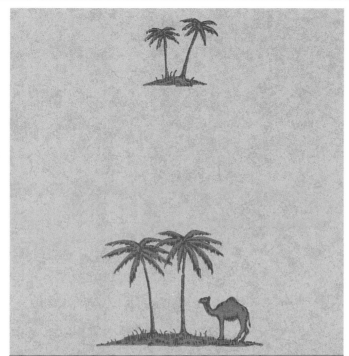

Andrew Martin/Khartoum Colour **red** Alt. colours **no** Width **52cm/20½in** Length **10m/11yd** Repeat **26cm/10¼in** Price ★

Alexander Beauchamp/Art Deco Fans Colour **special** Alt. colours **yes** Width **53cm/ 21in** Length **10m/11yd** Repeat **55cm/21½in** Price ★★★ ♣

Cole & Son/Alma Trellis 55/3062/PR Colour **yellow and gold** Alt. colours **yes** Width **52cm/20½in** Length **10m/11yd** Repeat **13.5cm/ 5¼in** Price ★

Nicholas Herbert/Sherwood W03-08 Colour **beige** Alt. colours **yes** Width **52cm/ 20½in** Length **10m/11yd** Repeat **13cm/5in** Price ★

8

9

10

8 Graham & Brown 13105 Colour **white** Alt. colours **no** Width **52cm/20½in** Length **10m/11yd** Repeat **8cm/3in** Price ★

9 Osborne & Little/Chantilly VW1223/04 Colour **terracotta** Alt. colours **yes** Width **52cm/ 20½in** Length **10m/11yd** Repeat **11cm/4¼in** Price ★

10 Zuber/Documents III/Grandes Abeilles 30118V0 Colour **green** Alt. colours **yes** Width **47cm/18½in** Length **10m/ 11yd** Repeat **24cm/9½in** Price ★★★

7

Motifs: **Late 20th–early 21st century**

During the 1950s and 1960s, wallpapers embellished with geometric and abstract motifs retained their popularity from earlier in the century. Apart from Cubist-inspired squares and oblongs, motif designs of the 1950s included diamonds, suns, stars, checks, "worm-casts", prisms, sound waves, sketchy squiggles and organic shapes based on amoeba and crystalline structures. In the 1960s, sunbursts, giant circles and even flying-saucer shapes appeared.

Plant-form motifs also remained prevalent during this period, especially in America and Scandinavia, where many designers were preoccupied with bringing nature indoors. Papers of this genre, designed to appeal to traditionalists, displayed patterns such as large-scale tropical flowers or leaves, single roses in cartouches, and Victorian sprigs or stylized flowers on diaper grounds derived from Persian art and ceramics, as well as sinuous Art Nouveau-style roots, stems and elongated blooms. More modern designs included wild strawberries, marine fauna and hogweed, while papers intended for kitchens featured not only fruits and vegetables, but also kitchenalia, recipes and bottles of "foreign" wine – the latter reflecting the substantial increase in international leisure travel at this time.

1

2

4

3

5

6

1 **Coloroll/Firenze Motif 27-108** Colour **beige** Alt. colours **yes** Width **52cm/20½in** Length **10m/11yd** Repeat **64cm/25in** Price ★

2 **Today Interiors/Zaniah ZW2800** Colour **0** Alt. colours **yes** Width **53cm/21in** Length **10m/11yd** Repeat **53cm/21in** Price ★

3 **Zoffany/Star 36ST05** Colour **05** Alt. colours **yes** Width **52cm/20½in** Length **10m/11yd** Repeat **32cm/12½in** Price ★

4 **Graham & Brown 91185** Colour **green** Alt. colours **yes** Width **18cm/7in** Length **5m/5½yd** Repeat – Price ★

5 **Sandberg/Mona 941** Colour **14** Alt. colours **yes** Width **3cm/1¼in** Length **10m/11yd** Repeat **9cm/3½in** Price ★

6 **Zoffany/Palm NC9802** Colour **peach** Alt. colours **yes** Width **52cm/20½in** Length **10m/11yd** Repeat – Price ★

7 **Today Interiors/Aymara/Saffir/
   AYW339** Colour **2** Alt. colours
   yes Width **53cm/21in** Length
   10m/11yd Repeat **52cm/20½in**
   Price ★

8 **Zoffany/Coppice WAL0100**
   Colour **2** Alt. colours **yes**
   Width **52cm/20½in** Length
   10m/11yd Repeat **52.5cm/
   20¾in** Price ★

8

9   **Zoffany/Blois Plain V43005**
    Colour **05** Alt. colours **yes**
    Width **52cm/20½in** Length
    10m/11yd Repeat **8.5cm/3¼in**
    Price ★

10 **Harlequin/Charm** Colour
    60307 Alt. colours **yes** Width
    52cm/20½in Length **10m/11yd**
    Repeat **2.5cm/1in** Price ★

11 **Laura Ashley/Rosie Border**
    Colour **lavender** Alt. colours
    yes Width **13cm/5in** Length
    10m/11yd Repeat **13cm/5in**
    Price ★

12 **Sandberg/Albin 711** Colour
    24 Alt. colours **yes** Width
    53cm/21in Length **10m/11yd**
    Repeat **32cm/12½in**
    Price ★

11

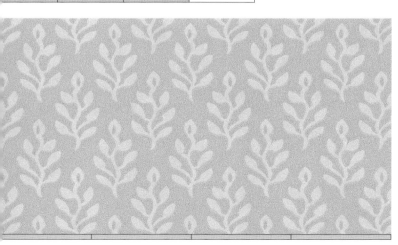

12

20th & 21st century

Motifs: Late 20th–early 21st century

While many new designs have been introduced since the 1970s, there has also been a major revival of interest in the wallpaper patterns of earlier periods. Favoured motifs have consequently been drawn from a rich catalogue of international ornament accumulated since the Middle Ages (*see* pages 212–225), with much of that imagery consisting of plant forms (especially floral motifs), geometric or abstract shapes, various emblems and imitations of architectural mouldings.

In many cases wallpaper companies have reproduced the original designs using traditional dyes and the original method of printing. In other cases, however, designers have adapted and updated the motifs by stylizing and recolouring them to suit a more modern aesthetic. Generally, this reworking has taken the form of a reduction in the numbers of colours used in any one design or pattern. There has also been a distinct favouring of colours that, although saturated, have a noticeably soft, chalky appearance.

1

2

1 **Today Interiors/Zaniah/Aphelion ZW280** Colour **1** Alt. colours **yes** Width **53cm/21in** Length **10m/11yd** Repeat **10.5cm/4in** Price ★

2 **Osborne & Little/Durbur/Catalp W1010** Colour **06** Alt. colours **yes** Width **52cm/20½in** Length **10m/11yd** Repeat **21cm/8¼in** Price ★

3 **Today Interiors/Aymara/Maya AYW340** Colour **3** Alt. colours **yes** Width **53.5cm/21in** Length **10m/11yd** Repeat **53.5cm/21in** Price ★

4

4 **Anna French/Chalice** Colour **CHAWP02** Alt. colours **yes** Width **52cm/20½in** Length **10m/11yd** Repeat **46cm/18in** Price ★

5 **Harlequin/Navari** Colour **355908** Alt. colours **yes** Width **52cm/20½in** Length **10m/11yd** Repeat **17.5cm/7in** Price ★

6 **Osborne & Little/Sundance Border B854/04** Colour **blue** Alt. colours **yes** Width **11cm/4¼in** Length **10m/11yd** Repeat – Price ★

7 **Designers Guild/Pushpa P243/03** Colour **ultramarine** Alt. colours **yes** Width **53cm/21in** Length **10m/11yd** Repeat **53cm/21in** Price ★

8 **Today Interiors/Samadhi/Tulipa SAW305** Colour **5** Alt. colours **yes** Width **53cm/21in** Length **10m/11yd** Repeat **26cm/10¼in** Price ★

5

6

7

8

9

10

11

Harlequin/Notebook Colour
35550 Alt. colours **yes** Width
52cm/20½in Length **10m/**
11yd Repeat **52cm/20½in**
Price ★

**Ornamenta/Elements/22 Carat
Gold Leaf** Colour **gold on
brown** Alt. colours **yes**
Width **50cm/19½in** Length
5m/5½yd Repeat **50cm/**
19½in Price ★★★★★ 👑

**Today Interiors/Samadhi/Arbus
SAW301** Colour **8** Alt. colours
yes Width **53cm/21in** Length
10m/11yd Repeat **26cm/**
10¼in Price ★

**Today Interiors/Aymara/Oasis
AYW342** Colour **0** Alt. colours
yes Width **53cm/21in** Length
10m/11yd Repeat **53cm/21in**
Price ★

Mulberry/Royal Palm FG038
Colour **H101** Alt. colours
yes Width **52cm/20½in**
Length **10m/11yd** Repeat
38cm/15in Price ★

**Jane Churchill/Book Eight/
Florian/Florian Leaf J034W-02**
Colour **green** Alt. colours **yes**
Width **52cm/20½in** Length
10m/11yd Repeat **20.5cm/**
8in Price ★

Anna French/Eden/Gobi Colour
GOBNW04 Alt. colours **yes**
Width **52cm/20½in** Length
10m/11yd Repeat **4cm/**
1½in Price ★

12

16

15

**16 Laura Ashley/Butterfly 3180
659** Colour **pink** Alt. colours
yes Width **26.5cm/10½in**
Length **10m/11yd** Repeat
26.5cm/10½in Price ★

17 Mulberry/Hedgerow FG037
Colour **S111** Alt. colours
yes Width **13cm/5in** Length
10m/11yd Repeat **13cm/5in**
Price ★

13   **14**   **17**

20th & 21st century

Floral Wallpapers

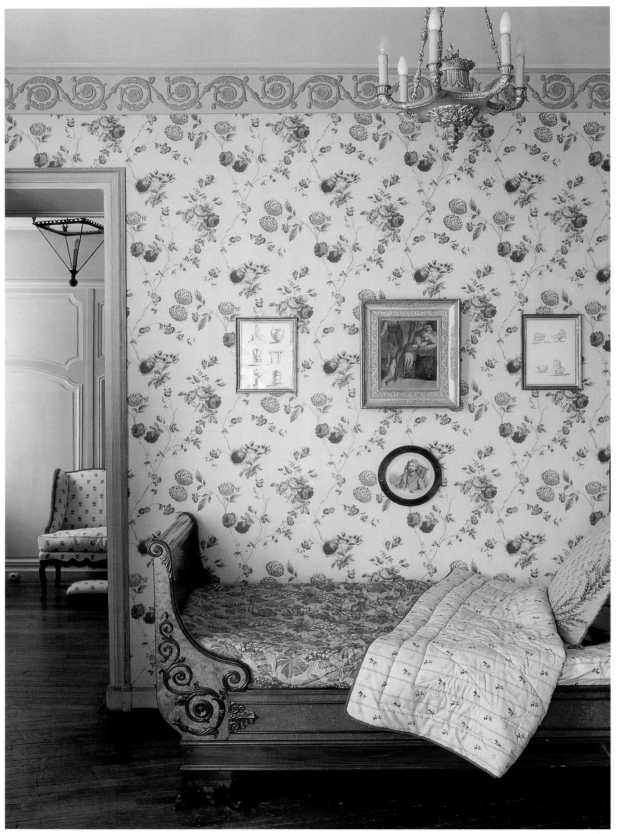

From the early Renaissance to the present day, flowers that are naturalistic and conventionalized in form have proved to be the most enduringly fashionable and universal form of imagery used on wallpapers. Only in the Modernist interiors of the first half of the 20th century were floral designs not prevalent.

Sources of inspiration for floral wallpaper patterns have been many and varied. For example, before the 19th century numerous papers replicated the floral designs found on textiles, particularly damasks and chintzes.

Throughout the 20th century and into the 21st, the wallpaper industry has avidly imitated the manner in which flowers have been depicted in fine art. Certain wallpaper designers have also produced floral patterns and motifs from their own observations of nature. However, the primary reference material for floral designs has been the pattern books and illustrated botanical studies that have been published since the 17th century, first in Europe and, later, also in America.

LEFT This provincial-style bedroom is in a late 18th-century Parisian townhouse. The wallpaper displays a naturalistic floral pattern printed in shades of red on a pale yellow ground. It echoes the other plant-form motifs on the bedding, and is typical of the horticultural and rustic imagery fashionable in many parts of Europe during the second half of the 18th century.

EMPIRE-STYLE FLORALS

This floral-patterned wallpaper is in a drawing room of the Jumel mansion, in New York, USA. The mansion was decorated and furnished in French Empire style during the 1820s after Madame Jumel returned from a trip to Paris with a collection of hand-blocked wallpapers and other furnishings that were considered the height of fashion and quality on both sides of the Atlantic. Naturalistic bouquets set against contrasting coloured grounds were among the most loved of Empire-style patterns.

KEY DESIGNS

1 Small repeats of native European flowers, such as larkspurs, roses, poppies, daisies, violets and anemones, were generally favoured over exotic oriental blooms in the late 18th century.

2 Uncomplicated floral patterns of delicately trailing flowers printed on pale grounds were very fashionable in France during the 1770s and 1780s, and remained popular until the 1840s.

3 Botanically accurate, large-scale floral patterns, characterized by realistic colours and subtle use of highlighting and shading, appeared in many Victorian interiors in the mid-19th century.

4 From the late 18th century onward, wallpaper manufacturers in both France and England have produced numerous floral-patterned papers that imitate *toile de Jouy* fabrics.

5 Since the early 18th century, many floral papers have been produced in imitation of floral-patterned, silk damask wall-hangings. This English example has a late 18th-century floral pattern.

6 Small repeat floral motifs are often used to embellish striped papers. This example is late 20th century, but floral-decorated stripes were also popular in the late 18th and early 19th century.

---

1 **Harlequin/Charm** Colour **30003** Alt. colours **yes** Width **52cm/20½in** Length **10m/11yd** Repeat **13cm/5in** Price ★

2 **Brunschwig & Fils/Georgette 16171-06** Colour **scarlet on white** Alt. colours **yes** Width **68.5cm/27in** Length **4.5m/5yd** Repeat **64cm/25in** Price ★★★★

3 **Nina Campbell/Zembla/Zembla NCW 2222/03** Colour **03** Alt. colours **yes** Width **52cm/20½in** Length **10m/11yd** Repeat **76cm/30in** Price ★

4 **Ornamenta/English Musick EMK702** Colour **blue** Alt. colours **yes** Width **53cm/21in** Length **10m/11yd** Repeat **92cm/36¼in** Price ★★ ♣

5 **Cole & Son/Pompadour/Cadora 58/1001** Colour **blue and cream** Alt. colours **yes** Width **52cm/20½in** Length **10m/11yd** Repeat **43cm/16¾in** Price ★★★★★

6 **Anna French/Daisy Rose Stripe** Colour **DAIWP077** Alt. colours **yes** Width **52cm/20½in** Length **10m/11yd** Repeat **64cm/25in** Price ★

Florals: Medieval to mid-18th century

Many of the black-and-white woodcut-printed papers of the late 16th and early 17th century featured floral patterns based on "black stitch" embroidery (black silk embroidery executed on a white ground). Sophisticated, stylized floral patterns derived from velvets and brocades were also highly fashionable during the 17th century (with many examples featuring additional hand-painted elements), as were naturalistically depicted flowers and fruit in imitation of "Spanish stitch" textiles.

Other 17th-century, floral-patterned papers of note displayed elaborate arrangements of flowers, such as tulips, narcissi, orchids and roses, set in classical vases and surrounded by stylized foliage and strapwork. Such designs were to remain in vogue for much of the 18th century, and became increasingly realistic as knowledge of plant forms grew (via illustrated pattern books) and methods of printing improved. Also fashionable in the first half of the 18th century were English flock papers styled in imitation of floral-patterned damasks, and Chinese and *chinoiserie* papers that displayed flowering shrubs, roses, chrysanthemums, poppies, peonies and bamboo, often accompanied by exotic birds and insects.

**1 Chameleon/Bayley Arms/
Acanthus** Colour **AND 019**
Alt. colours **no** Width **50cm/
19½in** Length **10m/11yd**
Repeat **50cm/19½in**
Price ★

2 Alexander Beauchamp/Ghintez
Colour **green** Alt. colours **yes**
Width **47cm/18½in** Length
10m/11yd Repeat **47cm/
18½in** Price ★★★ ♣

**3 Chameleon/Bayley Arms/
Damask** Colour **AND 009** Alt.
colours **yes** Width **53cm/21in**
Length **10m/11yd** Repeat
27cm/10½in Price ★

4 Alexander Beauchamp/Jacobean
Colour **special** Alt. colours
yes Width **39cm/15¼in** Length
10m/11yd Repeat **51cm/20in**
Price ★★★ ♣

**5 G.P. & J. Baker/Solomon's Seal
W0087-63** Colour **63** Alt.
colours **yes** Width **52cm/20½in**
Length **10m/11yd** Repeat
53cm/21in Price ★

3

2

4

5

6 **Sheila Coombes/Heversham W614** Colour **2** Alt. colours **yes** Width **53cm/21in** Length **10m/11yd** Repeat **53cm/21in** Price ★★★★

7 **Hamilton Weston/Twickenham** Colour **document grey, black and white on green** Alt. colours **yes** Width **52cm/20½in** Length **10m/11yd** Repeat **21cm/8¼in** Price ★★★ ♣

8 **Jane Churchill/Florian/Book Eight/Florian Damask J038W** Colour **02** Alt. colours **yes** Width **52cm/20½in** Length **10m/11yd** Repeat **41cm/16in** Price ★

9

9 **Alexander Beauchamp/Melton** Colour **green and white** Alt. colours **yes** Width **44cm/17in** Length **10m/11yd** Repeat **72.5cm/28½in** Price ★★★ ♣

10 **Nicholas Herbert/Bradenham W07** Colour **04 green and cream** Alt. colours **yes** Width **52cm/20½in** Length **10m/11yd** Repeat **27cm/10½in** Price ★

11 **Zoffany/Padova DWP3100** Colour **6** Alt. colours **yes** Width **68.5cm/27in** Length **10m/11yd** Repeat **51cm/20in** Price ★

12 **Brunschwig & Fils/Rêve du Papillon 12473.06** Colour **yellow** Alt. colours **yes** Width **69.5cm/27¼in** Length **4.5m/5yd** Repeat **98cm/38¾in** Price ★★★★ ♣

10

11

12

Florals: Late 18th century

Floral-patterned wallpapers, like floral-patterned textiles, were very fashionable in the second half of the 18th century. Chinese and European *chinoiserie* floral papers proved immensely popular, and many other papers displayed imagery that was half-Chinese and half-classical in origin – a typical example would combine oriental peacocks and parrots with classical vases of flowers.

Popular French papers included *papiers marbres* stencilled with floral patterns, floral flocks made from silk shearings in imitation of silk wall-hangings, floral arabesques (see page 247) and papers with patterns composed of flowers bound with ribbons. Fashionable English papers featured flowers with large petals, flowering bushes and diapered bouquets. Leading designers of the period included Jean-Baptiste Réveillon of France and the Englishman John Baptist Jackson. During this period, many papers by these designers, with others from France and Britain, were exported in large numbers to the increasingly prosperous American colonies.

1 Hamilton Weston/Mayfair 404 Colour **green** Alt. colours **yes** Width **52cm/20½in** Length **10m/11yd** Repeat **53cm/21in** Price ★

2 Jane Churchill/Country Garden/Book Seven/Rose Toile J026W Colour **02** Alt. colours **yes** Width **52cm/20½in** Length **10m/11yd** Repeat **17.5cm/7in** Price ★

3 Hamilton Weston/Kew Green Border Colour **pink, dark turquoise on cream** Alt. colours **yes** Width **6.5cm/2½in** Length **10m/11yd** Repeat **34cm/13½in** Price ★★★ ♣

4 Hamilton Weston/Kew Green Colour **pink, dark turquoise on cream** Alt. colours **yes** Width **50cm/19½in** Length **10m/11yd** Repeat **34cm/13½in** Price ★★★ ♣

5 Brunschwig & Fils/Suffield Arabesque 15690.06 Colour **white** Alt. colours **yes** Width **57cm/22½in** Length **4.5m/5yd** Repeat **55cm/21½in** Price ★★★★★ ♣

6 Zoffany/Qing Trellis WAL0600 Colour **1** Alt. colours **yes** Width **68cm/26¾in** Length **10m/11yd** Repeat **60cm/23¾in** Price ★

7 Brunschwig & Fils/Marianthi 13900.06 Colour **white** Alt. colours **yes** Width **68.5cm/27in** Length **4.5m/5yd** Repeat **68.5cm/27in** Price ★★★★★ ♣

8 Zoffany/Floraison Trail FRW030? Colour **7** Alt. colours **yes** Width **52cm/20½in** Length **10m/11yd** Repeat **64cm/25in** Price ★

FABRIC IMITATIONS

Many of the floral wallpapers that were produced during the 18th century derived their patterns from contemporary textiles – particularly Chinese silks, French and English printed floral chintzes and, above all, woven damasks and brocades. This is not surprising, given that during this period wallpapers were beginning to be employed as a less expensive alternative to textile wall-hangings in all but the grandest of houses. The paper shown here – a late 18th-century design – is an imitation of a typical stylized, floral-patterned damask (*see* pages 80–81).

Zoffany/Damask V2140 Colour **2** Alt. colours **yes** Width **52cm/20½in** Length **10m/11yd** Repeat **23cm/9in** Price ★

Zoffany/Floralie FRW0100 Colour **4** Alt. colours **yes** Width **52cm/20½in** Length **10m/11yd** Repeat **45.5cm/17¾in** Price ★

Zoffany/Tours DK0300 Colour **8** Alt. colours **yes** Width **68.5cm/27in** Length **10m/11yd** Repeat **64cm/25¼in** Price ★

Nobilis/Bagatelle Colour **BGL 316** Alt. colours **yes** Width **52cm/20½in** Length **10m/11yd** Repeat **52cm/20½in** Price ★

Nobilis/Bagatelle Colour **BGL 325** Alt. colours **yes** Width **52cm/20½in** Length **10m/11yd** Repeat **52cm/20½in** Price ★

Cole & Son/Paradise Tree 2630 1003 Colour **3** Alt. colours **yes** Width **52cm/20½in** Length **10m/11yd** Repeat **70cm/27½in** Price ★

9

14

14 Alexander Beauchamp/Genoa Colour **yellow** Alt. colours **yes** Width **53cm/21in** Length **10m/11yd** Repeat **72cm/28¼in** Price ★★★★ ♣

15 Cole & Son/Chippendale 58/1020/PR Colour **gold on coral** Alt. colours **yes** Width **52cm/20½in** Length **10m/11yd** Repeat **100cm/39¼in** Price ★★★

16 Zoffany/French/Bergère FWP4200 Colour **5** Alt. colours **yes** Width **52cm/20½in** Length **10m/11yd** Repeat **70cm/27½in** Price ★

18th century

15

1

12

13

16

Florals: Early 19th century

At the beginning of the 19th century, some British, French and American manufacturers produced stylized floral-patterned papers in imitation of fashionable glazed floral chintzes. More popular, however, were the naturalistically depicted floral patterns that had first come into vogue in the classical interiors of the late 18th century. Many of these were also inspired by contemporary textiles, such as elaborate floral-patterned silks.

The tendency to represent flowers in a naturalistic way, as opposed to conventionalizing them, became more marked as the century progressed. Apart from aesthetic considerations, the main factors that fuelled this greater realism were the publication of numerous illustrated botanical studies that provided designers with increasingly accurate reference material, and the development of new mineral dyes, including various oranges and greens, that closely resembled the vivid colours displayed in many natural plant forms. Also playing a part was the ever more sophisticated use of woodblock-printing (*see* opposite) to create subtle shading and "three-dimensionality" within patterns – a quality further, and literally, enhanced on the flocked papers that proved highly desirable during this period.

1 Hamilton Weston/Covent Garden Floral Colour **red on red** Alt. colours **yes** Width **52cm/ 20½in** Length **10m/11yd** Repeat **28.5cm/11in** Price ★★

2 Graham & Brown 51026 Colour **aubergine** Alt. colours **yes** Width **52cm/20½in** Length **10m/11yd** Repeat **53cm/ 21in** Price ★

3 Zoffany/Tulip Panel 326100 Colour **5** Alt. colours **yes** Width **52cm/20½in** Length **10m/11yd** Repeat **64cm/ 25in** Price ★

4 Hamilton Weston/Kingston Market Colour **8132** Alt. colours **yes** Width **53cm/ 21in** Length **10m/11yd** Repeat **26.5cm/10½in** Price ★★ 👑

5 Zoffany/Trianon 77010 Colour **03** Alt. colours **yes** Width **52cm/20½in** Length **10m/ 11yd** Repeat **64cm/25in** Price ★

6 Colefax and Fowler/Sudbury Park 7046/01 Colour **red on red** Alt. colours **yes** Width **52cm/ 20½in** Length **10m/11yd** Repeat **7.5cm/2¾in** Price ★

4

1

2

3

5

6

7 Cole & Son/Sweet Pea
54/4682/PR Colour **yellow**
Alt. colours **yes** Width **52cm/
20½in** Length **10m/11yd**
Repeat **38cm/15in**
Price ★

8 Chameleon/Traditional Style/
Sonja Colour **green** Alt. colours
yes Width **53cm/21in** Length
10m/11yd Repeat **76cm/30in**
Price ★

9 Hamilton Weston/Hortensia
Border Colour **document**
Alt. colours **yes** Width
10.5cm/4in Length **5m/
5½yd** Repeat **–** Price ★★ ♣

8

10

11

10 Nobilis/Bagatelle Colour **BGL
317** Alt. colours **yes** Width
52cm/20½in Length **10m/
11yd** Repeat **52cm/20½in**
Price ★

11 Hamilton Weston/Fuchsia
St. James Colour **8155** Alt.
colours **yes** Width **53cm/
21in** Length **10m/11yd**
Repeat **27.5cm/10¾in**
Price ★★ ♣

12 Chameleon/Traditional Style/
Lucy Anne Colour **mustard**
Alt. colours **yes** Width **53cm/
21in** Length **6.5m/7yd**
Repeat **50cm/19½in** Price ★

13 Zoffany/Hopetoun Flower
77040 Colour **04** Alt. colours
yes Width **52cm/20½in** Length
10m/11yd Repeat **26.5cm/
10½in** Price ★

HAND-BLOCKING

Despite the introduction of hand-operated cylinder printing in 1764, and machine-driven roller printing in the 1830s, the best-quality wallpapers were those that had been hand-blocked. The subtle shading, purity of colour and crispness of detail evident in this early 19th-century naturalistic floral border paper epitomizes traditional hand-blocking. The hand-blocking process involves each different colour of the pattern being allotted an individual wooden block (bearing part of the pattern in relief). The blocks are then skilfully pressed into position one at a time, each in perfect register with the previous colour.

Scalamandré/Prestwould Saloon Border WB81504/001 Colour **01** Alt. colours **no** Width **55.5cm/21¾in**
Length **6.5m/7yd** Repeat **110cm/43in** Price ★★ ♣

12

13

Florals: Mid-19th century

Although conventionalized flowers figured in the flat wallpaper patterns of internationally influential designers such as A.W.N. Pugin and Owen Jones around the middle of the 19th century, most of the floral-patterned papers produced during this period were naturalistically depicted, and subsequently given far greater depth either by shading and highlighting, or by flocking. Indeed, many floral designs were rendered realistic almost to the point of caricature. This effect was largely the result of designers favouring large coarse flowers, such as dahlias, hollyhocks and hydrangeas, and of manufacturers printing them with new synthetic aniline dyes that yielded sharp yellows, vivid blues and acid greens of a chemical intensity that did not always reflect the natural colouring of the real blooms and foliage. More authentically realistic were many of the popular "satin" papers made in imitation of floral silk hangings; their silk-like appearance was created by polishing the surface with french chalk.

1

2

3

1 Hodsoll McKenzie/Dorset Rose 502/607 Colour **red** Alt. colours **yes** Width **52cm/20½in** Length **10m/11yd** Repeat **46cm/18in** Price ★

2 Nobilis/Bagatelle Colour **BGL 326** Alt. colours **yes** Width **52cm/20½in** Length **10m/ 11yd** Repeat **52cm/20½in** Price ★

3 Cole & Son/Madras Violet 54/4625/PR Colour **cream ground** Alt. colours **yes** Width **52cm/20½in** Length **10m/11yd** Repeat **53cm/ 21in** Price ★

4 Graham & Brown 15559 Colour **pink** Alt. colours **no** Width **52cm/20½in** Length **10m/11yd** Repeat **64cm/25in** Price ★

5 Graham & Brown 91139 Colour **aubergine** Alt. colours **yes** Width **18cm/7in** Length **10m/11yd** Repeat – Price ★

6 Nobilis/Volubilis BOR3101 Colour **pink, yellow and green on cream** Alt. colours **yes** Width **23cm/9in** Length **9m/10yd** Repeat **47cm/ 18½in** Price ★★★ ♣

7 Jane Churchill/Country Garden/ Book Seven/Country Rose J023W Colour **01 red** Alt. colours **yes** Width **52cm/ 20½in** Length **10m/11yd** Repeat **61cm/24in** Price ★

8 Colefax and Fowler/Geranium Moiré 7402/01 Colour **coral and aqua** Alt. colours **yes** Width **52cm/20½in** Length **10m/11yd** Repeat **45.5cm/17¾in** Price ★

4

6

7

5

8

Laura Ashley/Melrose 023 127 Colour **old rose multi** Alt. colours **yes** Width 52cm/20½in Length 10m/11yd Repeat 32cm/12½in Price ★

Laura Ashley/Freshford 5255 575 Colour **sapphire** Alt. colours **yes** Width 13cm/5in Length 10m/11yd Repeat 13cm/5in Price ★

Hodsoll McKenzie/Faded Bouquet 610/601 Colour **pink** Alt. colours **yes** Width 52cm/20½in Length 10m/11yd Repeat 61cm/24in Price ★

Coloroll/Shayla Stripe 26-092 Colour **burgundy** Alt. colours **yes** Width 52cm/20½in Length 10m/11yd Repeat 53cm/21in Price ★

Crowson/Rosehill/Firle Colour **15** Alt. colours **yes** Width 52cm/20½in Length 10.5m/11½yd Repeat 26cm/10¼in Price ★

9

14

16

3

17

10

11

2

15

14 Hamilton Weston/Yellow Bedroom Colour **document** Alt. colours **yes** Width 52cm/20½in Length 10m/11yd Repeat 54.5cm/21½in Price ★★★ ♣

15 Watts of Westminster/Nimue W0031 Colour **grant** Alt. colours **yes** Width 47cm/18½in Length 10m/11yd Repeat 44cm/17in Price ★★

16 Colefax and Fowler/Camilla 7017/03 Colour **yellow and blue** Alt. colours **yes** Width 52cm/20½in Length 10m/11yd Repeat 23cm/9in Price ★

17 Chameleon/Bayley Arms/ Cabbage Rose Colour **AND 017** Alt. colours **yes** Width 53cm/21in Length 10m/11yd Repeat 25cm/9¾in Price ★

Florals: Late 19th century

Naturalistically depicted flowers continued to appear on wallpapers produced during the last 30 years of the 19th century. However, as a reaction to the overblown naturalism of many mid-19th-century papers, conventionalized floral patterns were more in evidence, especially in Arts and Crafts, Aesthetic and Art Nouveau interiors, where they were often employed as the field (filling) in a tripartite (frieze-field-dado) division of the walls. Undoubtedly the most popular were the Arts and Crafts papers of William Morris and his followers. These featured relatively simple flowers, such as poppies, daisies, marigolds and jasmine, hand-blocked with traditional vegetable dyes and contained within formal pattern structures.

Aesthetic papers, notably those by the influential English designer E.W. Godwin (publicized in Britain and America by Charles Eastlake), were also characterized by uncomplicated blooms, such as sunflowers, pinks and the Japanese lotus. Although many were botanically correct, they were generally highly stylized and rather static. These were in marked contrast to the sinuous poppy, wisteria and waterlily patterns of Art Nouveau designers, which, while conventionalized, had a marked rhythmical and sensuous quality.

4

4 **Brunschwig & Fils/Kyoto 15908-06** Colour **pongee** Alt. colours **yes** Width **68.5cm/ 27in** Length **4.5m/5yd** Repeat **91.5cm/36in** Price ★★★★ ♣

5 **Cole & Son/Special Block Print/Moss Rose 0139** Colour **dark green** Alt. colours **yes** Width **52cm/20½in** Length **10m/11yd** Repeat **12cm/ 4¾in** Price ★★★★ ♣

6 **Cole & Son/Dennis Hall/Pelham 63/7045** Colour **caramel** Alt. colours **yes** Width **52cm/20½in** Length **10m/11yd** Repeat **30.5cm/12in** Price ★★★★★

1

1 **Colefax and Fowler/Bowood 7401/04** Colour **yellow and blue** Alt. colours **yes** Width **52cm/20½in** Length **10m/11yd** Repeat **30cm/11¾in** Price ★

2 **Watts of Westminster/Sunflower W0055-01/P12** Colour **Xanthe** Alt. colours **yes** Width **54cm/21½in** Length **10m/11yd** Repeat **52cm/20½in** Price ★★

3 **Colefax and Fowler/Rose Damask 7407/03** Colour **yellow** Alt. colours **yes** Width **52cm/20½in** Length **10m/11yd** Repeat **61cm/24in** Price ★

5

3

6

Alexander Beauchamp/Oleander Trellis 161/20 Colour **multi** Alt. colours **yes** Width **47cm/18½in** Length **10m/11yd** Repeat **46cm/18in** Price ★★★★★ 🪣

Laura Ashley/Victoria Border 187 187 Colour **burgundy and stone** Alt. colours **yes** Width **13cm/5in** Length **10m/11yd** Repeat **13cm/5in** Price ★

7

8

9 **Graham & Brown/51022** Colour **aubergine** Alt. colours **yes** Width **52cm/20½in** Length **10m/11yd** Repeat **53cm/21in** Price ★

10 **Zoffany/Cottage Flowers WAL0300** Colour **4** Alt. colours **yes** Width **52cm/20½in** Length **10m/11yd** Repeat – Price ★

11 **Elizabeth Eaton/Chinese Poppy** Colour **blue and cream** Alt. colours **yes** Width **57cm/22½in** Length **10m/11yd** Repeat **47cm/18½in** Price ★★★ 🪣

12 **Bradbury & Bradbury/Antique Rose Panels ARP-550** Colour **550** Alt. colours **yes** Width **69cm/27in** Length **14m/15¼yd** Repeat **48cm/19in** Price ★★★★ 🪣

10

LINCRUSTA & ANAGLYPTA

Lincrusta was developed in 1877 by Frederick Walton, the inventor of linoleum. Made of linseed oil, gum, resins and wood-pulp spread over canvas, its surface was embossed with patterns produced by engraved metal rollers. Waterproof and durable, Lincrusta could be painted, stained or gilded to simulate traditional relief mouldings of wood, plaster, leather or tiles. A cheaper and lighter alternative – Anaglypta – was invented in 1886 by Thomas Palmer. Made from cotton fibre-pulp, its relief patterns were created by hollow moulding. Lincrusta and Anaglypta remain in demand in the 21st century, with both traditional and modern designs still being produced.

IHDG/Italian Renaissance RD1952 Colour **white** Alt. colours **no** Width **52cm/20½in** Length **102cm/40in** Repeat **102cm/40in** Price ★★★ 🔲

11

12

Marginal text

Florals: **Early 20th century**

Numerous floral-patterned wallpapers were manufactured during the first half of the 20th century. Designs included the stylized, long-stemmed lilies and poppies that were featured on Art Nouveau papers, and the cup-shaped blossoms favoured by the Deutscher Werkbund. Bizarre, dusty-coloured "magic flowers", with elongated, lancet-shaped leaves and slender blossoms, were characteristic of later Wiener Werkstätte papers, while Arts and Crafts floral patterns (*see* pages 238–239) retained their popularity from the previous century. Roses, daisies and dahlias were also among the floral motifs preferred in Art Deco interiors, their round heads stylized in a two-dimensional fashion, strongly outlined, densely packed and often presented in baskets, festoons or garlands.

Floral-patterned papers featured in early 20th-century interiors inspired by 18th-century French decoration, and took the form of fields in imitation of floral damasks, topped by friezes of swagged roses and ribbons, or of combined friezes and fields in which roses or wisteria cascaded down the wall. The "English country-house" look (fashionable in both Britain and America) also gave rise to many designs based on 18th- and 19th-century floral chintz patterns.

1 **Chameleon/Art Deco/Fleur** Colour **red on gold** Alt. colours **yes** Width **53cm/21in** Length **10m/11yd** Repeat **26cm/10¼in** Price ★

2 **Colefax and Fowler/Jessica 7403/01** Colour **yellow and blue** Alt. colours **yes** Width **52cm/20½in** Length **10m/11yd** Repeat **22.5cm/8¾in** Price ★

3 **Mauny/Bouquets** Colour **document** Alt. colours **yes** Width **55cm/21½in** Length **10m/11yd** Repeat **19cm/7½in** Price ★★★★ ♣

4 **Baer & Ingram/Cottage Rose** Colour **yellow** Alt. colours **yes** Width **52cm/20½in** Length **10m/11yd** Repeat **26.5cm/10½in** Price ★★★★

1

2

3

5 **Bradbury & Bradbury/Honeysuckle** Colour **HSW-900** Alt. colours **yes** Width **68.5cm/27in** Length **4.5m/5yd** Repeat **40cm/15¾in** Price ★★ ♣

6 **Colefax and Fowler/Lydia 7611/02** Colour **yellow and sage** Alt. colours **yes** Width **52cm/20½in** Length **10m/11yd** Repeat **4.5cm/1¾in** Price ★

7 **Jane Churchill/Tulip Sprig JY67W-02** Colour **blue on white** Alt. colours **yes** Width **52cm/20½in** Length **10m/11yd** Repeat **13cm/5in** Price ★

8 **Bradbury & Bradbury/Thistle Wall** Colour **THW-970** Alt. colours **yes** Width **68.5cm/27in** Length **to order** Repeat **53cm/21in** Price ★★ ♣

5

6

7

8

9 **Mauny/Tarterres 5044** Colour document Alt. colours **yes** Width **47cm/18½in** Length **10m/11yd** Repeat **68cm/ 26¾in** Price ★★★★ 🐞

10 **Bradbury & Bradbury/Glasgow Panel** Colour **GWP-970** Alt. colours **yes** Width **68.5cm/ 27in** Length **2m/2⅛yd** Repeat – Price ★★★ 🐞

11 **Jane Churchill/Country Garden/ Book Seven/Sweet Pea Sprig J025W** Colour **02** Alt. colours **yes** Width **52cm/20½in** Length **10m/11yd** Repeat **26cm/10¼in** Price ★

12 **Laura Ashley/Freshford Border 5094 677** Colour **pumpkin multi nutmeg** Alt. colours **yes** Width **13cm/5in** Length **10m/11yd** Repeat **13cm/5in** Price ★

13 **Mulberry/Honeysuckle FG036** Colour **soft gold T106** Alt. colours **yes** Width **52cm/ 20½in** Length **10m/11yd** Repeat **41cm/16in** Price ★

14

16

14 **Osbourne & Little/Wessex/ Buckton W1500** Colour **01** Alt. colours **yes** Width **52cm/ 20½in** Length **10m/11yd** Repeat **36cm/14in** Price ★

15 **Sanderson/Rose and Peony WR7670** Colour **1** Alt. colours **yes** Width **53cm/21in** Length **10.5m/11½yd** Repeat **53cm/ 21in** Price ★

16 **Crowson/Mackintosh Irvine** Colour **65** Alt. colours **yes** Width **52cm/20½in** Length **10m/11yd** Repeat **53cm/ 21in** Price ★

12

13

15

Florals: Late 20th–early 21st century

The years following the Second World War were characterized by innovative designs as much as by period ones. Frequently seen during the 1950s were large and flamboyantly coloured tropical flowers and, for feature walls, photo-engraved prints of single fantasy flowers; or screen-printed, freely spaced flowers embellished with metallic highlights and displayed on dark grounds. Floral damask and *chinoiserie* patterns were also fashionable, but often recoloured, rescaled and applied over textured grounds – brown, grey or pink flowers on white grass cloth being a typical example.

In the 1960s, Victorian sprigs and floral trails and sinuous Art Nouveau designs vied with sketchily realistic blooms and simplified flowers in bold, bright hues – the latter superseded during the romanticism of the mid-1970s by chalkily rendered, tiny floral repeats. Since the early 1980s there has been a significant growth of interest in documentary floral papers dating from the late Renaissance to the early 20th century; 18th- and 19th-century floral chintz patterns regained appeal (having fallen out of favour from 1945 until the late 1970s). More recently, bright, impressionistic floral designs – inspired by painters such as Monet and Matisse – have come into vogue.

Laura Ashley/Natile 3162 591 Colour **plum and lavender** Alt. colours **yes** Width **52cm/20½in** Length **10m/11yd** Repeat **32cm/12½in** Price ★★★

Jane Churchill/Country Garden/Book Seven/Rose Sprig J024W Colour **02** Alt. colours **yes** Width **52cm/20½in** Length **10m/11yd** Repeat **26.5cm/10½in** Price ★

Designers Guild/Quite Contrary Colour **orange** Alt. colours **yes** Width **52cm/20½in** Length **10m/11yd** Repeat **52cm/20½in** Price ★

Anna French/Eden/Decadence Colour **DECNW024** Alt. colours **yes** Width **52cm/20½in** Length **10m/11yd** Repeat **46cm/18in** Price ★

Brunschwig & Fils/Johanna 16140.06 Colour **ivory** Alt. colours **yes** Width **68.5cm/27in** Length **4.5m/5yd** Repeat **129cm/50¾in** Price ★★★★★ 🌳

Baer & Ingram/Daisy Border DSB16 Colour **blue** Alt. colours **yes** Width **10cm/4in** Length **10m/11yd** Repeat **9cm/3½in** Price ★

Coloroll/Life Border 355410 Colour **lilac** Alt. colours **yes** Width **13cm/5in** Length **5m/5½yd** Repeat **53cm/21in** Price ★

ina Campbell/Zembla/Kiku NCW 2226 Colour 08 Alt. colours yes
Width 52cm/20½in Length 10m/11yd Repeat 61cm/24in
Price ★

Anna French/T for Teddy/Rosebud Colour ROSWP071
Alt. colours yes Width 52cm/20½in Length
10m/11yd Repeat 15cm/6in Price ★

Anna French/Eden/Japonica Colour JAPWP025 Alt.
colours yes Width 52cm/20½in Length 10m/
11yd Repeat 61cm/24in Price ★

nna French/Isolde Colour ISOWP063 Alt. colours yes
Width 52cm/20½in Length 10m/11yd Repeat
cm/24in Price ★

Baer & Ingram/Cornflower CFW06 Colour blue Alt.
colours yes Width 52cm/20½in Length 10m/
11yd Repeat 53cm/21in Price ★★★★

Baer & Ingram/Rambling Rose RMW06 Colour blue Alt. colours yes Width 52cm/20½in
Length 10m/11yd Repeat 53cm/21in
Price ★★★★

nna Campbell/Rosenkavalier/Rosenkavalier NCW 2230
olour 04 Alt. colours yes Width 52cm/20½in
ength 10m/11yd Repeat 72cm/28½in Price ★

Anna French/Eden/Chinoiserie Colour CHIWP032
Alt. colours yes Width 52cm/20½in Length
10m/11yd Repeat 76cm/30in Price ★

Anna French/Ming Stripe Colour MINWP069 Alt. colours yes Width 52cm/20½in Length 10m/11yd
Repeat 76cm/30in Price ★

Pictorial Wallpapers

Pictorial wallpapers were first documented in 1481, when Louis XI paid Jean Bourdichon to paint 50 rolls of paper blue, and to add a Latin inscription held by three painted angels. Coloured papers with pictures of religious and allegorical subjects were also used in Europe during the 16th and 17th centuries. However, it was not until the 18th century that pictorial wallpapers were produced in quantity – many inspired by Chinese wall-hangings.

In England, John Baptist Jackson was the first to use papers in imitation of architectural features, but the finest pictorial papers were hand-printed in France during the late 18th and early 19th century, notably by paper-stainers such as Boulgard, Réveillon, Zuber and Dufour. Many of these papers were exported to Britain and America where, because of their high cost, they firmly remained as the preserve of the wealthy. The introduction of the cylinder-printing process in the 1850s then made possible the manufacture of mass-produced pictorials at more affordable prices thereafter.

LEFT A mid-19th-century Zuber pictorial wallpaper, hung in the Monmouth Mansion, in Natchez, Mississippi, USA. Never having visited America, the French designer painted this scene from his imagination, with Mississippi steamboats at Niagara Falls, Spanish moss at the Boston Tea Party and Native Americans in African dress.

ABOVE Hand-painted c. 1830, this paper uses images from the first volume of Audubon's Birds of America (1827); a facsimile was hung at Temple Newsam, England, in 1927.

PRINT ROOMS

The fashion for decorating rooms with prints pasted over painted walls originated in the mid-18th century. Many print rooms featured black-and-white prints and borders simply pasted in rows; others, such as those designed by Thomas Chippendale, were more flamboyant and incorporated trompe l'oeil paper cut-outs of swags, garlands, bows and chains "supporting" and embellishing the prints. This decorative convention continued well into the 19th century and has recently enjoyed a revival, with books of prints and borders being specifically designed for the purpose.

KEY DESIGNS

1 Human figures engaged in activities as diverse as military battles, hunting, shooting, harvesting, trading, sailing and taking tea have proved popular subject matter for pictorial papers.

2 Trompe l'oeil papers produced in imitation of luxuriously swagged, tailed and pleated textile hangings were often employed in grander late 18th- and early 19th-century Neo-classical interiors.

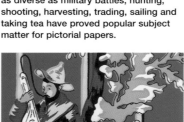

3 Chinoiserie-patterned papers were fashionable during the 18th century and early 19th. Much of the imagery was heavily Europeanized by designers who had only scant knowledge of the Orient.

4 Imported Chinese papers and artefacts provided much of the inspiration for bird motifs during the 17th and 18th centuries. Audubon's Birds of America (1827) was extremely influential in the 19th century.

5 Pictorial papers with naturalistic "still life" images of fruit and foliage were popular in the late 18th and mid-19th century, and have enjoyed a revival in the late 20th and early 21st century.

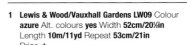

6 Nursery motifs were first introduced during the late 19th century. Subjects have included characters from children's tales and nursery rhymes and, since the late 1940s, from films and television.

1 **Lewis & Wood/Vauxhall Gardens LW09** Colour **azure** Alt. colours **yes** Width **52cm/20½in** Length **10m/11yd** Repeat **53cm/21in** Price ★

2 **Hamilton Weston/Regency Swag Border** Colour **yellow and umber** Alt. colours **yes** Width **32cm/12½in** Length **to order** Repeat **24cm/9½in** Price ★★ ♣

3 **Scalamandré/Ch'in Ling WP81212-10** Colour **old gold and bark on lacquer red** Alt. colours **yes** Width **61cm/24in** Length **5.5m/6yd** Repeat **96.5cm/38in** Price ★★★ ♣

4 **Cole & Son/Humming Birds** Colour **white** Alt. colours **yes** Width **52cm/20½in** Length **10m/11yd** Repeat **53cm/21in** Price ★★

5 **Brunschwig & Fils/Bartlett 16043-06** Colour **gold** Alt. colours **yes** Width **68.5cm/27in** Length **4.5m/5yd** Repeat **64cm/25in** Price ★★★★★ ♣

6 **Paper Moon/Peter Rabbit Border BPC 13045** Colour **sky** Alt. colours **yes** Width **16.5cm/6½in** Length **5m/5½yd** Repeat **24cm/9½in** Price ★ ⊞

Pictorials: **Pre-19th century**

Many pictorial papers of the 16th century and early 17th depicted subject matter similar to that of pictorial tapestries, including figures emblematic of the four seasons surrounded by coats-of-arms, hunting scenes, and characters and events from Christian history and classical mythology. Imported Chinese pictorial papers also became fashionable during the late 17th century. Typical patterns included landscapes of naturalistic flowering plants and trees; rivers and pools and exotic birds and insects; architectural images; and oriental figures engaged in diverse activities – both urban and rural, secular and religious.

These Chinese papers provided the inspiration for the European *chinoiserie* pictorials that proved popular throughout the 18th century, especially in Rococo interiors. Equally fashionable, however, were *chiaroscuro*-printed imitations of fine art (notably the paintings of Titian and Tintoretto) and of Graeco-Roman statuary and architecture. Also liked in the latter part of the century were French arabesques inspired by Roman wall paintings, Gothic ruins and exceptionally large panoramas or "panoramic papers" of subject matter as varied as the Grand Tour, the exploration of the South Pacific, *fêtes galantes* and scenes from the French Revolution.

1 Laura Ashley/Toile 1635 150
Colour **delphinium** Alt. colours
yes Width **52cm/20½in** Length
10m/11yd Repeat **53cm/21in**
Price ★

**2 Zoffany/Réveillon Landscape
81004** Colour **04** Alt. colours
yes Width **53cm/21in** Length
10m/11yd Repeat **98cm/38¼in**
Price ★★

3 Timney Fowler/Sphinx Border
Colour **black** Alt. colours **no**
Width **11cm/4¼in** Length
10m/11yd Repeat **61cm/24in**
Price ★

4 Scalamandré/Pillement Toile
Colour **4** Alt. colours **yes**
Width **69cm/27in** Length
4.5m/5yd Repeat **69cm/
27in** Price ★★★

5 Lewis & Wood/Print Room
Colour **legume** Alt. colours
yes Width **52cm/20½in** Length
10m/11yd Repeat **60cm/23¾in**
Price ★★★★★

6 Nobilis/L'Arbre Nantais Colour
red on cream Alt. colours **yes**
Width **55cm/21½in** Length
10m/11yd Repeat **75cm/29½in**
Price ★

1

2

3

5

6

Baer & Ingram/Summertime Toile SMW06 Colour **mid blue** Alt. colours **yes** Width **52cm/20½in** Length **10m/ 11yd** Repeat **53cm/21in** Price ★★★★

Cole & Son/Les Enfants Des Enfants 53/6074 Colour **parchment** Alt. colours **yes** Width **52cm/20½in** Length **10m/11yd** Repeat **53cm/ 21in** Price ★★

Schumacher/Jungle Kingdom 519011 Colour **document** Alt. colours **yes** Width **68.5cm/ 27in** Length **4m/4½yd** Repeat **93cm/36in** Price ★★

7

8

9

10

10 **Alexander Beauchamp/Hunting Scene** Colour **multi** Alt. colours **yes** Width **50cm/19½in** Length **10m/11yd** Repeat **39.5cm/15½in** Price ★★★★ ♣

11 **Zoffany/Réveillon Mini 8515004** Colour **04** Alt. colours **yes** Width **52cm/20½in** Length **10.5m/11½yd** Repeat **46cm/ 18in** Price ★

11

12 **Brunschwig & Fils/Yunnan 69344** Colour **190 cinnabar** Alt. colours **yes** Width **68.5cm/27in** Length **10.5m/11½yd** Repeat **182cm/71¾in** Price ★★★ ♣

13 **Hamilton Weston/Lambeth Saracen** Colour **8116** Alt. colours **yes** Width **51.5cm/ 20¼in** Length **10m/11yd** Repeat **20cm/8in** Price ★★ ♣

14 **De Gournay/Askew J-018** Colour **verdigris** Alt. colours **yes** Width **91cm/35¾in** Length **2.5m/2¾yd** Repeat – Price ★★★★★ ♣

12

13

ARABESQUES

The term "arabesque" refers to the stylized, interlaced foliage patterns derived from Islamic art. These patterns were introduced to Europe in the engraved metalwork of Muslim craftsmen, who emigrated to Venice during the 15th century, and they subsequently appeared on wallpapers from the 17th century to the early 21st. In the 18th century, however, arabesques acquired an additional meaning: French designers used the term to describe grotesque patterns, based on Roman wall-paintings, which incorporated figures, vases, bandwork, flowers and scrolling foliage.

Zuber/Documents V/Sully 2402N Colour **black** Alt. colours **yes** Width **47cm/ 18½in** Length **10m/11yd** Repeat **46cm/18in** Price ★★★

14

Pictorials: Early 19th century

The French panoramics produced during the late 18th century (*see* page 246) became even more popular during the early 19th century, although few were exported until the end of the Napoleonic wars in 1815. Apart from *chinoiserie* designs (*see* opposite), fashionable subject matter included classical deities (in *chiaroscuro*); views of English, European and American cities, monuments and landscapes; hunting and horseracing scenes; wars and battles; and episodes from literature.

Also widespread in the early 19th century were religious pictures portrayed in *grisaille,* and paper friezes designed in imitation of stucco work and sculpture depicting ancient Greek or Roman figures, legends and architectural elements. Of special note were the hand-blocked *trompe l'oeil* papers (*see* right), of mostly French manufacture, that simulated silk and velvet hangings realistically swagged and tailed, pleated or button-backed, and often embellished with decorative *passements,* such as cords, braids and tassels.

1

2

3

1 Zoffany/Empire Damask 36ED Colour 05 Alt. colours **yes** Width **52cm/20½in** Length **10m/11yd** Repeat **46cm/18in** Price ★

2 Brunschwig & Fils/Vaison 15760.06 Colour **sand** Alt. colours **yes** Width **68.5cm/27in** Length **4.5m/5yd** Repeat **46.5cm/18¼in** Price ★★★★ 🖌

3 Brunschwig & Fils/Bunny Business 15892-06 Colour **bluebell** Alt. colours **yes** Width **68.5cm/27in** Length **4.5m/5yd** Repeat **68.5cm/27in** Price ★★

TROMPE L'OEIL

A characteristic of many pictorial wallpaper designs produced for Neo-classical interiors of the early 19th century was an enhanced use of perspective. The realistic three-dimensional effect created by these *trompe l'oeil* papers, such as the pleated textile (right) and the Greek frieze (below), was primarily achieved by strengthening both the shadows and the highlights in the pattern.

Zuber/Document IV/Eugénie 9013 Colour **rouge** Alt. colours **yes** Width **47cm/18½in** Length **9m/10yd** Repeat **66.5cm/26¼in** Price ★★★

4

5

4 Zuber/Document V/Capiton 30023 Colour **rouge** Alt. colours **yes** Width **47cm/18½in** Length **10m/11yd** Repeat **20cm/8in** Price ★★★★

5 Zuber/Bordures VII/Bordure Draperie Empire 20047 Colour **vert** Alt. colours **yes** Width **34cm/13⅜in** Length **10m/11yd** Repeat **47cm/18½in** Price ★★★★★

Scalamandré/Prestwould Saloon Dado WB81504 Colour **document** Alt. colours **yes** Width **53cm/21in** Length **6.3m/7yd** Repeat – Price ★★ 🖌

19th century

7

6

8

During the first half of the 19th century, panoramic wallpapers were very fashionable on both sides of the Atlantic. Some papers were prodigiously large (up to 16m/52½ft long by 3m/10ft high), and the drops were designed to be placed in sequence around the four walls of a room. Some panoramic designs were so complicated that their production required up to 1,500 separate printing blocks. Especially desirable were *chinoiserie* designs, depicting scenes of everyday life in China, and landscapes populated with flowering trees and exotic birds, butterflies and insects.

De Gournay/Coutts Colour **antique finish** Alt. colours **yes** Width **91.5cm/36in** Length **3.5m/3⅞yd** Repeat – Price ★★★★★ (**hand-painted**) ⊞

De Gournay/Coutts Colour **painted paper** Alt. colours **yes** Width **91.5cm/36in** Length **3.5m/3⅞yd** Repeat – Price ★★★★★ (**hand-painted**) ⊞

Alexander Beauchamp/Regency Bamboo Border Colour **multi** Alt. colours **yes** Width **16.5cm/6½in** Length **10m/11yd** Repeat **68.5cm/27in** Price ★★★★★ ♣

Zuber 2369 Colour **blue** Alt. colours **yes** Width **53cm/21in** Length **10m/11yd** Repeat **70cm/27½in** Price ★★★ ♣

Coloroll/Pitcairn Border 750079 Colour **green** Alt. colours **yes** Width **17cm/6¾in** Length **5m/5½yd** Repeat **53cm/21in** Price ★

Brunschwig & Fils/Parc de Vincennes 69333 Colour **967 charcoal** Alt. colours **yes** Width **76cm/30in** Length **10m/11yd** Repeat **64cm/25in** Price ★

9

De Gournay/Earlham J040 Colour **dark blue** Alt. colours **yes** Width **91.5cm/36in** Length **3.5m/3⅞yd** Repeat – Price ★★★★★ (**hand-painted**) ⊞

Pictorials: Late 19th century

During the second half of the 19th century, the development of roller-printing and the introduction of new synthetic dyes made it much easier for wallpaper manufacturers on both sides of the Atlantic to produce sophisticated but reasonably inexpensive pictorial patterns. The favoured subject matter was diverse. Notable designs included three-dimensional depictions of animals, flowers, fruits and other plant forms – many indigenous to Europe and America, but others derived from more exotic *chinoiserie*, *japonaiserie*, and Indian and African imagery. Rural landscapes, scenes from industry and commemorative pictorials of significant military and political events also proved successful. Particularly fashionable in the various Classical Revival interiors of grander European and American homes were *trompe l'oeil* simulations of architectural elements, such as statuary, pillars, plaster mouldings and wood carvings. Favoured pictorial papers in Gothic Revival houses, on the other hand, were generally flatter-patterned and incorporated mMedieval imagery ranging from Gothic-arched windows with elaborate tracery to beasts-of-the-field, all invariably augmented with stylized or naturalistic plant forms, or with heraldic motifs, such as emblems and coats-of-arms.

5

6

1

3

1 Warner Fabrics/Temples of Antiquity Colour **cream** Alt. colours **yes** Width **52cm/ 20½in** Length **10m/11yd** Repeat **41cm/16in** Price ★

2 Morris & Co/Fruit WR8048 Colour **1** Alt. colours **yes** Width **53cm/21in** Length **10.5m/11½yd** Repeat **54cm/21½in** Price ★

3 Watts of Westminster/Bird Colour **blue** Alt. colours **yes** Width **64cm/25in** Length **10m/11yd** Repeat **59cm/ 23in** Price ★★

4 Bradbury & Bradbury/ Pomegranate Panel Colour **410** Alt. colours **yes** Width **68.5cm/ 27in** Length **to order** Repeat **68.5cm/27in** Price ★★★ ♣

5 Brunschwig & Fils/Bartlett 16043-06 Colour **gold** Alt. colours **yes** Width **68.5cm/ 27in** Length **4.5m/5yd** Repeat **64cm/25in** Price ★★★★★ ♣

6 Morris & Co/Trellis Colour **document** Alt. colours **no** Width **53cm/21in** Length **10.5m/11½yd** Repeat – Price ★★★★ ♣

7 Bradbury & Bradbury/Lion and Dove Frieze LDF Colour **001** Alt. colours **no** Width **67cm/ 26¼in** Length **to order** Repeat **117cm/46in** Price ★★★★★ ♣

2

7

11

12

13

8 **Brunschwig & Fils/Shimo 15414.06** Colour green Alt. colours **yes** Width **64cm/ 25in** Length **4.5m/5yd** Repeat **64cm/25in** Price ★★★

9 **Coloroll/Perfume Bottle Border 37375** Colour beige Alt. colours **yes** Width **17cm/ 6¾in** Length **5m/5½yd** Repeat **53cm/21in** Price ★

10 **Alexander Beauchamp/Etienne Frieze** Colour multi Alt. colours **yes** Width **53.5cm/21in** Length **10m/11yd** Repeat **25.5cm/10in** Price ★★★★ ♣

11 **Beaumont & Fletcher/Aubusson Rose** Colour rose and duck egg Alt. colours **yes** Width **52cm/ 20½in** Length **10m/11yd** Repeat **53.5cm/21in** Price ★★

12 **Sandberg/Altea 956** Colour **06** Alt. colours **yes** Width **3.5cm/1½in** Length **10m/ 11yd** Repeat **13.5cm/5¼in** Price ★

13 **Alexander Beauchamp/Moorish Dado** Colour **multi** Alt. colours **yes** Width **47cm/18½in** Length **10m/11yd** Repeat **56.5cm/22¼in** Price ★★★★★ ♣

CEILING PAPERS

Many wallpapers designed specifically for use on ceilings and adjacent cornices were made during the 19th century, and these were widely employed in Classical Revival interiors. As a result of new printing techniques, many examples, especially those of French origin, were sophisticated in terms of colour and shading – qualities exploited to produce *trompe l'oeil* simulations of both floral and faunal imagery, as well as plasterwork moulding, such as fan- and star-shaped roses and geometrical strapwork.

Bradbury & Bradbury/Renaissance Dado RED Colour **550** Alt. colours **yes** Width **68.5cm/ 27in** Length **4.5m/5yd** Repeat **68.5cm/27in** Price ★★★★ ♣

Bradbury & Bradbury/Gossamer Ceiling GSC Colour **610** Alt. colours **yes** Width **68.5cm/27in** Length **4.5m/5yd** Repeat **68.5cm/27in** Price ★★ ♣

Detail of an American Italianate or Second-Empire ceiling. Individual papers include a scrolling foliage Renaissance frieze, Italianate borders and Roman corner fans.

Pictorials: **Early 20th century**

Scenic wallpapers similar to those produced in early 19th-century France enjoyed a revival during the early 20th century, especially in America. Subject matter was diverse and ranged from horseracing to views of important cities and monuments, with woodland and hunting scenes favoured in dining rooms and seascapes appearing in bathrooms. Imitations of both medieval and Renaissance narrative tapestries also proved understandably popular in Arts and Crafts, Tudor and Jacobean Revival interiors.

Apart from nursery papers (*see* opposite), other pictorial-patterned wallpapers of note included designs inspired by 18th-century *chinoiserie* papers, Egyptian desert imagery, and exotic wild animals from the jungles and plains of central and southern Africa. In the 1940s, fine art exerted a strong influence, with manufacturers offering screen-printed mural copies of works by artists such as Henri Matisse, Jean Miró and Raphael, including the latter's decorations for the Loggia of the Vatican.

Osborne & Little/Jester Border B1210/05 Colour **yellow, red and blue** Alt. colours **yes** Width **13cm/5in** Length **10m/11yd** Repeat – Price ★

Scalamandré/Akbar's Stable WP81542-1 Colour **1** Alt. colours **yes** Width **70cm/27½in** Length **4.5m/5yd** Repeat **70cm/27½in** Price ★★★★

Osborne & Little/Toad Hall W1199-03 Colour **green** Alt. colours **yes** Width **52cm/20½in** Length **10m/11yd** Repeat **72cm/28¼in** Price ★★

Sandberg/Felicia 936 Colour **24** Alt. colours **yes** Width **10.5cm/4in** Length **10m/11yd** Repeat **32cm/12½in** Price ★

Mauny/Les Singes 5042 Colour **multi** Alt. colours **yes** Width **47cm/18½in** Length **10m/11yd** Repeat **52cm/20½in** Price ★★★★ ♣

Cole & Son/Pagoda 63/2010 Colour **tomato** Alt. colours **yes** Width **52cm/20½in** Length **10m/11yd** Repeat **61cm/24in** Price ★

ulberry/Flights of Fantasy FG034 Colour **F108**
t. colours **yes** Width **52cm/20½in** Length
m/11yd Repeat **53cm/21in** Price ★

Sandberg/Felicia 936 Colour **25** Alt. colours **yes**
Width **10.5cm/4in** Length **10m/11yd**
Repeat **32cm/12½in** Price ★

Mauny/Martin Pêcheur 5035 Colour **multi** Alt. colours **yes** Width **47cm/18½in** Length **10m/11yd**
Repeat **62cm/24¼in** Price ★★★ 🖌

ulberry/Naval Ensigns FG028/569 Colour **V113** Alt.
olours yes Width **52cm/20½in** Length **10m/11yd**
peat 59.5cm/23½in Price ★

Marthe Armitage/Willow Pattern Colour **multi** Alt.
colours **yes** Width **53cm/21in** Length **10m/11yd**
Repeat **42cm/16½in** Price ★

Mauny/Chinoiseries 5059 Colour **multi** Alt. colours **yes**
Width **47cm/18½in** Length **10m/11yd** Repeat **47cm/**
18½in Price ★★★★ 🖌

Nobilis/Zèbre et Léopard Colour **BOR2901 black and**
white Alt. colours **yes** Width **16cm/6¼in** Length
10m/11yd Repeat – Price ★★ 🖌

NURSERY PAPERS

Pictorial wallpapers designed
specifically for children's rooms first
appeared in the late 19th century,
when leading illustrators of the time
(including Walter Crane, Kate
Greenaway and Mabel Attwell)
devised patterns based on children's
stories and nursery rhymes. While
the nursery-paper genre was
established in the 19th century,
it proliferated in the 20th century.
Some early 20th-century designs,
notably those based on the tales of
Beatrix Potter and cartoon
characters such as Mickey Mouse™,
are still very popular today and
compete with subject matter as
diverse as soldiers, aeroplanes,
vintage cars, farm animals, humorous
vegetables and famous film and
television characters.

Osborne & Little/Lords and Ladies B1211/02 Colour **blue** Alt. colours **yes**
Width **13cm/5in** Length **10m/11yd** Repeat – Price ★

Nobilis/Borders No. 4/Fanny Colour **BOR2102** Alt.
colours **no** Width **26cm/10¼in** Length **10m/11yd**
Repeat – Price ★★★ 🖌

20th century

Pictorials: Late 20th–early 21st century

The revival of mural wallpapers that took place in the early 19th century has been largely sustained to the present day. However, there have been some significant changes of style and content that reflect the developments in both urban and rural life, and in printing techniques. For example, in America during the 1950s and 1960s fashionable photomurals showed subjects as diverse as the high-rise New York skyline, groups of commuting office workers, and Highway 66 winding its way through its desert landscape. Similarly, the Pop Art and Op Art of the 1960s was readily translated on to visually dramatic still-life pictorial papers.

Nursery papers have also been produced in increasing quantities in the late 20th and early 21st century. Many are photogravure murals designed to cover modern flush doors ("photodoors") in a child's bedroom, and, while some of the subject matter, such as the tales of Beatrix Potter, "life on the farm", Thomas the Tank Engine™ and Disney's Mickey Mouse™, is as popular today as it was earlier in the century, the genre has constantly accommodated new characters – familiar comic-book and cartoon figures including Barbie™, Action Man™, The Simpsons™ and Buzz Lightyear™ being very popular.

1

2

3

6

1 Crowson/Elephant Border
Colour **10** Alt. colours **yes**
Width **17.5cm/7in** Length
10m/11yd Repeat **17cm/
6¾in** Price ★★

**2 Nina Campbell/Ferronier/
Mirari NCW2195** Colour
04 Alt. colours **yes** Width
52cm/20½in Length **10m/
11yd** Repeat **72cm/28⅓in**
Price ★

3 Vymura/Teddies Border 29616B
Colour **natural medium** Alt.
colours **no** Width **26cm/
10¼in** Length **10m/11yd**
Repeat – Price ★

**4 Marthe Armitage/Italian
Garden** Colour **black and
white** Alt. colours **yes** Width
59cm/23in Length **10m/
11yd** Repeat **42cm/16½in**
Price ★

**5 Vymura/Thomas The Tank
Engine™ Border 19107**
Colour **multi** Alt. colours
no Width **17.5cm/7in** Length
10m/11yd Repeat – Price ★

**6 Baer & Ingram/Country Living/
Kitchen Garden KTW01** Colour
natural Alt. colours **no** Width
52cm/20½in Length **10m/
11yd** Repeat **53cm/21in**
Price ★★★★

7 Baer & Ingram/Country Living/
Woof! Woof! WFW10 Colour
tan Alt. colours yes Width
52cm/20½in Length 10m/
11yd Repeat 53cm/21in
Price ★★★★

8 Vymura/Buzz Lightyear™
09320 Colour bright blue
Alt. colours no Width 26cm/
10¼in Length 10m/11yd
Repeat – Price ★

9 Sandberg/Kaspar 708 Colour
blue 14 Alt. colours yes Width
53cm/21in Length 10m/11yd
Repeat 64cm/25in Price ★

10 Vymura/Action Man™ Border
09322 Colour extreme orange
Alt. colours no Width 26cm/
10¼in Length 10m/11yd
Repeat – Price ★

11 Vymura/Barbie™ Border 79111
Colour multi pastel Alt. colours
no Width 17.5cm/7in Length
10m/11yd Repeat – Price ★

12 Laura Ashley/Outer Space
Border 1180 793 Colour multi
blue Alt. colours no Width
26.5cm/10½in Length 10m/
11yd Repeat 26.5cm/10½in
Price ★

10   **11**

12

13 Vymura/Fairies Border 29614
Colour medium pink Alt.
colours no Width 26cm/
10¼in Length 10m/11yd
Repeat – Price ★

14 Laura Ashley/Lemon Grove
Border 664 888 Colour
cowslip/multi ivory Alt.
colours no Width 13cm/
5in Length 10m/11yd
Repeat 13cm/5in
Price ★

15 G.P. & J. Baker/Castle Street
Border W0117-01 Colour 01
Alt. colours available Width
18cm/7in Length 10m/11yd
Repeat 18cm/7in Price ★

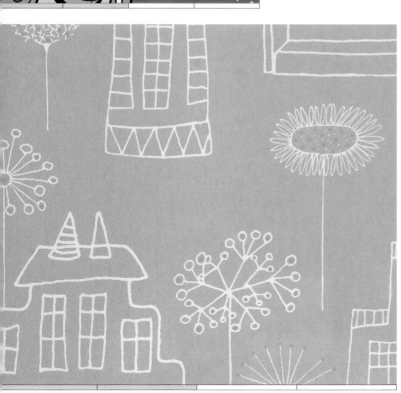

13

14   **15**

Overall Pattern Wallpapers

Of the countless patterns that have appeared on wallpapers from the late 15th century to the present day, a substantial number have been based on plant forms. Vying for popularity with floral designs have been patterns depicting fruits, nuts, vegetables and foliage. Since the Renaissance, the gradual assimilation of oriental, Middle Eastern, Asian and African styles of decoration into the vocabulary of European and, later, American ornament has resulted in a steady increase in the types of plant form available to wallpaper designers. The vagaries of fashion have also resulted in these organic forms being either conventionalized or depicted naturalistically during different periods. For example, naturalistic renderings were common for much of the 17th century, as well as in the late 18th and mid-19th century, while stylized representations were a feature of the late 19th and early 20th century.

Other popular overall patterns used since the 17th century include imitations of decorative plaster and wooden mouldings, simulations of the figuring and grain of various hardwoods, replicas of the random crazing found on craquelure-varnished panelling, and abstract designs inspired by microphotography and 20th- and 21st-century fine art.

PLANT-FORM REPEATS

Chinese wallpapers that displayed all kinds of exotic oriental imagery were highly sought after in Britain and Europe during the early years of the 18th century. However, they were generally confined to use in reception rooms. In bedrooms of this period it was much more usual to find wallpapers embellished with indigenous plant-form patterns. This example, in the Prince's Room at Temple Newsam, near Leeds, England, has a repeating pattern of leaves, fruit and vegetables, and is a reproduction of the original paper that was hung there in 1827.

ABOVE AND LEFT Large numbers of foliage-pattern papers, designed for use on both ceilings and walls, were produced throughout the 19th century and proved popular on both sides of the Atlantic. Early in the century, laurel-leaf and hart's-tongue patterns were fashionable. By the middle of the century, acanthus leaves, oak leaves, grapevines and ivy were popular, while in the later Aesthetic and Arts and Crafts interiors formalized oak, acanthus and lotus leaves were much in evidence. Colours – mostly shades of green and brown – remained realistic throughout the 19th century.

FAR LEFT Wallpapers produced to imitate stone blocking have been popular since the beginning of the 20th century, particularly in Medieval Revival interiors. Some examples are flat-patterned, and therefore little more than a pastiche of stonework, but others employ subtle highlights and shading in the areas of the mortar joints to achieve quite realistic *trompe l'oeil* effects.

KEY DESIGNS

1 Small-scale leaf patterns have been used on papers since the 17th century. This early 21st-century example is typical of many papers that have been inspired by period fabric designs.

2 The large-scale leaf pattern of this early 21st-century paper is derived from late 17th-century designs. As with many two-tone foliate patterns, it is produced in imitation of a silk damask.

3 Willow-pattern papers for walls and ceilings were especially fashionable during the second half of the 19th and the early 20th century, notably in Aesthetic and Arts and Crafts interiors.

4 Formal, stylized designs of Eastern and Middle-Eastern origin were very fashionable in the late 19th century. This example incorporates the scrolled leaf forms found in paisley patterns.

5 Abstract patterns have been popular since the end of the Second World War. Diverse sources of inspiration include rainwater, snowflakes and the microscopic organisms discovered by microphotography.

6 Many overall leaf patterns designed in the late 20th and early 21st century have had a pleasingly understated quality. In most cases this is achieved by using subtly different tones of the same colour.

---

1 **Graham & Brown 17393** Colour **green** Alt. colours **yes** Width **52cm/20½in** Length **10m/11yd** Repeat **32cm/12½in** Price ★

2 **Mulberry/Baroque Vine FG039** Colour **biscuit J115** Alt. colours **yes** Width **52cm/20½in** Length **10m/11yd** Repeat **76cm/30in** Price ★

3 **Morris & Co//Willow Bough** Colour **Morris 210** Alt. colours **yes** Width **53cm/21in** Length **10.5m/11½yd** Repeat **46cm/18in** Price ★ 🖌

4 **Mulberry/East of Suez FG024/633** Colour **gold T102** Alt. colours **yes** Width **52cm/20½in** Length **10m/11yd** Repeat **64cm/25in** Price ★

5 **Chameleon/Traditional Style/Warrington Puddle** Colour **WS3018** Alt. colours **yes** Width **53cm/ 21in** Length **10m/11yd** Repeat **53cm/21in** Price ★

6 **Today Interiors/Novus NV322** Colour **4** Alt. colours **yes** Width **53cm/21in** Length **10m/11yd** Repeat **17.5cm/7in** Price ★

Overall Pattern: **Pre-19th century**

From the mid-16th to the late 18th century, most overall-patterned papers depicted conventionalized or naturalistic fruit or foliage, with many of the designs produced in imitation of fashionable textiles such as damasks. Favoured plant forms during the Renaissance and the 17th century included grapevines, ivy, parsley, water leaves, oak leaves and palms, as well as pines and pomegranates (usually set within scrolling acanthus leaves). These were also used during the 18th century, when they vied with plants of oriental origin, such as lotus leaves and artichokes, Neo-classical anthemia, laurels and seaweed.

Apart from fruit and foliage, overall-patterned papers of the 18th century often imitated decorative architectural features traditionally made of plaster or wood. Typical examples, mostly *chiaroscuro*-printed to achieve the required three-dimensional imagery, included elements such as *grisaille* panelling and scrollwork, while in Sweden wood-effect designs were particularly popular.

1

2

5

4

6

1 **Hamilton Weston/Royal Crescent** Colour **grey, brown and white on blue** Alt. colours **yes** Width **52cm/20½in** Length **10m/11yd** Repeat **53cm/21in** Price ★★★ ♣

2 **Nina Campbell/Rosenkavalier/ Mandore NCW 2233** Colour **03** Alt. colours **yes** Width **52cm/20½in** Length **10m/11yd** Repeat **26.5cm/10½in** Price ★

3 **Alexander Beauchamp/Seaton** Colour **multi** Alt. colours **yes** Width **46cm/18in** Length **10m/11yd** Repeat **61cm/24in** Price ★★★★ ♣

4 **Alexander Beauchamp/ Gainsborough** Colour **white on blue** Alt. colours **yes** Width **43cm/16¾in** Length **10m/11yd** Repeat **46.5cm/18¼in** Price ★★★ ♣

5 **Coloroll/Mansfield Border 19-176** Colour **blue** Alt. colours **yes** Width **13cm/5in** Length **5m/5½yd** Repeat **53cm/21in** Price ★

6 **Hamilton Weston/Fynedon Gothick** Colour **document red** Alt. colours **yes** Width **47cm/18½in** Length **10m/11yd** Repeat **47cm/18¼in** Price ★★ ♣

7

**Sanderson/Chalfont Damask
WR8559** Colour **5** Alt. colours
yes Width **53cm/21in** Length
10m/11yd Repeat **61cm/24in**
Price ★

**Zuber/Venise Or/Damas Or
40068** Colour **red and gold** Alt.
colours **yes** Width **53cm/21in**
Length **10m/11yd** Repeat –
Price ★★★ ♣

**Alexander Beauchamp/
Holcombe** Colour **red and
gold** Alt. colours **yes** Width
50cm/19½in Length **10m/
11yd** Repeat **39.5cm/15½in**
Price ★★★ ♣

Nicholas Herbert/Lodge W01
Colour **01** Alt. colours **yes**
Width **52cm/20½in** Length
10m/11yd Repeat **18cm/7in**
Price ★

**Alexander Beauchamp/Urn
and Acanthus** Colour **red** Alt.
colours **yes** Width **53cm/
21in** Length **10m/11yd**
Repeat **47cm/18½in**
Price ★★★ ♣

**Alexander Beauchamp/Italian
Damask** Colour **green** Alt.
colours **yes** Width **53cm/
21in** Length **10m/11yd**
Repeat **60.5cm/24in**
Price ★★★★ ♣

8

10

11

9

SMALL-SCALE DESIGNS

The wallpaper shown here –
also known by its original
spelling "Sattin Grass" – was
one of 11 fine-quality papers
purchased from the English
paper-stainer James Duppa in
1799 by Lady Jean Skipworth
for her new house, Prestwould
Plantation in Clarksville,
Virginia, USA. It features a
striking, interlaced foliage
pattern on a highly polished
satin ground. It is typical of
the simple, small-scale
repeating designs (which also
included stripes and floral
patterns) that became
fashionable in grander English
townhouses and substantial
American mansions during
the 1790s and the first
decade of the 19th century.

Scalamandré/Satin Grass WP81527-7
Colour **07** Alt. colours **yes** Width **53cm/
21in** Length **4.5m/5yd** Repeat **53cm/21in**
Price ★★★ ♣

Overall Pattern: **Early 19th century**

In the 1830s and 1840s, cylinder-printed papers with patterns produced in imitation of arabesque-shaped plasterwork and set on *irisé* (blended colour) grounds proved very popular. Also fashionable were abstract-patterned papers in imitation of moiré silks. Nevertheless, as in previous centuries, the vast majority of overall-patterned papers produced during the first half of the 19th century were of the hand-blocked variety with their imagery derived from plant forms, particularly foliage.

In French, British and American Neo-classical interiors at the beginning of the century, favoured forms included laurels, hart's tongue (or water leaf), anthemia and "fibre" (seaweed). Most were conventionalized, but, as the century progressed, more naturalistic imagery, incorporating a greater use of shading (and sometimes flock), came into vogue. Oft-seen patterns included acanthus and oak leaves, parsley, thistles, grapevines, ivy and various fruits. However, by the 1840s, a reaction to highly naturalistic and three-dimensional imagery was beginning to set in, evidenced by the appearance during this period of many flat foliage patterns of stylized palmettes and anthemia derived from classical and Indian ornament.

5

4

5 **Hamilton Weston/Uppark Tapestry Room** Colour **unfaded document** Alt. colours **yes** Width **47cm/18¼in** Length **10m/11yd** Repeat **26cm/10¼in** Price ★★ ♣

6 **Hamilton Weston/Charlecote Strapwork** Colour **document orange on cream** Alt. colours **yes** Width **52cm/20½in** Length **10m/11yd** Repeat **91.5cm/36in** Price ★★★ ♣

7 **Graham & Brown 51063** Colour **yellow** Alt. colours **yes** Width **52cm/20½in** Length **10m/11yd** Repeat **53cm/21in** Price ★

8 **Crowson/Gallery/Matour Border** Colour **80** Alt. colours **yes** Width **17.5cm/7in** Length **10m/11yd** Repeat **17cm/6¾in** Price ★

9 **Nicholas Herbert/Bradenham W07** Colour **09** Alt. colours **yes** Width **52cm/20½in** Length **10m/11yd** Repeat **27cm/10½in** Price ★

10 **Hamilton Weston/Carlyle Damask** Colour **cream on yellow** Alt. colours **yes** Width **53cm/21in** Length **10m/11yd** Repeat **53cm/21in** Price ★★ ♣

11 **Today Interiors/Carlton Damask Ashridge CDV360** Colour **2** Alt. colours **yes** Width **53cm/21in** Length **10m/11yd** Repeat **26.5cm/10½in** Price ★

1

1 **Hamilton Weston/Jasmine** Colour **red and gold dots on olive green** Alt. colours **yes** Width **52cm/20½in** Length **10m/11yd** Repeat **30.5cm/12in** Price ★★ ♣

2 **Hamilton Weston/Covent Garden Floral** Colour **red on peach** Alt. colours **yes** Width **53cm/21in** Length **10m/11yd** Repeat **28.5cm/11in** Price ★ ♣

3 **Chameleon/Traditional Style/Lord Irvine Leaf** Colour **WS2358** Alt. colours **yes** Width **53cm/21in** Length **10m/11yd** Repeat **38cm/15in** Price ★

4 **Zoffany/Bokhara 9300** Colour **2** Alt. colours **yes** Width **53cm/21in** Length **10m/11yd** Repeat **64cm/25in** Price ★

2

3

8

9

10

11

12 Cole & Son/Clandon 52/7000
Colour **yellow and gold** Alt.
colours **yes** Width **53cm/
21in** Length **10m/11yd**
Repeat **14cm/5½in**
Price ★

**13 Jane Churchill/Colbrooke
Trellis JW62W-04** Colour
red Alt. colours **yes** Width
52cm/20½in Length **10m/
11yd** Repeat **17.5cm/7in**
Price ★★★★

**14 Zuber/Arabesques/Volutes
30005** Colour **20** Alt. colours
yes Width **47cm/18½in** Length
10m/11yd Repeat **47cm/18½in**
Price ★★★

**15 Hamilton Weston/Cyfarthfa
Damask** Colour **gold on red**
Alt. colours **yes** Width **52cm/
20½in** Length **10m/11yd**
Repeat **13cm/5in**
Price ★★ 🖌

**16 Watts of Westminster/
Kinnersley WW5025-01/B**
Colour **blue** Alt. colours **yes**
Width **54cm/21½in** Length
10m/11yd Repeat **89cm/35in**
Price ★★

17

18

17 Zuber/Moiré 1265 Colour **rouge**
Alt. colours **yes** Width **47cm/
18½in** Length **10m/11yd**
Repeat **66cm/26in**
Price ★★★

18 Coloroll/Kells Border 29-704
Colour **pink** Alt. colours
yes Width **13cm/5in** Length
5m/5½yd Repeat **13cm/5in**
Price ★

**19 Hamilton Weston/Chester
Square** Colour **green** Alt.
colours **yes** Width **52cm/
20½in** Length **10m/11yd**
Repeat **14cm/5½in**
Price ★

**20 Chameleon/Traditional Style/
Fern** Colour **autumn** Alt.
colours **yes** Width **53cm/
21in** Length **10m/11yd**
Repeat **76cm/30in**
Price ★

19

20

Overall Pattern: Late 19th century

Victorian designers Owen Jones and William Morris believed that, because wallpaper was intended to cover flat surfaces, the only appropriate form of pattern for it had to be two-dimensional in appearance; any *trompe l'oeil* and other three-dimensional effects were simply "dishonest". Their opinion was to prove remarkably influential during the second half of the 19th century: naturalistic foliage patterns continued to appear, but they were generally supplanted by conventionalized Arts and Crafts, Aesthetic and Art Nouveau designs in which any shading was usually limited to dots, lines and hatching. Arts and Crafts designs, notably those by Elbert Hubbard, were frequently based on willow and acanthus leaves. Aesthetic patterns, such as those by E.W. Godwin and Christopher Dresser, included formalized bamboo and lotus leaves, while many of C.F.A. Voysey's and the Silver Studio's Art Nouveau papers featured sinuously depicted pomegranates, thistles, various roots and leaf-like peacock feathers.

1

3

1 **Joanna Wood/Bourne Street L/W3354** Colour **Chinese yellow** Alt. colours **yes** Width **52cm/20½in** Length **10m/11yd** Repeat **27cm/10½in** Price ★

2 **Cole & Son/Owen Jones 52/7040** Colour **red** Alt. colours **yes** Width **53cm/21in** Length **10m/11yd** Repeat **7cm/2¾in** Price ★

3 **Alexander Beauchamp/Langley** Colour **blue** Alt. colours **yes** Width **46.5cm/18¼in** Length **10m/11yd** Repeat **48cm/19in** Price ★★★★♣

4 **Zuber/Venise 40068** Colour **130** Alt. colours **yes** Width **55cm/21½in** Length **10m/11yd** Repeat **66.5cm/26¼in** Price ★★★

2

4

19th century

9

5 Coloroll/Laurel Damask 21-027T Colour **red** Alt. colours **yes** Width **52cm/20½in** Length **10m/11yd** Repeat **53cm/21in** Price ★

6 Watts of Westminster/Melias W5028-02/A12 Colour **cream** Alt. colours **yes** Width **47cm/18½in** Length **10m/11yd** Repeat **35cm/13¾in** Price ★★

7 Bradbury & Bradbury/Eastlake Dado ELD Colour **550** Alt. colours **yes** Width **69cm/27in** Length **to order** Repeat **8cm/3in** Price ★★★ 🖌

8 Hodsoll McKenzie/Fern 616/602 Colour **yellow** Alt. colours **yes** Width **52cm/20½in** Length **10m/11yd** Repeat **53.5cm/21in** Price ★

9 Watts of Westminster/Clarence W0011 Colour **rose** Alt. colours **yes** Width **54cm/21½in** Length **10m/11yd** Repeat **26cm/10¼in** Price ★★

8

SANITARY PAPERS

In 1871 the English firm of Heywood, Higginbottom & Smith pioneered the first washable wallpapers. They were known as "sanitaries" because they could be kept clean. They were printed with engraved metal rollers that built up the pattern from a series of small dots of thin, oil-based inks or varnish colours. This technique produced a very smooth surface that was water-resistant, and also allowed for considerable subtlety in the shading and blending of colours.

Watts of Westminster/Cogges Manor Farm W5061-01/B13 Colour **Oxford** Alt. colours **yes** Width **54cm/21½in** Length **10m/11yd** Repeat **53cm/21in** Price ★★★

Overall Pattern: Early 20th Century

Botanic and organic forms continued to provide much of the inspiration for overall-patterned wallpapers during the first half of the 20th century. Scrolling acanthus, stylized thistles and sweeping and curving wisteria, and reed and waterlily patterns featured large in Art Nouveau designs, while small leaves with undulating stems articulated the surface of many Deutscher Werkbund papers. Stencilled leaf patterns were characteristic of the later Arts and Crafts papers of the 1920s and 1930s, and numerous early Art Deco designs consisted of fantastically stylized abstractions of plant forms. Also fashionable in the 1930s were realistic sketches of branches, leaves and blossom, and stylized, large-scale leaf patterns rendered in "teastain" colours and sometimes highlighted with silver or gold; in the 1940s ivy-leaf trellis papers proved especially popular.

Also much in evidence during the first half of the 20th century were papers displaying spattered patterns similar to those found on contemporary ceramics. In addition, papers were produced in imitation of 17th-century tooled-leather wall-hangings, classical mouldings, *faux*-marble paint finishes and panelling made of decoratively figured hardwoods such as maple and birch.

Hamilton Weston/Edwardian Damask Colour **document lustre on red** Alt. colours **yes** Width **61cm/24in** Length **10m/11yd** Repeat **61cm/24in** Price ★★ ♣

Chameleon/Art Deco/Suzzanne Colour **blue, black and gold on brown** Alt. colours **yes** Width **53cm/21in** Length **10m/11yd** Repeat **51cm/20in** Price ★

John Wilman/Figaro 170426 Colour **red** Alt. colours **yes** Width **52cm/20½in** Length **10m/11yd** Repeat **7.5cm/2¾in** Price ★

Osborne & Little/Madrigal W1441/10 Colour **green** Alt. colours **yes** Width **52cm/20½in** Length **10m/11yd** Repeat – Price ★

Zoffany/Viola Plain V21704 Colour **04** Alt. colours **yes** Width **52cm/20½in** Length **10m/11yd** Repeat **13cm/5in** Price ★

Zuber/Venise Or/Damas Or 10174 Colour **111** Alt. colours **yes** Width **47cm/18½in** Length **10m/11yd** Repeat **62cm/24¼in** Price ★★★

20th century

RAISED RELIEF DESIGNS

White or neutral-coloured wallpapers with raised relief patterns, intended for painting, proved popular throughout the 20th century. Being made of paper (or paper and vinyl), they proved cheaper to produce than Lincrusta and Anaglypta, and thus supplanted these earlier relief coverings in the mass market. Before the 1980s, all raised relief papers were produced by mechanical embossing, but thereafter "blown" vinyl techniques have also been employed. Favoured designs have ranged from traditional geometrics to abstracts such as bubble patterns, impasto-like doodlings and "cracked ice".

IHDG/Arundel RD100 Colour **white** Alt. colours **no** Width **52cm/20½in** Length **10m/11yd** Repeat – Price ★ 🖺

IHDG/Westminster RD101 Colour **white** Alt. colours **no** Width **52cm/20½in** Length **10m/11yd** Repeat **53cm/21in** Price ★

IHDG/Berkeley RD125 Colour **white** Alt. colours **no** Width **52cm/20½in** Length **10m/11yd** Repeat **13cm/5in** Price ★ 🖺

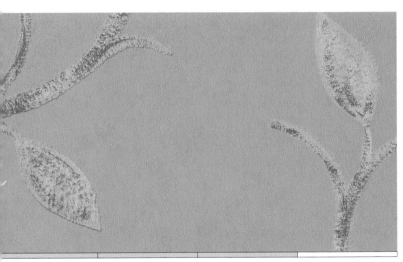

Today Interiors/Samadhi/Aritum SAW 302 Colour **4** Alt. colours **yes** Width **53cm/21in** Length **10m/11yd** Repeat **52cm/20½in** Price ★

Chameleon/Traditional Style/Oliver Colour **moss** Alt. colours **yes** Width **53cm/21in** Length **10m/11yd** Repeat – Price ★

Chameleon/Art Deco/Deco Merc Colour **stone** Alt. colours **yes** Width **53cm/21in** Length **10m/11yd** Repeat **26cm/10¼in** Price ★

Graham & Brown 15069 Colour **white** Alt. colours **no** Width **52cm/20½in** Length **10m/11yd** Repeat **32cm/12½in** Price ★

Crowson/Willowmead/Vine Colour **40** Alt. colours **yes** Width **52cm/20½in** Length **10m/11yd** Repeat **17cm/6¾in** Price ★

Marthe Armitage/Solomon's Seal Colour **orange** Alt. colours **yes** Width **53cm/21in** Length **10m/11yd** Repeat **43cm/16¾in** Price ★★★★★

Sheila Coombes/Belle Isle W607 Colour **10** Alt. colours **yes** Width **53cm/21in** Length **10m/11yd** Repeat **27cm/10½in** Price ★★★★

Overall Pattern: Late 20th–early 21st century

Conventionalized and naturalistic plant-form patterns seen in the previous century reappeared on numerous field and border papers produced during the 1950s and 1960s. For example, the late 19th-century rhythmical Arts and Crafts designs of William Morris and J.H. Dearle were hand-printed again with the original wooden blocks, and sinuous Art Nouveau vegetal patterns came back into fashion. American designers also created leaf patterns either overlaid with lines, dots, diamonds and checks, or combined with simulations of tweed textiles, while many Scandinavian and other American papers featured intricate patterns depicting marine flora and fauna.

Microphotographic views of the molecular structure of materials such as myoglobin and insulin provided additional inspiration for wallpaper designers during the 1950s and 1960s, and a general preoccupation with naturally occurring forms and phenomena was further evident in those patterns based on wormcasts, spiders' webs, amoeba and rainfall. Also fashionable since then, as in the early 20th century, have been printed replicas of the figuring and grain of various species of wood, as well as realistic and fantastic simulations of decorative stone finishes, such as those seen on marble and porphyry.

1

2

3

1 Maya Romanoff/Mica MR-SK-1402 Colour **Ishtar** Alt. colours **yes** Width **93cm/36in** Length **to order** Repeat – Price ★★★★

2 Donghia/Fluxus 2001 Colour **silver** Alt. colours **yes** Width **102cm/40in** Length **3m/3⅓yd** Repeat **15cm/6in** Price ★★★

3 Harlequin/Divine Colour **15255** Alt. colours **yes** Width **52cm/20½in** Length **10m/11yd** Repeat – Price ★

4

6

4 Marthe Armitage/Chestnut Colour **green** Alt. colours **yes** Width **59cm/23in** Length **10m/11yd** Repeat **81cm/32in** Price ★

5 Anna French/Fondant Colour **WP075BI** Alt. colours **yes** Width **52cm/20½in** Length **10m/11yd** Repeat **52cm/20½in** Price ★

6 Paint and Paper Library/David Oliver/Liberation/Opium 088-OP-DE-B3 Colour **duck egg** Alt. colours **yes** Width **52cm/20½in** Length **10m/11yd** Repeat **53cm/11yd** Price ★

7 Chameleon/Paisley/Dusty Border Colour **TC531** Alt. colours **yes** Width **9cm/3½in** Length **10m/11yd** Repeat – Price ★

8 Ornamenta/Arabesque Colour **bronze on silver** Alt. colours **yes** Width **53cm/21in** Length **10m/11yd** Repeat **30cm/11¾in** Price ★★★★★ ♣

5

8

Graham & Brown 91154 Colour **beige** Alt. colours **yes** Width **18m/7in** Length **5m/5½yd** Repeat – Price ★

Graham & Brown 91152 Colour **green** Alt. colours **yes** Width **18cm/7in** Length **5m/5½yd** Repeat – Price ★

Osborne & Little/Oratorio W1440/06 Colour **06** Alt. colours **yes** Width **52cm/ 20½in** Length **10m/11yd** Repeat **53cm/21in** Price ★

9

10

11

2

13

14

5

12 **Today Interiors/Novus/Saros NV320** Colour **2** Alt. colours **yes** Width **53cm/21in** Length **10m/11yd** Repeat – Price ★

13 **Nicholas Herbert/Celestria W04** Colour **03** Alt. colours **yes** Width **52cm/20½in** Length **10m/11yd** Repeat – Price ★

14 **Ornamenta/Curve** Colour **silver and pearl** Alt. colours **yes** Width **53cm/21in** Length **10m/11yd** Repeat – Price ★★★★★♣

15 **Anna French/Eden/Ritz** Colour **RITWP038** Alt. colours **yes** Width **52cm/20½in** Length **10m/11yd** Repeat **61cm/24in** Price ★

16 **Today Interiors/Novus NV318** Colour **4** Alt. colours **yes** Width **53cm/21in** Length **10m/11yd** Repeat **26cm/ 10¼in** Price ★

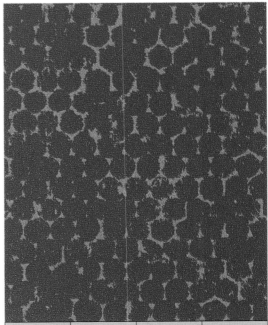

16

Overall Pattern: Late 20th–early 21st century

Many of the plant-form patterns favoured in the 1950s and 1960s (*see* pages 266–267) enjoyed a new lease of life during the late 20th century. This was largely as a result of manufacturers adapting them to suit more contemporary aesthetics. In the early 1970s, for example, some of these papers were reproduced in incandescent or muted colours on shiny or dull metallic grounds – a look that made them perfectly suited to what *Vogue* magazine described as "a Nickelodeon land of Art Deco with potted palms and mirrored halls".

Since the 1970s, metallic finishes have also served as patterns in their own right. Most of these finishes show random mottling across their surface that essentially replicates the appearance of tarnished metals and alloys, such as copper and bronze, in much the same way that some distressed paint finishes do. However, metallic finishes have not dominated wallpaper designs: abstract doodles, snowflakes under the microscope, wave-like patterns, small repeats of fruits and berries, and imitations of limed wood have also been much in evidence. Another trend has been a resurgence of documentary patterns dating back to the 17th century.

Ornamenta/Chinoiserie Colour **CHI 903 chinese red/straw** Alt. colours **yes** Width **52cm/20½in** Length **10m/11yd** Repeat – Price ★★★★★

Harlequin/Arc Colour **60356** Alt. colours **yes** Width **52cm/20½in** Length **10m/11yd** Repeat **52cm/20½in** Price ★

Paint and Paper Library/Hairpin 067-HP-RC-B3 Colour **red chalk** Alt. colours **yes** Width **52cm/20½in** Length **10m/11yd** Repeat **60cm/23¾in** Price ★

Jane Churchill/Esher JY66W-05 Colour **blue** Alt. colours **yes** Width **52cm/20½in** Length **10m/ 11yd** Repeat **27cm/10½in** Price ★

Paint and Paper Library/Emily Todhunter/Curves 015-CV-MO-S1 Colour **moss** Alt. colours **yes** Width **52cm/ 20½in** Length **10m/11yd** Repeat **60cm/23¾in** Price ★

Anna French/Eden/Olive Grove Colour **OLIWP096** Alt. colours **yes** Width **52cm/20½in** Length **10m/ 11yd** Repeat **26.5cm/10½in** Price ★

Today Interiors/Samadhi/Aritum SAW 303 Colour **3** Alt. colours **yes** Width **53cm/21in** Length **10m/11yd** Repeat **52cm/20½in** Price ★

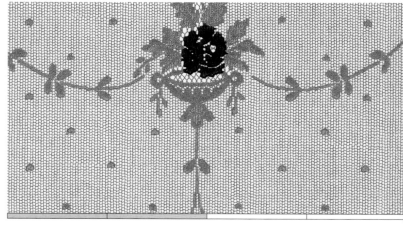

Anna French/Eden/Ritz Colour **RITWP088** Alt. colours **yes** Width **52cm/20½in** Length **10m/11yd** Repeat **61cm/24in** Price ★

Maya Romanoff/Crushed Pearl MR-P50-971 Colour medium peach Alt. colours yes Width 79cm/31in Length 3.6m/4yd Repeat 69cm/27in Price ★★★★★

Today Interiors/Novus NV321 Colour 3 Alt. colours yes Width 53cm/21in Length 10m/11yd Repeat – Price ★

Nobilis/Papiers Bois Couleur PBC103 Colour yellow Alt. colours yes Width 125cm/49¼in Length to order Repeat – Price ★★★★

IHDG/Tiger Eye RD841 Colour white Alt. colours no Width 52cm/20½in Length 10m/11yd Repeat 32cm/12½in Price ★

Coloroll/Wessex Border 29-710 Colour cream Alt. colours yes Width 17cm/6¾in Length 5m/5½yd Repeat 64cm/25in Price ★

Coloroll/Antonello Damask 16-279 Colour peach Alt. colours yes Width 52cm/20½in Length 10m/11yd Repeat 53cm/21in Price ★

Anya Larkin/Moondust Teapaper Colour 239 evergreen Alt. colours yes Width 102cm/40in Length 3m/3⅓yd Repeat – Price ★★★ ♣

Coloroll/Mosaic Border 37-372 Colour dark green Alt. colours yes Width 13cm/5in Length 5m/5½yd Repeat 53cm/21in Price ★

Geometric Wallpapers

Geometric and linear patterns appeared on wallpapers as soon as they were introduced as an alternative to textile wall-hangings during the late 15th century. Most of the geometric designs that were fashionable before the 18th century have been revived, particularly during the second half of the 19th century when designers on both sides of the Atlantic produced patterns based entirely on geometric principles of ornament. The catalogue of geometric patterns available to wallpaper designers has been extensive, steadily increasing since the Renaissance, as oriental, Islamic, African and South American geometric imagery was assimilated into Western culture. Favoured designs have included vertical stripes, checks, powdered ornament (stars and other geometric shapes), diaper patterns (trelliswork, latticework and strapwork) and, during the 20th century, mathematical and abstract shapes inspired by Cubist and Constructivist art. Some of these patterns have been augmented with, or provided the ground for, non-geometric imagery, such as stylized plant forms.

RIGHT Although vertical-striped wallpapers are closely associated with the Neo-classical interiors of the late 18th and early 19th century, they were often fashionable both before and after this period. This contemporary pale blue and white paper imitates painted stripes.

ABOVE The geometric wallpaper on the walls of this bathroom in a French Mediterranean villa is produced in imitation of blue and white gingham.

DIAPER PATTERNS

Trelliswork, latticework and strapwork patterns – collectively known as diaper patterns – have appeared on fabrics since the Middle Ages, and on wallpapers since the 17th century. Diaper patterns, original to both European and oriental decoration, often enclose small motifs. They also provide a ground for, and are often interlaced with, different types of plant-form or floral imagery. However, sometimes these geometric patterns remain unembellished – as with the blue-on-yellow latticework paper in this partly updated, early 19th-century, provincial English drawing room.

1 Diaper patterns have been used on papers since the Renaissance. This stylized flower-and-leaf trelliswork design is typical of both Regency and early 20th-century Classical Revival papers.

2 "Two-tone" striped papers made up of vertical bands of alternating solid colours were especially fashionable in Neo-classical interiors during the late 18th and early 19th century.

3 While many trelliswork patterns are unembellished, others are either entwined with or (as here) enclose or provide a ground for other motifs, such as naturalistic or stylized plant forms.

4 Many striped papers consist of vertical bands of alternating widths and colours. The bands are often embellished with small motifs, or show tonal configurations similar to those of moiré silk.

5 Diamond shapes have been an enduringly popular geometric motif on papers. An integral component of most diaper patterns, they are also often used as stand-alone repeat motifs.

6 Checked-and-striped papers produced in imitation of geometrically patterned fabrics, such as gingham and madras, became fashionable during the early years of the 20th century.

1 **Cole & Son/Tavistock 60/7045** Colour **green** Alt. colours **yes** Width **52cm/20½in** Length **10m/11yd** Repeat **20cm/8in** Price ★

2 **Laura Ashley/Colourwash Stripe 35089** Colour **taupe/ivory** Alt. colours **yes** Width **52cm/20½in** Length **10m/11yd** Repeat – Price ★

3 **Chameleon/Traditional Style/Gothic** Colour **HC 011** Alt. colours **yes** Width **50cm/19½in** Length **10m/11yd** Repeat **77cm/30¼in** Price ★

4 **Coloroll/Regency Stripe 694847** Colour **green** Alt. colours **yes** Width **52cm/20½in** Length **10m/11yd** Repeat **26.5cm/10½in** Price ★

5 **Today Interiors/Novus NV319** Colour **6** Alt. colours **yes** Width **53cm/21in** Length **10m/11yd** Repeat – Price ★

6 **Osborne & Little/Voyage/Parnasse W1120** Colour **01** Alt. colours **yes** Width **52cm/20½in** Length **10m/11yd** Repeat **27cm/10½in** Price ★

Geometrics: **Pre-19th century**

Some of the earliest woodcut-printed papers of the 16th century were patterned with simple repeats of spots or trelliswork, and many French papers of this period displayed rose motifs on vertical-striped grounds. Fashionable patterns of the 17th century included nailheads (small pyramid shapes), powdered ornament (sprinklings of stars or small flowers), trelliswork (often consisting of chevron-shaped pairs of leaves), strapwork (twisted and intertwined bands similar to ribbons or strips of leather), jewelled strapwork (in which the banding was enhanced with imitations of faceted jewels) and *guilloche* (Islamic in origin and consisting of interlaced, curved bands – some forming circular shapes – embellished with floral motifs).

Diaper patterns – mostly trellis- and latticework – were also featured in the Rococo and Gothick interiors of the 18th century. Some were flocked, and many provided the ground for, respectively, *chinoiserie* and heraldic imagery. However, the most prevalent geometric patterns in the Neo-classical interiors of the late 18th century were vertical stripes – consisting of plain bands of alternating widths and colours, or made up of stacked chevrons – or classical motifs, such as leaves, urns or figures.

5

6

7

5 **Colefax and Fowler/Juliana 7405/02** Colour **yellow** Alt. colours **yes** Width **52cm/ 20½in** Length **10m/11yd** Repeat – Price ★

6 **Hamilton Weston/Twickenham** Colour **grey, white and black or red** Alt. colours **yes** Width **52cm/20½in** Length **10m/ 11yd** Repeat **21cm/8¼in** Price ★★★ ♣

7 **Hamilton Weston/Strand Teardrop** Colour **8124** Alt. colours **yes** Width **52cm/ 20½in** Length **10m/11yd** Repeat **3cm/1¼in** Price ★★ ♣

8 **Today Interiors/Carlton Damask/Ashridge CDV359** Colour **8** Alt. colours **yes** Width **53cm/21in** Length **10m/11yd** Repeat **26.5cm/ 10½in** Price ★

1

2

3

1 **Chameleon/Traditional Style/ Trailing Vine** Colour **NF12** Alt. colours **yes** Width **50cm/ 19½in** Length **10m/11yd** Repeat **77cm/30¼in** Price ★

2 **Zoffany/Silk Stripe 245700** Colour **3** Alt. colours **yes** Width **52cm/20½in** Length **10m/11yd** Repeat **17cm/ 6¾in** Price ★

3 **Zoffany/Welbeck Trellis** Colour **gold and blue on beige** Alt. colours **yes** Width **52cm/20½in** Length **10m/11yd** Repeat **4.5cm/1¾in** Price ★

4 **Zoffany/Ticking Stripe 36TK03** Colour **03** Alt. colours **yes** Width **52cm/20½in** Length **10m/11yd** Repeat – Price ★

4

8

10

9 **Zoffany/Leaf Trellis V433** Colour **01** Alt. colours **yes** Width **52cm/20½in** Length **10m/11yd** Repeat **17cm/ 6¾in** Price ★

10 **Osborne & Little/Pipori W1013/05** Colour **blue/ pink** Alt. colours **yes** Width **52cm/20½in** Length **10m/ 11yd** Repeat **9cm/3½in** Price ★

11 **Zoffany/Venetian Grill V434** Colour **05** Alt. colours **yes** Width **52cm/20½in** Length **10m/11yd** Repeat **8cm/3in** Price ★

12 **Zoffany/Trellis V21502** Colour **02** Alt. colours **yes** Width **52cm/20½in** Length **10m/ 11yd** Repeat **52cm/20½in** Price ★

13 **Zoffany/Felbrigg Attic Paper NTW040** Colour **01** Alt. colours **yes** Width **52cm/20½in** Length **10m/11yd** Repeat **4.5cm/1¾in** Price ★

14 **Hamilton Weston/Bedford Stripe** Colour **303** Alt. colours **yes** Width **52cm/20½in** Length **10m/11yd** Repeat **15cm/6in** Price ★

15 **Zoffany/End Paper 8600** Colour **7** Alt. colours **yes** Width **53cm/21in** Length **10m/11yd** Repeat **21.5cm/ 8½in** Price ★

12

13

14

15

WALLPAPERS: *GEOMETRICS*   **273**

Geometrics: **Early 19th century**

Striped wallpapers inspired by contemporary textiles were highly fashionable in French Empire, English Regency and American Federal interiors during the early 19th century. In many cases the striped pattern consisted of solid vertical bands of alternating widths and colours, while in others some of the bands were made up of stylized foliage patterns or were edged with thin stripes that were similar in appearance to the decorative trimmings used as edgings on curtains.

Other popular geometric wallpaper designs of the first half of the 19th century included Greek-key borders; chequer patterns, brightly coloured in imitation of Indian ginghams and often embellished with small motifs; and oriental diaper patterns. One of the most significant examples of the latter was the three-dimensional *chinoiserie*-latticework design: set on a wave-pattern blue ground, this was devised by Robert Jones and J.G. Grace for the Royal Pavilion, in Brighton, England. Medieval and Renaissance diaper patterns, especially jewelled strapwork, also came back into vogue in Gothic Revival interiors during the 1840s, as did powdered ornament (evenly spaced scatterings of small, stylized motifs).

Osborne & Little/Alabaster/Ophite W5035 Colour 07 Alt. colours **yes** Width **52cm/20½in** Length **10m/11yd** Repeat – Price ★

Coloroll/Liberty Stripe 26-019 Colour **blue** Alt. colours **yes** Width **52cm/20½in** Length **10m/11yd** Repeat **26.5cm/10½in** Price ★

Hamilton Weston/Bloomsbury Square Colour **501** Alt. colours **yes** Width **52cm/20½in** Length **10m/11yd** Repeat **4cm/1½in** Price ★

Crowson/Gallery/Viliana Colour **80** Alt. colours **yes** Width **52cm/20½in** Length **10m/11yd** Repeat **52cm/20½in** Price ★

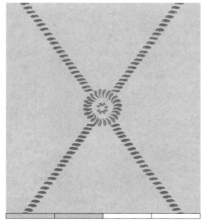

Cole & Son/Georgian Rope Trellis 59/3020 Colour **beige** Alt. colours **yes** Width **48cm/19in** Length **10m/11yd** Repeat **23.5cm/9¼in** Price ★

Hodsoll McKenzie/Scroll Stripe 615/601 Colour **pink** Alt. colours **yes** Width **52cm/20½in** Length **10m/11yd** Repeat **13.5cm/5¼in** Price ★

Hamilton Weston/Empire Stripe Colour **701** Alt. colours **yes** Width **52cm/20½in** Length **10m/11yd** Repeat – Price ★

Nicholas Herbert/Firle W08 Colour **01** Alt. colours **yes** Width **52cm/20½in** Length **10m/11yd** Repeat **12cm/4¾in** Price ★

Tiffany/Regency Trellis 36TR05 Colour 05 Alt. colours yes Width **52cm/20½in** Length **10m/11yd** Repeat **10cm/4in** Price ★

Zuber/Rayures à Auge Colour **190 jaune** Alt. colours **yes** Width **47cm/18½in** Length **10m/11yd** Repeat – Price ★★

Zoffany/Felbrigg Bedchamber NTW030 Colour **06** Alt. colours **yes** Width **52cm/20½in** Length **10m/11yd** Repeat **4cm/1½in** Price ★

...er & Ingram/Daisy Paper DSW04 Colour **yellow** Alt. colours **yes** Width **52cm/20½in** Length **10m/11yd** ...epeat **4.5cm/1¾in** Price ★

...milton Weston/Archway House Colour **blue, black** ...d white on brown Alt. colours **yes** Width ...cm/20½in Length **10m/11yd** Repeat **9cm/3½in** Price ★ ♣

Zoffany/Middle Hertford ZPH220 Colour **05** Alt. colours **yes** Width **52cm/20½in** Length **10m/11yd** Repeat – Price ★

Cole & Son/Brighton Pavilion/Bamboo Trellis Colour **traditional** Alt. colours **yes** Width **53cm/21in** Length **10m/11yd** Repeat **7cm/2¾in** Price ★★★★★

Geometrics: **Mid-19th century**

Although geometric-patterned wallpapers had proved fashionable during the early part of the 19th century, they were produced in far greater numbers following the publication of Owen Jones's *Grammar of Ornament* in 1856, in which he stipulated that "all ornament should be based on geometric construction". Jones had reached this conclusion partly as a result of a distaste for European pictorial and overblown naturalistic decoration, but mainly through his extensive studies of Egyptian, Turkish, Spanish, Chinese, Persian, Indian and Arabic styles of ornament. Jones's views, and the patterns he devised, proved highly influential with his design contemporaries. Among the numerous geometric patterns produced around the middle of the century were jewelled strapwork and lattice- and trelliswork grounds embellished with stylized plant-form motifs. However, ogival patterns were also successful, while stripes and powdered ornament retained their popularity from earlier in the century.

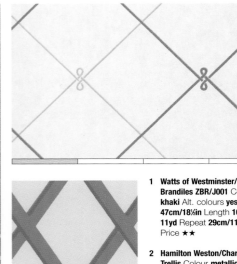

1

3

1 **Watts of Westminster/ Brandiles ZBR/J001** Colour **khaki** Alt. colours **yes** Width **47cm/18½in** Length **10m/ 11yd** Repeat **29cm/11¼in** Price ★★

2 **Hamilton Weston/Charlecote Trellis** Colour **metallic gold/ grey on white ground** Alt. colours **yes** Width **52cm/ 20¼in** Length **10m/11yd** Repeat **79.5cm/31¼in** Price ★★

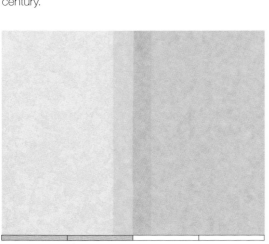

4

3 **Hamilton Weston/Richmond Trellis Border** Colour **8161** Alt. colours **yes** Width **17.5cm/7in** Length **3m/3⅓yd** Repeat – Price ★★ 👑

4 **Zoffany/Pemberley FRW0200** Colour **4** Alt. colours **yes** Width **52cm/20½in** Length **10m/11yd** Repeat – Price ★★

5 **Chameleon/Traditional Style/ Broad Stripe** Colour **SAW 3007** Alt. colours **yes** Width **50cm/19½in** Length **10m/ 11yd** Repeat – Price ★

6 **Today Interiors/Samadhi/Stripe** Colour **taupe** Alt. colours **yes** Width **53cm/21in** Length **10m/11yd** Repeat – Price ★

7 **Hamilton Weston/Victorian Leaf Quatrefoil** Colour **document (unfaded)** Alt. colours **yes** Width **52cm/20½in** Length **10m/11yd** Repeat **15cm/ 6in** Price ★★★★★ 👑

8 **Cole & Son/Plains and Stripes/ Oxford Stripe 57/2594** Colour **PR** Alt. colours **yes** Width **52cm/20½in** Length **10m/11yd** Repeat **15cm/6in** Price ★★★★★

6

5

7

8

19th century

12

13

14

10

11

BORDERS

Decorative paper borders were sometimes applied to the small area of wall space between the top of wooden panelling and the edge of the ceiling in houses during the 16th century. This makes them one of the oldest types of wallpaper. However, it was only during the 19th century that the use of borders became widespread. Used as friezes, and as alternatives to traditional dado and picture rails in fashionable tripartite divisions of walls, borders appeared in numerous and varied patterns. Among the most popular were the simple flat or *trompe l'oeil* stonework-style geometric repeats, which included Greek keys, dots, pearls, and peas framed by horizontal parallel stripes.

Geometrics: **Late 19th century**

Publications such as D.R. Hay's *Original Geometrical Diaper Designs* (1844) and, especially, Owen Jones's *Grammar of Ornament* (1856) continued to exert a tremendous influence on wallpaper designers during the last quarter of the 19th century. Their promotion of the view that geometry provided a fundamental basis for ornament was not only reflected in the striped, checked, chevron and diaper-patterned wallpapers produced during this period, but also underpinned the stylized organic patterns, devised by leading designers such as Christopher Dresser, in which considerable emphasis was placed on the hexagonal, octagonal and elliptical shapes to be found in natural plant forms.

The original source material for many of these geometric patterns was medieval, and therefore they were widely employed (often in stencilled form) in fashionable Gothic and Romanesque Revival interiors on both sides of the Atlantic. However, Islamic, Minoan, South Pacific and Celtic geometric ornament also figured large on many wallpapers, particularly borders. Typical designs incorporated abstract shapes, such as blocks, circles, dots and, from Celtic decoration, triquetra (triangular motifs of interlaced crescents) and triskele (Y-shaped sun motifs).

5

1

2 3

4

6

7

5 **The Arts & Crafts Home/Seddon LW5028** Colour **01** Alt. colours **yes** Width **52cm/20½in** Length **10m/11yd** Repeat **11cm/4¼in** Price ★

6 **Zoffany/Clarendon V21903** Colour **03** Alt. colours **yes** Width **52cm/20½in** Length **10m/11yd** Repeat – Price ★

7 **Baer & Ingram/Ticking Stripe TKW16** Colour **pale blue** Alt. colours **yes** Width **52cm/ 20½in** Length **10m/11yd** Repeat – Price ★

1 **Zoffany/Ditchley FRW0500** Colour **4** Alt. colours **yes** Width **52cm/20½in** Length **10m/11yd** Repeat – Price ★

2 **Watts of Westminster/Triad W0057** Colour **Northampton 05** Alt. colours **yes** Width **54cm/21½in** Length **10m/ 11yd** Repeat **80cm/31½in** Price ★

3 **Nicholas Herbert/Clara Stripe W02** Colour **pink 01** Alt. colours **yes** Width **52cm/ 20½in** Length **10m/11yd** Repeat **27cm/10½in** Price ★

4 **Zoffany/Fern 851200** Colour **6** Alt. colours **yes** Width **52cm/20½in** Length **10m/ 11yd** Repeat **5cm/2in** Price ★

8 Nina Campbell/Sackville Stripe NCW510/01 Colour **yellow** Alt. colours **yes** Width **52cm/20½in** Length **10m/11yd** Repeat – Price ★

9 The Arts & Crafts Home/Audsley LW5025 Colour **01** Alt. colours **yes** Width **52cm/20½in** Length **10m/11yd** Repeat **27cm/10½in** Price ★

10 Zoffany/Middle Hertford ZV07 Colour **01** Alt. colours **yes** Width **52cm/20½in** Length **10m/11yd** Repeat – Price ★

11 Alexander Beauchamp/Greek Key Border Colour **brown, black and shades of green** Alt. colours **yes** Width **18cm/7in** Length **10m/ 11yd** Repeat **56.5cm/22¼in** Price ★★★★★ ♣

12 Hamilton Weston/Uppark Trellis Colour **document** Alt. colours **yes** Width **53cm/21in** Length **10m/11yd** Repeat **11.5cm/4½in** Price ★★★ ♣

13

14   **15**

13 Cole & Son/Finsbury/Langley Stripe 59/8048 Colour **8** Alt. colours **yes** Width **52cm/ 20½in** Length **10m/11yd** Repeat – Price ★★★★

14 Jane Churchill/Langdale Stripe JY63W-08 Colour **red** Alt. colours **yes** Width **52cm/ 20½in** Length **10m/11yd** Repeat – Price ★

15 Zoffany/Pavilion 770800 Colour **3** Alt. colours **yes** Width **52cm/20½in** Length **10m/11yd** Repeat – Price ★

16 Colefax and Fowler/Wickham 7610/02 Colour **yellow** Alt. colours **yes** Width **52cm/ 20½in** Length **10m/11yd** Repeat – Price ★

1   **12**   **16**

Geometrics: **Early 20th century**

Wallpapers presenting geometric patterns were much in evidence during the first half of the 20th century. Many Art Deco papers featured highly mathematical forms, such as overlapping squares or oblongs derived from Cubist paintings, while some were inspired by Constructivist art – circles, triangles or rectangles appearing partly defined (on one side for example) and partly merged (on another side) into the background. Striped papers also proved fashionable during the 1920s, the stripes either plain, hatched or containing small repeat motifs. Also widely seen in the mid-1920s were pastel-coloured geometrics in which stripes, squares and triangles were harmoniously arranged in subtly balanced tones or gradations of a single colour.

In addition to a revival of Victorian striped and diaper-pattern designs, the 1930s witnessed the launch of the Bauhaus papers. Intended to encourage Modernist designers to use papered rather than painted finishes, they displayed shimmering cross-hatching; vertical, horizontal or wavy lines; or delicate latticework in closely related pastel tones. Many of these designs, together with patterns of sparsely arranged arrows, mazes and grids printed in bright colours on pale grounds, retained their popularity throughout the 1940s.

1 **Osborne & Little/Lamorna/Galena W1677** Colour **05** Alt. colours **yes** Width **52cm/20½in** Length **10m/11yd** Repeat **9cm/3½in** Price ★

2 **Anna French/Eden/Aquila** Colour **AQUNW03** Alt. colours **yes** Width **52cm/20½in** Length **10m/11yd** Repeat **53cm/21in** Price ★

3 **Cole & Son/Wide Moiré Stripe 55/3100** Colour **off-white** Alt. colours **yes** Width **52cm/20½in** Length **10m/11yd** Repeat **7cm/2¾in** Price ★

4 **Osborne & Little/Tangent/Index CW5162** Colour **03** Alt. colours **yes** Width **52cm/20½in** Length **10m/11yd** Repeat **2cm/¾in** Price ★

5 **Osborne & Little/Axiom/Calculus W1823** Colour **05** Alt. colours **yes** Width **52cm/20½in** Length **10m/11yd** Repeat **2.5cm/1in** Price ★

6 **Jane Churchill/Fernhurst JY61W** Colour **05 stone** Alt. colours **yes** Width **52cm/20½in** Length **10m/11yd** Repeat **7.5cm/2¾in** Price ★★★★

7 **Mauny/Grècque Frieze 506L** Colour **multi** Alt. colours **yes** Width **4cm/1½in** Length **10m/11yd** Repeat – Price ★ 🖌

8 **Paint and Paper Library/David Oliver/Liberation/Liberation 005-LIB-BF-S1** Colour **buff** Alt. colours **yes** Width **52cm/20½in** Length **10m/11yd** Repeat **53cm/21in** Price ★

9 **Cole & Son/Pinstripe 55/3043** Colour **PR yellow** Alt. colours **yes** Width **53cm/21in** Length **10m/11yd** Repeat – Price ★

15

16

17

11

12

13

14

15 Today Interiors/Novus NV317
Colour **0** Alt. colours **yes** Width **53cm/21in** Length **10m/11yd** Repeat – Price ★

16 Mauny/Pensée 5016 Colour **multi** Alt. colours **yes** Width **47cm/18½in** Length **10m/11yd** Repeat – Price ★★★ ♣

17 Colefax and Fowler/Candy Stripe 7409/02 Colour **pink** Alt. colours **yes** Width **52cm/20½in** Length **10m/11yd** Repeat – Price ★

18 Nicholas Herbert/Katie W05 Colour **12 cream on moss** Alt. colours **yes** Width **52cm/20½in** Length **10m/11yd** Repeat **5cm/2in** Price ★

Zoffany/Fresco Check V436 Colour **04** Alt. colours **yes** Width **52cm/20½in** Length **10m/11yd** Repeat **10.5cm/4in** Price ★

Jane Churchill/Tamora/Tamora Stripe JY98W Colour **08 aqua/cream** Alt. colours **yes** Width **52cm/20½in** Length **10m/11yd** Repeat – Price ★

Graham & Brown 51030 Colour **aubergine** Alt. colours **yes** Width **52cm/20½in** Length **10m/11yd** Repeat **4cm/1½in** Price ★

Nina Campbell/Zembla/Rick Rack NCW 2225 Colour **08** Alt. colours **yes** Width **52cm/20½in** Length **10m/11yd** Repeat – Price ★

Colefax and Fowler/Albemarle 7074/06 Colour **red** Alt. colours **yes** Width **52cm/20½in** Length **10m/11yd** Repeat **8.5cm/3¼in** Price ★

SIMULATIONS

Since the First World War, many manufacturers have produced patterned and plain wallpapers that are intended to simulate fabric or leather wall-hangings; notable examples include linen, cotton and (as here) snakeskin. Various methods have been employed to achieve the desired effect, including flocking, screen-printing and, more recently, photogravure printing – the latter building up the pattern and texture of the paper by means of a series of small coloured dots of varying degrees of translucency and opacity.

Today Interiors/FX/Snakeskin FXV3445 Colour **5** Alt. colours **yes** Width **53cm/21in** Length **10m/11yd** Repeat – Price ★

20th century

Geometrics: Late 20th–early 21st century

During the 1950s and 1960s, the link between wallpaper patterns and the designs employed in contemporary fine art that had been evident early in the 20th century was further consolidated by the appearance of the geometric papers produced by the British designer Lucienne Day, which featured linear patterns and ovoid shapes. The abstract, geometric shapes that appeared on the "Corbusier papers" launched in the late 1950s also revealed the influence of contemporary architecture. Other "modern" or "futuristic" designs of note included, from Scandinavia, giant circles and waving vertical bands displayed on rectangular grids in strong tone-on-tone colours and, in America, France and Britain, patterns made up of small geometric motifs rendered in reds, yellows, greys, mauves and black on dark backgrounds. For the more traditionally minded, striped-and-checked tartan patterns also proved popular during the 1950s and 1960s, while a mid-1960s' and 1970s' Art Deco revival provided more recent nostalgia. However, apart from a substantial increase in the production of documentary geometric papers dating from as early as the 17th century, the latter years of the 20th century were most notable for the arrival of naturalistic photogravure papers produced in imitation of brick walls and stone-blocking.

4

1

2

5

1 **Today Interiors/Zaniah ZB287** Colour **4** Alt. colours **yes** Width **53cm/21in** Length **10m/11yd** Repeat – Price ★

2 **Today Interoirs/Samadhi/Fino SAW304** Colour **3** Alt. colours **yes** Width **53cm/21in** Length **10m/11yd** Repeat **26cm/10¼in** Price ★

3 **Harlequin/Divine Border** Colour **35361** Alt. colours **yes** Width **13cm/5in** Length **5m/5½yd** Repeat – Price ★

4 **Baer & Ingram/Ticking Paper TKW11** Colour **black** Alt. colours **yes** Width **52cm/20½in** Length **10m/11yd** Repeat **4.5cm/1¾in** Price ★

5 **Nina Campbell/Ferronnier/ Chareau NCW2193** Colour **04** Alt. colours **yes** Width **52cm/ 20½in** Length **10m/11yd** Repeat – Price ★

6 **Coloroll/Harmony Stripe 86226** Colour **red and beige** Alt. colours **yes** Width **52cm/20½in** Length **10m/11yd** Repeat **53cm/21in** Price ★

7 **Osborne & Little/Lamorna/ Zennor W1670** Colour **01** Alt. colours **yes** Width **52cm/20½in** Length **10m/ 11yd** Repeat **18cm/7in** Price ★

8 **Anna French/T for Teddy/Rug** Colour **RUGWP034** Alt. colours **yes** Width **52cm/20½in** Length **10m/11yd** Repeat **2.5cm/1in** Price ★

3

7

8

9 **Ottilie Stevenson/Houndstooth
V0035** Colour **yellow** Alt.
colours **yes** Width **52cm/
20⅛in** Length **10m/11yd**
Repeat **3cm/1¼in**
Price ★★★★

10 **Anya Larkin/Artemis AR1**
Colour **grey and blue on gold
ingot** Alt. colours **yes** Width
76cm/30in Length **3m/
3⅓yd** Repeat **23cm/9in**
Price ★★★★★

11 **Today Interiors/Samadhi
SAW306** Colour **4** Alt.
colours **yes** Width **53cm/
21in** Length **10m/11yd**
Repeat **3cm/1¼in** Price ★

12 **Harlequin/Arc** Colour **35023**
Alt. colours **yes** Width
52cm/20⅛in Length **10m/
11yd** Repeat **26cm/10¼in**
Price ★

13 **Today Interiors/Zaniah/
Electrum ZW282** Colour **6**
Alt. colours **yes** Width **53cm/
21in** Length **10m/11yd** Repeat
52cm/20⅛in Price ★

14 **Today Interiors/Aymara/Leo
AYW336** Colour **1** Alt. colours
yes Width **53cm/21in** Length
10m/11yd Repeat **10.5cm/4in**
Price ★

15 **Anna French/Eden/Cupola**
Colour **CUPNW01** Alt. colours
yes Width **52cm/20⅛in** Length
10m/11yd Repeat **52cm/20⅛in**
Price ★

16 **Anna French/T for Teddy/Fairy
Stripe** Colour **FAIWP093** Alt.
colours **yes** Width **52cm/
20⅛in** Length **10m/11yd**
Repeat **52cm/20⅛in**
Price ★

17 **Nobilis/Tenor Border** Colour
BOR3604 Alt. colours **yes**
Width **14cm/5½in** Length
9m/10yd Repeat –
Price ★★ ♣

18 **Nobilis/Lousiaine** Colour
LOSA29 Alt. colours **yes**
Width **70cm/27½in** Length
10m/11yd Repeat – Price ★

19 **Anna French/T for Teddy/
Polka Dot** Colour **POLWP027**
Alt. colours **yes** Width **52cm/
20⅛in** Length **10m/11yd**
Repeat **11cm/4¼in** Price ★

20 **Osborne & Little/Jangala/
Aztec W5106** Colour **06** Alt.
colours **yes** Width **52cm/
20⅛in** Length **10m/11yd**
Repeat **53cm/21in** Price ★

Paints & Finishes

Paints

Prior to the mid-19th century, most paint pigments were derived from clays, vegetable matter and by-products of the mining industry such as copper carbonate, cobalt and iron, and chrome oxides. Until pharmacies began to sell phials of premixed pigments at the end of the 19th century, most paints were prepared onsite by itinerant craftsmen. Although a wide range of hues could be produced from these pigments, many proved unstable, or "fugitive", when exposed to moisture and sunlight. This instability caused bright colours to fade and blotch.

The invention of aniline dyes in the mid-19th century and, more significantly, of synthetic chemical pigments during the 20th century, resulted in more stable, durable paints, and an increase in the range of the colour palette. This mass-production also provided greater consistency of colour. However, recently there has been a reappreciation of the decorative qualities of some of the earlier paints – notably limewash and milk paint – with their constituents moderated to ensure greater stability and longevity than before.

LEFT The linear configuration of the colour scheme in this late 20th-century bathroom echoes some of the Art Deco interiors of the 1920s and 1930s (and revival Art Deco interiors of the 1960s). However, the pale yellow and lilac hues used here are lighter and cooler than the hot, saturated colours often employed in classic Art Deco rooms.

KEY COLOURS

1 Ox blood, burgundy and other dark red paints were a feature of decorative schemes from the Middle Ages to the early 18th century, and enjoyed numerous revivals thereafter.

2 Vegetable- and mineral-pigmented dark green paints were often used on woodwork from the early 17th to the mid-18th century. Acid greens became very fashionable in the Victorian era.

3 Lighter, more muted greens have included grey-green "drab" during the 18th century, olive green ("greenery-yallery") in the late 19th century and eau de Nil during the 1930s and 1940s.

4 Terracotta-coloured paints, tinted with clay pigments, have been produced for thousands of years, but stronger, more vivid mustard yellows emerged only with the invention of aniline dyes in the 1850s.

5 Pale blues, such as turquoise and Wedgwood blue, were fashionable from the 1750s until the 1840s, particularly on plasterwork. Light pastel blues have also proved popular since the 1930s.

6 Pale pinks were in vogue from the 1750s until the 1840s, while hotter, more vivid pinks (often combined with black) were a feature of Art Deco schemes of the 1920s and 1930s.

ABOVE The ambience in this southern Mediterranean hallway is created by the open archway and the juxtaposition of the quarry-tiled floor and staircase with a cool blue colourwash on the walls. Blue is often used in Mediterranean kitchens and hallways because of its cooling effect.

LEFT This is a typical 19th-century Shaker bedroom. The stone-coloured painted walls and the Shaker blue milk-painted joinery provide a cool, understated backdrop that enhances the warm, natural wood finishes of the exquisitely made pieces of Shaker furniture. Notable Shaker colours include yellow ochre, olive green and earthy shades of terracotta and pink.

1 **Finnaren & Haley** Colour **Mt. Vernon red 520315** Composition and finish *water-based:* **matt, semi-gloss** *oil-based:* **semi-gloss** Price ★★★ W 🎨 ⬜

2 **Sanderson/Spectrum** Colour **northern pine 56-1U** Composition and finish *water-based:* **matt, silk** *oil-based:* **eggshell, gloss** Price ★★ W C

3 **Sigma Coatings/BS4800 Colour Range** Colour **Westmorland 12B21** Composition and finish *water-based:* **matt, satin** *oil-based:* **gloss, satin** Price ★ W 🎨

4 **Annie Sloan** Colour **strong yellow 27** Composition and finish *water-based:* **matt** Price ★★ W 🎨

5 **Zest Essentials/Mediterranean Palette 113** Colour **Alexandria** Composition and finish *water-based:* **matt** Price ★★★ W

6 **Fired Earth/Kevin McCloud/English Palette** Colour **great house pink** Composition and finish *water-based:* **emulsion, eggshell, distemper** Price ★★ W C 🎨 🖼

Paints: **Pre-18th century**

Before the 18th century, limewash was the favoured medium for decorating masonry and plaster surfaces (*see* opposite). Limewash was also sometimes applied to woodwork, although if it was mixed incorrectly it tended to rub off on to clothing if brushed against. Milk paint provided a more stable medium for woodwork and furniture (*see* page 290), and was in widespread use, particularly in rural areas. By the beginning of the 17th century, durable oil paints and egg tempera (powder pigments mixed with linseed oil, water and egg yolk) were also increasingly employed on internal woodwork and furniture. However, being more costly to mix and apply, they tended to be confined to wealthier urban houses. Polychromatic colour schemes were highly fashionable until the end of the 17th century. Primary colours – rich reds, yellows and blues – were much in evidence, as were various shades of green and brown. Pigments were mostly derived from earth, clays and vegetable matter, although diverse materials such as ox blood, cattle urine and beetle juice were also utilized by colourists who, since the Middle Ages, had belonged to specialist guilds that jealously guarded the secrets of pigment production.

1

3

DARKER HUES

Prior to the 18th century, most softwood wall-panelling and other joinery found in the reception rooms of residential houses was painted in dark colours. While milk paint was often employed in rural areas and less affluent households, the favoured medium in urban areas and grander homes was oil paint, mixed on site from boiled linseed oil, ground chalk (whiting), turpentine and ground pigment. Oil versions were invariably in earth colours (mostly browns, reds and greens) derived from clays, plants and metal oxides.

J.W. Bollom/Bromel Colour **earthenware 08C39 JWB421** Composition and finish *water-based:* **matt, silk** *oil-based:* **eggshell, gloss** Price ★★★ Ⓦ Ⓒ Ⓢ

The plasterwork and wooden panelling and mouldings in Dennis Severs's authentically restored 17th-century house in London, England, have been painted with a gloss-finish, dark green oil paint typical of the period.

1 **Cole & Son** Colour **Strawberry Hill** Composition and finish *water-based:* **matt, emulsion** Price ★ Ⓦ Ⓒ

2 **Auro Organic Paints** Colour **cranberry 15D** Composition and finish *water-based:* **matt** Price ★★ Ⓦ Ⓕ 🏠

3 **Auro Organic Paints** Colour **tobacco** Composition and finish *water-based:* **gloss, eggshell** Price ★★★ 🏠🏠🏠🏠🏠🏠

4 **Dulux/Heritage Colours** Colour **90RR22/227** Composition and finish *water-based:* **matt, silk, soft sheen** *oil-based:* **dead flat, eggshell, gloss** Price ★ Ⓦ Ⓒ

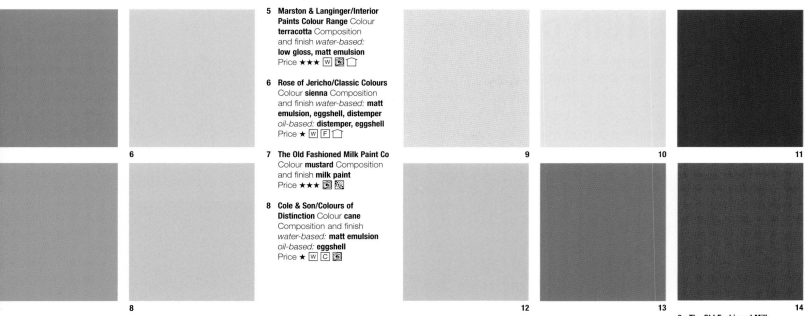

5 Marston & Langinger/Interior Paints Colour Range Colour **terracotta** Composition and finish *water-based:* **low gloss, matt emulsion** Price ★★★ W 🖉 ⬜

6 Rose of Jericho/Classic Colours Colour **sienna** Composition and finish *water-based:* **matt emulsion, eggshell, distemper** *oil-based:* **distemper, eggshell** Price ★ W F ⬜

7 The Old Fashioned Milk Paint Co Colour **mustard** Composition and finish **milk paint** Price ★★★ 🖉 🏵

8 Cole & Son/Colours of Distinction Colour **cane** Composition and finish *water-based:* **matt emulsion** *oil-based:* **eggshell** Price ★ W C 🖉

LIMEWASH PAINTS

First used *c.* 8000 BC, white limewash is made by mixing lime putty with water and raw linseed oil. Coloured versions are created by adding earth or metallic pigments. Applied to masonry and to lime renders and plasters, limewash dries to an opaque "pure" white or colour that appears bright and luminous under strong light but darker and matt under poor light. It also has the advantage of allowing moisture in the underlying surface to evaporate, thereby preventing structural deterioration.

1 Liz Induni Colour **terracotta** Composition and finish **limewash, distemper** Price ★ W 🖉

2 Liz Induni Colour **pale pink** Composition and finish **limewash, distemper** Price ★ W 🖉

3 Rose of Jericho Colour **eau de Nil** Composition and finish **limewash, distemper, emulsion, flat oil, eggshell** Price ★★ W F ⬜

4 Cy-Près Colour **Alice Grace** Composition and finish **limewash, distemper** Price ★ W F ⬜ 🏵

9 The Old Fashioned Milk Paint Co Colour **oyster white** Composition and finish **milk paint** Price ★★★ 🖉 🏵

10 Sanderson/Spectrum Colour **pheasant's feather 2-23M** Composition and finish *water-based:* **matt, silk** *oil-based:* **eggshell, gloss** Price ★★ W ⬜

11 Colourman Paints/ Reproduction Colours Colour **100** Composition and finish *water-based:* **matt** Price ★★ W 🖉

12 Craig & Rose/Authentic Period Colours Colour **pale Medici blue** Composition and finish *water-based:* **eggshell, chalk emulsion** Price ★★ W C F ⬜

13 Colourman Paints/Reproduction Colours Colour **115** Composition and finish *water-based:* **matt** Price ★★ W 🖉

14 Crown/RIBA Drawings Colour **Palladian 15** Composition and finish *water-based:* **matt emulsion, acrylic eggshell** Price ★★ T W F 🖉

Paints: 18th century

In the 18th century, limewash (*see* page 289) and milk paint (*see* below) remained in widespread use on plasterwork and woodwork respectively. However, as the century progressed matt, mid-sheen and gloss oil paints became the most frequently used finishes for plaster and wooden surfaces in more affluent households. As far as choice of colours was concerned, from the 1750s there was a general move from darker to lighter hues (*see* opposite), with bright, vivid colours, such as citron, violet, turquoise, pea green and cerise, proving especially popular toward the end of the century.

Underpinning the new aesthetic was a growing understanding of colour theory. An influential publication on the subject was Moses Harris's *The Natural History of Colours* (1766), which explained how to mix more than 300 tints from 15 basic colours. The consequences of this were that a wider choice of colours opened up, and decorators were able to employ varying shades of the same basic colour on adjacent flat and moulded surfaces to emphasize subtly the architectural proportions and details of a room.

1

MILK PAINTS

Casein ("milk") paint was used on woodwork and furniture throughout Europe, Scandinavia and America from the 16th to the 19th centuries, especially in rural areas. Cheap and durable, it was made by tinting buttermilk or skimmed milk with earth or vegetable pigments, and a little lime was added to inhibit insect infestation and fungal growth. Milk paint dries to a subtle sheen (somewhere between matt and mid-sheen) and displays a clarity and opacity of colour that is rarely matched by modern paints. Today, milk paint is available from specialist manufacturers.

1 **Old Village Paints/ Williamsburg** Colour **Virginia clock blue** Composition and finish **milk paint** Price ★★★★ 🖼🖼⌂

2 **The Old Fashioned Milk Paint Co** Colour **Lexington green** Composition and finish **milk paint** Price ★★★ Ⓦ Ⓕ 🖼

3 **Nutshell Natural Paints/ Casein Emulsion** Colour **turquoise** Composition and finish **milk paint** Price ★★ Ⓦ 🖼▦▦

4 **The Old Fashioned Milk Paint Co** Colour **buttermilk** Composition and finish **milk paint** Price ★★★ Ⓦ Ⓕ 🖼

5 **Nutshell Natural Paints/ Casein Emulsion** Colour **iron oxide-red 110 "strong"** Composition and finish **milk paint** Price ★★ 🖼▦▦

1

2

3

4

5

3

1 **Cole & Son** Colour **Georgian grey** Composition and finish *water-based:* **matt, emulsion** *oil-based:* **eggshell** Price ★ Ⓦ Ⓒ

2 **Dulux/Heritage Colours** Colour **dark stone** Composition and finish *water-based:* **matt, silk, soft sheen** *oil-based:* **dead flat, eggshell, gloss** Price ★ Ⓦ Ⓒ 🖼⌂

3 **Dulux/Heritage Colours** Colour **ash** Composition and finish *water-based:* **matt, silk, soft sheen** *oil-based:* **dead flat, eggshell, gloss** Price ★ Ⓦ Ⓒ 🖼⌂

5

4 **Sanderson/Spectrum** Colour **almond cream/11-1P** Composition and finish *water-based:* **matt, silk** *oil-based:* **eggshell, gloss** Price ★★ Ⓦ Ⓒ 🖼🖼⌂

6

5 **Dulux/Heritage Colours** Colour **DH white 0105 Y10R** Composition and finish *water-based:* **matt, silk, soft sheen** *oil-based:* **dead flat, eggshell, gloss** Price ★ Ⓦ Ⓒ 🖼⌂

6 **Sanderson/Spectrum** Colour **straw yellow 3-10M** Composition and finish *water-based:* **matt, silk** *oil-based:* **eggshell, gloss** Price ★★ Ⓦ Ⓒ 🖼🖼⌂

7

7 **Dulux/Heritage Colours** Colour **DH lemon 1643 YO5R** Composition and finish *water-based:* **matt, silk, soft sheen** *oil-based:* **dead flat, eggshell, gloss** Price ★ Ⓦ Ⓒ 🖼⌂

8 **Paint Magic/Quality Emulsion** Colour **haystack** Composition and finish *water-based:* **matt** Price ★★ Ⓦ

8

Dulux/Heritage Colours
Colour **DH pearl 1307G28Y**
Composition and finish *water-based:* **matt, silk, soft sheen** *oil-based:* **dead flat, eggshell, gloss** Price ★ W C 🔲 🗔

10 Farrow & Ball/National Trust
Colour **pea green** Composition and finish *water-based:* **distemper, matt** *oil-based:* **dead flat, eggshell** Price ★ W 🗔

11 Craig & Rose/Authentic Period Colours Colour **deep Adam green** Composition and finish *water-based:* **eggshell, chalk emulsion** Price ★★ W C F 🗔

12 Fired Earth/V&A Museum/Historic Colours Colour **terre vert 16** Composition and finish *water-based:* **emulsion, eggshell, distemper,** *oil-based:* **gloss** Price ★★ W C 🔲 🗔 🗔

13 Colourman Paints/Reproduction Colours Colour **104** Composition and finish *water-based:* **matt** Price ★★ W 🔲

9

11

13

15

17

19

10

12

14

16

18

20

14 Crown/Non-drip and Liquid Gloss Colour **Scottish pine** Composition and finish *oil-based:* **gloss** Price ★★ 🔲 🗔 🗔

15 Craig & Rose/Authentic Period Colours Colour **pompadour** Composition and finish *water-based:* **eggshell, chalk emulsion** Price ★★ W C F 🗔

16 The Old Fashioned Milk Paint Co Colour **Federal blue** Composition and finish **milk paint** Price ★★★ F 🔲 🗔

17 Pratt & Lambert/Interior Wall & Trim Colour **princely blue 1148** Composition and finish *water-based:* **matt, satin, eggshell, semi-gloss, gloss** Price ★★ W F 🔲

18 Colourman Paints/Reproduction Colours Colour **126** Composition and finish *water-based:* **matt** Price ★★ W 🔲

19 Paint and Paper Library/David Oliver Colour **Sophie Rose** Composition and finish *water-based:* **flat emulsion, acrylic eggshell, basecoat** *oil-based:* **dead flat, eggshell, basecoat** Price ★★★ W F 🔲 🗔

20 Paint and Paper Library/David Oliver Colour **bruno** Composition and finish *water-based:* **flat emulsion, acrylic eggshell, basecoat** *oil-based:* **eggshell, dead flat, basecoat** Price ★★★ W F 🔲 🗔

FROM DARK TO LIGHT

Lighter-coloured decorative schemes originated in the white-painted and gilded state rooms of French palaces during the late 17th century, but it took another 50 years for them to filter through to ordinary European, Scandinavian and American households. Consequently, for the first half of the 18th century, darker earth colours – muddy browns and greens ("drabs") – remained much in evidence on walls and joinery, but were gradually superseded by paler, brighter colours as the century progressed. Fashionable hues included pinks and light terracottas, pale greens and blues, and various yellows, such as "straw", "citron" and "Chinese".

1 Craig & Rose/Authentic Period Colours Colour **Swedish blue** Composition and finish *water-based:* **eggshell, chalk emulsion** Price ★★ W C 🔲 F

2 Berger Colour **pale lemon** Composition and finish *water-based:* **matt** Price ★★ W C

1

2

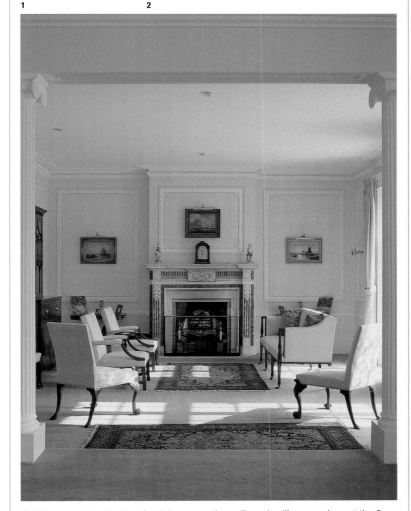

Subtly contrasting shades of pale lemon on the walls and ceiling complement the fine mahogany furniture, accentuate natural light and contribute to a general sense of spaciousness in this late 18th-century drawing room.

Paints: Early to mid-19th century

From the early 19th century until the 1830s, the late 18th-century drift toward the use of lighter hues (see page 290–291) continued in a number of fashionable colour schemes that combined cream, or sometimes white, with pale greys or blues. For the most part, however, Regency interiors were characterized by the use of stronger, more vivid hues. Notable examples, which were employed in fabrics and wallpapers as well as flat-painted finishes, included saffron and sulphur-yellows; emerald green; lilac and turquoise; deep pink; and cherry-, orange-, crimson- and Pompeiian reds. In the grandest Regency households, gilding was also much in evidence, primarily on decorative mouldings.

Such colours, many of which became fashionable in America, too (see opposite), were invariably applied flat and opaque. "Distressing" or "broken colour" techniques, such as sponging and ragging (see page 305), were not practised: their use in late 20th- and early 21st-century reproductions of Regency colour were an inauthentic, modern conceit.

1

2

3

4

1 Craig & Rose/Authentic Period Colours Colour **Regency white** Composition and finish *water-based:* **eggshell, chalk emulsion** Price ★★ W C F ☐

2 Crown/RIBA Drawings Colour **Regency 14** Composition and finish *water-based:* **emulsion, acrylic eggshell** Price ★★ W C ▣ ▦ T

3 Pratt & Lambert/Interior Wall & Trim Colour **osprey 1292** Composition and finish *water-based:* **matt, satin, eggshell, semi-gloss, gloss** Price ★★ W F ▣

4 Grand Illusions/Traditional Paints Colour **duck-egg blue** Composition and finish *water-based:* **matt** Price ★★ W F ▣

5 The Stulb Company Colour **Windsor Chair pink 81.2000.2** Composition and finish **milk paint** Price ★★★ W F ▣

6 Farrow & Ball/National Trust Colour **Eating Room red** Composition and finish *water-based:* **distemper, matt** *oil-based:* **distemper, dead flat, eggshell, gloss** Price ★★★ W ☐

7 Fired Earth/V&A Museum/Historic Colours Colour **Pompeiian red** Composition and finish *water-based:* **distemper, matt, eggshell** *oil-based:* **gloss** Price ★★ W C ▣

8 Dulux/Trade Colour Palette Colour **09YR 11/476** Composition and finish *water-based:* **matt, silk, soft sheen** *oil-based:* **dead flat, eggshell, gloss** Price ★ W C

9 J.W. Bollom/Bromel Colour **RAL 4005** Composition and finish *water-based:* **matt, silk** *oil-based:* **eggshell, gloss** Price ★★ W C ▣

10 Sanderson/Spectrum Colour **imperial purple 54-18U** Composition and finish *water-based:* **matt, silk** *oil-based:* **gloss** Price ★★ W C ▣ ☐

5

6

7

8

9

10

GOTHIC REVIVAL

Led by the architect Augustus Pugin and decorators such as John Gregory Crace, the Gothic Revival style became the height of fashion in Britain during the 1830s and 1840s. Based on studies of medieval design and decoration, it was characterized by deep, rich red, green, blue and yellow paint colours. These were echoed in tapestries and heavy, woven drapes, enlivened by brass candlesticks and wall sconces, and complemented by dark, heavy, ecclesiastical-style furniture mostly made of oak or mahogany.

1

2

3

4

1 Cole & Son Colour **Pugin blue** Composition and finish *water-based:* **emulsion** *oil-based:* **eggshell** Price ★★★ W C ▣ ▦ ☐

2 Crown/RIBA Drawings Colour **Gothic Revival 12** Composition and finish *water-based:* **emulsion, acrylic eggshell** Price ★★ W C ▣ ▦ T

3 Crown/RIBA Drawings Colour **Gothic Revival 3** Composition and finish *water-based:* **emulsion, acrylic eggshell** Price ★★ W C ▣ ▦ T

4 Crown/RIBA Drawings Colour **Gothic Revival 8** Composition and finish *water-based:* **emulsion, acrylic eggshell** Price ★★ W C ▣ ▦ T

| 11 | 12 | 13 | 14 | 15 | 16 |

| 17 | 18 | 19 | 20 | 21 |

THE FEDERAL PALETTE

During the 18th and 19th centuries, the colours employed in American interiors were strongly influenced by those that were fashionable at the time in Britain and France. This was especially so in the southern states of America, where rich plantation owners vied with one another to decorate their mansions in the most up-to-date Continental styles. Consequently, during the first half of the 19th century the "Colonial-Federal palette", which had combined earth colours, such as almond, rust-red and red-brown, with bright blues, greens and yellows, was gradually superseded by a later "Federal palette" that favoured terracottas, deep pinks, milky yellows, lavender and various stone colours, including several shades of grey.

1

2

1 Old Village Paints/Vintage Colours Colour **1752 lamplighter yellow** Composition and finish **milk paint** Price ★★★★ 🔳🔳🗁

2 Sawyer Finn Natural Milk Paint/River Valley Colour **terracotta** Composition and finish **milk paint** Price ★★★ Ⓦ Ⓒ Ⓕ 🔳

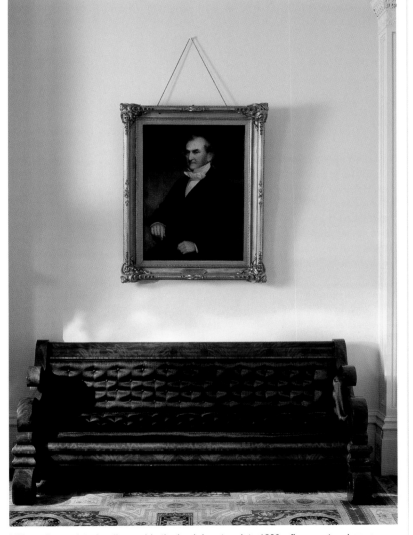

Milky-yellow painted walls provide the backdrop to a late 1830s, flame-cut mahogany settee in the Old Merchant's House, New York, USA. Yellow walls enlivened with gilt-framed paintings were particularly fashionable in the mid-19th century.

11 Finnaren & Haley/Shades of '76 Colour **Saybrook ivory 520800** Composition and finish *water-based:* **matt, satin, semi-gloss, gloss** *oil-based:* **semi-gloss** Price ★★★ Ⓦ 🔳 🗁

12 The Stulb Company Colour **Fancy Chair yellow 74.2000.1** Composition and finish **milk paint** Price ★★★ Ⓦ Ⓕ 🔳

13 Sherwin Williams/Preservation Palette Colour **rookwood clay SW2823** Composition and finish *water-based:* **matt, satin, semi-gloss** *oil-based:* **semi-gloss** Price ★★ Ⓦ 🔳

14 Sherwin Williams/Preservation Palette Colour **Downing sand SW 2822** Composition and finish *water-based:* **matt, satin, semi-gloss** *oil-based:* **semi-gloss** Price ★★ Ⓦ 🔳

15 Finnaren & Haley/Shades of '76 Colour **marblehead 520183** Composition and finish *water-based:* **matt, satin, semi-gloss, gloss** *oil-based:* **semi-gloss** Price ★ Ⓦ 🔳 🗁

16 Craig & Rose/Authentic Period Colours Colour **Sung yellow** Composition and finish *water-based:* **eggshell, chalk emulsion** Price ★★ Ⓦ Ⓒ Ⓕ 🗁

17 Dulux/Heritage Colours Colour **French grey 16BB50066** Composition and finish *water-based:* **matt, silk, soft sheen** *oil-based:* **dead flat, eggshell, gloss** Price ★ Ⓦ Ⓒ 🔳 🗁

18 Grand Illusions/Traditional Paints Colour **fresco pink** Composition and finish *water-based:* **matt** Price ★★ Ⓦ Ⓕ 🔳

19 Farrow & Ball/National Trust Colour **ointment pink** Composition and finish *water-based:* **distemper** *oil-based:* **distemper, dead flat, eggshell, gloss** Price ★★ Ⓦ 🗁

20 The Old Fashioned Milk Paint Co Colour **slate** Composition and finish *water-based:* **milk paint** Price ★★★ Ⓦ 🔳 🗁

21 Sherwin Williams/Preservation Palette Colour **Queen Anne lilac SW 0021** Composition and finish *water-based:* **matt, satin, semi-gloss** *oil-based:* **semi-gloss** Price ★★ Ⓦ 🔳

Paints: Mid- to Late 19th century

Most of the deeper, richer colours promoted by the Gothic Revival movement in the 1830s and 1840s (*see page 292*)) remained in vogue during the third quarter of the 19th century, and could still be found in many households 20 years later. In some respects this "High Victorian" palette was as much to do with technical innovation as fashionable aesthetics. The mid-century invention of aniline dyes derived from coal tar produced sharp yellows, deep blues, acid greens, lurid purples and mustards of an intensity not seen before – their sheer novelty an attractive quality in its own right. More traditional earthy reds and browns were still liked, but even these were usually brightened by eye-catching juxtapositions of gold or yellow. Not surprisingly, a reaction to this strong, eclectic and sometimes lurid palette soon set in – initially under the Aesthetic movement, and soon after among proponents and followers of the Arts and Crafts movement (*see*, respectively, below and opposite).

1 Craig & Rose/Authentic Period Colours Colour **Kashmir beige** Composition and finish *water-based:* **eggshell, chalk emulsion** Price ★★ W C F ⌂

2 Craig & Rose/Authentic Period Colours Colour **Winchester** Composition and finish *water-based:* **eggshell, chalk emulsion** Price ★★ W C F ⌂

AESTHETIC COLOURS

The richer and brighter hues favoured by the mid-to-late 19th-century Aesthetic movement (*see* above) included lustrous grape purples, plum-red, burgundy and lemon yellow. However, these were largely confined to soft furnishings. For painted woodwork and unpapered walls, paler or flatter colours were preferred. Flat olive green (known as "greenery-yallery") is probably the signature colour for Aesthetic woodwork, but white, ivory, stony greys and China blue were also popular, with shades of two or more often combined in the same room.

1 Craig & Rose/Authentic Period Colours Colour **moonstone grey** Composition and finish *water-based:* **eggshell, chalk emulsion** Price ★★ W C F ⌂

2 Morris & Co Colour **ivory** Composition and finish *water-based:* **matt emulsion** *oil-based:* **eggshell** Price ★ W C 🔲 🔲

3 Morris & Co Colour **olive** Composition and finish *water-based:* **matt emulsion** *oil-based:* **eggshell** Price ★★ W C 🔲 🔲

4 Fired Earth/V & A Museum/ Historic Colours Colour **china blue** Composition and finish *water-based:* **emulsion and eggshell** Price ★★ W C 🔲

3 Craig & Rose/Authentic Period Colours Colour **tapestry green** Composition and finish *water-based:* **eggshell, chalk emulsion** Price ★★ W C F ⌂

4 Craig & Rose/Authentic Period Colours Colour **jasper cane** Composition and finish *water-based:* **eggshell, chalk emulsion** Price ★★ W C F ⌂

5 Dulux/Heritage Colours Colour **crimson** Composition and finish *water-based:* **matt, silk, soft sheen** *oil-based:* **dead flat, eggshell, gloss** Price ★ W C 🔲 ⌂

6 Crown/RIBA Drawings Colour **Victorian eclectic** Composition and finish *water-based:* **emulsion, acrylic eggshell** Price ★★ W C 🔲 🔲 T

7 Craig & Rose/Authentic Period Colours Colour **Osborne maroon** Composition and finish *water-based:* **eggshell, chalk emulsion** Price ★★ W C F ⌂

8 Dulux/Heritage Colours Colour **yellow ochre** Composition and finish *water-based:* **matt, silk, soft sheen** *oil-based:* **dead flat, eggshell, gloss** Price ★ W C 🔲 ⌂

9 Craig & Rose/Authentic Period Colours Colour **grate black** Composition and finish *water-based:* **eggshell, chalk emulsion** Price ★★ W C F ⌂

12

13

14

15

10

11

ARTS AND CRAFTS MOVEMENT

Also partly a reaction to the stylistic eclecticism and rich palette of many High Victorian interiors (*see* page 294), the late 19th-century Arts and Crafts movement promoted a more coherent, generally lighter approach to decoration. The palette drew for inspiration on a number of sources, including medieval ones, but was ultimately characterized by the colours of flowers and plants indigenous to the English countryside. Notable among these were "greenery-yallery" (*see* Aesthetic colours, opposite) on woodwork, and old rose, burgundy red and hyacinth blue on walls.

1

2

3

1 Morris & Co Colour **rose** Composition and finish *water-based:* **matt emulsion** *oil-based:* **eggshell** Price ★ w C 🖼️🖌️

2 Fired Earth/V&A Museum/ Historic Colours Colour **Morris green** Composition and finish *water-based:* **emulsion, eggshell,** *oil-based:* **gloss** Price ★★ w C 🖼️🖌️🏠

3 Morris & Co Colour **mineral** Composition and finish *water-based:* **matt emulsion** *oil-based:* **eggshell** Price ★ w C 🖼️🖌️

Designed in the 1890s by Philip Webb, Standen House in Sussex, England, is a showpiece of the Arts and Crafts movement preserved by the National Trust. Its dining-room chimneypiece is painted sea green – another classic Arts and Crafts colour.

10 Fired Earth/V&A Museum/ Historic Colours Colour **Indian red** Composition and finish *water-based:* **emulsion, eggshell,** *oil-based:* **gloss** Price ★★ w C 🖼️🖌️🏠

11 Morris & Co Colour **wine** Composition and finish *water-based:* **matt emulsion** *oil-based:* **eggshell** Price ★ w C 🖼️🖌️

12 Morris & Co Colour **lichen** Composition and finish *water-based:* **matt emulsion** *oil-based:* **eggshell** Price ★ w C 🖼️🖌️

13 Holkham Linseed Paints Colour **wild sage** Composition and finish **linseed paint** Price ★★★ w C F 🖼️📊🖌️🏠

14 Morris & Co Colour **woad** Composition and finish *water-based:* **matt emulsion** *oil-based:* **eggshell** Price ★ w C 🖼️🖌️

15 Crown/RIBA Drawings Colour **Arts and Crafts 14** Composition and finish *water-based:* **emulsion, acrylic eggshell** Price ★★ w C 🖼️📊 T

Paints: Early 20th century

From the start of the 20th century to the outbreak of the First Word War, an element of continuity with late 19th-century Aesthetic colours was evident in Art Nouveau interiors (*see* below). However, the first four decades of the 20th century were largely dominated by three other, more innovative palettes. The first and most enduring of these centred on a fashion for "all-white" interiors, which emerged in the early 1900s and has coexisted alongside various other palettes to this day (*see* Quite White, page 300). The second palette, which largely consisted of pale, sophisticated hues, such as buff, beige, coffee, pastel blues and pinks and eau de Nil, became fashionable during the 1930s and in some respects was a forerunner of postwar–1950s' colour schemes (*see* page 298). In complete contrast, the third dominant palette – the height of fashion in Art Deco interiors of the late 1920s and 1930s – comprised striking combinations of hot, vivid colours (*see* opposite).

1

4

1 **Sherwin Williams/Preservation Palette** Colour **Burma jade SW 2862** Composition and finish *water-based:* **matt, satin, semi-gloss** *oil-based:* **semi-gloss** Price ★★ w c 🎨

2 **Dulux/Heritage Colours** Colour **eau de Nil 2127G36Y** Composition and finish *water-based:* **matt, silk, soft sheen** *oil-based:* **dead flat, eggshell, gloss** Price ★ w c 🎨 🏠

3 **Dulux/Heritage Colours** Colour **turquoise blue** Composition and finish *water-based:* **matt, silk, soft sheen** *oil-based:* **dead flat, eggshell, gloss** Price ★ w c 🎨 🏠

4 **Dulux/Heritage Colours** Colour **peacock blue** Composition and finish *water-based:* **matt, silk, soft sheen** *oil-based:* **dead flat, eggshell, gloss** Price ★ w c 🎨 🏠

5 **Crown/Emulsion for Walls and Ceilings** Colour **misty rose** Composition and finish *water-based:* **matt, silk** Price ★★ w c

6 **Fired Earth/V&A Museum/Art Nouveau** Colour **Cranston pink** Composition and finish *water-based:* **emulsion, eggshell** Price ★★ w c 🎨

7 **Fired Earth/V&A Museum/Art Nouveau** Colour **Glasgow grey** Composition and finish *water-based:* **emulsion, eggshell** Price ★★ w c 🎨

8 **Jane Churchill** Colour **primrose 12 grey** Composition and finish *water-based:* **matt** Price ★ w F 🎨

9 **Fired Earth/V&A Museum/Art Nouveau** Colour **Brussels orange** Composition and finish *water-based:* **emulsion, eggshell** Price ★★ w c 🎨

2

3

ART NOUVEAU

In many respects the palette for painted surfaces in Art Nouveau interiors (*see* above) can be seen as an extension of that of the Aesthetic movement (*see* page 294). Core colours included olive and sage green, pale blueish hues such as lilac and violet, pale yellow, and white and cream – both of the latter being particularly prevalent on walls in Charles Rennie Mackintosh interiors. However, stronger yellow-mustard and quirkier brown-mustard colours, and even black, were also sometimes used on woodwork.

1 **Fired Earth/V&A Museum/Art Nouveau** Colour **tearoom pink** Composition and finish *water-based:* **emulsion, eggshell** Price ★★ w c 🎨

2 **Fired Earth/V&A Museum/Art Nouveau** Colour **thistle** Composition and finish *water-based:* **emulsion, eggshell** Price ★★ w c 🎨

3 **Fired Earth/V&A Museum/Art Nouveau** Colour **maison jaune** Composition and finish *water-based:* **emulsion, eggshell** Price ★★ w c 🎨

4 **Fired Earth/V&A Museum/Art Nouveau** Colour **tervuren green** Composition and finish *water-based:* **emulsion, eggshell** *oil-based:* **gloss** Price ★★ w c 🎨 🎨 🏠

1

4

20th century

10 Dulux/Heritage Colours Colour **light buff** Composition and finish *water-based*: **matt, silk, soft sheen** *oil-based*: **dead flat, eggshell, gloss** Price ★ Ⓦ Ⓒ ▣ ⬠

11 Sanderson/Spectrum Colour **44-22M London grey** Composition and finish *water-based*: **matt, silk** *oil-based*: **eggshell, gloss** Price ★★ Ⓦ Ⓒ ▣ ▨ ⬠

12 Fired Earth/V&A Museum/Art Deco Colour **Silver screen** Composition and finish *water-based*: **metallic** Price ★★ Ⓦ ▣ Ⓢ ⬠

13 Dulux/Heritage Colours Colour **battleship grey** Composition and finish *water-based*: **matt, silk, soft sheen** *oil-based*: **dead flat, eggshell, gloss** Price ★ Ⓦ Ⓒ ▣ ⬠

14 Dulux/Heritage Colours Colour **slate** Composition and finish *water-based*: **matt, silk, soft sheen** *oil-based*: **dead flat, eggshell, gloss** Price ★ Ⓦ Ⓒ ▣ ⬠ *

10

11

12

HOT COLOURS

While predominantly white colour schemes have proved popular throughout the 20th century, there has also been a significant and contrasting vogue for employing combinations of hot, vivid colours. This can be traced back to the *Exposition des Arts Décoratifs*, held in Paris, France, in 1925, which launched the Art Deco movement internationally. Colours on show at the exhibition included ultramarine, sea green, deep blue, turmeric yellow, black, crimson, burnt orange and hot pink – tints that have remained fashionable ever since.

J.W. Bollom Colour **mandarin 06E51 JWB74** Composition and finish *water-based*: **matt, silk** *oil-based*: **eggshell, gloss** Price ★ Ⓦ Ⓒ ▣

John Oliver Colour **kinky pink** Composition and finish *water-based*: **matt** *oil-based*: **eggshell, gloss** Price ★★ Ⓦ ▣

This living room is painted and furnished in pink, beige, orange and black. The scheme is 1990s, but the colour combination originated in 1920s' Art Deco interiors.

15 Fired Earth/V&A Museum/Art Deco Colour **ocean liner** Composition and finish *water-based*: **emulsion, eggshell** Price ★★ Ⓦ Ⓒ ▣

16 Sherwin Williams/Preservation Palette Colour **pink flamingo SW0080** Composition and finish *water-based*: **matt, satin, semi-gloss** *oil-based*: **semi-gloss** Price ★★ Ⓦ Ⓒ ▣

17 Auro Organic Paints Colour **plum** Composition and finish *water-based*: **gloss, eggshell** Price ★★★ Ⓦ Ⓒ ▣ ▦ ▨ ⬠

18 Fired Earth/V&A Museum/Art Deco Colour **flapper pink** Composition and finish *water-based*: **emulsion, eggshell** Price ★★ Ⓦ Ⓒ ▣

19 Fired Earth/V&A Museum/Art Deco Colour **cabaret red** Composition and finish *water-based*: **emulsion, eggshell** Price ★★ Ⓦ Ⓒ ▣

20 Dulux/Heritage Colours Colour **brilliant green** Composition and finish *water-based*: **matt, silk, soft sheen** *oil-based*: **dead flat, eggshell, gloss** Price ★ Ⓦ Ⓒ ▣ ⬠

21 Crown/RIBA Drawings Colour **Art Deco 15** Composition and finish *water-based*: **emulsion, acrylic eggshell** Price ★★ Ⓦ Ⓒ ▣ ▩ Ⓣ

16

17

18

19

20

21

22

22 Fired Earth/V&A Museum/Art Deco Colour **jazz yellow** Composition and finish *water-based*: **emulsion, eggshell** Price ★★ Ⓦ Ⓒ ▣

23 Fired Earth/V&A Museum/Art Deco Colour **glamour gold** Composition and finish *water-based*: **metallic** Price ★★ Ⓦ ▣ Ⓢ ⬠

24 Crown/RIBA Drawings Colour **Art Deco 10** Composition and finish *water-based*: **emulsion, acrylic eggshell** Price ★★ Ⓦ Ⓒ ▣ ▩ Ⓣ

25 Crown/RIBA Drawings Colour **Art Deco 9** Composition and finish *water-based*: **emulsion, acrylic eggshell** Price ★★ Ⓦ Ⓒ ▣ ▩ Ⓣ

23

24

25

Paints: Mid-20th century

Underpinning the decorative styles that developed after 1945 was a universal need to leave behind the privations and gloom of the war years. This desire for a fresh start was strongly reflected in the colours favoured by decorators and homeowners. Initially, many looked back to the earlier years of the 20th century for inspiration – to bright, airy all-white or off-white schemes, and to the softer, paler colours of the 1930s (see pages 296 and 300).

By the 1960s and early 1970s, though, there was a widespread Art Nouveau revival, in which stronger Nouveau colours, such as peacock blues and greens, figured prominently (see page 296). Others took their inspiration from even earlier periods. For example, in some grander houses during the late 1950s and 1960s, late 18th- and early 19th-century schemes were recreated using opulent Neo-classical palettes (see pages 290–293). Far more innovative were the 'Op Art' interiors of the late 1950s and 1960s – notably those of influential designer David Hicks, who boldly combined an 18th-century sense of scale and form with saturated, contrasting colours, such as crimson, deep blue and violet.

THE 1950S PALETTE

For much of the 1950s, walls in many style-conscious homes were painted white. However, the chimneybreasts (or chimneybreast wall in its entirety) was invariably treated separately: either painted in a strongly contrasting primary colour, or lined with tongue-and-groove boards, usually of pine or stained in imitation of a darker wood. When white was not employed, fashionable alternatives included soft pinks, greens, blues and yellows, or pale, dusty reds, browns and greys.

1 Crown/RIBA Drawings Colour **50s sketchbook 1** Composition and finish *water-based:* **emulsion, acrylic eggshell** Price ★★ W C 🔲 🔲 T

2 Crown/RIBA Drawings Colour **50s sketchbook 4** Composition and finish *water-based:* **emulsion, acrylic eggshell** Price ★★ W C 🔲 🔲 T

3 Crown/RIBA Drawings Colour **50s sketchbook 9** Composition and finish *water-based:* **emulsion, acrylic eggshell** Price ★★ W C 🔲 🔲 T

4 Crown/RIBA Drawings Colour **50s sketchbook 11** Composition and finish *water-based:* **emulsion, acrylic eggshell** Price ★★ W C 🔲 🔲 T

5 Crown/RIBA Drawings Colour **50s sketchbook 15** Composition and finish *water-based:* **emulsion, acrylic eggshell** Price ★★ W C 🔲 🔲 T

1 Holkham Linseed Paints Colour **custard** Composition and finish **linseed paint** Price ★★★ W C F 🔲 🔲 🔲 🔲 🔲

2 Holkham Linseed Paints Colour **antique gold** Composition and finish **linseed paint** Price ★★★ W C F 🔲 🔲 🔲 🔲 🔲

3 Sawyer Finn Colour **peach** Composition and finish **milk paint** Price ★★★ W C F 🔲

4 Crown/RIBA Drawings Colour **50s sketchbook 8** Composition and finish *water-based:* **emulsion, acrylic eggshell** Price ★★ W C 🔲 🔲 T

5 Rose of Jericho/Classic Colours Colour **Pozzuoli red** Composition and finish **limewash** *water-based:* **matt emulsion, distemper, eggshell** *oil-based:* **flat oil, distemper, eggshell** Price ★ W C 🔲 🔲 🔲

6 Grand Illusions/Country Living Colour **708 Chinese leaf** Composition and finish *water-based:* **matt, acrylic** Price ★★ W 🔲

7 Grand Illusions/Country Living Colour **706 tourmaline** Composition and finish *water-based:* **matt, acrylic** Price ★★ W 🔲

8 Crown/RIBA Drawings Colour **50s sketchbook 14** Composition and finish *water-based:* **emulsion, acrylic eggshell** Price ★★ W C 🔲 🔲

20th century

9 Aalto Colour/Aalto Foundation Colour **Aalto turmeric** Composition and finish *water-based:* **matt** Price ★★ w C 🔲

10 Sherwin Williams/Preservation Palette Colour **holiday turquoise SW0076** Composition and finish *water-based:* **matt, satin, semi-gloss** *oil-based:* **semi-gloss** Price ★★ w C 🔲

11 Dulux/Trade Colour Palette Colour **72YY 47/743** Composition and finish *water-based:* **matt, silk, soft sheen** *oil-based:* **dead flat, eggshell, gloss** Price ★ w C

12 John Oliver Colour **Betty II blue** Composition and finish *water-based:* **matt** Price ★★ w 🔲

13 Paint Magic/Colour Collection Colour **Matisse blue** Composition and finish *water-based:* **matt** Price ★★ w C 🔲 ▨

14 Paint and Paper Library/ David Oliver Colour **hot lips** Composition and finish *water-based:* **flat emulsion, eggshell** *oil-based:* **eggshell, dead flat** Price ★★★ w 🔲

15 Paint and Paper Library/Nina Campbell Colour **raspberry** Composition and finish *water-based:* **flat emulsion, eggshell** *oil-based:* **eggshell, dead flat** Price ★★★ w 🔲

16 Auro Organic Paints Colour **beetle** Composition and finish *water-based:* **gloss, eggshell** Price ★★★ w C 🔲 ▨ ▨ ⌂

17 Grand Illusions/Country Living Colour **124 aubergine** Composition and finish *water-based:* **matt, acrylic** Price ★★ w 🔲

18 Designers Guild Colour **dandelion** Composition and finish *water-based:* **matt emulsion, eggshell** *oil-based:* **eggshell** Price ★★ w C F 🔲 ⌂

19 Designers Guild Colour **orchid** Composition and finish *water-based:* **matt emulsion, eggshell** *oil-based:* **eggshell** Price ★★ w C F 🔲 ⌂

KIDS COLOURS

Wallpapers and fabrics have been designed specifically for children's rooms since the 19th century (*see* Nursery Papers, page 253), but similarly designated paints are a more recent phenomenon. Early examples were lead-free and introduced in the mid-20th century when many standard paints still contained lead, which is harmful if ingested. However, from around the 1970s all bar some specialist paints have been formulated without this hazardous ingredient. Subsequently, therefore, kids' paints have been made and promoted on grounds of colour. Sometimes coordinated with wallpapers or fabrics from the same range, they are pale and restful or bright and energizing – dark, dense shades being held 'depressing' or 'unnerving' for young minds.

1 Designers Guild/Kids Paint Box Colour **daffodil** Composition and finish *water-based:* **matt emulsion, eggshell** *oil-based:* **eggshell** Price ★★ w C F 🔲 ⌂

2 Designers Guild/Kids Paint Box Colour **leaf** Composition and finish *water-based:* **matt emulsion, eggshell** *oil-based:* **eggshell** Price ★★ w C F 🔲 ⌂

3 Designers Guild/Kids Paint Box Colour **seashore** Composition and finish *water-based:* **matt emulsion, eggshell** *oil-based:* **eggshell** Price ★★ w C F 🔲 ⌂

4 Designers Guild/Kids Paint Box Colour **scarlet** Composition and finish *water-based:* **matt emulsion, eggshell** *oil-based:* **eggshell** Price ★★ w C F 🔲 ⌂

Paints: Late 20th–early 21st century

The decorative styles fashionable during the late 20th and early 21st century have been highly eclectic. This has resulted in a diverse range of colours being employed. As in the early and mid-20th century, white and off-white schemes have been in vogue (*see* below and pages 296–299). The practice of importing decorative palettes traditionally associated with the vernacular architecture of other countries or regions has also been prevalent, especially during the 1990s. Notable sources of inspiration have included cooling North African palettes; the hot, candy hues of the Mexican countryside; and the pure, vital metallic- and earth-pigment colours of the Mediterranean. At the same time, recreating and reinterpretating colour schemes from previous centuries has continued unchecked. Almost all periods have been referenced, although the medieval and Neo-classical periods (*see*, respectively, pages 288–289, and 290–293) have proved particularly rich mines for inspiration. Ultimately, this has been possible because of increased research into authentic period colours, and a dramatic increase in the range of colours produced by manufacturers following the development of new synthetic pigments and ever more sophisticated methods of manufacture.

1 2 3

4 5

QUITE WHITE

All-white colour schemes, or predominantly white schemes offset with stone colours, have been consistently in vogue during the late 20th and early 21st century. However, the fashion for them actually began around the turn of the 20th century. In 1904 English decorators Cowtan & Sons noted: "We seem to have done everything flatted white or enamelled white paint", while in the late 1920s Syrie Maugham created the influential "All-White Room" at her London home and Elsie de Wolfe produced similar interiors in America. The enthusiasm for white increased under the Modern movement and, subsequently, as manufacturers have produced increasingly "pure" brilliant whites. This enduring fashion is also underpinned by the gradual reduction of fossil-fuel-generated air pollution, which means whites no longer dirty as quickly as in the past'

Paint and Paper Library/David Oliver Colour **York stone** Composition and finish *water-based:* **emulsion, eggshell,** *oil-based:* **eggshell, oil, dead flat acrylic** Price ★★★ W C

Crown/Emulsion Colour **pure brilliant white** Composition and finish *water-based:* **matt, silk** Price ★★ W C

White-painted walls and ceilings provide an unobtrusive, neutral background for the natural colours and textures of a collection of functional and decorative wooden artefacts in designer Ivy Rosequist's 20th-century, cliffside Californian home.

1 **Dulux/Heritage Colours** Colour **0710 Y10R** Composition and finish *water-based:* **matt, silk, soft sheen** *oil-based:* **dead flat, eggshell, gloss** Price ★ W C 🏠

2 **Farrow & Ball/Off-Whites** Colour **blackened** Composition and finish *water-based:* **emulsion, eggshell, distemper** *oil-based:* **gloss, flat** Price ★★ W 🏠

3 **Farrow & Ball/Off-Whites** Colour **clunch** Composition and finish *water-based:* **emulsion, eggshell, distemper** *oil-based:* **gloss, flat** Price ★★ W 🏠

4 **Jane Churchill** Colour **oatmeal** Composition and finish *water-based:* **emulsion, eggshell** Price ★★ W

5 **Auro Organic Paints** Colour **ash** Composition and finish *water-based:* **gloss, eggshell** Price ★★★ W C 🏠

6 **Auro Organic Paints** Colour **mid-grey** Composition and finish *water-based:* **gloss, eggshell** Price ★★★ W C 🏠

7 Fired Earth/Kelly Hoppen/Indochine Colour **Zen** Composition and finish *water-based:* **matt emulsion, lacquer** Price ★★★ W C 🔲

8 Fired Earth/Kelly Hoppen/Indochine Colour **Chinese red** Composition and finish *water-based:* **matt emulsion, lacquer** Price ★★★ W C 🔲

9 Craig & Rose/Feng Shui Colour **bamboo** Composition and finish *water-based:* **emulsion, gentle sheen** Price ★ W C

10 Georgina Barrow/Cotswold Colours Colour **29 smock blue** Composition and finish *water-based:* **emulsion, flat** Price ★★ W C 🔲 🔲 🔲

MEDITERRANEAN PALETTE

Since the early 1990s, the distinctive palette of colours traditionally associated with the vernacular architecture of the Mediterranean has been increasingly employed in more northern climes. Essentially simple whitewash formulations coloured with earth pigments or by-products of the mining industry, such as chrome oxide, cobalt, copper carbonate and cadmium, their appeal is readily understandable. Not only do they display a vitality and purity of colour, and a mellowing with age, rarely matched by modern synthetic paints, they also change in appearance according to the light – acquiring an often dazzling luminosity in bright sunlight, and a darker, chalky quality under overcast conditions.

1 Zest Essentials/Mediterranean Palette Colour **Merseille 118** Composition and finish *water-based:* **emulsion** Price ★ W

2 Zest Essentials/Mediterranean Palette Colour **Seville 108** Composition and finish *water-based:* **emulsion** Price ★ W

3 Grand Illusions/Mediterranean Palette Colour **524 Giverny** Composition and finish *water-based:* **matt, acrylic** Price ★★ W 🔲

4 Grand Illusions/Mediterranean Palette Colour **115 olive** Composition and finish *water-based:* **matt, acrylic** Price ★★ W 🔲

11 Craig & Rose/Feng Shui Colour **aquamarine** Composition and finish *water-based:* **emulsion, gentle sheen** Price ★ W C

12 Craig & Rose/Feng Shui Colour **sulphur** Composition and finish *water-based:* **emulsion, gentle sheen** Price ★ W C

13 Aalto Colour/Aalto Foundation Colour **Aalto Clearing 82** Composition and finish *water-based:* **acrylic, gloss, satin, enamel** *oil-based:* **gloss enamel** Price ★★ W C 🔲 🔲 🔲 🔲 🔲

14 Old Village Paints/Couleurs de Provence Colour **2103 lavande** Composition and finish **milk paint** Price ★★★★ 🔲 🔲 🔲

15 Paint and Paper Library/Nina Campbell Colour **cinnabar** Composition and finish *water-based:* **flat emulsion, eggshell** *oil-based:* **eggshell, dead flat** Price ★★★ W 🔲

16 Old Village Paints/Couleurs de Provence Colour **2105 rouge royal** Composition and finish **milk paint** Price ★★★★ 🔲 🔲 🔲

Specialist Paints & Waxes

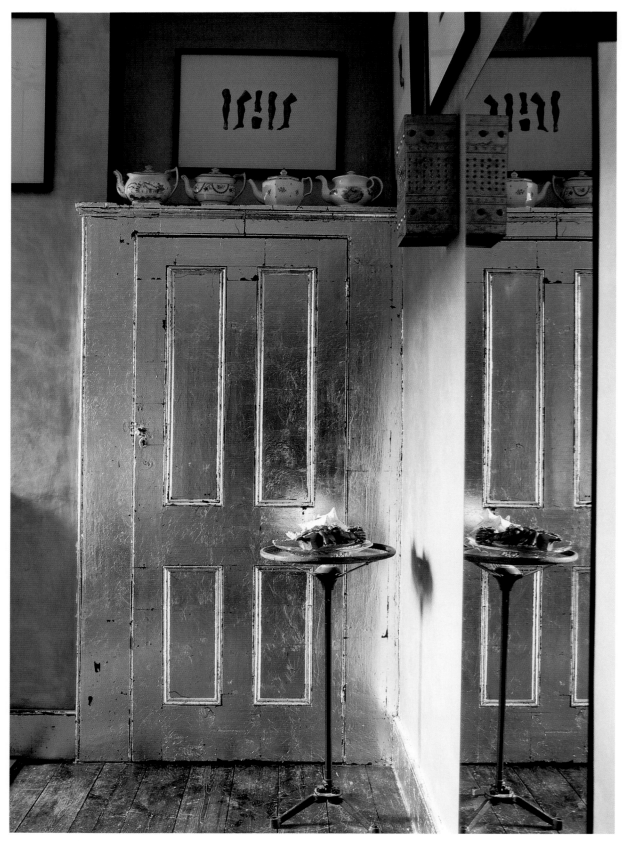

Whether hand-mixed by 18th-century itinerant craftsmen or mass-produced in 21st-century factories, the majority of paints have been designed to cover plaster, masonry or wooden surfaces with a smooth, opaque film of colour. In other words, most paints are simply used to decorate and protect a surface, and even though they mask the underlying material they do not disguise what it is, nor are they meant to.

However, there are some specialist paints and waxes that are intended visually to transform masonry, plaster or wood into a different material, or replicate another decorative medium. These include metallic paints and gilt creams, which simulate base or precious metals; liming pastes, which reproduce the bleaching effects of quick-lime on wood; textured paints that mimic decorative plasterwork; multi-coloured paints that resemble stonework or ceramics; and "broken colour" applications that imitate the fugitive pigmentation of early paints or the effects of ageing, or simply confer an abstract pattern upon a surface.

LEFT The built-in storage cupboard in the bathroom of this 19th-century townhouse in London, England, would have been painted originally or grained to match the woodwork. It now boasts a silver metallic paint finish more in keeping with the 1990s. The silver also works harmoniously with the wall mirror, serving to brighten the room.

ABOVE Set against a dark, terracotta-coloured, limewashed wall, this fire surround has been given a painted *faux*-marble finish. During the last quarter of the 20th century, many paint manufacturers produced paint kits (supplied with specialist applicators) for producing *faux*-marble, *faux*-porphyry and woodgrained finishes on plaster and wood.

ABSTRACT FINISHES

During the late 20th century, "broken colour" techniques – such as spattering, ragging, sponging, stippling, dragging and combing – were all the rage. Derived from fine art, they involve distressing paints and glazes applied over a contrasting-coloured ground to produce subtle patterns and gradations of colour. Manufacturers often supply paints and application tools specifically designed for the purpose. This example is an abstract pattern; others may simulate stone.

---

1 Many manufacturers supply paints designed to reproduce distressed finishes, such as ragging and rag-rolling, or to simulate materials such as porphyry.

2 Textured paints have been available since the early 20th century, and are mostly used to simulate the appearance of rustic plasterwork.

3 Gilt creams and waxes have been used since the Renaissance as an easy alternative to the traditional method of gilding wooden furniture and joinery with metal leaf or metallic powders.

4 Paints that produce a coating that imitates beaten and hammered metal became very popular during the late 20th century. They are available in a range of colours and finishes.

---

1 Dulux/Duette Colour **coral cascade** Composition and finish *water-based:* **matt** Price ★★ W C

2 Berger/Textures Colour **heavy texture with marble chips** Composition and finish *solvent-based:* **marble/stone** Price ★★★ W C

3 Liberon Waxes Colour **Fontainebleau** Composition and finish *spirit-based:* **satin sheen** Price ★★★★

4 Trimite/Hammer Finishes Colour **stoving red 811** Composition and finish *water-based:* **metallic** Price ★★

ABOVE The *chinoiserie* decoration on this four-poster bed has been executed in shades of gold metallic paint on a black oil-painted ground. The soft, flat finish was achieved by applying clear matt polyurethane varnish, lightly rubbed with fine-grade wire wool.

SPECIALIST PAINTS & WAXES **303**

Specialist Paints & Waxes

Metallic paints can be used on metal, wood and plaster, and are available in a wide range of colours. They are also produced in a range of different textures, including "smooth", "hammered" and "metallic cloth". Gilt creams and waxes, on the other hand, are always burnished smooth; used on mouldings, they replicate leaf- or powder-gilding. Colours include copper and shades of gold and silver.

Liming kits are available as hard waxes and soft pastes: the former are used on open-grained hardwoods, such as oak and ash; the latter on close-grained softwoods, such as pine. Some contain lime, which bleaches the wood a grey-white hue; others mimic this by depositing flecks of whiting in the grain.

Textured paints are mainly used to disguise cracked plaster, and are patterned with a serrated tool in imitation of the random swirls of rustic plasterwork. Similarly, most paints that mimic the appearance of ceramics (notably earthenware) and decorative stones (such as porphyry), or simulate the breakdown of pigments seen in pre-20th-century paints, are distressed with a specialist tool, or a brush or rag (*see* opposite). However, a few are supplied with an applicator that spatters colours randomly on top of one another.

1

2

3

4

5

6

1 **Aalto Colour/Aalto Precious Metals** Colour **Aalto void 14** Composition and finish *water-based:* **enamel** Price ★★★★ W C 🔲 🔳 🔳 🔳 🔳

2 **Tor Coatings/Ardenbrite** Colour **old penny bronze 35** Composition and finish *spirit-based:* **satin** Price ★★★★ 🔲 S 🔳 🔳 🔳

3 **Aalto Colour/Aalto Precious Metals** Colour **Aalto void 4** Composition and finish *water-based:* **enamel** Price ★★★★ W C 🔲 🔳 🔳 🔳 🔳

4 **Aalto Foundation/Aalto Precious Metals** Colour **Aalto starling 11** Composition and finish *water-based:* **enamel** Price ★★★★ W C 🔲 🔳 🔳 🔳 🔳

5 **Liberon Waxes** Colour **gilt cream chantilly** Composition and finish *spirit-based:* **satin sheen** Price ★★★★ 🔲 🔳

6 **Aalto Foundation/Aalto Precious Metals** Colour **Aalto zip 28** Composition and finish *water-based:* **enamel** Price ★★★★ W C 🔲 🔳 🔳 🔳 🔳

8

9

FAUX-STONE FINISHES

"Broken-colour" techniques such as ragging, sponging, stippling and spattering can be used to create abstract patterns in paint. However, since ancient Greek and Roman times these techniques have also been employed to simulate stones such as marble, limestone, granite and porphyry. *Faux*-stone finishes are used on architectural fixtures and fittings, and on furniture, when the natural material is unavailable, too expensive or structurally unsuitable. In the past, the authenticity of the finish was dependent on the skills of the decorator, but the specialist *faux*-stone paint kits now available have helped to guarantee effective results.

10

Paint Magic/Textures & Speciality Plasters/Marmorino Colour **white base (tint to colour)** Composition and finish **lime, marble** Price ★★★★ W C

7 **Berger/Luxatile Epoxy Polyurethane System** Colour **white** Composition and finish *solvent-based:* **high sheen, gloss** Price ★★ W C

8 **Paint Magic/Textures & Speciality Plasters/Craquelure** Colour **clear** Composition and finish *water-based:* **antique cracked varnish** Price ★★★★ W

9 **Berger/Textures** Colour **stoneshield** Composition and finish *solvent-based:* **marble/stone** Price ★★★ W C

10 **Trimite/Hammer Finishes** Colour **dark green 828** Composition and finish *water-based:* **metallic** Price ★★

11 **Artex/Decorative Textured Finishes** Colour **white** Composition and finish *water-based:* **textured** Price ★ W C

Dulux/Duette Classic Colour **springwater** Composition and finish *water-based:* **matt** Price ★★ W C

The Stencil Store/Paint Effects Colour **earthenware pink** Composition and finish *water-based:* **matt** Price ★★★ W

11

PAINTS & FINISHES: *SPECIALIST PAINTS & WAXES* **305**

Wood Finishes

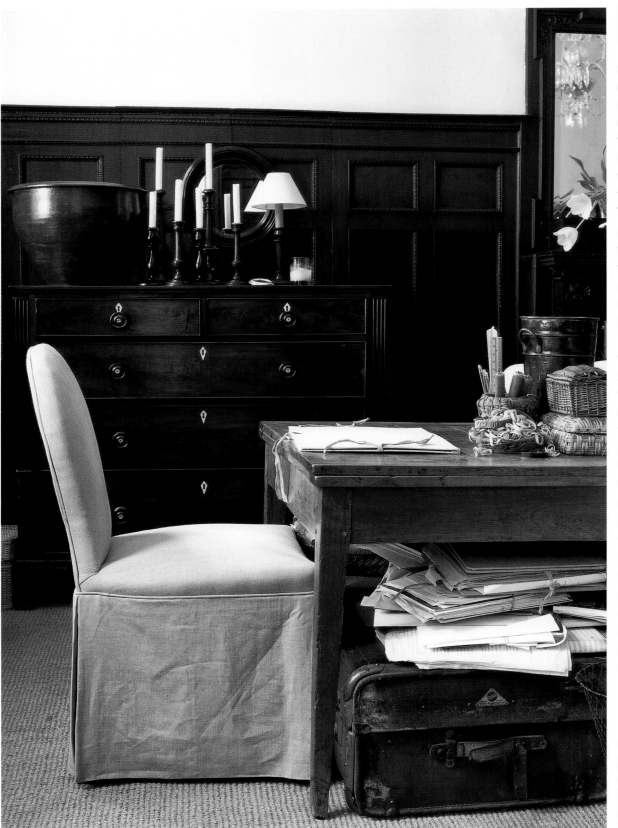

Unless they are heavily diluted, most paints dry to an opaque finish, and so obliterate the natural appearance of any wooden surface. For this reason, decorators have traditionally favoured translucent and semi-translucent stains and varnishes when highlighting the figuring and grain of a wood. This is particularly true in the case of hardwoods, such as walnut, oak and mahogany, which usually display more attractive markings than their softwood counterparts, which include pine and fir.

Wood stains are available in various formulations (*see* page 308–309). Some are intended for use on external woodwork, others for internal wood and furniture. Some offer protection against moisture and general wear and tear in a single coat, while others require an additional application of varnish or shellac and wax. However, the real versatility of wood stains lies in the colours available, which range from "natural" hues, such as brown or red mahogany, ebony and pine, to "non-naturalistic" tones, such as several shades of blue, green and grey.

LEFT An 18th-century chest of drawers, made of mahogany, has been restored using a dark brown, water-based mahogany stain that has then been shellacked and polished – the traditional finish. The half-height wall-panelling – typical of both Georgian and later Arts and Crafts interiors has been treated in the same manner.

1 Oil-based stains produce pure, transparent colours on timber, and since the 1970s have often been formulated to allow moisture to evaporate rather than remain trapped in the wood.

2 Many water-based stains require additional varnishing to make timber waterproof. However, those designed for exterior use are water-repellant and have anti-fungal properties.

3 Many chemical-based stains produce colour by reacting with the tannic acid that is present in wood. This light oak stain is designed for exterior use and formulated to resist cracking, peeling and flaking.

4 Nowadays, manufacturers often incorporate pigments in solvent- or spirit-based stains that help to filter out ultraviolet rays, thereby reducing the problem of fading in darker colours constantly exposed to sunlight.

1 Auro Organic Paints//Woodstains Colour **NR160-55 ultramarine blue** Composition and finish *oil-based:* **semi-translucent satin** Price ★★★ 📷 ⬜

2 Protim Solignum/Fencetone Colour **golden cedar** Composition and finish *water-based:* **matt** Price ★★★ 📷 ⬜

3 Dacrylate Paints/Nordac Wood Shades Colour **light oak** Composition and finish *chemical-based:* **natural** Price ★★ 📷 ⬜

4 Dulux/Weathershield Exterior Wood Stain Colour **ebony** Composition and finish *solvent-based:* **transparent satin** Price ★★★ 📷 ⬜

BOVE The cupboard, mirror surround, ngue-and-groove dado cladding and tt-jointed floorboards in this bathroom e made of pine. They have been coated ith clear varnish to protect them from the fects of moisture. The contrasting wooden n of the bath has been mahogany-stained d clear-varnished.

RIGHT This late 20th-century dining table stands on lightly limed, butt-jointed pine floorboards in the principal living area of a converted malt house built in the early 19th century in Somerset, England. The table is made of elm and has a clear beeswax-polish finish that allows the natural colour and figuring of the wood to show through.

Wood Finishes

There are four basic types of wood stain: water-, oil-, spirit- and chemical-based. Water-based stains produce clear, vivid colours that are well suited to light, close-grained woods, such as beech and pine. They raise the grain of the wood, which then needs sanding before varnishing, or treating with shellac and waxing.

Oil-based stains do not raise the grain of the wood, nor do they have to be varnished or treated with shellack; they also produce more even and transparent coloration on both hardwoods and softwoods. If the stains are spirit-based, the colours are usually muted and the grain raised. Spirit-based stains are best suited to oily or hard, fine-grained woods (especially before French polishing).

Chemical stains are many and varied. Notable types include biochromate of potash, which turns beech a light tan and walnut a pale yellow; and blue copperas, which gives most woods a light grey hue. However, exact coloration is unpredictable since it is affected by the level of tannic acid in the wood.

1 **Ronseal/All-in-One Quick & Simple/Woodstain** Colour **walnut** Composition and finish *oil-based:* **satin, gloss** Price ★★★

2 **Cabot Stains/O.V.T. Solid Color Stains** Colour **oracle sun** Composition and finish *oil-based:* **matt** Price ★★

3 **Cabot Stains/O.V.T. Solid Color Stains** Colour **chesapeake** Composition and finish *oil-based:* **matt** Price ★★

4 **Auro Organic Paints/Woodstain** Colour **NR160-74 grau** Composition and finish *oil-based:* **semi-translucent satin** Price ★★★

5 **Protim Solignum/Timbertone** Colour **petrol blue** Composition and finish *oil-based:* **translucent matt, translucent sheen** Price ★★★

6 **Liberon/Liming Wax** Colour **whit** Composition and finish *water-based:* **matt** Price ★★★

7 **Dulux/Protective Woodstain** Colour **elderberry** Composition and finish *solvent-based:* **transparent satin** Price ★★★

2

3

5

6

4

7

8

9

10

11

12

13

11 Dulux/Weathershield Exterior Woodstain Colour **antique pine** Composition and finish *solvent-based:* **matt** Price ★★★ 🖾 ⬜

12 Dulux/Protective Woodstain Colour **watermelon** Composition and finish *solvent-based:* **transparent satin** Price ★★ 🖾 ⬜

13 Rustins/Colorglaze Transparent Satin Colours Colour **grey** Composition and finish *oil-based:* **satin** Price ★★ 🖾 ⬜

14 Rustins/Colorglaze Colour **yellow** Composition and finish *oil-based:* **satin** Price ★★ 🖾 ⬜

8 Old Village Paints/Paste Woodstain Colour **brown mahogany** Composition and finish **milk paint** Price ★★★★ 🖾 ✐ ⬜

9 Old Village Paints/Paste Woodstain Colour **fruit wood** Composition and finish **milk paint** Price ★★★★ 🖾 ✐ ⬜

10 Auro Organic Paints/ Woodstains Colour **orangerot 80% NR160-26, 20% 160-33** Composition and finish *oil-based:* **semi-translucent satin** Price ★★★ 🖾 ⬜

MICROPOROUS WOOD STAINS

Anyone wishing to produce a durable, decorative finish on wooden surfaces has to contend with the fact that timber readily absorbs moisture from the atmosphere and from any material with which it is in contact. When the weather is warm and humidity levels fall, the moisture evaporates, causing traditional stains and varnishes that seal the surface to "bubble" and eventually to lift off. Fortunately, manufacturers have recently found ways to formulate microporous stains and varnishes that let moisture evaporate through them without causing damage.

Dacrylate Paints/Nordac Wood Shades Colour **pine** Composition and finish *chemical-based:* **natural** Price ★★ 🖾 ⬜

Dacrylate Paints/Nordac Wood Shades Colour **mahogany** Composition and finish *chemical-based:* **natural** Price ★★ 🖾 ⬜

14

Tiles

Plain Tiles

ABOVE This bathroom in the Rockcliffe Mansion in Hannibal, Missouri, USA is typical of a luxury bathroom installation of the late 19th century. It features plain white tiles that have been laid in brick fashion with relief-moulded capping. Similar arrangements of tiles were popular until the mid-1930s.

LEIGHTON HOUSE

Early mosaics, made up of thousands of small plain tiles, often featured Islamic-inspired patterns. The mosaic panel shown here, with a geometric floral pattern, is in the entrance hall of Leighton House in London, England. The artist Lord Leighton displayed his large collection of Islamic tiles in the "Arab Hall". The walls and ceiling were clad with original 16th- and 17th-century Iznik tiles, with the reproductions made by his friend William de Morgan to complete damaged panels.

During the mid-12th century, plain tiles were laid in large numbers on the floors of churches, cathedrals and royal palaces throughout Europe. Most were made locally using red-firing clays, often with a honey-coloured lead glaze to minimize wear. This was sometimes applied over a layer of white slip to produce yellow tiles, while the addition of a little copper to the glaze gave a range of greens.

Unglazed plain quarry tiles were very popular during the 18th and 19th centuries, but these were superseded by the flatter, smoother tiles produced by Herbert Minton using the dust-pressing technique invented by the Englishman Richard Prosser in 1840. Initially conceived as a method of making ceramic buttons from dried clay, this technique, Minton realized, could also be used to form ceramic *tesserae* and larger tiles. Plain tiles have been popular ever since. Art Nouveau schemes favoured pastel-shaded tiles, while red and black were dominant in Art Deco interiors of the late 1920s and the 1930s. More recently, the plain "rustic" tile has once again become fashionable.

RIGHT A simple but effective floor pattern has been achieved here by using just two colours of plain tile, laid alternately. This style of floor has its origins in Medieval cathedrals across Europe and was often re-created during the Renaissance using black and white marble.

KEY DESIGNS

1 Natural stone has always been used as a flooring material. Reclaimed limestone tiles and ceramic tiles imitating natural materials have recently become popular.

2 Geometric pavements, often consisting of combinations of triangular, hexagonal or rectangular plain tiles, have limitless permutations of patterns.

3 The humble, unglazed quarry tile has been used for centuries as a hard and durable floor covering. Plain terracotta tiles have become highly desirable in homes over the past few years.

4 Glazed tiles, with an uneven, slightly translucent appearance, were much liked in the mid-19th century. The Victorians favoured this "hand-made" look on their mass-produced tiles.

5 Light-reflective, easy-to-clean white tiles were widely seen during the mid-19th century, and have become almost universally popular in recent years.

6 Marble, a durable crystalline limestone, is available in an array of colours and patterns. Decorative and practical, it has remained a popular floorcovering.

---

1 Stonell/Bamboo Colour **grey with rust streak**
Alt. colours **yes** Composition **slate** Size
40 x 40 x 1.2cm/15¾ x 15¾ x ½in
Price ★★★ F ⊞

2 Elon/Carrillo Plain Colours Colour **natural**
Alt. colours **yes** Composition **ceramic**
Size **30 x 30cm/11¾ x 11¾in**
Price ★ F W

3 Elon/Saltillo Square Colour **terracotta**
Alt. colours **no** Composition **terracotta**
Size **30 x 30 x 2cm/11¾ x 11¾ x ¾in**
Price ★ F ⊞

4 Winchester Tile Co/Colours Colour **lime green**
Alt. colours **yes** Composition **ceramic**
Size **10.5 x 10.5cm x 7mm/4 x 4 x ¼in**
Price ★ W ⊞

5 H. & R. Johnson/Cotswold COTS 13 Colour **white
gloss** Alt. colours **yes** Composition **ceramic**
Size **15 x 15cm x 7mm/6 x 6 x ¼in**
Price ★ W ⊞

6 Pisani/Onyx Green Colour **green** Alt. colours
yes Composition **marble** Size **30.5 x
30.5 x 1cm/12 x 12 x ⅜in**
Price ★★★★★ special order F ⊞

Plains: **Pre-20th century**

Most early plain tiles were single-coloured, hand-made products, formed from local clays. A glaze was often applied to make a more durable surface or to add to the limited range of colours. These tiles were used on the floors of abbeys, cathedrals and parish churches throughout Europe.

In 1840, in England, the dust-pressing technique was invented by Richard Prosser. The technique used dry clay, which was ground into a fine powder, moistened with water and pressed into shape in a tile press. International interest in this process stemmed from the fact that tiles could now be produced with smoother surfaces and more accurate dimensions. A greater range of colours was also made possible, as pigments could be added much more easily to dry clay. Huge quantities of dust-pressed tiles were produced for constructing geometric pavements, which relied on the many different and newly available colours for their decorative effect.

The mid-19th century saw a large increase in the production of plain-glazed wall tiles. This was triggered by the construction of railway stations and by new demands for hygiene in hospitals, which created a need for light-reflective, easy-to-clean, durable surfaces.

1

2

5

6

7

4

8

9

1 Fired Earth/Venetian Marble (2 tiles) Colour **Rosso** Alt. colours **yes** Composition **marble** Size **10 x 10cm/4 x 4i**n Price ★ F

2 Kievel Stone/Fossil Stone Colour **cream** Alt. colours **no** Composition **limestone** Size **40 x 20cm/15¾ x 8in** Price ★★★★★ F ⊞

3 Walker Zanger/Metallismo/ Rhomboid Finish 877 611 0199 Colour **smooth** Alt. colours **yes** Composition **metal** Size **2 x 4cm/¾ x 1½in** Price ★★★★★

4 Fired Earth/VM Travertino Colour **travertino** Alt. colours **yes** Composition **Venetian marble** Size **10 x 10cm/4 x 4**in Price ★ F ⊞

5 Fired Earth/Turin Stone/Aosta Green Colour **green** Alt. colours **yes** Composition **terracotta** Size **15 x 15cm/6 x 6in** Price ★ F

6 Marble Flooring Specialists/ Labrador Blue Pearl Colour **blue pearl** Alt. colours **no** Composition **granite** Size **30 x 30cm/11¾ x 11¾in** Price ★★ F ⊞

7 Kirkstone/Pavia Toscana Colour **roman light** Alt. colours **yes** Composition **Itallian travertine** Size **40 x 40cm/15¾ x 15¾in** Price ★★★★★ ⊞

8 Original Style/Skirting Tile G9903 Colour **royal blue** Alt. colours **yes** Composition **ceramic** Size **15 x 15cm/6 x 6in** Price ★ W

9 Stonell/Mountain Green Slate Colour **mountain green** Alt. colours **no** Composition **slat**e Size **30 x 30cm/11¾ x 11¾in** Price ★ F ⊞

12

10 Fired Earth/Valencia Dado
Colour **cream** Alt. colours
yes Composition **ceramic**
Size **12 x 5cm/4¾ x 2in** Price
★★ W

**11 Fired Earth/Antique
Reclaimed Terracotta/Classic
Melange Hexagonals** Colour
natural Alt. colours **yes**
Composition **terracotta** Size
various Price ★★★★★
(£/m²) F

12 Elon/Natural Marble Colour
snow white Alt. colours **yes**
Composition **marble** Size
30 x 30cm/11¾ x 11¾in
Price ★ ⊞

**13 Paris Ceramics/Antique
Parrefeuille Terracotta**
Colour **terracotta** Alt.
colours **no** Composition
terracotta Size **35 x 21cm/
13¾ x 8¼in** Price ★★★★★
(special order) F

**14 Fired Earth/Roman Mosaic
Natural Floor** Colour
natural Alt. colours
yes Composition **stone**
Size **20 x 20cm/8 x 8in** Price
★★ F ⊞

13

14

NATURAL STONE

The colours available to the tile-maker were once limited to those of the natural materials at hand. These materials had a wealth of subtle tones and natural patterning that are still appreciated today. Stone provides a rich variation of subtle hues according to locality, from dark slate or granite to pale, warm sandstones. Marble, with its distinctive, veined appearance, is a more costly alternative. In the case of stone and marble, most of the durable materials are of neutral, earthy tones, while naturally occurring clays generally fire to a red or a buff colour.

Villeroy & Boch/Villostone/Indian Stone Colour **2104 8335**
Alt. colours **yes** Composition **porcelain stonework**
Size **30 x 30cm/11¾ x 11¾in** Price ★★★★ F

15

16

17

18

19

20

21

**15 Fired Earth/Pre-sealed
Encaustic** Colour **olive** Alt.
colours **yes** Composition
encaustic Size **20 x 20cm/8 x
8in** Price ★ F

16 Elon/Carrillo Plain Colours
Colour **terracotta** Alt. colours
yes Composition **ceramic**
Size **20 x 20cm/8 x
8in** Price ★ W F ⊞

17 Froyle Tiles/Vellum Colour
vellum Alt. colours **yes**
Composition **stoneware**
Size **10 x 10cm/4 x 4in**
Price ★ W F ▢ ▣ ⊞

18 Winchester Tile Co/Colours
Colour **yellow** Alt. colours
yes Composition **ceramic** Size
12.5 x 12.5cm/5 x 5in Price
★★ W ⊞

**19 Original Style/Victorian
Floor Tiles/Conway Triangle**
Colour **buff** Alt. colours **no**
Composition **ceramic** Size
5 x 3.5cm/2 x 1⅓in Price ★★
▢ F ⊞

20 Original Style/KK5903 Colour
foxglove Alt. colours **yes**
Composition **ceramic** Size
14 x 10cm/5½ x 4in Price ★ W

**21 H. & R. Johnson/Minton
Hollins/Victoria Blue Border
Tile MH1B** Colour **blue** Alt.
colours **yes** Composition
ceramic Size **15 x 7.5cm/
6 x 2⅞in** Price ★ W F ⊞

Plains: 20th–early 21st century

At the beginning of the 20th century, the Art Nouveau influence began to manifest itself in tile design. Most Art Nouveau tiles were individual designs that were intended to be set among plain tiles within a scheme. However, by the 1920s the plain tiles had become dominant and entire rooms were decorated with these in pastel shades, sometimes with a narrow row of simple black and white geometric border tiles set at dado height. Highly glazed tiles gradually became less popular, and manufacturers responded by producing eggshell and matt-glazed plain tiles.

Stronger colours, including red and black, were used in the late 1920s and early 1930s as Art Deco schemes became increasingly favoured. The popularity of strong colours on plain tiles was further enhanced as tile-makers employed chemists to develop new glaze colours and effects. During the 1960s and 1970s, there was a move towards using not only strong colours but textures and mottling in the decoration of tiles.

During the late 20th and early 21st century, "rustic" plain tiles, made by hand or in imitation of hand-production, have become popular, the variations in shape and shade extending the range of plain tiles available.

1

1 **Saloni/Eternity/Vidriado** Colour **miel** Alt. colours **yes** Composition **porcelain ceramic** Size **30 x 30cm/ 11¾ x 11¾in** Price ★★★★★ W F ⊞

2 **Elite Tiles/Porcelain Tile** Colour **polish** Alt. colours **yes** Composition **porcelain** Size **30 x 30cm x 9mm/ 11¾ x 11¾ x ⅛in** Price ★★★★ F

3 **Cinca/Arquitectos/Azulejo de Faianca/Vidruda de Parta/Branca Matt 0190** Colour **beige** Alt. colours **yes** Composition **white biscuit** Size **15 x 15cm/6 x 6in** Price ★★★ W ⊞

2

3

4

5

6

7

8

4 **Kenneth Clark Ceramics/Plain Colours** Colour **honey** Alt. colours **yes** Composition **ceramic** Size **10 x 10cm/ 4 x 4in** Price ★ ⊞

5 **Domus Tiles/Interni Ghiaccio Satin Finish** Colour **white** Alt. colours **yes** Composition **ceramic** Size **10 x 10cm x 7mm/4 x 4 x ¼in** Price ★ F ⊞

6 **Winchester Tile Co/Colours** Colour **grey** Alt. colours **yes** Composition **ceramic** Size **10.5 x 10.5cm x 7mm/ 4 x 4 x ¼in** Price ★★ W

7 **Elon/Carrillo Plain Colours** Colour **red** Alt. colours **yes** Composition **ceramic** Size **10 x 10cm x 7mm/4 x 4 x ¼in** Price ★ W F

8 **H. & R. Johnson/Pennines/ Profile Strip** Colour **yellow** Alt. colours **yes** Composition **ceramic** Size **10 x 5cm/4 x 2in** Price ★ W

10

11

12

16

17

13

14

15

9 **Villeroy & Boch/Non-Vitreous Walls/Granicolour 0016 D341** Colour **green** Alt. colours **yes** Composition **non-vitreous ceramic** Size **15 x 15cm/6 x 6in** Price ★★★★ W

10 **Marble Flooring Specialists/ Marghestone Grigio Plata M234** Colour **multi** Alt. colours **yes** Composition **marble** Size **60 x 40 x 2cm/23¾ x 15¾ x ¾in** Price ★ F +

11 **Winchester Tile Co/Colours** Colour **turquoise** Alt. colours **yes** Composition **ceramic** Size **10.5 x 10.5cm x 7mm/ 4 x 4 x ¼in** Price ★ W +

12 **Winchester Tile Co/Colours** Colour **amethyst** Alt. colours **yes** Composition **ceramic** Size **10.5 x 10.5cm x 7mm/ 4 x 4 x ¼in** Price ★★ W +

13 **Carocim/Palette U15** Colour **violet** Alt. colours **yes** Composition **cement/ marble (encaustic)** Size **20 x 20 x 1cm/8 x 8 x ⅜in** Price ★ W F +

14 **Simmy Ceramics/Crackle Glaze** Colour **ice** Alt. colours **yes** Composition **ceramic** Size **10 x 10cm/4 x 4in** Price ★★★★★ F

15 **Daltile/Semi-Gloss** Colour **vermilion** Alt. colours **yes** Composition **ceramic** Size **10.8 x 10.8cm x 7mm/ 4 x 4 x ¼in** Price ★ W 🗑 +

16 **Elon/Carrillo Plain Colours** Colour **lime green** Alt. colours **yes** Composition **ceramic** Size **10 x 10cm x 7mm/4 x 4 x ¼in** Price ★ W F

17 **Original Style/Ocean Deep/Midwater Tile 6773A** Colour **blue** Alt. colours **no** Composition **ceramic** Size **15 x 15cm/6 x 6in** Price ★★★ F

TILES: *PLAINS* **317**

Motif Tiles

ABOVE This view of the hallway of Hall Place in London, England, indicates just how strong the Gothic Revival influence was on interior design in the mid-19th century. The inlaid tiles on the floor of the room enhance the Gothic look. They feature striking, Islamic-inspired medieval motifs.

TILED STOVES

In Eastern Europe and Scandinavia, tiled stoves were very common from the 15th century onward. The tiles were functional as well as decorative, helping to retain the heat and distributing it evenly to the room. Although such tiled stoves were not particularly common in England, A.W.N. Pugin designed one in 1850 for the Minton Company to display at the Great Exhibition of 1851. After the exhibition, the stove was destroyed, leaving behind only a few tiles and a contemporary engraving.

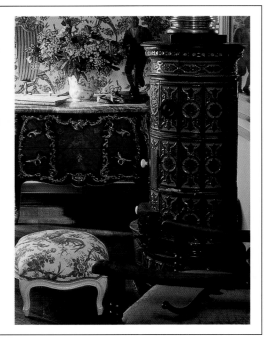

Symbolism was an essential component of medieval art, and many tiles of the period reflected this in the motifs chosen for inlaid patterns. Large numbers of motif tiles were used in churches, and featured the religious symbols that would be familiar to their congregations. Arabesques were common motifs on delftware tiles from the late 16th century to the mid-17th century, but gradually gave way to the more simply painted corner motifs that are a feature of later tiles.

In the 1770s, with the rise of interest in Neo-classicism, swags, drapes and urns all appeared on tiles. The Gothic Revival of the 1830s and 1840s brought about a return to the symbolism of medieval tiles but in an updated form, while the Aesthetic movement in the 1860s saw the use of prunus blossom and Chinese *mons* on tiles. Military or musical emblems became popular images on tiles during the 1880s.

By the 1920s motifs were seldom used in tile design owing to the influence of the Art Deco movement, which relied on strong geometric images. The late 20th and early 21st century has seen a return to motif-decorated tiles, with traditional designs being produced alongside "New Age" motifs, such as the sun, the moon and the stars.

ABOVE The use of natural materials pressed into an unfired clay tile has its origins in the animal footprints that are sometimes found on Roman roof tiles. The example shown here is modern, although the technique was first used by J. & J.G. Lowe in America in the 1880s.

LEFT The floor tiles in this bathroom in a house in Suffolk, England, feature strongly Islamic-inspired motifs. They form the perfect foil for the plainer, Victorian-style sanitary ware and wall tiles.

KEY DESIGNS

1 In the 1830s and 1840s, architects were inspired by motifs on medieval tiles, such as those on this Gothic Revival design panel.

2 Corner motifs are a particular feature of tin-glazed and delft tiles. When placed together, the corner patterns join to form another design.

3 Neo-classical imagery, such as this scrolling leaf pattern, has been popular on tiles since the 1770s. Swags, trophies and drapes have also been much used.

4 Tiles for cast-iron hearth surrounds proliferated in the late 19th century. This floral and foliate motif example is by Arts and Crafts designer William de Morgan.

5 Floral motifs on tiles have been popular since the Middle Ages. Monochromatic examples have been fashionable since the mid-19th century.

6 Of all the floral motifs, the fleur-de-lis, or Burgundian lily, is perhaps the most widely recognized. In the Middle Ages, it was a symbol of the Holy Trinity.

1 Original Style/Gladstone 6260 (4-tile panel) Colour **blue/brown** Alt. colours **yes** Composition **ceramic** Size **15 x 15cm/ 6 x 6 in** Price ★★★★ F

2 Winchester Tile Co/English Delft/Ship and House W.DE1519HP Colour **blue and white** Alt. colours **no** Composition **ceramic** Size **12.5 x 12.5cm/ 5 x 5in** Price ★★★★★ W F

3 Candy/Vivaldi Florentine CAN32316 Colour **grey** Alt. colours **yes** Composition **ceramic** Size **20 x 10cm/8 x 4in** Price ★ W

4 Kenneth Clark Ceramics/Hermitage/William de Morgan/Wightwick Colour **green blue** Alt. colours **yes** Composition **ceramic** Size **15 x 15cm/6 x 6in** Price ★★★★ W

5 Craven Dunnill Jackfield/Leighton Colour **cream** Alt. colours **yes** Composition **ceramic** Size **15 x 15cm/6 x 6in** Price ★ W

6 Daltile/Metal Signatures/Fleur de Lis MS10 Colour **aged iron** Alt. colours **yes** Composition **Questech™** Size **5 x 5cm/2 x 2in** Price ★★ W

Motifs: **Pre-19th century**

The tradition of motifs on tiles began in the Middle Ages, when symbolism was used as a way of educating the people and focusing their thoughts on God. As a result, the motifs that adorned early tiles were strongly based on Christian beliefs and ideals. Typical examples from the period were the fish (a mystical symbol of the church), the fleur-de-lis (representing the Holy Trinity) and the circle (symbolizing eternity). Following on from this, certain symbols also became strongly associated with heraldry.

As Islamic influences spread across Europe via Spain, arabesques, which had originated as cloud scrolls on Chinese porcelain, became popular motifs. By the early 17th century, these had been reduced to a simple corner motif on the delftware tiles produced in the Netherlands, Germany, England and other European countries. There are a great many variations of these corner motifs, rejoicing in such names as spider's head, ox-head, fleur-de-lis and oak leaf. Delftware tiles, imported from the Netherlands, were equally successful in colonial America. The popularity of classical ornamentation in Europe during the late 18th century was reflected in tile design; many classical motifs, including urns and birds, were to be found as decorative designs on tiles.

6

1

2

3

1 **Daltile/Metal Signature/ Floral Dot MS10** Colour **aged iron** Alt. colours **yes** Composition **Questech** Size **5 x 5cm/2 x 2in** Price ★★ W

2 **Fired Earth/Roman Mosaic/ Wave Scroll Border** Colour **black** Alt. colours **yes** Composition **stone/ceramic** Size **10 x 40cm/4 x 15¾in** Price ★★★★ F

3 **H. & R. Johnson/Cotswold Fairford (4-tile panel)** Colour **multi** Alt. colours **no** Composition **ceramic** Size **20 x 20cm/8 x 8in** Price ★★ W

4 **Daltile/Passagio/Universal Stone Corner PA40** Colour **natural** Alt. colours **yes** Composition **glazed porcelain** Size **15 x 15cm/ 6 x 6in** Price ★ W F

5 **Villeroy & Boch/Athos/Border Corner 2349-VA6100 1077** Colour **55C6** Alt. colours **yes** Composition **polished porcelain stone** Size **30 x 30cm/11¾ x 11¾in** Price ★★★★ W

4

5

9

10

11

6 **Carocim/Gothic** Colour **red and blue** Alt. colours **yes** Composition **cement/ marble (encaustic)** Size **20 x 20cm/8 x 8in** Price ★ W F ⊞

7 **Fired Earth/Antieke Delft/ Fish 4** Colour **blue and white** Alt. colours **no** Composition **ceramic** Size **13 x 13cm/5 x 5in** Price ★★★ W

8 **Ann Sacks/Batchelder Lion** Colour **stoneware** Alt. colours **yes** Composition **ceramic** Size **10 x 10cm x 9mm/4 x 4 x ⅛in** Price ★★★ W

9 **Elon/Carillo Wall Tiles/ Anita B** Colour **blue** Alt. colours **no** Composition **ceramic** Size **10 x 10cm/ 4 x 4in** Price ★ W ⊞

10 **H. & R. Johnson/Ravenna/ Mariona** Colour **natural** Alt. colours **yes** Composition **ceramic** Size **33 x 25cm/ 13 x 9¾in** Price ★★ W

11 **Walker Zanger/Avignon/ Décoratif/Fleur de Lis** Colour **chamois** Alt. colours **yes** Composition **ceramic** Size **13 x 13cm/5 x 5in** Price ★★ W F ⊞

12 Walker Zanger/Venezia Di Pinto/Duomo Liner Colour **natural** Alt. colours **no** Composition **stone** Size **31 x 9.5cm/12 x 3¾in** Price ★★★★ W

13 Carré/Sols/Terres Cuites/ Antiquare/2733 Série C Colour **red and cream** Alt. colours **no** Composition **terracotta** Size **13 x 13 x 1.5cm/5 x 5 x ⅝in** Price ★ W

14 Winchester Tile Co/English Delft/Boats/Trinitie of London W.DE1527HP Colour **blue and white** Alt. colours **no** Composition **ceramic** Size **12.5 x 12.5cm/5 x 5in** Price ★★

15 Fired Earth/Puebla/Damask B Colour **blue and white** Alt. colours **no** Composition **terracotta** Size **10 x 10cm/4 x 4in** Price ★ W

16

17

18

19

20

16 Lowitz & Co/Talisman Panel Beginnings Border (2 tiles) Colour **white** Alt. colours **yes** Composition **ceramic** Size **15 x 10cm x 7mm/6 x 4 x ¼in** Price ★★★ W ⬠

17 Paris Ceramics/Thera Star/ Hand Decorated Colour **pale blue, russet and cream** Alt. colours **yes** Composition **ceramic** Size **15 x 15cm/6 x 6in** Price ★★★★ W

18 Walker Zanger/Venezia Di Pinto/Medici Border Colour **natural** Alt. colours **no** Composition **stone** Size **41 x 9.5cm/16 x 3¾in** Price ★★★★ W F

19 Walker Zanger/Intarsio Romano/Villa Nova Corner/ Deco Colour **natural** Alt. colours **no** Composition **stone** Size **13.5 x 13.5cm/5¼ x 5¼in** Price ★★★★★ W F

20 Fired Earth/Roman Mosaic/ Green Butterfly Colour **green** Alt. colours **yes** Composition **stone/ceramic** Size **20 x 20cm/8 x 8in** Price ★★★★ F

Motifs: **19th century**

By the mid-19th century, A.W.N. Pugin and other Gothic Revival architects were finding inspiration in the Christian and heraldic symbols used on medieval tiles. Such motifs became icons for these architects, and they soon added new symbols of their own to the repertoire; these included the chalice and wafer, the Paschal Lamb and the Alpha and Omega.

The opening up of trade routes to the Orient led to an influx of porcelain and metal goods from the Far East that was to serve as a source of inspiration for the followers of the Aesthetic movement later in the century. Tiles featuring motifs such as the *prunus* blossom, often as a background to Japanese *mons* or armorial seals, proved particularly popular. Also widely used as a highly stylized motif in tile decoration was the sunflower, which was to become one of the Aesthetic movement's chief symbols (*see* page 332). The fan, too, was a favourite symbol on tiles, and inspired a variety of different designs. Toward the end of the century, the use of very stylized military or musical motifs became a trend throughout Europe and America. These were often combined with stylized swags or ribbons that served to unify the image and provide an extra, decorative element.

3

1

2

4

5

7

8

1 **Original Style/Victorian Border Tile 6034** Colour **colonial white** Alt. colours **no** Composition **ceramic** Size **15 x 15cm x 7mm/6 x 6 x ¼in** Price ★ W

2 **New Castle Delft/Gallery/ Coat-of-Arms** Colour **blue and white** Alt. colours **yes** Composition **ceramic** Size **13 x 13cm/5 x 5in** Price ★★ W

3 **Tiles of Stow/Gothic Reliefware/Fleur de Lys** Colour **cream** Alt. colours **yes** Composition **terracotta** Size **13 x 13cm x 11mm/ 5 x 5 x ¼in** Price ★★★

4 **H. & R. Johnson/Babylon/ Nineveh Inset** Colour **natural** Alt. colours **no** Composition **ceramic** Size **15 x 15cm/6 x 6in** Price ★ W

5 **Winchester Tile Co/Ironbridge Rope Moulding W.AN1217** Colour **anthracite** Alt. colours **yes** Composition **ceramic** Size **25 x 21.5cm/ 9¾ x 8½in** Price ★ W

6 **Walker Zanger/Venezia Di Pinto/Cascina Liner** Colour **natural** Alt. colours **no** Composition **stone** Size **31 x 4.5cm/12 x 1¾in** Price ★★★ W F

7 **Original Style/Victorian Floor Tiles/Liverpool 6283** Colour **white/buff** Alt. colours **yes** Composition **ceramic** Size **15 x 15cm/6 x 6in** Price ★ W ▱

8 **Walker Zanger/Venezia de Pinto/Pompeii Medallion** Colour **natural** Alt. colours **no** Composition **stone** Size **93 x 93cm/36 x 36in** Price ★★★★★★ W F

9

Original Style/Victorian Floor Tiles/Elgin Border 6582 Colour **blue on white** Alt. colours **yes** Composition **ceramic** Size **15 x 7.5cm/6 x 2⅞in** Price ★★ W ⌂ F

The Arts & Crafts Home/ **Pugin Floor** Colour **multi** Alt. colours **yes** Composition **ceramic** Size **15 x 15cm x 7mm/6 x 6 x ¼in** Price ★★★ W F

Kenneth Clark Ceramics/ **William de Morgan/Ruby Lustre/Winged Serpent** Colour **ruby lustre** Alt. colours **no** Composition **ceramic** Size **15 x 15cm/ 6 x 6in** Price ★★★★★ W

10

13 14 15

16

1

12 **Kenneth Clark Ceramics/ William de Morgan/Ruby Lustre/Galleon West and Galleon East (2 tiles)** Colour **ruby lustre** Alt. colours **no** Composition **ceramic** Size **15 x 15cm/ 6 x 6in** Price ★★★★★ W

13 **H. & R. Johnson/Malverns Newland/Newland Inset** Colour **marine, blue and platinum** Alt. colours **yes** Composition **ceramic** Size **15 x 15cm x 6.5mm/6 x 6 x ¼in** Price ★ W

14 **Original Style/Victorian Floor Tiles/Wellesley 6568** Colour **green on buff** Alt. colours **yes** Composition **ceramic** Size **15 x 15cm/6 x 6in** Price ★★ F ⌂

15 **H. & R. Johnson/Papyrus Idfu** Colour **beige** Alt. colours **yes** Composition **ceramic** Size **15 x 15cm/6 x 6in** Price ★ W

16 **Original Style/Evening Reverie 6046** Colour **multi** Alt. colours **no** Composition **ceramic** Size **15 x 4cm x 7mm/6 x 1½ x ¼in** Price ★ W

ARTS AND CRAFTS DESIGNS

In 1860, when William Morris was looking for tiles for his new home "Red House" in Kent, England, he lamented the fact that no company in England was manufacturing hand-made tiles. He decided to buy hand-made, white, glazed Dutch tiles and decorated them with the enamels he used for stained glass. The tile shown below is based upon one of Morris's own designs, known as "Swan". Not currently reproduced, it is often available from antique and reclaimed tile merchants.

Swan Repeat Colour **blue** Alt. colours **yes** Composition **ceramic** Size **15 x 15cm x 7mm/6 x 6 x ¼in** W

Motifs: Early 20th century

Perhaps as a reaction to the designs of the Art Nouveau movement, some tile manufacturers returned to Neo-classical imagery at the beginning of the 20th century. However, as labour costs rose, manufacturers sought methods of production that were cheaper and faster than the traditional printing and hand-colouring, and this led to the development of machine-moulded relief tiles. Tiles moulded with drapes, wreaths, bowls or baskets of fruit, shells and other still-life compositions were arranged as borders along the tops of walls, the remainder of the tiling being plain. Moulded tiles were used in commercial buildings, especially butcher's shops and dairies, as well as in domestic halls and porches.

In the 1920s and 1930s, many companies – such as Carter & Co in Dorset, England – produced tiles that featured small motifs, to be used in conjunction with their pictorial tiles; subjects might be a clump of grass or a bunch of flowers. During this period in America, companies such as Malibu Tiles and Gladding McBean were making tiles decorated with a range of boldly coloured, Catalan-inspired motifs, designs that were frequently in relief. In addition, the influence of Art Deco in Europe and America inspired graphic, linear motifs based on objects such as fans and stylized flowers.

1 **Ann Sacks/Topiary Tree** Colour **SW05** Alt. colours **yes** Composition **ceramic** Size **15 x 7.5cm/6 x 2¾in** Price ★★★ W

2 **Original Style/Shell Frieze 6991B (2 tiles)** Colour **multi** Alt. colours **no** Composition **ceramic** Size **15 x 7.5cm/6 x 2¾in** Price ★★ W

3 **Fired Earth/Cherry** Colour **red, cream and green** Alt. colours **no** Composition **ceramic** Size **11 x 11cm/4¼ x 4¼in** Price ★★★ W 🗐

4 **Walker Zanger/Ceramica Alhambra/Chaparral Border** Colour **natural** Alt. colours **no** Composition **ceramic** Size **10 x 10cm/4 x 4in** Price ★★★ W

5 **Winchester Tile Co/Designer Flowers/Stem Vase W.HP1490** Colour **off-white** Alt. colours **no** Composition **ceramic** Size **21 x 10.5cm/8¼ x 4in** Price ★★★ W

6 **Kenneth Clark Ceramics/ Shells S3** Colour **black on white** Alt. colours **yes** Composition **ceramic** Size **10 x 10cm/4 x 4in** Price ★ W 🗐 ⊞

7 **Winchester Tile Co/ Cockerel WHP1052** Colour **white** Alt. colours **yes** Composition **ceramic** Size **10.5 x 10.5cm x 8mm/4 x 4 x ⅓in** Price ★★ W

8 **Walker Zanger/Ceramic Alhambra/Alamedilla Deco Border** Colour **multi** Alt. colours **no** Composition **ceramic** Size **10 x 10cm/ 4 x 4in** Price ★★★ F

9 **Winchester Tile Co/Cherry Border WHP1052** Colour **off-white** Alt. colours **yes** Composition **ceramic** Size **10.5 x 10.5cm/4 x 4in** Price ★★ W

10 **Fired Earth/Anita B** Colour **blue** Alt. colours **yes** Composition **ceramic** Size **10 x 10cm/4 x 4in** Price ★ W F +

11 **Minton Hollins/Baroque ANFI** Colour **blue** Alt. colours **yes** Composition **ceramic** Size **15 x 15cm/6 x 6in** Price ★ W

12

9

10

13

12 **Fired Earth/Puebla Wall Tiles/Guadalajara** Colour **multi** Alt. colours **no** Composition **terracotta** Size **10 x 10cm/4 x 4in** Price ★ W

13 **Ann Sacks/Celtic Deer** Colour **springwheat** Alt. colours **yes** Composition **ceramic** Size **10 x 10cm/4 x 4in** Price ★★★ W

14 **Kenneth Clark Ceramics/ Doves Relief** Colour **primrose yellow** Alt. colours **yes** Composition **ceramic** Size **15 x 7.5cm/6 x 2¾in** Price ★★ W

11

14

TILES: *MOTIFS* **325**

Motifs: Late 20th–early 21st century

The years following the Second World War were a time of austerity, and very few tiles other than plain pastels and simple mottles were produced. However, by the mid-1950s companies were experimenting with new techniques to meet a demand for decorated tiles. Carter & Co in England introduced the world's first automated screen-printing production line for tiles, enabling the company to supply popular kitchen and bathroom tiles with motifs such as fruits, kitchen utensils, seashells, fish and the signs of the zodiac (these tiles were generally inset at random in a field of matching plain tiles). By the mid-1970s, tiles were being mass-produced with simple overall patterns, while the late 20th and early 21st century has seen a return to motif-decorated tiles, with the tile industry becoming more craft-orientated. As well as traditional tile motifs, many of these modern tiles feature motifs such as the sun, moon and stars, which have been popularized by the New Age movement.

3

5

6

7

1

4

2

8

1 **Original Style/Sands of Time/Caledonian KHP5642** Colour **natural** Alt. colours **no** Composition **ceramic** Size **20 x 5.5cm/8 x 2¼in** Price ★★ W

2 **Carocim/Grenouille** Colour **blue and green** Alt. colours **yes** Composition **cement/ marble (encaustic)** Size **20 x 20cm/8 x 8in** Price ★ W ⊞

3 **Kenneth Clark Ceramics/ Magic Lantern/Blue Bird** Colour **blue** Alt. colours **yes** Composition **ceramic** Size **15 x 15cm/6 x 6in** Price ★★★ W ⊞

4 **Original Style/Seashells/ Yoka Star KHP5429T** Colour **clematis** Alt. colours **no** Composition **ceramic** Size **10 x 10cm/4 x 4in** Price ★★★ W

5 **Winchester Tile Co/Dragonfly WHP1290** Colour **white** Alt. colours **yes** Composition **ceramic** Size **10.5 x 10.5cm/ 4 x 4in** Price ★★ W

6 **Tiles of Stow/Heraldic Star** Colour **multi** Alt. colours **yes** Composition **ceramic** Size **10 x 10cm/4 x 4in** Price ★★ W

7 **Carocim/Hilton McConnico/ Pepper HMC20** Colour **U4** Alt. colours **yes** Composition **cement/marble (encaustic)** Size **20 x 20cm/8 x 8in** Price ★ W F

8 **Reptile/Sealife No. 29** Colour **multi** Alt. colours **yes** Composition **ceramic** Size **15 x 15cm/6 x 6in** Price ★★★ W ⊞

9 Kenneth Clark Ceramics/
Woodland Colour **white
and green** Alt. colours
no Composition **ceramic**
Size **15 x 15cm/6 x 6in**
Price ★★ W ⊞

10 Winchester Tile Co/Borders/
**Blue Crabapple Frieze
W.HPLB1056** Colour **off-
white** Alt. colours **yes**
Composition **ceramic**
Size **21 x 4.5cm/8¼ x
1¾in** Price ★★ W

11 Winchester Tile Co/**Grapes
WHP1042** Colour **off-
white** Alt. colours **yes**
Composition **ceramic**
Size **10.5 x 10.5cm
x 8mm/4 x 4 x ⅓in**
Price ★★ W

12 Fired Earth/Fruits de Mer/
Fossil Colour **cream** Alt.
colours **yes** Composition
ceramic Size **13 x 13cm/5 x
5in** Price ★★★ W

13 Simmy Ceramics/Versace/
Mirror Diamond Tile Colour
black Alt. colours **yes**
Composition **quartzite**
Size **30 x 30cm/11¾ x 11¾in**
Price ★★★★★ W ⊞

14 Kenneth Clark Ceramics/
Angela Evans/Star Colour **1**
Alt. colours **no** Composition
ceramic Size **5 x 5cm/2 x 2in**
Price ★★ W

15 Kenneth Clark Ceramics/
Magic Lantern/Bee Colour
multi Alt. colours **yes**
Composition **ceramic**
Size **10 x 10cm/4 x 4in**
Price ★★★ W ⊞

16 Carocim/Hilton McConnico/
Cactus Haut HMC07 Colour
multi Alt. colours **yes**
Composition **cement/marble
(encaustic)** Size **20 x 20cm/
8 x 8in** Price ★ W F

Floral Tiles

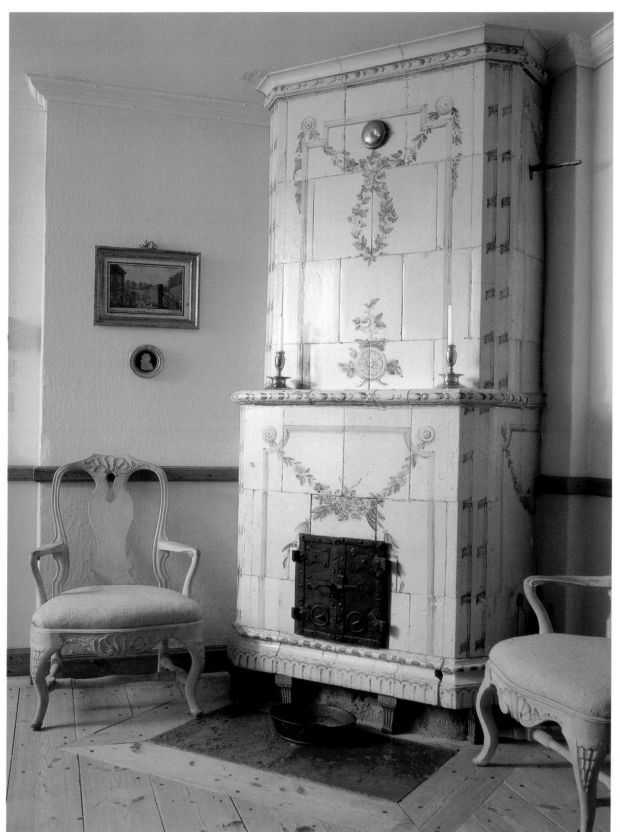

Floral designs have been a recurrent theme on tiles from earliest times. Styles have varied over the years, ranging from the simple lotus and daisy patterns of ancient Egypt to the elaborate flowers on Islamic tiles that were echoed in the 19th century by the Arts and Crafts designer William de Morgan. Flowers have featured as backgrounds in Islamic calligraphic tiles, as borders and corner ornaments and as individual specimen varieties on delftware tiles, and as vases or pots of flowers on large Dutch and Portuguese tile panels. They have also been seen as repeating designs on late 18th- and 19th-century tiles, in highly stylized form on Art Nouveau tiles and as posies and bunches on mid-20th century tiles.

Designs have been taken from a variety of sources including nature itself, herbals and florilegia in the late Middle Ages, and even bulb growers' catalogues, a source much used by the early 17th-century delftware painters. Flowers featured have ranged from the naturalistic to the highly stylized, where the original species is indeterminable.

LEFT The light, uncluttered style of this typically Swedish tiled stove was especially popular in Scandinavia. While the tiles on most Eastern European stoves were decorated with darker, lead-based glazes, the Scandinavian stoves invariably featured tiles based on white tin-glazes, similar to those used on delft tiles.

ABOVE A corner of a bathroom in La Heredia near Malaga, Spain, which, although decorated in the late 20th century, captures the spirit of a 16th-century Spanish tiled interior. There is an almost unbroken history of the manufacture of these richly glazed tiles, decorated with bold floral motifs, both in and around Seville.

BATHROOM TILING

In the late 19th century, bathrooms in wealthier homes often contained elaborate mahogany-panelled baths decorated with insets of tiles. These tiles were sometimes arranged in large panels of naturalistic or stylized floral patterns. Wash-basins were often housed in matching mahogany cabinets, with a marble surround and tiled splashbacks echoing those set behind the bath. The example shown here includes tiles set into the doors and a tip-up basin, which is inverted to dispose of the water.

KEY DESIGNS

1 The image of a flower as a botanical specimen was popular on early delftware tiles, the inspiration for which was often taken from bulb growers' catalogues.

3 Floral designs in particular lend themselves to the imagination of the designer, and stylization reached its height during the Art Nouveau period in the late 19th century.

5 Floral tile designs have been taken from both nature and printed sources, with some naturalistic images rendered in the style of botanists' drawings.

6 Magnificent arrangements of flowers in vases or pots either on a single tile or a large panel of tiles were popular in 17th-century Portugal and the Netherlands, as well as on some English delft tiles.

2 Abstract designs – where the flower is depicted as a geometric pattern – have been frequently used on tiles since the Victorian era.

4 Flowers have frequently featured as ornament on border tiles. This is largely thanks to their form being suitable for both vertical and horizontal extension.

1 **Fired Earth/Antieke Delft Tulips 3** Colour **blue, white, red, and green** Alt. colours **no** Composition **ceramic** Size **13 x 13cm/5 x 5in** Price ★★★★ Ⓦ

2 **Elon/Seville B** Colour **B** Alt. colours **yes** Composition **ceramic** Size **10 x 10cm/4 x 4in** Price ★ Ⓦ ⊞

3 **Craven Dunnill Jackfield/Art Nouveau/Iris (2 tiles)** Colour **violet on merganser** Alt. colours **yes** Composition **ceramic** Size **15 x 15cm/6 x 6in** Price ★★ Ⓦ

4 **Winchester Tile Co/Red Clover Border WKHP1356** Colour **multi** Alt. colours **yes** Composition **ceramic** Size **20 x 10cm/8 x 4in** Price ★ Ⓦ

5 **Welbeck Tiles/English/Flora 3** Colour **charcoal** Alt. colours **yes** Composition **ceramic** Size **13.5 x 13.5cm/5¼ x 5¼in** Price ★★ Ⓦ

6 **H. & R. Johnson/Minton Hollins/Lilies TRP1 (2 tile panel)** Colour **ivory** Alt. colours **yes** Composition **ceramic** Size **15 x 15cm/6 x 6in** Price ★★★ Ⓦ

Florals: **Pre-19th century**

The flower was an important element of early Egyptian culture, and fragments of tile dating from about 1370BC have been excavated from Tell-el-Amarna (north of Thebes) bearing lotus-blossom and daisy patterns. Floral themes recur on Islamic tiles from about AD1200, when they were used as a background for calligraphic inscriptions.

Tulips, carnations, daisies and leaf shapes were predominant themes on Iznik pottery (*see opposite*) of the 15th to 17th centuries. Tulips also appear on early polychrome delftware tiles, but, by 1625, the fashion for coloured ceramics declined as the trade in Chinese blue-and-white porcelain brought about a change in taste. A few large tile panels featuring vases of flowers were made toward the end of the 17th century; some fine examples can be seen in the kitchens at the Rambouillet Palace in France. Small quantities of polychrome, purple or blue-and-white flower-vase tiles were produced in Liverpool, Bristol and London in England, as well as in some areas of Germany, during the mid-18th century.

1

1 **Fired Earth/Margarite B/Y** Colour **yellow and green** Alt. colours **yes** Composition **ceramic** Size **10 x 10cm/ 4 x 4in** Price ★ W

2 **Fired Earth/Puebla/Bouquet** Colour **multi** Alt. colours **no** Composition **terracotta** Size **10 x 10cm/4 x 4in** Price ★ W

3 **Fired Earth/Early English Delft/Daisy** Colour **blue/ white** Alt. colours **no** Composition **ceramic** Size **13 x 13cm/5 x 5in** Price ★★★ W

2

3

6

8

7

SEALING-WAX RED

Probably some of the finest examples of the tile-maker's art were the beautiful floral tiles produced in Iznik, the modern-day Turkish town of Nicea, between about 1575 and 1600. One of the most striking features of these tiles is the rich sealing-wax red, so called because it stands proud of the surface of the glaze. The secret ingredients of this colour are still unknown and elude modern potters, although contemporary glazes have achieved a good approximation to the distinctive, rich red.

Fired Earth/Izmir Border
Colour **multi** Alt. colours **no** Composition **ceramic** Size 20 x 5cm x 8mm/8 x 2 x ⅓in Price ★★ W

9

4 **Fired Earth/Delft Archive Carnation** Colour **blue and white** Alt. colours **yes** Composition **ceramic** Size 11 x 11cm/4¼ x 4¼in Price ★★★ W

5 **Fired Earth/Iznik/Adana Silk Border A09L2** Colour **blue, green and red** Alt. colours **no** Composition **ceramic** Size 20 x 10cm/8 x 4in Price ★★ W

6 **Winchester Tile Co/Swag Flower Border W.HP1234** Colour **rosa** Alt. colours **yes** Composition **ceramic** Size 21.5 x 7.5cm/8½ x 2¾in Price ★★★ W

7 **Carré/Aquarelle/Les Majoliques Paniers cx 5254** Colour **blue** Alt. colours **yes** Composition **alabaster** Size 14 x 14cm/5½ x 5½in Price ★★ W F

8 **Marlborough Tiles/Georgian Flowers** Colour **blue on ivory** Alt. colours **yes** Composition **ceramic** Size 11 x 11cm/4¼ x 4¼in Price ★★ W

9 **Fired Earth/Foundry Art/Lotus** Colour **white bronze** Alt. colours **no** Composition **bronze** Size 7.5 x 7.5cm/2⅝ x 2⅝in Price ★★★★★ F

Florals: 19th century

Floral designs were seldom used on tiles in the late 18th and early 19th centuries, but they enjoyed a renaissance in the 1860s as designers were inspired by the new Aesthetic movement that drew heavily upon Japanese and other oriental designs and forms. William de Morgan, the English Arts and Crafts potter and friend of William Morris, revived interest in Islamic-influenced floral designs in the 1870s. It also became fashionable to make realistic drawings of flowers such as sunflowers from which to create more abstract decorative motifs; this can be seen in the work of tile designers such as C.F.A. Voysey in England, J. & J.G. Low in America and Rafael Bordallo Pinheiro in Portugal.

Floral tiles were used in cast-iron fireplaces. Traditionally, each side of the fireplace held five tiles, and many panels depicting a pot or vase of flowers were designed to suit this specification. These tiles were usually transfer-printed, but hand-painted versions were available for wealthier clients. Toward the end of the century, relief-moulded tiles gave a three-dimensional look to floral designs.

1

1 Kenneth Clark Ceramics/ William Morris/Primrose
Colour **green** Alt. colours **yes** Composition **ceramic** Size **15 x 15cm/6 x 6in** Price ★★ W

2 Kenneth Clark Ceramics/ William Morris/Columbine
Colour **blue** Alt. colours **yes** Composition **ceramic** Size **15 x 15cm/6 x 6in** Price ★★ W

3 Original Style/Floral Garland/ Meadow Cranesbill 5962
Colour **clematis** Alt. colours **no** Composition **ceramic** Size **10 x 10cm/4 x 4in** Price ★★★ W

4 Kenneth Clark Ceramics/ William Morris/Findon Daisy
Colour **green** Alt. colours **yes** Composition **ceramic** Size **15 x 15cm/6 x 6in** Price ★★★★ W

2

3

4

5 H. & R. Johnson/Minton Hollins/Persia/Persepolis Border Colour **multi** Alt. colours **no** Composition **ceramic** Size **15 x 2.5cm/ 6 x 1in** Price ★★ W

6 H. & R. Johnson/Minton Hollins/Kew/White Border Colour **white** Alt. colours **yes** Composition **ceramic** Size **15 x 7.5cm/6 x 2¾in** Price ★ W

7 H. & R. Johnson/Minton Hollins/Blenheim/Ivory Inset Colour **ivory** Alt. colours **yes** Composition **ceramic** Size **15 x 15cm/6 x 6in** Price ★ W

6

10

8 H. & R. Johnson/Minton Hollins/Transfers/Poppies Colour **multi** Alt. colours **yes** Composition **ceramic** Size **15 x 15cm/6 x 6in** Price ★★ W

9 Original Style/Blue Iris 6080A (5-tile panel) Colour **multi** Alt. colours **no** Composition **ceramic** Size **15 x 15cm x 7mm/6 x 6 x ¼in** Price ★★★★ W

10 Original Style/Rose and Trellis 6970A (2 tiles) Colour **multi** Alt. colours **no** Composition **ceramic** Size **15 x 15cm x 7mm/ 6 x 6 x ¼in** Price ★ W

9

Florals: **Early 20th century**

With the advent of the Art Nouveau movement, the floral tile became increasingly abstract and stylized in its design. In Continental Europe, Art Nouveau-style tiled panels were used to create complete interiors, while in America and England such floral designs tended to be on individual tiles or arranged as small panels up to dado height. In the early 20th century, many tiles were produced by tube-lining. In this technique the linear elements of a design are applied to stand out from the surface of the tile, enabling designers to create fluid, sinuous shapes with positive outlines separating the coloured glazes.

In Portugal, Spain, Belgium and the Netherlands, highly elaborate Art Nouveau floral panels were often used to cover the façades of buildings, while in Britain tiles were largely confined to interiors. By the 1920s, floral tiles were becoming noticeably less stylized once again; naturalistic flowers were frequently shown in small posies or within larger arrangements. Many floral tiles in this style were made by Carter & Co in England, closely echoing the brightly coloured pots made at Poole Pottery in Dorset, England. Meanwhile, in America, the Rookwood Pottery (based in Cincinatti, Ohio), which was also well known for its pots, produced a wide range of spectacular floral tiles and tile panels.

1

2

3

6

4

5

7

1 **Original Style/Spring Border 6062** Colour **lilac** Alt. colour **no** Composition **ceramic** Size **15 x 15cm x 7mm/ 6 x 6 x ¼in** Price ★ ⓦ

2 **Kenneth Clark Ceramics/ Tubeline Flowers GTF1** Colour **green** Alt. colours **yes** Composition **ceramic** Size **10 x 10cm x 6mm/4 x 4 x ¼in** Price ★★★ ⓦ ⊞

3 **Fired Earth/Bluebells** Colour **multi** Alt. colours **no** Composition **ceramic** Size **15 x 15cm x 8mm/6 x 6 x ¼in** Price ★★★ ⓦ

4 **Minton Hollins/Kew/ Marguerite** Colour **multi** Alt. colours **no** Composition **ceramic** Size **15 x 15cm/ 6 x 6in** Price ★★ ⓦ

5 **Welbeck Tiles/Platinum/ Botanicals 4** Colour **black on cream** Alt. colours **yes** Composition **ceramic** Size **13.5 x 13.5cm/5¼ x 5¼in** Price ★★★ ⓦ

6 **Craven Dunnill Jackfield/ Victorian/Claverley** Colour **burgundy** Alt. colours **yes** Composition **ceramic** Size **30 x 10 x 1.5cm/11¾ x 4 x ⅝in** Price ★★ ⓦ

7 **Tiles of Newport & London/ Decorated Tozzetto TNL414A** Colour **multi** Alt. colours **no** Composition **ceramic** Size **4 x 4cm x 7mm/1½ x 1½ x ¼in** Price ★ ⓦ

8 **Original Style/Rose and Bud (5-tile panel)** Colour **colonial white** Alt. colours **no** Composition **ceramic** Size 15 x 15cm x 7mm/6 x 6 x ¼in Price ★★★★ W

9 **Craven Dunnill Jackfield/ Victorian/Hope** Colour **cream** Alt. colours **yes** Composition **ceramic** Size 7.5 x 7.5cm/2¾ x 2¾in Price ★ W

10 **Original Style/Sunflower KHP5826B** Colour **clematis** Alt. colours **yes** Composition **ceramic** Size 10 x 10cm x 7mm/4 x 4 x ¼in Price ★★★ W

11 **Original Style/Orchid (Orchidée) 1902 6054** Colour **multi** Alt. colours **no** Composition **ceramic** Size 15 x 15cm x 7mm/ 6 x 6 x ¼in Price ★ W

9

0

11

ART NOUVEAU

The opening of the shop L'Art Nouveau in Paris, France in 1896 heralded the beginning of a new style movement that was to shape the decorative arts for the next 25 years. This was a period of highly stylized, curvilinear designs, which were often based on sinuous floral motifs and glamorous female figures. Such designs lent themselves particularly well to tube-lining, a technique similar to piping icing on to a cake. The raised lines give a three-dimensional appearance to the design as well as containing the coloured glazes used.

Kenneth Clark Ceramics/Tubeline Tulip Border Colour **green** Alt. colours **yes** Composition **ceramic** Size 10 x 10cm/ 4 x 4in Price ★★★ W ⊞

Florals: **Late 20th–early 21st century**

Government restrictions in Britain, and to some extent in Continental Europe, inhibited the production of decorative tiles in the years following the Second World War. At this time, most building construction was government-commissioned and plain tiles, rather than decorated ones, were considered more appropriate, given limited resources. In Europe, this restriction affected some countries more than others but, overall, this period saw a temporary lull in the production of decorative tiles.

By the 1960s, tile production in Europe and America was increasing rapidly but was chiefly in the hands of a few large companies, such as Villeroy & Boch in Germany and H. & R. Johnson in England, which specialized in mass-production. Floral tiles tended to be simple, pastel-coloured designs that could be made quickly and easily by screen-printing or wax-resist techniques. Perhaps spotting a gap, many small companies emerged during the 1980s, 1990s and early 2000s in both Europe and America specializing in hand-made and decorated tiles. At the same time, the colourful tiles traditionally used in European countries, notably Spain and Italy, became more widely sought after, and were exported to other European countries and America.

4

1

2

3

5

1 Tiles of Stow/Summer Flowers Border Colour **multi** Alt. colours **yes** Composition **ceramic** Size **15 x 15cm/6 x 6in** Price ★★ W

2 Tiles of Stow/Summer Flowers Colour **multi** Alt. colours **yes** Composition **ceramic** Size **15 x 15cm/6 x 6in** Price ★★★ W

3 Tiles of Stow/Fleur Antique Border Colour **multi** Alt. colours **yes** Composition **ceramic** Size **10 x 10cm/4 x 4in** Price ★ W

4 Carocim/Glamour Fleur M432 (4 tiles) Colour **U4** Alt. colours **yes** Composition **cement/marble (encaustic)** Size **20 x 20cm/8 x 8in** Price ★ W F

5 Elon/Carillo/Bouquet Colour **multi** Alt. colours **no** Composition **ceramic** Size **10 x 10cm/4 x 4in** Price ★ W

6 **Winchester Tile Co/Clematis and Fuschia WHP1336** Colour **pure white** Alt. colours **yes** Composition **ceramic** Size **10.5 x 10.5cm/4 x 4in** Price ★★ W

7 **Original Style/Wild Rose 5964** Colour **clematis** Alt. colours **no** Composition **ceramic** Size **10 x 10cm/4 x 4in** Price ★★★ W

8 **Original Style/La Belle/Dried Bouquet Plaque KHP5698B** Colour **clematis** Alt. colours **no** Composition **ceramic** Size **20 x 30cm/8 x 11¾in** Price ★★★★★ W

9 **Fired Earth/Impressions/ Flowers/Amaryllis** Colour **cream** Alt. colours **yes** Composition **ceramic** Size **13 x 13cm/5 x 5in** Price ★★★ W

10 **Kenneth Clark Ceramics/ Hydrangea Border** Colour **rosemary** Alt. colours **yes** Composition **ceramic** Size **15 x 15cm/6 x 6in** Price ★★

9

10

Pictorial Tiles

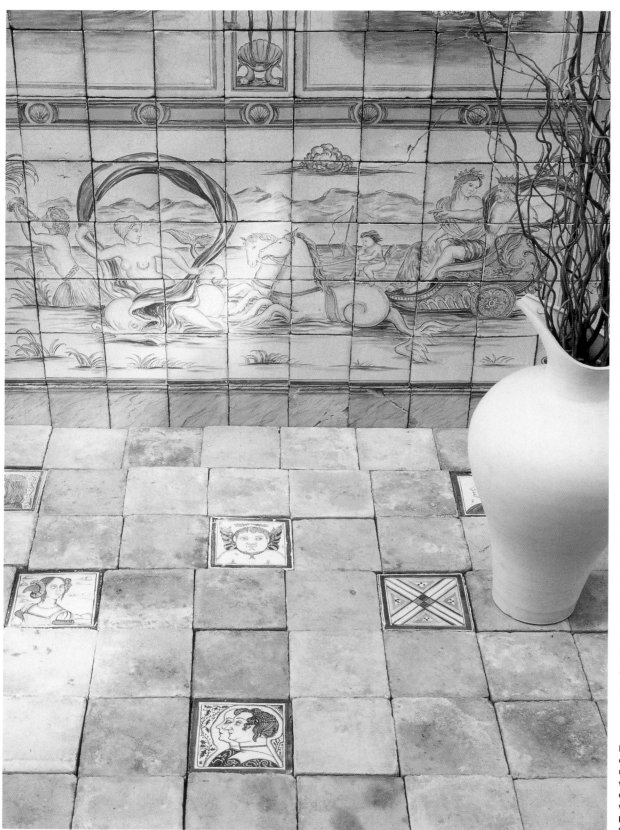

Since the earliest times, pictorial tiles have been an important element of the tile-maker's repertoire. Displaying mythical creatures and warriors in tile work on the walls of the city of Babylon, built in about 580BC, was intended to frighten potential invaders. The medieval romance and hunting scenes on many 13th- and 14th-century tile installations reflect the lifestyle of the noblemen who were the tile-makers' patrons.

In the deeply religious countries of Spain and the Netherlands, tiles often depicted saints and biblical scenes. The tile-makers of the Netherlands, influenced by the nation's connections with the sea, also created maritime scenes on their tiles.

By the mid-19th century, there was a great interest in literary subjects, reflected in the numerous series of tiles presenting scenes from the works of writers and artists such as William Shakespeare and Albrecht Dürer. The advent of photography provoked a new enthusiasm for pictorial subjects, and many tile companies reproduced actual photographs on their tiles.

LEFT In Italy during the 15th and 16th centuries, tin-glazed tiles were commonly used on the floors as well as the walls of wealthy homes. On the floors, pictorial designs or motifs were often interspersed with areas of plain tiling. On the walls, pictorial panels, often featuring mythological subjects, were common.

BOVE An original 18th-century tiled stove sits in Lars Sjoberg's home at Odenslunda in tockholm, Sweden. The individual tiles are quite big, and combine to form an impressive ictorial design. Swags feature at the top and bottom of the stove, while the central image that of a large urn.

POWDER-GROUND

The English delft tiles shown here were made in London between 1730 and 1750. They surround a niche decorated in plain tiles and marble. The border on the octagonal tiles is known as a powder- ground and was produced by spattering pigment through a metal stencil. Most of powder- ground tiles have a purple border produced from manganese ore, but occasionally English delft tiles are found with red, green or blue borders. These colours were never used on Dutch powder- ground tiles.

1 Ancient cultures have proved a rich source of imagery for tiles. Typical examples include scenes from ancient Greece, Rome and Egypt.

2 Marine-themed tiles were loved among the seafaring Dutch, and were a favourite subject for the Arts and Crafts potter William de Morgan.

3 Pictorial scenes of children's games and sporting activities have been popular since the 17th century, especially on delft tiles. Allegorical and symbolic designs were much used in the 19th century.

4 Landscape tiles and tile panels (often featuring people) have been widely seen since the 17th century. In the Victorian era, stylized imagery as well as naturalistic scenes were common.

5 Since the middle of the 19th century, tiles depicting scenes from literary works, such as this *Alice in Wonderland* design, have remained fashionable.

6 Animals have long been a favourite subject for tile designers. This late 20th-century kitchen tile is typical of a modern, cartoon-like scene.

1 **Original Style/Egyptian Wedding Banquet KHP5475** Colour **black on terracotta** Alt. colours **no** Composition **ceramic** Size **20 x 20cm/8 x 8in** Price ★★★ W

2 **Original Style/Viking Longship 6966B** Colour **multi** Alt. colours **no** Composition **ceramic** Size **15 x 15cm/6 x 6in** Price ★★ W

3 **Fired Earth/Delft Archive/Golfing/St. Andrews** Colour **sepia** Alt. colours **yes** Composition **ceramic** Size **11 x 11cm/4¼ x 4¼in** Price ★★★ W

4 **Winchester Tile Co/English Delft/Lady and Mansion WDE1512** Colour **blue and white** Alt. colours **no** Composition **ceramic** Size **12.5 x 12.5cm/5 x 5in** Price ★★★★ W

5 **The Arts and Crafts Home/Voysey "Alice"** Colour **multi** Alt. colours **no** Composition **ceramic** Size **15 x 15cm/6 x 6in** Price ★★★★ W

6 **Tile Productions/Farmyard: Sheep** Colour **multi** Alt. colours **yes** Composition **ceramic** Size **11 x 11cm/4¼ x 4¼in** Price ★★ W

Pictorials: **Pre-19th century**

In the 13th century, many inlaid floor tiles were produced with designs that depicted dogs, stags and huntsmen. Although made as individual tiles, they were often laid in groups to give the effect of a chase. In about 1500, the potter Francisco Niculoso moved from Pisa in Italy to Seville in Spain, where he introduced the art of painting ceramics in tin-glaze. From Spain the art spread to the Low Countries and, by the 17th century, many fine picture tiles and tile panels were being produced in Antwerp, Rotterdam and Delft. The tin-glaze technique gave the tile-maker a wider palette of colour, facilitating freer, more realistic designs.

Large-scale panels consisting of 400 to 500 tiles – such as those by the Dutch artist Cornelis Bouwmeester (1651–1733), best known for his shipping scenes – were expensive, but even the most humble of homes were decorated with single pictorial tiles. In 1756, in Liverpool, England, Sadler and Green perfected a method of transferring an image from a printing plate to a tile by means of a transfer tissue, to allow consistent reproduction of very fine detail. The majority of Sadler and Green's output was pictorial, with designs taken mainly from Rococo prints. In colonial America, delftware tiles imported from the Netherlands were favoured, particularly those showing figures or moral or religious themes.

4

1

2

3

1   **Simmy Ceramics/Cherubs
    (6-tile panel)** Colour **blue
    on white** Alt. colours **yes**
    Composition **ceramic** Size
    20 x 20cm/8 x 8in Price
    ★★★★★ W ⊞

2   **Winchester Tile Co/Balloon
    6 W.HP1418** Colour **off-
    white** Alt. colours **yes**
    Composition **ceramic**
    Size **12.5 x 12.5cm/5 x
    5in** Price ★★★ W

3   **Fired Earth/Early English
    Delft/Fisherman** Colour **blue
    and white** Alt. colours **no**
    Composition **ceramic** Size
    13 x 13cm/5 x 5in Price
    ★★★ W

4   **Paris Ceramics/Hand-
    Painted Decorative/Mappa
    Mundi (35-tile panel)** Colour
    multi Alt. colours **no**
    Composition **ceramic**
    Size **12.5 x 12.5cm/5 x 5in**
    Price ★★★★★ F ♣

DELFTWARE
These tiles usually feature a central picture framed by a decorative border and a small ornamental motif at each corner. The delft tile-painter faces a task akin to painting a watercolour on blotting paper. After the tile has been biscuit-fired, it is dipped in a liquid tin-glaze; the tile absorbs the moisture, leaving a thin layer of powdered glaze. The outline is marked on this glaze by dabbing powdered charcoal through a pricked paper pattern, and the tile-painter then follows this outline, using a very fine brush to apply the colour.

1

2

1   **Fired Earth/Delft/Windmill 2**
    Colour **blue and white** Alt. colours
    no Composition **ceramic** Size
    13 x 13cm/5 x 5in
    Price ★★★ W

2   **Fired Earth/Early English Delft/
    Pottery** Colour **blue and white** Alt.
    colours **no** Composition **ceramic**
    Size **13 x 13cm/5 x 5in**
    Price ★★★ W

5 **Walker Zanger/Deruta/ Pergola Border** Colour **multi** Alt. colours **no** Composition **ceramic** Size **15 x 15cm/6 x 6in** Price ★★★★★ W

6 **Original Style/Masterpiece/ Botticelli, Birth of Venus 6364** Colour **multi** Alt. colours **yes** Composition **ceramic** Size **36 x 56cm/ 14 x 22in** Price ★★★★★ W

6

7 **Winchester Tile Co/King of Diamonds** Colour **multi** Alt. colours **no** Composition **ceramic** Size **15 x 10.5cm/ 6 x 4in** Price ★ W

8 **Welbeck Tiles/English/ Figures 10** Colour **charcoal** Alt. colours **yes** Composition **ceramic** Size **13.5 x 13.5cm/5¼ x 5¼in** Price ★★★★ W

9 **Winchester Tile Co/English Delft/Exotic Birds/Bird in Tree W.DE1522** Colour **multi** Alt. colours **no** Composition **ceramic** Size **12.5 x 12.5cm/5 x 5in** Price ★★ F

10 **Fired Earth/Natural History/ Crab Apple (12 tile panel)** Colour **multi** Alt. colours **no** Composition **ceramic** Size **40 x 30cm/15¾ x 11¾in** Price ★★★★★ W

11 **Fired Earth/Antieke Delft/ Childrens Games 2** Colour **blue/white** Alt. colours **no** Composition **ceramic** Size **11 x 11cm/4¼ x 4¼in** Price ★★★ W

12 **Reptile/Birds and Bees** Colour **multi** Alt. colours **no** Composition **ceramic** Size **15 x 15cm/6 x 6in** Price ★★★ W +

8

9

10

11

12

Pictorials: 19th century

Comparatively few tiles were made in the first 40 years of the 19th century, but by 1845 the master British ceramicist Herbert Minton had introduced his first series of picture tiles, based on the romantic paintings of the French artist Jean-Antoine Watteau. These were so successful that they were still in production in the early 20th century. By the 1870s, his company, Minton China Works of Stoke-on-Trent, was one of the largest commercial potteries in the world.

Also produced in the 19th century were pictorial tiles in the style of the Aesthetic movement, echoing the renewed interest in the Orient. These tiles were all mass-produced, which was anathema to William Morris and the other leaders of the Arts and Crafts movement in Britain and America. Morris made tiles himself for a few years, before turning to his friend William de Morgan to make and paint decorative tiles for his company. Galleons, and real and mythical animals, such as sea monsters, all appear on the de Morgan tiles, which were painted in monochrome, full colour or his own wonderful lustres. Meanwhile, in America, tile-makers such as Henry Chapman Mercer and William H. Grueby, who formed part of the American Arts and Crafts movement, achieved an interesting range of pictorial relief tiles, including the distinctive floor tiles made by Mercer for Wellington House in New York.

1 **H. & R. Johnson/Natural Selection/Cotswold Kelmscott** Colour **mushroom** Alt. colours **yes** Composition **ceramic** Size **30 x 20cm/11¾ x 8in** Price ★★ W

2 **Winchester Tile Co/De Morgan/Fish Frieze W.HP1261/2 (2-tile panel)** Colour **multi** Alt. colours **no** Composition **ceramic** Size **10.5 x 10.5cm/4 x 4in** Price ★★ W

3 **Fired Earth/Heritage/Hare and Hound (2 tiles)** Colour **natural** Alt. colours **no** Composition **ceramic** Size **11 x 6cm/4¼ x 2½in** Price ★★ W

4 **New Castle Delft/Gallery/Stein-bass (18 tiles)** Colour **blue and white** Alt. colours **yes** Composition **ceramic** Size **20 x 10cm/8 x 4in** Price ★★ W

5

6

7

12

5 **Original Style/Masterpiece/ Alma-Tadema, Silver Favourites 6360** Colour **multi** Alt. colours **yes** Composition **ceramic** Size **56 x 38cm/22 x 15in** Price ★★★★★ W

6 **Fired Earth/Natural History/ Fish/Chetodon/Maille** Colour **natural** Alt. colours **no** Composition **ceramic** Size **10 x 10cm/4 x 4in** Price ★★★ W

7 **Original Style/Nocturnal Slumber 6042 (3-tile panel)** Colour **multi** Alt. colours **no** Composition **ceramic** Size **15 x 15cm/6 x 6in** Price ★★★ W

8 **Welbeck Tiles/Victorian Jelly** Colour **cream crackle** Alt. colours **no** Composition **ceramic** Size **13.5 x 13.5cm/5¼ x 5¼in** Price ★★★ W

9 **Winchester Tile Co/Animals and Bugs/Cow W.HP1293** Colour **brown on white** Alt. colours **no** Composition **ceramic** Size **10.5 x 10.5cm/4 x 4in** Price ★★ W

10 **Original Style/Cameo Carousel 6006 (5-tile panel)** Colour **imperial ivory** Alt. colours **no** Composition **ceramic** Size **15 x 15cm/6 x 6in** Price ★★★★ W

11 **Original Style/Exotic Birds (Left) 6968A (3-tile panel)** Colour **multi** Alt. colours **no** Composition **ceramic** Size **15 x 15cm/6 x 6in** Price ★★★ W

12 **Original Style/Peacock Border 6960A (2-tile panel)** Colour **multi** Alt. colours **no** Composition **ceramic** Size **15 x 7.5cm/6 x 2¾in** Price ★★ W

9

10

11

Pictorials: **20th–early 21st century**

The Art Nouveau movement generated a wealth of wonderful tiled interiors, particularly in Belgium and France – many in the style of the graphic illustrations by Czech artist Alphonse Mucha. In Britain, few pictorial tiles were made until the 1920s and 1930s when Carter & Co produced several series of brightly coloured, hand-painted picture tiles in the Art Deco style, covering a number of subjects ranging from "Nursery Rhymes" to "Water Birds". Packard and Ord, established in London in 1935, specialized in hand-painted pictorial sets.

In America, the influence of the Arts and Crafts movement continued, and many small tile-makers offered striking relief landscapes and other pictorial tiles. In more recent years, tile murals, often in *trompe l'oeil* form, have regained their popularity. There is also a trend for manufacturers to commission fashion houses, such as Fendi and Kenzo, to provide ideas for tiles – hence Fendi's white-on-white relief-tile series, "Astrologia".

1

1 Winchester Tile Co/Copper Engravings/Sunbather W.1850HP Colour **off-white** Alt. colours **no** Composition **ceramic** Size **10.5 x 10.5cm/ 4 x 4in** Price ★★ W

2 Original Style/Laurel (Le Laurier) 6052 Colour **multi** Alt. colours **no** Composition **ceramic** Size **15 x 15cm/6 x 6in** Price ★★ W

3 Paris Ceramics/Four Seasons/ Summer Colour **multi** Alt. colours **no** Composition **ceramic** Size **25 x 25cm/9¾ x 9¾in** Price ★★★★★ W

4 Fired Earth/Natural History Crab Apple (2-tile panel) Colour **natural** Alt. colours **no** Composition **ceramic** Size **20 x 10cm/8 x 4in** Price ★★★★ W

5 Ann Sacks/Algonquin Tent Colour **earthenware** Alt. colours **yes** Composition **ceramic** Size **10 x 10cm/ 4 x 4in** Price ★★★ W

6 Reptile/4 Fishes No. 21 Colour **multi** Alt. colours **yes** Composition **ceramic** Size **15 x 15cm/6 x 6in** Price ★★★ W ⊞

7 Surving Studios/Vine Tree Frog Triptych (3-tile panel) Colour **green** Alt. colours **yes** Composition **ceramic** Size **10 x 10cm/4 x 4in** Price ★★★★★ W

8 Tiles of Stow/Sixpence Bird Colour **multi** Alt. colours **yes** Composition **ceramic** Size **15 x 15cm/6 x 6in** Price ★★★ W

3

4

5

6

7

20th & 21st century

9

Reptile/Seal No. 17 Colour
multi Alt. colours **yes**
Composition **ceramic**
Size **15 x 15cm/6 x 6in**
Price ★★★ Ⓦ ⊞

0 Candy/Reflection Marine
Inset CAN32569 Colour **blue**
Alt. colours **no** Composition
ceramic Size **25 x 20cm/
9¾ x 8in** Price ★★ Ⓦ

1 Kenneth Clark Ceramics/
Magic Lantern/Animal
Assembly Colour **multi** Alt.
colours **yes** Composition
ceramic Size **10 x 10cm/4 x
4in** Price ★★★ Ⓦ ⊞

0

11

12

16

13

14

15

12 Kenneth Clark Ceramics/
Tubeline Tiles/Boats Colour
multi Alt. colours **yes**
Composition **ceramic**
Size **10 x 10cm/4 x 4in**
Price ★★★ Ⓦ ⊞

13 Winchester Tile Co/Sweetcorn
and Mushroom W.HP1085
Colour **multi** Alt. colours
no omposition **ceramic**
Size **10.5 x 10.5cm/4 x 4in**
Price ★★ Ⓦ

14 Simmy Ceramics/The
International Restaurant
Range Colour **white** Alt.
colours **yes** Composition
ceramic Size **20 x 20cm
x 8mm/8 x 8 x ⅛in**
Price ★★★★ Ⓦ ⊞

15 Carocim/Dé Jeté H.M.C. 08
Colour **green** Alt. colours
yes Composition **cement/
marble (encaustic)** Size
20 x 20cm/8 x 8in
Price ★ Ⓦ Ⓕ ⊞

16 Original Tiles/Fruits
Exotiques/Star Fruit to
Melon Border KHP5737B
Colour **multi** Alt. colours
no Composition **ceramic**
Size **20 x 7.5cm/8 x 2⅜in**
Price ★★ Ⓦ ♣

17 Original Style/A La Ferme/
Geese Border KHP5797B
Colour **clematis** Alt. colours
no Composition **ceramic**
Size **20 x 5cm/8 x 2in**
Price ★★ Ⓦ

18 Kenneth Clark Ceramics/
Magic Lantern/Elephant
Colour **ML2** Alt. colours
no Composition **ceramic**
Size **10 x 10cm/4 x 4in** Price
★★ Ⓦ ⊞

19 Tiles of Stow/Grasslands
Tiger Colour **white**
Alt. colours **yes**
Composition **ceramic**
Size **13 x 13cm/5 x 5in**
Price ★★★ Ⓦ

TILES & ADVERTISING

Because of their durability and
ease of cleaning, tiles have
frequently been used to advertise
products and services. It was once
common to see butcher's shops
and dairies with tile panels
depicting sheep, cattle and
poultry, although many of these
have now disappeared behind
modern laminated surfaces. In the
1920s and 1930s, W.H. Smith, the
English stationer and bookseller,
used a number of Carter & Co's
tiles to advertise their products,
while the Santa Fe Railroad in
America used tiled logos on its
principal stations.

Rye Tiles/Rooster Panel (12-tile panel) Colour **multi** Alt. colours **yes** Composition **ceramic**
Size **11 x 11cm/4¼ x 4¼in** Price ★★★★★

17

18

19

Overall Pattern Tiles

By their very nature, tiles make an overall pattern when laid. Even when the design extends across a large number of tiles, the basic grid pattern is visible in the joints. To try to hide this, delft tile-painters used various forms of corner ornament to carry the design to adjacent tiles, so that the corners themselves create an additional element in the overall pattern.

Individual tiles have also been designed with an overall pattern. By covering the tile with a repeated pattern of small motifs, often organic and vegetal in nature, an effect approaching that of wallpaper is achieved. The application of printing techniques to tile manufacture in the 1750s enabled such overall designs to be produced accurately and cheaply. Marble effects were also very popular on tiles, particularly in the Netherlands. These finishes subsequently reappeared in modified form during the 1920s and 1930s as the mottled tiles so beloved of fireplace manufacturers. The advent of Pop Art in the 1950s and 1960s brought a wave of tiles with simple designs that consisted of dots, squiggles, lines and other patterns; many of these are designed by computer today.

ABOVE This modern fireplace incorporates tiles that are essentially based on traditional designs and patterns. The inspiration is derived from the "Masters of Tabriz", from the dado of the Muradiye in Edirne, Turkey, which dates from the middle of the 15th century. The border tiles in the fireplace are based on later Iznik tiles of the 17th century.

RIGHT The strong geometric shapes in Charles Jencks's Post-Modernist home are characteristic of the Art Deco period. The patterns in which the simple, mottled tiles are laid in the bathroom reflect this style. Brightly coloured tiles of this kind were a particular feature of Art Deco schemes. The stepped window surround is also in keeping with the distinctive feel of the room.

KEY DESIGNS

1 Tile designs have often imitated architectural features. This is particularly true of border tiles where the overall pattern simulates plaster or stone mouldings.

2 The repeated use of a small floret or other motif can create an overall effect that almost produces the impression of "ceramic wallpaper".

3 Earthenware tiles with *faux* finishes were first seen in the Netherlands in the 17th century. This *faux* stone porcelain tile is a modern example.

4 Dots, squiggles and a variety of other small-scale decorations have often been used since the mid-20th century as a background for a feature tile or tile panel, and also as patterns in their own right.

1 **Candy/Suzy Florentine 32583 (2 tiles)** Colour **dusk** Alt. colours **yes** Composition **ceramic** Size **20 x 10cm/8 x 4in** Price ★ W

2 **Elon/Terracotta Frieze** Colour **terracotta** Alt. colours **yes** Composition **ceramic** Size **10 x 10cm/4 x 4in** Price ★ W

3 **Daltile/La Costa/ColorBody Porcelain/Field** Colour **rust LC04** Alt. colours **yes** Composition **porcelain** Size **15 x 15cm/6 x 6in** Price ★ W F ⊞

4 **Carocim/Souleiado-Tortillon S510** Colour **blue** Alt. colours **yes** Composition **ceramic** Size **20 x 20cm/8 x 8in** Price ★ W F ⊞

Overall Pattern: **Pre-20th century**

Early ceramic tiles rarely featured overall patterns, largely because of the difficulty of producing regular designs by hand-painting. Some medieval tiles did feature overall patterns, but the tiles were invariably divided up into panels of four, nine or 16 by additional lines of plain tiles.

In the Netherlands, a number of tiled rooms still exist that show how the corner ornaments on 17th- and 18th-century delft tiles created a cohesive pattern when used *en masse*. The marble patterns that appear on delft tiles from the end of the 17th century were produced before the tiles were fired, by splashing pigments on to the surface or by swirling colour into the glaze with a comb. The printing technique developed by Sadler and Green in England during the 1750s lent itself to the production of tiles with repeated small motifs and patterns, similar to those seen on wallpapers.

During the 19th century, more heavily patterned designs were used on tiles, many of them based on stylized, rhythmical, organic and vegetal forms. This was particularly true of the second half of the 19th century, and reflected the generally busy, cluttered feel of Victorian interiors. Classical patterns such as scrollwork also remained popular.

1

2

3

5

6

4

7

1 **Fired Earth/Ironbridge Spinney** Colour **Prussian blue** Alt. colours **yes** Composition **ceramic** Size **15 x 7.5cm/6 x 2¾in** Price ★★ W

2 **Fired Earth/Roman Mosaic Rope Border** Colour **black** Alt. colours **yes** Composition **stone** Size **40 x 10cm/15¾ x 4in** Price ★★★★ F

3 **Walker Zanger/Alhambra Algiers Border** Colour **multi** Alt. colours **yes** Composition **ceramic** Size **10 x 10cm/4 x 4in** Price ★★ W

4 **Carocim/Victoria** Colour **black and white** Alt. colours **yes** Composition **cement/ marble (encaustic)** Size **20 x 20cm/8 x 8in** Price ★ W F +

5 **Tiles of Stow/Tozetto Inset** Colour **blue on white** Alt. colours **yes** Composition **ceramic** Size **4 x 4cm/1½ x 1½in** Price ★★ W F

6 **Candy/Cararra Troy CAN32767** Colour **white** Alt. colours **no** Composition **ceramic** Size **25 x 10cm/9¾ x 4in** Price ★★ W

7 **Fired Earth/Iznik/Arabesque (4 tiles)** Colour **multi** Alt. colours **no** Composition **ceramic** Size **20 x 20cm/8 x 8in** Price ★★ W

MEXICAN TILES

Although there had been an indigenous pottery industry in Mexico for many centuries, the Spanish Conquistadores introduced the technique of painting on tin-glaze. Colourful tiles were produced during the 17th and 18th centuries combining Spanish and native Mexican designs, and were used to decorate the façades of churches. The traditional centre for tile-making was Puebla, where there has been a recent revival of the craft. Most of the Spanish influence has now disappeared and modern production has a more traditional feel.

Elon/Carrillo Arbor G Colour **Mexican white and green** Alt. colours **no** Composition **ceramic** Size **10 x 10cm x 8mm/4 x 4 x ⅓in** Price ★ W

Elon/Carillo Wall/Martha Colour **multi** Alt. colours **yes** Composition **ceramic** Size **10 x 10cm/4 x 4in** Price ★ W

12

8

9

10

11

13

14

8 **Carocim/Souleiado/Ronce Frieze S507 (2 tiles)** Colour **U2/U8** Alt. colours **yes** Alt. colours **yes** Composition **cement/marble (encaustic)** Size **20 x 20cm/8 x 8in** Price ★ W F

9 **Daltile/Village Bend/ Decorative Border** Colour **olive VB04** Alt. colours **yes** Composition **glazed ceramic** Size **31 x 15cm/ 12 x 6in** Price ★ W F

10 **Original Style/Cornice K9904** Colour **Baltic blue** Alt. colours **yes** Composition **ceramic** Size **15 x 7.5cm/ 6 x 2¾in** Price ★ W

11 **Winchester Tile Co/Acanthus Leaf Moulding Trim W.SF1214** Colour **saffron** Alt. colours **yes** Composition **ceramic** Size **21.5 x 19cm/8½ x 7½in** Price ★★ W

12 **Candy/Suzy Florentine CAN32286** Colour **dawn** Alt. colours **yes** Composition **ceramic** Size **20 x 10cm/ 8 x 4in** Price ★ W

13 **Fired Earth/Anatolia 2** Colour **blue and white** Alt. colours **no** Composition **ceramic** Size **17.5 x 17.5cm/ 7 x 7in** Price ★★ W

14 **Kenneth Clark Ceramics/ William de Morgan/Ruby Lustre/Berries and Leaves** Colour **ruby lustre** Alt. colours **no** Composition **ceramic** Size **15 x 15cm/ 6 x 6in** Price ★★★★★ W

Overall Pattern: 20th–early 21st century

The use of overall tile patterns declined markedly at the beginning of the 20th century; this was largely as a result of the Art Nouveau movement sweeping across Europe, and to some extent, America. In keeping with this movement, plain tiles were preferred for room schemes, with patterned tiles being restricted to a mere dado-height row or a random insert.

By the 1920s, plain tiles had given way to mottles, often produced in the newly developed matt or eggshell glazes. Tile-makers began to investigate the chemistry of glazes, so that new and varied glazes were developed – many having small random crackle or star-burst effects. These and the mottled tiles were popular choices for decorating fireplaces, but they were also used to cover entire walls, especially in bathrooms and kitchens.

Increased mechanization in the 1950s and 1960s led to the simplification of tile design and the subsequent introduction of the many bland and repetitive patterns that swamped the market during the 1970s. Overall pattern designs featuring small floral motifs, in the style of Laura Ashley, were produced during the late 1970s and early 1980s, while in recent years computer-generated tile designs have become commonplace, although hand-made tiles have retained their appeal.

3

1

2

5

1 Kenneth Clark Ceramics/ Border Tiles/Blue Waves Colour **blue** Alt. colours **yes** Composition **ceramic** Size **10 x 10cm/4 x 4in** Price ★ W

2 Original Style/Laurel Quarter Tile Colour **multi** Alt. colours **no** Composition **ceramic** Size **15 x 4cm/6 x 1½in** Price ★ W

3 Tile Productions/Wave Border Colour **multi** Alt. colours **yes** Composition **ceramic** Size **11 x 11cm/4¼ x 4¼in** Price ★★★ W

4 Kirkstone/Minoan Liner Colour **avalon** Alt. colours **no** Composition **glass** Size **19.5 x 6.5cm/7¾ x 2½in** Price ★★★★ W

5 Carocim/Poétique Foncé M282 Colour **U9** Alt. colours **yes** Alt. colours **yes** Composition **cement/ marble (encaustic)** Size **20 x 20cm/8 x 8in** Price ★ W F

6 **Daltile/Keystones** Colour **corallin** Alt. colours **yes** Composition **ceramic** Size **5 x 5cm/2 x 2in** Price ★ W F C ⊞ 🗐 🏠

7 **Fired Earth/Planets/Jupiter** Colour **browntone** Alt. colours **yes** Composition **ceramic** Size **10 x 10cm/4 x 4in** Price ★ W

8 **Winchester Tile Co/Leaf Border WHP.1051** Colour **white** Alt. colours **yes** Composition **ceramic** Size **10.5 x 10.5cm/4 x 4in** Price ★★ W

9 **Candy/Silver Leaf CAN31364** Colour **blue** Alt. colours **yes** Composition **ceramic** Size **20 x 7cm/8 x 2¾in** Price ★★ W

10 **Carocim/Music** Colour **yellow and black** Alt. colours **yes** Composition **cement/ marble (encaustic)** Size **20 x 20cm/8 x 8in** Price ★ W F ⊞

11 **Fired Earth/Heritage/Sunflower Leaves** Colour **green** Alt. colours **no** Composition **ceramic** Size **11 x 11cm/4¼ x 4⅛in** Price ★★★ W

12 **Carocim/Asie Mineure F551** Colour **U8** Alt. colours **yes** Alt. colours **yes** Composition **cement/marble (encaustic)** Size **20 x 20cm/8 x 8in** Price ★ W F

10

11

12

Geometric Tiles

Tiles are essentially geometric in form and, even when the design extends across a number of them, the geometric pattern of the tiling is still evident.

Since medieval times, geometry has also been a basis for tile decoration, often in the form of checks, trellises and overlapping circles. Designs of this nature are fundamental to Islamic culture and this is reflected in the tiles and mosaics of Spain, North Africa and the Middle East.

In 18th-century Portugal, so-called "pombaline" tiles, which have a diagonal pattern of foliage, were placed together to form a trellis pattern. Geometric patterns were also very popular on the tin-glazed tiles produced in France, and to a lesser extent in the Netherlands, toward the end of the 19th century. At the same time, pavements composed of geometrically shaped tiles in various colours were thought appropriate for hallways, porches and public buildings throughout Europe. In the 20th century movements such as Pop Art expanded the possibilities of geometrically patterned tiles.

RIGHT Designs composed of overlapping circles have been used on tiles since medieval times, and relieve the square effect of the tile itself. This 18th-century-style Spanish kitchen is an excellent example of this. Such geometric patterns have appeared in many eras, notably in Art Deco interiors of the early 20th century.

BOVE The tiles positioned around the cooking range in the Scottish home of Annie and achlan Stewart have all been hand-made and hand-painted. The ever-popular tartan attern, here in various shades of green, fits in perfectly with the style of this farmhouse itchen, with its Aga and painted woodwork.

ZILLIJ DESIGNS

Zillij is the name given to traditional North African cut-mosaic tilework. Originally, large square tiles were cut after firing into the individually shaped pieces required to make up these elaborate patterns. However, nowadays the pieces are shaped before firing and glazing. The shapes of the pieces and the arrangements of the colours are traditional and have varied surprisingly little over the past 500 years.

KEY DESIGNS

1 The use of interlocking shapes dates back to the medieval period, but it reached its height in Moorish Spain when extremely complex patterns were produced from very simple geometric shapes.

2 Some tiles give the illusion of having interlocking components, such as this geometric *trompe l'oeil* design. The visual effect is heightened when several tiles are placed together.

3 Perhaps the simplest and most popular of geometric designs is the square arranged in alternating colours, either straight or diagonally as a diamond pattern.

4 Some modern tiles are trimmed top and bottom with a contrasting material. The result, as on this chrome-trimmed 21st-century border tile, is a strongly defined linear pattern.

5 Tartan designs have been popular since the 19th century, and are still employed by tile designers in the 21st century – often updated with new colour combinations.

1 H. & R. Johnson/Kerastar/Puzzle Border Colour **grey and white** Alt. colours **no** Composition **porcelain** Size **30 x 15cm/11¾ x 6in** Price ★★★ F ▨ ⌂

2 Carocim/Cube Moyen M063 Colour **U1** Alt. colours **yes** Alt. colours **yes** Composition **cement/marble (encaustic)** Size **20 x 20cm/8 x 8in** Price ★ W F

3 Carocim/Petit Carré M201 Colour **U2** Alt. colours **yes** Alt. colours **yes** Composition **cement/marble (encaustic)** Size **20 x 20cm/8 x 8in** Price ★ W F

4 Saloni/Alesia/Stella Border/Celta Colour **green** Alt. colours **yes** Composition **rectified porcelain** Size **30 x 5cm/11¾ x 2in** Price ★ ⊞ W F

5 Tiles of Stow/Check Colour **green and purple** Alt. colours **yes** Composition **ceramic** Size **10 x 10cm/4 x 4in** Price ★★★ W

Geometrics: **Pre-19th century**

During the period of the Roman Empire, geometric mosaic floors were laid in domestic buildings as well as in public ones, particularly in Britain and Italy. From the 10th century, the use of cut geometric mosaics was brought to Spain by the Moors from North Africa during their 500-year occupation. This style still survives in such buildings as the 14th-century Alhambra in Granada.

In the early 13th century, a number of abbeys in the north of England were tiled with elaborate pavements of geometrically shaped interlocking tiles. By the end of that century, however, these had been superseded by inlaid tiles, often with intricate geometric patterns, which were used in abbeys and churches across Europe. Owing to the difficulty of producing cut geometric mosaics, these designs were soon reproduced on tiles. Painted geometric tiles were used on walls in many Portuguese interiors during the 14th and 15th centuries, often creating a *trompe l'oeil* three-dimensional box effect. By the 17th century, the Portuguese were also applying tiles to the exteriors of buildings, often to resemble ornate trelliswork.

1

1 **H. & R. Johnson/Natural Selection/Chilterns Checkendon** Colour **sand** Alt. colours **yes** Composition **ceramic** Size **15 x 15cm/6 x 6in** Price ★ W

2 **Candy/Suzy Diamond Border/CAN33931** Colour **dawn** Alt. colours **yes** Composition **ceramic** Size **20 x 7cm/8 x 2¾in** Price ★ W

3 **Walker Zanger/Intarsio Romana/Tarquina Border** Colour **natural** Alt. colours **no** Composition **stone** Size **30 x 13.5cm/11¾ x 5¼in** Price ★★★★ W F ☐

4 **Saloni Ceramics/Ocana Blanco** Colour **multi** Alt. colours **no** Composition **ceramic** Size **25 x 5cm/9¾ x 2in** Price ★ W

5 **Carré/Sols/Terres Cuites/ Antiquaire/Damiers 2736** Colour **red terracotta and cream** Alt. colours **no** Composition **terracotta** Size **13 x 13cm/5 x 5in** Price ★ W F

2

4

3

5

8

10

6 **Elon/Trellis G** Colour **green and cream** Alt. colours **yes** Composition **ceramic** Size **10 x 10cm/4 x 4in** Price ★ Ⓦ

7 **Candy/London Chelsea Cream Field CAN34297** Colour **cream** Alt. colours **yes** Composition **ceramic** Size **33 x 25cm/13 x 10in** Price ★★ Ⓦ

8 **Winchester Tile Co/Painted Edge Lines** Colour **red** Alt. colours **yes** Composition **ceramic** Size **10.5 x 10.5cm/4 x 4in** Price ★ Ⓦ ⊞

9 **Walker Zanger/Intarsio Romano/Viejo Deco** Colour **natural** Alt. colours **no** Composition **stone** Size **12 x 12cm/4¾ x 4¾in** Price ★★★★ Ⓦ

10 **Elon/Daisy May II G** Colour **green** Alt. colours **yes** Composition **ceramic** Size **10 x 10cm/4 x 4in** Price ★ Ⓦ

11 **Carocim/Grec** Colour **brown and white** Alt. colours **yes** Composition **cement/ marble (encaustic)** Size **20 x 20cm/8 x 8in** Price ★ Ⓦ Ⓕ ⊞

12

13

14

15

12 **Carocim/Tanger** Colour **multi** Alt. colours **yes** Composition **cement/ marble (encaustic)** Size **20 x 20 cm/8 x 8in** Price ★★ Ⓦ Ⓕ ⊞

13 **Villeroy & Boch/Villostone/ Geometric Border Electra 2154 845G** Colour **green and beige** Alt. colours **yes** Composition **porcelain stoneware** Size **30 x 7.5cm/11¾ x 2¾in** Price ★★★ Ⓦ Ⓕ

14 **Candy/Tripoli Rombi CAN33382** Colour **cream** Alt. colours **yes** Composition **ceramic** Size **25 x 8cm/ 9¾ x 3in** Price ★ Ⓦ

15 **Carocim/Petit Latti M172** Colour **blue and black** Alt. colours **yes** Composition **cement/marble (encaustic)** Size **20 x 20 cm/8 x 8in** Price ★ Ⓦ Ⓕ ⊞

Geometrics: **19th century**

When the Gothic Revival took place in the early 19th century, architects in Britain and elsewhere in Europe rediscovered the geometric designs of the Middle Ages. Chief among these in England was A.W.N. Pugin, who collaborated with the potter Herbert Minton to create a range of encaustic tiles based on Gothic designs. Many of these were strongly geometric in form. In 1840 Herbert Minton purchased the rights to Richard Prosser's patent for dust-pressing clay products (*see* page 314) and realized that the process could be used to form ceramic *tesserae* and tiles. He was soon able to produce hundreds of geometric shapes based on fractions of a 15cm/6in square. The technique also made it easier to stain the clay different colours, and the tiles were used to create elaborate geometric pavements suitable for public as well as residential buildings. In France, intricate geometric patterns were stencilled on to tin-glazed tiles, particularly in the Pas de Calais region toward the end of the century.

1

1 **Carré/Les Classiques/Carré Bleu 3891** Colour **blue and white** Alt. colours **yes** Composition **glazed stoneware** Size **11 x 11cm/4¼ x 4¼in** Price ★★ W F

2 **Original Style/Royal Stewart Tartan Border 6795A** Colour **multi** Alt. colours **no** Composition **ceramic** Size **15 x 7.5cm/ 6 x 2¾in** Price ★ W

3 **Original Style/Culloden Stirling Tartan Border 6791A** Colour **multi** Alt. colours **no** Composition **ceramic** Size **15 x 7.5cm/ 6 x 2¾in** Price ★ W

2

3

4

5

4 **Kenneth Clark Ceramics/ Gingham** Colour **black and white** Alt. colours **yes** Composition **ceramic** Size **15 x 7.5cm/6 x 2¾in** Price ★ W

5 **Daltile/Tajah/Natural Slate Borders/Autumn Mist** Colour **California gold TS91** Alt. colours **yes** Composition **slate** Size **23 x 13cm/9 x 5in** Price ★★ F W

7

6 Tiles of Stow/English Lattice
Colour **blue** Alt. colours
no Composition **ceramic**
Size **15 x 15cm/6 x 6in**
Price ★ W

7 Original Style/Melbourne
Border 6680 Colour **black
spot** Alt. colours **yes**
Composition **ceramic**
Size **15 x 2.5cm/
6 x 1in** Price ★ F

8 Carocim/Grand Carré M191
Colour **U4/U2** Alt. colours **yes**
Alt. colours **yes** Composition
cement/marble (encaustic)
Size **20 x 20cm/8 x 8in**
Price ★ W F

9 Carocim/Pliage Mariella
Frieze F063 (3 tiles) Colour
U2/U4, U6/U9 Alt. colours
yes Composition **cement**
Size **20 x 20cm/8 x 8in**
Price ★ F

10 Carocim/Petit Carré M201
Colour **red and yellow** Alt.
colours **yes** Composition
cement/marble (encaustic)
Size **20 x 20cm/8 x 8in**
Price ★ W F ⊞

10

11 Kenneth Clark Ceramics/
Fircone Colour **various
(4 tiles)** Alt. colours **yes**
Composition **ceramic**
Size **10 x 10cm/4 x 4in**
Price ★ W

12 Kenneth Clark Ceramics/
**Stripes/Verdant Stripes
(4 tiles)** Colour **multi** Alt.
colours **yes** Composition
ceramic Size **15 x 15cm/
6 x 6in** Price ★★ W ⊞

13 Carocim/Game/Corner
F202 (2 tiles) Colour **U8** Alt.
colours **yes** Composition
cement/marble (encaustic)
Size **20 x 20cm/8 x 8in**
Price ★ W F

14 Carocim/Game/Frieze
F202 (3 tiles) Colour **U8**
Alt. colours **yes** Alt. colours
yes Composition **cement/
marble (encaustic)** Size **20 x
20cm/8 x 8in** Price ★ W F

12

13

14

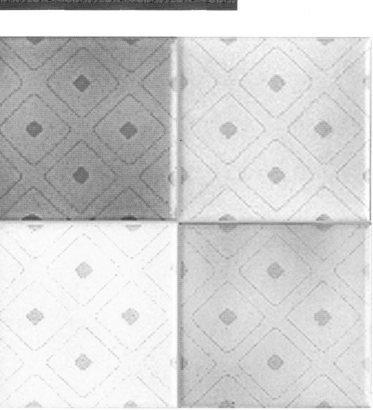

Geometrics: 20th–early 21st century

Perhaps as a reaction to the excesses of Victorian design, early 20th-century tiles were often plain or simply moulded with a geometric effect that resembled bricks in a wall. During the 1920s and 1930s, bold geometric shapes in tilework were often applied to Art Deco buildings. This style was hugely popular in America, and was also used to decorate a number of buildings in England – for example, the Hoover Building in Perivale designed by the architects Wallis, Gilbert & Partners, which opened in 1933. Not only did tiles form dramatic designs on the exteriors of such buildings, they were used inside as well.

On a smaller scale, some geometric tube-lined tiles were produced for domestic use around fireplaces – by the English firm of Maw & Co, for example. Geometric designs became even more desirable during the 1950s and 1960s with the advent of Pop Art, with its designs of squares, circles and triangles that were often overlaid and printed in bright colours. The recently developed technique of screen-printing on tiles lent itself particularly well to this style of decoration. In the late 20th and early 21st century, geometric tiles have often featured a single design element, such as a diagonal line or a quadrant, which can be combined in different ways to create a wide range of patterns.

1

2

3

4

5

6

7

1 **Carocim/Horta** Colour **purple and white** Alt. colours **yes** Composition **cement/ marble (encaustic)** Size **20 x 20cm/8 x 8in** Price ★ Ⓦ Ⓕ ⊞

2 **Kenneth Clark Ceramics/ Squares/Mellow Squares** Colour **peach and white** Alt. colours **yes** Composition **ceramic** Size **10 x 10cm/ 4 x 4in** Price ★★ Ⓦ ⊞

3 **Carocim/Souleiado/Madras Frieze S514 (2 tiles)** Colour **U15/U3/U9** Alt. colours **yes** Composition **cement/marble (encaustic)** Size **20 x 20cm/ 8 x 8in** Price ★ Ⓦ Ⓕ

4 **Mosquito/Dichroic Sparkle Tile** Colour **turquoise** Alt. colours **yes** Composition **ceramic/glass** Size **20 x 20cm/8 x 8in** Price ★★★★★ Ⓦ ⊞

5 **Carocim/Casson M221** Colour **multi** Alt. colours **yes** Composition **cement/ marble (encaustic)** Size **20 x 20cm/8 x 8in** Price ★ Ⓦ Ⓕ ⊞

6 **Kenneth Clark Ceramics/ Peppercorn Sands** Colour **multi** Alt. colours **yes** Composition **ceramic** Size **15 x 15cm/6 x 6in** Price ★★ Ⓦ

7 **Winchester Tile Co/Little Snap Pattern** Colour **blue and white** Alt. colours **no** Composition **ceramic** Size **15 x 10.5cm/6 x 4in** Price ★ Ⓦ

8

**H. & R. Johnson/Alpine
White/Metallica Inset
MET 1D** Colour **platinum**
Alt. colours **no** Composition
ceramic body, chrome coating
Size **20 x 20cm/8 x 8in**
Price ★ W

9

10

**Candy/Jazz Bebop/Satin
Gloss/CAN33177** Colour **blue**
Alt. colours **no** Composition
ceramic Size **20 x 7.5cm/
8 x 2¾ in** Price ★ W

**Original Style/Manhattan
Border 6490** Colour
multi Alt. colours **no**
Composition **ceramic**
Size **15 x 5cm/6 x 2in**
Price ★ W

**Fired Earth/Glass Art/Optics/
Decor 5** Colour **multi** Alt.
colours **no** Composition
glass Size **14.5 x 14.5cm/5¾
x 5¾in** Price ★★★★ W

11

12

13   **14**

15   **16**

17

**12 Candy/Reflections Geo
CAN32552** Colour **black** Alt.
colours **no** Composition
ceramic Size **20 x 7.5cm/8 x
2¾in** Price ★ W

**13 The Digitile Showroom/
Dominic Crinson/Glitz/
Glaterre 5** Colour **blue** Alt.
colours **yes** Composition
ceramic Size **15 x 15cm/
6 x 6in** Price ★★ W ⊞

**14 Original Style/Satin Glazed
Decorative/Odeon Border/
Double Diamond** Colour
salmon Alt. colours **yes**
Composition **ceramic**
Size **15 x 8cm/6 x 3in**
Price ★ W

**15 Tiles of Stow/Kingham
Border** Colour **blue** Alt.
colours **yes** Composition
ceramic Size **15 x 15cm/6 x
6in** Price ★ W

**16 Tiles of Newport & London/
Check** Colour **yellow**
Alt. colours **yes**
Composition **ceramic**
Size **20 x 20cm/8 x 8in**
Price ★ W

**17 Fired Earth/Shadows/
Spirits 5** Colour **grey/silver**
Alt. colours **no** Composition
ceramic Size **6.5 x 6.5cm/2½
x 2½in** Price ★★★ W

ART DECO DESIGNS

The Art Deco movement was
particularly influential in Germany,
Austria and America, where it was
a major source of inspiration in the
architecture of the day. Tiles were
designed with bold geometric
patterns, often based on objects
including fans, bows and flowers.
The origin of the pattern is not
always apparent at first glance,
especially if the tiles are viewed
en masse. The tile shown here is
based on a fan but, when placed
with other tiles, a zig-zag effect is
the result.

Original Style/Salmon 6481 Colour **multi** Alt. colours
no Composition **ceramic** Size **15 x 15cm/6 x 6in**
Price ★★ W

Wooden Flooring

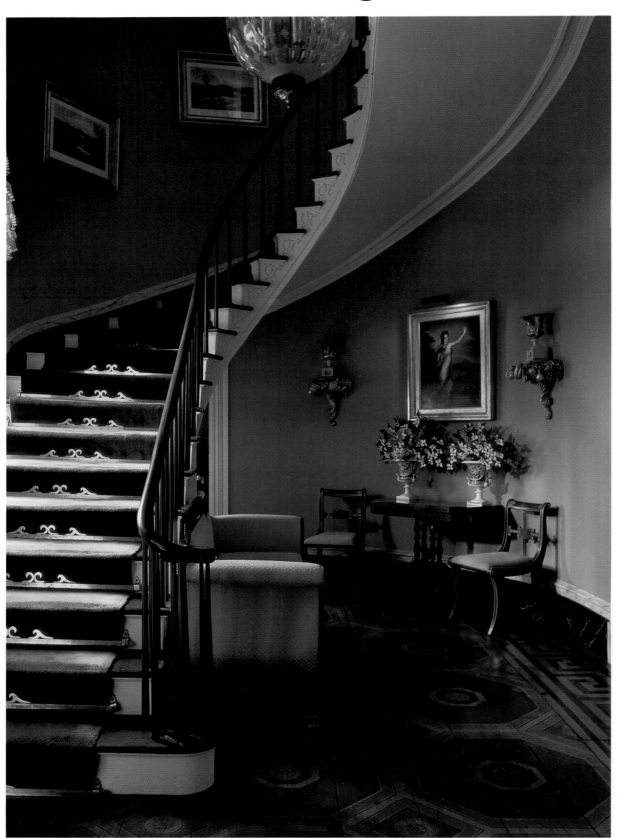

The use of wood as a flooring material predates the classical civilizations of ancient Greece and Rome. However, before the late 17th century wooden boards were usually confined to upper storeys; thereafter they were increasingly employed at ground level as well. Until the 16th century, the types of wood used were generally restricted to locally available species, but subsequently the expansion of international trade enabled housebuilders to use imported timber as well.

Fashionable alternatives to plain, solid boards have included marquetry (*see* page 369), which originated in Persia and was brought to Europe in the 14th century, and parquetry (*see* opposite), a cheaper and more practical alternative. Favoured patterns include lozenges and diamonds. Stencilled patterns have also been much in evidence, especially during the 18th and 19th centuries. In the 20th century and early 21st, hardwood and softwood laminates have provided more affordable alternatives to solid wooden flooring, although reclaimed solid floors are now much sought after.

LEFT The hall of Richard Jenrette's house in New York State, USA, is dominated by a sweeping staircase and an inlaid wooden floor. Copied from a floor in the Tsar's Palace in St Petersburg, Russia, the design has big octagonal motifs and an Islamic-inspired geometric border. The furniture and colour scheme complete the early 19th-century look.

ABOVE The wide, uneven oak floorboards in this American kitchen typify the rustic simplicity of the Colonial look. Usually, boards of varying widths were laid, with the widest in the middle and the narrowest at the edges. Simple and practical, these boards were neatly tacked down with headless nails.

PARQUET FLOORS

Parquetry originated in France in the 17th century, and was first applied to small areas such as half-landings and stair treads. It involves the use of hardwood blocks arranged in geometric patterns, echoing the three-dimensional and *trompe l'oeil* effects of inlaid and paved stone. The parquet floor in this 18th-century French interior consists of a basic geometric pattern, although lozenge arrangements were very popular in France at this time. Other patterns include stars, diamonds and latticework.

1 These butt-jointed boards are made with reclaimed Bordeaux oak. Reclaimed wood has become increasingly popular as much for its period authenticity as for environmental reasons.

2 Basic geometric parquetry patterns have been popular since the early 17th century. This configuration, in walnut, has been one of the most popular parquet patterns since the early 20th century.

3 Marquetry patterns inlaid into wooden floors can consist of many different types of wood in addition to other materials, such as ivory and pewter, offering the decorator a choice of designs.

4 By the early 20th century, floorboards of the same width were usually laid in each room. A more recent alternative consists of a thin top layer of laminated hardwood glued to a plank of softwood.

5 The chevron, or herringbone, pattern is a popular parquet design. In Europe Rhodesian teak was used extensively for this at the end of the 19th century and beginning of the 20th.

6 Cork tiles, first developed in the 1920s, are made from the bark of the cork oak. The bark is stripped every nine years, granulated, then made into blocks from which the tiles are cut.

---

1 LASSCO/Bordeaux Oak (Patinated) OB020 Colour **natural** Alt. colours **no** Composition **oak** Width **15cm/6in** Repeat – Price ★★★★ ⊞

2 Historic Floors of Oshkosh/Marie Antoinette 151 Colour **natural** Alt. colours **yes** Composition **walnut** Width **76cm/30in** Repeat – Price **on application** ⊞

3 Historic Floors of Oshkosh/Border 149 Colour **natural** Alt. colours **yes** Composition **red oak, maple, walnut and Brazilian cherry** Width **11.5cm/4½in** Repeat – Price **on application**

4 Boen Parkett/Ash Sheet Colour **natural** Alt. colours **yes** Composition **ash** Width **14cm/5½in** Repeat – Price ★★

5 LASSCO/Herringbone Colour **natural** Alt. colours **yes** Composition **antique Rhodesian teak** Width **to order** Repeat – Price ★★★ ⊞

6 Siesta Cork Tiles/Harlequin Colour **green** Alt. colours **yes** Composition **cork** Width **30 x 30cm/11¾ x 11¾in (tile)** Repeat – Price ★

Wooden Flooring: **Pre-19th century**

The choice of wood as a flooring material stemmed as much from its availability as its intrinsic beauty. Initially, wide boards were used, although they were often covered by matting or loose rushes. It was not until the 17th century that ornate designs in wood became common in Europe. Parquet flooring (*see* page 363) was popular in grander houses in the mid-17th century, particularly in France. This brought about the use of more unusual woods, and resulted in an increase in the importation of exotic woods – such as mahogany from the West Indies – into Europe. In the early 18th century, floorboards were sometimes decorated by painting or stencilling, a practice thought to have originated in Scandinavia. More elaborate designs often imitated the patterns and *trompe l'oeil* effects of marble, stone paving or garden parterres.

During the 17th and 18th centuries in America, floors were considered to be strictly functional, and floorboards were invariably left bare. Pine was laid in broad planks, and was scrubbed, not waxed or polished. Occasionally, the boards were painted or stencilled with floral patterns, animals or folk-art motifs. At this time in both Europe and America, fine parquet floors were still considered to be the preserve of the wealthy.

4 **Sinclair Till/Greek Key Border** Colour **natural** Alt. colours **yes** Composition **walnut and maple** Width **28.5cm/11in** Repeat – Price ★★

5 **Historic Floors of Oshkosh/ Medallion 306** Colour **natural** Alt. colours **yes** Composition **American cherry, walnut, red oak and mahogany** Width **to order** Repeat – Price **on application**

6 **Berti Pavimenti Legno/Bonfadini Border** Colour **natural** Alt. colours **yes** Composition **jatoba and maple** Width **to order** Repeat – Price ★★★★★

1

2

1 **Berti Pavimenti Legno/Trissino Border** Colour **natural** Alt. colours **yes** Composition **French walnut, sycamore, oak, wenge, ipe and mahogany** Width **to order** Repeat – Price ★★★★★

2 **Fired Earth/Planche Antique de Quercy** Colour **natural** Alt. colours **no** Composition **oak** Width **14cm/5½in** Repeat – Price ★★★ ⊞

3 **Historic Floors of Oshkosh/ Marseille 145** Colour **natural** Alt. colours **yes** Composition **American cherry** Width **to order** Repeat – Price **on application**

3

5

6

7

9

10

7 Historic Floors of Oshkosh/Rose Border 130 Colour **natural** Alt. colours **yes** Composition **bubinga, mahogany, walnut, green poplar and maple** Width **to order** Repeat **10.5cm/4in** Price **on application**

8 Historic Floors of Oshkosh/ Château 152 Colour **natural** Alt. colours **yes** Composition **ipe** Width **to order** Repeat – Price **on application**

9 Berti Pavimenti Legno/ Giustinian Border Colour **natural** Alt. colours **yes** Composition **walnut, ipe, maple and oak** Width **to order** Repeat – Price ★★★★★

10 Berti Pavimenti Legno/ Todeschini Border Colour **natural** Alt. colours **yes** Composition **doussie, walnut, gatambu and wenge** Width **to order** Repeat – Price ★★★★★

11 Historic Floors of Oshkosh/ Louve 154 Colour **natural** Alt. colours **yes** Composition **white oak** Width **to order** Repeat – Price **on application**

12 LASSCO/Baltic Pine PN101 Colour **natural** Alt. colours **no** Composition **pine** Width **20cm/8in** Repeat – Price ★★ ⊞

13 Historic Floors of Oshkosh/ Fontainebleau Colour **natural** Alt. colours **yes** Composition **red oak and white oak** Width **to order** Repeat – Price **on application**

11

12

MAHOGANY

Since the 16th century, mahogany has been recognized as one of the world's finest timbers for flooring and cabinet-making. Less subject to shrinking, swelling or warping than many other hardwoods, it ranges in colour from a light tan to a dark reddish-brown and displays aesthetically pleasing grain and figuring. The latter varies – curly, wavy, speckled or "ostrich-plume", depending on how it is cut. In the 17th and 18th centuries it was mostly imported from the West Indies and Cuba.

Pergo/PO 26001 Colour **Mahogany Blocked** Alt. colours **no** Composition **mahogany** Width **19.5cm/7¾in** Repeat – Price ★★

13

Wooden Flooring: **19th century**

During the 19th century in Europe and America, narrower floorboards came into use, especially in wealthier homes. Such floorboards were often only 10cm (4in) in width – in contrast to the 23cm- (9in-) wide floorboards used in poorer homes. In the 1820s, tongued-and-grooved wooden boards were introduced. As the century progressed, these were increasingly prepared by machine and, as a result, became more even in width.

In America, the practice of painting wooden floors developed into a popular craft, although plain-coloured versions were as liked as stencilled ones. In Europe, the tradition of floor painting continued, as did the trend for staining wood with different oils. However, now that carpets had become more common, floors were generally painted or glazed in a single colour, and the designs for parquet floors became simpler. At the same time, it was discovered that thin boards could be glued, nailed or screwed down on to a solid backing to produce a good imitation of a floor composed of solid wood blocks. This was the forerunner of the modern parquet floor. By the end of the 19th century, American manufacturers were offering intricate, ready-made examples consisting of oak blocks glued to cloth or softwood in a closely woven pattern.

Historic Floors of Oshkosh/110 and 106 Colour **natural** Alt. colours **yes** Composition **plainsawn white oak and walnut** Width 30.5 x 30.5cm/12 x 12in (panel) Repeat – Price **on application**

Historic Floors of Oshkosh/Monticello 155 Colour **natural** Alt. colours **yes** Composition **ash** Size 25.5 x 25.5cm/10 x 10in (panel) Repeat – Price **on application**

Boen Parkett/Ship's Deck Colour **natural** Alt. colours **yes** Composition **merbau** Width **14cm/5½in** Repeat – Price ★★★

LASSCO/Norse Oak NS009 Colour **dark oil stain** Alt. colours **yes** Composition **oak** Width **2m/2⅙yd** Repeat – Price ★★

Kentucky Wood Floors/Trinity Colour **natural** Alt. colours **yes** Composition **oak** Width **to order** Repeat – Price ★★★★★ (special order)

Historic Floors of Oshkosh/Border 137 Colour **natural** Alt. colours **yes** Composition **Santos mahogany, maple and red oak** Width **to order** Repeat – Price **on application**

Historic Floors of Oshkosh/Border 135 Colour **natural** Alt. colours **yes** Composition **ash, mahogany, bubinga and walnut** Width **to order** Repeat – Price **on application**

Historic Floors of Oshkosh/Wave Border 168 Colour **natural** Alt. colours **yes** Composition **red oak, maple and American cherry** Width **11.5cm/4½in** Repeat – Price **on application**

LASSCO/Re-Milled Bordeaux Oak Colour **natural** Alt. colours **no** Composition **oak** Width **to order** Repeat – Price ★★★★ ⊞

The Hardwood & Natural Stone Flooring Company/Antiqued English Oak Colour **antiqued** Alt. colours **yes** Composition **oak** Width **17cm/6¾in** Repeat – Price ★★★

LASSCO/Burmese Teak Parquet Colour **natural** Alt. colours **yes** Composition **teak** Width **23cm/9in** Repeat – Price ★★★ ⊞

Kentucky Wood Floors/Florentine Colour **natural** Alt. colours **yes** Composition **Brazilian cherry, walnut, bird's-eye maple and brass** Width **to order** Repeat – Price ★★★★★

Wooden Flooring: 20th–early 21st century

Although parquet borders were popular in the early 20th century as an accompaniment to loose-laid carpet, it was not until the 1930s that complete parquet floors enjoyed a resurgence in Europe; this was to last until the 1950s. The designs were extremely basic, with the polished hardwood blocks or strips being laid in clear, simple patterns.

By the 1970s, a revival of appreciation for the qualities of wood sparked a fashion for revealing and restoring old wooden floorboards, as well as laying new ones. This led to the development of new types of wooden flooring systems that catered to a growing international market. By the 1990s, the different options included prefinished floors of oiled wood planks and floors with a wooden laminate surface laid over a high-density fibreboard or chipboard base. Wood-laminate flooring is easy to lay, as it is glued at the tongue-and-groove and does not need to be secured to the sub-floor. In addition, tongued-and-grooved parquets are available in many different woods of various colours, grades and thicknesses. Marquetry designs have remained popular, and replicas of old parquet floors – made by gluing thin panels of oak, beech or birch to a solid backing – have also become widely available.

7

1

2

3

4

5

8

6

10

9

1 **Boen Parkett/Natural Dark Beech** Colour **dark** Alt. colours **yes** Composition **beech** Width **14cm/5½in** Repeat – Price ★★

2 **Westco/C480012** Colour **natural** Alt. colours **no** Composition **Rhodesian teak** Size **47.5 x 47.5cm/18¾ x 18¾in (panel)** Repeat – Price ★

3 **Natural Wood Floor Co/African Walnut Planks** Colour **natural** Alt. colours **yes** Composition **African walnut** Width **9cm/3½in** Repeat – Price ★ ⊞

4 **Junckers/Merbau Plank 065300-189** Colour **natural** Alt. colours **yes** Composition **merbau** Width **13cm/5in** Repeat – Price ★★★

5 **LBC/Solid Elm Planks** Colour **natural** Alt. colours **yes** Composition **elm** Width **to order** Repeat – Price ★★

6 **Historic Floors of Oshkosh/ Oxford 150** Colour **natural** Alt. colours **yes** Composition **Santos mahogany, ipe, maple and American cherry,** Width **to order** Repeat – Price **on application**

7 **Historic Floors of Oshkosh/ Nautical Compass 319** Colour **natural** Alt. colours **yes** Composition **wenge, jatoba, purple heart, maple and brass** Width **to order** Repeat – Price **on application**

8 **LBC/Pitch Pine Planks** Colour **natural** Alt. colours **no** Composition **pine** Width **10cm/4in** Repeat – Price ★★ ⊞

9 **Kahrs/Alder Monte Carlo** Colour **natural** Alt. colours **no** Composition **alder** Width **20cm/8in** Repeat – Price ★★

10 **Kahrs/Rotterdam Diagonal Pattern 3215 OB 50** Colour **natural** Alt. colours **yes** Composition **birch and oak** Width **15cm/6in** Repeat – Price ★

1 **Bruce Hardwood/Dakota Plank E-153** Colour **harvest** Alt. colours **yes** Composition **oak** Width **7.5cm/2¾in** Repeat – Price ★★

2 **Bruce Hardwood/Dakota Plank E150** Colour **toast** Alt. colours **yes** Composition **oak** Width **7.5cm/2¾in** Repeat – Price ★★

3 **Wicanders/LS06 & LS13** Colour **ruby and coal** Alt. colours **yes** Composition **cork** Width **30.5 x 30.5cm/12 x 12in (tile)** Repeat – Price ★

4 **Pergo/PC 14592** Colour **green maple** Alt. colours **no** Composition **maple** Width **20cm/8in** Repeat – Price ★

11

12

MARQUETRY

The skilled art of inlaying wood with pieces of wood or other materials, such as ivory and metal, to form mosaics, arabesques or pictures is the basis of marquetry. First seen in Italy in the 14th century, marquetry was mainly used to decorate furniture. By the early 17th century, it was widespread in France and the fashion rapidly spread to the rest of Europe. Today, many marquetry firms use a laser beam to cut the veneer, thus ensuring a precision previously attained only through the very time-consuming hand-cutting of wooden shapes.

Historic Floors of Oshkosh/Medallion 340 Colour **natural** Alt. colours **yes** Composition **maple and ipe** Width **to order** Repeat – Price **on application**

3

4

15

16

17

18

19

15 **Junckers/Sylvaket Plank** Colour **natural** Alt. colours **yes** Composition **sylvaket** Width **13cm/5in** Repeat – Price ★★

16 **Wicanders/Walnut 3 Strip PT57** Colour **natural** Alt. colours **yes** Composition **walnut** Width **13cm/5in** Repeat – Price ★★

17 **Boen Parkett/Oak Dutch Pattern** Colour **natural** Alt. colours **yes** Composition **oak** Width **14cm/5½in** Repeat – Price ★★

18 **Pergo/PO 25401** Colour **Bali walnut** Alt. colours **no** Composition **walnut** Width **19.5cm/7¾in** Repeat – Price ★★

19 **Seri Parquet/Bamboo Light** Colour **natural** Alt. colours **yes** Composition **bamboo** Width **17.5cm/7in** Repeat **2.2m/2¼yd** Price ★★

Matting

ABOVE This medieval-style room features an elegant coir-matting floor covering. Coir is harvested in two main seasons: the freshwater season, when the fibre lying in the lagoons is washed daily, and the saltwater season. The fibre is then beaten from the coconut husks before being spun and woven into patterns such as this herringbone design.

GRASSES

The different grasses used in matting depend on where it is produced. Sisal is the fibre produced from the leaf of the Mexican agave plant, coir is harvested from the husks of coconuts, while jute is derived from the stalk of a herb of an Indian *Tiliaceae* family. With the expansion of maritime trade, these fibres gradually replaced the rush (shown here) as the traditional component of matting in Europe. All can be woven into a variety of patterns and are particularly suitable for early period homes.

Matting evolved from the spreading of rushes, straw and herbs over floors for both insulation and comfort. By the 17th century in Europe, braided rush strips sewn together to cover the whole floor were common in wealthier houses, although the matting was often covered by oriental carpets. As trade with North Africa opened up in the 17th century, more lightweight mattings – made from narrow strips of braided bullrushes – became popular. These finely woven and delicately patterned floor coverings were known as Africa, Barbary or Portugal mats and largely superseded the traditional European rush matting, which was heavy and needed replacing every few years. The introduction of mass-produced carpets led to a decline in the use of matting, although it was still laid in informal areas of houses. In America, matting was popular in the early 19th century, as importers brought in mats from India and Africa.

Contemporary production techniques mean matting can be machine-woven and given a latex backing. This has increased its durability and made it reasonably stain-proof.

RIGHT Forms of rush matting have been woven for centuries. The ancient Egyptians used bullrushes from the Nile to weave floor-coverings. Today, methods have changed little and rush matting is equally suited to contemporary interiors.

1 Jute has been used as a floor covering since the 18th century. Once harvested, it is tied together, soaked in water and then pounded with wooden mallets. This provides a very soft matting.

2 Wool is often mixed in varying proportions with durable but coarser sisal to give the matting a softer texture underfoot. The 80/20 per cent ratio of wool to sisal in this example is typical.

3 As well as having a wide variety of weaves, sisal is available in numerous colourways. Blues, reds and greens have proved very fashionable in the late 20th and early 21st century.

4 Throughout the years, matting has been decorated with different patterns – such as this medieval design – using either paints or dyes, and it can be printed, stencilled or hand-painted.

5 Modern weaving techniques make it easier for different materials and colours to be combined. The mixture of coir and sisal shown here displays an appealing abstract-motif repeat.

6 Coir matting, produced from coconut fibre that is spun and then woven, varies in colour depending on the time at which it is harvested. It became very popular in the late 20th century.

---

1 **Carpet Innovations/Panama Jute** Colour **natural** Alt. colours **yes** Composition **100% jute** Width **3.9m/4½yd** Repeat – Price ★

2 **Fired Earth/Hungerford/Ribbed** Colour **natural** Alt. colours **yes** Composition **80% wool, 20% sisal** Width **4m/4½yd** Repeat – Price ★★

3 **Crucial Trading/Accents/Fine Bouclé C712** Colour **blue** Alt. colours **yes** Composition **100% sisal** Width **4m/4½yd** Repeat – Price ★★

4 **Sinclair Till/Wrought Iron** Colour **black** Alt. colours **yes** Composition **100% sisal** Width **to order** Repeat – Price ★★★

5 **Ruckstuhl/Pur/Dots** Colour **727** Alt. colours **yes** Composition **48% coir, 52% sisal** Width **2m/2⅛yd** Repeat – Price ★★

6 **Reeve Flooring/Herringbone** Colour **natural** Alt. colours **yes** Composition **100% coir** Width **4m/4½yd** Repeat – Price ★

Matting

Thick rush matting (*see* opposite), which was common in Europe in the 16th century, was largely replaced during the 17th century by imported North African matting. During the 1970s and 1980s plant-fibre matting, especially varieties made from sisal and coir, and mostly in natural colours (*see* pages 370–371), became hugely fashionable. Indian matting was tremendously popular in the late 18th and early 19th centuries. Made of reeds or grass, it was often woven into yard-wide strips and then bound with linen twill. In the latter part of the 19th century, mats from China and Japan were widespread. They were made from grass but had a jute warp, and they invariably featured tight chevron patterns in bright colours with the ends bound with oil cloth.

In the early part of the 20th century, popular colours for matting included natural, white, olive, and red-and-white checks. More recently, there has been a renewed interest in plant-fibre matting, including varieties made from sisal and coir.

3

1 **Crucial Trading/Coir/Herringbone Contrast HBC** Colour **natural** Alt. colours **yes** Composition **100% coir** Width **4m/4½yd** Repeat – Price ★

2 **Crucial Trading/Accents/Big Bouclé E680** Colour **black** Alt. colours **yes** Composition **100% sisal** Width **4m/4½yd** Repeat – Price ★★

3 **Ruckstuhl/Pur/Step** Colour **726** Alt. colours **yes** Composition **100% sisal** Width **2m/2½yd** Repeat – Price ★★★

4 **Crucial Trading/Papa/Papaflat PFN** Colour **natural** Alt. colours **yes** Composition **100% paper** Width **3.6m/4yd** Repeat – Price ★★

5 **Ruckstuhl/Fondato/Jaipur** Colour **50038** Alt. colours **yes** Composition **100% sisal** Width **2m/2½yd** Repeat – Price ★★★

6 **Ruckstuhl/Webside/Upside** Colour **20303** Alt. colours **no** Composition **100% sisal** Width **4m/4½yd** Repeat – Price ★★

1

2

4

5

6

7 **The Alternative Flooring Co/ Buckingham Basketweave AFC 102** Colour **natural** Alt. colours **no** Composition **100% seagrass** Width **4m/ 4½yd** Repeat – Price ★★

8 **Carpet Innovations/Tecwoven** Colour **603** Alt. colours **yes** Composition **90% polyester, 10% wool** Width **4m/4½yd** Repeat – Price ★

9 **Sinclair Till/Giraffe** Colour **giraffe** Alt. colours **yes** Composition **100% sisal** Width **to order** Repeat – Price ★★★

10 **Carpet Innovations/Recife** Colour **chestnut** Alt. colours **yes** Composition **100% sisal** Width **4m/4½yd** Repeat – Price ★★

8

9

10

12

11 **Fired Earth/Rousham Seagrass** Colour **natural** Alt. colours **no** Composition **100% seagrass** Width **4m/4½yd** Repeat – Price ★

12 **Sinclair Till/Stars** Colour **black and blue** Alt. colours **yes** Composition **100% sisal** Width **to order** Repeat – Price ★★★

13 **The Alternative Flooring Co/ Sisal Panama AFC 503** Colour **Donegal** Alt. colours **yes** Composition **100% sisal** Width **4m/4½yd** Repeat – Price ★★

14 **Stark/Water Hyacinth/Andiamo** Colour **natural** Alt. colours **yes** Composition **100% water hyacinth** Width **to order** Repeat – Price ★★★★★

1

13

TRADITIONAL RUSH MATTING

Used since Medieval times, rush matting is still manufactured in the traditional way. The rushes are soaked in cold water to make them pliable, squeezed dry, then plaited into strips, each consisting of 9 strands. (This is known as a 9-ply weave.) These strips are then sewn together with string using a sailmaker's curved needle. The use of string is the only deviation from traditional methods. Edged with a finer, 11-ply strip, the matting must be sprinkled with water every 6–8 weeks in order to keep it supple.

Waveney Rush Industry/Rush Medieval Matting Colour **natural** Alt. colours **no** Composition **100% rush** Width **to order** Repeat – Price ★★★★

14

Matting

Since the 1990s, matting has become an increasingly fashionable alternative to fitted carpets, although it is often augmented with loose-lay kilims and rugs. Pure sisal and coir weaves have remained popular choices, but other materials have also figured prominently. Notable examples include seagrass, and hard, durable bamboo-strip matting – the latter, reasonably resilient to water and moisture, has been much employed in shower rooms and bathrooms. Compositional matting, in which different fibres and materials are combined, has also become more prevalent. These include paper and viscose; paper, wool and goathair; and wool and sisal – the two latter combinations providing a softer texture underfoot particularly suited to bedrooms.

Plain, solid colours, most notably natural hues and shades of red, blue and green, have remained in vogue, although there has been a discernible increase in patterned examples. Invariably geometric designs, they are mostly two-tone, but occasionally polychromatic.

1 Crucial Trading/Basket/ **Basket T300** Colour **gold** Alt. colours **yes** Composition **100% sisal** Width **4m/4½yd** Repeat – Price ★★

2 Crucial Trading/Bamboo/ **Bamboo for Rugs BBN** Colour **natural** Alt. colours **yes** Composition **100% bamboo** Width **2m/2½yd** Repeat – Price ★★

3 Ruckstuhl/Webside/Check Colour **395** Alt. colours **yes** Composition **66% sisal, 34% linen** Width **4m/4½yd** Repeat – Price ★★

1

2

3

5

6

4 Carpet Innovations/Multicolor **Coir** Colour **M7 candy stripe** Alt. colours **no** Composition **100% coir** Width **2m/2½yd** Repeat – Price ★★

5 Ruckstuhl/Spirit/Capra Colour **283** Alt. colours **yes** Composition **30% wool, 30% goathair, 40% paper** Width **2m/2½yd** Repeat – Price ★★★★

6 Carpet Innovations/Diamond **Coco** Colour **712** Alt. colours **no** Composition **100% coir** Width **2m/2½yd** Repeat – Price ★★

7

8

7 Ruckstuhl/Webside/Fresco
Colour **361** Alt. colours **yes**
Composition **100% sisal**
Width **4m/4½yd** Repeat –
Price ★★

8 Carpet Innovations/Santorini
Colour **3045** Alt. colours **yes**
Composition **100% sisal**
Width **4m/4½yd** Repeat –
Price ★

9 Ruckstuhl/Webside/One One
Colour **251** Alt. colours **yes**
Composition **100% sisal**
Width **4m/4½yd** Repeat –
Price ★★

10 Ruckstuhl/Fondato/Jaipur
Colour **10098** Alt. colours
yes Composition **100% sisal**
Width **2m/2⅛yd** Repeat –
Price ★★★

9

10

11

11 Ruckstuhl/Fondato/Manila
Colour **20155** Alt. colours
yes Composition **100% sisal**
Width **2m/2⅛yd** Repeat –
Price ★★★

12 Carpet Innovations/Tree Bark
Colour **maize** Alt. colours
no Composition **100%
seagrass** Width **4m/4½yd**
Repeat – Price ★

13 Ruckstuhl/Pur/Scotch
Colour **234** Alt. colours
yes Composition **100%
sisal** Width **1.68m/1¾yd**
Repeat – Price ★★★

14 Ruckstuhl/Spirit/Shine
Colour **271** Alt. colours **no**
Composition **70% paper,
30% viscose** Width **2m/2⅛yd**
Repeat – Price ★★★

15 Fired Earth/Woodstock Colour
Blenheim Alt. colours **no**
Composition **100% sisal**
Width **4m/4½yd** Repeat –
Price ★★

12

13

14

15

Carpets

Carpets are highly decorative textiles manufactured on a horizontal or vertical loom. A knotting technique is used to create an artificial pile that hides the supporting grid of horizontal and vertical strands. The yarns and fibres used range from wool, silk and cotton to modern synthetics, such as nylon and viscose.

The earliest known knotted carpet, the Altai carpet, was found preserved in the ice of Siberia and dates from approximately 500BC. From the 11th century, carpets were used in Europe to cover walls, chairs and tables, but it was only in the late 17th century that they began to be used regularly as a floor covering. During the 16th century, European imitations of oriental carpets, such as "turkeywork" (see page 378), emerged, but it was the development of European and American looms in the 19th century that made carpets widely available. By the mid-20th century, fitted wall-to-wall carpets were widespread.

Designs and decorative motifs have varied throughout the centuries, although abstract or stylized geometric designs have remained consistently popular.

ABOVE This carpet in Richard Jenrette's house in New York State, USA, combines strong, symmetrical lines with simple motifs, a combination that epitomizes the American Empire style in carpets. This mirrors the French Empire and English Regency styles, but lacks the opulence and elaboration that characterizes European carpets of the period.

WILTON CARPET
Developed from Brussels carpet, Wilton has a velvety surface formed by the cutting of the looped pile. It was first produced in the mid-18th century in Wilton, England, but the method soon spread to Europe and America. Wilton carpets were woven in 69cm/27in strips with repeating patterns so the pieces could be laid wall-to-wall. The introduction of the Jacquard loom in 1805 meant that Wilton soon became cheaper than hand-knotted carpets and as a result much more widespread.

RIGHT The principal staircase in Sir John Soane's London, UK, house is covered by a sumptuous, deep red-and-gold stair runner. The scrolling leaf border in gold and the red moiré-effect pile reflect the influence of the French Neo-classical movement.

KEY DESIGNS

1 Small, symmetrical motif patterns are typical of North African carpets and have often been adopted in European carpets. Many of the motifs were originally ancient tribal and religious emblems.

2 Stylized and naturalistic floral designs originated in Persia and India in the 16th century and have always been popular. Here, small floral vignettes are interspersed among strips of geometric motifs.

3 Geometric diaper patterns are a recurring design on carpets. The patterns include trelliswork, latticework and strapwork, and often enclose floral motifs or plant-form imagery.

4 When introduced in the 1860s, chemical dyes produced only strong, often virulent solid colours, but nowadays they can create softer tones previously given only by traditional vegetable dyes.

5 The pile in this monochromatic tufted carpet consists of long strands of wool stitched into a prewoven backing. Deep-pile carpets have proved particularly popular in the 20th century.

6 The mottled colouring of this carpet is typical of the late 20th and early 21st century. In this example synthetic (nylon) fibres have been woven to create a texture similar to that of woollen fibres.

---

1 Stoddard/Cathiness/Traditional Axminster 4/4556 Colour **zanzibar** Alt. colours **no** Composition **80% wool, 20% nylon** Width **91cm/35¾in** Repeat **81cm/32in** Price ★★ ⊞

2 Ulster Carpets/Glenmoy/Persian Garden Colour **10-2160** Alt. colours **no** Composition **80% wool, 20% nylon** Width **3.66m/4yd** Repeat **91.5cm/36in** Price ★★ ⊞

3 Stoddard Templeton/Midnight Embroidery Colour **4** Alt. colours **no** Composition **80% wool, 20% nylon** Width **3.66m/4yd** Repeat **76cm/30in** Price ★★

4 Ollerton Hall/Solid Extra Colour **7510** Alt. colours **yes** Composition **100% danaklon** Width **4m/4½yd** Repeat – Price ★

5 Ollerton Hall/Shag Pile Colour **pink** Alt. colours **yes** Composition **100% wool** Width **3.66m/4yd** Repeat – Price ★

6 Mannington/Aspects II Modular Colour **bellflower** Alt. colours **yes** Composition **100% DuPont nylon** Width **3.66m/4yd** Repeat – Price ★★ ▣ ⊞ Ⓣ

Carpets: **Pre-19th century**

In Europe during the Middle Ages, oriental carpets were the preserve of the wealthy. However, during the 15th and 16th centuries English workshops were producing "turkeywork", a cheap hand-knotted pile cloth used for chair upholstery and tablecloths. Some of these were later introduced into America by British settlers. Embroidered carpets were commissioned in America, featuring heraldic motifs and floral patterns.

By the middle of the 18th century, the carpet industry was thriving in Europe, the two main centres for carpet production being Britain and France. In Britain, the Earl of Pembroke gave his patronage to the Wilton factory in 1740; the carpet weavers Thomas Whitty and Thomas Moore were working in Axminster and London respectively; and there was great activity in Scotland, the north of England and Kidderminster. In France at this time, Henry IV supported Pierre Dupont in establishing a workshop in the Louvre to produce carpets in "the manner of the Orient". This later moved to the Savonnerie site. At Aubusson, the long-established tapestry weavers turned their skills to producing tapestry carpets, which were less costly than Savonneries. With their delicate floral patterning, these carpets became extremely popular during the reigns of Louis XV and Louis XVI.

5

1

4

7

1 Stark/Dartmouth Colour **multi** Alt. colours **no** Composition **100% wool** Width **68.5cm/ 27in** Repeat **35cm/13¾in** Price ★★★★

2 Stark/Brissac Border Colour **white and gold** Alt. colours **yes** Composition **80% wool, 20% viscose** Width **23cm/ 9in** Repeat **22cm/8½in** Price ★★★

3 Stark/Czardis Border Colour **spice** Alt. colours **no** Composition **100% wool** Width **17cm/6¾in** Repeat **16cm/6¼in** Price ★★

4 Stark/Czardis Colour **spice** Alt. colours **no** Composition **100% wool** Width **372cm/12ft 2in** Repeat **30.5cm/12in** Price ★★★★

5 Axminster Carpets/Turkish Splendour 380/01803 Colour **oriental gold** Alt. colours **yes** Composition **100% wool** Width **3.66m/4yd** Repeat **91cm/35¾in** Price ★★ ⊞

6 Stark/Dover Colour **stock** Alt. colours **yes** Composition **100% wool** Width **3.66m/ 4yd** Repeat **30.5cm/12in** Price ★★★★

7 Hugh Mackay/Ribbon 100089- 910953 Colour **multi** Alt. colours **yes** Composition **100% wool** Width **69cm/ 27in** Repeat **11cm/4¼in** Price ★★

**8 Stoddard Templeton/Cathiness
1/4558** Colour **turkey red**
Alt. colours **no** Composition
80% wool, 20% nylon Width
91cm/35¾in Repeat **41cm/16in**
Price ★★ ⊞

9 Brintons/Flake 1/2455 Colour **1**
Alt. colours **yes** Composition
80% wool, 20% nylon Width
4m/4½yd Repeat **50cm/19½in**
Price ★★★ ⊞

**10 Hugh Mackay/Fleur de Lys
126893-910063** Colour **multi**
Alt. colours **yes** Composition
80% wool, 20% nylon Width
69cm/27in Repeat **9cm/3½in**
Price ★★★ ⊞

**11 Brintons/Regina International
16/19714** Colour **coronet
apricot** Alt. colours **yes**
Composition **80% wool,
20% nylon** Width **3.6m/
4yd** Repeat **23cm/9in**
Price ★★ ⊞

**12 Hugh Mackay/Balmoral 99956-
910984** Colour **multi** Alt.
colours **yes** Composition
100% wool Width **69cm/
27in** Repeat **43cm/16¾in**
Price ★★

13 Stark/Brissac Colour **white/
gold** Alt. colours **yes**
Composition **80% wool,
20% viscose** Width **68.5cm/
27in** Repeat **53cm/21in**
Price ★★★★

8

CLASSICAL WREATHS
Used in ancient Rome and Greece to laud the
achievements of emperors, heroes, poets and
athletes, the wreath symbolizes eternity,
sovereignty, honour and glory. It usually consists
of a garland of leaves (usually laurel, but oak
or olive are also seen), often bound with ribbon.
Wreaths became popular in carpet designs in
the mid-18th century as the Neo-classical style
spread throughout Europe.

Brintons/Wreath 9/13710 Colour **9** Alt. colours **yes** Composition
80% wool, 20% nylon Width **4m/4½yd** Repeat **50cm/19½in**
Price ★★★ ⊞

9

10

11

14

**14 Axminster Carpets/Panel Persian
142/11397** Colour **green** Alt.
colours **yes** Composition
100% wool Width **3.66m/
4yd** Repeat **91cm/35¾in**
Price ★★ ⊞

15 Stark/Filigrane et Fleurs
Colour **pastel** Alt. colours
yes Composition **100%
wool** Width **101cm/39¾in**
Repeat **131cm/51½in**
Price ★★★★★

12

13

15

Carpets: **Early 19th century**

The early 19th century saw Jacquard machines largely supplanting the old hand looms, and greatly expanding carpet production. In Britain, Kidderminster remained the major manufacturing centre, with at least 1,000 carpet looms in operation. Brussels carpet, where a worsted warp is brought to the surface to form a pile, and Wilton, where the looped pile is cut to create a more velvet-like surface, were especially popular at this time, being both versatile and cheap. In America, non-pile, reversible carpets, such as "ingrain" and "Scotch", were being produced in large numbers. These were made in strips and laid to cover the whole room.

Desirable designs sought after in America and Europe at this time included those based on architectural panels, as well as paisley and Indian motifs, naturalistic floral designs and *verdure* patterns of ferns, foliage and palms. Heraldic motifs were also popular. In France, delicate floral carpets in soft colours became fashionable.

5

5 Chatsworth/Buckingham Colour **constitution gold** Alt. colours **yes** Composition **100% wool** Width **4m/4½yd** Repeat **90cm/35½in** Price ★★★

6 Stark/Houles Colour **floral black** Alt. colours **yes** Composition **100% wool** Width **3.66m/4yd** Repeat **99cm/39in** Price ★★★★

7 Stark/Fontainebleau Ribbon Border Colour **creme** Alt. colours **yes** Composition **100% wool** Width **35cm/13¾in** Repeat **44cm/17in** Price ★★★

8 Stark/Clichy Colour **yellow** Alt. colours **yes** Composition **100% wool** Width **101cm/39¾in** Repeat **25cm/9¾in** Price ★★★★

9 Hugh Mackay/142974–7282 Colour **multi** Alt. colours **yes** Composition **100% wool** Width **91cm/35¾in** Repeat **86cm/33¾in** Price ★★ ⊞

1

2

1 Stark/Summer Flowers Border Colour **yellow** Alt. colours **no** Composition **100% wool** Width **23cm/9in** Repeat **6cm/2⅜in** Price ★★★★★

2 Stark/Kingston Border Colour **blue** Alt. colours **yes** Composition **100% wool** Width **17cm/6¾in** Repeat **18cm/7in** Price ★★

3 Brintons/Annabelle Classique 136/16668 Colour **summer spray harvest** Alt. colours **yes** Composition **80% wool, 20% nylon** Width **3.6m/4yd** Repeat **91cm/35¾in** Price ★★ ⊞

4 Woodward Grosvenor/Emblem 36/5681 Colour **36** Alt. colours **yes** Composition **100% wool** Width **4m/4½yd** Repeat **13cm/5in** Price ★★★

6

7

3

4

8

9

10

10 Hugh Mackay/Brampton 7426
Colour **62273** Alt. colours **yes**
Composition **100% wool** Width
91cm/35¾in Repeat **12cm/4¾in**
Price ★★★ ⊞

**11 Brintons/Regina International
44/19784** Colour **rosette
green** Alt. colours **yes**
Composition **80% wool,
20% nylon** Width **3.66m/
4yd** Repeat **45cm/17½in**
Price ★★ ⊞

12 Zoffany/Richmond RIC21004
Colour **speedwell** Alt. colours
yes Composition **80% wool,
20% nylon** Width **4m/4½yd**
Repeat – Price ★★★ ⊞

13 Stark/Navarre Border
Colour **olive** Alt. colours
no Composition **100% wool**
Width **17cm/6¾in** Repeat
17cm/6¾in Price ★★

12

11   **13**

15

**14 Stoddard Templeton/Cathiness
4/4540** Colour **midnight
embriodery** Alt. colours **no**
Composition **80% wool,
20% nylon** Width **91cm/
35¾in** Repeat **78cm/30¾in**
Price ★★ ⊞

15 Stark/Small Star Colour
cobalt blue Alt. colours
yes Composition **100%
wool** Width **3.66m/4yd**
Repeat **15cm/6in**
Price ★★★

16 Stark/Small Star Border
Colour **cobalt blue** Alt.
colours **yes** Composition
100% wool Width **17cm/
6¾in** Repeat **29.5cm/
11½in** Price ★★

17 Bosanquet Ives/Icicles
Colour **01** Alt. colours
yes Composition **100%
wool** Width **69cm/27in**
Repeat – Price ★★

18 Stark/Kingston Colour **blue**
Alt. colours **yes** Composition
100% wool Width **372cm/
12ft 2in** Repeat **8cm/3in**
Price ★★★★

16

14

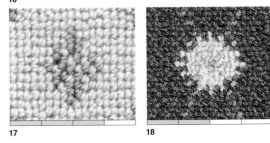

17   **18**

Carpets: **Late 19th century**

Factors such as the development of synthetic dyes and the power loom, along with the increased wealth of the middle class, gave great impetus to the British and American carpet industries. Engineers in America developed the Axminster loom, and Brintons of Kidderminster, England, introduced the Gripper version in 1890. The Kleitos Axminster Broadloom, brought from America and patented by Tomkinson Ltd in Kidderminster in 1896, enabled the production of large carpets with no colour limitation, giving full rein to the floral chintz that became a hallmark of the British industry. A mid-19th-century exhibition of oriental carpets in Berlin triggered a revival in Persian and Indian designs. Many carpets were based on Baroque themes using crimsons and blues. Other influences at this time were Owen Jones's *Dictionary of Ornament* (1856) and Christopher Dresser's *Principles of Design* (1879). The Great Exhibition of 1851 in Britain inspired carpet designs by Morris and Company, C.F.A. Voysey, and other members of the Arts and Crafts movement. William Morris's floral designs, such as the acanthus and poppy Axminsters of the 1870s, were reinterpretations of Persian designs. In America, the Arts and Crafts designs of Frank Lloyd Wright and Greene & Greene were more restrained.

5

1

1 Stark/Winford Rose Border
Colour **yellow** Alt. colours
no Composition **100% wool**
Width **23cm/9in** Repeat **61cm/
24in** Price ★★★★★

**2 Woodward Grosvenor/Pearl
Damask 26/5687** Colour **26**
Alt. colours **yes** Composition
100% wool Width **4m/4½yd**
Repeat **74.5cm/29¼in**
Price ★★★

3 Stark/Chambone Border
Colour **stock** Alt. colours
no Composition **100% wool**
Width **23cm/9in** Repeat
47cm/18½in Price ★★★

4 Stark/Flanders Border
Colour **stock** Alt. colours
no Composition **100% wool**
Width **23cm/9in** Repeat –
Price ★★★

2

6

7

5 Ulster Carpets/Glenavy/Overture
Colour **2-2162** Alt. colours
no Composition **80% wool,
20% nylon** Width **3.66m/
4yd** Repeat **94cm/36½in**
Price ★★

6 Stark/Buisson des Roses
Colour **stock** Alt. colours
no Composition **100% wool**
Width **101cm/39¼in** Repeat
11.5cm/4½in Price ★★★★

7 Stark/Fontaine de Bleu
Colour **black and white**
Alt. colours **no** Composition
100% wool Width **69cm/
27in** Repeat **85cm/33½in**
Price ★★★★

**8 Axminster Carpets/Torbay
100/Silk Chintz 152/11008**
Colour **shadow green** Alt.
colours **yes** Composition
100% wool Width **3.66m/
4yd** Repeat **91cm/35¾in**
Price ★★ ⊞

3

4

8

Bosanquet Ives/Wool Linen
Colour **multi** Alt. colours
yes Composition **80% wool,
20% linen** Width **4m/4½yd**
Repeat – Price ★

0 Stark/Villandry Colour **green
and peach** Alt. colours
yes Composition **100%
wool** Width **69cm/27in**
Repeat **76cm/30in**
Price ★★★★★

9

1 Stark/Kenshire Colour
gold/green Alt. colours **yes**
Composition **100% wool**
Width **68.5cm/27in** Repeat
18cm/7in Price ★★★★

2 Stark/Petite Diagonal Border
Colour **navy blue** Alt. colours
yes Composition **100%
wool** Width **23cm/9in**
Repeat **55cm/21½in**
Price ★★★★

10

11

3 Stark/Polo Colour **stock**
Alt. colours **no** Composition
100% wool Width **68.5cm/
27in** Repeat **18cm/7in**
Price ★★★★

4 Stark/Chambone Colour **stock**
Alt. colours **no** Composition
100% wool Width **101cm/
39¾in** Repeat **105cm/41¼in**
Price ★★★★★

5 Woodward Grosvenor/21/7051
Colour **red** Alt. colours **yes**
Composition **100% wool**
Width **69cm/27in** Repeat –
Price ★★

6 Woodward Grosvenor/19–7050
Colour **green** Alt. colours
yes Composition **100%
wool** Width **69cm/27in**
Repeat **29.5cm/11½in**
Price ★★★

13

14

12

DESIGN PAPERS

Carpets have traditionally been designed using "point-paper". Point-paper is divided into inch squares, each redivided into tiny blocks representing one tuft. The transferring of the design to the paper has to be precise, and applied in a semi-transparent form so that each square can be counted (so as to calculate the exact amount of yarn for each colour). In spite of computerization, which is now universal, many companies retain the services of a designer who understands these techniques.

The design paper shown above was used to produce the carpet shown below, which is an interpretation of an historic Persian design.

Stoddard Templeton/Antiquarian 1/8312 Colour **multi** Alt. colours **no** Composition **80% wool, 20% nylon** Width **137cm/54in** Repeat **93cm/36in** Price ★★ ⊞

5

16

Carpets: **Early 20th century**

In Britain the transition from Art Nouveau to Art Deco can be seen most clearly in the work of Charles Rennie Mackintosh, who stripped away gratuitous ornament and pointed the way to cleaner, simpler lines. This simplicity was reflected in carpet designs of the early 20th century. Geometric patterns, reflecting the Modernist preoccupation with the machine, were particularly favoured, as were plain, wall-to-wall carpets. In Britain, Scotland and America, brilliantly coloured abstracts were woven for the new cinemas and department stores. Large hotels and ocean liners were treated to soft, muted designs with large repeats, intended to create a mood of calm. In France, highly formal, stylized floral carpets were in demand.

More inspiration for designs on both sides of the Atlantic came from the Ballet Russe, the discovery of the tomb of Tutankhamun and the popularity of African art. However, at the same time, the tradition of Persian, Turkish and chintz designs also remained an important part of carpet ranges (*see* opposite).

1

2

3

4

1 **Stark/Navarre** Colour **olive** Alt. colours **yes** Composition **100% wool** Width **372cm/ 3ft 2in** Repeat **10cm/4in** Price ★★★★

2 **Bosanquet Ives/Trellis** Colour **olive and khaki** Alt. colours **yes** Composition **100% wool** Width **69cm/27in** Repeat – Price ★★★

3 **Stark/La Seine** Colour **cocoa** Alt. colours **no** Composition **100% wool** Width **372cm/ 3ft 2in** Repeat **93cm/36in** Price ★★★★

4 **Axminster Carpets/Honeycomb 40/2505** Colour **champagne** Alt. colours **yes** Composition **100% wool** Width **3.66m/ 4yd** Repeat **23cm/9in** Price ★★ ⊞

5

6

7

5 **Ulster Carpets/Glenmoy/Royal Stewart** Colour **10-2754** Alt. colours **no** Composition **80% wool, 20% nylon** Width **3.66m/4yd** Repeat **45.5cm/ 17¾in** Price ★★ ⊞

6 **Stark/Floral Vine** Colour **azure yellow** Alt. colours **yes** Composition **100% wool** Width **4m/4½yd** Repeat – Price ★★★★★

7 **Stoddard Templeton/Cathiness 2/4541** Colour **lorenzo green** Alt. colours **no** Composition **80% wool, 20% nylon** Width **91cm/35¾in** Repeat **88cm/34½in** Price ★★ ⊞

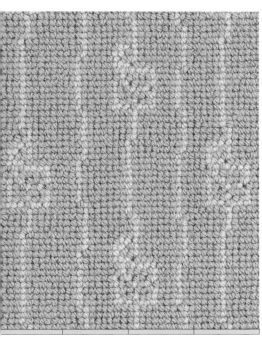

8 Bosanquet Ives/Woodlands
Colour **multi** Alt. colours
yes Composition **100%
wool** Width **69cm/27in**
Repeat – Price ★★★

**9 Woodward Grosvenor/Strata
26/5677** Colour **26** Alt.
colours **yes** Composition
100% wool Width **4m/
4½yd** Repeat **10cm/4in**
Price ★★★

10 Stark/Bristol Border Colour
sienna gold Alt. colours
yes Composition **100%
wool** Width **17cm/6¾in**
Repeat – Price ★★

**11 Woodward Grosvenor/Rambling
Rose 16/5684** Colour **16** Alt.
colours **yes** Composition
100% wool Width **4m/4½yd**
Repeat **43cm/16¾in**
Price ★★★

**12 Ulster Carpets/Glenavy/White
Shirzar** Colour **1-2467** Alt.
colours **no** Composition
80% wool, 20% nylon Width
3.66m/4yd Repeat **94cm/
36½in** Price ★★ ⊞

13 Stark/Havorford Colour
black and white Alt. colours
no Composition **100%
wool** Width **3.66m/4yd**
Repeat **30cm/11¾in**
Price ★★★★★ ⊞

14 Stark/Nouvelle Colour **stock**
Alt. colours **no** Composition
100% wool Width **68.5cm/
27in** Repeat **11.5cm/4½in**
Price ★★★★

15 Stark/Calla Lilies
Colour **red** Alt. colours **no**
Composition **100% wool**
Width **3.66m/4yd** Repeat
15cm/6in Price ★★★★★

12

13   14   15

PERSIAN INFLUENCE

The influence of richly
coloured Persian carpets on
contemporary European and
American designs has been
profound. Although Art Deco
and Modernist schemes
largely eschewed the complex
Persian-style designs, such
carpets were arguably more
popular in the early 20th
century than ever before.
Carpets from Sarouk in
Persia – which were salmon
pink in colour and featuring
geometric or floral decoration
– were particularly loved in
America at this time.

Stoddard Templeton/Cathiness 20/4520 Colour **Persian lattice**
Alt. colours **no** Composition **80% wool, 20% nylon** Width
91cm/35¾in Repeat **57cm/22½in** Price ★★ T ⊞

0   11

20th century

Carpets: Mid-20th century

From the mid-20th century onward, there has been a great increase in the use of man-made fibres. Although wool has always been the traditional fibre for carpet (owing to its natural resilience and ability to absorb dye), it is comparatively more expensive than man-made fibres. Wool is frequently blended with nylon in a ratio of 4:1 to improve durability, and synthetic fibres are also blended in various combinations.

In terms of patterning, there was a new range of influences on carpet design in the mid-20th century. In 1951 the Festival of Britain had a profound impact on the industry, which produced for the first time delicate, linear "spot" designs. In the late 1950s and 1960s there was a noticeable response to the leading painters and designers, with, for example, the painter Jackson Pollock greatly influencing domestic Axminster and Gripper ranges. At this time, Middle Eastern and African ornament – including animal-print patterns – was fashionable in Europe and America, but plain carpets were also popular.

Ollerton Hall/Berber Colour **sea green** Alt. colours **yes** Composition **100% wool** Width **4m/4½yd** Repeat – Price ★ ⊞

Ollerton Hall/Sovereign Colour **106250** Alt. colours **yes** Composition **100% polypropylene** Width **4m/4½yd** Repeat – Price ★ ⊙⊞

Brintons/Bell Twist 9582 Colour **dianthus** Alt. colours **yes** Composition **80% wool, 20% nylon** Width **3.66m/4yd** Repeat – Price ★★ ⊞

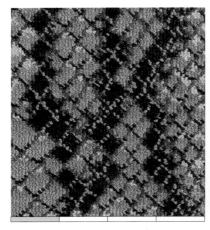

Hugh Mackay/Indian River Snake 1377/7152 Colour **multi** Alt. colours **yes** Composition **80% wool, 20% nylon** Width **69cm/27in** Repeat **30cm/11¾in** Price ★★★

Zoffany/Paintbox Border Colour **sable with porridge** Alt. colours **yes** Composition **80% wool, 20% Woolbond** Width **12cm/4¾in** Repeat – Price ★

Stark/Somali Panther Colour **stock** Alt. colours **no** Composition **100% wool** Width **3.66m/4yd** Repeat **1.87m/2yd** Price ★★★★★

Chatsworth/Leopard Skin Colour **multi** Alt. colours **no** Composition **100% nylon** Width **3.66m/4yd** Repeat **90cm/35½in** Price ★★

Chatsworth/White Tiger Colour **black and white** Alt. colours **no** Composition **100% nylon** Width **3.66m/4yd** Repeat **90cm/35½in** Price ★★

Zoffany/Windsor WIN0000 Colour **4** Alt. colours **yes** Composition **100% wool** Width **4m/4½yd** Repeat – Price ★★★

Ulster Carpets/York Wilton/Paprika Colour **Y1025** Alt. colours **yes** Composition **80% wool, 20% nylon** Width **3.66m/4yd** Repeat – Price ★★

Ollerton Hall/Graphics Colour **dark blue** Alt. colours **yes** Composition **100% polypropylene** Width **4m/4½yd** Repeat – Price ★ 🔘

Mannington Carpets/Sorata RERI Colour **red river** Alt. colours **yes** Composition **100% nylon** Width **3.66m/4yd** Repeat **5.5cm/2¼in** Price ★ ⊞

Hugh Mackay/MacBeth Tartan 1389-7104 Colour **multi** Alt. colours **yes** Composition **80% wool, 20% nylon** Width **69cm/27in** Repeat **69cm/ 27in** Price ★★★

Brintons/Zenith Club Class Calypso 23/12740 Colour **multi** Alt. colours **no** Composition **80% wool, 20% nylon** Width **69cm/27in** Repeat **85cm/33½in** Price ★★ T

Stoddard/New England 3/8334 Colour **multi** Alt. colours **no** Composition **80% wool, 20% nylon** Width **3.66m/4yd** Repeat **65cm/ 25½in** Price ★★ ⊞

Ollerton Hall/Princess 6TCP Colour **burgundy** Alt. colours **yes** Composition **80% wool, 20% nylon** Width **4m/4½yd** Repeat – Price ★★ ⊞

Hugh Mackay/Wilton 210455 Colour **308891** Alt. colours **yes** Composition **100% wool** Width **91m/35⅜in** Repeat – Price ★★★ ⊞

Axminster Carpets/French Impressions 232/15020 Colour **Erica pink** Alt. colours **yes** Composition **100% wool** Width **3.66m/4yd** Repeat **91cm/ 35¾in** Price ★★ ⊞

Hugh Mackay/127864-942416 Colour **multi** Alt. colours **yes** Composition **80% wool, 20% nylon** Width **69cm/27in** Repeat – Price ★★ ⊞

Carpets: Late 20th–early 21st century

The majority of carpets are now mass-produced using a tufting process; the machines that create them resemble gigantic sewing machines with hundreds of needles. Unlike woven carpet, where the backing is an integral part of the cloth, tufted yarn is machine-sewn to a ready-woven backing that is then covered with latex. The continuing development of synthetic fibres, an expanding range of textures and industry computerization have all contributed to the success of such carpets. They are often produced in soft, modulated colours, achieved by using space-dyed yarns or screen-printing. There has been experimentation recently with injection dyeing, which involves each tuft receiving its own jet of dye; this provides complete freedom for designers and can produce highly colourful ranges.

Lately, too, the popularity of the loose carpet square – available in sizes as large as a square metre or yard – has provided designers with many opportunities. Contemporary designers in Europe and America have continued to draw inspiration for the patterning of carpets from the bold influences of Africa, India and South America and from a wide range of styles from the past, as well as creating exciting new designs and experimenting with colours and patterns.

1

2

6

7

8

9

3

4

5

1 **Chatsworth/Pebbles** Colour **silver grey** Alt. colours **yes** Composition **100% wool** Width **4m/4½yd** Repeat **–** Price ★★★★★ ⊞

2 **Stark/Broadway** Colour **ocean** Alt. colours **yes** Composition **80% wool, 20% nylon** Width **4m/4½yd** Repeat **–** Price ★★★

3 **Chatsworth/Keyboard** Colour **multi** Alt. colours **yes** Composition **100% wool** Width **to order** Repeat **–** Price ★★★★★

4 **Ruckstuhl/Jack Lenor Larsen/ Get Up** Colour **486** Alt. colour **yes** Composition **100% wool** Width **4m/4½yd** Repeat **–** Price ★★★

5 **Zoffany/Pastiche** Colour **spin drift** Alt. colours **yes** Composition **100% wool** Width **4m/ 4½yd** Repeat **5cm/2in** Price ★★

6 **Bosanquet Ives/Sinfonie** Colour **54** Alt. colours **yes** Composition **100% wool** Width **4m/4½yd** Repeat **–** Price ★★★★

7 **Ollerton Hall/Ultimate Shag Pile** Colour **pink** Alt. colours **yes** Composition **100% wool** Width **to order** Repeat **–** Price ★★

8 **Atlas Carpet Mills/Tintoretto TT01** Colour **Danube** Alt. colours **yes** Composition **100% nylon** Width **3.66m/ 4yd** Repeat **4cm/1½in** Price ★★

9 **Chatsworth/Dakee SP121** Colour **multi** Alt. colours **yes** Composition **100% wool** Width **to order** Repeat **–** Price ★★★★★

10 Chatsworth/Link Border (carved) Colour **blue and green** Alt. colours **yes** Composition **100% wool** Width **to order** Repeat – Price ★★★★

11 Bosanquet Ives/Woollen Chord Colour **multi** Alt. colours **yes** Composition **100% wool** Width **to order** Repeat – Price ★★

12 Ulster Carpet/Metro/Hemp Colour **11-2987** Alt. colours **yes** Composition **80% wool, 20% nylon** Width **3.66m/4yd** Repeat **91.5cm/36in** Price ★★ ⊞

13 Chatsworth/Foresta 8520 Colour **white** Alt. colours **yes** Composition **100% wool** Width **to order** Repeat – Price ★★★★

10

11

12

13

14

15

16

17

18

19

14 Atlas Carpet Mills/Cipriani 35 Colour **R947 Lapis** Alt. colours **yes** Composition **100% nylon** Width **3.66m/4yd** Repeat **2cm/¾in** Price ★★

15 Ruckstuhl/Jack Lenor Larsen/ Diva Colour **179** Alt. colours **yes** Composition **97% wool, 3% lurex** Width **2m/2⅛yd** Repeat – Price ★★★★★

16 Westbond/8L Colour **curry, Bastille grey, white Russia** Alt. colours **yes** Composition **100% nylon** Width **50 x 50cm/ 19½ x 19½in (tile)** Repeat – Price ★★ ⊞

17 Mannington Carpets/Strategies ZENI Colour **zenith** Alt. colours **yes** Composition **100% nylon** Width **3.8m/4⅛yd** Repeat **47cm/18½in** Price ★★

18 Chatsworth/Greek Key Border Colour **black and beige** Alt. colours **yes** Composition **100% wool** Width **to order** Repeat – Price ★★★★★

19 Brintons/Marrakesh 22/11894 Colour **22** Alt. colours **yes** Composition **80% wool, 20% nylon** Width **3.66m/ 4yd** Repeat **18cm/7in** Price ★★ ⊞

COMBINATION WEAVES

Owing to the increased sophistication of looms and tufting machines, a very wide range of textures is now available in carpets. For example, high and low piles, cut and uncut loops, and "carved" effects can all be employed within a single carpet, giving it a mixture of several different textures. New yarns can also provide "pebble" surfaces, while space-dyed yarns provide a speckled effect. Modern tufted carpets are extremely hardwearing, and any number of colours can be used.

Monterey/Presidio 6021-384 Colour **general** Alt. colours **yes** Composition **100% nylon** Width **3.66m/4yd** Repeat – Price ★★

Hugh Mackay/Brampton 210482 Colour **308904** Alt. colours **yes** Composition **100% wool** Width **91cm/36in** Repeat **4cm/1½in** Price ★★★ ⊞

Sheet Flooring

Sheet flooring refers to a wide range of highly practical floor coverings. These include floorcloths, linoleum, vinyl and rubber.

Sheet flooring refers to a wide range of highly practical floor coverings. These include floorcloths, linoleum, vinyl and rubber.

Floorcloths first appeared in the late 17th century as groundsheets for marquees, but they were soon integrated in interiors as an economical and decorative means of covering floors. Often made from oil cloth, they came into use as a result of the availability of large expanses of sailcloth from the shipbuilding industry. Stemming from the older practice of painting floorboards, the patterns often simulated stone and marble pavings.

The rapid growth of industrial mass-production in Britain during the 19th century brought with it the invention of linoleum (*see* page 393). Made from relatively cheap materials, it remained the most popular form of domestic sheet flooring until the mid-20th century. The social changes since have brought an increased demand for easy-to-clean, mass-produced flooring. Major developments in the plastics industry led, in the 1950s, to the introduction of vinyl and resin floorings that imitated wood, stone and terracotta. The late 20th and early 21st century has seen a move into the domestic market of contract flooring materials such as rubber and metal.

ABOVE Modern vinyl flooring can replicate the most intricate of designs found on traditional floor coverings, and can be coloured to complement any interior. This bold geometric design is based on a classical pattern.

LEFT The white vinyl floor tiles in this modern interpretation of a 17th-century interior give the appearance of a polished marble floor, yet provide a surface that is easy to clean and warm to the touch.

FAR LEFT Cushion vinyl, invented in America in 1963, cleverly simulates a wood finish in this modern interior. Today, cushion vinyl is produced in many different designs and textures. It also has the advantage of being much quieter underfoot than its wooden equivalent.

1 Popular since the middle of the 19th century, linoleum is now available in a wide range of colours. However, the traditional colours – browns, reds and yellows – are still very fashionable.

2 Rubber is a highly durable 20th-century floor covering. Particularly suitable for public areas and airports, it can now be produced in a variety of colours and textures thanks to new technology.

3 Traditional stone or terracotta slabs are just one of the styles imitated by vinyl flooring. Available as rolls or tiles, this can simulate most natural materials; modern abstract designs are also used.

4 Composite laminates that imitate wood are a durable, easy-care and cheaper alternative to natural boards. A wide range of different grains, colours and board sizes is available.

5 Modern techniques can reproduce the look of natural stone to a highly accurate degree, as seen on this *faux*-stone vinyl. The benefits of this include ease of installation and lower cost.

6 Metal sheet flooring became increasingly popular in the late 20th century. Being both durable and stylish, it is now found in domestic as well as commercial settings.

1 **Armstrong DLW/Linoleum/Marmorette 121** Colour **48** Alt. colours **yes** Composition **linoleum** Width **2m/2⅓yd** Repeat – Price ★

2 **Dalsouple/Uni** Colour **pêche** Alt. colours **yes** Composition **rubber** Width **34 x 34cm/ 13⅓ x 13⅓in (tile)** Repeat – Price ★★

3 **Westco/Cobble Gold Embossed** Colour **cobble gold** Alt. colours **yes** Composition **PVC** Width **30.5 x 30.5cm/12 x 12in (tile)** Repeat – Price ★

4 **Armstrong DLW/Scala/Scala Wood 20040** Colour **52** Alt. colours **yes** Composition **synthetic** Width **91.5 x 7.5cm/36 x 2¾in (tile)** Repeat – Price ★★

5 **Armstrong DLW/Scala/Scala Stone 20258** Colour **85** Alt. colours **yes** Composition **synthetic** Width **30.5 x 30.5cm/12 x 12in (tile)** Repeat – Price ★★

6 **Deralam/Footplate AD866** Colour **pewter tone** Alt. colours **no** Composition **aluminium laminate** Width **122cm/48in** Repeat – Price ★

Sheet Flooring: **Pre-20th century**

In the 18th century, floors were often covered by painted, stencilled or printed floorcloths. Canvas was stretched and nailed down so that it would hold its shape; it was then soaked with water, primed and painted several times on each side with finely ground ochres or leads and linseed oil to give it a base coat before being decorated. Much employed in imposing Neo-classical entrance halls, floorcloths were either painted one colour or decorated – much as were painted floorboards – to look like stone or marble paving or mosaic. Other patterns popular in the 18th century included the simulation of elaborate Roman floors. The patterns of Eastern carpets were also copied, while in America geometric chequer patterns were common.

In Britain, painted floorcloths were being mass-produced in factories by the late 18th century. The introduction of a printing process in about 1770, as well as improvements in colouring pigments, made more elaborate designs possible. Although waterproof, painted floorcloths were quite fragile and could not withstand a great deal of wear and tear. However, in spite of the advent of harder-wearing linoleum in 1860 (*see* opposite), production of floorcloths continued until after the First World War.

1 **Sinclair Till/Tartan** Colour **multi** Alt. colours **yes** Composition **linoleum** Width **to order** Repeat – Price ★★

2 **Sinclair Till/Chequerboard with Inlaid Stars** Colour **multi** Alt. colours **yes** Composition **linoleum** Width **to order** Repeat – Price ★★★

3 **Armstrong DLW/Linoleum/ Marmorette 121** Colour **70** Alt. colours **yes** Composition **linoleum** Width **2m/2⅕yd** Repeat – Price ★ ⬚ ⊞

4 **Karndean/Desert Clay Terracotta and Midnight Black Marble T74** Colour **red and black** Alt. colours **yes** Composition **vinyl** Width **30.5 x 30.5cm/ 12 x 12in (tile)** Repeat – Price ★

5 **Karndean/Carrara Marble and Diamond T90 & B300 Border** Colour **white and black** Alt. colours **yes** Composition **vinyl** Width **30.5 x 30.5cm/ 12 x 12in (tile)** Repeat – Price ★

6 **Armstrong DLW/Linoleum/ Granette 111** Colour **59** Alt. colours **yes** Composition **linoleum** Width **2m/2⅕yd** Repeat – Price ★ ⊞ ⬚

7 **Sinclair Till/Inlaid Curlicue and Star Border** Colour **multi** Alt. colours **yes** Composition **linoleum** Width **to order** Repeat – Price ★★

8

9

18th century
19th century

8 **Jane Knapp/Fossil Stone Marble Floorcloth** Colour **multi** Alt. colours **yes** Composition **paint on canvas** Width **to order** Repeat – Price ★★★★★

9 **Amtico/Norwegian Slate SN36** Colour **silver** Alt. colours **no** Composition **vinyl** Width **30.5 x 30.5cm/12 x 12in (tile)** Repeat – Price ★★★ ⊞

10 **Armstrong DLW/Linoleum/ Linodur 151** Colour **42** Alt. colours **yes** Composition **linoleum** Width **2m/2⅕yd** Repeat – Price ★ ⊞ ⬚

11 **Karndean/Granite Dove and Raven D202/D203** Colour **grey** Alt. colours **yes** Composition **vinyl** Width **30.5 x 30.5cm/ 12 x 12in (tile)** Repeat – Price ★

12 **Marley/Leaf Border** Colour **MBF4MPC** Alt. colours **yes** Composition **vinyl** Width **15cm/6in** Repeat **90cm/35½in** Price ★

10

11

12

LINOLEUM

Cheap and easy to produce, linoleum was first patented by Frederick Walton in Scotland in 1860, and was originally the trade name for a canvas floor cloth covered in solidified linseed oil, resin and kauri gum. The ingredients were pressed through heated rollers on to the canvas or jute backing, then hung and left to dry for several days. Today, linoleum is made in much the same way, apart from slight changes in the composition to incorporate hardwearing, man-made fibres and a wider selection of pigments. The demand for natural-based products means that linoleum is now reclaiming some of the market lost to vinyl since the 1950s.

Armstrong DLW/Linoleum/Marmorette 121 Colour **71** Alt. colours **yes** Composition **linoleum** Width **2m/2⅕yd** Repeat – Price ★ ⊞ ⬚

Sheet Flooring: 20th–early 21st century

The first half of the 20th century saw little change in the sheet-flooring market. Floorcloths were factory-produced until after the First World War, while linoleum continued to dominate the market until the introduction of vinyl-based products in the 1950s. The Art Deco and Modernist movements influenced linoleum design in the 1940s and early 1950s, and soon inspired designs on vinyl. Imitation brick, tile, wood and even carpet designs were all possible on vinyl, and this resulted in a reduction in sales of linoleum. The new vinyl sheet flooring was sound- and shock-absorbent, slip-resistant, gave good heat insulation and was easy to clean. In the late 20th century, a small, specialist market for floorcloths appeared, with designs based on traditional as well as modern patterns. There has also been a renewed interest in linoleum – its use of natural ingredients making it desirable again in the environmentally aware 21st century. Other types of sheet flooring have emerged, including traditional contract floorings (such as rubber) which have been adapted slightly to offer designs suited to domestic use. Such flooring became the keynote of the late 1970s' and early 1980s' high-tech style (see page 397). Metal sheet flooring in a variety of finishes has also become fashionable in recent years, as have resin laminates.

1

2

3

5

6

1   **Armstrong DLW/Linoleum/ Linorette 124** Colour **18** Alt. colours **yes** Composition **linoleum** Width **2m/2¼yd** Repeat – Price ★ ⊞ ⊠

2   **Westco/Aristocrat** Colour **London brick** Alt. colours **yes** Composition **PVC** Width **30.5 x 30.5cm/12 x 12in (tile)** Repeat – Price ★

3   **Armstrong DLW/Linoleum/ LinoArt Star 144** Colour **72** Alt. colours **yes** Composition **linoleum** Width **2m/2¼yd** Repeat – Price ★ ⊞ ⊠

4   **Marley/Eclipse BEF528** Colour **sunflower** Alt. colours **yes** Composition **vinyl** Width **2m/2¼yd** Repeat – Price ★★★★ ⊞

5   **Armstrong DLW/Scala/Scala Wood 20015** Colour **65** Alt. colours **yes** Composition **synthetic** Width **91.5 x 7.5cm/ 36 x 2¾in (tile)** Repeat – Price ★ ⊞

6   **Karndean/Knight Plank D504** Colour **beech** Alt. colours **yes** Composition **vinyl** Width **91.5 x 10.5cm/36 x 4in (tile)** Repeat – Price ★

7

8

9

7 Bonar Floors/Newlyn
146010 Colour **ocean spray**
Alt. colours **yes** Composition
flotex flooring Width **2m/2⅙yd**
Repeat – Price ★★ [◻] [T]

8 Bill Amberg/Leather Floor
(Tile) Colour **light tan** Alt.
colours **yes** Composition
leather Width **to order**
Repeat – Price ★★★★★

9 Bill Amberg/Leather Floor
(Stitch) Colour **tan** Alt. colours
yes Composition **leather**
Width **to order** Repeat –
Price ★★★★★

10 Westco/Floral Colour **multi**
Alt. colours **no** Composition
PVC Width **30.5 x 30.5cm/12 x**
12in (tile) Repeat – Price ★

10

11

12

11 Bonar Floors/Orkney 120020
Colour **summer sand** Alt.
colours **yes** Composition
flotex flooring Width **2m/2⅙yd**
Repeat – Price ★★ [◻]

12 Armstrong DLW/Scala/Scala
Stone 20045 Colour **43** Alt.
colours **yes** Composition
synthetic Width **30.5 x 30.5cm/**
12 x 12in (tile) Repeat –
Price ★★ [⊞]

13 Armstrong DLW/Scala/Scala
Metal 20063 Colour **06** Alt.
colours **yes** Composition
synthetic Width **30.5 x 30.5cm/**
12 x 12in (tile) Repeat –
Price ★★ [⊞]

14 Amtico/Tilewood TW 714
Colour **warm maple** Alt.
colours **yes** Composition
vinyl Width **30.5 x 30.5cm/**
12 x 12in (tile) Repeat –
Price ★★★ [⊞]

15 Armstrong DLW/Heterogeneous/
Protech 518 Colour **223** Alt.
colours **yes** Composition
heterogeneous vinyl Width
2m/2⅙yd Repeat –
Price ★ [◻] [⊞] [▨]

16 Westco/Diamond Black
Embossed Colour **diamond**
black Alt. colours **yes**
Composition **PVC** Width
30.5 x 30.5cm/12 x 12in
(tile) Repeat – Price ★

13

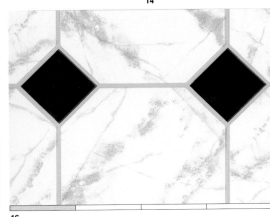

14

15

16

Sheet Flooring: 20th–early 21st century

During the late 20th and early 21st century, patterns on sheet flooring have often been derived from classical designs, such as the ancient Greek key pattern. Some manufacturers provide ready components, including borders and key squares, for constructing formal classical patterns. Recent designs have also included 1950s' café-revivalist flooring; semi-flexible PVC tiles with sparkling silica quartz; and sheet flooring consisting of coloured vinyl chips suspended in clear vinyl to produce a three-dimensional effect.

The art of mimicking other, more costly materials in synthetic flooring has become increasingly sophisticated in the early 21st century. Imitation wood is produced using a material with a fibreboard core, laminated with a wood-textured photoprint overlay and bonded with melamine resin. Marble, granite and terracotta are still extremely popular effects, as they were on floorcloths, and offer the look of the original material but with the added advantages of being hardwearing and washable.

1

2

4

1 **Dalsouple/Martelé** Colour **rose indien** Alt. colours **yes** Composition **rubber** Width **68cm/26¾in** Repeat – Price ★★

2 **Deralam/Antique Copper CD490** Colour **copper** Alt. colours **no** Composition **copper laminate** Width **122cm/48in** Repeat – Price ★★★★

3 **Deralam/Copper Relief CD710** Colour **green/black** Alt. colours **no** Composition **copper laminate** Width **122cm/48in** Repeat – Price ★★★★

4 **Deralam/Stainless Steel Wheels SS600** Colour **stainless steel** Alt. colours **no** Composition **stainless steel laminate** Width **102cm/40in** Repeat – Price ★★★★

5 **Armstrong DLW/Homogeneous/ Conductive/Pastell LG2 2815** Colour **40** Alt. colours **yes** Composition **synthetic** Width **1.8m/2yd** Repeat – Price ★

6 **Armstrong DLW/Homogeneous/ Conductive/Royal LG1/LG2 1422/2422** Colour **41** Alt. colours **yes** Composition **synthetic** Width **1.8m/2yd** Repeat – Price ★★

7 **Armstrong DLW/Scala/Scala Borders/Stream 2 23206/23106** Colour **60** Alt. colours **yes** Composition **synthetic** Width **91.5 x 7.5cm/36 x 2¾in** Repeat – Price ★

5

6

7

3

8 Jaymart/Fishface Colour **black** Alt. colours **no** Composition **rubber** Width **100cm/39¼in** Repeat – Price ★★★ 🔲 🔯

9 Armstrong DLW/Scala Borders/ Cube 1 23204/12104 Colour **40** Alt. colours **yes** Composition **synthetic** Width **91.5 x 7.5cm/ 36 x 2¾in** Repeat – Price ★

10 Amtico/Treadplate Colour **silver** Alt. colours **yes** Composition **vinyl** Width **30.5 x 30.5cm/12 x 12in (tile)** Repeat – Price ★★★ ⊞

11 Armstrong DLW/Scala/Scala Uni 20023 Colour **30** Alt. colours **yes** Composition **synthetic** Width **30.5 x 30.5cm/12 x 12in (tile)** Repeat – Price ★

12 Jaymart/Astroturf Colour **classic green** Alt. colours **yes** Composition **vinyl** Width **91cm/35¾in** Repeat – Price ★★ 🔲

8

9

10 11 12

13

RUBBER FLOORING

First produced in the 1930s, sheet rubber flooring has been used regularly in the contract market. It is tough, hardwearing and easy to clean, and, thanks to developments in the 1990s, available in virtually any colour. Popular designs include terrazzo effects as well as a variety of studded surfaces. The high-tech style of the late 1970s and early 1980s introduced rubber into a domestic setting. "Ecologically friendly" rubber flooring has also been produced recently using recycled car tyres.

Dalsouple/Metro Colour **vert pomme** Alt. colours **yes** Composition **rubber** Width **68 x 68cm/26¾ x 26¾in (tile)** Repeat – Price ★★ 🔲 🔯

14

15

13 Armstrong DLW/Scala/Scala Metal 20052 Colour **20** Alt. colours **yes** Composition **synthetic** Width **30.5 x 30.5cm/ 12 x 12in (tile)** Repeat – Price ★

14 Amtico/Florentine NM-97 Colour **blue** Alt. colours **yes** Composition **vinyl** Width **30.5 x 30.5cm/12 x 12in (tile)** Repeat – Price ★★★ ⊞

15 Armstrong DLW/Heterogeneous/ Contract Interior Acoustic/ Strata 333 Colour **61** Alt. colours **yes** Composition **heterogeneous vinyl** Width **2m/2⅕yd** Repeat – Price ★

Glossary

 Asterisked terms have a separate entry

A

acanthus Foliage ornament based on the serrated leaves of the *Acanthus spinosus* plant. Similar to thistle, parsley or poppy leaves and sometimes used for *scrolling foliage. Originally used in *Classical Greek and Roman architecture and ornament.

Adam style A *Neo-classical style pioneered by the English Adam brothers during the late 18th century, inspired by *Classical Roman and Greek and *Renaissance ornament. Characterized by motifs such as *swags, *guilloche, *friezes, *anthemia and *palmettes.

Aesthetic movement See p.43.

aniline dyes Synthetic dyes made from coal tar. Formulated in the late 1820s, but not developed for general use until the 1850s.

anthemion A floral motif similar to the *palmette and primarily associated with the Classical vocabulary of ornament. Based on either the flower of the *acanthus, the flower and leaf of the honeysuckle or the Egyptian lotus.

appliqué Technique of applying cut-out patterns of fabric on to a ground cloth using either plain or embroidery stitches.

arabesque A stylized, interlaced foliage pattern of Near-Eastern origin, probably based on laurel leaves. In Western ornament often combined with *bandwork or *strapwork. In the 18th century, French designers used the term to describe panels of *grotesque designs incorporating figures, bandwork and *scrolling foliage.

Art Deco See pp.49–51.

Art Nouveau See p.46.

Arts and Crafts movement See pp.42–48.

Aubusson French town where, in the "Royal Manufactury", flat-weave tapestries were made from c.1665, and thick- and short-pile carpets were made from c.1742.

Axminster English town where Thomas Whitty established a carpet factory in 1755 (the factory moved to Wilton in 1835). Before 1860 it made hand-woven, woollen pile carpets ("Axminsters"); later, machine-woven equivalents were also produced.

B

bandwork An 18th-century term for *strapwork.

Baronial style Mock-*Gothic style of architecture and decoration inspired by the castles and manor houses of medieval feudal overlords, the barons. Popular during the late 19th and early 20th centuries.

Baroque Style of architecture and ornament prevalent during the 17th century. A *Classical style characterized by elaborate sculptural forms, painted decoration, marble inlays, carved gilding, and architectural elements applied purely ornamentally. Typical motifs included human figures, angels, *putti, scrolls, *swags, urns and flaming torches.

batik See Indonesian style p.126.

Bauhaus School of arts and crafts founded at Weimar in Germany in 1906, and moved to Berlin in 1932. Closed by the German Nazi party in 1933. Initially inspired by the *Arts and Crafts movement, but from the 1920s focused on industrial designs characterized by a stark, cubic simplicity.

bed-hangings Collective term for fabrics draped above or around beds. Includes canopies, valances, drapes and coronas.

Biedermeier See p.29.

"black stitch" *Embroidery worked in black thread on a white or ivory-coloured ground fabric. Also known as "blackwork".

block-printing See *hand-blocking.

braid Decorative woven ribbon made of almost any fibre. Used for trimming and edging seams, especially on upholstered furniture.

brocade Heavyweight fabric with elaborately figured patterns raised against a ground cloth by the addition of supplementary *wefts.

brocatelle A variant of *damask, with raised areas of pattern.

Brussels carpet A flat-weave carpet woven from *linen and *worsted with a looped, uncut pile. Typically decorated with bold patterns in two or three colours (but sometimes more).

bullion fringe See p.197.

buttonhole stitch A looped outline stitch used to finish the raw edges of fabric, and to create straight or curved lines in embroidery patterns.

C

calico A *plain-weave cotton fabric, originally from India but also produced in the West from the 17th century. Naturally cream-coloured, but can also be bleached white, dyed and printed with motifs and patterns.

cambric A fine, slightly stiff, plain-weave cotton fabric.

campaign fringe See p.191.

canvas A coarse, hardwearing fabric woven from fibres of hemp or flax. It can be unbleached, bleached white or dyed.

cartouche A decorative panel consisting of a scroll-shaped frame with a plain, decorated or inscribed centre. Much used in *Renaissance, *Baroque and *Rococo decoration.

casein paint See *milk paint.

chenille "Caterpillar" in French. A velvet-like fabric woven from a soft, fuzzy-textured woven yarn of natural or synthetic fibre.

chequer A geometric pattern consisting of regularly spaced squares of alternating colour.

chevrons V-shaped motifs, traditionally symbolizing water and lightning. Usually stacked singly in a vertical series or strung together horizontally to form a zig-zag.

chiaroscuro Originally a fine-art technique employing shades of black, grey and white to introduce areas of light and shade (and therefore a sense of depth and perspective) into a painting. Since the 17th century also used on fabrics and wallpapers.

chiffonier A wooden cupboard with twin doors, surmounted by drawers and a flat top sometimes supporting one or two shelves.

chimera A fire-breathing creature from classical mythology with the head, mane and legs of a lion, the body of a goat, the tail of a dragon and the wings of an eagle.

chinoiserie Western adaptations of traditional Chinese artefacts and styles of ornament.

Classical style Revivals of the principles and forms of ancient Greek and Roman architecture and ornament. There have been numerous reinterpretations and revivals, beginning with the late 14th- to late 16th-century *Renaissance, when illustrated treatises, engravings and pattern books of the monuments and ruins of the Roman Empire first became widely available. Notable and influential 17th-century examples include the architecture of Perrault and Mansart in France, and Inigo Jones in England – the latter inspired by the work of Palladio (see *Palladianism). During the 18th century, the classical vocabulary was expanded (and better understood) following excavations at Pompeii and Herculaneum. This resulted in the *Neo-classicism of *Adam style, *Empire style, *Federal style and the *Greek Revival. Late 19th- and early 20th-century Classicism took the form of various *Renaissance, *Baroque and *Empire revivals, while 20th-century *Modernism was also partly inspired by classical forms.

coir Fibre made from coconut husks and woven into matting.

Colonial style The styles of architecture and decoration prevalent in the North American colonies during the 17th and 18th centuries. The primary sources of inspiration were contemporary or recent English and, to a lesser extent, European designs (see pp.14–21).

combing A *distressed paint finish that involves dragging a comb through a wet *glaze to produce vertical, horizontal or wavy stripes that allow a contrasting-coloured ground coat to ghost through. Sometimes employed in woodgraining.

Constructivism An early 20th-century Russian style of architecture and design, based on the principles of utilitarian simplicity and logical use of materials, notably glass and metal, in construction and decoration.

cord A form of rope, of various thicknesses, made from twisted threads (of any fibre). Primarily used for *tie-backs and as a trim on upholstered seating.

corduroy A pile fabric (see pp.70–75) with regularly spaced, parallel ridges (or ribs).

cornice A decorative moulding used to cover the join between the walls and the ceiling.

cotton Lightweight fabric woven from spun fibres from the boll (the fruit) of the cotton plant.

cotton duck See p.59.

crewelwork See p.113.

Cubism Abstract art movement of the early 20th century that analysed the interrelation of forms. In practice, several views of the subject were combined and superimposed on one another to provide an account of the entire structure of the subject, rather than simply one view of it.

cypher See p.93.

D

dado Lower section of a wall, running from floor to waist height, the latter often defined by a wooden or plaster dado rail. Also see tripartite division.

damask See pp.76–85.

damascening A decorative technique, originally applied to metalwork, in which gold, silver and copper are inlaid in *arabesque patterns into base metal. Developed in the Near East, it was brought in the 15th century to Europe where the patterns were also applied to other decorative media.

deal Collective term for softwoods (pine and fir) used in the construction of furniture and architectural fixtures and fittings.

delftware Pottery made in England from the late 17th century, in imitation of the Dutch *tin-glazed earthenwares named after the town of Delft, the principal centre of production. Typical decoration included *chinoiserie and European (mostly Dutch) landscapes.

dentils *Classical ornament consisting of a row of small, regularly spaced blocks. Originally applied along a *cornice, but from the early 17th century also applied to furniture.

Deutscher Werkbund An association of manufacturers, architects, artists and designers founded in Munich, Germany, in 1907. Its purpose was to create a national style of art, architecture and design without any stylistic imitation and based on sound principles of construction. Their ideas were taken over by the *Bauhaus during the 1920s.

diaper patterns Collective term for patterns incorporating a geometric framework, such as *latticework or *trelliswork.

distemper Alternative English term for whitewash: a water-based paint made from whiting (ground chalk) and animal glue. Forerunner of modern latex emulsion paints.

distressed finishes Collective term for paint finishes, mostly derived from fine art, in which semi-translucent paints or *glazes are applied over a contrasting-coloured, opaque ground coat, and then distressed while wet to produce patterns and subtle gradations of colour over a surface. See: *combing, *dragging, *ragging, *spattering, *sponging and *stippling.

dobby A mechanical attachment for a loom that facilitated the production of patterns made up of regularly repeated small motifs, particularly geometric shapes. Invented in the early 19th century.

documentary fabrics See p.117.

dogtooth A star-shaped motif, developed from the *nailhead, applied in regular repeats and popular in *Gothic and *Renaissance decoration.

dragging A *distressed paint finish that involves dragging a brush through a wet glaze in parallel sweeps to produce a striped finish in simulation of the figuring and grain of wood.

drawboy Type of loom, named after the weaver's assistant (a young boy) who operated the harness that raised the *warp threads when weaving patterns. Introduced to Europe from the Near East during the *Middle Ages, and a forerunner of the *Jacquard loom.

E

earthenware Porous (unless glazed) pottery produced by firing earth or clays at low temperatures.

egg-and-dart A decorative moulding consisting of alternating egg and V shapes. Originated in *classical Greek architecture.

egg tempera A paint made by mixing powder pigments with linseed oil, water and egg yolk. Primarily used on furniture.

embroidery Decorative stitching applied to the surface of a fabric.

Empire style See pp.29–33.

encaustic tiles *Earthenware tiles patterned with inlays of coloured clay *slips.

enfield An *heraldic beast, with the body of a dog, the head, hindquarters and tail of a fox and the claws of an eagle.

F

Federal style The predominant style of architecture and decoration in America between 1776, following the Declaration of Independence, and c.1830. Initially based on *Adam style, but superseded by the adoption of *Empire style – in turn, gradually supplanted by the *Greek Revival.

felt A dense cloth made from compressed wool or animal fur.

fêtes galantes Pictorial decoration showing fashionably dressed men and women in romantic landscapes. Originated in mid-18th-century France, and widely used in *Rococo style.

field The section of a wall that extends down from the *cornice or *frieze to the top of the *dado. Also see *tripartite division.

flame stitch See p.155.

fleur-de-lis A stylized three- or five-petal lily. Originally a symbol of purity, the motif has been used since the early *Middle Ages, notably in *heraldic ornament.

flock Wallpaper with a raised, textured pattern formed by sprinkling fine particles of *wool (or other fibres) over the paper. These stick to an adhesive applied to the paper in the shape of the pattern.

floorcloth A floorcovering made from *canvas stiffened with linseed oil, and then either painted or *stencilled (often to resemble more expensive floorcoverings such as carpet, *parquet or tiles).

formalized See *stylized.

French knots Decorative embroidery knots worked on the show side of a fabric to create textured dots of colour.

frieze Section of wall extending from the ceiling or *cornice down to the top of the *field. Also see *tripartite division.

fringe A trimming for upholstery and curtains. Consists of threads or decorative shapes made from materials such as fabric, wood, glass or metal, hung from a heading (such as *braid).

fustian Collective term for a group of coarse, usually patterned fabrics woven from *wool, *worsted, or *cotton and wool.

gaufrage French for stamping, and a method of embossing patterns on to the surface of fabrics with heated metal rollers. Often applied to velvets.

galloon A decorative tape or ribbon primarily used to disguise the stitched or glued seams between joined sections of fabric.

gimp A type of *braid traditionally made from strands of *silk, *worsted or *cotton, plaited or twisted around a cord or wire.

gingham A light *cotton fabric with a geometric check pattern of two alternating colours on a white or off-white ground.

glaze In ceramics, a clear or coloured vitreous coating fired over the body of the object. In painting, a semi-translucent paint applied over an opaque ground. (Also see *distressed finishes.)

Gothic The predominant style of architecture and ornament during the *Middle Ages. Also see p.13.

Gothic Revival A late 18th- and 19th-century revival of *Gothic architectural forms and ornament.

Gothick See p.19.

grass cloth See p.207.

Greek key pattern A regular repeat of interlocking right-angled and vertical lines. Used as a border ornament in *Classical architecture and decoration.

Greek Revival See p.61.

grisaille A *trompe l'oeil technique in which figures and patterns are rendered in shades of black, grey and white to produce a three-dimensional effect.

grotesques Decorations based on ancient Roman wall paintings (*grottesche*) discovered in buried ruins in Rome in the late 15th century. Subsequently also applied to ceramics, fabrics and wallpapers. Typical motifs included animals, birds and fishes. Grotesques provided the inspiration for 18th-century, Neo-classical *arabesques.

grotto ornament Decorative elements, including stalactite- and shell-encrusted ceilings and walls, water cascades and pools of ornamental fishes, frogs, lizards and snakes. Originally used in ancient Roman grottoes. Revived in the 17th and 18th centuries.

guilloche A decorative repeat of interlacing curved bands, sometimes forming circles embellished with floral motifs. Used in *Classical ornament.

hand-blocking See p.235.

half-tester A bed with an overhead canopy extending from the headboard to partway along the bed.

hemp Coarse fabric woven from fibres of plants such as *Cannabis sativa*. The fibres can also be twisted and plaited into rope.

heraldic motifs See p.95.

herbals Illustrated accounts of plants. Circulated in Europe during the late *Middle Ages and the *Renaissance.

herringbone Geometric pattern consisting of alternating diagonal lines similar in appearance to the spine and ribs of a herring fish.

hieroglyphics Picture characters developed by the ancient Egyptians and accommodated within Classical Roman ornament.

holland Generic term for fine-woven linen cloth, available unbleached, bleached white, dyed or patterned (usually with stripes), and glazed or unglazed. Produced since the 16th century, notably for upholstery and window blinds.

ikat Indonesian fine cotton or silk fabric decorated with blocks, circles or stripes softened by a vegetable-dyeing process that blends the edges of the colours into one another.

indiennes See p.132.

Iznik pottery *Earthenware of Turkish origin. Either *tin-glazed or coated with white *slip. Decorated with brightly coloured designs.

Jacquard loom A mechanical loom, invented in the early 19th century. Did away with the need for a *drawboy by employing a system of punch-cards (similar to a piano roll) to control the harness mechanism that raised the *warp threads during weaving. Now often computer-controlled.

japonaiserie English, European and American furniture, ceramics, metalwares, wallpapers and fabrics decorated in the style of imported Japanese equivalents. Typical motifs include blossoms, chrysanthemums, bamboo, exotic birds and animals, and *diaper patterns. Especially fashionable during the last quarter of the 19th century.

jewelled strapwork See *strapwork.

jute Fibre derived from Asian plants. Woven into a floor matting.

lacquerware *Oriental furniture and wooden artefacts coated with numerous polished layers of sap of the lacquer tree. Untreated, the lacquer dries to a lustrous black colour. However, it can also be dyed various colours, notably red, and inlaid with shells or decorative powders. European and American pieces have also been produced, in imitation of the oriental originals.

lambrequin A stiff, shaped *pelmet similar in shape to a horse's harness. First used in the 17th century; in the 18th and 19th, it was often extended over halfway down the sides of the window.

latticework A grid-like design made up of open diamond shapes. The pattern for leading in late 16th-century glazed windows. Also worked in stone or wood as an architectural and furniture embellishment, and used as a pattern on ceramics, fabrics, wallpapers and metalwares.

limewash See p.289.

linen Strong fabric woven from fibres of flax plant stalks. Mostly used for bedsheets, pillowcases, tablecloths and upholstery.

linenfold panelling Wooden panelling in which the individual panels are carved to resemble the vertical folds of draped linen.

lit-en-bateau French term meaning "boat bed". A bed with outwardly curving wooden head- and foot-boards (of equal height), their shape approximating to the bow and stern of a boat.

lustreware Ceramics or glass wares with a metallic sheen, produced by firing them with a thin coating of metallic *glaze.

madras Brightly coloured checked and *plaid *cotton or *silk cloth from Madras in India.

Manchester velvet A *cotton velvet with a pile that simulated the sheen of expensive silk velvets. Made in a wide range of colours and patterns (woven or *gaufrage). Manufactured in Manchester, England, during the late 18th century and for most of the 19th. Popular in Britain, Europe and America.

marquetry See p.369.

matelassé See p.85.

medieval style See pp.12–13.

Middle Ages Historical period extending from the fall of the Western Roman Empire in the 5th century AD to the beginning of the Renaissance in the 15th century.

milk paint See p.290.

mille fleurs French for a thousand flowers. A flower-studded pattern originally used on medieval pictorial tapestries. Favoured flowers, naturalistically depicted, include roses, anemones, pinks and violas.

Modernism See pp.49–52.

moiré See p.65.

monochrome One-colour (or shades of one colour).

moquette A woollen velvet, either plain or patterned, the patterns either woven or *gaufrage. Used for upholstery and carpeting.

moresques Alternative name for *arabesque patterns from the late 16th to the early 17th centuries.

mosaic A pattern constructed from small pieces of coloured stone, ceramic or glass. Originally used in Roman architecture.

mottle tiles Tiles decorated with spots of varying shades of colour. Introduced in the 1920s.

mullions Vertical bars used to divide windows into sections.

muslin A lightweight, *plain-weave cotton gauze. Either left plain or patterned with motifs.

nailheads Small pyramid-shaped motifs, often regularly repeated to create an overall pattern.

naturalistic Realistic depictions of organic or inorganic forms.

Neo-classical style See p.22.

noil *Silk fabric with a shimmery surface created by the presence of tiny balls made from the waste products of spun silk mixed with *cotton or wool.

ogival Pointed arch formed by pairs of serpentine-shaped curves.

oil cloth See *floorcloth.

Op Art A 20th-century style of art and decoration in which geometric forms are precisely arranged so that the movement of the observer's eye, or loss of focus, creates an illusion of movement in the painting or pattern.

organza A fine, *plain-weave, sheer *cotton fabric. Produced either plain or printed with motifs.

oriental Collective term used in the West for Eastern artefacts and styles of decoration and ornament. Includes Arabian, Chinese, Indian, Japanese, Persian and Turkish styles.

paisley See p.154

Palladianism See pp.18–23.

palmette Foliate motif loosely based on a formalized palm leaf. Often indistinguishable from the *anthemion and much used in *Classical decoration.

parquetry See p.363.

passementerie Collective term for decorative trimmings applied to soft furnishings. Includes ribbons, bows, braids, tassels and fringes.

pastoral Romanticized imagery of life in the countryside. Also see *Picturesque.

paterae Oval- or circular-shaped form or motif based on dishes or wine holders used in religious ceremonies. Usually decorated with a stylized flower and/or fluting. In Neo-classical ornament often designed as *rosettes.

pelmet Fabric-covered wooden fitting, or a stiffened section of fabric, fixed above a window and designed to conceal the curtain pole and the tops of the curtains.

petit point Form of *embroidery using very fine, small stitches.

photogravure A method of machine-printing wallpaper using metal rollers photochemically engraved with tiny cells or dots that together make up the design. Coloured inks are scraped into the cells and the paper is then forced between the rollers and a rubber cylinder, which forces the surface of the paper into the cells to take up the inks.

picot A decorative furnishing trim that is made up of small loops of thread.

Picturesque A late 18th- and early 19th-century taste for *pastoral imagery combined with theatrical architectural forms (especially *Gothick).

plaid A *plain- or *twill-weave cloth, such as Scottish tartan, with a pattern of intersecting stripes in both the *warp and the *weft.

plain weave A simple weave in which the *warp and the *weft yarns cross at right angles to each other, are spaced at roughly equal intervals and the wefts are passed alternately over and under the warps in one direction and vice versa in the other direction. Also known as "tabby" weave.

plush A velvet-like fabric, but with a longer, less dense pile. Mostly used for upholstery.

point-paper Paper used for designing carpets. Divided into small squares, these being further divided into tiny blocks – each block representing one tuft in the pile of the carpet.

Pointillism Style of painting, developed in France during the late 19th century, in which images are gradually built up through the application of small dots of colour. In the 20th century, also applied to fabrics and wallpapers.

polychromatic Multi-coloured.

polyester Durable, crease-resistant, synthetic fibre.

pombaline A form of tile decoration prevalent in Portugal during the 18th century, in which individual tiles are decorated with a diagonal band of foliage so that a *trellis pattern is formed when the tiles are placed together.

Pop Art An art movement of the 1960s, producing graphic images of everyday figures and objects using techniques employed in film, television and advertising.

poplin Lightweight fabric traditionally woven with fine *silk *warps covering coarser *worsted *wefts to produce a ribbed effect.

portière A curtain designed to be hung over an archway or door.

Post-Modernism An architectural and design movement that began in the mid-1960s as a reaction to the plain, unadorned forms of Modernism, and revived traditional *Classical forms of ornament.

powder ground Tile decoration created by *spattering fine sprays of pigment through a stencil.

powdered ornament Patterns consisting of evenly spaced scatterings of small motifs such as flower sprigs and stars. Originated in *heraldic ornament.

print room See p.245.

putti Images of children based on cherubs and the infant attendants of Cupid or Eros (gods of classical mythology).

quarries Small panes of glass, usually diamond-shaped, supported by *latticework leading in 16th-century glazed windows.

quarry tile An unglazed floor tile made from fired clay.

R

ragging or **rag-rolling** A *distressed paint finish that involves brushing a semi-translucent glaze over an opaque, contrasting-coloured ground coat and dabbing it with a rag to remove random patches of glaze.

Regency See pp.29–35.

relief tiles Tiles decorated with a moulded pattern that stands proud of the surface.

Renaissance Historical period and a term used to describe the movement in art, architecture, design and ornament that originated in Italy in the late 14th

century and spread across Europe during the course of the next 200 years. At its heart lay a revival of the architecture and ornament of ancient Rome and Greece (see *Classical style).

rep *Plain-weave, ribbed fabric mainly used for upholstery. Made from *silk, *wool, or silk and wool, and sometimes *cotton.

rocaille A form of ornament prevalent in *Rococo style. Based on asymmetrical rock and shell forms found in *grotto decoration.

Rococo See p.19.

rosette A circular, formalized floral ornament of Mesopotamian and ancient Greek origin, widely employed in *Classical decoration since the Renaissance. Also used to describe any circular ornament with decorative elements, such as fluting, radiating from its centre.

rush Grass-like, marshland plant, the dried stalks of which are plaited into strips and sewn together to form floor matting.

S

sanitary papers See p.263.

sash window A window made of glazed wooden frames (sashes) that slide up and down in vertical grooves by means of counterbalanced weights.

saturated colour Dense, opaque colour, as opposed to thin, semi-transparent colour.

screen printing A method of transferring a design on to fabric or paper by squeezing dyes or inks through a mesh screen placed on the surface. The screen is masked in those areas where a colour is not required for the design.

scrolling foliage Naturalistic plant forms presented in abstract, curving lines (see p.147).

seersucker Originally an Indian striped fabric of mixed *silk and *cotton, but from the 17th century also manufactured in the West. Characterized by a rippled or puckered texture formed by weaving the cotton *warps at a looser tension than the silk *wefts.

shellac A transparent varnish with a red-brown tint, made from a resin secreted on the twigs of trees by Asian lac insects.

silk Luxury cloth woven from the shiny, smooth filaments spun from the cocoons of the silkworm.

singerie From the French for monkey, and a style of pictorial decoration showing monkey figures engaged in human

activities (often set within *scrolling foliage or *bandwork). Popular in *Rococo interiors.

sisal A fibre produced from the leaf of the Mexican agave plant. Woven into rope or floor matting.

slip A creamy mixture of clay and water used to decorate pottery. Also a fascia, usually of marble or glazed tiles, set into a fireplace.

slub silk Raw silk fabric with a textured surface produced by incorporating small flecks of the silkworm cocoon in the weave.

Spanish stitch Embroidery characterized by naturalistic floral, fruit and insect patterns.

spattering A *distressed paint finish that involves flicking flecks of wet *glaze from the bristles of a brush over an opaque, contrasting-coloured ground coat to create a pattern of random specks of colour. Used to simulate stones such as porphyry and granite.

sponging *Distressed paint finish that involves dabbing a sponge over a *wet glaze applied to a contrasting coloured ground coat. The resulting pattern of random specks and gradations of colour is often incorporated in *faux* marble and stone finishes.

stem stitch An overlapping embroidery stitch particularly suited to producing curving lines, and so often employed for plant-form patterns (especially florals).

stencilling A technique for applying motifs and patterns to a surface by dabbing paints, glazes or dyes through cut-outs made in a stencil (a thin card usually made of oiled paper, but sometimes wood, metal or plastic).

stippling *Distressed paint finish that involves tapping the bristle tips of a brush over wet glazes applied to an opaque, contrasting-coloured ground coat. Used to blend different coloured glazes and to create subtle shading and gradations of colour.

strapwork Form of ornament consisting of twisted and intertwined bands (similar in appearance to strips of leather or ribbons). Sometimes combined with *arabesques or serving as the framework for *grotesques. Also often studded with *rosettes, *nailheads or faceted jewel-like forms – the latter known as jewelled strapwork.

strié A mottled effect produced on the surface of a fabric by dyeing the yarns with two different colours before weaving.

stucco A fine cement or plaster made from sand, slaked lime and gypsum. Applied to the surface of walls, mouldings and other architectural ornaments. By the 19th century, generally used as a term for exterior rendering.

stylized Non-*naturalistic depictions of organic or inorganic forms, the original subject matter merely providing inspiration for the final design.

swag Both a loop of drapery and a pendant garland made up of, or depicting, flowers, vegetables, fruit, leaves or shells.

swag-and-tail A style of hanging curtains in which the main body of the fabric is looped horizontally along the top of a window or door, and the ends, or tails, are allowed to hang down at the sides.

Swedish style In the 20th-century, a simple style of interior decoration characterized by the use of muted colours such as cobalt blue, grey and white, restrained ornamentation and the extensive use of natural materials, notably wood and glass. However, in the 18th century, Swedish "Gustavian" style based on *Rococo was far more elaborate.

T

taffeta A firm, closely woven *silk or *linen fabric with an identical glossy surface on both sides.

tassel See p.192-195.

terracotta A red-coloured *earthenware, usually unglazed.

terrazzo A decorative finish for walls and floors, made of chips of marble or other stones set into mortar and then polished smooth.

tesserae The small cubes of coloured stone, ceramic or glass used to make *mosaic patterns.

ticking See p.161.

tie-back A length of rope, *cord or fabric used to secure a curtain to one side of a window.

tin-glaze A glassy white *glaze made by adding tin oxide to lead glaze. Used to decorate pottery such as *delftware.

toile de Jouy See p.135.

tongue-and-groove A method of jointing boards, in which the edge of one board has a tongue, or lip, that fits into a groove cut into the edge of the next board.

tours de cheminées Plain or decorative lengths of fabric hung from the leading edge of the mantelshelf of a fireplace.

transfer printing A method of printing designs on ceramics by first printing an engraved design on paper, using an oil-based ink. The paper is then laid over the body of the ceramic and burnt off during firing, to leave an outline design (which can be coloured in by hand).

Tree of Life An English pattern developed during the late 16th century, possibly from ancient Persian or Indian ornament, and symbolizing the life force. Much used on fabrics, it usually consisted of a central trunk, branches, sinuous stems and tendrils, fantastical flowers and exotic fruits, all woven around exotic birds and insects.

trelliswork A crisscross wooden support for plants, and a decorative pattern devised in imitation of it. Notably popular in *medieval, *Regency and *Arts and Crafts decoration.

tripartite division The horizontal division of a wall into three sections – *frieze, *field and *dado – for the purposes of decoration.

triquetra A three-lobed, triangular motif made up of interlaced crescent shapes. Of Celtic origin.

triskele A Y-shaped sun motif, originally used in ancient Greek and Celtic ornament.

trompe l'oeil French for "trick the eye". A decorative technique in which paints or dyes are applied to stone, plaster, wood, fabric or paper to create the appearance, form (and often texture) of three-dimensional scenes or objects. Typical examples included marbling, woodgraining, *grisaille* and architectural components or vistas rendered in perspective.

tube-lining A method of decorating tiles in which raised lines of *slip are piped on to the surface through a thin tube. The lines define the pattern by separating subsequently applied coloured glazes.

tufting A technique used in the mass-production of carpets, in which a pile is created by sewing tufted yarn on to a ready-woven backing fabric (the backing is then coated in latex to secure the yarn).

tulle Fine, *muslin-like material made of silk. First produced in France during the 18th century.

turkeywork An inexpensive woollen pile fabric produced in imitation of expensive Turkish and Persian carpets. Used for upholstery and table and floor coverings during the 17th century.

tweed A coarse-textured, *twill-weave cloth made from different coloured woollen yarns.

twill-weave A variation of a *plain-weave. Has a diagonal grain produced by floating the *weft threads diagonally over and under groups of, rather than alternating, *warps.

V, W, Y, Z

valance A short, soft curtain, either used at the top of a window to hide the curtain pole and the tops of the main curtains, or hung from the canopy or base of a bed.

velour Heavyweight, velvet-like fabric with a thick pile that lies in one direction. Woven from wool, cotton or synthetic fibres.

verdure French for "greenness", and for tapestry with a green colour cast and displaying predominantly plant-form imagery.

vinyl A man-made polymer used in resin form to produce sheet flooring. Also used for vinyl wallpapers (see p.243).

voile A fine, crisp, sheer fabric woven from *cotton, *silk, *wool or synthetic fibres.

warp The threads that run lengthways in a piece of cloth. They are set and spaced on a loom and the *wefts are woven through them from side to side.

water leaf A motif consisting of a broad, blade-shaped leaf with crimped edges and curling tip. Probably based on the waterlily leaf and widely used in *Gothic and *Neo-classical ornament.

weft The threads in a piece of cloth that are woven from side to side through the *warps.

Wiener Werkstätte A studio founded in Vienna, Austria, in 1907. Specialized in hand made fabrics, furniture and metalwork in the *Art Nouveau style.

Wilton Generic name for a type of carpet first produced in Wilton, England, in the mid-18th century. Similar to *Brussels carpet, but with a cut pile.

wool A yarn spun from the fibrous coat of an animal, most often a sheep or a goat.

worsted Smooth, strong woollen cloth made from carded and combed wool yarn.

ypotryll An *heraldic beast with the head of a boar, the body of an antelope and the tail of a lion.

zillij Traditional North African *mosaic tile work.

Directory

All items featured in the book are available via a store, a distributor or by mail order, and the majority of manufacturers will ship overseas. If a supplier in your area or country is not listed, please contact the company for details of local suppliers or how to order. Company web sites offer a wealth of information and some provide on-line ordering. Before visiting suppliers, please telephone or check the website since not all outlets are open to the public or require an appointment. Note that toll-free (freephone) numbers usually work in originating country only.

Please refer to these addresses whenever the Chelsea Harbour Design Centre (UK) or the D&D Building (New York) are listed:

Chelsea Harbour Design Centre
Chelsea Harbour
London SW10 0XE
UK
Tel: +44 (0)20 7225 9100
Fax: +44 (0)20 7352 7868
www.chdc.co.uk

The D&D Building
979 Third Avenue
New York, New York
USA 10022
Tel: +1 212 759 5408
www.ddbuilding.com

For further information, Canadian readers should contact:

Designers Walk
160 Pears Street, Suite 311
Toronto, Ontario
Canada M5R 2K9
Tel: +1 416 961 1211
Tel Toll-free: +1 888 707 9255
Fax: +1 416 928 9683
www.designerswalk.com

Ontario Design Centre
260 King Street East, #414
Toronto, Ontario
Canada M5A 1K3
Tel: +1 416 594 9310
Fax: +1 416 594 9313

Telio & Cie
1407 rue de la Montagne
Montreal, Quebec
Canada H3G 1Z3
Tel: +1 514 842 9116
Fax: +1 514 842 2748
www.telio.com

A

Aalto Country Colours
Head office: 8 Railway Street
Newmarket, Auckland
New Zealand
Tel: +64 9 522 2019
Fax: +64 9 522 2149
www.aaltocolour.com
(Ships worldwide.)
and
Aalto Advisory
29 Leslie Hills Drive
Christchurch
New Zealand
Tel: +64 3 348 8015
Fax: +64 3 348 2408
and
34 Grosvenor Street
Neutral Bay
Sydney, NSW 1585
Australia
Tel: +61 2 9953 0933
Fax: +64 92 9953 0944

Abbott & Boyd
1/22 Chelsea Harbour
Design Centre
UK
Tel: +44 (0)20 7351 9985
Fax: +44 (0)20 7823 3127
www.abbottandboyd.co.uk
(Distributed in USA by Brunschwig & Fils.)

Ace Hardware Corporation
Paint Division
2200 Kensington Court
Oak Brook, Illinois
USA 60523-2100
Tel: +1 630 990 6600
www.acehardware.com

A. Elder Reed & Co. Ltd.
(trade as Reed Harris)
Riverside House
27 Carnworth Road
London SW6 3HR
UK
Tel: +44 (0)20 7736 7511
Fax: +44 (0)20 7751 2988
www.reedharris.co.uk
(UK distributor of Carré.)

Alexander Beauchamp
Appleby Business Centre
Appleby Street
Blackburn
Lancashire BB1 3BL
UK
Tel: +44 (0)1254 691133
Fax: +44 (0)1254 691199
www.alexanderbeauchamp.com
and
Fonthill Ltd.
D&D Building, USA
Tel: +1 212 755 6700
Fax: +1 212 371 2358

The Alternative Flooring Co.
Unit 3b, Stephenson Close
East Portway Industrial Estate
Andover
Hampshire SP10 3RU
UK
Tel: +44 (0)1264 335111
Fax: +44 (0)1264 336445
www.alternative-flooring.co.uk

Altfield Ltd.
2/22 Chelsea Harbour
Design Centre
UK
Tel: +44 (0)20 7351 5893
Fax: +44 (0)20 7376 5667
www.altfield.com
(UK distributors of Maya Romanoff, Blumenthal and van Schelle & Gurland.)
and
Suite 605
9 Queen's Road Central
Hong Kong
Tel: +852 2523 9356
(Distributor of Henry Newbery.)

(The) Amtico Company Ltd.
Solar Park, Southside
Solihull B90 4SH
UK
Tel: +44 (0)121 745 0800
Fax: +44 (0)121 745 0888
Brochures: 0800 66 77 66
www.amtico.com
and
Amtico International Inc.
The Amtico Studio
6480 Roswell Road
Atlanta, Georgia
USA 30328
Tel: +1 404 267 1900
Fax: +1 404 267 1901
and
Amtico International Pty. Ltd.
PO Box 297, Chatswood
Sydney 2057, NSW
Australia
Tel: +61 2 9415 0200
Fax: +61 2 9417 3344
and
Irvine International Floors Ltd.
68 Falsgrave Street
PO Box 7545
Christchurch
New Zealand
Tel: +64 3 377 7537
Fax: +64 3 377 7547
and
Novel Building Supplies Ltd.
10/F Kam Fung Commercial Building
2–4 Tin Lok Lane
Wan Chai
Hong Kong
Tel: +852 2892 2232
Fax: +852 2893 2262
and
Kagawa & Company Ltd.
8–17 5 Chome
Nishiawaji
Higashiyodogawa-Ku
CPO Box 871
Osaka
Japan
Tel: +816 6 323 6598
Fax: +816 6 324 3930
and
Deco Expression Pte. Ltd.
74/74a Neil Road
Singapore 0408
Tel: +65 225 8433
Fax: +65 225 8455
and

Taaf Hamman Trading Pty. Ltd.
22 Dublin Road
Bramley View Ext 6 2090
Johannesburg
South Africa
Tel: +27 11 882 1000
Fax: +27 11 882 5403

Andrew Martin International Ltd.
200 Walton Street
London SW3 2JL
UK
Tel: +44 (0)20 7225 5100
Fax: +44 (0)20 7589 8502
and
Unique Fabrics Ltd.
6 Mt Eden Road
Eden Terrace, Auckland
New Zealand
Tel: +64 9 306 1580
(Distributed in USA by Kravet.)

Anna French
343 Kings Road
London SW3 5ES
UK
Tel: +44 (0)20 7351 1126
Fax: +44 (0)20 7351 0421
www.annafrench.co.uk
and
Sanderson
D&D Building, USA
Tel/Fax: +1 212 759 5408
and
Interior Textiles Corporation
(trading as Anna French)
275 Swan Street
Richmond 3121
Melbourne, Vic.
Australia
Tel: +61 39 428 1800
Fax: +61 39 428 0053
and
Crescendo, Annestarr Agencies
3–611 Alexander Street
Vancouver, British Columbia
Canada V6A 1E1
Tel: +1 604 254 3376
Fax: +1 604 254 3336

Ann Sacks Tile and Stone
5 East 16th Street
New York, New York
USA 10003
Tel: +1 800 278 8453
Fax: +1 212 463 0067
www.annsacks.com
and
Yaletown Tileworks
1009 Cambie Street
Vancouver, British Columbia
Canada V6B 5L7
Tel: +1 604 682 3060
Fax: +1 604 681 5997

Anne and Robert Swaffer
Bakewell Road
Orton Southgate
Peterborough PE2 6WQ
UK
Tel: +44 (0)1733 371727
Fax: +44 (0)1733 371247

Annie Sloan Practical Style
117 London Road

Headington
Oxford OX3 9HZ
UK
Tel: +44 (0)1865 768666
www.anniesloan.com

Anta Scotland Ltd.
Fearn, Tain
Ross-shire IV20 1XW
UK
Tel: +44 (0)1862 832477
Fax: +44 (0)1862 832616
www.anta.co.uk

Antico Setificio Fiorentino
50124 Firenze
Via L. Bartolini 4
Italy
Tel: +39 055 213 861
Fax: +39 055 218 174
www.anticosetificiofiorentino.it
(Distributed in USA by Kravet.)

Anya Larkin
39 West 28th Street,
8th Floor
New York, New York
USA 10001
Tel: +1 212 532 3263
Fax: +1 212 532 2854
www.anyalarkin.com
(Distributed in UK by Donghia.)

Apenn
Head office: 33 Kensington
Park Road
London W11 2EU
UK
Tel: +44 (0)20 7792 2457
Fax: +44 (0)20 7727 4719
and
Showroom:
1/11 Chelsea
Harbour Design Centre
UK
Tel: +44 (0)20 7349 9100
Fax: +44 (0)20 7351 7056

Armstrong DLW
Hitching Court
Abingdon Business Park
Abingdon OX14 1RB
UK
Tel: +44 (0)1235 444010
Fax: +44 (0)1235 444011
www.armstrongdlw.co.uk
and
Armstrong World Industries
2500 Columbia Ave. (17603)
PO Box 3001
Lancaster, PA
USA 17604
Tel: +1 800 233 3823/
Tel: +1 877 ARMSTRONG
www.armstrong.com
and
Armstrong World Industries
6911 Decarie Blvd.
Montreal, Quebec
Canada H3W 3E5
Tel: +1 800 233 3823/
Tel: +1 877 ARMSTRONG
www.armstrong.com
and
Armstrong World Industries
(Australia) Pty. Ltd.
29–39 Mills Road
PO Box 109

Braeside 3195
Mordialloc
3195 Vic.
Australia
Freephone: +1800 632 624
Fax: +61 3 9586 5634
www.armstrong-aust.com.au
and
Armstrong World Industries
(H.K.) Ltd.
19/FL Neich Tower
128 Gloucester Road
Wan Chai
Hong Kong
Tel: +852 2585 7800
Fax: +852 2598 7181

Artex
Pasture Lane
Ruddington
Nottinghamshire NG11 6AG
UK
Tel: +44 (0)115 984 5679
Fax: +44 (0)115 940 5240
www.artex-bluehawk.co.uk

The Arts & Crafts Home
25a Clifton Terrace
Brighton BN1 3HA
UK
Tel: +44 (0)1273 327774
Mobile: +44 (0)777 55 33 453
www.achome.co.uk
(Web-based company.)

Atlas Carpet Mills
2200 Saybrook Avenue
Los Angeles, California
USA 90040
Tel: +1 323 724 9000
Toll-free: +1 800 367 8188
Fax: +1 323 724 4526/
Toll-free: +1 800 272 8527
(Distributed in the UK, Europe and the Middle East by Christy Trading).

Auro Organic Paints
Unit 2, Pamphillions Farm
Purton End
Debden
Saffron Walden
Essex CB11 3JT
UK
Tel: +44 (0)1799 543077
Fax: +44 (0)1799 542187
www.auroorganic.co.uk
and
1340-G Industrial Avenue
Petaluma, California
USA 94952
Tel: +1 707 763 0662
and
Eco Solves Systems
4 Kitson Street
Frankston
Vic. 3199
Australia
and
Inui Corporation
2-5, 2-chome
Doshomachi
Chuo-ku
Osaka 541-0045
Tel: +816 6 231 2971

Axminster Carpets Ltd.
Woodmead Road
Axminster
Devon EX13 5PQ
UK
Tel: +44 (0)1297 32244
Fax: +44 (0)1297 35241
www.axminster-
carpets.co.uk
and
6th Floor, 150 East 55th Street
New York, New York
USA 10022
Tel: +1 212 421 1050/
Toll-free: +1 800 356 5013
Fax: +1 212 935 6690
www.axminster-carpets.com

B

Baer & Ingram
Dragon Works
Leigh on Mendip
Radstock BA3 5QZ
UK
Hotline: +44 (0)1373 813800
Tel: +44 (0)1373 812552
Fax: +44 (0)1373 813601
www.baer-ingram.com
and
Davan Port Ltd.
404 Pleasant View Court
Copaigue, New York
USA 11726
Tel: +1 631 225 1811
Fax: +1 631 225 0879

H.T. Barnes Co., Inc.
PO Box 1327
Foley, Alabama
USA 36536
Toll-free: +1 800 211 5018
Fax: +1 251 943 8310
*(Distributes Conso trim,
including Imperial Collection,
Wendy Cushing trims, and
British Trimmings.)*

Beaumont & Fletcher
Showroom: 261 Fulham Road
London SW3 6HY
UK
Tel/Fax: +44 (0)20 7352 5594
www.beaumontandfletcher.com
*(Distributed in USA by F.
Schumacher & Co.)*
and
Office: 71 Warriner Gardens
The Old Imperial Laundry
London SW11 4XW
UK
Tel: +44 (0)20 7498 2642
Fax: +44 (0)20 7498 2644

Belinda Coote Tapestries
(see Watts of Westminster)

Bennett Silks
Crown Royal Park
Higher Hillgate
Stockport SK1 3HB
UK
Tel: +44 (0)161 476 8600
Fax: +44 (0)161 480 5385
www.bennett-silks.co.uk
and
Garin 1820 Showroom

2–9 Chelsea Harbour Design
  Centre
UK (see p401)
Tel: +44 (0)20 7351 6496
Fax: +44 (0) 20 7351 3761
and
Elijah Slocum
8360 Melrose Avenue
Los Angeles, California
USA 90069
Tel: +1 323 655 1263
Fax: +1 323 655 0936

Bennison Fabrics
16 Holbein Place
London SW1W 8NL
UK
Tel: +44 (0)20 7730 8076
Fax: +44 (0)20 7823 4997
and
Bennison Inc. (trade shop)
The Fine Arts Building
232 East 59th Street
New York, New York
USA 10022
Tel: +1 212 223 0373
Fax: +1 212 223 0655

Bentley & Spens
1–2 Mornington Street
London NW1 7QD
UK
Tel/Fax: +44 (0)20 7387 7374
www.fabenglish.com
and
Christopher Hyland Inc.
D&D Building, Suite 1710
USA (see p401)
Tel: +1 212 688 6121
Fax: +1 212 688 6176
and
Designers International
77a Parnell Road
Auckland
New Zealand
Tel: +64 9 309 1589
Fax: +64 9 309 1591
and
E & Y Co. Ltd.
4-3-25 Tenjin
Chuo-ku
Fukuoka 819-0001
Japan
Tel: +81 92 771 9688
Fax: +81 92 752 3176

Berger Paints
Berger Paints Emirates Ltd.
PO Box 27524
Dubai
United Arab Emirates
Tel: +971 4 3391 000
Fax: +971 4 3391 322/323
www.bergeronline.com
and
Berger Paints Singapore PTE
22 Benoi Sector
Singapore 629854
Tel: +65 6261 5224
Fax: +65 6265 6356
and
Lewis Berger Overseas
Holdings
77 Marlowes
Hemel Hempstead
Hertfordshire HP1 1LF
UK

Tel: +44 (0)1442 260075
Fax: +44 (0)1442 254600

Bernard Thorp & Co.
Trade showroom:
6 Burnsall Street
London SW3 3ST
UK
Tel: +44 (0)20 7352 5745
Fax: +44 (0)20 7376 3640
*(Distributed in USA by Stark
Carpet Corporation.)*
and
Shop:
53 Chelsea Manor Street
London SW3 5RZ
UK
Tel: +44 (0)20 7352 5457
Fax: +44 (0)20 7376 3640

Berti Pavimenti Legno
Via Rettilineo 81
35010 Villa del Conte
Padova
Italy
Tel: +39 049 93 25011
Fax: +39 049 93 23639
www.berti.net
and
Paul Meakin
PM Hardwoods
5 Nelson Street
Southend-on-Sea
Essex SS1 1ES
UK
Tel: +44 (0)1702 348877
Fax: +44 (0)1702 334851

Bill Amberg
The Shop
10 Chepstow Road
London W2 5BD
UK
Tel: +44 (0)20 7727 3560
Fax: +44 (0)20 7727 3541
www.billamberg.com
and
The Workshops
23 Theatre Street
London SW11 5ND
UK
Tel: +44 (0)20 7924 4296
Fax: +44 (0)20 7924 4002

Boen Parkett
Boen Bruk AS
4658 Tveit
Norway
Tel: +47 3806 6600
Fax: +47 5806 6601
www.boen.no
and
Hardwood Flooring Supplies
Unit 1, Kestrel Way
Goldsworth Park Trading
  Estate, Woking
Surrey GU21 3AZ
UK
Tel: +44 (0)870 770 4322
Fax: +44 (0)870 770 4340
www.hfsltd.co.uk
and
Floorworks International Ltd.
365 Dupont Street
Toronto, Ontario
Canada M5R 1W2
Tel: +1 416 961 6891

Fax: +1 416 961 3881
and
Nova Hardwood Flooring
6-170 Joseph Zatzman Drive
Dartmouth, Nova Scotia
Canada B3B 1L9
Tel: +1 902 468 5154
Fax: +1 902 468 1917
and
Coast Hardwood Floors
12540 Bridgeport Road,
  Suite 100
Richmond, British Columbia
Canada V6V 1J5
Tel: +1 604 214 9663
Fax: +1 604 273 3000
and
Boen Hardwood Flooring Inc.
350 Hollie Drive
Bowles Industrial Park
Martinsville, Virginia
USA 24112
Tel: +1 276 638 3700
Fax: +1 276 638 3066
www.boen.com

Bonar Floors
High Holborn Road
Ripley
Derbyshire DE5 3NT
UK
Tel: +44 (0)1773 744121
Fax: +44 (0)1773 744142
www.bonarfloors.com
and
Bonar Floors Inc.
Suite 100
365 Walt Sanders Memorial
  Drive
Newnan, Georgia
USA 30265
Tel: +1 770 252 4890
Fax: +1 770 252 4894

Borderline
2/7 Chelsea Harbour Design
  Centre
UK (see p401)
Tel: +44 (0)20 7823 3567
Fax: +44 (0)20 7351 7644
www.borderlinefabrics.com
*(Distributed in USA by
Classic Revivals.)*

Bosanquet Ives
Bank Chambers
29 High Street
Ewell
Surrey KT17 1SB
UK
Tel: +44 (0)20 8786 4107
www.bosanquetives.co.uk

Bradbury & Bradbury
PO Box 155
Benicia, California
USA 94510
Tel: +1 707 746 1900
Fax: +1 707 745 9417
www.bradbury.com
*(Distributed in the UK by
Hamilton Weston.)*

Brian Yates (Interiors) Ltd.
Lansil Way, Caton Road
Lancaster LA1 3QY
UK

Tel: +44 (0)1524 35035
Fax: +44 (0)1524 32232
*(Distributor of Sheila
Coombes; distributed in USA
by Sanderson; only Sheila
Coombes collection
exported internationally.)*
and
Showroom:
G27 Chelsea Harbour
  Design Centre
UK (see p401)
Tel: +44 (0)20 7352 0123
Fax: +44 (0)20 7352 6060
and
Telio & Cie
1407 rue de la Montagne
Montreal, Quebec
Canada H3G 1Z3
Tel: +1 514 842 9116
Fax: +1 514 842 3728
and
Ascraft Fabrics
19a Boundary Street
Rushcutters Bay 2011
Australia
Tel: +61 2 9360 2311
Fax: +61 2 9360 5335
and
Vivace
16 Railway Street
Newmarket
Auckland
New Zealand
Tel: +64 95 230625
Fax: +64 95 230627
and
Silk Company
3rd Floor, R B C Building
8 Kramer Road
Kramerville
2148 Johannesburg
South Africa
Tel: +27 114 482578
Fax: +27 114 482522

Brintons
Design office:
PO Box 16, Exchange Street
Kidderminster
Worcestershire DY10 1AG
UK
Tel: +44 (0)1562 820000
Fax: +44 (0)1562 515597
www.brintons.co.uk
and
Brintons US Axminster
1856 Artistry Lane
PO Box 877
Greenville, Mississippi
USA 38702-0877
Tel: +1 662 332 1581
Fax: +1 662 332 1594
and
150 East 58th Street,
New York, New York
USA 10155
Tel: +1 212 832 0121
Toll-free: +1 800 941 9884
Fax: +1 212 980 1505
www.brintonsusax.com
and
Showroom & sales office
2/67 Palmerston Crescent
South Melbourne
Vic. 3205
Australia

Tel: +61 3 9 645 0088
Fax: +61 3 9 645 0655
and
Showroom & sales office
18d Level 2
125 The Strand
Parnell
Auckland
New Zealand
Tel: +64 9 379 9205
Fax: +64 9 379 9003

Bruce Hardwood
185 Milton Park
Abingdon OX14 4SR
UK
Tel: +44 (0)1235 515100
Fax: +44 (0)1235 862255
www.brucefloors.com
and
16803 Dallas Parkway
Addison, Texas
USA 75001
Toll-free: +1 800 722 4647
Tel: +1 214 887 2000

Brunschwig & Fils Inc.
C10 The Chambers
London SW10 0XF
UK
Tel: +44 (0)20 7351 5797
Fax: +44 (0)20 7351 2280
www.brunschwig.com
(Distributor of John Boyd.)
and
D&D Building, Suite 1200
USA (see p401)
Tel: +1 212 838 7878
Fax: +1 212 838 5611
and
320 Davenport Road
Toronto, Ontario
Canada M5R 1K6
Tel: +1 416 968 0699
Fax: +1 416 968 6500
and
751 High Street
Armadale
Vic. 3143
Australia
Tel: +61 3 9509 6766
Fax: +61 3 9509 6866
and
Icon Textile Ltd.
Level 2
155–165 The Strand
Parnell, Auckland
New Zealand
Tel: +64 9375 9850
Fax: +64 9375 9855
and
Halogen International
8 Kramer Road
Kramerville 2148
South Africa
Tel: +27 11 448 2060
Fax: +27 11 448 2065
and
Textile Iida Co. Ltd.
1-1150-0011
1-25-11 Higashi
Shibuya-Ku
Tokyo 151
Japan
Tel: +81 3 5468 5001
Fax: +81 3 5468 5075
www.textileiida.co.jp

Busby & Busby
The Old Stables
Winterborne Whitchurch
Blandford Forum
Dorset DT11 9AW
UK
Tel: +44 (0)1258 881211
Fax: +44 (0)1258 881351
www.busbyfabric.com

C

Cabot Stains
33360 Central Avenue
Union City, California
USA 94587
Toll-free: +1 800 877 8246
Fax: +1 978 462 2720
www.cabotstain.com

Candy
(British Ceramic Tiles)
Heathfield
Newton Abbot
Devon TQ12 6RF
UK
Tel: +44 (0)1626 834774
Fax: +44 (0)1626 834775
www.bctltd.co.uk

Carocim
BP 10
1515 rte du Puy Ste
  Reparade
13540 Puyricard
France
Tel: +33 442 92 20 39
Fax: +33 442 92 20 96
www.carocim.com

Carpet Innovations
(Clodan Carpets Inc.)
588 Broadway
Space 803
New York, NewYork
USA 10012
Tel: +1 212 966 9440
Fax: +1 212 941 8467
www.carpetinnovations.com
and
Object Carpet UK
The Studio, Little Manor
Staplehurst Road
Frittenden
Kent TN17 2EA
UK
Tel: +44 (0)1580 852585
Fax: +44 (0)1580 852586

Carré
91 quai de Valmy
75010 Paris
France
Tel: +33 146 07 03 26
Fax: +33 146 07 37 61
www.carre.fr
*(Distributed in the UK by A.
Elder Reed.)*

Cath Kidston
Head office:
9a Penzance Place
London W11 4PE
UK
Tel: +44 (0)20 7221 4248
Fax: +44 (0)20 7221 4388
www.cathkidston.co.uk
and

shop: 8 Clarendon Cross
London W11 4AP
UK
Tel: +44 (0)20 7221 4000
Orders: +44 (0)20 7229 8000
Fax: +44 (0)20 7229 1992
(Distributed outside the UK
by the Designers Guild.)

Celia Birtwell
71 Westbourne Park Road
London W2 5QH
UK
Tel: +44 (0)20 7221 0877
Fax: +44 (0)20 7229 7673

Chase Erwin
Head office: River House
43 Lydden Grove
London SW18 4LW
UK
Tel: +44 (0)20 8875 1222
Fax: +44 (0)20 8875 1444
www.chase-erwin.com
(Distributed in USA by
Tiffany.)
and
Showroom: 22 Chelsea
Harbour Design Centre
UK (see p401)

Chatsworth Carpets
Head office: Unit 1
Greasley Place
Burrough Gardens
Hendon
London NW4 4AJ
UK
Tel: +44 (0)20 7584 1386
Fax: +44 (0)20 8457 9500

Chelsea Textiles
13 Walton Street
London SW3 2HX
UK
Tel: +44 (0)20 7584 5544
Fax: +44 (0)20 7584 4844
www.chelseatextiles.com
and
D&D Building, Suite 914
USA (see p401)
Tel: +1 212 319 5804
Fax: +1 212 319 1492

Christy Trading
1 Danbury Court
Winford Wood
Milton Keynes MK14 6PL
UK
Tel: +44 (0)1908 308777
Fax: +44 (0)1908 265224
www.christy-carpets.co.uk
(UK distributor of Atlas and
Monterey Carpet Mills.)

Cinca
Rua Principal 39
apartado 12
P-4535-908 Fiães VFR
Portugal
Tel: +351 22 747 6400
Tel (export): +351 22 747 6462
Fax: +351 22 747 6490
Fax (export): +351 22 747 6494
www.cinca.pt
and
Lisbon Showroom

Rua Abranches Ferrão 3b
P-1600-001 Lisboa
Portugal
Tel: +351 21 727 53 04
Fax: +351 21 727 48 64

Claremont (Furnishing
Fabrics Co. Ltd.)
35 Elystan Street
London SW3 3NT
UK
Tel: +44 (0)20 7581 9575
Fax: +44 (0)20 7581 9573
www.claremontfurnishing.com
and
The Claremont Furnishing
Fabrics Co. Inc.
2nd Floor
1059 Third Avenue
New York, New York
USA 10021
Tel: +1 212 486 1252
Fax: +1 212 486 1253

Claremont Fabrics
Glossop Brook Road
Glossop
Derbyshire SK13 8GF
UK
Tel: +44 (0)1457 866927
Fax: +44 (0)1457 854669
www.claremontfabrics.com
and
International Design Source
(IDS)
7 Hills, NSW
Australia
Tel: +61 2 9674 7600
Fax: +61 2 9674 7196
and
Irvine Merchant Holdings
Christchurch
New Zealand
Tel: +64 3 366 5113
Fax: +64 3 366 5024
and
Air Fair Fabrics
Rm. 809-810 Paramount
Building
12 Ka Yip Street
Chaiwan
Hong Kong
Tel: +852 2898 3903
Fax: +852 2556 6690

Clarence House (UK) Ltd.
3/10 Chelsea Harbour
Design Centre
UK (see p401)
Tel: +44 (0)20 7351 1200
Fax: +44 (0)20 7351 6300
www.clarencehouse.com
and
211 East 58th Street
New York, New York
USA 10022
Toll-free: +1 800 221 4704
Tel: +1 212 752 2890
Fax: +1 212 755 3314
and
c/o Telio
160 Pears Avenue,
Suite 400
Toronto, Ontario
Canada M5R IT2
Tel: +1 416 968 2020
and

South Pacific Fabrics
195 Paddington Street
Paddington, NSW 2021
Australia
Tel: +61 29 327 7222
Fax: +61 29 327 7686
and
St Leger & Viney
St Leger & Viney House
8 Kramer Road, Sandton
South Africa
Tel: +27 11 444 6722
Fax: +27 11 444 6759

Classic Revivals
Suite 534
1 Design Centre Place
Boston, Massachusetts
USA 02210
Tel: +1 617 574 9030
Fax: +1 617 574 9027
www.classicrevivals.com
(Distributor of Borderline, Guy
Evans, John Boyd and
Mauny.)

Cole & Son
Lifford House
199 Eade Road
London N4 1DN
UK
Tel: +44 (0)20 8442 8844
Fax: +44 (0)20 8802 0033
www.cole-and-son.com
(Distributed in USA by Lee Jofa.)
and
G10 Chelsea Harbour
Design Centre
UK (see p401)
Tel: +44 (0)20 7376 4628
Fax: +44 (0)20 7376 4631

Colefax and Fowler
Head office:
19-23 Grosvenor Hill
London W1K 3QD
UK
Tel: +44 (0)20 7493 2231
Fax: +44 (0)20 7499 9910
For stockists:
+44 (0)20 8887 6400
(Distributor of Manuel
Canovas, Jane Churchill and
Larsen.)
and
G2 Chelsea Harbour Design
Centre
UK (see p401)
Tel: +44 (0)20 7351 0666
Fax: +44 (0)20 7351 0655
and
For details of US showrooms
(trade only):
Cowtan & Tout
76 9th Avenue
New York, New York
USA 10011
Tel: +1 212 647 6900
and
For UK & worldwide
distributors:
Tel: +44 (0)20 8874 6468

Coloroll
CWV Group Ltd.
PO Box 15
Talbot Road, Hyde

Cheshire SK14 4EJ
UK
Tel: +44 (0)161 368 4000
Fax: +44 (0)161 368 3430
www.cwvgroup.com

Colourman Paints
The Bowjy
Trevowhan
Morvah
Penzance
Cornwall TR20 8YT
UK
Tel: +44 (0)1736 787420
Fax: +44 (0)1736 788518

(G.) Comoglio
22 rue Jacob
Paris 75006
France
Tel: +33 143 54 65 86
Fax: +33 140 51 70 56

Craig & Rose
Unit 16/17 Stewartfield
Newhaven Road
Edinburgh EH6 5RQ
UK
Tel: +44 (0)131 555 3773
Fax: +44 (0)131 555 5777
and
Unit 8
Halbath Industrial Estate
Crossgates Road
Halbeath
Dunfermline
Fife KY11 7EG
UK
Tel: +44 (0)1383 740000
Fax: +44 (0)1383 740010

Craven Dunnill Jackfield
Jackfield Tile Museum
Ironbridge Gorge
Shropshire TF8 7LJ
UK
Tel: +44 (0)1952 882840
Fax: +44 (0)1952 884487
www.cravendunnill-jackfield.co.uk

Création Baumann Fabrics
World's End Studios
134 Lots Road
London SW11 ORJ
UK
Tel: +44 (0)20 7349 7022
Fax: +44 (0)20 7349 7024
www.creationbaumann.com
and
Création Baumann USA Inc.
114 North Centre Avenue
Rockville Centre
New York, New York
USA 11570
Tel: +1 516 764 7431
Fax: +1 516 678 6848
and
Tessuti Uno
Création Baumann
Designer's Walk Bldg 2
320 Davenport Road
Toronto, Ontario
Canada M5R 1K6
Tel: +1 416 922 0126
Fax: +1 416 922 0441
and
Création Baumann Pty. Ltd.

214 Nicholson Street
PO Box 89
Fitzroy, 3065
Melbourne Vic.
Australia
Tel: +61 39 419 6799
Fax: +61 39 417 4213
and
James Dunlop Textiles Ltd.
PO Box 1636
Christchurch
New Zealand
Tel: +64 3366 8681
Fax: +64 3366 8790
and
Swisstime Hong Kong Ltd.
19th Floor
Lee Fund Centre
31 Wong Chuk Hang Road
Aberdeen
Hong Kong
Tel: +852 2870 0096
Fax: +852 2554 2590
and
Tokyo Design Center 25-19
Higashi-Gotanda
5 chome
Shinagawa-ku
Tokyo 141-0022
Japan
Tel: +81 35 423 5036
Fax: +81 35 423 5047

Crown
Crown House
PO Box 37
Hollins Road
Darwen
Lancashire BB3 0BG
UK
Tel: +44 (0)1254 704951
Fax: +44 (0)1254 774414
www.crownpaint.co.uk
(Owned by Akzo Nobel
Decorative Coatings Ltd.)
www.akzonobel.com
and
Akzo Nobel Decorative
Coatings Inc
117 Brush Street
Pontiac, Michigan
USA 48341
Tel: +1 248 253 2495
Fax: +1 248 333 8775

Crowson
Crowson House
Bellbrock Park
Uckfield
East Sussex TN22 1QZ
UK
Tel: +44 (0)1825 761044
Fax: +44 (0)1825 764283
www.crowsonfabrics.com
(Distributor of Monkwell, The
Design Archives and Hill &
Knowles.)
and
Showroom:
227 Kings Road
London SW3 5EJ
UK
Tel: +44 (0)20 7823 3294
Fax: +44 (0)20 7376 7767
and
Monkwell in the USA:
Tel: +1 516 752 7600

and
Monkwell and Crowson in
Australia and New Zealand:
Tel: +61 295 189 911
and
Crowson (Australia) Pty. Ltd.
35-39 Mountain Street
Ultimo 2007
NSW
Australia
Tel: +61 29 211 7751
Fax: +61 29 211 7752
and
Crowson (New Zealand) Ltd.
PO Box 1303
Auckland
New Zealand
Tel: 0800 440 559
Fax: 0800 440 576

Crucial Trading
PO Box 10469
Birmingham B46 1WB
UK
Tel: +44 (0)1675 743747
Fax: +44 (0)1675 433521
www.crucial-trading.com
and
Concepts International
83 Harbour Road
Port Washington, New York
USA 11050
Tel: +1 516 767 1110
Fax: +1 516 767 3019
(Also distributed in USA and
Canada by Stark Carpet
Corporation.)
and
Prestige Carpets (VIC) Pty. Ltd.
PO Box 334
Doveton
Vic. 3175
Australia
Tel: +61 39 792 1655
Fax: +61 39 792 1686
and
Fine Craft Co.
206012 Ebisu-Minami
Shibuya-Ku
Tokyo 150-0022
Japan
Tel: +81 33 792 3571
Fax: +81 33 792 3572
and
Deco Expression Private Ltd.
74/74a Neil Road
088839 Singapore
Tel: +65 6 225 8433
Fax: +65 6 225 8455

Cuprinol
Wexham Road
Slough
Berkshire SL2 5DS
UK
Tel: +44 (0)1753 550555
www.cuprinol.co.uk

Cy-Près
14 Bells Close
Brigstock
Kettering
Northamptonshire NN14 3JG
UK
Tel: +44 (0)1536 373158
Fax: +44 (0)1536 373431

D

Dacrylate Paints
Lime Street
Kirkby in Ashfield
Nottingham NG17 8AL
UK
Tel: +44 (0)1623 753845
Fax: +44 (0)1623 757151
www.dacrylate.co.uk

Dalsouple Direct Ltd.
PO Box 140
Bridgewater
Somerset TA5 1HT
UK
Tel: +44 (0)1984 667233
Fax: +44 (0)1984 667366
www.dalsouple.com
(Some suppliers do mail
order.)

Daltile
7834 CF Hawn Frwy
Dallas, Texas
USA 75217
Tel: +1 214 398 1411
Fax: +1 214 309 4480
www.daltile.com
and
470 Rowntree Dairy Road
Woodbridge, Ontario
Canada L4L 8H2
Tel: +1 905 850 4390
Fax: +1 905 850 4398

David Oliver Ltd.
5 Elystan Street
London SW3 3NT
UK
Tel: +1 44 (0)20 7823 7755
Fax: +1 44 (0)20 7823 7766
www.paintlibrary.co.uk
and
Fonthill Ltd.
979 Third Avenue
New York, New York
USA 10022
Tel: +1 212 755 6700
Fax: +1 212 371 2358
(Distributes Etro, Ottilie
Stevenson, Thomas Dare;
Alexander Beauchamp;
Neisha Crosland; Paper
Library; Wendy Cushing)
and
Hinson & Company
Space B-690
8687 Melrose Avenue
Los Angeles, California
USA 90069
Tel: +1 310 659 1400
Fax: +1 310 659 0104
and
Primavera
160 Pears Avenue #210
Toronto, Ontario
Canada M5R 1T2
Tel: +1 416 921 3334
Fax: +1 416 921 3227

De Gournay
112 Old Church Street
Chelsea
London SW3 6EP
UK
Tel: +44 (0)20 7823 7316

Fax: +44 (0)20 7823 7475
www.degournay.com
and
Christopher Norman Inc.
10th Floor
41 West 25th Street
New York, New York
USA 10010
Tel: +1 212 647 0303
Fax: +1 212 647 0369

De Le Cuona Designs
Head office:
The Old Stables
9–10 Osborne Mews
Windsor SL4 3DE
UK
Tel: +44 (0)1753 830301
Fax: +44 (0)1753 620455
www.delecuona.co.uk
and
Shop and trade showroom:
150 Walton Street
London SW3 2JJ
UK
Tel: +44 (0)20 7584 7677
Fax: +44 (0)20 7838 1059

Dedar
(Distributed by Mary Fox Linton.)

Deralam Laminates
West Coast Park
Bradley Lane, Standish
Wigan
Lancashire WN6 0YR
UK
Tel: +44 (0)1257 478540
Fax: +44 (0)1257 478550

The Design Archives
Crowson House
Bellbrock Park, Uckfield
East Sussex TN22 1QZ
UK
Tel: +44 (0)1825 747901
Fax: +44 (0)1825 764517
(Distributed by Crowson.)

Designers Guild
Head office:
3 Olaf Street
London W11 4BE
UK
Tel: +44 (0)20 7243 7300
Fax: +44 (0)20 7243 7320
www.designersguild.com
(Distributed in USA by Osborne & Little; distributor of Cath Kidston outside the UK.)
and
Designers Guild Fabric & Wallpaper (Australia)
Head office and showroom:
79 Frenchmans Road
Randwick NSW 2031
Australia
Tel: +61 2 9326 5111
and
Icon Textiles Ltd.
Level 2 155–165 The Strand
Parnell, Auckland
New Zealand
Tel: +64 9302 1652
Fax: +64 9375 2855

Dominic Crinson
The Digitile Showroom
15 Redchurch Street
London E2 7DJ
UK
Tel: +44 (0)20 7613 2783
Fax: +44 (0)8700 468 198
www.digitile.co.uk
(Showroom visits by appointment.)

Domus Tiles
1 Canterbury Court
6 Camberwell New Road
London SE5 0TG
UK
Tel: +44 (0)20 7091 1500
Fax: +44 (0)20 7091 1501
www.domustiles.co.uk

Donghia
G23 Chelsea Harbour Design Centre
UK (see p401)
Tel: +44 (0)20 7823 3456
Fax: +44 (0)20 7376 5758
www.donghia.com
(Distributor of Anya Larkin.)
and
Donghia Furniture/Textiles Ltd.
485 Broadway
New York, New York
USA 10013
Tel : +1 212 925 2777
Fax: +1 212 925 4819
and
South Pacific Fabrics
195 Paddington Street
Paddington
NSW 2021
Australia
Tel: +61 2 9327 7222
Fax: +61 2 9327 3311
and
Atelier Textiles
55 Boston Road
Mt Eden
Auckland
New Zealand
Tel: +64 9373 3866
Freephone: 0800 283 543
Fax: +64 9373 3566
and
Mavromac Pty. Ltd. (Textiles)
PO Box 76178
Wendywood 2144
South Africa
Tel: +27 11 444 1584
Fax: +27 11 444 1541
and
Altfield Enterprises
Nine Queen's Road
#605 Central
Hong Kong
Tel: +852 2524 3318
Fax: +852 2524 5676
and
Tomita & Co. Ltd.
2-3-16 Kyobashi
Chuo-Ku
Tokyo 104-0031
Japan
Tel: +81 33 273 7555
Fax: +81 33 273 7577

Dulux
Customer Care Centre

ICI Paints
Wexham Road
Slough SL2 5DS
UK
Tel: 01753 550 000/555
www.dulux.co.uk
www.dulux.com
and
925 Euclid Avenue
Cleveland, Ohio
USA 44115
Tel: +1 216 344 8000
www.iciduluxpaints.com

E

Elite Tiles
Elite House
The Broadway
London NW9 7BP
UK
Tel: +44 (0)20 8202 1806
Fax: +44 (0)20 8202 8608

Elizabeth Eaton
85 Bourne Street
London SW1W 8HF
UK
Tel: +44 (0)20 7730 2262
Fax: +44 (0)20 7730 7294

Elon
Head Office:
12 Silver Road
White City
London W12 7SG
UK
Tel: +44 (0)20 8932 3000
Fax: +44 (0)20 8932 3001
www.elon.co.uk
and
Showroom:
66 Fulham Road
South Kensington
London SW3 6HH
UK
Tel: +44 (0)20 7460 4600
Fax: +44 (0)20 7460 4601

F

Fardis
Omnova Solutions France SA
Touranjou/Fardis
33 quai de Dion Bouton
92814 Puteaux, Cedex
France
Tel: +33 149 07 86 20
Fax: +33 149 06 02 77

Farrow & Ball
Uddens Trading Estate
Wimborne
Dorset BH21 7NL
UK
Tel: +44 (0)1202 876141
Fax: +44 (0)1202 873793
www.farrow-ball.com
(Search online for local suppliers.)
and
Farrow & Ball Inc., USA
Tel: +1 845 369 4912
Fax: +1 845 369 4913
usasales@farrow-ball.com
and
Farrow & Ball (Canada)
1054 Yonge Street

Toronto, Ontario
Canada
Tel: +1 416 920 0200
Toll-free: +1 877 363 1040
Fax: +1 416 920 1223

Finnaren & Haley
901 Washington Street
Conshohocken,
Pennsylvania
USA 19428-2390
Tel: +1 610 825 1900
Fax: +1 610 825 1184
www.fhpaint.com

Fired Earth p.l.c.
Twyford Mill
Oxford Road
Adderbury
Oxon OX17 3HP
UK
Tel: +44 (0)1295 812088
Fax: +44 (0)1295 812189
www.firedearth.com
(Distributor of Froyle Tiles and Lowitz & Company.)
and
2404 Dominion Center
43–59 Queens Road East
Wanchai
Hong Kong
Tel: +852 286 13864

Froyle Tiles
Froyle Pottery
Lower Froyle
Alton
Hampshire GU34 4LL
UK
Tel: +44 (0)1420 23693
Fax: +44 (0)1420 22797
www.froyletiles.co.uk
(Distributed by Fired Earth and Paris Ceramics.)

G

G.P. & J. Baker
2 Stinsford Road
Poole
Dorset BH17 0SW
UK
Tel: +44 (0)1202 266 700
Fax: +44 (0)1202 266 701
www.gpjbaker.co.uk
(Distributor of Parkertex; distributed in USA by Lee Jofa.)
and
Showroom:
G18–19 Chelsea Harbour Design Centre
UK (see p401)
Tel: +44 (0)20 7351 7760
Fax: +44 (0)20 7351 7752
and
Charles Radford Furnishings Pty. Ltd.
8–18 Glass Street
Richmond 3121
Australia
Tel: +61 39 429 6122
Fax: +61 39 427 1587
and
Icon Textiles
PO Box 9832
Newmarket
Auckland

New Zealand
Tel: +64 9302 1652
Fax: +64 9375 2855
and
Textile Iida Co. Limited
150-0011
1-25-11 Higashi
Shibuya-KLL
Tokyo
Japan
Tel: +81 03 5468 5001
Fax: +81 03 5468 5075
www.textileiida.co.jp

Gainsborough Silk Weaving
Alexandra Road
Sudbury
Suffolk CO10 2XH
UK
Tel: +44 (0)1787 372081
Fax: +44 (0)1787 881785
and
16 Coda Centre
189 Munster Road
London SW6 6AW
UK
Tel: +44 (0)20 7386 7153
Fax: +44 (0)20 7386 9220
and
Travers & Company
504 East 74th Street
New York, New York
USA 10021
Tel: +1 212 772 2778
Fax: +1 212 888 7800
(Also distributed in USA by Lee Jofa.)
and
Bilbrough & Co. Ltd.
Designers Walk
326 Davenport Road
Toronto, Ontario
Canada M5R 1K6
Tel: +1 416 960 1611
Fax: +1 416 960 5742
and
St James (Wardlaw) Pty. Ltd.
230–232 Auburn
Hawthorn, Vic. 3122
Australia
Tel: +61 39 819 1569
Fax: +61 39 819 4179
and
Claremont House Ltd.
35 Sherwood Road
off Camp Road
Singapore 1025
Tel: +65 474 0377
Fax: +65 474 0316

Galbraith & Paul
116 Shurs Lane
Philadelphia, Pennsylvania
USA 19127
Tel: +1 215 508 0800
Fax: +1 215 508 0866
(Distributed in the UK by Nina Campbell.)

Garin
2/9 Chelsea Harbour Design Centre
UK (see p401)
Tel: +44 (0)20 7351 6496
Fax: +44 (0)20 7351 3761
www.garin1820.com
and

C/Quart 45–49 Moncada
CP 46113 Valencia
Spain
Tel: +34 96 130 90 23
Fax: +34 96 139 58 64

George Spencer Designs
29 Chapel Street
London SW1X 7DD
UK
Tel: +44 (0)20 7235 1501
Fax: +44 (0)20 7235 1502
www.georgespencer.com
(Distributed in USA by Claremont Furnishing Fabrics.)

Glant
(Distributed in the UK by Mary Fox Linton.)

Graham & Brown
Harwood Street
Blackburn
Lancashire BB1 3BR
UK
Tel: +44 (0)1254 661122
Fax: +44 (0)1254 680849

Grand Illusions
41 Crown Road
St Margaret's
Twickenham TW1 3EJ
UK
Tel: +44 (0)20 8607 9446
Fax: +44 (0)20 8744 2017
www.grandillusions.co.uk

Guy Evans
(Distributed by Classic Revivals.)

H

H. & R. Johnson
Harewood Street
Tunstall
Stoke-on-Trent ST6 5JZ
UK
Tel: +44 (0)1782 575575
Fax: +44 (0)1782 577379
(Distributor of Minton Hollins.)
and
W. May & Co.
PO Box 234
Brielle, New Jersey
USA 08730
Tel: +1 732 528 2248
Fax: +1 732 528 2249
and
PO Box 50518
Dubai
United Arab Emirates
Tel: +971 4 398 6004
Fax: +971 4 398 7006

Hamilton Weston Wallpapers
18 St Mary's Grove
Richmond
Surrey TW9 1UY
UK
Tel: +44 (0)20 8940 4850
Fax: +44 (0)20 8332 0296
www.hamiltonweston.com
(Distributed in USA by Classic Revivals; distributor of Bradbury & Bradbury.)
and

Brook Street Trading
50 Bayswater Road
Elizabeth Bay
Sydney 20011
NSW
Australia
Tel: +61 29 380 6502
Fax: +61 29 380 6503

The Hardwood & Natural Stone Flooring Company
Fisherton Mill
59–61 Fisherton Street
Salisbury
Wiltshire SP2 7SU
UK
Tel: +44 (0)1722 415000
Fax: +44 (0)1722 414816
www.woodstonefloors.co.uk
(Online shopping; overseas delivery.)

Harlequin
Ladybird House
Beeches Road
Loughborough
Leicestershire L11 2HA
UK
Tel: +44 (0)1509 225000
Fax: +44 (0)1509 225001
www.harlequin.uk.com
and
Harlequin USA
5100 Highlands Parkway
Smyrna, Georgia
USA 30082
Tel: +1 678 303 9999
Fax: +1 678 303 8250
and
Beauport Wallcoverings
1400 Graham Bell
Boucherville, Quebec
Canada J4B 6E5
Tel: +1 450 641 4477
Fax: +1 450 641 4585
and
Wilson Fabrics & Wallcoverings
Level 1
10–14 Waterloo Street
Surrey Hills NSW 2010
Australia
Tel: +61 2 597 7200
Fax: +61 2 597 7211
and
Malcolm Fabrics Ltd.
PO Box 5460
Papanui
Christchurch
New Zealand
Tel: +64 3352 8668
Fax: +64 3352 6622
and
Pandora
12–14, 8th Floor Block A
Eldex Industrial Building
21 Ma Tau Wei Road
Hung Hom Kowloon
Hong Kong
Tel: +852 2773 6113
Fax: +852 2764 5125
and
Phoenix International
3-26-20 Shibuya-Ku
1500-0002 Tokyo
Japan
Tel: +81 35 778 3511

Fax: +81 35 778 3512
and
Bilchik Wallpapers Pty. Ltd.
33 Height Street
Doorn Fontaine 2094
Johannesburg 2000
South Africa
Tel: +27 11 402 2800
Fax: +27 11 402 1151
and
Goodrich
Goodrich Building
16 Tampines Street
92 Singapore 528873
Tel: +65 787 8787
Fax: +65 788 7733

Henry Newbery & Co.
18 Newman Street
London W1T 1AB
UK
Tel: +44 (0)20 7636 5970
Fax: +44 (0)20 7436 6406
www.henrynewbery.com
and
Christopher Hyland Inc.
Suite 1710, D&D Building
USA (see p401)
Tel: +1 212 688 6121
Fax: +1 212 688 6176
and
Davan Port Ltd.
404 Pleasant View Court
Copaigue, New York
USA 11726
Tel: +1 631 225 1811
Fax: +1 631 225 0879
(Also distributed in USA by Lee Jofa.)
and
Bilborough & Co. Ltd.
326 Davenport Road
Toronto, Ontario
Canada M5R 1K6
Tel: +1 416 960 1611
Fax: +1 416 960 5742
and
Innovations
14 Kembla Way
Willetton
Perth
WA 6155
Australia
Tel: +61 89 457 5522
Fax: +61 89 354 3094
(Distributed in Hong Kong by Altfield Ltd.)

Hill & Knowles
(Distributed in the UK only by Crowson.)

Historic Floors of Oshkosh
911 East Main Street
Winneconne, Wisconsin
USA 45986
Tel: +1 920 582 9977
Fax: +1 920 582 9971
www.oshkoshfloors.com

Hodsoll McKenzie
52 Pimlico Road
London SW1W 8LP
UK
Tel: +44 (0)20 7254 9940
Fax: +44 (0)20 7254 2033
www.hodsollmckenzie.com

and
Christopher Norman Inc.
41 West 25th Street,
10th Floor
New York, New York
USA 10010
Tel: +1 212 647 0303
Fax: +1 212 647 0369

Holkham Linseed Paints
The Clock Tower
Longlands
Holkham Park
Wells-Next-The-Sea
Norfolk NR23 1RU
UK
Tel: +44 (0)1328 711 348
Fax: +44 (0)1328 710 368
www.holkhamlinseedpaints.co.uk

Howe
93 Pimlico Road
London SW1W 8PH
UK
Tel: +44 (0)20 7730 7987
Fax: +44 (0)20 7730 0157
www.howelondon.com

Hugh Mackay
PO Box 1
St Johns Road
Meadowfield Industrial Estate
Durham DH7 8YQ
UK
Tel: +44 (0)191 378 4444
Fax: +44 (0)191 378 4141
www.hughmackay.com
and
Maeve Fegan
767 Lexington Avenue,
Suite 402
New York, New York
USA 10021
Tel: +1 212 355 7053
Fax: +1 212 355 6722
(See website for list of outlets)
and
Wes Friesen & Associates
Suite 367
151–32500 South Fraser Way
Abbotsford, British Columbia
Canada V2T 4W1
Tel: +1 604 855 5186
Fax: +1 604 855 6071
and
Austpacific Investments Ltd.
Carpet Consultants Division
16th Floor Tianjin Building
167 Connaught Road West
Hong Kong
Tel: +852 2527 2125
Fax: +852 2861 3225
and
Contract Carpets Japan Ltd.
Checker Building
5–29 Akasaka, 8 Chrome,
Minato-Ku
Tokyo 107
Japan
Tel: +81 33 405 5281
Fax: +81 33 405 6823

Ian Mankin
109 Regents Park Road
London NW1 8UR
UK

Tel: +44 (0)20 7722 0997
Fax: +44 (0)20 7722 2159
and
Showroom:
271 Wandsworth Bridge Road
London SW6 2TX
UK
Tel: +44 (0)20 7371 8825

Ian Sanderson
PO Box 148
Newbury
Berkshire RG15 9DW
UK
Tel: +44 (0)1635 33188
Fax: +44 (0)1635 45070
and
Showroom:
2/23 Chelsea Harbour
    Design Centre
UK (see p401)
Tel: +44 (0)20 7352 6919

The Imperial Home Décor
Group (IHDG)
Belgrave Mills
Belgrave Road
Darwen
Lancashire BB3 2RR
UK
Tel: +44 (0)1254 870700
Fax: +44 (0)1254 873340
www.ihdg.co.uk
and
IHDG Inc.
23645 Mercantile Road
Cleveland, Ohio
USA 44122
Tel: +1 888 608 5943
Fax: +1 800 444 7865
www.ihdg.com

Interdesign UK
G30 Chelsea Harbour
    Design Centre
UK (see p401)
Tel: +44 (0)20 7376 5272
Fax: +44 (0)20 7376 3020
www.interdesignuk.com

The Isle Mill Ltd.
Tower House
Ruthvenfield Road
Inveralmond
Perth PH1 3UN
UK
Tel: +44 (0)1738 609000
Fax: +44 (0)1738 604010
(A division of MacNaughton Holdings Ltd.)
and
Macnaughtons of Pitlochry
Mail Order Department
Station Road
Pitlochry
Perthshire
Scotland PH16 5AF
UK
Tel: +44 (0)1796 472722
Fax: +44 (0)1796 474266
www.macnaughton-group.com

Ivo Prints
Unit 3 Trident Way
International Trading Estate
Southall
Middlesex UB2 5LF

UK
Tel: +44 (0)20 8574 7943
Fax: +44 (0)20 8571 7664
www.ivo.co.uk

J

J. Robert Scott
Corporate office:
500 North Oak Street
Inglewood, California
USA 90302
Tel: +1 310 680 4300
Customer service:
Toll-free: +1 800 322 4910
Fax: +1 310 680 4424
www.jrobertscott.com
and
Showroom:
D&D Building, 2nd Floor
USA (see p401)
Tel: +1 212 755 4910
Fax: +1 212 755 4957
and
Telio et Cie
1407 rue de la Montagne
Montreal, Quebec
Canada H3G 1Z3
Tel: +1 514 842 9116
Fax: +1 514 842 3728
and
2/19 Chelsea Harbour
    Design Centre
UK (see p401)
Tel: +44 (0)20 7376 4705
Fax: +44 (0)20 7376 4706

J.W. Bollom
PO Box 78
Croydon Road
Beckenham
Kent BR3 4BL
UK
Tel: +44 (0)20 8658 2299
Fax: +44 (0)20 8658 8672
www.bollom.com

Jab International
Furnishings Ltd.
1/15–16 Chelsea Harbour
    Design Centre
UK (see p401)
Tel: +44 (0)20 7349 9323
Fax: +44 (0)20 7349 9282
www.jab.de
and
Stroheim & Romann Inc.
155 East 56th Street
New York, New York
USA 10022
Tel: +1 212 486 1500
Fax: +1 212 980 1782
and
JAB Anstoetz Inc.
326 Davenport Road
Toronto, Ontario
Canada M5R 1K6
Tel: +1 416 927 9192
Showroom: +1 416 920 3020
Fax: +1 416 927 7510
and
Seneca Textiles Ltd.
317 High Street
3181 Prahan
Vic.
Australia
Tel: +61 3 9529 2788
Fax: +61 3 9529 4388

and
Seneca Textiles (NZ) Ltd.
14 Heather Street, Parnell
37–702 Auckland
New Zealand
Tel: +64 9309 6411
Fax: +64 9309 8866
and
National Trading Inc.
4-5-2, Minami-Azab 4-chome
106 Minato-ku
Tokyo
Japan
Tel: +81 33 442 4791
Fax: +81 33 447 4048
and
TD Fabrics Pte. Ltd.
No. 21 Orchard Boulevard
#01-25 Park House
248645 Singapore
Tel: +65 6295 5115
Fax: +65 6295 5132
and
Chelsea Harbour Fabrics
Unit 17, Gallagher Place
Suttie Road, Midrand
1683 Midrand
South Africa
Tel: +27 11 315 9822
Fax: +27 11 315 9824

Jack Lenor Larsen
(see Larsen)

Jane Churchill
151 Sloane Street
London SW1X 9BX
UK
Tel: +44 (0)20 7730 9847
Fax: +44 (0)20 7259 9189
(Distributed in the UK and USA by Colefax and Fowler.)

Jane Knapp
6 Chatham Row
Walcot, Bath
Avon BA1 5BS
Tel/Fax: +44 (0)1225 463468
www.janeknapp.com
and
Walcot Inc.
108 Walcot Street
Bath, BA1 5BG
UK
Tel: +44 (0)122 544 4404
Fax: +44 (0)122 544 8163

Jason D'Souza
1/6 Chelsea Harbour Design
    Centre
UK (see p401)
Tel: +44 (0)20 7351 4440
Fax: +44 (0)20 7351 4396
www.jasondsouza.co.uk
and
Nancy Corzine
256 West Ivory Avenue
Inglewood, Los Angeles,
California
USA 90302
Tel: +1 310 672 6775
Fax: +1 310 672 7160

Jaymart Rubber & Plastics
Ltd.
Woodlands Trading Estate
Eden Vale Road

Westbury
Wiltshire BA13 3QS
UK
Tel: +44 (0)1373 864926
Fax: +44 (0)1373 858454
Jaymart@compuserve.com

Jim Thompson
(Distributed by Mary Fox Linton.)

Joanna Wood
(see Lewis & Wood)

John Boyd Textiles
Higher Flax Mills
Castle Cary
Somerset BA7 7DY
UK
Tel: +44 (0)1963 350451
Fax: +44 (0)1963 351078
www.johnboydtextiles.co.uk
and
Alton-Brooke
2/25 Chelsea Harbour
    Design Centre
UK (see p401)
Tel: +44 (0)20 7376 7008
Fax: +44 (0)20 7376 7009
(Distributed in USA by Classic Revivals, F. Schumacher & Co., Scalamandré, Stark Carpet Corporation, Lee Jofa and Brunschwig & Fils.)
and
Herbert J. Stein & Richard
    Gladstein
979 Third Avenue
New York, New York
USA 10022
Tel: +1 212 688 1802
Fax: +1 212 759 7565
and
William Switzer & Associates
6–611 Alexander Street
Vancouver, British Columbia
Canada V6A 1E1
Tel: +1 604 255 5911
Fax: +1 604 255 5931
and
Telio & Cie
1407 rue de la Montagne
Montreal, Quebec
Canada HG3 1Z3
Tel: +1 514 842 9116
Fax: +1 514 842 3728
and
South Pacific Fabrics
195 Paddington Street
Paddington
NSW 2021
Australia
Tel: +61 2 9327 7222
Fax: +61 2 9327 3311
and
Rata
44 Ghuznee Street
Wellington
New Zealand
Tel/Fax: +64 4801 9589

John Lewis
Head office:
John Lewis p.l.c.
171 Victoria Street
London SW1E 5NN
UK
Tel: +44 (0)20 7828 1000

(Distributor of Louis de Poortere.)
and
Customer Services:
John Lewis Direct
PO Box 369
Exeter EX1 1DH
UK
Tel: +44 (0)8456 049 049
Fax: +44 (0)8456 049 050
www.johnlewis.com
(See website for list of stores.)

John Oliver Ltd.
33 Pembridge Road
London W11 3HG
UK
Tel: +44 (0)20 7221 6466
Fax: +44 (0)20 7727 5555

John Wilmans
(See Wilman Interiors.)

Junckers
Wheaton Court Commercial
    Centre
Wheaton Road
Witham
Essex CM8 3UJ
UK
Tel: +44 (0)1376 534700
Fax: +44 (0)1376 514401
www.junckers.co.uk
and
Junckers Hardwood Inc.
4920 E. Landon Drive
Anaheim, California
USA 92807
Toll-free: +1 800 878 9663
Tel: +1 714 777 6430
Fax: +1 714 777 6436
www.junckershardwood.com

K

Kährs UK Ltd.
Unit 2 West
68 Bognor Road
Chichester
West Sussex PO19 2NS
UK
Tel: +44 (0)1243 778747
Fax: +44 (0)1243 531237
www.kahrs.se
and
Kährs International Inc.
Oasis Office Center,
Suite 1000
940 Center Circle
Altamonte Springs, Florida
USA 32714
Tel: +1 407 260 9910
Fax: +1 407 260 9933
and
ABC Trading Co. Ltd.
12–14, 2-Chome
Nagata-Cho
JP-Chiyoda-Ku
Tokyo 100
Japan
Tel: +81 3 3507 7077
Fax: +81 3 3581 4819
and
Jocels Marketing Pte. Ltd.
Blk 6003 #01-556
Ang Mo Kio Industrial Park 3
SG 569455
Singapore
and

Interior Wooden Floors CC.
Konsulentvägen 17
SE-237 32 Bjärred
South Africa
Tel: +46 46 29 12 60
Fax: +46 46 29 24 40

Karndean Ltd.
Crabapple Way
Vale Business Park
Evesham
Worcestershire WR11 1GP
UK
Tel: +44 (0)1386 49902
Fax: +44 (0)1386 761249
www.karndean.com
and
Karndean International LLC
1951 Lincoln Highway
North Versailles,
Pennsylvania
USA 15137
Tel: +1 412 829 3922
Fax: +1 412 829 3920
and
Karndean Australia Pty. Ltd.
91 Rushdale Street
Knoxfield
Vic. 3180
Australia
Tel: +61 3 9763 5588
Fax: +61 3 9763 1625
and
Karndean International NZ
Unit A, 73 Greenmount Drive
East Tamaki
Auckland
New Zealand
Tel: +64 9273 5430
Fax: +64 9273 5435

Kenneth Clark Ceramics
The North Wing
Southover Grange
Southover Road
Lewes
East Sussex BN7 1TP
UK
Tel: +44 (0)1273 476761
Fax: +44 (0)1273 479565
www.kennethclarkceramics.co.uk
(Mail order available.)

Kentucky Wood Floors
15412 Highway 62
Charlestown, Indiana
USA 47111
Tel: +1 502 451 6024
Fax: +1 502 451 6027
www.kentuckywood.com
and
Burnside Flooring
31 Sterns Court
Dartmouth, Nova Scotia
Canada B3B 1W7
Tel: +1 902 468 5576
www.burnsideflooring.com
and
Rainleaf Flooring
1 Bridge Street
Bures
Suffolk CO8 5AD
UK
Tel: +44 (0)1787 229 986
www.rainleaf.com

Kievel Stone
Lower Farm
Lower Farm Lane
Ampfield
Hampshire S051 9BP
UK
Tel: +44 (0)17994 368865
Fax: +44 (0)1794 368914

Kirkstone
Head Office:
Kirkstone Quarries Ltd.
Skelwith Bridge
Ambleside
Cumbria LA22 9NN
UK
Tel: +44 (0)1539 433296
Fax: +44 (0)1539 434006
and
Showroom:
128 Walham Green Court
Moore Park Road
Fulham
London SW6 4DG
UK
Tel: +44 (0)20 7381 0424
Fax: +44 (0)20 7381 0434
www.kirkstone.com
(Distributed in USA by Walker
Zanger.)
and
Domestic Marble and Stone
Corporation
145 Hudson Street
New York, New York
USA 10013-2195
Tel: +1 212 343 3300
Fax: +1 212 343 3301
and
Acme Slate & Tile Company
780 Birchmont Road
Units 8/9
Scarborough, Ontario
Canada M1K 5H4
Tel: +1 416 293 3664
Fax: +1 416 293 3232
and
Artisan Marble Pty. Ltd.
Nirvana Street
Pendle Hill
NSW 2145
Australia
Tel: +61 2 9631 5038
Fax: +61 2 9631 2717

Knowles & Christou
116 Lots Road
London SW10 ORJ
UK
Tel: +44 (0)20 7394 2101
Fax: +44 (0)20 7394 2131
www.knowles-christou.com

Kravet London
G/17 Chelsea Harbour
Design Centre
UK (see p401)
Tel: +44 (0)20 7795 0110
Fax: +44 (0)20 7349 0678
www.kravet.com
and
Kravet Inc .
Corporate Headquarters:
225 Central Avenue South
Bethpage, New York
USA 11714
Tel: +1 516 293 2000

Toll-free: 1 800 645 9068
Fax: +1 516 293 2737
(Distributor of Andrew Martin
International.)
and
Tritex Fabrics Ltd.
106–611 Alexander Street
Vancouver, British Columbia
Canada V6A 1E1
Tel: +1 604 255 4242
Fax: +1 604 255 9255
and
Mokum Textiles
98 Barcon Avenue
Rushcutters Bay
Sydney NSW 2000
Australia
Tel: +61 2 9380 6188
Fax: +61 2 9380 6476
and
Mokum Textiles Ltd.
11 Cheshire Street
Parnell, Auckland
New Zealand
Tel: +64 9 379 3041
Fax: +64 9 377 5385
and
Ionia Ltd.
4th Flr 3-1-7 Yushima
Bunkyo-Ku, Tokyo 113 0034
Japan
Tel: +81 3 383 77792
Fax: +81 3 383 77793

L

Larsen
(previously known as Jack
Lenor Larsen.)
1/12–13 Chelsea Harbour
Design Centre
UK (see p401)
Tel: +44 (0)20 7352 0047
Fax: +44 (0)20 7349 0700
Stockists: +44 (0)20 8877 6400
(Distributed by Colefax and
Fowler.)
and
Cowtan & Tout Larsen
20 Vandam Street
New York, New York
USA 10013
Tel: +1 646 638 4201

LASSCO
Maltby Street, Bermondsey
London SE1 3PA
UK
Tel: +44 (0)20 7394 2101
Fax: +44 (0)20 7394 2131
www.lassco.co.uk

Laura Ashley Ltd.
27 Bagleys Lane
Fulham
London SW6 2QA
UK
Tel: +44 (0)20 7880 5100
Fax: +44 (0)20 7880 5200
and
Customer Services
Freepost SY1225
PO Box 19
Newtown
Powys SY16 1DZ
UK
Tel: +44 (0)870 562 2116

Fax: +44 (0)1686 622 183
www.lauraashley.com

LBC Hardwood Flooring
Unit 9, Knutsford Way
Sealand Road
Chester CH1 4NS
UK
Tel: +44 (0)1244 377811
Fax: +44 (0)1244 373678

Lee Jofa
Head Office:
Unit 5
Knighton Heath Industrial
Estate
851 Ringwood Road
Bournemouth
Dorset BH11 8NE
UK
Tel: +44 (0)1202 575457
Fax: +44 (0)1202 575723
www.leejofa.com
and
G/18–19 Chelsea Harbour
Design Centre
UK (see p401)
Tel: +44 (0)20 7351 7760
Fax: +44 (0)20 7351 7752
and
Lee Jofa Inc.
201 Central Avenue South
Bethpage, New York
USA 11714
Tel: +1 516 752 7600
Fax: +1 516 752 7623
and
D&D Building
USA (see p401)
Tel: +1 212 688 0444
Fax: +1 212 759 3658
(Distributor of Cole & Son,
G. P. & J. Baker,
Gainsborough Silk Weaving,
Henry Newbery & Co., John
Boyd, Monkwell and
Mulberry Home in the USA.)
and
Lee Jofa Canada
Donovan & Associates Inc.
Designers Walk
Suite 200
320 Davenport Road
Toronto, Ontario
Canada MSR 2K9
Tel: +1 416 921 1262
Fax: +1 416 921 7875
(Distributor of Mulberry Home.)
and
Mokum Textiles (Lee Jofa)
98 Barcon Avenue
Rushcutters Bay
Sydney NSW 2000
Australia
Tel: +61 2 9380 6188
Fax: +61 2 9380 6476

Lelièvre
1/19 Chelsea Harbour
Design Centre
UK (see p401)
Tel: +44 (0)20 7352 4798
Fax: +44 (0)20 7352 9569
www.lelievre-tissus.com
and
Stark Old World Weavers
979 Third Avenue

New York, New York
USA 10022
Tel: +1 212 752 9000
Fax: +1 212 758 4342
and
Telio & Cie
1407 rue de la Montagne
Montreal, Quebec
Canada HG3 1Z3
Tel: +1 514 842 9116
Fax: +1 514 842 3728
and
Order Imports Ltd.
11a Boundary Street
Rushcutter Bay
NSW 2011
Australia
Tel: +61 2 9360 3565
Fax: +61 2 9360 3572
and
Vivace Textiles
125 The Strand
Parnell
Auckland
New Zealand
Tel: +64 9 309 6271
Fax: +64 9 302 4833

Lennox Money Antiques Ltd.
93 Pimlico Road
London SW1W 8PH
UK
Tel: +44 (0)20 7730 3070
Fax: +44 (0)20 7259 9563
and
Classic Revivals Inc.
IDesign Center Place
Suite 534
Boston, Massachusetts
USA 02210
Tel: +1 617 574 9030
Fax: +1 617 574 9027
and
Boyac Decorative Furnishings
537 High Street
Prahran East
Vic. 3181
Australia
Tel: +61 3 9533 7833
Fax: +61 3 9533 8911
www.boyac.com.au

Lewis & Wood
(also known as Joanna Wood)
5 The Green
Uley
Gloucestershire GL11 5SN
UK
Tel: +44 (0)1453 860080
Fax: +44 (0)1453 860054
www.lewisandwood.co.uk

Liberon Waxes
Mountfield Industrial Estate
Learoyd Road
New Romney
Kent TN28 8XU
UK
Tel: +44 (0)1797 367555
Fax: +44 (0)1797 367575
www.woodfinishsupply.com
and
Liberon/Star Wood Finish
Supply
PO Box 86
Mendocino, California
USA 95460

Tel: +1 707 962 9480
Fax: +1 707 962 9484
www.liberonsupply.com

Liberty Furnishings
(Distributed by Osborne &
Little.)

Liz Induni Traditional Paints
11 Park Road
Swanage
Dorset BH19 2AA
UK
Tel: +44 (0)1929 423776

Louis de Poortere
William House
Clarendon Court, The Parade
Leamington Spa CV32 4AH
UK
Tel: +44 (0)1926 431200
Fax: +44 (0)1926 431525
www.finerugs.co.uk
(Distributed in the UK by
John Lewis.)
and
45 rue de la Royenne
B-7700 Mouscron
Belgium
Tel: +32 56 393 393
Fax: +32 56 393 317
and
136 Cass Street
Adairsville, Georgia
USA 30103
Tel: +1 866 537 7847
Fax: +1 866 537 2329

Lowitz & Company
4401 N. Ravenswood Avenue
Chicago, Illinois
USA 60640
Tel: +1 773 784 2628
Fax: +1 773 784-2656
www.lowitzandcompany.com
(Distributed in the UK by Fired
Earth.)

M

The Malabar Cotton Co. Ltd.
31–33 The South Bank
Business Centre
Ponton Road
London SW8 5BL
UK
Tel: +44 (0)20 7501 4200
Fax: +44 (0)20 7501 4210
National stockists:
+44 (0)20 7501 4200
www.malabar.co.uk
and
US stockists:
+1 877 MALABAR
and
Australian stockists:
+61 2 9660 5588
and
WH Bilbrough & Co. Ltd.
Designers Walk
362 Davenport Road
Toronto, Ontario
Canada M5R 1K6
Tel: +1 416 960 1611
Fax: +1 416 960 5742
and
Choi Designs
Unit 408

4/F Dominion Centre
43–59 Queens Road East
Wanchai
Hong Kong
Tel: +852 2866 0781
Fax: +852 2866 6099
and
The Penny Wise
5-3-6 1F Shiroganedai
Minato-Ku
Tokyo
Japan
Tel: +81 3 3449 4568
Fax: +81 3 3443 4312
and
Just The Place
19 Tanglin Road
02-03 Tanglin Shopping
Centre
1024 Singapore
Tel: +65 735 3389
Fax: +65 735 9959
and
Halogen International
8 Kramer Road
Kramerville
Johannesburg 2148
South Africa
Tel: +27 11 448 2060
Fax: +27 11 448 2065

Mannington Carpets
International
Unit 19
Leafield Trading Estate
Corsham
Wiltshire SN13 9SW
UK
Tel: +44 (0)1225 811476
Fax: +44 (0)1225 811427
www.mannington.com
and
Mannington Commercial
1844 U.S. Highway 41 S.E.
Calhoun, Georgia
USA 30701
Tel: +1 706 629 7301
Fax: +1 706 629 0705

Manuel Canovas
(Distributed by Colefax and
Fowler.)

Marble Flooring Specialists
Verona House
Filwood Road
Fishponds
Bristol BS16 3RY
UK
Tel: +44 (0)117 965 6565
Fax: +44 (0)117 965 6573
www.marbleflooring.co.uk
and
Mitre House
177 Regent Street
London W1R 7FB
UK
Tel: +44 (0)20 7287 1500
Fax: +44 (0)20 7287 1600

Marlborough Tiles
Head office & factory:
Elcot Lane
Marlborough
Wiltshire SN8 2AY
UK
Tel: +44 (0)1672 512422

Fax: +44 (0)1672 515791
www.marlboroughtiles.co.uk
(Search online for local supplier.)

Marley Floors
Dickley Lane
Lenham
Maidstone
Kent ME17 2QX
UK
Tel: +44 (0)1622 854040
Fax: +44 (0)1622 858549
www.marley.com
and
Floor Supply Distributing
N1802 Langley
Spokane, Washington
USA 99212
Tel: +1 509 535 9707
Fax: +1 509 535 0558
and
George Low Pty. Ltd.
PO Box 314
114 Woodlands Drive
Braeside
Vic. 3195
Australia
Tel: +61 395 874 222
Fax: +61 395 874 525
and
Compass Flooring Ltd.
The Flooring Technology
Centre
6580 Kestrel Road
Mississauga, Ontario
Canada L52 123
Tel: +1 905 564 1330
Fax: +1 905 564 0750
www.compassfloor.com
and
Nuplex Industries Ltd.
721 Great South Road
Penrose
Auckland
New Zealand
Tel: +64 579 2029
Fax: +64 525 3709
www.nuplex.co.nz

Marston & Langinger
192 Ebury Street
London SW1W 8UP
UK
Tel: +44 (0)207 881 5783
Fax: +44 (0)207 881 5755
www.marston-and-langinger.com
and
Factory shop:
George Edwards Road
Fakenham
Norfolk NR21 8NL
UK
Tel: +44 (0)1328 852540
Fax: +44 (0)1328 852552
and
105 Regency Park Drive
Agawam, Massachusetts
USA 10010
Tel: +1 212 575 0554
Fax: +1 212 840 0236

Marthe Armitage
1 Strand-on-the-Green
London W4 3PQ
UK
Tel: +44 (0)20 8994 0160

Marvic Textiles
Unit 11 Westpoint Trading
Estates
Alliance Road
London W3 0RA
UK
Tel: +44 (0)20 8993 0191
Fax: +44 (0)20 8993 1484
and
G26 Chelsea Harbour
Design Centre
UK (see p401)
Tel: 020 7352 3119
Fax: 020 7352 3135
www.marvictextiles.co.uk
and
Roger Arlington Inc.
D&D Building, Suite 1411
USA (see p401)
Tel: +1 212 752 5288
Fax: +1 212 935 5195
and
Seneca Textiles
317 High Street
Prahan
Melbourne
Vic. 3181
Australia
Tel: +61 3 9529 2788
Fax: +61 3 9529 4388
and
W. H. Bilbrough & Co. Ltd.
Designers Walk
326 Davenport Road
Toronto, Ontario
Canada M5R 1K6
Tel: +1 416 960 1611
Fax: +1 416 960 5742
and
Seneca Ltd.
14 Heather Street
PO Box 37–702
Parnell
Auckland
New Zealand
Tel: +64 9 309 6411
Fax: +64 9 309 8866

Mary Fox Linton
1/8–10 Chelsea Harbour
Design Centre
UK (see p401)
Tel: +44 (0)20 7351 9908
Fax: +44 (0)20 7351 0907
(Distributor of Jim Thompson, Glant and Dedar.)

Mauny
(Distributed in USA by Classic Revivals.)

The Maya Romanoff Corporation
1730 West Greenleaf
Chicago, Illinois
USA 60626
Tel: +1 312 465 6909
Fax: +1 312 465 7089
www.mayaromanoff.com
(Distributed in the UK by Altfield Ltd.)

Minton Hollins
(Distributed by H. & R. Johnson.)

Monkwell
Crowson House
Bellbrock Park
Uckfield
East Sussex TN22 1QZ
UK
Tel: +44 (0)1825 747901
Fax: +44 (0)1825 764517
(Distributed in the UK by Crowson; distributed in USA by Lee Jofa.)

Monterey Carpet Mills
3030 South Susan Street
Santa Ana, California
USA 92704
Toll-free: +1 800 678 4640
Fax: +1 714 557 0292
www.montereycarpets.com
(Distributed in the UK by Christy Trading.)

Montgomery Tomlinson Ltd.
Broughton Mill Road
Bretton
Cheshire CH4 0BY
UK
Tel: +44 (0)1244 661363
Fax: +44 (0)1244 661167
www.montgomery.co.uk
and
Marco Fabrics
155 Auburn Road
Hawthorn
Vic. 3122
Australia
Tel: +61 3 9882 7238
Fax: +61 3 9813 1568
and
Irvine Merchant Holdings Ltd.
116 Buchan Street
PO Box 2039
Christchurch
New Zealand
Tel: +64 3366 5113
Fax: +64 3366 5024

Morris & Co.
(95% of their archive is distributed by Sanderson.)

Mosquito
Amy Cushing
62 Lower Ham Road
Kingston-upon-Thames
Surrey KT2 5AW
UK
Tel: +44 (0)20 8715 5611
Fax: +44 (0)20 8949 4490

Mulberry Home
Kilver Court, Shepton Mallet
Somerset BA4 5NF
UK
Tel: +44 (0)1749 340500
Fax: +44 (0)1749 345532
www.mulberry.com
(Distributed in Canada and USA by Lee Jofa.)
and
Mulberry Home
322 Kings Road
London SW3 5UH
UK
Tel: +44 (0)20 7823 3455
Fax: +44 (0)20 7823 3329
and

Boyac Decorative Furnishings
537 High Street
Prahran East
Vic. 3181
Australia
Tel: +61 39 533 7833
Fax: +61 39 533 8911
www.boyac.com.au
and
St Leger & Viney Pty. Ltd.
(Lee Jofa)
PO Box 55508
Northlands 2116
Transvaal
South Africa
Tel: +27 11 444 6722
Fax: +27 11 444 6756
www.leejofa.com

N

Natural Wood Floor Co.
20 Smugglers Way
Wandsworth
London SW18 1EQ
UK
Tel: +44 (0)20 8871 9771
Fax: +44 (0)20 8877 0273
www.naturalwoodfloor.co.uk
Email:
sales@naturalwoodfloor.co.uk

New Castle Delft
Charles S. Allen
25b Hoult's Estate
Walker Road
Newcastle upon Tyne NE6 1AB
UK
Tel/Fax: +44 (0)191 224 2323
www.newcastledelft.com

Nice Irma's
Unit 2
Finchley Industrial Centre
879 High Road
London N12 8QA
UK
Tel: +44 (0)20 8343 9766
Fax: +44 (0)20 8343 9590
www.niceirmas.co.uk
(Online ordering.)

Nicholas Herbert
118 Lots Road
London SW10 0RJ
UK
Tel: +44 (0)20 7376 5596
Fax: +44 (0)20 7376 5572
www.nicholasherbert.com
and
Travers & Co.
D&D Building
USA (see p401)
Tel: +1 212 888 7900
Fax: +1 212 752 3837
(fabric 'Le Pecheur 113' only)
and
Claremont Inc.
139 East 57th Street
New York, New York
USA 10022
Tel: +1 212 486 1252
Fax: +1 212 486 1253
(Fabric 'Corinthia 109' only.)
and
Ascraft & Decortex
19a Boudary Street
Rushcutters Bay

NSW 2011
Australia
Tel: +61 2 9360 2311
Fax: +61 2 9360 5335
and
St Leger & Viney Ltd.
PO Box 55508
Northlands 2116
South Africa
Tel: +27 11 444 6722
Fax: +27 11 444 6758

Nina Campbell
Trade showroom:
Bridge Studios
318–26 Wandsworth Bridge
Road
London SW6 2TZ
UK
Tel: +44 (0)20 7471 4270
Fax: +44 (0)20 7471 4274
www.ninacampbell.com
and
9 Walton Street
London SW3 2JD
UK
Tel: +44 (0)20 7225 1011
Fax: +44 (0)20 7225 0644
(Distributed by Osborne & Little; distributor of Galbraith & Paul.)

Nobilis
29 rue Bonaparte
75006 Paris
France
Tel +33 143 29 21 50
Fax +33 143 29 77 57
www.nobilis.fr
and
Bellevue House
Althorp Road
London SW17 7ED
UK
Tel +44 (0)20 8767 0774
Fax +44 (0)20 8682 4904
and
Nobilis Inc.
20 Locust Avenue
Berkeley Heights,
New Jersey
USA 07922
Tel +1 908 464 1177
Fax +1 908 464 4272
and
Telio & Cie
1407 rue de la Montagne
Montreal, Quebec
Canada HG3 1Z3
Tel: +1 514 842 9116
Fax: +1 514 842 3728
and
Redelman & Son Pty. Ltd.
96 Dalmeny Avenue
Roseberry
2018 NSW
Australia
Tel: +61 29 313 6811
Fax: +61 29 313 7334
and
Vivace Textiles Ltd.
16 Railway Street
Newmarket
Auckland
New Zealand
Tel: +64 9523 0325
Fax: +64 9523 0326

and
Cetec
128 Wellington Street
Hong Kong
Tel: +852 2522 0832
Fax: +852 2810 1954
and
Inter Fabrics Corporation
1-27.5 Sendagaya
Shibuya-Ku
Tokyo 151
Japan
Tel: +81 33 479 4552
Fax: +81 33 479 4368
and
Mavromac
PO Box 76178
12d Kramer Road
Wendywood 2144
Kramerville
Sandton
Johannesburg
South Africa
Tel: +27 11 444 1584
Fax: +27 11 444 1541

Northwood Designs
Trinity Gask
Auchterarder
Perthshire PH3 1LG
UK
Tel: +44 (0)1764 683334
Fax: +44 (0)1764 683462

Nutshell Natural Paints
PO Box 72
South Brent
Torquay TQ10 9YR
UK
Tel: +44 (0)1364 73801
Fax: +44 (0)1364 73068
www.nutshellpaints.com
(Online ordering. Contact for overseas delivery.)

Nya Nordiska
2/26 Chelsea Harbour
Design Centre
UK (see p401)
Tel: +44 (0)20 7351 2783
Fax: +44 (0)20 7352 5305
www.nya-nordiska.de
and
Randolph & Hein
979 Third Avenue,
Suite 1640
New York, New York
USA 10022
Tel: +1 212 826 9898
Fax: +1 212 826 1033
and
Ascraft and Decortex
Albion House
PO Box 407
1335 Potts Point
NSW
Australia
Tel: +61 29 360 2311
Fax: +61 29 360 5335

O

The Old Fashioned Milk Paint Co.
436 Main Street
PO Box 222
Groton, Massachusetts
USA 01450

Tel: +1 978 448 6336
Fax: +1 978 448 2754
www.milkpaint.com
and
The Shaker Kitchen and
Furniture Workshop
The Workshop
Barcham Farm
Soham
Ely
Cambridgeshire CB7 5TU
UK
Tel: +44 (0)1353 624616
Fax: +44 (0)1353 721089
and
Nitty Gritty Reproductions
170 King Street East
Toronto, Ontario
Canada M5A 1J4
Tel: +1 416 364 1393
Fax: +1 416 364 1170
and
Waiohine Woodware
Waiohine Gorge Road
Wairarapa
New Zealand
Tel: +64 6379 5288

Old Village Paints
PO Box 1030
Fort Washington,
Pennsylvania
USA 19034-1030
Tel: +1 610 238 9001
Fax: +1 610 238 9002
www.old-village.com
(Distributor of The Stulb Company.)
and
Bespoke Country Collection
18 Bar Street
Scarborough
North Yorkshire YO11 2HT
UK
Tel: +44 (0)1723 378728
Fax: +44 (0)1723 378728
www.bespokecountry
collection.com

Old World Weavers
D&D Building, 10th Floor
USA (see p401)
Tel: +1 212 355 7186
Fax: +1 212 593 0761
www.old-world-weavers.com
and
Stark Carpet
Chelsea Harbour Design
Centre
3rd Floor South Dome
UK (see p401)
Tel: +44 (0)20 7352 6001
Fax: +44 (0)20 7376 4908
and
Crown Wallpaper and Fabric
88 Ronson Drive
Rexdale, Ontario
Canada M9W 1B9
Tel: +1 416 245 2900
Fax: +1 416 245 8572

Olicana
Brook Mills Crimble
Slaithwaite
Huddersfield
West Yorkshire HD7 5BQ
UK

Tel: +44 (0)1484 847666
(for international stockists)
Fax: +44 (0)1484 847735
and
ZG Design
Zina Glazebrook
PO Box 144
Sagaponack, New York
USA 11962
Tel: +1 631 537 4454
Fax: +1 631 537 4453

Les Olivades
Chemin des Indienneurs
13103 Saint Etienne-du-Grès
France
Tel: +33 490 491919
Fax: +33 490 491920
www.les-olivades.com
and
Concorde FLP
8 Skye Close
Maidstone
Kent ME15 9SJ
UK
Tel: +44 (0)1622 682122
Fax: +44 (0)1622 691922
and
Pierre Deux
40 Enterprise Avenue
Secausus, New Jersey
USA 07094-2517
Tel: +1 201 809 2500
Fax: +1 201 319 0719
and
2 Transvaal Avenue
Sydney
Australia
Tel: +61 2 9327 8073
and
Chogin
1319 Nihonbashi
Horidomecho
Chuo Ku
1038560 Tokyo
Japan
Tel: +81 33 665 8641

Ollerton Hall
Ollerton
Knutsford
Cheshire WA16 8SF
UK
Tel: +44 (0)1565 650222
Fax: +44 (0)1565 754411
www.ollertonhalldiscount
carpets.co.uk

Original Style
Falcon Road
Sowton Industrial Estate
Exeter
Devon EX2 7LF
UK
Tel: +44 (0)1392 474011
Fax: +44 (0)1392 473003
www.originalstyle.com
*(The parent company of
Winchester Tiles.)*
and
Roma Tile Company Inc.
400 Arsenal Street
Watertown, Massachusetts
USA 02472
Tel: +1 617 926 7662
and

Cercan Tile Inc.
241 Hanlan Road
Woodbridge, Ontario
Canada L4L 3R7
Tel: +1 905 851 7923
and
Old Blagowalah Restorations
375 Sydney Road
Balgowalah
NSW 2093
Australia
Tel: +61 29 949 6266
and
Designa Ceramic Tiles Ltd.
PO Box 17475
Greenalne
Auckland
New Zealand
Tel: +64 9579 0714

Ornamenta
Tel: +44 (0)20 7591 0077
Fax: +44 (0)20 7591 0055
www.ornamenta.co.uk
and
Stark Wallcovering
979 Third Avenue
New York, New York
USA 10022
Tel: +1 212 355 7135
Fax: +1 212 753 3761

Osborne & Little
49 Temperley Road
London SW12 8QE
UK
Tel: +44 (0)20 8675 2255
Fax: +44 (0)20 8673 8254
www.osborneandlittle.com
*(Distributes Liberty
Furnishings, Nina Campbell
and Designers Guild.)*
and
304 Kings Road
London SW3 5UH
UK
Tel: +44 (0)20 7352 1456
Fax: +44 (0)20 7351 7813
and
D&D Building, Suite 520
USA (see p401)
Tel: +1 212 751 3333
Fax: +1 212 752 6027
and
Primavera
160 Pears Avenue,
Suite 110
Toronto Ontario
Canada M5R 3P8
Tel: +1 416 921 3334
Fax: +1 416 921 3227
(Distributes Designers Guild.)
and
Mokum Textiles Pty. Ltd.
98 Barcom Avenue
Rushcutters Bay
NSW 2011
Australia
Tel: +61 2 9380 6188
Fax: +61 2 9380 6476
www.mokumtextiles.com
and
Mokum Textiles Ltd.
11 Cheshire Street
Parnell
New Zealand
Tel: +64 9379 3041

Fax: +64 9777 5385
www.mokumtextiles.com
and
Osborne & Little/Liberty
Kinsan Collections Ltd.
56 d'Aguilar Street Central
Hong Kong
Tel: +852 2526 2309
Fax: +852 2840 1652
and
The Fabric Library
PO Box 912
Halfway House
1685 Johannesburg
South Africa
Tel: +27 11 265 9000
Fax: +27 11 315 1068

Ottilie Stevenson
Unit F8
Birch House, Birch Walk
Fraser Road, Erith
Kent DA8 1QX
UK
Tel: +44 (0)1322 441181
Fax: +44 (0)1322 441187

P

Paint and Paper Library
5 Elystan Street
London SW3 3NT
UK
Tel: +44 (0)20 7823 7755
Fax: +44 (0)20 7823 7766
www.paintlibrary.co.uk

Paint Magic
Bedec Products
Units 1/2 Poplars Farm
Aythorpe Roding, Dunmow
Essex CM6 1RY
UK
Tel: +44 (0)1279 876657
Fax: +44 (0)1279 876008
www.paintmagic.net
and
61 Walcot Street
Bath BA1 5BN
UK
Tel: +44 (0)1225 469966
Fax: +44 (0)1225 423040
and
Desmond International
412 Pebble Creek Court
Pennington, New Jersey
USA 08534-1945
Tel: +1 609 730 0445
and
Paint Effects Ltd.
Shop 279
Grand Central Plaza
138 Rural Committee Road
Shatin N.T.
Hong Kong
Tel: +852 2377 0388
*(See website for list of
stockists.)*

Paper Moon
The Paddocks
29 Bragbury Lane
Bragbury End
Hertfordshire SG2 8TJ
UK
Tel: +44 (0)1438 211770/1
Fax: +44 (0)1438 211772
and

Design and Press Office:
The Studio
3 Hill Road
London NW8 9QE
UK
Tel: +44 (0)20 7286 9455
Fax: +44 (0)20 7286 9502
www.papermoon.co.uk
(Online ordering available.)

Paris Ceramics
583 Kings Road
London SW6 2EH
UK
Tel: +44 (0)20 7371 7778
Fax: +44 (0)20 7371 8395
www.parisceramics.com
(Distributor of Froyle Tiles.)
and
150 East 58th Street,
7th Floor
New York, New York
USA 10155
Tel: +1 212 644 2782
Fax: +1 212 644 2785

Parkertex
(Distributed by G.P. & J. Baker.)

Pergo
19 Blacklands Way
Abingdon Business Park
Abingdon
Oxon OX14 1DY
UK
Tel: +44 (0)1235 556300
Fax: +44 (0)1235 556350
Freephone: 0800 374771
www.pergo.com
and
Pergo Inc.
PO Box 1775
Horsham, Pennsylvania
USA 19044-6775
Toll-free: +1 800 337 3746
and
Floored! Australia Pty. Ltd.
PO Box 6456
Shepparton
3632 Vic.
Australia
Tel: +61 3 5821 0733
Fax: +61 3 5821 0755

Pierre Frey
253 Fulham Road
London SW3 6HY
UK
Tel: +44 (0)20 7376 5599
Fax: +44 (0)20 7352 3024
www.pierrefrey.fr
and
15 East 32nd Street,
6th Floor
New York, New York
USA 10016
Tel: +1 212 213 3099
Fax: +1 212 213 3296
and
Milgate Fabrics Pty. Ltd.
533 High Street
Prahran
Vic. 3181
Australia
Tel: +61 395 109 822
Fax: +61 395 109 833
and

Altfield
617 Prince's Building
Central Hong Kong
Tel: +852 2524 3318
Fax: +852 2525 8751

Pippa & Hale
*(Distributed by Today Interiors
Ltd.)*

Pisani Ltd.
Unit 12, Transport Avenue
Great Western Road
Brentford
Middlesex TW8 9HF
UK
Tel: +44 (0)20 8568 5001
Fax: +44 (0)20 8847 3406
www.pisani.co.uk

Pratt & Lambert Paints
101 W. Prospect Avenue
Cleveland, Ohio
USA 44115
Toll-free: +1 800 289 7728
Fax: +1 216 566 1655
www.prattandlambert.com

Protim Solignum (Osmose)
Fieldhouse Lane
Marlow
Buckinghamshire SL7 1LS
UK
Tel: +44 (0)1628 486644
Fax: +44 (0)1628 476757
www.protimsolignum.com
*and similar products
available from:*
Osmose Holdings Inc.
980 Ellicott Street
Buffalo, New York
USA 14209
Tel: +1 716 882 5905
Fax: +1 716 882 5134
www.osmose.com

R

Ramm, Son & Crocker
Chiltern House
The Valley Centre
Gordon Road
High Wycombe
Buckinghamshire HP13 6EQ
UK
Tel: +44 (0)1494 474741
(for international stockists)
Fax: +44 (0)1494 603400
(Owned by Robert Allen.)
and
G28–29 Chelsea Harbour
Design Centre
UK (see p401)
Tel: +44 (0)20 7352 0931
Fax: +44 (0)20 7352 0935
and
D&D Building
USA (see p401)
Tel: +1 212 759 5408

Reeve Flooring
Valley Farm
Brancaster Staithe
Norfolk PE31 8DB
UK
Tel: +44 (0)1485 210754
Fax: +44 (0)1485 210910
www.reeveflooring.com

Reptile
Gwaith Meyn
Llanglydwen
Whitland
Carmarthenshire SA34 0XP
UK
Tel/Fax: 01994 419402

Ronseal Ltd.
Thorncliffe Park
Chapeltown
Sheffield S35 2YP
UK
Tel: +44 (0)114 246 7171
Fax: +44 (0)114 245 5629
www.ronseal.co.uk
(Online ordering available.)

Rose of Jericho
Horchester Farm
Holywell
Dorchester
Dorset DT2 0LL
UK
Tel: +44 (0)1935 83676
Fax: +44 (0)1935 83903
www.rose-of-jericho.demon.co.uk

Roses Mill
14 Stoneygate Road
Newmilns
Ayrshire KA16 9AL
UK
Tel/Fax: +44 (0)1560 322285
www.rosesmill.co.uk
(Online shopping available.)

Rubelli
H.A. Percheron Ltd.
G6 Chelsea Harbour Design
Centre
UK (see p401)
Tel: +44 (0)20 7349 1590
Fax: +44 (0)20 7349 1595
www.rubelli.it
and
USA head office:
Tel: +1 914 665 0800
Fax: +1 914 665 7900
www.bergamofabrics.com
and
Bergamo Fabrics Inc.
D&D Building, 17th Floor
USA (see p401)
Tel: +1 212 888 3333
Fax: +1 212 888 3877

Rucksthul
Head office:
St. Urbanstrasse 21
4901 Langenthal
Switzerland
Tel: +41 62 919 86 00
Fax +41 62 922 48 70
www.ruckstuhl.net
and
Bill Nunn Manufacturers
Pardix House
Cadmore Lane
Cheshunt
Hertfordshire EN8 9LQ
UK
Tel: +44 (0)1992 642 753
Fax: +44 (0)1992 642 690
and
Ruckstuhl USA Ltd.
PO Box 50

Allendale NJ
USA 07401
Tel: +1 239 573 3400
Fax: +1 239 573 3415

Rustins
Waterloo Road
London NW2 7TX
UK
Tel: +44 (0)20 8450 4666
Fax: +44 (0)20 8452 2008
www.rustins.co.uk
and
The Woodsmith Pty. Ltd.
1 Burgess Road
North Bayswater
Vic. 3153
Australia
Tel: +61 3 9761 4622
Fax: +61 3 9761 4544
www.thewoodsmith.com.au
and
Latimer Marketing Ltd.
5a Victoria Park Road
Christchurch
New Zealand
Tel: +64 3337 0445
and
Hardware Centre
PO Box 3760
Johannesburg 2000
South Africa
Tel: +27 11 791 0850

Ryalux Carpets Ltd.
Ensor Mill
Queensway
Castleton
Rochdale
Lancashire OL11 2NU
UK
Tel: +44 (0)1706 716000
Fax: +44 (0)1706 860618
www.ryalux.com

Rye Tiles
The Old Brewery
Wishward
Rye
East Sussex TN31 7DH
UK
Tel: +44 (0)1797 223038
Fax: +44 (0)1797 224834

S

Sahco Hesslein
G24 Chelsea Harbour
Design Centre
UK (see p401)
Tel: +44 (0)20 7352 6168
Fax: +44 (0)20 7352 0767
www.sahco-hesslein.com
and
Bergamo Fabrics
PO Box 231
256 Washington Street
Mount Vernon
New York, New York
USA 10553
Tel: +1 914 665 0800
Fax: +1 914 665 7900
www.bergamofabrics.com
and
South Pacific Fabrics
195 Paddington Street
Paddington
NSW 2021

Australia
Tel: +61 2 9327 7222
Fax: +61 2 9327 7686
www.southpacificfabrics.com
and
Atelier Fabrics
55 Boston Road
Mount Eden
Auckland
New Zealand
Tel: +64 9 3733 866
Fax: +64 9 3733 566
and
Home Fabrics
60 Old Pretoria Road
PO Box 5207
Halfway House
Midrand 1685
South Africa
Tel: +27 11 266 3700
Fax: +27 11 266 3900
www.homefabrics.co.za

Saloni Ceramica
Carretera Alcora 12130
San Juan de Moro
12080 Castellon
Spain
Tel: +34 96 434 3434
Fax: +34 96 434 3473
www.saloni.com
and
Saloni UK Ltd.
Unit 23 City North
Fonthill Road
London N4 3HN
UK
Tel: +44 (0)20 7263 5550
Fax: +44 (0)20 7561 1611
and
2001 Mabeline Road
North Charleston,
South Carolina
USA 29406-4656

Sandberg Tapeter AB
Box 69
SE-52322
Ulricehamn
Sweden
Tel: + 46 321 53 16 60
Fax: +46 321 53 16 61
www.sandbergtapeter.com
and
For stockists: +44 0800 967 222
and
Country Swedish Showroom
D&D Building, Suite 1409
USA (see p401)
Tel: +1 212 838 1976
and
Appel Ltd.
321 Davenport Road
Toronto, Ontario
Canada
Tel: +1 416 922 3935
and
Ascraft Fabrics
19a Boundary Street
Rushcutters Bay
NSW 2011
Australia
Tel: +61 29 360 2311
and
Atelier Textiles
55 Boston Road
Mount Eden

Auckland
New Zealand
Tel: +64 9 3733 866
Fax: +64 9 3733 566
and
Kinsan Collections Ltd.
56 d'Aguilar Street
Central Hong Kong
Tel: +852 2526 2309
Fax: +852 2840 1652

Sanderson
100 Acres
Sanderson Road
Uxbridge
Middlesex UB8 1DH
UK
Tel: +44 (0)1895 830044
Fax: +44 (0)1895 830055
www.sanderson-online.co.uk
*(Distributes 95% of the
Morris & Co. archive.)*
and
Sanderson Store
233 Kings Road
London SW3 5EJ
UK
Tel: +44 (0)20 7351 7728
and
D&D Building, Suite 409
USA (see p401)
Tel: +1 212 319 7220
Fax: +1 212 593 6184
*(Distributor of Brian Yates
and Sheila Coombes.)*
and
Telio & Cie
160 Pears Avenue, Suite 400
Toronto, Ontario
Canada M5R 3P8
Tel: +1 514 842 9116
Fax: +1 514 842 3728
and
Australian Domestic Textile
Corporation Pty. Ltd.
95 Albert Street
Brunswick
Vic. 3056
Australia
Freephone: 1800 177 170
Fax: +61 3 9387 3338
and
Instyle Interior Products
37–41 Carbine Road
Mount Wellington
Auckland
PO Box 2312
New Zealand
Tel: +64 9574 3220
Fax: +64 9574 3221
and
Kinsan Collections Ltd.
56 d'Aguilar Street
Central Hong Kong
Tel: +852 2526 2309
Fax: +852 2840 1652
and
Mitsui & Co. Ltd.
Head Office:
2-1 Ohtemachi 1-chome
Chiyodu-Ku
Tokyo, Japan
Tel: +81 3 3285 6314
Fax: +81 3 3285 9967
and
The Fabric Library
PO Box 912, Halfway House

1685 Johannesburg
South Africa
Tel: +27 11 265 9000
Fax: +27 11 315 1068

Sawyer Finn
1600 Genessee 555
Kansas City, Missouri
USA 64102
Tel: +1 816 421 4717
www.sawyerfinn.com

Scalamandré
300 Trade Zone Drive
Ronkonkoma, New York
USA 11779-7381
Tel: +1 631 467 8800
Fax: +1 631 467 9448
www.scalamandre.com
*(Distributed in the UK by Altfield
Ltd.; distributor of John Boyd.)*
and
Fabric Unlimited
158 North Third St.
Danville, Kentucky
USA 40422
Tel: +1 859 238 2289
(Online mail order.)
and
Primavera Interior Furnishings, Ltd.
160 Pears Avenue, Suite 110
Toronto, Ontario
Canada M5R 3P8
Tel: +1 416 921 3334
Fax: +1 416 921 3227
www.primavera.ca
and
Golia Color Centre
6710 Drummond Road
Niagara Falls, Ontario
Canada L2G 4P1
Tel: +1 905 354 7447
Fax: +1 905 354 3480
www.ont.net/don/golia/wall/
wallpaper.htm
and
G4 Chelsea Harbour Design
Centre
UK (see p401)
Tel: +44 (0)20 7795 0988
Fax: +44 (0)20 7795 0989

F. Schumacher & Co.
D&D Building, Suite 832
USA (see p401)
Tel: +1 212 415 3900
Fax: +1 212 415 3907
www.fschumacher.com
*(Distributed in the UK by
Turnell & Gigon; distributor of
Beaumont & Fletcher and
John Boyd in the USA.)*
and
Designer's Gallery
354 Davenport Road
Toronto, Ontario
Canada M5R 1K6
Tel: +1 416 964 3714
Fax: +1 416 964 2015
and
Seamoor Fabrics
512 Wallace Down Road
Bournemouth
Dorset BH11 8PT
UK
Tel: +44 (0)1202 598000
Fax: +44 (0)1202 598010

and
Fabrics Direct UK
Tel: +44 (0)800 975 7296
Fax: +44 (0)800-975 7297
Email:
info@fabricsdirect.co.uk
www.fabricsdirect.co.uk
*(Online ordering, ships
worldwide.)*

Seri Parquet
BP60ZI du Centre 12300
Decazeville, France
Tel: +33 565 430574
Fax: +33 565 433980

Sheila Coombes
*(Distributed in the UK by
Brian Yates; distributed in
USA by Sanderson.)*

Sherwin Williams
101 Prospect Street
Cleveland, Ohio
USA 44115-1075
Tel: +1 216 566 2000
Fax: +1 216 566 2318
www.sherwin-williams.com
and
Sherwin Williams (Canada)
170 Brunel Road, Unit #A
Mississauga, Ontario
Canada L4Z 1T5
Tel: +1 905 507 0166
Fax: +1 905 507 4198

Siesta Cork Tile Co.
Unit 21 Tate Road
Gloucester Road
Croydon CR0 2DP
UK
Tel: +44 (0)20 8683 4055
Fax: +44 (0)20 8683 4480
www.siestacorktiles.co.uk

Sigma Kalon
Sigma Coatings
Unit C
Tingewick Road
Buckingham MK18 1ED
UK
Tel: +44 (0)1280 812081
Fax: +44 (0)1280 815656
www.sigmakalon.com
and
Decorative Coatings UK
Kalon Ltd.
Huddersfield Road
Birstall
Batley
West Yorkshire WF17 9XA
UK
Tel: +44 (0)1924 354000
Fax: +44 (0)1924 354601
and
Sigma Coatings USA
1401 Destrehan Avenue
Harvey, Louisian
USA 70058
Tel: +1 504 347 4321
Fax: +1 504 341 9120
www.sigmacoatings.com
and
Prominent Paints
Alberton
Johannesburg

South Africa
Tel: +27 11 389 4600
www.prominentpaints.co.za

The Silk Gallery
G25 Chelsea Harbour
Design Centre
UK (see p401)
Tel: +44 (0)20 7351 1790
Fax: +44 (0)20 7376 4693
www.thesilkgallery.co.uk
(Mail order available.)

Simmy Ceramics
Sayer House
Oxgate Lane
London NW2 7JN
UK
Tel: +44 (0)20 8208 0416
Fax: +44 (0)20 8450 1140
www.simmyceramics.com
(Online shopping forthcoming.)

Sinclair Till
793 Wandsworth Road
London SW8 3JQ
UK
Tel: +44 (0)20 7720 0031
Fax: +44 (0)20 7498 3814

Stark Carpet Corporation
D&D Building
USA (see p401)
Tel: +1 212 752 9000
Fax: +1 212 758 4342
www.starkcarpet.com
*(Distributor of Bernard Thorp
& Co., Crucial Trading and
John Boyd.)*
and
3/6–7 Chelsea Harbour
Design Centre
UK (see p401)
Tel: +44 (0)20 7352 6001
Fax: +44 (0)20 7376 4908

The Stencil Store
4a Heronsgate Road
Chorleywood
Hertfordshire WD3 5BL
UK
Tel: +44 (0)1923 285577
Fax: +44 (0)1923 285136
and see also
Designer Stencils
c/o The Stencil Shoppe Inc.
3364 Silverside Road
Wilmington, Delaware
USA 19810
Toll-free: +1 800 822 7836
Fax: +1 302-477-0170
www.designerstencils.com
*(Online ordering, custom
stencils.)*

Stoddard Carpets Ltd.
Glenpatrick Road
Elderslie
Johnstone
Renfrewshire PA5 9UJ
UK
Tel: +44 0845 272 0032/
+44 0845 272 0034
Sample/brochure hotline:
0800 0274888
Fax: +44 (0)845 272 0033/
+44 0845 272 0035

www.stoddardcarpets.com
and
Stoddard USA
PO Box 11080
Boulder, Colorado
USA 80301
Toll-free: +1 800 742 1244
Tel: +1 303 516 9620
Fax: +1 303 527 1662

Stonell
Forstal House
Beltring, Paddock Wood
Kent TN12 6PY
UK
Tel: +44 (0)189 283 3500
Fax: +44 (0)189 283 3600
www.stonell.com
and
521/525 Battersea Park Road
London SW11 3BN
UK
Tel: +44 (0)207 738 9990
Fax: +44 (0)207 738 0660

Stuart Interiors
Barrington Court
Barrington
Ilminster
Somerset TA19 ONQ
UK
Tel: +44 (0)146 024 0349
Fax: +44 (0)146 024 2069
www.stuart-interiors.com

The Stulb Company
*(Distributed by Old Village
Paints.)*

Surving Studios
17 Millsburg Road
Middletown, New York
USA 10940
Toll-free: +1 800 768 4954
Tel: +1 845 355 1430
Fax: +1 845 355 1517
www.surving.com
and
Dealer:
Creekside Tile Co.
161 West 2nd Avenue
Vancouver, British Columbia
Canada V5Y1B8
Tel: +1 604 876 4900
Fax: +1 604 876 4902

Textra Ltd.
Sheephouse Barn
Allins Lane
East Hundred
Oxon OX12 8HR
UK
Tel: +44 (0)870 241 4949
Fax: +44 (0)870 241 4950
www.textra.co.uk

Thomas Dare
Unit 11
Saxon Business Centre
Windsor Avenue
London SW19 2RR
UK
Tel: +44 (0)20 8542 1160
Fax: +44 (0)20 8542 1180
and
Fonthill Ltd.

979 Third Avenue
New York, New York
USA 10022
Tel: +1 212 755 6700
Fax: +1 212 371 2358
and
The Silk Company
PO Box 1738
Parkland 2121
South Africa
Tel: +27 11 482 8073
Fax: +27 11 448 2522

Tile Productions
Technique House
New Garden Street
Blackburn
Lancashire BB2 3RE
UK
Tel/Fax: +44 (0)1254 673003
www.tileproductions.co.uk

Tiles of Newport & London
326 Chepstow Road
Newport
South Wales NP19 8NP
UK
Tel: +44 (0)1633 273399
Fax: +44 (0)1633 270404
www.tilesofnewport.co.uk
and
51–5 Stirling Road
Chiswick
Off Bollo Lane
London W3 8DJ
UK
Tel: +44 (0)20 8993 5545
Fax: +44 (0)20 8752 0281

Tiles of Stow
Langston Priory Workshops
Station Road
Kingham OX7 6UP
UK
Tel: +44 (0)1608 658993
Fax: +44 (0)1608 658951
www.tilesofstow.co.uk

Timney Fowler
355 King Street
London W6 9NH
UK
Tel: +44 (0)20 8748 3010
for US stockists
Fax: +44 (0)20 8748 3007
www.timneyfowler.com
and
WH Bilbrough & Co. Ltd.
326 Davenport Road
Toronto, Ontario
Canada M5R 1K6
Tel: +1 416 960 1611
Fax: +1 416 960 5742
and
Cheshire Pty. Ltd.
100 Auburn Road
Hawthorn 3122, Vic.
Australia
Tel +61 3 9818 8799
and
Atelier Textiles
PO Box 5017
Wellesley Street, Auckland
New Zealand
Tel: +64 9 3733 866
Fax: +64 9 3733 566
and

Kinsan Collections
56 d'Aguilar Street
Central Hong Kong
Tel: +852 2526 2309
Fax: +852 2840 1652
and
St Leger & Viney Pty. Ltd.
PO Box 55508
Northlands 2116
Gauteng
South Africa
Tel: +27 11 444 6722
Tel: +27 11 444 6756

Today Interiors Ltd.
Hollis Road
Grantham
Lincolnshire NG31 7QH
UK
Tel: +44 (0)1476 574401
Fax: +44 (0)1476 590208
www.today-interiors.co.uk
(Distributor of Pippa & Hale.)
and
Gaetano Ltd.
186 Sherman Avenue
Berkeley Heights,
New Jersey
USA 07922
Tel: +1 908 508 9006
Fax: +1 908 508 9797
and
Charles Radford Furniture
8–18 Glass Street
Richmond 3121
Australia
Tel: +61 3 9429 6122
Fax: +61 3 9427 1587
and
Malcolm Fabrics Ltd.
PO Box 5460
Papanni, New Zealand
Tel: +64 3 352 8668
Fax: +64 3 352 6622
and
Mercer House Interiors
G/F Wilson House
19–27 Wyndham Street
Central Hong Kong
Tel: +852 2524 2000
Fax: +852 2525 2280

Tor Coatings Ltd.
Portobello Industrial Estate
Birtley
Chester le Street
Co. Durham DH3 2RE
UK
Tel: +44 (0)191 410 6611
Fax: +44 (0)191 492 0125

Trimite Ltd.
Arundel Road
Uxbridge
Middlesex UB8 2SD
UK
Tel: +44 (0)1895 251234
Fax: +44 (0)1895 256789
www.trimite.com
and
Trimite Powders Inc.
5680 North Blackstock Road
Spartanburg, South Carolina
USA 29303
Toll-free: +1 800 866 8666
Fax: +1 864 587 6152

Turnell & Gigon
Unit 2 Wellington Works
Wellington Road
London SW19 8EQ
UK
Tel: +44 (0)20 8971 1711
Fax: +44 (0)20 8971 1716
*(UK distributor of F.
Schumacher & Co.)*
and
G20 Chelsea Harbour
Design Centre
UK (see p401)
Tel: +44 (0)20 7351 5142
Fax: +44 (0)20 7376 7945

U

Ulster Carpets
Castleisland Factory
Craigavon BT62 1EE
Northern Ireland
UK
Tel: +44 (0)28 3833 4433
Fax: +44 (0)28 3833 3142
www.ulstercarpets.com
and
Ulster Carpet Mills (NA) Inc.
81 Whitlock Avenue
Marietta, Georgia
USA 30064
Tel: +1 770 514 0707
Fax: +1 770 514 1006
and
Carpet Design Solutions
42 Heath Street East
Toronto, Ontario
Canada M4T 1S3
Tel/Fax: +1 416 966 3332
and
Tascot Templeton Carpets
Pty.
119 Church Street
Richmond 3121
Vic.
Australia
Tel: +61 3 9428 4925
Fax: +61 3 9429 6234
and
Ulster Carpet Mills Pty. Ltd.
PO Box 72253
Mobeni 4060
Reunion, Natal
South Africa
Tel: +27 31 912 1310
Fax: +27 31 902 5557

V

V. V. Rouleaux
54 Sloane Square
Cliveden Place
London SW1W 8AW
UK
Tel: +44 (0)20 7730 3125
Fax: +44 (0)20 7730 9985
www.vvrouleaux.com
(Online ordering available.)

Villeroy & Boch (UK) Ltd.
Building Ceramic Division
267 Merton Road
London SW18 5JS
UK
Tel: +44 (0)20 8871 4028
Fax: +44 (0)20 8870 3720
www.villeroy-boch.com
and

Corporate Headquarters:
PO Box 1120
D-66688 Mettlach
Germany
Tel: +49 6864 81 1020
Fax: +49 6864 81 2305
and
1600 Cottontail Lane
Somerset, New Jersey
USA 08873
Tel: +1 732 302 0987
Fax: +1 732 302 1544

Vymura (CWV Group)
PO Box 15
Talbot Road
Hyde
Cheshire SK14 4EJ
UK
Tel: +44 (0)161 368 8321
Fax: +44 (0)161 367 9128
www.vymura.com

W

Walker Zanger
8901 Bradley Avenue
Sun Valley, California
USA 91352
Tel: +1 818 504 0235
Fax: +1 818 504 2057
www.walkerzanger.com
(Distributor of Kirkstone.)
and
World Mosaic Ltd.
1665 West 7th Avenue
Vancouver, British Columbia
Canada V6J 1S4
Tel: +1 604 736 8158
Fax: +1 604 736 9908

Warner Fabrics
Head Office:
Unit 2
Wellington Works
Wellington Road
London SW10 OXE
UK
Tel: +44 (0)20 8971 1711
Fax: +44 (0)20 8971 1716
and
G11 Chelsea Harbour
Design Centre
UK (see p401)
Tel: +44 (0)20 8971 1713
Fax: +44 (0)20 8971 1716
and
D&D Building, Suite 1403
USA (see p401)
Tel: +1 212 593 9787
and
Charles Radford Furnishings
Pty. Ltd.
8–18 Grass Street
Burnley
Melbourne
Vic. 3121
Australia
Tel: +61 3 9429 6122
Fax: +61 3 9427 1587
and
Icon Textiles Ltd.
PO Box 9832
Newmarket
Auckland
New Zealand
Tel: +64 9302 1652
Fax: +64 9375 2855

and
Choi Design
Unit 408
4F Dominion Centre
43–59 Queens Road East
Wanchai
Hong Kong
Tel: +852 2866 6861
Fax: +852 2866 6099
and
Sente Studio Corporation
6–21 Tamagawa-Denenchofu
2 Chome
Scragaya-ku
Tokyo 158
Japan
Tel: +81 334 424 501

Warwick
Hackling House
Bourton Industrial Park
Bourton-on-the-Water
Gloucestershire GL54 2EN
UK
Tel: +44 (0)1451 833383
Fax: +44 (0)1451 822369
www.warwick.co.uk
and
55 Bridge Road
Glebe
Sydney NSW 2037
Australia
Tel: +64 9 518 8688
Fax: +64 9 518 8699
and
12 Apollo Drive
Mairangi Bay
Auckland
New Zealand
Tel: +64 9 479 6466
Fax: +64 9 479 6313

Watts of Westminster
3/14 Chelsea Harbour
Design Centre
UK (see p401)
Tel: +44 (0)20 7376 4486
Fax: +44 (0)20 7376 4636
www.wattsofwestminster.com
and
Christopher Norman Inc.
41 West 25th Street,
10th Floor
New York, New York
USA 10010
Tel: +1 212 647 0303
Fax: +1 212 647 0369
www.christophernorman.com

Waveney Rush Industry Ltd.
The Old Maltings
Caldecott Road
Oulton Broad
Lowestoft
Suffolk NR32 3AH
UK
Tel: +44 (0)1502 538777
Fax: +44 (0)1502 538477
www.waveneyrush.co.uk
*(Online ordering; overseas
delivery.)*

Welbeck Tiles
1 East Building
Tan Gallop
Welbeck

Nottinghamshire S80 3LW
UK
Tel: +44 (0)1909 476539
Fax: +44 (0)1909 472772
www.welbeck-tiles.co.uk

Wemyss (Houlès)
1/20 Chelsea Harbour
Design Centre
UK (see p401)
Tel: +44 (0)20 7376 4430
Fax: +44 (0)20 7376 4465

Wendy Cushing Trimmings
G7 Chelsea Harbour Design
Centre
UK (see p401)
Tel: +44 (0)20 7351 5796
Fax: +44 (0)20 7351 4246
*(Distributed in USA by
Fonthill Ltd. and H.T.
Barnes.)*

Westbond
1 Home Farm
Luton Hoo
Bedfordshire LU1 3TD
UK
Tel: +44 (0)1582 876161
Fax: +44 (0)1582 876151
www.westbond-carpets.com

Westco
Penarth Road
Cardiff
Wales CF1 8YN
UK
Tel: +44 (0)29 203 76700
Fax: +44 (0)29 203 83573
www.westcofloors.co.uk
and
Gerflor Australasia Pty. Ltd.
17 Cato Street
Hawthorn East
Vic. 3123
Australia
Tel: +61 3 9832 1333
and
Young & Robins Ltd.
51 Druces Road
Wiri
Manukua City
SAMC
Auckland
New Zealand
Tel: +64 9 262 4260

Wicanders
Amorim (UK) Ltd.
Suite 1EA
Bishops Weald House
Albion Way
Horsham
West Sussex RH12 1AH
UK
www.wicanders.com
and
Amorim Cork America Inc.
2557 Napa Valley
Corporate Drive
Napa, California
USA 94558
Tel: +1 707 224 6000
Fax: +1 707 224 7616

Wilman Interiors
(also known as John Wilmans)
Heasand Ford Industrial Estate
Widow Hill Road
Burnley
Lancashire BB10 2TJ
UK
Tel: +44 (0)1282 727238
Fax: +44 (0)1282 727454
www.wilman.co.uk

Winchester Tile Co.
Falcon Road
Exeter
Devon EX2 7LF
UK
Tel: +44 (0)1392 474011
Fax: +44 (0)1392 219932
www.winchestertiles.com
*(See Original Style for
distributors.)*

Woodward Grosvenor
Stourvale Mill
Green Street
Kidderminster
Worcestershire DY10 1AT
UK
Tel: +44 (0)1562 820020
Fax: +44 (0)1562 820042
and
J.R. Burrows & Company
PO Box 522
Rockland, Massachusetts
USA 02370
Toll-free: +1 800 347 1795
Tel: +1 781 982 1812
Fax: +1 781 982 1636
www.burrows.com

Z

Zest Essentials
(formerly Brats Paints)
38 Upper Street
Islington
London N1 OPN
UK
Tel: +44 (0)20 7226 6138
Fax: +44 (0)20 7226 7001
www.zestessentials.com
*(Online ordering; overseas
shipping.)*

Zimmer & Rohde
G13–15 Chelsea Harbour
Design Centre
UK (see p401)
Tel: +44 (0)20 7351 7115
Fax: +44 (0)20 7351 5661
www.zimmer-rohde.com
and
D&D Building, Suite 1616
USA (see p401)
Tel: +1 212 758 7925
Fax: +1 212 758 4372
and
Tessuti Uno
320 Davenport Road, B12
Toronto, Ontario
Canada M5R 1K6
Tel: +1 416 922 0126
Fax: +1 416 922 0441
and
Mokum Textiles Pty. Ltd.
98 Barcom Avenue
Rushcutters Bay
Sydney

NSW 2011
Australia
Tel : +61 29 357 0555
Fax: +61 29 380 6476

Zoë Barlow Passementerie
17 Oak Road
Hale
Altrincham
Cheshire WA15 9JA
UK
Tel: +44 (0)161 929 1255

Zoffany
G9 Chelsea Harbour Design
Centre
UK (see p401)
Tel: +44 (0)20 7349 0043
Fax: +44 (0)20 7351 9677
www.zoffany.com
and
979 Third Avenue,
Suite 1403
New York, New York
USA 10022
Tel: +1 212 593 9787
Fax: +1 212 593 9771
*(Distributor of Chase Erwin in
the USA.)*
and
Tessuti Uno
320 Davenport Road, B12
Toronto, Ontario
Canada M5R 1K6
Tel: +1 416 922 0126
Fax: +1 416 922 0441
and
Charles Radford Furniture
8–18 Glass Street
Richmond 3121
Australia
Tel: +61 3 9429 6122
Fax: +61 3 9427 1587
and
Icon Textiles Ltd.
Level 2
155–165 The Strand
Parnell
PO Box 9832
New Market
Auckland
New Zealand
Tel: +64 9302 1652
Fax: +64 9375 2855

Zuber
42 Pimlico Road
London SW1H 8LP
UK
Tel: +44 (0)20 7824 8265
Fax: +44 (0)20 7824 8270
www.zuber.fr
and
D&D Building
USA (see p401)
Tel: +1 212 486 9226
Fax: +1 212 754 6166

Index

Companies in *italic* appear in the Directory

A

Aalto Colour 299, 301, 304
Abbott & Boyd 67, 101, 105, 107, 109, 113, 131, 134, 139, 140, 179, 191, 193, 195, 200
Adam style 80, 96
Adam 54, 80, 82, 98, 108, 116, 118, 128, 134, 138, 152, 154, 168, 169, 174, 176, 182, 184
Adams, James 23
Adams, Robert 23
Aesthetic 43, 102, 122, 124, 138, 140, 154, 170, 198, 220, 238, 262, 318, 332, 342
  colour schemes 294, 296
Afia 385, 386, 388
Africa 37, 49, 57, 128, 138, 140, 170, 176, 300
Alencon, France 180
Alexander Beauchamp 217, 222, 223, 230, 233, 239, 247, 249, 251, 258, 259, 262
Alhambra, Granada, Spain 354
alloys 53
Alternative Flooring Co., The 373
America (USA) 14, 19, 23, 29, 43,
Amtico 395, 397
Andrew Low House, Georgia, USA 160
Andrew Martin 74, 80, 94, 145, 153, 207
animal skin fabric 159
Ann Sacks 320, 324, 325, 344
Anna French 109, 125, 145, 177, 179, 182, 187, 211, 215, 226, 227, 229, 242, 243, 266, 267, 268, 280, 282, 283
Anne & Robert Swaffer 117, 134, 153
Annie Sloan 287
Anta 163
Antico Setificio Fiorentino 68, 78, 170, 171
  history 167
Antwerp 180
Anya Larkin 207, 269, 283
Apenn 97, 129, 151
arabesques 247, 318
Arabia 37, 132
Argenton, France 180
armchairs 17, 19, 49
Armstrong DLW 391, 392, 393, 394, 395, 396, 397
Art Deco 49, 54, 194, 198, 280, 282, 296, 297, 384, 385, 394
  floral fabrics 124
  floral wallpaper 240
  geometric fabrics 172
  motif fabrics 104
  motif wallpaper 222
  overall pattern fabrics 156
  overall pattern wallpaper 264, 268
  pictorial fabrics 142

tiles 312, 316, 318, 322, 344, 358, 359
Art Nouveau 46, 54, 384
  colour schemes 296, 298
  floral fabrics 122
  floral wallpaper 238, 240, 242
  motif fabrics 102, 104, 106
  motif wallpaper 220, 222
  overall pattern wallpaper 262, 264, 266, pictorial fabrics 140, 154, 156, 158
  tapestry 91
  tiles 312, 316, 324, 328, 334, 335, 344, 350
Artex 305
Arts and Crafts 43, 382
  colour schemes 294, 295
  floral fabrics 111, 122, 123, 124
  floral wallpaper 238, 240
  geometric fabrics 170
  motif fabrics 102, 104, 108
  motif wallpaper 220, 222
  overall pattern fabrics 154, 156, 158
  overall pattern wallpaper 262, 264, 266
  pictorial fabrics 138, 140, 142
  pictorial wallpaper 252
  tiles 323, 328, 332, 342, 344
Arts and Crafts Home, The 104, 278, 279, 323, 339
Atlas Carpet Mills 388, 389
Attwell, Mabel 253
Aubusson, France 23, 88, 90
Auro Organic Paints 288, 297, 299, 300, 307, 308, 309
Australia 184
Austria 29
Axminster 378, 379, 382, 384, 387
Aztec influence 104, 172, 176

B

Baer & Ingram 168, 240, 243, 247, 254, 255, 282
Ballet Russe 384
Balmoral, Scotland 170
Banks-Pye, Roger 110
Baronial style 90, 172
Baroque 14, 94, 130, 132, 382
Baroque Revival 37, 100, 218
bathroom tiling 329
batik 128, 130
Bauhaus 280
Beaumont & Fletcher 72, 80, 113, 114, 120, 122, 251
Beauvais, France 88
beds 13, 32
benches 13
Bennett Silks 111, 164, 167, 173, 179, 181, 183, 188
Bennison Fabrics 97, 102, 116, 117, 119, 121, 129, 147, 151, 155, 172
Bentley & Spens 74, 85, 139, 144, 176, 183, 186, 187
Berger 291, 303, 305
Bernard Thorp & Co. 95, 113, 148, 181

Berti Pavimenti Legno 364, 365
Biedermeyer 29
Bill Amberg 395
Blass, Bill 57
bleaching 64
blinds 32, 64, 172
block-printing 146
Bodley, G. F. 213
Boen Parkett 363, 366, 368, 369
Bonaparte, Napoleon 29, 39, 92, 98, 99, 136, 169, 198, 216
Bonar Floors 395
Borderline 100, 119, 120, 122, 141, 155
borders 277
Bosanquet Ives 381, 383, 384, 385, 388, 389
Boulgard 244
Bourdichon, Jean 244
Bouwmeester, Cornelis 340
Bradbury & Bradbury 213, 221, 222, 239, 240, 241, 250, 251, 263
braids 190–1, 200–1
brick 13, 14
Brintons 379, 380, 381, 382, 386, 387, 389
Britain 23, 29, 46, 54, 76, 80, 116, 118, 168, 169
brocade 76–85
brocatelle 76, 78, 82, 84
brown Holland 64
Bruce Hardwood 369
Brunschwig & Fils 65, 75, 77, 87, 88, 91, 93, 96, 97, 98, 105, 106, 109, 116, 117, 118, 121, 122, 125, 127, 130, 131, 132, 133, 134, 135, 136, 137, 140, 151, 152,155, 157, 169, 173, 174, 198, 199, 201, 229, 231, 232, 238, 242, 245, 247, 248, 249, 250, 251
Brussels 180, 380
bullion fringe 191
bureau-bookcases 19
Busby & Busby 96, 133, 137, 139, 153

C

cabinets 40
Cabot Stains 308
Calhoun Mansion, South Carolina, USA 43, 190, 191
calico 62, 64, 110, 112, 114, 128, 132, 134
cambric 62, 64
campaign fringe 191
Candy 319, 347, 348, 349, 351, 354, 355, 359
canvas 62, 63
Carocim 317, 320, 326, 327, 336, 345, 347, 348, 349, 350, 351, 353, 355, 357, 358
Carpet Innovations 371, 373, 374, 375
carpets 13, 17, 19, 23, 40, 46, 49, 376–89
  combination weaves 389
  design papers 383

fitted 29
  types 377
Carré 321, 331, 354, 356
Carter & Co. 324, 326, 334, 344, 345
carving 14
Cedar Grove, USA 37
ceilings 251
  eighteenth century 19, 23
  medieval 13
  nineteenth century 29, 40
  sixteenth century 14
  twentieth century 49
Celia Birtwell 105, 131, 143
Celtic influence 170, 278
ceramics 46, 132, 150
chairs 19, 32, 40, 82, 87
chaises longues 32
Chameleon 230, 235, 237, 240, 257, 260, 261, 264, 265, 266, 271, 272
chandeliers 29
Chantilly, France 180
Chase Erwin 147, 189
Château de Compiègne, France 22, 23
Château de Morsan, France 20, 110
Chatsworth 380, 386, 388, 389
Chelsea Textiles 112, 115
chenille 70, 72, 74
chestnut 13
chiaroscuro 246, 248
chiffoniers 32
Chilperic I of France 99
China 14, 37, 43, 114, 128, 132, 150, 170, 244, 246, 256
chinoiserie 19, 23, 29, 49, 88, 96, 114, 132, 134, 136, 138, 140, 166, 232, 248, 249
chintz 32, 54, 94, 108, 114, 116, 118, 124, 126, 128, 136, 142, 150, 234, 240
  carpet design 384
  faded chintz 121
Chippendale 64, 245
Christianity 13, 111, 246, 318, 320, 322
chrome 49
Cinca 316
Claremont 78, 84, 194, 195, 196, 197, 200, 201
Claremont Fabrics 127, 130, 180
Clarence House 124, 132, 143, 158, 191, 197, 198
Classical 13, 14, 19, 29, 37, 54, 87, 98, 144, 216, 248
Classical Revival 100, 250, 251
coir matting 370, 372, 374
Cole & Son 210, 214, 217, 218, 219, 221, 223, 229, 233, 235, 236, 238, 245, 247, 252, 261, 262, 271, 274, 275, 276, 277, 279, 280, 288, 289, 290, 292
Colefax and Fowler 96, 115, 120, 140, 167, 234, 236, 237, 238, 240, 273, 277, 279, 281
Colefax, Sybil 126
Colonial style 54

Acknowledgments

I would very much like to thank the editorial, design and production team for all the long hours, dedication and skill they have committed to the new *Style Sourcebook*: Emma Clegg for calmly and efficiently overseeing this complex project from start to finish; Catherine Emslie for her editorial skills, co-ordinating with suppliers and design and, especially, for her unflagging good humour and encouragement in her constant dealings with this author; Caroline Dyas for researching a wealth of detailed information on the samples shown; Libby Willis for her eagle-eyed proof-reading; Helen Snaith for her essential index; and Juanne Branquinho for contacting suppliers. Also many thanks to Auberon Hedgecoe for overseeing the design; Peter Gerrish and John Round for transforming an enormous volume of fresh material into an informative visual treat; Roger Dixon for excellent new photography; Emma O'Neil for researching new interiors pictures; and Gary Hayes and Julie Young for marshalling the complex process of production.

I would also like to acknowledge again the team who created the first *Style Sourcebook* over five years ago. Their pioneering work still resonates in our new title: Emma Boys, Kenny Grant, Estelle Bayliss, Penelope Cream, Julia North, Claire Musters, Anna Nicholas, Patrick Evans, Steve Tanner, Judith More, Janice Utton, Samantha Gray, Jane Royston, Hilary Bird, Jo Wood, Glen Watkins, and the late and much-missed Arlene Sobel.

Heartfelt thanks to the following for kindly allowing location photography: Lee Anderson; Andrew Lowe House; Sue Andrews; Roger Banks-Pye; Cornelia Bayley; Alison & Kip Bertram; Calhoun Mansion; Cedar Grove; Château de Compiègne; Comoglio Showroom; Colline Covington; Clifford Ellison; John Evert; Ruth Fane; Garth Woodside Mansion; Geffrye Museum; Christophe Gollut; Jacques Granges; Richard Gray; Paul & Lisa Grist; Richard Hampton Jenrette; Amelia Handegan; Michael Harris;

Thierry & Agnès Hart; La Heredia; Jonathon Hudson; Charles Jencks; Mr & Mrs Michael Keehan; Wendy Kidd; Lyn von Kirsting; Leeds Castle; Ian Lieber; Linley Sambourne House; Lord & Lady McAlpine; The Malt House; Marshall Schule Associates; Justin Meath Baker; Jim & Debbie Millis; Janet Milner; Issey Miyake; Mor Jumel Mansion; Monmouth Mansion; Françoise Lafon; Nathaniel Russell House; The Old Merchant's House; Eileen O'Neill; Jaime & Janetta Parlade; Parham House; Tom Parr; Jack & Tasha Polizzi; Rockliffe Mansion; Rosalie Mansion; Ivy Rosequist; Jackl Sadoun; Dennis Severs; Shaker Museum; Lars Sjöberg; Keith Skeel; Sir John Soane Museum; Annie & Lachlan Stewart; Eric & Gloria Stewart; St Mary's, Bramber; Temp Newsam House; Maryse and Michel Trama; David Warbeck; West Green House; Lou de Wet; Lillian Williams.